Acclaim for *A Prelude to Immortality*

'This fascinating biography of a biography essentially explains to the reader how Winston Churchill's thought processes worked when he wrote *My Early Life*, one of the books that deservedly won him the Nobel Prize for Literature. A vital part of the Churchill myth as well as being a beautiful piece of writing in itself, *My Early Life* has always been something of an enigma – until now.'

– Andrew Roberts, author of *Churchill: Walking with Destiny*

'A superb study of Churchill the writer. Meticulously researched, highly readable, and offering unique insights into his life, ambitions and character.'

– Katherine Carter, historian, curator at Chartwell and author of *Churchill's Citadel: Chartwell and the Gatherings Before the Storm*

'This is a well-crafted and lavishly illustrated deep dive into Churchill's most revealing book; illuminating how and why he wrote it and showing how it was received by his contemporaries and later historians.'

– Allen Packwood OBE, Director, Churchill Archive Centre, Cambridge University

---

'Color coded, profusely illustrated, citations, appendices, and a wealth of information all thoroughly indexed! Stiles has produced an encyclopedic study of Winston Churchill's most beloved book. From brief biographies of everyone mentioned in the text to a record of every language in which *My Early Life* has been published, *A Prelude to Immortality* immediately becomes a classic study of a classic book.'

– David Freeman, editor for the International Churchill Society

---

'Most of what is written about Churchill just tells us who he was and what he did. Stiles shows us how and why Churchill became who he was. In Stiles' hands, Churchill's single most popular work not only entertains the reader, as it has done for nearly a century since it was first published, but now illuminates its author as never before. Stiles brilliantly uses Churchill's own – and only – retrospective on his origins as a kind of skeleton key to access Churchill's voice and vitality, his animating attitudes and ambitions. A true sense of Churchill ramifies and resonates in these pages. Not only has this never been done before, but it is hard to imagine it being done better. *A Prelude to Immortality* is silver-tongued scholarship – part rigorous analysis, part reference compendium, all held within a gripping narrative.'

– Marc Kuritz, Proprietor, Churchill Book Collector, ABAA | ILAB

A Prelude to Immortality

CHURCHILL'S 'MY EARLY LIFE'

Gary L. Stiles

UNICORN

Published in 2025 by Unicorn,
an imprint of Unicorn Publishing Group
Charleston Studio
Meadow Business Centre
Lewes BN8 5RW
www.unicornpublishing.org

The author has asserted his moral right under the Copyright, Designs and Patents Act 1988 to be identified as the author of this work.

All rights reserved. No part of the contents of this book may be reproduced, stored in or introduced into a retrieval system, or transmitted, in any form or by any means (electronic, mechanical, photocopying, recording or otherwise), without the prior written permission of the copyright holder and the above publisher of this book.

Every effort has been made to trace copyright holders and to obtain their permission for the use of copyrighted material. The publisher apologises for any errors or omissions and would be grateful to be notified of any corrections that should be incorporated in future reprints or editions of this book.

Excerpts reproduced with permission of Curtis Brown, London on behalf of Portland Churchill Ltd © Winston S. Churchill / Portland Churchill Ltd

ISBN 978-1-917458-27-6

10 9 8 7 6 5 4 3 2 1

Designed by Matthew Wilson

Printed and Bound in Great Britain by Bell and Bain Ltd, Glasgow

Dedication

For Alexis,
my wife, my love, my best friend, my muse

Contents

Acknowledgements	8
Abbreviations	11
Introduction	12
Chapter 1 Early Influences	17
Chapter 2 Becoming a Writer	26
Chapter 3 Writing *My Early Life*	67
Chapter 4 Creation of *My Early Life* text from Churchill's Earlier Publications	146
Chapter 5 Launch of the Book	149
A. Gifted Inscribed Copies of My Early Life	149
B. Book Reviews of My Early Life	178
C. Launch, Advertising and, Sales	209
Chapter 6 Previously Unrecorded English and Non-English Editions	235
Chapter 7 Global Impact of *My Early Life*	256
A. Analysis of My Early Life *by Historians*	273
B. Analysis of the Writing Style	285
C. Churchill's Nobel Prize for Literature	297
Chapter 8 Conclusions	308
Appendices	
Appendix 1 Brief Biographies	313
Appendix 2 Chapter 4: Childhood	322
Appendix 3 Chapter 4: War in Cuba	347
Appendix 4 Chapter 4: Cavalry Charge	353
Appendix 5 Chapter 4: Armoured Train	383
Appendix 6 Chapter 4: Escape	400
Appendix 7 Chapter 5: Bibliography	486
Appendix 8 Chapter 6: Unrecorded Books and Other Media	493
Index	567

Acknowledgements

Winston Churchill's *My Early Life* is a book that captured my imagination more than forty years ago. The action, the drama, the larger-than-life character of Churchill, the magnificent writing, and the unapologetic challenging charge to a 'new generation' to grasp life at its fullest and to change the world leaves little more to be desired in any individual book. To more completely understand and grasp the scope of what Churchill accomplished and how impactful the book has been for more than ninety years, I embarked on a journey of discovery of the why and how Churchill came to write this book – his one and only autobiography and one that carries his life only up to the age of about 28. My journey turned out to take much longer than expected and took me through more realms of intellectual pursuit than I ever could have envisaged. I traveled from politics to philosophy, military strategy to horsemanship, biography to bibliography, creative writing to learning disabilities, finance to publishing, advertising to grammar and with a seemingly endless uncovering of new facts in libraries and databases around the world. It has been a fulfilling journey and one that I certainly could not have been made without the help and prior intellectual accomplishments of a large number of people to whom I am indebted for making this journey possible.

First and foremost, I would like to most heartily thank the late Richard M. Langworth CBE, friend and colleague, who for more than forty years was always willing to advise and assist with his limitless knowledge of all things Churchill. He kindly wrote the Foreword for my last book, *Churchill in Punch*. The last thing we communicated about, just 10 days before his death, was his willingness to write something for this book. Alas, it was not to be. The world will miss you Richard!

ACKNOWLEDGEMENTS

As anyone who writes about Churchill, I am indebted to those writers/historians who have provided the classic texts about Churchill and his life and without whose works this book would not have been possible. I am particularly indebted to Martin Gilbert, Randolph S. Churchill, and Larry P. Arnn for the official biography and companion volumes of Winston S. Churchill. I would be remiss if I didn't acknowledge Lord Roberts, the superb historian, for all of his books on Churchill but most especially *Churchill: Walking With Destiny*. The magnificent *Bibliography of the Writings of Sir Winston Churchill* by Ronald I. Cohen MBE was the underpinning for much of what appears in this book. Ron Cohen's willingness to always answer questions about Churchill's books is much appreciated. His encyclopedic knowledge of Churchill's books is unequalled.

The late Mark Weber of *The Churchill Book Specialist* and Marc Kuritz, proprietor of *Churchill Book Collector*, have provided much critical information and guidance through long discussions and never-ending emails. Their willingness to engage is much appreciated. They have both taught me an enormous amount about Churchill and his books. Dave Turrell, proprietor of *Nineveh & Tyre*, likewise, has provided much information and was willing and very helpful in reviewing sections of the book. These three have likewise provided many books by and about Churchill for my collection.

A special thanks goes to Allen Packwood OBE, director of the Churchill Archive Centre, at Cambridge University who provided access and information that was critical to so many sections of this book. This Centre is such a treasure trove of Churchill materials and so helpful in finding the materials needed. A true understanding of the journey Churchill made in actually writing *My Early Life*, and bringing it to market would not have been possible without information in the Churchill archives.

Permission to quote from the works of Sir Winston Churchill was obtained from Curtis Brown Ltd., on the behalf of the estate of Winston S. Churchill.

I wish to thank Lucie Teegarden for her expert editorial assistance. She was not only critical to the production of my last two books on the artist William Hart and *Churchill in Punch* but likewise contributed significantly to the production of this book. It is always a pleasure to work with her.

Without the help and input of Lord Strathcarron and Ryan Gearing of Unicorn Publishing Group, this book simply would not have happened. I am forever grateful.

The scope, accuracy, and readability of the book owe much to all of those who helped as noted above, and any errors of fact or other inaccuracies, whether by omission or commission, are solely the responsibility of the author.

Finally, as in all work I have done, the most important inspiration and support comes from my wife, Alexis, a talented professional executive, and loving partner. I appreciate and love her more than she will ever know and this book is dedicated to her.

Gary L. Stiles
New York, New York
September 2025

Abbreviations for *My Early Life*

Am.	American
Br.	British
C of E	Chancellor of the Exchequer
dj	dust jacket
ed.	edition, editor, edited
L to L	*London to Ladysmith*
MEL	*My Early Life*
MP	Member of Parliament
PM	Prime Minister
SA	South Africa
Scribner	Charles Scribner (individual)
Scribner's	Charles Scribner's Sons (Book Company)
WSC	Winston S. Churchill
WWI	First World War
WWII	Second World War

Introduction

WINSTON CHURCHILL'S NAME HAS BEEN CONSISTENTLY RECOGNISABLE around the world for more than 125 years. He has been named the 'Greatest Briton' and 'Man (or Person) of the Century' in a variety of popular polls and by distinguished authors.[1] He is best known for his leadership as Prime Minister of Great Britain during the Second World War. His unequalled oratorical skills in defending and inspiring the British people (and the rest of the world) leading up to the war and throughout the war's duration are legendary. This skill was succinctly and elegantly highlighted by Edward R. Murrow when he said Churchill 'mobilized the English language and sent it into battle'.[2]

The indefatigable Churchill is not one-dimensional in his skill sets: he has been recognised for the diversity of his talents, including his military endeavours as a young man, sixty years as a noted global and outspoken politician, and as an artist and, importantly, a writer and newspaper correspondent. Churchill, in fact, has been known, both during his life and continuing to the present, as an extremely prolific and noted author. He produced more than 50 books, 260 pamphlets, 840 articles and more than 9,000 pages of speeches.[3]

Although more than a thousand books have been written about Churchill, very few have focused on his writing skills and techniques, and none have focused entirely on Churchill the autobiographer. This book will focus on him as an autobiographer and the impactful book he wrote. Here, the term 'writer' is used in its broadest sense: that is, it encompasses all the aspects that surround writers, from their educational backgrounds and life experiences to their writing and researching techniques. In addition, Churchill's interactions with editors and publishers and how they engage in the launch and advertising campaigns are probed. He was deeply involved in all these aspects of his books. Important questions not previously studied include why he chose to write an autobiography when he was in his fifties, what he hoped to achieve, and how he wanted the world (electorate?) to perceive him.

This author believes Churchill's writings will be remembered for a very long time, certainly as long as he is remembered as the heroic leader of the Second World War. To understand Churchill the writer, it is necessary to consider how and why he became a writer and to study the life experiences that influenced him and shaped his mind and writing style and techniques. To this end, Churchill's only book-length autobiography, *My Early Life*, was chosen as the focus of this study. In many ways, the studies of Churchill and *My Early Life* are so intertwined that to separate them would do a tremendous disservice to both. Thus, this book is equally the story of Churchill the writer as well as the story of the book *My Early Life*.

My Early Life provides several unique attributes and characteristics compared to all Churchill's other works. Yet it is still representative in many aspects of the whole of his entire canon in terms of the processes he employed to write most of his books and his very hands-on approach to the entire creative process.

My Early Life is the only one of Churchill's books that focuses entirely on himself and provides the story of his life and career from his birth to the time he entered Parliament and a few years after (1874–1903). It is not only a prime example of his method and style of writing, but it also provides key insights into his experiences and the life events that shaped him into the writer he became. Churchill's bestselling single-volume book, *My Early Life* has received widespread acclaim since its release in 1930.

Additional aspects of *My Early Life* that make it the appropriate choice to study include, first, the fact that reviewers have deemed it Churchill's most readable, endearing, and personal book; and, secondly, that Churchill tells his own story in his own words. He shares what he considers to be the most impactful experiences that molded his life and character, as well as his hopes and goals for his life. This revealing story is enhanced by the fact that Churchill writes in the voice and thought processes that were inherent to his age at the time of each episode. That is to say, you hear the voice of the fearful young boy going off to boarding school for the first time; the voice of the young soldier as he is about to participate in his first cavalry charge in war; and the quizzical voice of the student attempting to digest the classical languages, such as Latin, and questioning why they should be required. Thus, you don't hear Churchill the man in his fifties telling the story: it is himself translated back to the appropriate age. He provides powerful and engaging stories in which readers can fully immerse themselves and empathise with him, even if they have not experienced similar episodes. The stories are written in a warm and conversational prose approaching lyric poetry, where the words are chosen carefully not only for their meaning but also for the sound and voice they provide the reader. Many sections sing off the page and so engross the reader that they are unable to put the book down.

My Early Life is also of literary interest concerning how Churchill created the manuscript from his research materials. It is the only book for which he had previously published a significant body of work related to the experiences he would retell in *My Early Life*. In fact, he had already published four books (containing his newspaper reports as a war correspondent in Cuba, India, the Sudan and South Africa) and more than thirteen major articles about his life, and numerous war correspondence reports.[4] Thus, when he decided to write his autobiography, he had not only his personal memories but a large collection of printed and archival materials upon which to draw and weave into a coherent and readable story.

How he melded these publications into a coherent manuscript provides insight into what Churchill hoped to gain in writing the book. In fact, he had multiple goals, including personal recognition both as a writer and political leader; creation of the image of himself he wanted the public to accept; not unimportantly, enhancement of his income; and, finally, inspiration of the next generation. To this end, Churchill dedicated his book 'To a New Generation.' This phrase has several implications. First, Churchill recognises that the story of his youth is a Victorian-age story with life experiences, values and politics that will never be seen again. Yet, human nature and the personality traits of people and their desire to succeed are universal and timeless. Thus, his stories are applicable to any generation and are timeless, much in the manner of Shakespeare's plays. Churchill recognises that there is a new generation who are becoming the movers and shakers of the country, and he is challenging and imploring them not to be timid or to retreat from life and be afraid of action as a consequence of the great upheaval that was the First World War. As he states in Chapter 3 of *My Early Life*,

INTRODUCTION

Come on now all you young men, all over the world. You are needed more than ever now to fill the gap of a generation shorn by the War. You have not an hour to lose. You must take your places in life's fighting line. Twenty to twenty-five! These are the years! Don't be content with things as they are. 'The earth is yours and the fulness thereof.' Enter upon your inheritance, accept your responsibilities. Raise the glorious flags again, advance them upon the new enemies, who constantly gather upon the front of the human army, and have only to be assaulted to be overthrown. Don't take No for an answer. Never submit to failure.[5]

For all these reasons, *My Early Life* has been chosen as the example to be used to study Churchill the writer.

This book is divided into chapters that address the individual components of what made Churchill become a writer and how he wrote, launched, and publicised his books. In addition, it describes how the quality and impact of his storytelling made *My Early Life* a success not only commercially and in the opinion of reviewers but also as a work which has been widely quoted in lay and academic publications. Chapter 2 ('Becoming a Writer') discusses his education; his love of the English language; the financial needs that drove him to write; his time as a war correspondent; and his need to have multiple manuscripts in various states of preparation at all times. Chapter 3 focuses on the writing of his autobiography, including his creation of organised writing teams, his use of consultants, secretaries and reviewers, as well as his interactions with publishers and editors. Chapter 4 describes how he wove all the previous published material into the new book and how he decided what to include or exclude. Next, Chapter 5, covers the launch of *My Early Life*, tells how he gifted books as a token of thanks and for publicity, how he was intimately involved in the advertising and sales of the book, and what reviewers said about the book. Chapter 6 focuses on the book's success, as attested by the numerous editions, reprints, serialisations and multimedia formats of his story since the book was first published in 1930. There are now known to be more than ninety variations of *My Early Life* published in English and printed around the world. More than a hundred non-English versions have been published. These versions of the book and representations of it in other media forms are catalogued in Appendix 8 Chapter 6 Unrecorded Books and Other Media.

Chapter 7 describes *My Early Life*'s worldwide impact as measured by the frequency of its citation in the literature and how regularly the episodes from his life contained therein are now quoted in textbooks, journals and other literature as 'real-life' examples from which to learn or emulate. These examples span a wide range of topics as varied as nannies, soldiering, politics, polo and English composition. In addition, an analysis of his writing from both a historical point of view and a literary assessment are provided. This includes a discussion of his winning the Nobel Prize in Literature in 1953. *My Early Life* was one of only a few books mentioned in the presentation speech in Stockholm.[6] To read the translated transcript of the presentation speech and hear the logic and justification of why Winston Churchill was worthy of the Nobel Prize in Literature is to be enriched by a paean to the majesty of Churchill's writing and oratory. My hope is that this book will provide further insight into Churchill the autobiographer and his timeless book, *My Early Life*.

Notes

1. Charles Krauththammer, 'Person of the Century', *Washington Post*, 31 December 1999, p. A31; John Ramsden, *Man of the Century: Winston Churchill and His Legend Since 1945*, New York, Columbia University Press, 2003; Neil Ferrier, Churchill, *The Man of the Century*, Garden City, LI, Doubleday, 1965; 'Greatest Briton', London, BBC poll, 2002.
2. Edward R. Murrow, broadcast, 30 November 1954, *In Search of Light*, New York, Knopf, 1967, p. 276.
3. Marc Kuritz, *Churchill Book Collector*, https://www.churchillbookcollector.com/
4. Ronald I. Cohen, *Bibliography of the Writings of Sir Winston Churchill*, London, Thoemmes Continuum, 2006.
5. Winston S. Churchill, *My Early Life*, London, Thornton Butterworth, 1930, p. 74.
6. *Nobel Lectures, Literature 1901-1967*, ed. Horst Frenz, Amsterdam, Elsevier Publishing, 1969, pp. 487–495.

CHAPTER 1

Early Influences

Winston S. Churchill, in his only autobiography, *My Early Life*, tells his personal story from his first memories of childhood through his very early experiences in the House of Commons at age twenty-eight. From the beginning to the end, Churchill had a message he wanted to deliver to his readers: *This is who I am, and here are the experiences and adventures that moulded me into the person I am*. Naturally, the story is told from his perspective, and, of necessity, it includes his biases to frame a coherent and exciting tale. He provides a story full of facts, emotions, and scenarios that he desires the reader to believe are truthful and accurate and conveying what he actually experienced and believed to be true at the time. However, as with any autobiography, an understanding of what was actually true and real and what the author might have thought was real needs careful evaluation by the reader or reviewer. Certain embellishments or alterations of facts are noted in this book. However, this book is not intended to be a 'fact checker' of *My Early Life*, and it is neither a biography nor a psychoanalysis of Churchill. There are many such written works, and the reader is referred to them.[1] This is the how and why Churchill wrote *My Early Life*; and the success he had with the book in telling his story, the literary acclaim it received and the impact it had.

An individual's character and personality are impacted by their childhood and family environment. Therefore, it is important to provide some pertinent information on Churchill's early life and his personal, familial, and experiential interactions. These interactions, and Churchill's view of them, influenced Churchill tremendously, including the storytelling approaches he took and the message he wanted to convey to his readers. For many years, scholars have asserted that Churchill was capable of telling his story in the manner that best met his needs and the vision of himself that he wanted to portray. This vision, as mentioned above, was at times an embellishment of what reality might have been.[2]

This dichotomy between reality and Churchill's vision of reality is certainly discernible throughout his book. This does not make Churchill unique among autobiographers. Neither does it detract from his literary style and the value of the book. However, keeping this perspective in mind while reading *My Early Life* is quite essential to a more complete understanding of Churchill's book, his writing acumen and his character. In addition, as will become clear in subsequent chapters, Churchill wrote *My Early Life* in a powerful and unusual voice: that of himself at the age he was during the described events – not the voice of a man in his mid-fifties telling the story as a later observer. Thus, the author's point of view is coloured by the beliefs and background knowledge of, for example, a schoolboy or a young soldier, not through the lens of the composite experience of a mature adult.

Churchill always thought that he was different from most people; while he believed we are all but worms, he thought he was at least a 'glow worm'.[3] He believed that he was preordained to do great things on the world stage, including being Prime Minister, and that he would lead his nation to greatness and/or salvation. In many ways, he always thought that he was Saint George slaying the dragon. Whatever the issue or situation, Churchill wanted to portray himself as the underdog, always having to fight against great odds to earn recognition. Therefore, it was always required of him to display the utmost strength, bravery and skill to be successful. This point of view, or personal mandate, certainly extends to his interactions with his parents and his school life, from being home-schooled by his nanny, Mrs. Everest, and his private tutor while in Ireland, all the way through his public schools and Sandhurst. The unquenchable need for self-promotion (in both written and oral form) of his bravery, risk-taking, and daring throughout his military and correspondent experiences are just another example of what he believed he must do to be successful.

PARENTING

There were three people early in Churchill's life who dominated his world and had the most significant impact on the moulding of his character: his father, his mother, and his nanny. According to him, he desperately wanted to please all three, and in return, he desired to receive praise and support. These three would be the subjects of extensive discussions in his autobiography. Only one of them met these needs unhesitatingly, creating a lifelong bond with him: Mrs Elizabeth Everest, his nanny. She was, for all intents and purposes, his surrogate mother, and she provided the most parenting of the three. Churchill describes this relationship when he states, 'My nurse was my confidant. It was to her I poured out my many troubles.'[4] And as was aptly described by Andrew Roberts, 'One doesn't have to embrace Freudianism to find his nick-names for her – "Woom" or "Woomany" – poignant in a child looking for a mother-surrogate while his real mother was dazzling the Prince of Wales's Marlborough House Set with her beauty, high spirits, and sexual allure.'[5] This is all one needs to remember about 'Woomany' when reading Churchill's endearing descriptions of her.

Churchill loved and, in many ways, idolised his parents, but he always wanted more from them. He wanted more of their time; for them to display more interest in him; and most importantly, he wanted to be praised by them. He portrays them as aloof, uncaring, critical and, at times, uninterested in him. Thus, he was always fighting to gain their interest. His actions took multiple forms, including writing to them frequently, asking to spend more time with them, and certainly acting out with bad behaviour in a misguided manner to attract their attention. It must be said, however, that for higher-society children in the Victorian era, this was not a rare complaint or vision for children, as many were mostly cared for by nannies, not their parents. Parents often led lives quite separate from their children. William Manchester, in his introduction to the 1996 new American edition of *My Early Life*, discusses this issue directly, highlighting the fact that Churchill's vision of his parents was often at odds with reality, even if, at times, Manchester is harsher than reality might require:

> His descriptions of his parents, Lord and Lady Randolph Churchill, are gravely flawed. He enshrines both. 'My mother,' he writes here, 'always seemed to me a fairy princess: a radiant being possessed of limitless riches and power. She shone for me like the Evening Star.' In reality Lady Randolph, the American-born Jennie Jerome, was a beautiful, shallow, diamond-studded panther of a woman who neglected him shamefully. … Churchill's recollection of Lord Randolph was even more

distorted. In *Amid These Storms* he wrote: 'The greatest and most powerful influence in my early life was of course my father. … He saw no reason why the old glories of church and state, of King and country, should not be reconciled with modern democracy; or why the masses of working people should not become the defenders of these ancient institutions by which their liberty and progress had been achieved.' History's verdict is very different. Randolph was a shallow political demagogue whose star briefly crossed the parliamentary firmament in the mid-1880s, when he became the Chancellor of the Exchequer and then, within six months, owing to his extraordinary bad judgment, plunged out of sight.

Emotionally abandoned by both, young Winston blamed himself. Needing outlets for his own welling adoration, he created images of them as he wished they were, and the less he saw of them, the easier the transformation became. His suppressed resentment at their neglect had to be directed elsewhere. Thus he became a difficult child and a wretched student.[6]

Richard M. Langworth, the noted historian, editor and Churchillian expert, is less harsh in his analysis:

He was not nearly so ignored and abandoned by his parents as he implies. His nephew, Peregrine Churchill, aided by Lady Randolph Churchill's archives, concluded that Winston's mother spent a surprising amount of time with him and his brother Jack before they left for school—and that Winston 'was a very naughty boy; his parents were very concerned about him'.[7]

The important lesson here is that, in his mind, Churchill needed to fight against all odds to be successful in life – even in his quest for parental love and affection. Thus, he is likely to portray a situation as more dire than it may actually be so as to ensure that he appears to display Herculean efforts to overcome his perceived disadvantage.

SCHOOLING

Churchill had a variety of types of schooling during his childhood and youth. He had home-schooling with a private instructor, then a series of private schools, and then Harrow, the well-known public school, followed by military training at Sandhurst, Britain's equivalent of West Point. In Churchill's view, he was a lonely, poor student who received little recognition but many whippings, which would have often drawn blood. Much has been written about Victorian public education. From a modern perspective, it was narrow-minded, regimented and filled with cruel treatment of students.[8] Churchill regarded his school years as the most unpleasant and painful period of his life. He felt very strongly that the academic approach he was offered provided little incentive for him to work hard and that it fully stifled any educational curiosity he had. The schools focused on the classical languages, mathematics and rote memorisation. Churchill could certainly do the last one well, but the first two were of little interest to him, and so he did not engage in them. Churchill portrays himself as a poor student and problem child. According to him, he was always in the lowest form, he received no praise for his work, and, at best, he was left alone to be unhappy and lonely.

Churchill's description of his education in *My Early Life* is compelling and wonderful (if at times painful) to read. He makes many cogent arguments about educational reform that needed to be made. However, the truth is probably that his education was not what it should have been; he was at times mistreated; his academics were better than he confessed (he does praise one master for teaching him English); and his isolation was not quite as dramatic as he suggests. Roberts again provides worthwhile insights: 'For all his later denials, Churchill was something of a success at Harrow. At fourteen he won a prize for reciting no fewer than 1,200 lines of Macauley's *Lays of Ancient Rome* without error, and a contemporary recalled that "he could quote whole scenes of Shakespeare's plays and had no hesitation in correcting his masters if they misquoted."'[9] It is clear Churchill invokes literary licence to embellish his storytelling so as to strengthen his point and highlight that he always had to overcome obstacles, but this does not in any way detract from his literary skills. (For additional discussion about his education process, see Chapter 2.)

MILITARY EXPERIENCE

For a man with no long-term military career goals, Churchill had more global military action than could be expected in any short military career. He saw action in Cuba, India, the Sudan and South Africa, and he wrote about his experiences as both a war correspondent and soldier simultaneously. Churchill believed firmly that the most direct way to be successful and move up the social, political and career ladders was to win recognition as a soldier who displayed bravery and was recognised in military and newspaper dispatches. Just as important to him was the need to wear war medals on his chest. Thus, he expended all of his energy and effort from 1895 to 1900 to be sure he was directly involved in military actions.

In addition, it was critical that he be observed in action and then written about, regardless of whether the writer was Churchill himself or another reporter. Since he was the only writer he could be sure was writing what he wanted to be promulgated, he needed to position himself in harm's way around the world and write of his experiences – which he did, profusely, in both newspapers and books. As Roberts has stated, 'Few have set out with more cold-blooded deliberation to become first a hero and then a great man.'[10]

Many of his contemporaries fully recognised the approach Churchill was taking. His mother even warned him about what he was doing. Writing to him in January 1897, she admonished him not to be too pushy or sing his own praises; that was for others to do:

> You will be glad to hear that Col. Brab [Reginald Brabazon] sent me a letter from Sir Bindon Blood in which he speaks of you in the praise & says he mentioned you in dispatches. You have done more than well my darling boy & I am as always proud of you. Forgive a piece of advice – which may not be needed – but *be modest* [emphasis added]. All your feats of valour are sure to come out & people will know. Let it be from others & not from yourself. One must be tempted to talk of oneself in such a case – but resist. Let them drag things out.[11]

This advice was given to Churchill many times over the years. It was never accepted.

Churchill explicitly admitted and explained his approach numerous times in multiple letters. For example he wrote this to his mother on 5 September 1897, from India:

> I am at present correspondent for the *Pioneer* – to which I have to telegraph 300 words a day. At the first opportunity I am to be put

on the strength of the force – which will give me a medal if I come through.... I have faith in my star – that is I am intended to do something in the world. If I am mistaken – what does it matter? My life has been a pleasant one and though I should regret leaving it – it would be a regret that perhaps I should never know.[12]

He wrote to her again on 2 October 1897:

I hope you will talk about this [the battles he was in] to the Prince and others – as if any fuss is made, they may give a special clasp for Mahmoud Valley. This has been the hardest fighting on the frontier for forty years. I have been attached as a matter of extreme urgency – to the 31st Punjaub Infantry. A change from British cavalry to the Native Infantry! Still it means the medal and also that next time I go into action I shall command a hundred men – and possibly I may bring off some 'coup.' Besides I shall have some other motive for taking chances than merely love of adventure.[13]

Another letter followed on 12 October:

Since I last wrote I have seen two or three sharp skirmishes and have now been 10 complete times under fire. *Quite a foundation for a political life* [emphasis added]. ... I intend or rather am seriously contemplating writing 'The Story of the M.F.F.' [Malakand Field Force] ... the idea has filled my mind. ... I have earned my medal and clasps fully. [Sir Bindon] Blood [the commanding general] says not one in a hundred have seen as much fighting as I have – and mind you – not from the staff or distance but from the last company of the rearguard every time. A splendid episode.[14]

In a letter to his brother (John Churchill) on 13 January 1898, Churchill states:

Now if all goes well I shall get to Egypt and then I shall have enough of war. I am now on my way to Calcutta – to ask for employment should the spring campaign take place now – in case I do not get to

Egypt – but you will understand the latter would be much better as I should get a least 2 fresh medals out of it. [Drawing in the letter of four medals with 'Frontier Egypt Cuba' written underneath.][15]

Finally, in a letter dated 18 December 1898 to Aylmer Haldane, who was aide-de-camp to General Sir William Lockhart, Commander-in-Chief in India at the time – and who later would fight with Churchill in South Africa – Churchill writes:

There is another matter about which I want to ask you. I am leaving the army in April. I have come back merely for the Polo Tournaments. I naturally want to wear my medals while I have a uniform to wear them on. They have already sent me the Egyptian one. I can not think why the frontier one has not arrived. Young Life Guardsmen on Sir B. Blood's staff in Buner have already got theirs. Do try and get mine for me as soon as possible. Otherwise it will never be worn.[16]

With his formal military career at an end, for now, Churchill moved on to the next phase in his life, journalism and a further search for notoriety and glory. It is hoped that these perspectives will be useful to the reader in understanding Churchill's motivation in all he did and why he chose to act, speak and write as he did.

Notes

1. Martin Gilbert, *Winston S. Churchill* (Boston, MA: Houghton Mifflin Company, 8 vol., 1966–1988); Andrew Roberts, *Churchill: Walking with Destiny* (London: Allen Lane, 2018); Jonathan Rose, *The Literary Churchill* (New Haven, CT: Yale University Press, 2014); Martin Gilbert, *The Power of Words* (Boston, MA: Da Capo, 2012).
2. Richard M. Langworth, *A Connoisseur's Guide to the Books of Sir Winston Churchill* (London: Brassey's, 1998), pp. 129–30.
3. Violet Bonham Carter, *Winston Churchill as I Knew Him* (London, Reprint Society, 1966), p. 16.
4. Winston S. Churchill, *My Early Life* (London: Thornton Butterworth, 1930), p. 19.
5. Andrew Roberts, *Churchill: Walking with Destiny* (London: Allen Lane, 2018), p. 15.
6. William Manchester, 'Introduction', in Winston S. Churchill, *My Early Life* (New York: Touchstone, 1996), pp. vii–xix.
7. Langworth, *A Connoisseur's Guide*, p. 129.
8. Jonathan Gathorne-Hardy, *The Old School Tie* (New York: The Viking Press, 1978), pp. 140–142; Morton A. Kaplan, ed., *Character & Identity: The Sociological Foundation of Literary and Historical Perspective* (St. Paul, MN: Paragon House, 2000): Chapter 6 'Winston Churchill at School,' by James W. Muller, pp. 83–111; Henry E. Armstrong, 'Mr. Winston Churchill on Miseducation,' *Nature*, 27 December 1930, pp. 983–5.
9. Roberts, *Churchill: Walking with Destiny*, p. 20.
10. Roberts, *Churchill: Walking with Destiny*, p. 31
11. Randolph S. Churchill, *Winston S. Churchill*, Companion Vol. 1, part 2, 1896–1900, p. 832.
12. Randolph S. Churchill, *Winston S. Churchill*, Companion Vol. 1, part 2, 1896–1900, p. 784.
13. Randolph S. Churchill, *Winston S. Churchill*, Companion Vol. 1, part 2, 1896–1900, p. 797.
14. Randolph S. Churchill, *Winston S. Churchill*, Companion Vol. 1, part 2, 1896–1900, p. 804.
15. Randolph S. Churchill, *Winston S. Churchill*, Companion Vol. 1, part 2, 1896–1900, p. 858.
16. Randolph S. Churchill, *Winston S. Churchill*, Companion Vol. 1, part 2, 1896–1900, p. 995.

CHAPTER 2

Becoming a Writer

THE HARROW YEARS

While at Harrow, his well-regarded secondary school, Churchill developed an interest in and love of the English language and English composition. He realised for the first time the wonderful possibilities of combining words to create stories and convey information in a pleasing and impactful style. He found that the thoughtful combining of words was applicable to both the spoken and written word. Churchill noted in *My Early Life* that Mr Somervell, his English master, had a unique manner of teaching English composition and of instilling an appreciation for words and how to write effectively and meaningfully:

> Mr. Somervell – a most delightful man, to whom my debt is great– was charged with the duty of teaching the stupidest boys the most disregarded thing – namely, to write mere English. He knew how to do it. He taught it as no one else has ever taught it. Not only did we learn English parsing thoroughly, but we also continually practiced English analysis. Mr. Somervell had a system of his own. He took a fairly long sentence and broke it up into its components by means of black, red, blue, and green inks. Subject, verb, object: Relative Clauses, Conditional Clauses, Conjunctive and Disjunctive Clauses! Each had its colour and its bracket. It was a kind of drill. We did it almost daily. As I remained in the Third Fourth three times as long as anyone else, I had three times as much of it. I learned it thoroughly. Thus I got into my bones the essential structure of the ordinary British sentence – which is a noble thing. And when in after years my schoolfellows who had won prizes and distinction for writing such beautiful Latin poetry and pithy Greek epigrams had to

come down again to common English, to earn their living or make their way, I did not feel myself at any disadvantage.[1]

Another of Churchill's mentors at Harrow was Mr Moriarty. He commented on Winston's strong interest in English, noting how unusual it was for a young lad of fourteen to show 'such love and veneration for the English language'.[2] Churchill certainly distinguished himself at Harrow for his writing skills. He won at least two awards for history compositions and, in addition, won a prize for his poem *Influenza*.[3] It was also at Harrow that Churchill began writing to and for newspapers. His outspoken and direct opinions were evident even at this early phase of his writing 'career'. Using the pen name 'Junius Junior', he wrote a series of letters to *The Harrovian*, the school newspaper. These letters were critical of the school administration and their policies. The student editor of the paper, Leo Amery, was an older student who had had a humorous interaction with Churchill, who had pushed him into the swimming pool. (This episode will be described in more detail later.) Amery was now in a position as editor of the newspaper to get his revenge on Churchill. Churchill's letters were so strong and opinionated that they were almost vitriolic. Amery edited them significantly and then added the editorial comment: 'We have omitted a portion of our correspondent's letter, which seemed to us to exceed the limits of fair criticism.'[4] This and other letters by Churchill certainly weren't received well by the headmaster, who knew who had written them.[5] This is but one example of Churchill sending letters to the school newspaper; he sent many more using a variety of pseudonyms, such as De Profundis, Aequitas Junior and Truth. (See Companion Volume 1 Part 1 of the Churchill Biography for a more complete listing.)[6]

The thrill and recognition that Churchill received from writing to the school newspaper made an important impression on him. He completely grasped the impact his letters could have on his reputation, as well as influencing others. He would continue to write for newspapers for the rest of his life. In fact, his first paying job outside of the army was as a newspaper correspondent.

Churchill's love of history was also nurtured while at Harrow. He particularly enjoyed lectures on the battles of Waterloo and the Sudan.[7,8] As Andrew Roberts notes, Churchill combined his love of history with his writing skills – something he would do to great advantage for the remainder of his life – to produce remarkable documents. As Roberts states,

> The Harrow Archives contain an extraordinary document written when Churchill was fourteen, a 1,500-word essay set in the future about a British invasion of Russia, complete with six pages of battle plans. Written in the first person by 'Colonel Seymour' and dated 7 July 1914, it is full of military maneuvers, 'glittering bayonets,' 'dark clouds of Cossacks,' heroic derring-do and aides-de-camp charging across limb-strewn battlefields, carrying vital orders between commanders. 'The fields which this morning were green,' Churchill wrote, 'are now tinged with the blood of seventeen thousand.'[9]

Churchill's writing had already become remarkably mature, advanced and colourful. His choice of vocabulary had also progressed beyond his years.

Churchill became enamoured with words themselves and the use of word play while at Harrow. William Manchester provides in his biography of Churchill an apt description of this process:

> At Harrow his lifelong fascination with words grew. He was thirteen, and Somervell was introducing him to literature. Except for best-sellers like Wilkie Collins's *Moonshine,* few Harrovians read for pleasure. Winston was soon deep into Thackeray, Dickens, Wordsworth, and every biography he could get his hands on. He knew what was good and found he liked it. Inevitably, his vocabulary increased. In his letters he wrote of a toy given him by his aunt as 'a source of unparalleled amusement,' his funds needed 'replenishing,' welcoming news was 'pleasing intelligence.' The bookseller Moore whose shop was near Harrow saw him almost daily and noticed that he was displaying evidence of his unusual command of words. He would argue in the shop on any subject, and, as a result of this, he was, I am afraid, often left in sole position on the floor.'[10]

These experiences at Harrow certainly planted the seeds of excellent writing and public speaking in Churchill's mind, seeds that would grow and flourish in him for the rest of his life. Writing and speechmaking would remain central elements in Churchill's daily life from that time forward.

His future readers would owe a debt of gratitude to Mr Somervell and his teaching techniques.

THE ROLE OF FINANCES IN SHAPING CHURCHILL'S WRITING CAREER

Another aspect of Churchill's life and character that would promote and require that he write not only for pleasure but also for financial compensation was his unquenchable need for cash. As a young man, he was always in need of money, for his lifestyle was beyond what he could afford on his meagre salaries from any of the positions or occupations he ever held. This began with his first position as a subaltern in the army after he graduated from Sandhurst, the British military academy. His army pay scale in the mid-1890s was not large – certainly not large enough to support his lifestyle and expensive hobbies such as polo. As noted by David Lough, 'Subalterns in the 4th Hussars earned ten pounds a month, but they were expected to equip themselves for hunting and polo.' Ever the resourceful individual, Churchill was able to acquire a horse from his aunt Duchess Lily (Lady Lily Spencer-Churchill, Duchess of Marlborough) and a $500 allowance from his mother so he could 'maintain his position'.[11] As would become evident to all, including his family, friends, bankers, and later to his beloved wife, Clementine, these resources were quite insufficient to meet his needs. He would begin to borrow significant money from individuals and banks. Churchill's lifelong struggle with finances is described in detail in Lough's book *No More Champagne*. Lough notes that, in the best of times, Churchill was barely able to keep his finances in order, and for much of his life until his very last years, he was continually in debt. Importantly, for significant periods, he was desperately in debt and near bankruptcy.[12] This fact weighed heavily on Churchill, though it almost never kept him from wanting the best in terms of material objects and services. The underlying issue was not only that he wanted expensive things but also that he actually could not, or would not, restrain himself from purchasing them. Thus, writing for pay was an essential adjuvant to his income. It is fair to say that the vast preponderance of his income throughout his life was from his writing and that he lived 'pen to mouth'.

Churchill's approach to financial budgeting was not what most of us would term prudent. He never really envisaged the need to decrease expenditure; rather, he always sought enhanced income to solve his financial issues. The concept of a balanced personal budget never really concerned him. With his love of and proficiency in the English language, writing was a natural avenue for generating income. Peter Clarke described the situation cogently:

> One thing is consistent in Winston's lifelong financial strategy – if it can be called that. This was to seek any means of boosting current income rather than to effect significant cuts in expenditure. And here his mother really did help him – belatedly, improbably, spasmodically, but, on the whole, effectively. She helped her son fashion a career that paralleled and supported his political ambitions; that paid the bills; and that by most ordinary tests became his primary occupation and source of income – not so much a subsidiary career as one in which he was to achieve professional recognition and satisfaction as well as financial reward.[13]

The third important factor in Churchill's diligent pursuit of writing was that he recognised it could bring him name recognition not only from the voting public (he always knew that politics was his long-term goal), but also, more importantly, from people of influence in government, the military, and high society, including royals. These were the ones who could provide the right introductions, assure his inclusion in important social, business and political associations, and generally improve his chances of success. In addition, by reporting his military exploits as a war correspondent in dispatches to newspapers as he did in Cuba, India, the Sudan and South Africa, he might win medals or be named in official military dispatches to the press – recognition seen by him as essential to a burgeoning career. Churchill decided early in his military career that politics would be his professional goal and that he would not pursue a long-term military career.

ACTIVE-DUTY WAR CORRESPONDENT

Churchill joined the 4th Queen's Own Hussars in January 1895. At that time, the British army had seen little active military combat since the early 1880s, so very few young soldiers had been able to display bravery under fire or win medals. In Churchill's mind there seemed little reason to be in the army if one could not experience active war, win medals and obtain recognition as a stepping stone to additional pursuits. He saw bravery and heroism as the core requirements, and he stated as much in *My Early Life*:

Rarity in a desirable commodity is usually the cause of enhanced value; and there has never been a time when war service was held in so much esteem by the military authorities or more ardently sought by officers of every rank. It was the swift road to promotion and advancement in every arm. It was the glittering gateway to distinction. It cast a glamour upon the fortunate possessor alike in the eyes of elderly gentlemen and young ladies.[14]

Thus, in need of finding active service, Churchill characteristically and, as described in his own words, took action: 'I searched the world for some scene of adventure or excitement.'[15] Cuba was the answer; it was the only scene of active military fighting. Churchill continues the story:

> Accordingly it was to Cuba that I turned my eyes. I unfolded the project [to seek action] to a brother subaltern – Reginald Barnes – who afterwards long commanded Divisions in France, and found him keen.[16]
>
> Thus fortified, I wrote to my father's old friend and Fourth Party colleague, Sir Henry Wolff, then our Ambassador at Madrid, asking whether he could procure us the necessary permissions from the Spanish military authorities. … Excellent introductions, formal and personal, soon arrived in a packet, together with the Ambassador's assurance that we had only to reach Havana to be warmly welcomed by the Captain-General and shown all there was to see. Accordingly at the beginning of November 1895, we sailed for New York, and journeyed thence to Havana.[17]

This is the approach Churchill would take for his entire military career: find action somewhere in the world; use personal contacts to get permission to travel there; and then create as much press coverage as possible. He also desired to be mentioned in miliary dispatches, gain military experience, establish himself as a war correspondent, be recognised for his valour, and win medals. In addition, he recognised that the written reports could, at a later stage, be the kernels for more extensive manuscripts and books.[18] This, Churchill believed, was the best possible way to not only become successful in the army but also set a strong foundation for a political career – which was, in reality, his end game. This turned out to be an enormously successful approach.

In November 1895, it must be remembered, Churchill was just turning twenty-one years of age; he had very recently joined the army with no experience; and was virtually unknown in the press and in the world. His advantages were that he had a famous name, well-positioned relatives, and a long list of distinguished contacts through those relatives. He also had an unquenchable thirst for recognition and success.

Churchill and his friend Reginald Barnes set sail from Liverpool on the steamship *Etruria* for adventure in New York and then Cuba. Just before embarking, he secured a contract as a war correspondent with the *Daily Graphic*, a London newspaper, to send back reports from the front in Cuba.[19] This was his first paying position as a writer. He was to be paid five guineas a letter. He would send a total of ten letters. As noted by Frederick Woods, Lady Randolph Churchill certainly helped to make this arrangement possible.[20] Thus, prior to leaving, he had alerted the press to his plans of being an observer and war correspondent covering the Spanish forces in Cuba who were attempting to squelch a rebel uprising.

When they arrived in New York City, the two young men stayed with Bourke Cockran, an old friend of Churchill's mother's who was a very well-placed lawyer and politician, and well connected to New York society – and, more importantly, to the American press. On their first night in town, Cockran hosted a large dinner party for Churchill and Barnes with the leading personalities of New York. They stayed in New York for a week and were wined and dined the entire time, with side trips to West Point, to the naval base in Brooklyn, and to fire stations in the city.[21]

The press coverage in the United States began even before he arrived. On 8 November, it was reported that 'one of the passengers on the *Etruria*, which is due today, is Winston Churchill, eldest son of the late Lord Randolph Churchill, and eldest grandson of the late Leonard Jerome. Winston Churchill will not only make his first visit to the United States, but he will be the first of the grandsons of Mr. Jerome to come to this country. Young Churchill will go to Cuba in order to go up country with the Spanish troops.'[22]

A few days later, more information on Churchill is reported: '…on his way to Cuba to observe the maneuvers of modern warfare as practiced between the Cubans and the Spaniards. ... He said today that his visit to Cuba was without diplomatic significance and that he would be simply an onlooker of any important engagements which might occur.'[23]

Churchill, never one to be a passive observer, rides into action with the commanding generals, and it is reported in early December: 'In the reports of the battle received here [the US] especial mention is made of the *valorous* [emphasis added] conduct of the English officers, Lieu. Winston Churchill ... and Lieu. Barnes, both of the Fourth Hussars of the British army, who recently joined the Spanish forces in Cuba.'[24]

On this same day, the *Chicago Tribune* published an article entitled 'Churchill in a Fight'. They not only reported that Churchill was in the battle but also reprinted a full letter that Churchill had sent to the *New York World* newspaper in which he had described the battle and praised the Spanish army for their valour.[25]

Churchill is clearly successful at getting his name in the press as both a brave and valorous soldier and a news correspondent. Churchill's activities are widely covered both in the UK and North America. The *Tribune* article also suggests his presence will create diplomatic problems for England, the concern being why is a young, inexperienced British officer actively engaging in military combat and taking sides in an insurrection against a foreign power? However, counterbalancing quotations, including one by Churchill's mother, state that he is only observing and not participating actively in the Spanish army.[26] No major diplomatic issues ever arose.

By mid-December, New York newspapers are printing articles with titles such as 'They Cannot Win'. These are reports by Churchill assessing and critiquing the Spanish army and its chances of success. With incredible audacity, he reports,

> I think that owing to the nature of the country, the Spanish have before them a very difficult task in the suppression of the rebellion. Although I believe them to be brave and energetic, I do not think there is sufficient combination in the movement of their several columns to catch the insurgents or inflict upon them serious defeat. ... If when the spring rains set in, Spain is in the same position that she is now, the probabilities are that the insurgents will win.[27]

This from a twenty-one-year-old soldier seeing his first battle action and who is supposed to be a neutral observer.

Importantly, the ten letters (military reports) Churchill sent back to London brought him for the first time to the attention of the *Daily Graphic* readers as having been involved in a serious military action and as a war correspondent. Furthermore, the fact that his story was picked up by a multitude of media outlets who then reported his activities further enhanced the impact he had been hoping to gain. The positive feedback that Churchill received from his coverage spurred him on to report on additional wars. All of this was pretty heady stuff for a twenty-one-year-old.

Throughout this chapter, excerpts from contemporaneous newspaper accounts will be provided to illustrate just how the public read about Churchill and his exploits. The clippings highlight the significant impact a young man can have on his fellow citizens and on the global landscape. A few examples of the reports in London newspapers concerning his Cuba trip are shown in in Figures 1 and 2. In these newspaper articles it is, again, striking how boldly Churchill provided strong recommendations, criticism and unsolicited advice to the politicians and military leaders of Spain and Cuba.

Churchill's next 'assignment' was to be a correspondent when he was on active duty in India on the North-West Frontier. He is patently clear on what he hopes to attain as a correspondent. He wrote to his mother to obtain help in achieving it:

> Herewith two letters for the D. T. [*Daily Telegraph*]. I do not know what terms you have made with them, but it should certainly not be less than £10 per letter. Having read please forward – and decide whether they should be signed or not. I am myself very much in favour of signing – as otherwise I get no credit for the letters. It may help me politically to come before the public in this way.[28]

Much to his chagrin, Churchill's mother had accepted £5 per letter and no byline. He berated his mother for her choices but in the end had to live with those terms. While in India, he wrote dispatches in 1897 not only for the *Daily Telegraph* but also for the *Pioneer Mail and Indian Weekly News*, published in both the UK and India. Churchill's agreement with the *Pioneer* was to cable them 300 words a day. In total, he would send thirty-two reports.[29]

THE INSURRECTION IN CUBA.
MR. WINSTON CHURCHILL ON THE WAR.

NEW YORK, Tuesday.—Mr. Winston Churchill has arrived at Tampa, Florida, from Cuba. In an interview on the subject of the insurrection he is reported to have said : "The Spaniards do not quite grasp the Cubans' method of fighting. Apart from England, I do not believe there is a country which could suppress this revolution, unless those in command arranged a brilliant coup. I cannot see how reinforcements can help the situation."—*Reuter*.

Figure 1. News article in *Pall Mall*, London, 10 December 1895, p. 6.

Everybody will be glad to learn, both for his own sake and for the sake of the name he bears, that Mr. Winston Churchill—Lord Randolph's eldest son—is, or was as late as Saturday, safe and sound in Cuba. Nor has he been exposed to any of those terrible dangers which the imagination of enterprising American journalists conjured up for him. It is true that he ran the risks incurred by a war correspondent, but he was never in danger of being strung up as a rebel or treated as an offender against the provisions of the Foreign Enlistment Act. "I came," he telegraphs to New York, "to witness the war. There is no truth in the statement that I have taken part in the fighting against the Cubans. I have not even fired a revolver. I am a member of General Valdez's staff by courtesy only, and am decorated with the Red Cross only by courtesy. I start for home to-day." We hope, therefore, to have some accurate information on the state of affairs in Cuba. They seem pretty hopeless to judge by the close of Mr. Churchill's letter. "The military situation," he says, "is a difficult one. It seems to me the war will never end, nor even that Spain will be able to suppress or harm the Cubans to any extent."

Figure 2. News article in *Pall Mall*, London, 9 December 1895, p. 2.

Although Churchill was dissatisfied with the terms reached with the *Daily Telegraph* (he grumbled about it for months), he had accomplished most of his initial goals: he had a national byline, even if it was 'By a Young Officer' rather than his name, and he had a national voice for his opinions; and his mother 'ensured that everyone of note – from the Prince of Wales down – knew the identity of the young officer.'[30]

It should come as no surprise that Churchill's dispatches were well written, full of action and filled with Churchillian verse, and although they covered what normally would be included in battlefield reporting, they were not bereft of opinion and commentary far beyond normal reporting. He was not averse to criticising generals, government officials or the Cabinet. Thus, he not only engendered praise from the reading public for his writing skills but was also regarded with disdain by officials both in the army and the government. Those officials did not appreciate a junior subaltern criticising and publicly challenging the decisions made by their leaders. These feelings would continue throughout Churchill's reporting of the conflicts in the Sudan and South Africa. Churchill wrote the way he thought best, and he would never stop espousing his views. He always kept his long-range goals in mind. To that end, even before all his dispatches to the *Daily Telegraph* were published, he had already begun to write a manuscript about the Indian campaign which, in short order, would become his first book, *The Story of the Malakand Field Force*.

This multitasking set the stage for the approach to writing that Churchill would embrace for the next fifty years and more; he typically had several books actively under construction or in editing, along with numerous articles for periodicals or newspapers. He would come to create a veritable writing machine staffed by multiple secretaries, researchers and proofreaders, all completely overseen and actively managed by Churchill with his prodigious mind, memory and work ethos.

The publication of *The Story of the Malakand Field Force* was well received. Many newspapers printed positive reviews (see Figures 3 and 4). This was exactly the type of press coverage that Churchill craved. This first book and its reviews had a particularly important impact on his self-esteem, and they provided a great impetus for him to continue writing. When reminiscing about this time, Churchill would write in *My Early Life*, 'The reader must remember I had never been praised before. The only comments which had

The Story of the Malakand Field Force*

No more vivid picture of the recent frontier war has yet been afforded than that given by Mr. Winston Churchill in his vigorously written and intensely interesting narrative under the above name, just published by Messrs. Longmans. Mr. Churchill is a lieutenant in the 4th Queen's Own Hussars. He was not with the force in an official capacity, but, scenting fighting from afar, he obtained six weeks' leave of absence from his regiment and posted to the frontier as correspondent of the *Daily Telegraph* and *Pioneer*. This book is, to a certain extent, made up of letters from the front to those papers, but worked up into a complete and detailed account of the operations, with numerous digressions, which are, perhaps, the most interesting part of the whole. In the opening chapter is given a sketch of the people with whom we have had to contend and their characteristics, which sheds much light on the difficulties of the operations. "The tribesmen of the Afghan border," he writes, "afford the spectacle of a people who fight without passion, and kill one another without loss of temper." They are born to warfare as the sparks fly upward. They perhaps make an attack and are repulsed—

From their point of view the incident is closed. There has been a fair fight, in which they have had the worst fortune. What puzzles them is that "the Sirkar" should regard so small an affair in a serious light. Thus the Mohmands cross the frontier, and the action of Shabkadr is fought. They are surprised and aggrieved that the Government are not content with the victory, but must needs invade their territories, and impose punishment. Or, again, the Mamunds, because a village has been burnt, assail the camp of the second brigade by night. It is a drawn game. They are astonished that the troops do not take it in good

Figure 3. Review of *The Story of the Maland Field Force* in *Colonies and India*, London, 19 March 1898, p. 20 (excerpt).

> **The Story of the Malakand Field Force: An Episode of the Frontier War.** By WINSTON L. SPENCER-CHURCHILL. (*London: Longmans, Green & Co.*)
>
> LIEUT. WINSTON CHURCHILL, of the 4th Queen's Own Hussars, is one of those officers who, wishing to gain some experience of the warfare on the Indian Frontier—an opportunity seldom afforded to cavalry regiments—joined the Malakand Field Force as a newspaper correspondent. Hence the recent appearance of a series of interesting letters from his pen in the columns of the *Daily Telegraph*. The favourable reception these letters received encouraged him to reproduce them in substantial book form, a wise proceeding, for the stirring narrative well repays portrayal. In this work the author makes no pretence to deal with the complications of the Frontier Question, nor to present a complete summary of its phases and features. He claims simply to have recorded the facts as they occurred, and his impressions as they arose, without any regard for policy, with the hope that his pages may stimulate the growing interest in the Imperial Democracy. In the first chapter he discourses on the general character of the numerous tribes on the Indian Frontier. In the second he describes the road from Nowshera to the Malakand, the Malakand Camps, and life on the Frontier. The third is devoted to "The Outbreak," its causes and preparations. The officers were just returning from polo when the news of the unexpected outbreak reached them. We read—"At 9.30 the officers sat down to dinner, still in their polo kit, which there had been no time to change. At 10 o'clock they were discussing the prospects of the approaching skirmish march; and eagerly weighing the

Figure 4. Review of *The Story of the Malakand Field Force* in *The Graphic, An Illustrated Weekly*, London, 19 March 1898, p. 23 (excerpt).

ever been made upon my work at school had been "indifferent", "Untidy", "Slovenly", "Bad", "very bad", etc.'[31] Although this statement is an obvious exaggeration, it demonstrates how much the adulation regarding the book meant to him and spurred him on to continue writing. He recognised that writing brought him three things critically important for his career: money, recognition and, now, praise for his literary skills. Churchill's multifaceted skill set was recognised by important personages including the Prince of Wales and Ian Hamilton, an important military leader who wrote in 1898, 'You have in you the raw materials for several successful careers.'[32]

Savrola, begun while he was in transit to India to join the Malakand operation, was Churchill's only 'serious' foray into fiction. He began the book before he created *The Story of the Malakand Field Force* but did not finish it until after *Malakand* was complete and while he was completing *The River War*. *Savrola* would hardly be remembered were it not written by Winston Churchill. Its characters are thinly disguised, based on people in Churchill's life. In addition to Lucile, a character who suggests Lady Randolph, and Savrola, one who is similar to Churchill himself, there is even a nurse who has many of the characteristics of Mrs Everest, his beloved nanny.[33] The goal of the book was, again, to attract press coverage and name recognition for Churchill. As he wrote to his mother in September 1897,

> In my novel I develop the idea that a 'politician' very often possesses mere physical courage. Military opinion is of course contrary. But at any rate whatever I do afterwards, no one can say anything against me on this score. I rode on my grey pony all along the skirmish line where everyone else was lying down in cover. Foolish perhaps, but I play for high stakes and given an audience there is no act too daring or too noble. Without the gallery things are different. … Still I should like to come back and wear my medals at some big dinner or some other function.[34]

Here he is describing battle behaviour that is simply not smart or appropriate: riding a bright colored horse in full view of the enemy. He is, of course, playing up to his fellow soldiers, hoping to be noticed and get named in dispatches back in London, and to be awarded medals for bravery. The novel would be published in 1900, but before its release, Churchill would serialise the book in eight parts, from May to December 1899, in *Macmillan's Magazine*. This was another approach Churchill would use frequently throughout his career; he would publish components of a new book in magazine form before the book's release. This not only gave greater exposure and advertising for the book but also generated additional income.

Churchill's next notable duty as a correspondent came when, following all the political influence he and his mother could muster, he was appointed to Kitchener's army in the Sudan. The tone of the notice he received for this appointment speaks volumes to how unwelcome he was:

> You have been attached as a supernumerary Lieutenant to the 21st Lancers for the Sudan campaign. You are to report at once at the Abassiyeh Barracks, Cairo, to the Regimental Headquarters. It is understood that you will proceed at your own expense and that in the event of your being killed or wounded in the impending operation, or for any other reason, no charge of any kind will fall on the British Army Funds.[35]

One of the promises made to political and military leaders in order to obtain Churchill's appointment was that he would refrain from actively writing about the campaign. This, however, was not to be. The ruse Churchill employed was to send the reports as those of an unnamed soldier to a friend. That friend just happened to be Oliver Borthwick, the owner of the *Morning Post*. It was agreed that, when they were published, the newspaper would conveniently, if not quite truthfully, describe the reports as being sent from a private soldier to a friend. Churchill, however, was not above letting friends know who wrote the reports, as he stated in a letter to Aylmer Haldane: 'If you look in the *Morning Post* it is possible you will see that one of my friends has committed and continues to commit an unpardonable breach of confidence by publishing letters of mine. Don't give away the pious fraud as I do not want to be recalled….'[36] From August through October 1898, Churchill would write sixteen published reports in the *Morning Post*.[37] For this assignment, Churchill was paid £15 per article. As he had done previously, he not infrequently criticised Kitchener, the army and politicians. This inflamed Kitchener and even offended the Prince of Wales, who felt compelled to admonish him:

I fear that in matters of discipline in the army I may be old-fashioned and I must say that I think an officer serving in a campaign should not write letters for the newspapers or express strong opinions of how the operations were carried out. If the Sirdar [Kitchener], as you say, viewed your joining his force with dislike – it is I am sure merely because he knows you write, for which he has the greatest objection I understand – and I cannot help agreeing with him….[38]

Although this was a significant rebuke by the Prince, Churchill likely took some delight in the letter, knowing that his commentary was being read by those whom he had wanted to read it and that the Prince thought it important enough to write to him about it. Even as is often held to be the case today, many personages believed that when it came to advertising, all news was good news. Churchill's involvement in the battle at Omdurman and his reports in the press concerning the cavalry charge led to further press coverage, as he was frequently invited to speak about these experiences. (See Figure 5 for an example of this type of coverage.)

His experience in the Sudan with the 'exhilarating' cavalry charge and the publication of his newspaper reports led Churchill to fulfil his larger goals of national recognition with the publication of a substantial two-volume book, *The River War*. This book was much more than an amalgamation of his newspaper pieces. It was a historically important and academic effort that required much in-depth research. It was the first publication for which Churchill adopted academic-type research approaches. He certainly had not been formally trained in such endeavours; he had had no university experience. The book placed this specific military operation in the broader context of the events leading up to the need for this battle. These included all the political, social, religious and territorial rights battles which resulted in the death of General Charles George Gordon at Khartoum in 1885. His death, and the British response to it, provided the impetus for the later Sudan campaign in 1898 known as the Battle of Omdurman, where the combined forces were led by Kitchener. Churchill was in the cavalry charge of this battle as a member of the 21st Lancers.

Churchill's book provides an in-depth discussion of the political and religious history of the region. It is worth noting that at this time Churchill was writing his books without the aid of paid researchers. He spent

MR. WINSTON CHURCHILL AT ROTHERHITHE.—Last night, Lieutenant Winston Churchill, who was present at the battle of Omdurman, spoke at a crowded meeting at Rotherhithe Town-hall, convened by the Rotherhithe Conservative Association. He said that the position occupied by the Unionist Government was of tremendous strength, and during the past 10 days all that was best and noblest in Radicalism had made speeches in support of that Government. We lived in very troublesome times; for the last three years guns had hardly ceased firing in one or other quarter of the globe, and the British Empire had been involved in dispute with nearly every one of the great Powers. But we had gained in them all and we had to look to the Continent of Africa to begin to see the brilliant success of the Tory foreign policy. By a series of extraordinary, successful, and brilliant campaigns on the Upper Nile we claimed to have become possessed of the whole of the Nile Valley, and we were resolved not to be robbed of the fruits of our victories. A Power with whom we had long lived on terms of friendship had deliberately crossed our path—a path which we had set our hearts upon to pursue—and had brought upon us what he could not call less than a personal affront. It was fortunate that the Government was strong; it was fortunate that those who composed it were possessed of the confidence of the country, for in the course of a few days, perhaps even a few hours, we might be called upon to make a great effort to hold what really belonged to us. War clouds were hovering over us. He thought it probable—and they all hoped that it would be probable—that these clouds might pass away. But if they should not pass away, if by any misfortune it should be found impossible to conduct Fashoda negotiations successfully, and should it be necessary to carry that debate into the field, then we should have to face the question firmly and with the traditional courage of the English people. We must take good heart, look the future well in the face, hold our heads very high, and be determined to act, and then, by God's help, we should find the way to success. A resolution approving of the Government's foreign policy, especially in Egypt, was carried with acclamation. Lady Randolph Churchill was also present at the meeting.

Figure 5. Speech, press coverage, *The Times*, London, 25 October 1898, p. 10.

considerable time researching and travelling back to the Sudan to obtain material for the book. *River War*, which runs to more than 900 pages, provides a massive amount of material on the geopolitics, religion and historical background leading up to Kitchener's Sudan campaign. The creation of this book markedly expanded Churchill's experience and approach to writing, in general. More specifically, it set a precedent: his future books would require significant levels of research. An excellent and comprehensive description of how Churchill wrote the book is provided by Cohen in his *Bibliography*.[39] The book would command excellent reviews, and reviews of the book would begin to note Churchill's previous military exploits and publications, which must have pleased Churchill immensely and further energised his writing. It is notable that when these reviews (see Figures 6 and 7) were published, Churchill was deeply involved in the Boer War.

CIVILIAN REPORTER AND PRISONER OF WAR

His next and by far most impactful role as a reporter came in the Boer War. Churchill was first invited by the founder of the *Daily Mail* to become their reporter in South Africa. At this time, he had resigned from the army, and so he would be a civilian reporter. By now, Churchill felt empowered by the success that he had had as a reporter. As he described, Oliver Borthwick

> …came to offer me an appointment as principal War Correspondent of the *Morning Post*, £250 a month, all expenses paid, entire discretion as to movements and opinions, four months' minimum guarantee of employment – such were the terms; higher, I think, than any previously paid in British journalism to War Correspondents, and certainly attractive to a young man of twenty-four with no responsibilities but to earn his own living. The earliest steamer, the *Dunottar Castle,* sailed on the 11th [October 1899], and I took my passage forthwith.[40]

Churchill had now achieved another level of recognition as a reporter and writer. Further fame would shortly follow. This is not the place to recount all of Churchill's audacious adventures during the Boer War. While Churchill was riding in an armoured train to gather information for his dispatches, the train was derailed by the Boers. He was assumed (for good reason) to be a combatant and was captured and kept as a prisoner of war. He escaped, to

"THE RIVER WAR."*

MR. WINSTON CHURCHILL'S BOOK.

A special interest attaches at this moment to anything from the pen of Mr. Winston Churchill, whose praises for his plucky conduct at the recent armoured-train fight have been in everybody's mouth. Mr. Churchill's account of the Soudan campaigns is, on the whole, the most complete and the most accurate history of the rise and fall of Mahdism which has appeared. It is divided into two volumes. The first deals with the early history of the Soudan, and of those phases of the war which preceded the final advance on Omdurman. It traces carefully and thoughtfully the rise of the Dervish power, the overthrow of the Egyptian rule, the shrinking and slow recovery of Egyptian territory, the steady advance southwards. The author's facts, carefully culled from every source of information, edited by Colonel Frank Rhodes, an officer of almost unrivalled experience in Soudanese warfare, are told conscientiously and picturesquely. The first volume of the "River War" is a careful history of political conditions and military movements. It is the work of a military historian, who weighs his words, into which, here and there, thoughts of a less strategical than philosophical character are introduced. The truth of these reflections may not always be approved, but the form in which they are spoken is attractive. In endeavouring to weigh the responsibility of Ministers in the spring of 1885 for the fall of Khartoum, the author says: "A majority voted for them. This must be their defence at the bar of History. . . . The Ministry was representative of the nation in an hour when its spirit was tame and sluggish, its courage and its fortunes low." In rehearsing the motives which induced Egypt to first conquer the Soudan, the author says: "To give peace to warring tribes, to administer justice, to strike the chains from the slave, to plant the seeds of commerce and learning, what more beautiful ideal? The act is virtuous, the exercise invigorating, the result often extremely profitable." In paying a tribute to the ability of Sir Alfred Milner, Mr. Churchill refrains from quoting more from "England in Egypt," because "it were incongruous to patch the garb of a wayfarer with the raiment of a king."

Figure 6. Review of *The River War*. *Daily News*, London, 23 November 1899, p. 6.

The River War; an Historical Account of the Reconquest of the Soudan. By WINSTON SPENCER CHURCHILL. Edited by Colonel F. RHODES, D.S.O. Longmans. 36s.

Mr. Winston Churchill has proved himself a good writer by his narrative of the Malakand campaign of 1897. That he is a good soldier also we have been lately learning from South African telegrams, which speak highly of his exertions in the calamity which befell an armoured train near Estcourt, and which ended by leaving him a prisoner in the hands of the Boers. But as he has managed to escape his captivity may only add some special information to the book that he will certainly write when the war is over. If he can describe the South African War as fully and graphically as he has described that in North-East Africa, we shall all be much indebted to him. *The River War*—as he appropriately names the latter, because it runs along the enormous length of the Nile which dominates and restricts all the strategy—is treated from the beginning. The first five chapters deal with the rise of the Mahdi and the Dervish Empire, which on his death was consolidated by the Khalifa Abdullahi. They include the tragedy of Gordon's slaughter in Khartoum, and the silent but steady commencement of the reorganisation of Egypt under British control. The actual narrative of the war begins with the advance beyond the frontier of Wady Halfa and the occupation of Akasha on March 20th, 1896. Three months later the engagement at Firket showed that the new Egyptian army was capable of encountering and defeating the Dervishes. But a long task lay before it. Slowly but surely the army crept along by the river bank, dragging after it the railway, on which it relied for its communications, its supplies, and its mobility, and which was, in fact, the indispensable instrument of its victorious march. Calamities of all kinds beset its path. Sandstorms whirled away the tents; tempests of rain, almost unknown before in Egypt, deluged the camp; the Nile delayed beyond its usual time the flood which was needed to float the steamers and gunboats; and, to crown all, the cholera claimed its victims and weakened the whole force. Nothing, however, could stop the stern determination of the Sirdar. The army toiled on, and were rewarded in September by a victory at Dongola, which restored the whole of the province to Egyptian rule. Abu Hamed—the terminus of the railway striking across the desert to avoid the great curve of the river from Wady Halfa—and Berber were seized in the following year, and early in 1898 the march was resumed southward. The battle of Atbara—near the junction of the river of that name with the Nile—was fought on April 8th, 1898, and was followed by the closing victory of Omdurman on September 2nd.

Figure 7. Review of *The River War*, *Guardian*, London, 28 December 1899, p. 21.

international acclaim, then rejoined the army, serving in the South African Light Cavalry until he finally resigned to come home and begin his political career. From November 1899 until December 1900, Churchill would file and publish more than 130 articles in the *Morning Post*. In addition, excerpts from these articles would appear in a large number of British newspapers such as *The Times*, *Standard*, *Daily News*, and *Daily Telegraph*.[41]

It is important to highlight the dramatic turn in media focus following Churchill's capture by the Boers, from Churchill as war reporter to Churchill as deeply engaged in the action of the war. This new press coverage was truly remarkable in terms of the number of dispatches published in newspapers around the world and also the sizes of the headlines and how positive and laudatory the reports of his actions and bravery were. The *Morning Post* went so far as to reprint summaries of what other newspapers had written about Churchill. For example, on 18 November 1899, the *Morning Post* published a summary of articles reprinted from eighteen other British newspapers.[42] (See Figure 8 for an excerpt of this article.) Each paper had breathlessly described his capture with terms such as 'hero', 'greatest coolness and courage', 'most gallantly', 'fearlessly', 'hero of the hour', 'courageous conduct', 'most brilliant', and 'hereditary gallantry'. The story of his capture was reported worldwide (see Figures 8–11). These praises would surely ring loudly in Churchill's mind and would be just the sort of public praise he had always striven for. In addition, the newspapers would link these heroics with Churchill's literary skills, as reported in the *Daily Telegraph*: 'Mr. Churchill is the well-known author of a recent book on the Soudan Expedition, as well as of a work on the Malakand Campaign, the son of the late Randolph Churchill, and a young man of brilliant promise.'[43]

If the story of his capture produced an abundance of press, his escape created an even greater frenzy of acclaim and plaudits, raising his status to almost hero worship. More than a hundred years on, it is difficult to capture how large an event this was and how international the coverage was. To attempt to capture some idea of the scope of the coverage, the commercial electronic newspaper archive *Newspapers.com* was searched for reports of Churchill's escape in newspapers in 1899. A number of qualifying caveats need to be understood. First, although this is an international newspaper database, it certainly is not inclusive of all or even the majority of newspapers worldwide. It is United States–centric and does not include non-English

OUR CAPTURED CORRESPONDENT.
MR. WINSTON CHURCHILL'S GALLANTRY.

The gallantry displayed by Mr. Winston Churchill, one of our War Correspondents, in the fight at Chieveley, has excited the greatest admiration, as the following extracts show :

The *Times* Correspondent : " Mr. Winston Churchill behaved most gallantly."

The *Standard* in a leading article : " Mr. Winston Churchill is said to have behaved during the skirmish with the greatest coolness and courage."

The *Daily News* Correspondent : " Mr. Winston Churchill's heroic conduct is the general subject of conversation. He rallied the party frequently, and fearlessly exposed himself."

The *Daily Telegraph* Correspondent : "Mr. Winston Churchill, who was the only Correspondent out with the train, set to work heroically with the engine hands and cleared the debris, and put many of our wounded men upon the locomotive and tender, which, though shelled,

Figure 8. 'Reports of Heroism', *Morning Post*, London, 18 November 1899, p. 5.

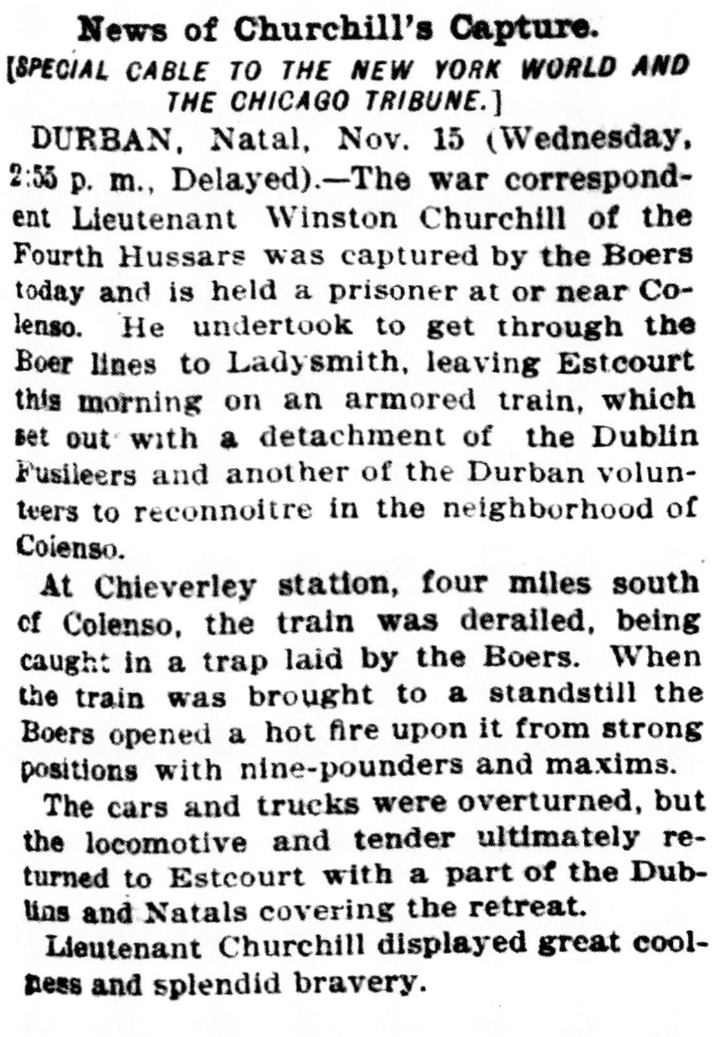

News of Churchill's Capture.

[SPECIAL CABLE TO THE NEW YORK WORLD AND THE CHICAGO TRIBUNE.]

DURBAN, Natal, Nov. 15 (Wednesday, 2:55 p. m., Delayed).—The war correspondent Lieutenant Winston Churchill of the Fourth Hussars was captured by the Boers today and is held a prisoner at or near Colenso. He undertook to get through the Boer lines to Ladysmith, leaving Estcourt this morning on an armored train, which set out with a detachment of the Dublin Fusileers and another of the Durban volunteers to reconnoitre in the neighborhood of Colenso.

At Chieverley station, four miles south of Colenso, the train was derailed, being caught in a trap laid by the Boers. When the train was brought to a standstill the Boers opened a hot fire upon it from strong positions with nine-pounders and maxims.

The cars and trucks were overturned, but the locomotive and tender ultimately returned to Estcourt with a part of the Dublins and Natals covering the retreat.

Lieutenant Churchill displayed great coolness and splendid bravery.

Figure 9. 'Churchill's Capture', Chicago, *Chicago Tribune*, 17 November 1899, p. 3.

SECOND EDITION.

MORNING POST. Nov. 17. 6.25 A.M.

THE TRANSVAÁL WAR.

ARMOURED TRAIN TRAPPED.

MR. CHURCHILL CAPTURED.

HIS COOLNESS AND BRAVERY.

Figure 10.' Churchill's Bravery', London, *London Morning Post*, 17 November 1899, p. 5 (excerpt).

> **CHURCHILL AT CHIEVELY.**
> **HE STUCK TO THE MEN IN THE FIX.**
>
> Further news about the armored train fight at Chievely shows that it was a particularly gallant affair.
>
> Mr. Churchill, the "Morning Post's" war correspondent, who failed to return to Estcourt with the train, could have escaped, but declined to do so, declaring that he would stick with the men who could not be rescued, and take his chances with them.
>
> He was at the train, but returned to the men, and was accordingly left behind.

Figure 11. 'Churchill's Loyalty', *The Sunday Times*, London, 19 November 1899, p.7 (excerpt).

newspapers. Recognising all of these disclaimers, the search produces 3,729 citations of Churchill's escape. Of these, 2,579 are in US newspapers, 818 in the UK, and 163 are in Canada. Figures 12 to 14 show excerpts from representative international articles. They highlight the types of headlines he was receiving – and their sizes – as well as the people who were lauding his courage and character. Through his efforts and exploits, Churchill had now become a significant personage who was recognised worldwide at the age of twenty-five. He now felt ready to launch himself into politics. This was all brought about by his skills as a reporter and his gallant military exploits. He was clearly a professional writer who could support himself quite nicely if he so chose. Churchill had achieved the goals he had set for himself when he had set out to be a writer: international recognition and acclaim.

Churchill, as was his wont, turned his experiences and these dispatches into additional articles and two full books, *London to Ladysmith Via Pretoria* and *Ian Hamilton's March*. Thus, by the age of twenty-six, he had established himself as a writer of note and an international personage, and he had developed an occupation which would help sustain him financially. In addition, in 1900, he was elected to Parliament.

Churchill was proud of the new occupation and the financial remuneration associated with it.

He later stated in *My Early Life* that 'the sales of the *River War* and of my two books of war correspondence from South Africa, together with the ten months salary amounts to £2500 from the *Morning Post*, had me in possession of more than £4000.'⁴⁴ To put this amount in perspective, this would be the equivalent of about £640,000 in today's money.

READING AS A PREREQUISITE TO WRITING

The South African War would be the last time Churchill covered a war as a full-time reporter, though he certainly continued to write of his personal experiences concerning war. He was now launching his career as a politician. Woods summed up his position *vis à vis* his writing occupation when he commented:

> Henceforth, journalism always loomed large in Churchill's life, but from now on the major impetus was political. Professional journalism had served its purpose for the time being. But in so doing, it had started one of the twentieth century's greatest writers on one of his several careers. And if Churchill's literary verve succumbed from time to time to the extended purple patches of rhetoric, at least it started – and succeeded – in the toughest sphere of all.[45]

Although Churchill's penchant and need for reading began early in life, his reading habits from childhood on (at least up until the time he wrote *My Early Life*) are worthy of mention for the purposes of this book. What one reads and studies shapes one's world view and approach to writing. Churchill was no exception, but there is no comprehensive list of the books that Churchill read, and his impressive library had, by and large, dispersed at the time of his death, although there are some remnants at Chartwell.

Referring to his early schooling, Churchill noted that 'The greatest pleasure I had in those days was reading. When I was nine and a half my father gave me *Treasure Island*, and I remember the delight with which I devoured it.'[46] A recent article notes that the young Churchill enjoyed the popular novels of Henry Rider Haggard and that he specifically requested his new novel, *Jess* (1887), from his mother. The article provides much additional insight into Churchill the reader and book collector.[47]

After leaving school, while serving in the army in India, Churchill realised that, having not gone to university, he had not been exposed to much of the great literature and thinkers. He resolved to correct the deficit

WINSTON CHURCHILL HEARD FROM.

The Plucky Soldier-Correspondent Tells How He Escaped From His Boer Prison at Pretoria—He Has Gone to Aid Buller in Natal.

LIEUT. WINSTON CHURCHILL,
As He Appears in His Uniform of the Fourth, Queen's Own, Hussars.

LORENZO MARQUES, December 22.—Mr. Winston Churchill arrived here late last night, and left for Durban by the steamer Induna. His intention is to join General Buller at the seat of operations in Natal, where the knowledge he has gained during his passage from Estcourt to Pretoria as a prisoner and from Pretoria to this place as a refugee will be invaluable.

A THRILLING NARRATIVE.

the unflinching and uncompromising prosecution of the war.

"On the afternoon of December 12 the Transvaal's Secretary of War informed me that there was little chance of my release. I therefore resolved to escape, and the same night I left the State Schools prison in Pretoria by climbing the wall when the sentries' backs were turned momentarily. I walked through the streets of the town without disguise, meeting many burghers, but was not challenged in the crowd. I got through the pickets of the town guard and struck the Delagoa Bay railway. I walked along it, evading the watchers at the bridges and culverts and waited for a train beyond the first station.

"The 11.10 goods train from Pretoria had arrived before I reached the place, and was moving at full speed. I boarded it with great difficulty and hid under coal sacks. I jumped from the train before dawn, and was sheltered during the day in a small wood, in company with a huge vulture, who displayed a lively interest in me.

"I walked on at dusk. There was no more trains that night. The danger of meeting the guards of the line continued, but I was obliged to follow it as I had no compass or map. I had to make wide detours to avoid bridges, stations and huts, and so my progress was very slow.

"Chocolate is not a satisfying food. The outlook was gloomy, but I persevered with God's help. For five days my food supply was very precarious. I was lying up by daytime and walking by night.

"Meanwhile my escape had been discovered and my description telegraphed everywhere. All trains were searched, and

Figure 12. 'Churchill's Escape', Montreal, *Montreal Star*, 27 December 1899, p. 8 (excerpt).

CHURCHILL TELLS OF HIS ESCAPE.

Sixty Hours of Misery Endured Before He Cleared the Watchful Eyes of His Boer Hunters.

Figure 13. 'Churchill's Escape', Montreal, *Evening Mail*, 27 December 1899, p. 1 (excerpt).

"THE STORY OF MY ESCAPE."

TELEGRAPHED BY

WINSTON SPENCER CHURCHILL,

OUR WAR CORRESPONDENT.

LOURENÇO MARQUES, DEC. 21, 10 P.M.

On the afternoon of the 12th the Transvaal Government's Secretary for War informed me that there was little chance of my release.

I therefore resolved to escape.

The same night I left the State Schools Prison in Pretoria by climbing the wall when the sentries' backs were turned momentarily.

I walked through the streets of the town without any disguise, meeting many Burghers, but I was not challenged.

In the crowd I got through the pickets of the Town Guard and struck the Delagoa Bay railroad.

I walked along it, evading the watchers at the bridges and culverts.

I waited for a train beyond the first station out of the town.

Figure 14. 'The Story of My Escape', *Morning Post*, London, 28 December 1899, p. 5 (excerpt).

by his own hard work. He embarked on an impressive self-education and improvement programme. As he states in *My Early Life*,

> So I resolved to read history, philosophy, economics, and things like that; and I wrote to my mother asking for such books as I had heard of on these topics. She responded with alacrity, and every month the mail brought me a substantial package of what I thought were standard works. In history I decided to begin with Gibbon. Someone had told me that my father had read Gibbon with delight; that he knew whole pages of it by heart, and that it had greatly affected his style of speech and writing. So without more ado I set out upon the eight volumes of Dean Milman's edition of Gibbon's *Decline and Fall of the Roman Empire*. I was immediately dominated both by the story and the style. All through the long glistening middle hours of the Indian day, from when we quitted stables till the evening shadows proclaimed the hour of Polo, I devoured Gibbon.[48]

He would go on to read Macaulay, Plato, Aristotle, Darwin, Malthus – and the list goes on and on. He was clearly absorbing and critiquing various styles of writing and forming his own concepts of how he would meld them into his own unique style. Churchill considered this self-education in India to be the most impactful education he received.

After Churchill's army days, he continued to read voraciously for the rest of his life. The scope of literature that he enjoyed was wide-ranging. However, it excluded hard-core science, which he never really embraced – although he certainly was captivated by science fiction, particularly the works of H.G. Wells. A brief mention of some of his favourite topics and books will be provided here. The reader is also directed to the recent article noted above for more detail.[49]

History and military history were what he most frequently read, including everything on Napoleon and Marlborough, Gibbon's *The Rise and Fall of the Roman Empire* and Hallam's multi-volume *Constitutional History of England*. In the realm of poetry he enjoyed Keats, Milton, Tennyson, Housman, Wordsworth and Burns. He enjoyed much French literature; he amassed a very large collection of literature and history in French. He liked reading in French, particularly original editions. He also enjoyed conversing in French – although his facility with conversational French, according to most sources, was less than adequate. Churchill recognised this fact and even made jokes about it. When he met with native French speakers, he always desired to speak French with them, much to their chagrin. At one conference, as the French were struggling to understand him, a gentleman who was attempting to help the conversation had Churchill turn to him and say, 'Would you please stop translating my French into French!'[50]

Novels by both American and British authors, including Hardy, Dickens, Austen, Twain, Harriet Beecher Stowe and Steinbeck were of great interest to him, and he enjoyed reading them to relax. Works of philosophy, such as Plato's *Republic* and Aristotle's *Ethics* and *Politics,* were among those he read less frequently. Dramatic plays from Greek, Roman and modern times, especially Shakespeare, were frequently read. The great breadth of his readings surely impacted his writing and provided him a wealth of knowledge from which to recall the many quotes and allusions to literature that he included in all he wrote. As would be expected, when Churchill was writing one of his myriad books, the topic being written about took front stage in his reading repertoire. To say that Churchill was extremely well read would be an understatement; the frequency with which he quoted the world's literature attests to that fact.

That Churchill was a serious reader (and collector) of books with a prodigious memory and detailed recall of content has been ably documented by a wide range of observers. A few vignettes and stories will suffice to make the point.

In a letter to his wife that was written in February 1924 while he was working on his book *The World Crisis,* Churchill notes, 'I continue to read a great deal about the war, consuming on average a book a day.'[51]

Churchill was a lifelong admirer and voracious reader of Shakespeare. His recall of what he had read in Shakespeare would significantly disturb Richard Burton, the magnificent Shakespearean actor. Burton recalled that in 1953, Churchill came to see him perform *Hamlet* at the Old Vic. He notes, 'I came on stage, feeling absolutely diabolical [he had been in hospital], and I hear this diabolical rumble in the front rows of the stalls. I wondered what it was. It was Winston speaking the lines with me. I could not shake him off … in "To be or not to be" he was with me to the death.'[52] For those who are curious, that is twenty-four lines of verse! A much longer demonstration of his recall was exhibited when, as a student, he recited from memory 1,200 lines of Macaulay's *Lays of Ancient Rome* to win a school prize.[53]

A final vignette: during Churchill's visit to Washington in 1943, he and Roosevelt and their entourage were travelling to Shangri-La (now called Camp David) when Harry Hopkins, advisor to Roosevelt, recited the first two lines of John Greenleaf Whittier's poem *Barbara Frietchie*, an 1863 Civil War poem about an elderly woman challenging a Confederate general and supporting the American flag. No one else in the entourage continued on with the poem, so Churchill picked up the lines from memory and continued to the end of the poem with others chiming in on the chorus. Churchill noted that the group, including Roosevelt, was astonished that he knew the entire poem. Churchill later noted that no one had corrected his errors, even though he was sure he had made some mistakes.[54] Understandably so, as Churchill certainly hadn't read the poem in years prior to his recitation.

In a 1929 article, *Politicians and Their Books*, Walter T. Roberts describes the books in the libraries of major political figures, as well as those leaders' current reading interests. He includes Stanley Baldwin, David Lloyd George and Winston Churchill. Roberts's article was published while Churchill was writing *My Early Life*. According to the author, Churchill 'is probably the most widely read man in political life today'. He continues:

> In Mr. Winston Churchill's library, at his home near Westerham, there is to be found one of the most varied collections of books possessed by any book-lover. Modern fiction, French and English, English classics, the Greek and Latin classics, books on philosophy, all kinds of memoirs, histories of all kinds, poetical works, dramatic works, all jostle on the bookshelves. And it is safe to say that the owner has read every book in his curiously assorted collection.[55]

It is apparent that Churchill's only novel, *Savrola*, written when he was twenty-three, contains much autobiography. At this time, he was only beginning his library in earnest, but through his discussion of Savrola's library we can easily picture the type of library he imagined for himself (the below quote was written by Churchill in *Savrola* and quoted by Roberts in his article):

The room was lit by electric light in portable shaded lamps. The walls were covered with shelves filled with well-used volumes. To that Pantheon of Literature none were admitted till they had been read and valued. It was a various library – the philosophy of Schopenhauer divided Kant from Hegel, who jostled the memoirs of St. Simon and the latest French novel; *Rasselas* and *La Curée* lay side by side; eight substantial volumes of Gibbon's *History* were not perhaps inappropriately prolonged by a fine edition of *Decameron*; the *Origin of Species* rested by the side of a black-letter *Bible* [this speaks volumes about Churchill's beliefs]; the *Republic* maintained an equilibrium with *Vanity Fair* and the *History of Modern European Morals*. A volume of Macaulay's *Essays* lay on the writing-table itself. The library of the imagination of a young man of twenty-three has become, on a much more extensive scale, the actual library of the Chancellor of the Exchequer. The rapidity with which Mr. Churchill has always been able to read allows him to indulge in general reading more extensively than any other man actively engaged in public affairs finds time to do.[56]

As noted above, Churchill wrote extensively about his early war experiences in both articles for the press and book format. Churchill always envisaged that these publications would later be used in the creation of an autobiography. Thus, they presaged the publication of *My Early Life*. There were two types of publications created from Churchill's life experiences: the group that were published shortly after the events described (1895–1900), and those that were written more than twenty years later (1920s). The latter group would not only enhance his income but, more importantly, also be used directly, as will be seen in the next chapter, as the backbone framework for certain sections of his autobiography. As was often Churchill's custom with his latter books, some publications were created specifically as prepublication market-enhancers for *My Early Life*.

The following is a list of all the Churchill publications containing materials used directly in the creation of *My Early Life*.

BOOKS AND COLLECTIONS OF WAR CORRESPONDENCE AND HISTORIC VOLUMES

1. *The Story of the Malakand Field Force,* London, Longmans, Green and Co., 1898, 1st Br. ed.
2. *The River War*: *An Historical Account of the Reconquest of the Sudan*, London, Green and Co., 1899 (2 volumes), 1st Br. ed.
3. *London to Ladysmith Via Pretoria*, London, Longmans and Co., 1900, 1st Br. ed.
4. *Ian Hamilton's March*, London, Longmans, Green and Co., 1900, 1st Br. ed.

ANTHOLOGIES OF WAR CORRESPONDENCE PUBLISHED POST RELEASE OF *MY EARLY LIFE*

It should be noted that Churchill had access to all the original correspondence (dispatches) later published in these anthologies listed below at the time of the writing of *My Early Life*.

5. *Frontiers and Wars*, London, Eyre & Spottswood, 1962. This is a condensed version of war correspondence from his first four frontier wars.
6. *Young Winston's Wars: The Original Dispatches of Winston S. Churchill War Correspondent 1897-1900*, Frederick Woods, ed., London, Leo Cooper, London, 1972. Covers India, Sudan and South Africa.

PUBLISHED ARTICLES ABOUT WAR EXPERIENCES, 1923–1925

From December 1923 through August 1925, Churchill would publish a series of thirteen articles about the exciting experiences he had had in India, the Sudan and South Africa for prominent periodicals in both the UK and the US, such as the *Strand Magazine, Cosmopolitan, and Nash's Pall Mall.* These are listed below.

1. 'My Escape From the Boers'
   a. *Strand Magazine*, December 1923, Vol. LXVI, 537–40, 542–4, 546–7
   b. *Strand Magazine*, January 1924, Vol. LXVII, 14–18, 20–23
   c. *Cosmopolitan*, January 1924, Vol. LXXVI, No. 1, 30–34, 161–6
2. 'The Eve of Omdurman'; 'Omdurman'
   a. *Nash's Pall Mall*, February 1925, Vol. LXXIV, No. 382, 46–7. 124–7

    b. *Nash's Pall Mall*, March 1925, Vol. LXXIV, No. 283, 42–3, 124–7
3. 'A Trapped Armored Train'
    a. *Cosmopolitan*, January 1925, Vol. LXXVIII, No. 7, 70–72
4. 'In an Indian Valley'
    a. *Nash's Pall Mall*, September 1927, Vol. LXXIX, no. 412, 20–23, 95–7
5. 'When I Was Young'; 'A Hand-To-Hand Fight with Desert Fanatics'
    a. *Strand Magazine*, December 1924, Vol. LXVIII, 604–12
    b. *Cosmopolitan*, December 1924, Vol. LXXVII, No. 6, 94–5, 152–5
6. 'My Difference with Kitchener'; 'A Difference With Kitchener'
    a. *Cosmopolitan*, November 1924, Vol. LXXVII, No. 5, 60–61, 135–7
    b. *Nash's Pall Mall*, January 1925, Vol. LXXIV, No. 381, 46–7, 111–14
7. 'When I Risked Court Martial in Search of War'
    a. *Cosmopolitan*, October 1924, Vol. LXXVII, 80–81, 112–13
8. 'How Rt. Hon. Winston Churchill, MP and General Botha First Met'
    a. *Nash's Pall Mall*, August 1925, Vol. LXXV, 48–49, 134, 136, 138

These articles were written in 1923–1925, during the remarkably busy period of Churchill's life when he was attempting to return to Parliament following the loss of his seat in late 1922; doing major renovations on Chartwell; and frantically writing to generate income. Shortly after Churchill lost his seat, he moved his family to Cannes, where he spent his time painting and writing part of *The World Crisis*, his multivolume history of the First World War. Churchill's financial status in this period was disastrous. The costs of renovations for Chartwell had been grossly underestimated and did nothing but climb, climb, and climb again as it was discovered just how dilapidated and deteriorated all the components of the ancient house were. As Roberts has stated, 'The costs of renovating and running Chartwell were debilitating.'[57] Churchill's characteristic response was to talk about cost-cutting but never implement it, while borrowing more money and working harder at writing more to increase inward cash flow. For those interested in the gory but fascinating details of Churchill's finances, please see David Lough's excellent book *No More Champagne: Churchill and His Money*.[58] By November 1924, he was not only back in Parliament but had also been appointed Chancellor of the Exchequer. This appointment only made his life busier and more hectic, yet it did not slow his writing or his output of articles and books.

There are a number of reasons Churchill began this series of articles retelling the story of his dramatic adventures as a young soldier and reporter. First, as was just mentioned, Churchill was in dire need of money and writing is what he did for money. Secondly, as Churchill states in the preamble to the first instalment in the *Strand Magazine* in December 1923,

> During the Boer War, in which I acted as War Correspondent for the *Morning Post* and later served as a Lieutenant in the South African Light Horse, I gave some account of my escape from Pretoria. It was not, however, possible for me to tell the full story. To have done so would have been to compromise the liberty and perhaps the lives of those who helped me, and also to aggravate needlessly the difficulties of other British prisoners then still in captivity. For many years these reasons have disappeared; but I have not found the time or inclination to return to those exciting days, having since then been plunged almost continuously in strife and stress. Now for the first time having recovered that leisure [he was not a member of Parliament anymore] and freedom from worry and anxiety to which we look forward as a sequel to stirring times, I have found it possible again to turn over the records and memoranda of this vanished epoch in British affairs, and to complete an account which when it had been written had necessarily to be mutilated and mysterious.[59]

This is the main reason Churchill provides for the rewriting of his early wartime experiences, and the one he wants us all to believe. However, a third reason is that he was preparing and gathering material needed to write his autobiography, which would be an even more extensive and action-filled rendition of his youthful exploits. He would excerpt heavily from these articles. Substantial sections were transcribed *in toto* into the autobiography. (This will be discussed in detail in Chapter 4.) Churchill would start writing the book in earnest in 1928.

Finally, a less-recognised, but still important, fourth reason to republish the events – particularly his escape from the Boers – was Churchill's desire to get into print his full and complete version of what transpired during his escape. Following his initial presentation of his escape in the newspaper reports and, subsequently, in book form, Captain Haldane, a colleague and senior officer, challenged Churchill's version of his escape both behind the scenes and, sometimes, quite publicly. Haldane said that Churchill had escaped using Haldane's plan and had then left Haldane in the lurch while escaping alone. Haldane believed that Churchill had not thought or worried about the others who had been part of the plan but had been selfish and uncaring. Churchill did not agree. A full discussion of this topic can be found in Roy Jenkins's book *Churchill: A Biography*.[60] Churchill and Haldane would never fully agree on what had actually happened. For additional information on this topic, see Appendix 6 Chapter 4 Escape.

From Churchill's perspective, publishing his full version of his escape had the effect on the public that he had desired. The two-part *Strand* article published in 1923-24 and a similar article published in 1924 in North America in *Cosmopolitan* were highly advertised and very well received by the public, if not by Haldane.[61] Newspapers by the dozens across the UK, the US and Canada carried articles about the periodical story as well as advertisements promoting the publications. In the UK, one newspaper stated that

> In Mr. Churchill's article, 'My Escape from the Boers' – now told in full for the first time, the Christmas 'Strand Magazine' has an exceptionally attractive feature. It will be remembered that during the Boer War Mr. Churchill gave some account of his escape from Pretoria, though it was not possible for him to tell the full story. It is a thrilling story, most graphically told.[62]

Advertisements carried large-letter headlines such as 'The Rt. Hon. Winston S. Churchill – The First of the Exciting Chapters from his dramatic life – My Escape From the Boers.'[63] The later article 'A Trapped Armored Train' was also widely advertised.[64] Churchill's version of the story thus received the worldwide coverage he had desired.

As will be seen, large sections of all the articles listed above were excerpted and placed in the autobiography. Churchill's approach to writing books and articles was always to have them reviewed by professional friends, experts and literati. He followed this same pattern for his article 'My Escape From the Boers'.

In a 27 September 1923 letter to Edward (Eddie) Marsh, private secretary, friend and frequent reviewer of much of his literary work, Churchill wrote:

My dear Eddie,

You are always so kind in looking over my other stuff and I have such confidence in your English and punctuation, that I should be grateful to you if you would look through the proof of one or two articles I have written lately. The first is about my escape from the Boers which I have written for the Strand Magazine. I will send you the second portion of it if you will let me.

Yours ever,

W[65]

This literary relationship between Churchill and Marsh would bear much fruit over the years. Another interaction between them, which took place shortly after the publication of *My Early Life*, illuminates much of Churchill's thinking about his approach to writing. In 1932, Churchill's friend the newspaper magnate Lord Riddell, who had received an inscribed *My Early Life* as a gift in 1930, asked Churchill if he would be willing to write six articles on some of the world's great literature 'as retold by Winston Churchill'. These were not to be summaries (à la York Notes or CliffsNotes) concerning the themes and take-home points but, rather, Churchill's own spin on the story. Churchill was thrilled; he thought the idea fabulous. Not surprisingly, Churchill would be well compensated for his work. Churchill hired Marsh to help with this project. Marsh created first drafts of about 2,500 words on books such as *Ben-Hur*, *The Count of Monte Cristo*, and *Jane Eyre*, among many others. These would be published in newspapers such as the *News of the World* and the *Chicago Tribune*.[66]

Churchill wrote to Marsh, 'If I had read about 2,500 words of your ideas on each of the selected books, it would be a foundation of which I could tell my story. I shall of course be writing them all again myself.'[67] This would be the start of another of Churchill's writing 'cottage industries', and it would fit in well with the other works in which he was constantly engaged. His staff would eventually term these pieces 'potboilers', as they were relatively short pieces, quick to produce, quick to get out the door, and quick to return good money.[68]

Churchill's approach to these 'retellings' was to make them new and exciting – not just boring condensations or summaries of facts. In his correspondence with Marsh, Churchill made it clear that his goal was to have each article submitted to the publisher total about 5,000 words. Marsh created a draft of the *Count of Monte Cristo* for review and discussion with Churchill. Churchill was quick to reply: '[W]e are not writing great stories summarised, but great stories retold.' (Obviously, retold in Churchill's voice and manner, full of excitement and word play.) Churchill continued: 'It is essential to select the salient features of the tale and make them live in their fullness, leaving the rest in darkness. In *Monte Cristo* I shall give 1000 words to the plot against Dantès and 2500 to the terrific prison drama and 1500 to the revenge. That well fixes the dimensions.'[69] The retellings would use Churchill's words and phrasing and his selection of the storyline to highlight what he thought was most important and interesting about these great works, not necessarily what the author might have thought most important. This approach makes these works still worthy of reading and able to be enjoyed.

These works ended up being extremely popular and well received. In total, there would be eighteen such pieces published. A full description of them in provided in Cohen's *Bibliography*.[70] Churchill had developed a distinctive personal voice and style in all his written works. This approach, especially as it relates to *My Early Life*, will be further described throughout this book.

Finally, Phyllis Moir, one of Churchill's private secretaries who wrote of her experiences with Churchill as a writer, commented upon Churchill's pathway to success:

> The solid foundation of these achievements has been a boundless zest for living, a keen sense of personal integrity, and an infinite capacity for taking pains. The lad who was at the bottom of the bottom class at Harrow made himself into one of the finest authors and orators of the English language. How? By years of eager, purposive reading; years of reading not the good but the best; years devoted to thinking about words, sounding them out to himself; years of endlessly polishing and repolishing everything he wrote until he could do no better. He disciplined a 'brilliant but erratic' mind until its tidiness was the envy of every civil servant.[71]

Notes

1. Winston S. Churchill, *My Early Life*, London, Butterworth, 1930, pp. 30–31.
2. E.D.W. Chaplin, *Winston Churchill and Harrow: Memories of the Prime Minister's School Days 1888-1892*, Harrow, Harrow School Bookshop, 1941, p. 34.
3. Douglas S. Russell, *Winston Churchill Soldier: The Military Life of a Gentleman at War*, London, Brassy's, 2005, p. 28.
4. Randolph S. Churchill, *Winston S. Churchill CV I part I*, Boston, Houghton Mifflin Company, 1967, p. 311.
5. Russell, *Winston Churchill Soldier*, p. 29.
6. Randolph S. Churchill, *Winston S. Churchill CV 1 part 1*, pp. 308–319.
7. Andrew Roberts, *Churchill: Walking with Destiny*, London, Allen Lane, 2018, p. 21.
8. Churchill, *My Early Life*, p. 55.
9. Roberts, *Churchill Walking with Destiny*, p. 21–2.
10. William Manchester, *The Last Lion: Winston Spencer Churchill: Visions of Glory, 1874-1932*, Boston, Little Brown and Company, 1983, pp. 161–2.
11. David Lough, *No More Champagne: Churchill and His Money*, New York, Picador, 2015, p. 37.
12. Lough, *No More Champagne*, pp. 49, 73, 118, 124, 136–7.
13. Peter Clarke, *Mr. Churchill's Profession*, New York, Bloomsbury Press, 2012, p. 37.
14. Churchill, *My Early Life*, p. 88.
15. Churchill, *My Early Life*, p. 89.
16. Churchill, *My Early Life*, p. 90.
17. Churchill, *My Early Life*, p. 90–91.
18. Frederick Woods, *Young Winston's Wars*, New York, Viking Press, 1972, p. XV.
19. Randolph S. Churchill, *Winston S. Churchill Youth 1874-1900*, Boston, Houghton Mifflin, 1966, p. 256.
20. Woods, *Young Winston's Wars*, p. XV.
21. Churchill, *Youth 1874-1900*, pp. 259–60.
22. 'A Churchill in Cuba', *The Akron Beacon-Journal*, Akron, OH, 8 November, 1895, p.1.
23. 'Young Churchill Going to Cuba', *Buffalo Courier*, Buffalo, NY, 11 November 1895, p. 1.
24. 'Another Big Battle', *The Sun*, New York, NY, 6 December 1895, p. 2.
25. 'Churchill in a Fight', *Chicago Tribune*, Chicago, IL, 6 December 1895, p. 4.
26. *Brooklyn Daily Eagle*, Brooklyn, NY, 8 December 1895, p. 4; 'Mr. Churchill in Cuba', *Birmingham Evening Mail*, West Midlands, UK, 9 December 1895, p. 4; *Buffalo News*, Buffalo, NY, 8 December 1895, p. 2; 'Far From Hopeless', *Buffalo*

Courier, Buffalo, NY, 15 December 1895, p. 1; and 'Can't Cope With the Cubans', *The Sun*, New York, NY, 15 December 1895, p. 3.
27. 'They Cannot Win', *Democrat and Chronicle*, Rochester, NY, 16 December 1895, p. 2.
28. Randolph S. Churchill, Winston S. *Churchill Companion Volume 1 part 2 1896-1900*, p. 784.
29. Ronald I. Cohen, *Bibliography of the Writings of Sir Winston Churchill*, New York, Thoemmes, 2006, pp. 1282–7.
30. Woods, *Young Winston's Wars*, p. xvi.
31. Churchill, *My Early Life*, p. 170.
32. Clarke, *Mr. Churchill's Profession*, p. 43.
33. Churchill, *My Early Life*, pp. 16–20, 86, and 140.
34. Randolph S. Churchill, *Youth 1874-1900*, p. 346.
35. Churchill, *My Early Life*, p. 182.
36. Randolph S. *Churchill, Companion vol 1*, 1896-1900, p. 964.
37. Cohen, *Bibliography*, pp. 1289–91.
38. Churchill, *Youth 1874-1900*, p. 182.
39. Cohen, *Bibliography*, pp. 35–40.
40. Churchill, *My Early Life*, p. 244.
41. Cohen, *Bibliography*, pp. 1295–1314.
42. 'Our Captured Correspondent', *Morning Post*, London, 15 November 1899, p. 2.
43. *The Daily Telegraph*, London, 17 November 1899, p. 9.
44. Churchill, *My Early Life*, p. 374.
45. Woods, *Young Winston's Wars*, p. xxiv.
46. Churchill, *My Early Life*, pp. 26–7.
47. Christopher C. Harmon, 'The Books that Churchill Read: The Self-Education of a Statesman', *American Spectator*, 21 May 2022, https://spectator.org/the-books-that-churchill-read/
48. Churchill, *My Early Life*, p. 125.
49. Churchill, *My Early Life*, p. 372.
50. Christopher C. Harmon, 'The Books that Churchill Read'.
51. Mary Soames, *Winston and Clementine: The Personal Letters of the Churchills*, Boston, Houghton Mifflin, 2001, p. 278.
52. 'Theatre', *The Guardian*, 31 July 2015.
53. Churchill, *My Early Life*, pp. 32–3.
54. Winston S. Churchill, *The Second World War, Vol IV The Hinge of Fate*, London, Cassell & Co., 1951, pp. 711–12.

55. Walter T. Roberts, 'Politicians and Their Books', *Windsor Magazine*, London, January 1929, pp. 149–156.
56. Roberts, *Politicians and Their Books*, pp. 150–51.
57. Andrew Roberts, *Churchill: Walking with Destiny*, London, Allan Lane, 2018, pp. 294, 299.
58. David Lough, *No More Champagne: Churchill and His Money*, New York, Picador, 2015.
59. Winston S. Churchill, 'My Escape From the Boers', *Strand Magazine*, December 1923, p. 537.
60. Roy Jenkins, *Churchill: A Biography*, New York, Farrar, Straus and Giroux, 2001, pp. 51–
61. *Country Life*, London, 14 December 1923, p. lvi.
62. *Newquay Express and Cornwall County Chronicle*, Newquay, UK, 14 December 1923, p. 6.
63. *The Daily Telegraph*, London, 1 December 1923, p. 13; *The Philadelphia Inquirer*, Philadelphia, PA, 14 December 1923, p. 3; *Chicago Tribune*, Chicago, 12 December 1923, p. 15; *The Province*, Vancouver, BC, 19 December 1923, p. 3.
64. *The Cincinnati Enquirer*, Cincinnati, OH, 12 December 1924, p. 9.
65. Gilbert, *Winston S. Churchill, Companion Volume V, Part 1*, p. 61.
66. Richard M. Langworth, 'Winston Churchill Retells the World's Great Stories, Part 1', *The Churchill Project*, 3 August 2023, https://winstonchurchill.hillsdale.edu/worlds-great-stories/
67. Martin Gilbert, ed., *The Churchill Documents, vol. 12, The Wilderness Years 1929-1935*, Hillsdale, MI, Hillsdale College Press, 2009, p. 463.
68. Richard M. Langworth, ed., *Churchill by Himself: In His Own Words*, New York, NY, Rosetta Books, 2016, p. 60.
69. Gilbert, *The Wilderness Years*, p. 473.
70. Cohen, *Bibliography*, pp. 1383–8.
71. Phyllis Moir, 'Why Churchill', *Current History and Forum*, Vol. 52, No. 12, May 1941, p. 12.

CHAPTER 3

Writing *My Early Life*

Before describing the writing of *My Early Life*, it is prudent to describe the process Churchill utilised to write his books by the late 1920s or early 1930s. Although Churchill produced a prodigious quantity of books, articles, pamphlets, short stories – and even a screen play – he was never a full-time or professional writer in the classic sense. That is, he was not trained academically as a writer, historian or journalist. He was, in fact, mostly self-educated in literature, history, and politics through the extensive reading that began when he was a student at Harrow and then, in an accelerated self-designed programme, as a young officer in India. In spite of his suggestion that he was a poor student, Churchill did indeed learn much history and certainly learned how to write well while at Harrow. He won a number of awards for his academic prowess in English. His lack of an academic diploma at university would trouble Churchill himself – or, at least, so he claimed – and would tarnish his career in the minds of some academics and professional newspaper editors and even at the Royal Academy. Woods cites examples of this biased and not infrequently held opinion.[1] For example, Colin Coote, the managing editor of the *Daily Telegraph*, wrote of Churchill in 1953, 'Churchill is certainly the King of the Freelancers, but he is not a professional.'[2] This would seem to be a bit petty in its pronouncement, as Churchill had been one of the highest, if not *the* highest, paid correspondents in his early career, and he would continue to be paid vast sums for his articles and praised widely for his writings.[3] Not only was he paid well, but, as has been described previously, his writings were also widely sought after and published in newspapers and periodicals around the world. In addition, he had created multiple books from his wartime reporting which had been well received, as was his biography of his father,

Lord Randolph Churchill. It is unclear what Churchill would have had to do to have been considered a professional in Coote's mind.

Another example is this comment by Professor J.H. Plumb: 'In those fields where his work challenges comparison with professional history, Churchill remains, by the most generous assessment, a gifted amateur.'[4] Certainly, none of these types of comments detracted from Churchill's appeal to the non-academic and wider public or his success in publishing and selling his books. It is widely accepted that he was one of the most successful and profitable writers of the twentieth century.[5] Nor did the lack of a university degree prevent the Nobel Committee from awarding him the Nobel Prize in Literature in 1953.

Recognising that he was not a full-time writer, how did someone who was obviously talented, with a prodigious memory and an apparently indefatigable work ethic, create so many excellent manuscripts for publication while performing his duties as a politician, parliamentarian and speaker? Churchill's duties when he was a cabinet minister were especially time-consuming, yet he still managed to be a prolific writer at those times. The most senior of these positions included being the First Lord of the Admiralty (twice), Chancellor of the Exchequer, and Prime Minister (twice).

The only way to accomplish this task was to create an effective and high-performing writing organisation that had a flexibility responsive to Churchill's schedule, and sufficient structure and people to work continually and in harmony – much like an orchestra, with Churchill as the supreme conductor. This is exactly what Churchill did at Chartwell, beginning in the 1920s. According to Woods, '*Lord Randolph Churchill* was the first and last major work that Churchill tackled single-handedly; it was the last he physically wrote.'[6] Beginning with his work on *The World Crisis*, his writing organisation was composed of paid research assistants (usually young men just out of university); his personal secretaries, such as Mrs Pearman, who was with Churchill as he wrote *My Early Life*; typists and stenographers to take dictation; and a large cadre of friends, associates, noted experts and colleagues to whom Churchill would turn when in need of particular facts or skill sets. In addition, when he was nearing the final set of galley proofs, he would enlist leading military and political leaders to provide feedback. The size and scope of the group of contributors was highly variable, depending on the book. It was also not uncommon for there to be more than one "team" functioning at any given time. The common focal point was always Churchill. The 1930s would see Churchill create his most comprehensive and long-lasting team, one that would – with breaks during the Second World War – serve him until the mid-1950s. A few comments on this team, which came to be known as the 'Syndicate', are certainly warranted here.

CREATION OF THE WRITING TEAM

In 1936, while Churchill was still working on *Marlborough*, he needed to add a new researcher to the team. As usual, he wanted a young man with First Class Honours from Oxford's graduate programme in History.[7] William Deakin, a twenty-two-year-old recent graduate, was to become a key player in the production of the last volume of *Marlborough*, as well as *The History of the English-Speaking Peoples* and the *Second World War* memoirs. The team would remain active and functioning until the early 1950s, with several interruptions for war and other emergencies, and the team would expand, and contract as was necessary relating to changes in the work and topics and people moving on to other careers. The many mainstays of the Syndicate included Deakin, Edward Marsh, Sir Henry Pownall, Dennis Kelly, Lord Ismay, Maurice Ashley, C.C. Wood and G.M. Young, among many others.

Deakin tells an amazing story of the diligence of Churchill and the team, as well as Churchill's incredible ability to focus on the task at hand and block out everything else when he needed to. This event occurred in April 1940 when Churchill was First Lord of the Admiralty. The team at the time was working on *A History of the English-Speaking Peoples*, and Churchill had just finished a long day of meetings and planning for the war effort. It was eleven o'clock that night in an Admiralty room where Deakin picks up the story:

> Naval signals awaited attention, Admirals tapped impatiently on the door of the First Lord's room, while on one occasion talk inside ranged round the spreading shadows of the Norman invasion and the figure of Edward the Confessor who, as Churchill wrote 'comes down to us faint, misty, frail.'
>
> I can still see the map on the wall, with the disposition of the British Fleet off Norway, and hear the voice of the First Lord as he grasped with his usual insight the strategic position of 1066. But this was no lack of attention to current business. It was a measure of the

man with the supreme historical eye. The distant episodes were as close and real as the mighty events on hand.[8]

This was to be the last meeting of the team for the duration of the war. After the war, Deakin and the team reassembled and continued on with the writing of Churchill's war memoirs.

Dennis Kelly, the Syndicate's factotum, remarked in 1985 that he was often asked how much of Churchill's books did the great man really write himself. That, said Kelly, was

> …almost as superficial a question as asking a master chef: 'Did you cook the whole banquet with your own hands?' It was an apt analogy. Churchill did not chop the vegetables, and he did not lay the tables or mix all the sauces, but he knew how to get a six-course meal on the table in the right order and at more or less the right time —not just a meal but a feast.[9]

A few people should be singled out as having contributed significantly to the editorial processes of multiple books. Deakin became the leader of the group and also became very close to Churchill. Another was Charles (C.C.) Wood who was the head of Harrap's Editorial Department and who first began working with Churchill during the production of *Marlborough*. After Wood retired from Harrap's in 1940, he became Churchill's proofreader for many years. Another was Edward Marsh, his long-time private secretary and friend. Marsh collaborated with Churchill for more than fifty years. Much more about him later.

How much Churchill appreciated the Syndicate can be gleaned from the following story:

> "During the Summer of 1952, Kelly reworked numerous chapters [of the *Second World War*], trying to reduce the documents and tighten the prose, and this gave Churchill plenty to deal with while vacationing with Beaverbrook on the French Riviera in September – so much so that he felt able to wind up the 'Syndicate' (and stop paying Allen, Deakin, and Pownall) at the end of October. 'There will be no more group work on the book after this month,' Churchill told his assistants,

'as I shall not be able to do anything more it until just before it is published.' As a token of his appreciation, he invited Allen, Deakin, and Powell to dinner at Number 10 on 27 October. It was a splendid evening, to judge by their letters of appreciation, and in the afterglow all three volunteered to do anything they could, gratis, to see the volume through to publication.[10]

The writing of *My Early Life* may not have always followed the exact paradigm described above, as it was an autobiography, not a history like *Marlborough* or *Lord Randolph Churchill* or a wartime memoir such as *Memoirs of the Second World War*, but, still, the core of the process was similar. Although *My Early Life* did require much fact-checking and research, the storyline is all about events that Churchill personally experienced. In addition, it will become obvious in this chapter how Churchill transmuted his early war correspondence, books and the bevy of articles on his early life that he had written in the early 1920s into significant sections of *My Early Life* by selectively weaving texts from those works into the new book.

DICTATION: THE PREFERRED METHOD

Churchill's preferred method for creating his manuscripts was dictation. He liked to walk around the room and think, gesture and listen to the words as they came forth from his mouth and reverberated around the room. Perhaps one of the main reasons Churchill favoured this method had little to do with the speed with which the manuscript could be created but, rather, it was that he wanted to hear the sound of the words and how they resonated and embellished the scene he was creating and the meaning he wanted to convey. He wanted to create what the American poet Robert Frost called 'the sound of sense'. There are numerous examples in *My Early Life* where the importance of the sounds of words becomes clear. (This theme will be developed in Chapter 7, 'Global Impact of *My Early Life*'. Suffice it here to say that the sounds of the words reflect and embellish the story being told and make the sentences and the action come alive.) As will be seen later, Churchill even commented on the sounds of the words in sentences when he wrote to one of his favourite reviewers, Edward Marsh – who had been reviewing the text for *Marlborough* – that he was 'delighted with the way you have increased in some instances the precision, in others the euphony of a sentence.'[11]

Maurice Ashley, an Oxford graduate, joined Churchill in 1929 as a half-time researcher. He was Churchill's lead researcher on *Marlborough*. Ashley would become a noted historian, newspaperman and editor, as well as an author in his own right with his special interest centred on Cromwell. He also wrote *Churchill as Historian*, from which we can learn much about Churchill's process of writing and researching.[12] When Ashley joined Churchill, the work on *My Early Life* was well underway and was proceeding contemporaneously with *Marlborough*; thus, one can be fairly sure that what he describes about Churchill as a writer and his methodologies reflects his general approach on both projects. Ashley has described how he liked to do his dictation:

> He would walk up and down the room (when I worked for him it was usually his bedroom) puffing at a cigar while a secretary patiently took it all down as best she could in Pitman [shorthand system]. Occasionally he would pause to say, 'scrub that start again.' At times he would stop while he contemplated the next point he wanted to make; at others he would be entirely swept on by the stimulus of his imagination; he had perceived how like what had happened was to something else he had read about or even experienced himself.[13]

Churchill was not one to wait for all the research to be completed before starting the process of getting words on paper. As Ashley noted:

> Churchill always preferred to get something down on paper and to fill in the gaps later. I always remember my astonishment to find myself listening to him dictating an introductory chapter about *Marlborough* before, as far as I could make out, he knew anything at all about him beyond the skeleton of his career as it was familiar to every schoolboy (in fact the chapter never saw the light). Brought up as I had been, in the most rigorous atmosphere of Oxford historical research – in the world of venerable scholars like Sir Charles Firth and Reginald Lane Poole – I found it difficult to envisage how anyone could start writing an important work of history without previously mastering all possible sources, comparing them, and sorting out the wheat from the chaff. For Churchill had an incredible memory and once he had read a book or

committed to mind a quotation or absorbed an historical episode, he stored it up for future use and rarely got it wrong.[14]

Churchill himself commented on his approach to writing: 'I write a book the way they built the Canadian Pacific Railway. First I lay the track from coast to coast, and then I put in all the stations.'[15]

The use of dictation, as it turns out, was not new for Churchill; it had actually begun in his school days. When Churchill was a senior at Harrow, dictation became a useful, value-adding skill. Churchill relates the story of this dictating as an amusing anecdote in *My Early Life* when he describes how he and a friend helped each other with their schoolwork:

> My Sixth-Form friend for his part, was almost as much troubled by the English essays he had to write for the Head-master as I was by these Latin crossword puzzles. We agreed together that he should tell me my Latin translations and that I should do his essays. The arrangement worked admirably. The Latin master seemed quite satisfied with my work, and I had more time to myself in the mornings. On the other hand, once a week or so I had to compose the essays of my Sixth-Form friend, I used to walk up and down the room dictating – just as I do now – and he sat in the corner and wrote it down in long-hand. For several months no difficulty arose; but once we were nearly caught out. One of these essays was thought to have merit. It was 'sent up' to the Head-master, who summoned my friend, commended him on his work and proceeded to discuss the topic with him in a lively spirit. 'I was interested in this point you make here. You might, I think, have gone even further. Tell me exactly what you had in your mind.' Mr. Welldon in spite of very chilling responses continued in this way for some time, to the deep consternation of my confederate. However, the Head-master, not wishing to turn an occasion of praise into one of cavilling, finally let him go with the remark, 'You seem to be better at written than at oral work.' He came back to me like a man who has had a very narrow squeak, and I was most careful ever afterwards to keep to the beaten track in essay-writing.[16]

Churchill learned from this near disaster, and in future essays, he was careful not to make them too 'interesting'; however, his penchant for thoughtful and soaring composition had clearly been established at an early age.

Churchill expected much from his research assistants. He tasked them with specific duties including gathering background material such as documents and pertinent books, which he preferred to have bought and added to his library rather than just borrowed. The assistants were also to mark the specific pages or sections for Churchill to read, along with a fully fleshed-out bibliography. Churchill always seemed to find time to read and learn all the material presented to him. The researcher was also expected to know the material completely so as to be able immediately answer any question Churchill might conjure. Another duty, according to Ashley, 'was to make sympathetic and co-operative noises while Churchill dictated. They were required to sit by and if possible, to fill in the gaps in his knowledge; but they were not expected immediately to criticise his line of argument or form of presentation.'[17] Once Churchill had set the plan for the section to be dictated, he wanted to proceed full speed ahead and did not tolerate interruptions well. After the dictation had been transcribed, the research assistant was then expected to check the piece for any errors of fact and get them corrected.

Churchill involved the printers much earlier and more extensively than most writers. Churchill not only liked to get something down on paper as soon as he possibly could, but he demanded to see at once how what he had dictated looked like in type. He was unenthusiastic about reading even original letters and documents in manuscript form. Thus, as soon as a chapter had been finished – and sometimes even before the facts in it had been fully checked – it would be sent off to the printer. The printer's reader would then make the obvious marks on the galley proofs and they would be sent back to Churchill ready for the next treatment.[18]

Most authors are not accommodated with such extravagances by their publishers unless the author is known to be highly successful. As will be seen later in this book, Churchill, during the writing and publication of *My Early Life*, would be required to reimburse his publishers for overuse of this service. Churchill directly addressed the value he found by working with the galley proofs early in a project and recognised the cost of doing so in a letter to George Harrap, his publisher for *Marlborough*, in 1932 when he was working on the first volume of that book:

The great advantage of working on these large galley proofs is that one sees practically three pages of typescript at a glance. This enables the structure to be much more easily shaped. You must not however suppose that I attach any finality to the proofs, because they are printed. I always knock them about a great deal and incorporate the criticisms of any authorities who may have read them … I am only expecting you to give me the usual allowance for an author's corrections, namely £50 for each volume. The rest of the expense for proof corrections I bear myself, though I rely on you to get the best terms from the printers.[19]

As will be seen in the discussion of the writing of *My Early Life*, Churchill would use the printer extensively. He would require from the printer many revised copies and edited versions.

Once a section or chapter of a book was available in draft form, he would begin circulating it to a group of people for comment and review. He wanted to edit continually to improve the writing and, very importantly, ensure that he had not missed something important or created a major misstatement of fact. As Ashley comments,

> Churchill's early books were circulated in the form of draft chapters for the advice and criticism of his friends and knowledgeable acquaintances. … He learned at an early stage how necessary that was and how important it was to find experts to assist him at every stage of the writing and the book production. The busy and successful man who elects to write a book – notably a book of memoirs – always employs assistants; though not ghosts [ghost-writers, that is], for unless he is in desperate need of money [which Churchill often was] there is little joy in projecting a book and then hiring others to put it together.[20]

A key individual in the review and publication of many of Churchill's books, including *My Early Life*, was Edward (Eddie) Marsh. Marsh had been his private secretary at the Colonial Office in 1905, and he would follow him through many of Churchill's offices. In addition, he became a close friend and trusted advisor on prose and grammar. Woods describes his importance to the Churchill writing machine as being the 'indefatigable arbiter on style and punctuation'. Marsh 'was still deeply involved in the preparation of Churchill's books when he died in 1953'.[21] He read all of Churchill's galley proofs, and, as will be seen in the section on the direct writing of *My Early Life*, the two of them carried on a lively correspondence. Additional insights into just how much Churchill depended on Marsh can be seen in their correspondence on the writing and editing of *Marlborough*, the early part of which was contemporaneous with *My Early Life*. Churchill wrote to Marsh,

> I now send you twenty-seven of the twenty-nine or thirty chapters of the first volume of *Marlborough*. ... These form a complete narrative and have already undergone two or three revisions… The points I want you to particularly mark are:
>
> 1. Clumsy sentences where the meaning is obscure or the grammar questionable.
> 2. Repetition of words. I have a good many favourites and they may crop up too often, e.g., vast, bleak, immense, formidable, etc.…
> 3. Repetition of arguments…
> 4. Dull, boring, stodgy passages…
> 5. Cheap, vulgar, undignified references…
> 6. Hyphens … capitals and punctuation throughout…[22]

As can readily be seen, Churchill always asked much of Marsh, and Marsh always responded with detailed and useful comments, paying attention to such qualities as precision and euphony.[23]

Churchill was ever the competitor on all issues, and his writing was no exception. He liked to 'keep score' and relate how well he was performing to all his confidants, his family and members of the writing team. As Ashley has noted,

> Churchill enjoyed counting the number of words that he had produced in any given space of time. In the early hours of the morning, after an exhausting session which he had begun not long before midnight, he would observe with deep satisfaction: 'Well, we must have done three thousand words.' 'We' – that is to say the tired secretary and anyone else

who had been watching the performance and trying to avoid falling asleep – might not have experienced the same sense of pleasurable achievement.[24]

Churchill also kept his wife fully informed of the 'score' when he was writing. In a letter to her in 1928, he writes, 'Nearly 3000 words in the last two days! … I do not conceal from you that it is a task. But it is not more than I can do.'[25]

No discussion of how Churchill wrote would be complete without quoting Churchill himself, on how he felt about writing a book. By the time of this quotation, he had already published multiple books. Churchill wrote,

> It was great fun writing a book. One lived with it. It became a companion. It built an impalpable crystal sphere around one of interests and ideas. In a sense one felt like a goldfish in a bowl, but in this case the goldfish made his own bowl. This came along everywhere with me. It never got knocked about in travelling, and there was never a moment when agreeable occupation was lacking. Either the glass had to be polished, or the structure extended or contracted, or the walls required strengthening. I have noticed in my life deep resemblances between many different kinds of things. Writing a book is not unlike building a house or planning a battle or painting a picture. The technique is different, the materials are different, but the principle is the same. The foundations have to be laid, the data assembled, and the premises must bear the weight of their conclusions. Ornaments or refinements may then be added. The whole when finished is only the successful presentation of a theme. In battles however the other fellow interferes all the time and keeps upsetting things, and the best generals are those who arrive at the results of planning without being tied to plans.[26]

THE CREATION OF *MY EARLY LIFE*

With this as background, we can now begin the story of the birth and development of *My Early Life*. The exact date when Churchill first considered writing an autobiography is unknown. However, recognising the fact that he was always a self-promoter and even thought of himself as a 'glow worm' compared to the rest of humanity, who were simply 'worms', it is difficult to believe that, by the time he was first hired as a war correspondent for his trip to Cuba in 1895, plans weren't already being formed in his mind to write one. Churchill was always thinking of schemes to get his name in front of the general public and, in particular, important people who could advance his career. He was never shy in promoting himself to gain notoriety. In addition, he certainly archived for later use all the materials he had written from Cuba, India, the Sudan and South Africa.

There is a curious note in an article titled 'Under Cover' in the periodical *The Bookseller and the Stationery Trades Journal* in July 1925 that states,

> There is sure to be a rush for Mr. Winston Churchill's forthcoming volume of recollections, to which he is giving the expansive title, "A Roving Commission'. But there is no truth in the rumour that, in graceful allusion to the Chancellor of the Exchequer's recent financial activities, there is to be an *edition de luxe*, calf-bound with artificial silk wrappers. Such an edition would hardly be worth stocking![27]

The writer here is making a joke about a controversy in Parliament over the Finance Bill of 1925, over which Churchill presided as Chancellor of the Exchequer. The controversary related to what international taxes were to be collected by the general commercial agents in the UK who were considered to have a 'roving commission' and no specific ties or relationships with foreign buyers.[28] The article is intended to be humorous. It relates to the government agents, but it is also prescient in that it turns out to be the earliest published account of what Churchill would actually consider as the title 'A Roving Commission' for his autobiography. That title was Churchill's first choice, but after much consideration, debate and acrimony with at least with one of his publishers, Scribner's, Churchill, Butterworth and Scribner's agreed to two separate and distinct titles for the British and American editions.

In the preface to *My Early Life*, Churchill writes that he has published various accounts of his early life and adventures in newspapers, magazine articles and books. In about 1926 or 1927, he

> …thought it right to bring the whole together in a single complete story; and to tell the tale, such as it is, anew. I have therefore not only

searched my memory, but have most carefully verified my facts from the records which I possess. I have tried, in each part of the quarter-century in which this tale lies, to show the point of view appropriate to my years, whether as a child, a schoolboy, a cadet, a subaltern, a war-correspondent, or a youthful politician.[29]

This later goal of telling his story in the words, thoughts, and perspective of the appropriate age of his character at the time was completely successful, as reflected in later reviews of *My Early Life*.

By 1927, Manchester notes in his biography of Churchill that 'between the Exchequer and his publishers' deadlines, nearly all of his holidays were working holidays. He meant to take most of the summer of 1927 off, painting at Chartwell, entertaining friends there, and sweating over walls, dams, and ponds, but then he decided to start writing an account of his youth. It is his most delightful book.[30] This date is confirmed by Gilbert, as he notes, in the summer of 1927, 'He also began work on a new literary venture, an autobiography, telling the story of his childhood, youth, and military career, from 1874 to 1900.'[31] From this time forward until what would become *My Early Life* was published in October 1930, Churchill would spend time writing and dictating material for the book. As Churchill was wont to do, his vacations were always working ones, and Gilbert notes that during a break in Venice in October 1927, 'he swam, painted and wrote more of his autobiography'.[32]

Churchill almost never worked on only a single manuscript; he would typically have several books and multiple articles at various levels of completion at all times. His commentary about the process he employed to write – and how he lived his life to accommodate his writing – makes for interesting reading, and I shall cite relevant anecdotes throughout this chapter. By the summer of 1928, he was in full swing working on *My Early Life*, as he notes in a letter to Clementine in August: 'I have averaged about 1,200 words a day on the book as well as finishing the Savinkov article.'[33] This later article would be published in *Nash's Magazine* in 1929 as 'Boris Savinkov: The Story of a Man Who Was Not Without Honour Except in His Own Country'.[34] Savinkov was a Russian Empire writer and dissident. Churchill would expand this article and use it as a chapter in his 1937 book, *Great Contemporaries*.

It appears that a significant proportion of *My Early Life* was written during the parliamentary recess in the summer of 1928. Churchill wrote to Stanley Baldwin on 2 September, 'I have had a delightful month – building a cottage and dictating a book: 2000 bricks and 2000 words per day.'[35] In addition to these manuscripts, Churchill was actively working on the fifth volume of *The World Crisis* and was under much pressure from his publisher, Thornton Butterworth, to deliver on time what had been promised. As noted in Churchill's letter to Baldwin, not all of his time at Chartwell was devoted to writing. A visitor to Chartwell comments on Churchill's routine at this time:

> He works at bricklaying four hours a day, and lays 90 bricks an hour which is a very high output. He also spends a considerable time on a history of post-war Europe which he is writing. His ministerial work comes down from the treasury every day, and he gives some hours to that. It is a marvel how much time he gives to his guests, talking sometimes for an hour after lunch and much longer after dinner.'[36]

By the fall of 1928, Churchill and his Conservative colleagues had come to believe that they would not retain a majority after the 1929 election. Churchill realised that if and when he lost his cabinet position as Chancellor of the Exchequer, his income would plummet. To address this issue, Churchill began negotiations for additional writing contracts. His first thought was to contract for the autobiography he was currently writing. However, in late October of 1928, his agent Curtis Brown suggested 'a fortnightly newspaper column written for worldwide syndication that would make £300–£400 per article … providing the subjects were of international interest, and providing you had, meanwhile, made a visit to America.'[37] For an interesting and robust description of Churchill's finances at this time, the reader is referred to David Lough's excellent book *No More Champagne*.[38]

Churchill's heavy work schedule continued throughout 1928. In November he wrote to Clementine, 'I have had very busy days, trying to push the book forward and at the same time with heaps of engagements and politics.'[39] By December, he was frantically attempting to finish the latest volume of *The World Crisis* and obtain feedback from friends who were integral to Britain's input to the aftermath of the First World War.

For example, on 17 December he wrote this to James Headlam-Morley, a British historian who was involved in drafting the Treaty of Versailles:

> I send you a copy of the sketch I have made of Chapter XI on the Peace Treaties. … I should be extremely grateful for any help you can give me in clothing the skeleton or straightening any deformities in its bones. You know the field so well. What I should really like would be if you would take my skeleton as a text and run through the points verbally with me; give me in fact a short lecture. You would find me very apt to learn. After all I have got to compress it into perhaps six or seven thousand words at the outside.[40]

On 27 December, Churchill wrote the following to Lord Cecil of Chelwood (lawyer, politician, diplomat, and one of the architects of the League of Nations):

> I have a chapter in my new book dealing with the Covenant of the League of Nations, in which I find you played a most important part. I wonder whether you would care to read it through and let me know whether I have done justice to the topic. If so, I should be very much obliged. I presume I am right in attributing to you the first written conception of Articles XIV and XV, and that Phillimore followed on this and Wilson built on both.[41]

This correspondence illustrates several important points on how Churchill created his books. First, he frequently sought advice and criticism of topics in which he was not expert; secondly, he had no hesitancy in writing to the world's experts and seeking their help and opinions. Churchill also frequently hired academically trained researchers to spend all or a significant part of their time researching topics for him.

A final example of letters written to help with the book is one sent to his good friend David Lloyd George, the former Prime Minister. Churchill wrote to him in December:

> I am so pressed in finishing my book that I shall not have a complete copy for you to read before the Closure. I therefore send you those passages – not very numerous – in which I have either quoted or

described opinions you expressed to me verbally, or which contains extracts from letters or telegrams sent by you to me. ... Pray let me know as soon as possible what you think of these extracts.[42]

These are but a few of the many such letters sent.

Building on the comments above concerning Churchill's seeking help from noted experts on his manuscripts, several points are worth making. First, Churchill possessed a remarkable ability to multitask. Secondly, he had a remarkable ability to manage version control. He always had multiple manuscripts in various stages of completion, and he regularly put significant factual detail into each one while working with multiple consultants and versions of the manuscript. It should be remembered, especially by those readers under the age of forty to fifty, that there were no computers, no Microsoft Word; therefore, version control would have been an absolute nightmare. To add new facts or edit manuscripts, authors would have had to have pages retyped or literally cut paper sections and scotch-tape them in. The writing and editing of multiple books and articles would seem like a full-time job to most people. Thirdly, Churchill had more than a full workload as Chancellor of the Exchequer, and he was frequently making political speeches. Then, in his spare time, he was working as a bricklayer on the 'little' house and the walls at Chartwell. Working in his favour was his absolutely stunning memory of all he read and the things he heard from others; he could recall these details quite accurately and place them in major publications.

By March 1929, *Aftermath*, the latest volume of *The World Crisis*, was published. Many letters of thanks rolled into Chartwell acknowledging the receipt of inscribed copies of the new book. (It was a routine practice for Churchill to send copies of his new books to friends and colleagues.[43])

LAST DAYS AS A CABINET MEMBER AND A SPEAKING TOUR OF USA AND CANADA

In early 1929, Churchill was extremely busy with preparing his fifth and final budget as Chancellor of the Exchequer and with party politics in preparation for the upcoming election. The budget was presented in April, and the election was held on 30 May, with Labour winning 287 seats to the Conservatives' 260. So, as anticipated, though he retained his personal seat in Parliament, Churchill would lose his ministerial position. This dramatically changed Churchill's life and how he would prioritise his time. Churchill's former literary agent, A.P. Watt, had suggested that Churchill write a biography of his ancestor the Duke of Marlborough, a topic that much interested him.[44] Negotiations were undertaken, and after much kerfuffle, successful and lucrative contracts were signed in both the US and the UK, as well as a contract to serialise each volume in the *Daily Telegraph*.[45] This linking of a book publication with a just-prior release of its serial publication in a newspaper or a magazine would be the norm for Churchill throughout his writing career.

With no ministerial duties, Churchill decided it was a good time to take an extended break from routine and travel. As was his wont, it had to be a working break. Previously, Churchill had met with Paul Reynolds, a New York agent, to probe what approaches he might take to enhance his presence in the American publication arena. Reynolds had suggested that Churchill make a trip to the United States to tour, lecture and meet important personages who could help enhance his readership.[46] A plan was developed whereby Churchill and his brother Jack and their sons Randolph and John, respectively, would travel across Canada and the United States by train. (John [Jack] Churchill was Winston's younger brother and only sibling. They were close friends throughout their lives.) Along the way, Churchill would lecture and be wined and dined by the Canadian and American Who's Who in society, business and politics. Churchill would then write his impressions for a number of newspapers and periodicals.

Churchill left London on 3 August 1929 and would not return until 5 November. The trip was filled with non-stop action including a myriad of speeches (for which he was paid), the tremendous financial disaster of the October stock market crash, and frantic activity with his investment team in response to that crash. In addition, he was meeting, greeting and cajoling every important person he could get on his schedule, while at the same time reading books on Marlborough in anticipation of the upcoming book he had contracted to write. As the story of his North American trip is well described in numerous excellent books, only events that directly relate to the production of *My Early Life* will be described here.[47-49]

Near the end of August, in a letter to Thornton Butterworth concerning all the projects he had underway, Churchill wrote, 'About the future, I think Reminiscences [the working title for what would become *MEL*] might well come out in the Autumn of 1931, but I have no definite plan at the moment.'⁵⁰ Thus, *My Early Life* was not at the top of Churchill's list: his proposed publication date was two years off. Just how weary Churchill was with politics is made clear in a very poignant letter to Clementine that he sent from Banff Springs Hotel in Canada:

> Darling, I am greatly attracted to this country. There are fortunes to be made in many directions. The tide is flowing strongly. I have made up my mind that if N Ch [Neville Chamberlain] is made leader of the CP [Conservative Party] or anyone else of that kind, I clear out of politics & see if I cannot make you and the kittens a little more comfortable before I die. Only one goal still attracts me [Prime Minister], & if that were barred I should quit the dreary field for pastures new. As Daniel Peggotty says, 'There's mighty lands beyond the seas.' However the time to take decision is not yet.⁵¹

STILL MORE PROJECTS, AND A CONTRACT FOR MEMOIRS

During the remainder of 1929 (November and December), it appears that Churchill spent most of his time researching *Marlborough* and writing a myriad of articles in *Colliers Magazine*, including 'Crucial Crises of the Great War'. Research for these articles had spurred his interest in what had occurred in the Eastern theatre of the First World War. By January 1930, Churchill was contemplating another volume for *World Crisis*. He wrote to Butterworth that

> …as a result of the books I have been reading for this purpose [i.e. writing articles on the Great War for *Colliers Magazine*], I have become much interested in the story of the Eastern Front … But now I think I might write a volume called 'The Eastern Front'… While I have not made up my mind whether I can fit this in with all my other work, I am at present quite favourably disposed to the idea.⁵²

The idea for this new volume gelled quickly in Churchill's plans. By 22 February, he was writing to his New York publisher Charles Scribner, informing him of this new volume and telling him that Butterworth had already contracted with Churchill for its production. He was hoping that

Scribner's would offer a similar contract for the American rights. In addition, Churchill had already contracted with a military researcher to prepare the military part of the book. Almost unbelievably, Churchill ends the letter with 'The preparation of this volume will not in any way conflict with or delay the "Marlborough" book, on which work is steadily proceeding and which forms the staple of my reading. This is, however, as you know a very much longer business.'[53] That this is unbelievable relates to the fact that Churchill was not only working on *Marlborough* and a number of articles for periodicals, but during this month he had also reactivated the memoirs project as a priority, as will be seen below – and now he suggests yet another book, *The Eastern Front*!

Roy Jenkins, one of Churchill's esteemed biographers, writes:

> Thus when, in February 1930, he was proposing to add about 40,000 new words to the 50,000 or more of *My Early Life* which he had already written (the number of literary balls he had in the air at that stage is staggering), he insisted that, at his own expense if necessary, the already written text must be set up in print – 'until I see the existing material in type I cannot make progress'! Associated with this was his increasing desire to work standing up, for which purpose he acquired a sloping desk of appropriate height at the side of his Chartwell study. He needed the feel and look of printed proofs for his literary teeth, but he rarely worked at them seated at a writing table. It was nearly all done either upright or in bed.[54]

Six days after writing to Scribner about contracting for *The Eastern Front*, Churchill writes to Butterworth:

> I am anxious to have my memoirs of *My Early Life* set up in proof. There are perhaps 50,000 words in the articles I have already reassembled. I was on the point of sending them to Butler and Tanner[*] to print at my expense when it occurred to me that possibly the arrangements we might make for the book would involve a different type, and instead of your being able to take over the work by Butler & Tanner in the event of our agreeing upon a contract for the book it

would all have to be set up again. It is therefore important to settle this matter as soon as possible.

The book would vary from 100,000 to 125,000 words. It should be published at not less than a guinea. It could come out in the autumn publishing season of 1931.

Pray let me know your views.

I should probably write 30,000 or 40,000 new words, but until I see the existing material in type I cannot make progress. Perhaps pending any definite arrangements or contract being made you will telephone me whether the type of 'The World Crisis' will do.[55]

*Printer at the Selwood Printing works in Somerset.

This letter is stunning for a number of reasons. It is the first indication that Churchill has reactivated the memoirs project, and now it seems to have skyrocketed to being a top priority. Churchill is already asking for a quick decision on what the type should be for the publication. Never mind that he doesn't have a contract with Butterworth for the book yet. In addition, he is suggesting a price for the book, the date it should be published, and how long it should be. To say that this process is not standard practice in the publishing industry would be an understatement. But then Churchill never did anything but in his own way. Churchill was back in the harness for this project and would remain so until October 1930, when it would be published – a year earlier than he had originally anticipated. Butterworth answered Churchill's letter within a week:

> Herewith I have the pleasure to send you a draft of the agreement for your memoirs, which I trust you will find in order and satisfactory in every respect. If that be so, will you please sign it and I will immediately sign and send the counterpart for your files. We are very pleased to have arranged with you for the publication of this work, and from the little you read to me I found it very interesting. We shall do our best to make it a success.[56]

Churchill returned the signed contract two days later. Eager to get on with the project, he immediately wrote to Butler and Tanner:

> I have arranged with Mr. Thornton Butterworth that my memoirs should be set up in type forthwith. I send you therefore the first installment approximating 50,000 words. Mr. Butterworth will advise you of the type and style to-day or tomorrow. Triplicates will be required on the usual broad paper. I shall be glad to know when they may be expected.[57]

Note the level of detail and control and the expectations Churchill provides to all who work with him on a writing project. The typescript of 'Reminiscences' (another working title for *MEL*) was returned to Churchill on 9 April.[58] Churchill is working not only on these memoirs but also on research (along with a dedicated researcher) for the manuscript of *The Eastern Front*, research for *Marlborough* (along with a separate dedicated research assistant), and several articles as well. With all these projects swirling in his head, he starts to prioritise. He writes to Butterworth twice on 16 April to lay out his thoughts:

> Now that the proofs of my memoirs (about 30,000 words) have come to hand, I should be glad if you could find time to glance at them. They seem to me to read extremely well and, when woven into the texture of a continuous narrative, they will I believe make a book of adventure, *possibly of some permanent merit* [emphasis added].
>
> It occurred to me that it might be better to publish these memoirs in the spring of 1931 instead of *The Eastern Front*, and to publish the latter at the beginning of the autumn session of 1931. I feel very ready to go on with these memoirs now and my mind is full of ideas about them. On the other hand, *The Eastern Front* requires a great amount of new study and will gain if more time is taken over it. … *The Eastern Front* is of course a massive production, which has to be quarried out, whereas the Memoirs are all in my head, or actually finished. … Pray let me know so that I can notify Scribner of the transposition of the order of publication.
>
> Now, this very weekend, I will send you the blurb for the abridged edition [*The World Crisis*] from Scribner, but as soon as I do I will send you the explanatory note you wished me to write about it.[59]

In this same letter, Churchill suggests how a number of articles to be published should be arranged to optimise the negotiations for the serial rights for *The Eastern Front*, and at the end he mentions that he will send the materials requested for the abridged edition of *The World Crisis*, on which he was also working. In the second letter to Butterworth on the same day, Churchill proposes additional work, which he thinks will not be a problem:

> A friend of mine is anxious that I should publish, for a moderate fee, an extract of about 1,500 words, from one of my articles previously published in the *Strand* about my escape from Pretoria. The article is one which will be required for the memoirs. My friend says that the weekly in question circulates among a class who would never dream of buying such a book and he is anxious that I should oblige him. Do you see any harm in it in view of our forthcoming publication next year? I do not myself.[59]

Butterworth answers both letters in the affirmative. He believes that moving up the date of publication to the spring of 1931 is a good idea:

> In the first place the Memoirs being of a lighter and more popular nature will accord well with Spring publication. … We will, therefore, arrange accordingly, and should be very glad indeed if you would let us have a note of about 200 words more or less, as you wish, concerning the Memoirs that we may circulate to our agents, at the earliest moment convenient to your goodself.

Butterworth is, thus, fully on board with the extra article to be published in the spring.[60]

With this issue agreed upon by Butterworth, Churchill now needed to negotiate a deal with Charles Scribner for the American publication rights and an agreement that Scribner will change the date they will publish *The Eastern Front*. As usual, Churchill takes a very upbeat approach. In a letter titled 'My Early Life' he writes:

> I hope you will not mind a slight alteration in our programme, which Butterworth and I are agreed will be for the best. As you know, I have in the last five or six years written a series of articles on my past adventures, covering broadly speaking the first thirty years of my life.

About 70,000 words, of which more than 50,000 have been set up in book print, will be directly available for publication in book form. I shall write another 30,000 or 40,000 words so as to make a continuous homogeneous narrative. This is easy for me as I have it all in my head. I send you herewith 50,000 words in proof which will give you a far better indication of the character and scope of the work. I think there is no doubt it will have a wide value.

We think it would be best to publish these memoirs in the Spring of 1931 and postpone 'The Eastern Front' until September 1931….

I have not hitherto written to you about the memoirs. I shall be very glad to know what you think of them and whether you will wish to publish them. Perhaps you will cable me your views on receipt of this.

I send you a synopsis of the whole of the Memoirs. A great deal, in addition to the 50,000 words now sent you, has already been printed, and of course I should not necessarily follow the plan exactly; 100,000 words being my limit, of which perhaps 30,000 will be new material. I think myself it would have a very large sale as a book of real adventures, and of a young man's struggle with life. However I shall leave the sample to speak for itself.[61]

On 7 May, Churchill received a telegram from Charles Scribner: WELCOME MEMOIRS ACCEPTING CHANGE IN PLAN STOP COULD PAY FIFTEEN PERCENT ROYALTY TO FIVE THOUSAND AND TWENTY PERCENT THEREAFTER.[62]

With that response, Churchill writes to Butterworth the next day:

I have now heard from Scribner that he welcomes the Memoirs and that he accepts the change in plans. I am making rapid progress, having written above 20,000 words in the last ten days. I hope to finish them quite soon now, so as to have my hands free for further progress on 'The Eastern Front' in the summer holidays.[63]

By the end of May, Churchill writes to one of his literary agents, Nancy Pearn, asking her to try to obtain serial rights for what he had previously written but with the caveat that he does not wish these to interfere with future sales of *My Early Life*:

> The book of 'Memoirs' to be published in February by Thornton Butterworth will comprise all the articles upon my early life and adventures, including much that appeared in the 'Strand' and 'Nash's' magazines – the Indian, Soudan, and South African adventures. These together amount approximately to 60,000 words. In addition, I am writing about an equal amount of new matter making the whole into a complete story. It is probable that this tale will end either in the year 1900 when I got into Parliament, or in the year 1905 when I first took office. All articles and adventures in the air, in the Great War, or on other topics later than 1906, will be excluded from the scope of this volume. I do not wish to take the bloom off this publication by reprinting serials of the articles to be included in this book. There would however be no objection to Colonial publication or West African rights, and I shall be glad to receive any offer for any of the articles from the Elder Dempster Company which you may be able to procure.[64]

Churchill continued writing additional sections for his memoirs. He sent off another 25,000 words of the draft to Scribner, indicating that the book would be about 120,000 words in total.[65] (It should be noted that when referring to Churchill writing sections, in fact, many of the sections were dictated to his secretary.[66]) Churchill always liked to hear the sounds of the words in a sentence. Chapters 2 and 7 contain full discussions of why Churchill liked to dictate and how it helped shape the structure of his sentences and how they fit together, as well as speeding up the process of writing.

Churchill followed up on 3 June with a letter to Scribner: 'I hope you will be interested in this new chapter of memoirs which I sent. Perhaps you will send me a cable when you have read them, to let me know whether you and your colleagues think this kind of material will be interesting to the wide circle of American readers to whom I hope to appeal.[67]

CHURCHILL ADVANCES TIME FRAME FOR MEMOIRS

Churchill was now contemplating advancing the publication of his memoirs to an even earlier date. He writes to Butterworth on 5 June:

> Our present plans are to publish the abridged edition [*World Crisis*] in September. The Memoirs in February 1931 and *The Eastern Front* in

> September 1931. I am making such good progress with the Memoirs that it would be possible to publish them in September of this year if you wished. It is possible then that I might be able to keep my original date about *The Eastern Front*. Before coming to any conclusion or opening a suggestion with Scribner, I should like to know from you whether the publication of the Memoirs in September would interfere with the abridged edition. It seems to me that they run on quite separate lines, one being only a new edition of an already published work, and the other a new book. Let me know what you think. I believe I could make sure of letting you have the copy of the Memoirs so as to go to press early in August.[68]

Butterworth was not enthusiastic about Churchill's suggestions, as they were currently juggling the timing of three separate books of his. Butterworth replied:

> Thank you for putting the suggestion contained in your letter of the 8th instant before us. I at once took the matter up with Sir Tresham Lever, my sales manager, and my advertising manager, and independently of each other, they confirmed most definitely my own feelings in the matter, namely that it would be a mistake to publish two books in the same season. The abridged edition, as you know, will be more of a booksellers' book than a library book, and we shall have to do everything possible to get the public interested to make it a success. To publish it alone this autumn, as originally arranged, would ensure not only the concentration of newspapers, but public interest during the months of Christmas sales. Published with your memories, we feel that reviewers would pay more attention to the latter and, again, would be divided between the two books.
>
> You will gather here from that our strong advice is to keep the original plan to publish the abridged edition of *The World Crisis* in September; your Memoirs in January or February, reserving *The Eastern Front* for the Autumn of 1931. I do hope you feel our advice is sound.[69]

This would not be last of this discussion. Now, for the first time, Churchill is beginning to seek input and editorial comments on the drafts of the memoirs from trusted friends and colleagues. This was a practice he would repeat over and over again with all of his publications.

By 13 June, Butterworth had sixteen chapters in galley proof form, although they were not yet final, and some of the chapter titles would be modified.[70] (At publication, there would be twenty-nine chapters.)

CHURCHILL SEEKS INPUT ON TEXT OF MEMOIRS
Churchill wrote to his close friend and confidant Brendan Bracken on 16 June:

> Herewith the proofs of the Memoirs, so far as they have yet progressed. The Chapters, 'Sandhurst,' 'The Fourth Hussars,' and 'Cuba 1898' are all new, and there will probably be about four more, making 40,000 words, now, in all. The text has appeared, the bulk of it five years ago, in either the *Strand Magazine* or *Nash's*, but I am quite free to use the second serials if they are desired.
>
> It must be understood that the stories will ultimately make one connected narrative, and that there are at present both gaps and overlapping.
>
> Many thanks for interesting yourself in this matter.[71]

On 17 June, Churchill received a telegram from Scribner:

> MOST ENTHUSIASTIC ABOUT TEXT OF MEMOIRS AND HOPEFUL OF OUTCOME BUT CANNOT PREDICT RECEPTION UNDER PRESENT UPSET CONDITIONS* STOP ADVANCE SALES WOULD BE LIGHT STOP BELIEVE PRICE SHOULD BE THREE AND ONE HALF DOLLARS AND WOULD EXPECT FIRST PRINTING FIVE THOUSAND.[72]

* The reference is apparently to the price war which has broken out among American publishers.

Churchill continued to write and edit the manuscript, and various sections were cycled between Churchill, the printers and his publishers. As noted by Cohen,

A batch of hand typescripts were sent by Churchill's secretary Violet Pearman to Messrs. Butler & Tanner on Monday, 7 July, with the request that 'the usual second revise proofs' be returned to him, if possible by the end of the week. Three weeks later she sent 'the last bundle of proofs' with the request that the printers return 'early on the Friday next' [8 August] twelve copies of everything, including two chapters in second revise and the chapter sent earlier this morning in first revise. 'This will enable Mr. Churchill to have twelve copies which he can circulate to various people before finally going into page proof. He would particularly like the proofs on Friday as he wishes to send one to America urgently. …

The British publisher [Thornton Butterworth] agreed to pay him a royalty of 25% up to 5000 copies, 27 ½% over 7500 copies, and 30% over 10,000.

The final text was about 130,000 words and Butterworth was torn between leaving the price at 21s. and raising it to 25s.[73]

The telegram from 17 June noted above was followed up a few days later with a letter from Scribner which heaped praise on the nascent book but noted the market would need to be developed:

> I do not see how any one can fail to find pleasure in the candor and life you have given to the narrative, and I believe it will give the American Public a new and most pleasing conception of your character. Memoirs have not had the popularity here that they seem to enjoy in England, and it is far more difficult to guess at their reception than that of a book on a historical or scientific subject. Anything you say naturally attracts immediate attention in England, but you may realize that although your name is well known here as that of any public character outside of America, there is not the same prompt curiosity to induce an American to purchase your book. Therefore, the market has to be made …[74]

These precautions were likely a pre-emptive offensive in dealing with Churchill because Churchill, always in need of cash, would negotiate fiercely for an advance on each of his books. Scribner was well aware that he had already paid Churchill a large total advance on all the books they were working on simultaneously.

DISCORD WITH SCRIBNER

In June 1930, Scribner received a confidential cable from another London publishing house (i.e. not Butterworth) asking if Scribner would join them in bidding for yet another book Churchill was interested in writing, a one-volume publication of *The History of the English- Speaking Peoples*. This prompts a very long letter from Scribner to Churchill in which he lays out his views on what a good partner Scribner has been and will continue to be. He then goes through each of the arrangements they have with Churchill, including the abridged *World Crisis* and *A Roving Commission*, and now a newly suggested large one-volume work – *The History of the English-Speaking Peoples*, which would come out in 1933 in the midst of finishing *Marlborough* and a US lecture tour that Churchill was planning. He is incredulous that Churchill could possibly deliver on all of this and that he would offer it to another publisher. He also notes that they had agreed on adding his memoirs, *A Roving Commission,* 'coming on when it did seem to us to have such unusual possibilities of establishing your popularity among American readers before the publication of the one-volume *World Crisi*s that we advertised it to the limit.'[75]

The letter continues:

> The sum of the whole matter is that we believe in your work and in its future, and we also believe that it would be very detrimental to your interests as well as our own if your American book rights were divided between two or more publishers. It has always worked out that neither publisher is then as keen to wholeheartedly push an author's books, as his efforts may only result in bearing fruit for a rival and prevents combination in sets. I might add that if at anytime you may wish £1000 we should be glad to advance it against your account, but naturally we would like some assurance you will give us the option on your next book, provided we make terms satisfactory to you.[75]

Churchill's response to this letter has not been uncovered. However, Churchill's *History of the English-Speaking Peoples* would not be published for another twenty-five years; and it was not published by Scribner. If all this turmoil were not enough, Churchill further inflamed Scribner when he sent this cable to him on 20 June: 'Now considering publication Memoirs towards end October. Butterworth advises this will not affect publication of abridged edition [*The World Crisis*] as planned in middle of September/ STOP/ Pray cable how this strikes you before I decide. Winston Churchill.'[76]

Scribner's response was swift and clear: WOULD GREATLY DEPLORE PUBLICATION MEMOIRS THIS FALL STOP WOULD CONFLICT BEYOND QUESTION WITH SALES OF CRISIS STOP MEMOIRS TOO IMPORTANT AND PROMISING TO ISSUE AT END OF SEASON WITHOUT OPPORTUNITY OF FULL AND UNDIVIDED EXPLOITATION.[77]

Churchill tries again on 26 June. sending another telegram: BUTTERWORTH KEEN OCTOBER PUBLICATION MEMOIRS FOR CHRISTMAS SALES.[78]

Scribner still opposed, but he adds some flexibility: BELIEVE FALL PUBLICATION BOTH BOOKS INJURIOUS YOUR BEST INTERESTS HERE STOP IF BUTTERWORTH INSISTENT FALL PUBLICATION MEMOIRS WE ASK DEFERMENT ABRIDGED EDITION CRISIS BOTH COUNTRIES TO EARLY NINETEEN THIRTY ONE.[79]

Churchill and Butterworth agree. Churchill then negotiates final financial terms with Scribner in yet another cable: BUTTERWORTH AGREES YOUR SUGGESTIONS POSTPONE ABRIDGED TILL 1931 AND PUBLISH MEMOIRS EARLY OCTOBER 1930 AM SERIALIZING NEW MATTER DURING SEPTEMBER STOP I ACCEPT 15-0/0 TO 5000 [copies sold] AND 20-0/0 THERAFTER [sic] BUT PROPOSE IF I WAIVE ADVANCE ON LINES YOUR LETTER THAT ROYALTY SHOULD BE 25-0/0 AFTER 10,000. STOP WRITING TO CONFIRM.[80]

In a letter dated 28 June to Churchill, Butterworth follows up on a telephone conversation he had had with Churchill on the timing of the publications:

> With reference to our telephone conversation in regard to Scribner's views concerning the prospects of bringing out your Memoirs and the Abridged Edition of 'The World Crisis' this autumn; I would like to say in advance of the meeting with you on Monday afternoon that if it comes to alternative between the two books, I would plump wholeheartedly for your memoirs! At the same time, I can see no reason

why we should not publish the two books here this autumn, as I feel quite sure that the publication of the Abridged Edition of 'The World Crisis' here in advance of Scribner's would in no wise affect their market. On both sides of the Atlantic, I believe and expect that the book will have a long run and will be in demand for some years to come.

I have pleasure to enclose herewith preliminary announcement of the Abridged Edition, which I think will interest you. This has already gone to Australia and to the exporters.

Although your book is announced for September, it will not affect the situation if it is finally decided to postpone publication until the turn of the year. It is merely a question of cabled advice.

I shall wait your telephone call informing me of whether it is more convenient to you that I should meet you at the House of Commons or Eaton Terrace [emphasis added].[81]

This last sentence brings to the fore just how busy Churchill was and how complicated his schedule must have been. Here his publisher is willing to meet Churchill wherever he wished to get the work completed. Following this scheduled meeting, Butterworth follows up with a letter on 1 July:

With reference to our conversation of yesterday concerning the publication of your memoirs and the popular edition of *The World Crisis*: I have the pleasure to confirm that we will publish your Memoirs in October next – we would like it to be on Thursday the 2nd, so as to give a long a run as possible before the Christmas sales – and *The World Crisis* early in the new year, on say Thursday the 22nd January.

To accomplish this change in publication now agreed upon we are making some sacrifice, as we have already broadcasted the Trade Overseas with some thousands of the Prospectus of *The World Crisis*, which will now have to be scrapped; have spent a certain amount of forward advertising; and we shall have to pay some months in advance our Travellers' Commission on orders already booked. For this reason among others, we would have greatly preferred to have both books published this Autumn; but we are willing to meet Scribner's wishes as our relations with that Firm have always been of the friendliest nature. … We have every hope of a great success with this book, and shall leave no stone unturned to that end.

In regard to the Serial portion of this work in *The Daily News*, I enclose a copy of the notices, which *The Times* gave us at the head and foot of each article. We hope you will be able to arrange for *The Daily News* to give similar advertising to Volume publication.
P.S. May we use the following as the preliminary title: -
'The Autobiography of Winston Churchill'
'From Boyhood to Manhood'[82]

It is now set that *My Early Life* (still not yet its title) is to be published in October 1930; the one-volume abridged *World Crisis* is pushed back to 1931.
Churchill now writes a long letter to Scribner summarising the positions of all parties and advising that Butterworth is very much interested in accommodating the needs of Scribner. All agree that the memoirs will be published in October and *World Crisis* in 1931. Cohen comments:

Churchill agreed to waive the advance as proposed by Scribner. He also expressed concern that without the advance Scribner would be less motivated to promote the book. 'I rely upon you to do your very best for the book, although there is no advance to spur the publisher. If their arrangements suit you, will you kindly have a contract drawn out in our usual form and send it to me for signature.'[83]

In the long letter noted above, Churchill tells Scribner,

I have sold the English serial rights of the Memoirs for $7500 to the *Daily News*, and I am also selling them in the United States. The serials must be completed in time for publication on the first, or at least the second Thursday in October. Everyone here who has seen the copy seems very keen and the *Daily News* have gone far beyond any price they have previously paid for serials.
The book will amount to between a hundred thousand and a hundred and twenty thousand words. We are publishing here at 1 pound.[84]

Churchill then provides a page of the suggested financial arrangements including the fact that he will waive the upfront advance even though he fears this will lead to Scribner not being motivated to promote the book.

Churchill asks for reassurance that this will not be the case. He also asks Scribner to please send him a contract to sign if these financial arrangements are agreeable. He ends the letter with,

> *The Eastern Front* will not come out until the autumn of 1931. I hope for 'Marlborough' in the autumn of 1932.
>
> P.S. I should like to emphasize the fact that Mr. Butterworth was most anxious to co-operate in every way with you, and to fit all the plans to suit our various but common interests.[84]

Here again, it is worthy of note that Churchill is actively engaged on four separate books with two publishers. By 7 July, Churchill is sending a batch of proofs and typescript to his printer and asking if he can have all of them in proof form by the end of the week, as he will be at Chartwell for the weekend and wants to work on them.[85] Churchill is amending chapters as well as creating new ones to fill in the gaps in the story and to weave the story into a more smoothly running narrative. He is also working with Butterworth to create the flow of the book and clarify chapter names and content. As can be seen in the table below, the chapters as of 10 July, and those that will appear at publication, are not yet set. On 10 July, Butterworth asks for clarification of the chapters and structure:

> I now beg to send your copy of your Chapter headings. We have received proof of Chapters 1, 4, 5, 6, 10, 13, 14, 17, 19, 20 and 21. In addition, we have received proofs of the following Chapter headings:
> 'Myself When Young' [Presumably, Chapter 1, which is now titled 'Childhood'.]
>   'The Lure of War'
>   'In an Indian Valley'
>   'General Botha'
>   '1896'
>   'How I placated Lord Roberts'
>
> and I should be glad if you would let me know: What are the present titles of the other five Chapters?[86]

Below, in the left column, is how Butterworth listed the chapters as of 10 July. On the right is how the chapters would appear in October at publication.

Chapters as of July 1930	In book at publication
1. Childhood	Childhood
2. Harrow	Harrow
3. Examinations	Examinations
4. Sandhurst	Sandhurst
5. The 4th Hussars	The Fourth Hussars
6. Cuba	Cuba
7. Hounslow	Hounslow
8. India	India
9. Bangalore	Education at Bangalore
10. The Malakand Field Force	The Malakand Field Force
11. The Mamud Valley	The Mamud Valley
12. The Tirah Expedition	The Tirah Expedition
13. A Difference with Kitchener	A Difficulty with Kitchener
14. The Eve of Omdurman	The Eve of Omdurman
15. The Sensations of a Cavalry Charge	The Sensations of a Cavalry Charge
16. I Leave the Army	I Leave the Army
	17. Oldham
17. With Buller to the Cape	18. With Buller to the Cape
18. The Armoured Train	19. The Armoured Train
19. In Durance Vile	20. In Durance Vile
20. I Escape from the Boers	21. I Escape From the Boers
21. I Escape from the Boers (contd)	22. I Escape from the Boers (contd)
22. On the Tugela	
	23. Back to the Army
	24. Spion Kop
	25. The Relief of Ladysmith
23. In the Orange Free State	26. In the Orange Free State
24. A Ride through Johannesburg	27. Johannesburg and Pretoria
25. Pretoria	
26. The Khaki Election	28. The Khaki Election
27. The House of Commons	29. The House of Commons

That Churchill is actively adding new material is verified in a letter to the printers from his secretary, Pearman, in which she states,

> Mr. Churchill wishes me to send to you herewith a further chapter of the Memoirs in typescript etc. The separate sheets marked 'xyz' are to go to the end of the chapter which was sent to you last evening (the 10th). Mr. Churchill will be at Chartwell till Tuesday morning next (the 15th) and will be glad to receive proofs in the usual way as soon as possible.[87]

A very similar letter with new typescript material was sent to the printers two days later. Pearman then sends a letter on 14 July which provides some insights into what Churchill is modifying, adding, 'I am desired by Mr. Churchill to forward herewith two further chapters. The chapter entitled "With Buller to the Cape" supersedes where it differs from the copy already sent to you (see Mr. Churchill's note on top). There is another chapter i.e. XVII Oldham.'[88]

Here we can see Churchill has added the chapter ('Oldham') that did not exist before, as seen in the above Table, while modifying the other chapter.

Churchill and Scribner had still not reached agreement on financial contract, as Scribner couldn't accept Churchill's suggestion. They cabled him on 16 July: TWENTY-FIVE PERCENT ROYALTY MEMOIRS IMPOSSIBLE WITH AMERICAN DISCOUNT STOP HOPE YOU WILL ACCEPT TWENTY-FIVE HUNDRED DOLLARS ADVANCE AND TWENTY PERCENT ROYALTY AFTER TEN THOUSAND AS A COMPROMISE STOP SUGGESTED DATES FOR BOOKS PERFECTLY SATISFACTORY.[89]

Churchill agreed. On 30 July, Scribner sent him a contract dated 28 July. In it, Scribner included sole rights in the US and Canada. Churchill struck out Canada, signed it 'WSC', and sent it back. The contract was not finally signed and executed until 26 October 1930. It provided for a royalty of 15 per cent on the published price on the first 5000 copies and 20 per cent thereafter.[90]

ITERATIVE FACT-CHECKING

As Churchill was writing and editing, he continued researching specific elements of the work and asking for original material he had written earlier in his career. This can be seen in his letter to H.A. Gwynne, editor of the *Morning Post*, on 17 July 1930:

> I wonder if you could send me a copy of the telegram I sent the *Morning Post* at the beginning of March 1900, advocating clement treatment for Natal rebels. I remember that I got into some trouble about this telegram and I should like to see what it was I actually said. I should be much obliged if you could help me in this.[91]

(The *Morning Post* sent him a copy. It had been published on 27 March 1900.)

As has been indicated previously, *My Early Life* was an amalgamation of his earlier newspaper war correspondence; the four books he had written on India, the Sudan and the South African War; and the articles on his early life published in the early 1920s. The next chapter will provide in detail examples of just how he wove all of these together along with new text to create the book. The issue of who owned the copyright to all of his previous publications was dealt with at this time. On 23 July, he wrote to Longman's, his publisher for the books in question:

> Dear Sirs, Several books you have published for me, namely, *The Malakand Field Force, London to Ladysmith via Pretoria, Ian Hamilton's March*, and *The River War* have, I understood, been long out of print and therefore I assume that your copyright has lapsed.
>
> I have already arranged to publish some memoirs of *My Early Life* which draw upon some of the incidents and adventures recounted in those books. I wish to make use of the original books only to the extent of about twelve pages from *London to Ladysmith via Pretoria* about my escape, and about seven pages from *Ian Hamilton's March* about the adventure I had at De Wetsdorf [South Africa]. For these incidents I prefer to use the exact words in which I recorded them while the events were fresh in my memory. I trust this will be agreeable to you.
>
> It has however occurred to me that it might be more satisfactory to you if the copyright of these four books, or at any rate some of them, should revert to me, and I should like to know whether you would care to mention any sum which I should pay you for them.[92]

Longmans answers Churchill that he can use any material he desires from the books of his that they published and that they are happy to transfer all rights to him as they don't anticipate reissuing any of them.[93]

Churchill was seeking wide input on what he had written thus far. He asked a very disparate group of experts to review and comment on the manuscript. The first response noted was from John Buchan, a well-known Scottish novelist, historian and Unionist politician. Churchill much admired Buchan's *A History of the Great War* and had written to him congratulating him on his books.[94] Buchan wrote to Churchill on 23 July:

> Your proofs have given me most enormous entertainment. You have written the most original, and one of the most delightful books of reminiscences I have ever come across. Without doubt it will be a great success. As a mere matter of writing I do not think you have ever surpassed some of the passages – e.g. the Lancers' charge at Omdurman.
>
> I have not attempted to correct any of the printers' errors and as for finding longueurs, the thing is not possible.
>
> I have only two things to suggest. The first is the question of fact. In Chapter XIII, you have not got the Grenfell family quite right. The twins were younger, not older brothers of Robert, and only one, Francis, got the V.C., though both were killed.
>
> The other is a matter of taste, on which I may offer my views with humility. It is in connection with Chapter IX, 112c-112g. My own feeling is that the little discussion about religion and philosophy is not quite in proper perspective. It is either too short or too full. It seems to me to not be in the same tone as the rest of the book. I should be inclined to leave it out; but I offer that suggestion with some trepidation. Many thanks for letting me see the proofs. They have given me great pleasure.[95]

Buchan certainly enjoyed what he read. His comments on religion and philosophy most likely relate to the chapter 'Education at Bangalore', where Churchill is voraciously reading history, philosophy and religion to educate himself. (See, for example, pp. 127–9 in *MEL*.) This section would come to vex Churchill, and we shall see further on how he would deal with it. We do not have all the revisions this section went through, so it is impossible to know which version Buchan read. Churchill continued to send chapters to Buchan. He received another letter stating, 'This is an excellent chapter. I hope the book does not finish with your first election, but sees you safely in Parliament. This is the natural close of the first part of your career.'[96]

Churchill also wrote to King George V to obtain permission to include an 1898 letter from King Edward (then Prince of Wales) concerning Churchill's book *The Story of the Malakand Field Force*. He received permission.[97]

Churchill was now sending so many new proofs and revised proofs to his printer that the printer became overwhelmed, so much so that he cabled Churchill to push back on when Churchill would receive the amended pages.[98]

A few days later, Pearman wrote to the printer:

> I am desired by Mr. Churchill to send herewith the last bundle of proofs, and to say that he would like to have early on Friday morning next, if possible, here at Chartwell, twelve copies in all of everything including the chapters 'Orange Free State' and 'Johannesburg and Pretoria' which can come back in second revise; also new chapter sent to you early this morning which can come back in first revise. This will enable Mr. Churchill to have twelve copies which he can circulate to various people before going into page proof. He would particularly like the proofs on Friday as he wishes to send one copy to America urgently.[99]

One can only imagine the pressure and frustration that the printers, publishers and reviewers must have felt in the face of Churchill's prodigious output and demands. When one considers that there were no computers and there were twelve copies of chapters in various stages of editing circulating to large numbers of people, how any of the parties could hope to have any semblance of version control is simply beyond comprehension.

On 25 July, Churchill wrote to Buchan on the comments he had received:

> Thank you so much for your letter and for so kindly reading my proofs. I will certainly carefully consider what you say about my religious and philosophical excursions. I was doubtful about them myself on the very grounds you mention. They are of course intended to be the opinions of a subaltern officer thinking things out for himself without the advantage which students enjoy at a University. Do you remember

a chapter called 'In Durance Vile'? This is all about a plan which never came off. It is therefore hypothetical and one, I had bound it over to come up for judgment when called upon. How did it strike you?

Again, did you think the chapter called 'Cuba' required compression? Did it flag and seem to run less easily than the rest? I always try to jettison ten per cent of a book and many hundred adjectives in the last run over. It is so awful to have padding! But a new eye can measure so much better than the author. Once more thanking you.[100]

Churchill never lost sight of the fact that he had not attended university and was self-educated. As noted in the above letter, when describing how he discussed philosophy and religion, he feels he doesn't have the academic grounding to make the discussion as robust and academic as a university graduate might have. Churchill hardly needed to apologise for his intellectual skills, but this lack of formal education always gnawed at him a little.

MARKETING BEGINS

When Butterworth began their marketing plans, he sent Churchill a letter asking for his input:

I have pleasure to send you preliminary prospectus we are rushing out mainly for Australasian buyers. Final prospectus will be in four page form. Meanwhile would you be so good as to go over the 'blurb' now it is in print and make any alterations you think fit for its improvement. Personally speaking I don't like the last four words in the expression 'from the dust of the desert to the grassy plains.' The words 'grassy plains' do not appear to me to mark the venue so clearly as the expression, 'lonely days and nights on the veld.' There may, of course, be other points that occur to you, when you have time to consider it.

In view of the unexpected length of the book, as you informed me over the telephone, we have taken the precaution to put the price at 21/- or 25/-. Our desire and yours is, I think, that the book should be published at 21/-; but it is impossible for us at the present time to advise you whether that will be practicable or not, – we must await the final cast-off and the costing of the illustrations that will be selected.

I am looking forward with the keenest interest to the revised proofs, which I shall read immediately they are sent in. Could you give me an idea when that will be?[101]

Churchill continues to ask former colleagues for information about their common experiences. Lieutenant-Colonel Sir Cecil Levita, a Captain of the Royal Artillery in South Africa, sends Churchill an eight-page letter describing what he remembers happening, especially concerning Spion Kop.[102]

Edward Marsh was a British polymath, translator, arts patron, and, as stated previously, he was a private secretary to Churchill and a trusted friend and confidant of his. Churchill frequently sought Marsh's advice in literary issues. Here, Marsh responds to Churchill's request in a letter: 'Could you let me have your proofs here by Thursday? I am going to Bowood [his family estate in Wiltshire] on Friday & shall be there until Tuesday next week, so they would be a delightful occupation for the mornings.'[103] Churchill replies the next day:

I hope to have a third revise virtually complete for you on Friday, and will send them to Bowood. It is no good you're reading the earlier versions. It will be very kind of you if you will read it in sequence and keep an eye on the following:

1. Punctuation
2. Grammar and Style
3. Longueurs (I could afford to cut out 10,000 words if necessary)
4. Repetitions of words and phrases
5. John Buchan thought the religious and philosophical disquisition either too long or too short, and out of focus. I do not quite feel this. It is of course intended to be a subaltern's outlook. Let me know what you feel about it after having read the book as a whole.

There are about 3,000 more words to come at the end about the 'Hooligans' and the first threats of tariff reform, ending up with marrying and living happily ever after.

PS. The first 12 chapters have just come in and so I send them now.[104]

Here again, Churchill is worried about his discussion of religion and philosophy. Over the years, there would be many lively exchanges between Churchill and Marsh on punctuation, style, and grammar (see below). They both thoroughly enjoyed the details, correctness and flair of the English language.

DEBATE ON THE TITLE BEGINS

In a letter from Scribner which provided the final contract, Scribner also raises the issue of what the title should be: 'I am not certain if you intend to use "Memoirs" as the title or not. We should prefer another but if it is the best title for the English market we are perfectly content to abide by it. To me it rather suggests a book written at the close of life.'[105]

Churchill replied on 1 August that he would suggest as the American title 'A Roving Commission' Scribner cabled back on 8 August: ALL HEARTILY FAVOR ROVING COMMISSION WITH SOME SUBTITLE CABLE WHETHER BUTTERWORTH APPROVES.[106] This was not the end of the discussion, as will be seen.

On 31 July Churchill writes to Marsh:

I sent you yesterday the first twelve chapters but found afterwards – they are not the latest revise. These I will send you sometime tomorrow. There is not much difference between the two versions, but it will save trouble if you will read the latest. I am also sending you today to Bowood all the rest of the book after the twelve. This is the third revise and should be worked on.[107]

Churchill continues to seek input on the book. On 2 August, he sent proofs to Stanley Baldwin, former and future Conservative Prime Minister, writing, 'Any comments which occur to you, either favourable or unfavourable, or any advice, will always be received by me with customary respect!' Baldwin sent a quick note on 18 August: 'This is only a line: I will write you at length in a few days from Aix. I am half-way through your book which I am savouring as if it were a delicious vintage. I am enjoying every word of it. It is too good to gulp.'[108] Baldwin sent a more complete review on 4 September:

My dear Winston,

You asked for criticism. There really isn't much to be said. Of course there are minor things to be attended to such as cutting one or two duplications and the natural corrections you would make yourself, but generally I think the whole book is admirable. You have got a delightful touch running through it all, and I am inclined to agree with Buchan as to the philosophic meditation being a bit out of place.

I like the part of the chapter on books and your reading them like a young lion tasting meat for the first time: that all helps to explain and illuminate the personality that emerges as quite an engaging one!

No, my dear Winston, it is a remarkable production and I have read it with real delight. I kept saying 'My wig' or words to that effect 'that is GOOD.'

And it is jolly good. I wish I could write anything half that good. One thing is certain. You will be read, and annotated, and examined and compared, by every one who studies or attempts to write the history of these times, and that will be fun although we shan't be there to see it.

The public will clamour for more.[109]

On 2 August, Churchill sent out a number of proofs to be reviewed by friends and colleagues, and it is interesting to read what he asked each of them. Some are quite specific questions directed to those who shared some common experiences; other are repeatedly nagging questions such as his description of philosophy and religion; while still others are general questions like 'How does it read?' or 'Does it flow?'

To General James Edmonds, an officer in the Royal Engineers who worked in Intelligence section during the Boer War, Churchill wrote:

You very kindly said you would like to look at these proofs. They are practically in a finished condition, though of course there is a certain amount of checking of facts and style yet to be done. I should be grateful if you would let me know whether you find any part drags particularly, and also what you think about the religious and philosophical excursions in Chapter 9. Buchan thought them out of focus, either too long or too short. Any comments which occur to you, favourable or unfavourable, or any advice, will always be received by me with customary respect.[110]

To General Sir Ian Hamilton, a good friend, a general in the Boer War and a writer, he writes:

> I send you forthwith a copy of my early memoirs. You figure a good deal in them, and all the events with which they deal are well known to you. I shall be most grateful if you will read the proofs for me and write freely upon them any comments, corrections, criticisms, embellishments or omissions which may suggest themselves. It would be most kind of you also to give me your judgment on the general literary aspect of this work. For instance, are there any parts that drag and could be jettisoned? Do you think the chapter on Cuba requires compression? Do you think my philosophical or religious disquisitions – intended to be those of a subaltern – in Chapter 9 are out of focus, whether too long or too short and might well be omitted? Do you think the chapter 'In Durance Vile' might be cut out as it deals only with that what never came off?[111]

The saga of deciding whether to select one or two titles (British and American) continues when Churchill sends a letter to Butterworth: '… Title. I cannot think of anything better than *A Roving Commission* – if you like it with a sub-title "The Memoirs of My Early Life". I rather like the new title *A Roving Commission*. Have you any suggestions? This is a matter in which your advice would be especially valuable.'[112]

Butterworth quickly replied:

> In regard to the title *A Roving Commission*: I would say at first blush that the sub-title 'The Memoirs of My Early Life' even with it does not sound sufficiently important for your book or really sufficiently embracing, as of course your autobiography covers your early years. But may I make enquiries elsewhere, both inside and outside the office, as I should be sorry to be dogmatic and run the risk, perhaps, of making a mistake. I feel, as I am sure you do, that the right title is all important.[113]

Feedback on the book was now coming back to Churchill. Eddie Marsh writes, on 5 August,

> I am delighting in the book, which is most interesting, amusing, & in parts enthralling. It was a very pleasant occupation for my mornings at Bowood & this evening I can go on with it & just finished the Escape – so seven chapters remain, which I hope to get through tomorrow evening, in which case I will post the whole on Thursday morning to Chartwell unless you say otherwise.
>
> I have made a number of small suggestions, and cannot think of any general criticisms & I didn't myself feel any consciousness of longueurs I have suggested no omissions.
>
> John Buchan's criticism would not have occurred to me – the passage on Bangalore is very slightly pretentious & as you say it is only supposed to give yr youthful notions. As however the objection has occurred to him, it may occur to others; and if you wish to meet it you might leave out the paragraph about the sun on p. 112 – the discussion is well rounded without it.[114]

This last comment likely relates to the paragraph about the sun on pages 131 and 132 in *My Early Life*, which contains a sort of philosophical stream of consciousness. However, we have no way of knowing what paragraphs Churchill kept in or deleted.

In a follow-up letter the next day, Marsh continues:

> I've finished the chapter in a canter & will send them off in the morning. The S. African part is all most spirited & entertaining & I've enjoyed the whole thing immensely. I suppose you'll be sending me the last 2 chapters. I don't know if you will like my punctuation. I've respected your wish to do with as few stops as possible, but perhaps you will still think I've put in too many. It all depends on one's own individual ear for the run of a sentence. I feel I can justify all my suggestions, but perhaps only to myself!
>
> There are two inconsistencies in spelling, which I have left – about half way through I realized that you said, 'my mother' and sometimes 'my Mother.' I didn't know which you would prefer & anyhow I didn't go back and find all the places. The same applies to the spelling of

verbs ending -ize or -ise & nouns in -ization or – isation. My personal preference is for the Z forms; but at the beginning the printer always seemed to have used the 's' ones and I let him have his way. Then I found that the 'Z's were creeping in & there are a good many scattered about. But again I didn't go back. Perhaps in both these matters you can tell the printer what to do in his final proof reading.[115]

Butterworth writes on 6 August:

I read your Autobiography very carefully. I read it through on Sunday and Monday last and I became so engrossed in it that I begrudged any interruption.

Nevertheless, I do feel that, with the exception of the more Adventurous Chapters, it would be improved by compression here and there. The early Chapters would gain by some cutting, as one wants to get on to your Adventures, and, in this connection, I would particularize the Ormiston Chant episode. The Cuban Chapter, while tremendously improved, does not in my opinion compare with the interest of the Egyptian and Boer Chapters. It might also be worth your consideration whether the Political Chapters curtailed or not. More than this I cannot say, without reading the works through again. Moreover, I feel sure that you have friends, whose advice would be more valuable than mine.

I see that the book will now run to 384 pages all told, that is counting in the prelims and index; in other words, it makes twelve sections of 32 pages each, namely two sections more than the usual ten sections or 320 pages. To bring it within the desired length, it would require cutting by about twenty thousand words. At first blush, you will probably consider this too much but, possibly, and I hope that as you go through it you will feel that such cutting would be all to the good.

There are three reasons why I recommend this should be done, if you can see your way:

1) The interest of the book, as a whole, would I believe gain by compression.
2) It would enable us to bring the book out at 21/-, which I feel sure is the price we should aim at in these hard times.

3) It would allow us to bring the book out, later on, at a reasonably cheap price, and thereby enable the younger generation to read it side by side with 'Treasure Island' and possibly the Schools would take it up as a reader. Every section over ten sections, 320 pages, means additional costs for Moulds, for Stereos, for paper, for printing and for binding. This means much.

I am afraid I have not been so helpful as I could have wished, but nevertheless I trust that the points I have put before you may be of some little service, when you come to final revision.[116]

Churchill does not appear to have accepted many of Butterworth's suggestions, as the 'Ormiston Chant' section, which refers to Churchill's interaction at the Empire Theatre when a cadet at Sandhurst, remains in the final book (pp. 64–6). The book was brought out in school editions, as suggested by Butterworth. In Sweden, a school edition (in English) was first published by Albert Bonniers Forlag in 1936, with three additional printings in 1944, 1946 and 1950. In the UK, Oldhams published a school edition in 1958 followed by twelve reprints from 1959 to 1964. In Germany, Brandstetter Verlag published in 1958 an abridged *My Early Life*, in English with extensive German comments, for students to learn English. (See Appendix 8 Chapter 6 Unrecorded Books and Other Media.) The chapter on Cuba remains, and the book ended up being even longer: 392 pages. This reluctance to shorten the book is confirmed in a letter to Butterworth on 9 August:

1. Title. I await your suggestions.
2. Abridged edition. These dates will be quite satisfactory.
3. Photographs and maps. These will be sent to you by Sunday's post.
4. I am taking several opinions about Memoirs copy and whether any of it should be jettisoned. I will then read it finally again from this point of view.

With regard to the Mrs. Ormiston Chant episode, your reference to the future use in schools makes me think that perhaps you are a little afraid of the topics round which this incident is built. Others, when they read these proofs, seemed to like it very much. …

> I am rather reluctant to scrap as much as 20,000 words. Indeed now I see it coldly, I think it is all fairly readable. I have telegraphed to Scribner asking for suggestions about a title.[117]

As might be expected with so many individuals and corporate entities handling various versions of the proofs which were divided into chapters, there came a time in early August when Churchill's agent Curtis Brown sent a frantic, complex letter to Churchill's secretary, Pearman, noting that 'we are still without certain chapters'. In addition, he notes that 'the printer has numbered some of the later chapters wrongly'. He includes a new contents page with the correct order of the chapters and information needed so that the chapters can be reordered correctly and informs her that certain chapters are completely missing. He further asks if a new chapter is being written, as his total doesn't match the number he was told there would be.[118]

After much mayhem, the disparities are deciphered and corrected. This would have been a good day not to be at Chartwell.

The plan had been to publish excerpts from the book in serial form in newspapers prior to the release of the book to prepare the market and provide advertising for the book. In a letter dated 9 August, Churchill addresses this issue and provides Butterworth with justifications as to why he didn't accept any of his previous recommendations:

> Mr. Tom Clark, the Editor of the *Daily News*, visited me today. He had picked out rather over 25,000 words from the hitherto unpublished material. The *Daily News* appears to be quite excited about the publication. I was told, in confidence, that they intend to spend 3,500 pounds on advertising what they consider 'my finest book.' I send you the two papers which Mr. Clark left with me. I should be glad if you would get in touch with him early next week, in order that common interests may be studied to the highest advantage. He particularly likes the Mrs. Ormiston Chant incident, praises 'Cuba,' and strongly urged that nothing should be cut. [Churchill never let an issue drop until he was absolutely convinced that his point was accepted.]
>
> I have received the copy back from Eddie Marsh with the punctuation and the grammar thoroughly scrutinized. He does not recommend any omissions. …

> Scribner's have telegraphed 'All heartily favour Roving Commission with some sub-title: 'cable whether Butterworth approves.' I think it will be difficult to beat 'A Roving Commission,' with the subtitle 'Memories of My Youth.'
>
> Pray let me know what you think about this as soon as possible.
>
> Maps and photographs should reach you Monday.
>
> I am much encouraged by the impression this has made on those who have read it.
>
> We must settle the *bulk* of the book this week.[119]

The *Daily News* noted in the above letter is the parent company. They had purchased the serial rights to be published in their publication the *News Chronicle*.

Churchill followed up the next day with another letter to Butterworth:

> I send you herewith the maps and photographs. There are twenty-five in all, of which two pairs go on a page, and two or three print in the text. They spread very evenly through the book, and I think illustrate it extremely well. If you wish to omit any, the one in Chapter XVII Oldham, the Dutch postcard for Chapter XIX, the half page one to Chapter XXIII marked X, and the Lady Randolph gun Chapter XXV, could be omitted. There would be some advantage in having 22Y, of me speaking under the Union Jack at Durban, a full page.
>
> *I am very disinclined to cut the book. Please give me your final view after you have had a talk with Mr. Tom Clark and have seen what he intends to do in advertisement. The majority of our purchasers at a guinea or 25/- do not read the 'Daily News' but all will see the placards and advertisements, and so will the libraries during the month of September. Then I expect there will be a fine demand for the book, and I am sure it will hold its own with the reviewers.* [emphasis added]
>
> I plan to send the complete text for page proofs as soon as I hear from you, and final decisions are taken on bulk. You will certainly be able to go to press by the end of this month, which gives forty days and forty nights for you to accomplish your labours.
>
> I am really most hopeful about this book. The extracts which the *Daily News* are so enthusiastic about, do not convey its real staple, namely

the adventures up the Nile and at the Cape. I would not be surprised if you sold 15,000 of the expensive edition, and I am sure that if a year later we can get into a 5/- or a 3/6, there will be a very large sale.

I have yet to do the preface. I should like to see the proofs of the maps and reproductions. *Note*. I am sending you separately by parcel post the original of the £25 Reward proclamation.

I should be much obliged if you would arrange with Scribner to let them have the blocks of the illustrations and maps as soon as made, making whatever arrangement is proper with him thereafter. I have no duplicates of many of these photographs, and therefore cannot send him a complete set.

After you have seen Mr Tom Clark I can give you lunch any day here [Chartwell] if you will come. It is one hour's motor drive, and you will find it a pleasant drive. We can then settle everything finally.[120]

When published, the book had a total of twenty-nine photographs and illustrations and nine maps, including a pull-out map. Some of the photographs are combined on one page. In the letter above, Churchill states there are twenty-five photographs and maps 'in all'. It is possible to comment on the specific ones he mentions. The Dutch postcard image remains in. The photograph from Chapter XVII ('Oldham') is out. The half-page photograph in Chapter XXVII ('Back to the Army') is in. The photograph in Chapter XXV of the Lady Churchill gun was removed. The photograph of Churchill speaking in Durban was made a full page. What other changes may have been made to the maps and photographs are unknown.

Churchill truly enjoyed the writing of this book. He was quite playful in his responses to his appointed reviewers, for example, Marsh, who, as can be seen by the manner in which Churchill signs the letter, is quite dear to him. On 10 August, Churchill writes,

> I am enormously obliged to you for the great pains you have taken in correcting my proofs. I have adopted your punctuation although I had been inclined to let 'and' play the part of a comma as well as itself. I am really startled at your hyphens! Parade-ground, riding-school, thorn-bushes etc. On those lines you would write party politics with a hyphen. Surely nobody does that. Could you let me know what is the

rule about hyphens, and whether there is not an option in a great many of these cases.

I will send the other two chapters as soon as they come back from the printer.

Once more thanking you,
Yours Affectionately,
W[121]

Marsh replied the next day:

I'm very glad you're pleased with my proof-reading. As for the comma after 'and' my feeling is not to have a comma unless the readers' mind should pause & you certainly don't after those 'and' I found the commas pulling me up in the wrong place.

Hyphens are very tricky. I will try to remember to bring you *Modern English Usage* when I come on the 23rd, it contains an interesting disquisition on them. The rule I was following in the cases you question was that one puts a hyphen when the second component has lost all or some of its normal accent. I certainly say parade ground, not parade-ground, riding school not riding-school, thorne bushes, not thorne-bushes. … looking forward to the last 2 chapters.[122]

Ian Hamilton, another of his reviewers, writes the following on 10 August:

Although my hands are pretty full I'm real sorry to part with your gay memoirs. Don't cut the philosophy & religion: the adventures of the spirit are even more Xciting [*sic*] than those of the body. Don't cut Cuba but here (if you care to take the very great sweat of giving each sentence) a little pruning – say 7 % – might repay you. Preserve 'In Durance Vile.' It shows the effect of the prison atmosphere in producing megalomania just as mushrooms and 'Pilgrims Progress' are produced in Dungeons. You end where you are just about to enter upon the mist –shaky sketch of you on the tight-rope. … all this time what industry being developed in 105 Mount Street: and so, *Labor omnia vincit*, as I may permit myself to say now that old Squiff, that 'Big Dog,' is no more.

Anyway in what follows – be careful. Throw as much as you can of your differences with the Tories onto what in your last para [*sic*] you call your 'sentimental view' about the Boers. Actually in its application, it was high living Statesmanship, as opposed to a vindictive obscurantist outlook.[123]

Hamilton agrees with Churchill on what to save. He suggests that he do some pruning and distance himself from the Tories on the issue of the Boer War. Churchill writes back three days later and thanks him for his comments.[124]

Ian Hamilton sends Churchill a fascinating letter on 13 August, enclosing an article Hamilton wrote about Churchill in 1921 containing Hamilton's recollections of their interactions in the army. The article is certainly worth reading in its entirety. Hamilton writes:

I have just received from London a book of newspaper cutting … In it is my article in *MacLean's Magazine* (Canada) on you. It is dated 1921 [*MacLean's Magazine*, 15 June 1921, pp. 12–14]. If you have never seen it or have forgotten it I think I ought to send you down the volume for it gives another rendering (but not in any way contradictory) of many of the matters treated in your M.S.S. Your visit & manner of life for the 2 or 3 days you spent with me in the Gala Kadai (Thieves Den) camp in the Barer Valley. The [*illegible*] of your letter to me written after you got back to the regiment.[125]

Hamilton continues:

May we meet again when rifles are loaded and sword sharp-ended, if possible before an audience which will include 40 centuries (and so we did!). Then there is your long letter written on the train on 16 September 1899 giving a variant of your type script story. It is very good & of course the effect of a contemporary letter in inverted commas is much more convincing than a reminiscence. The answer given you by the Sargent 21st Lancers after the charge is too good to be lost. You asked him if he had enjoyed himself. He replied, 'Well, I don't exactly say I enjoyed it, Sir, but I think I'll get more used to it next time.[126]

(This last exact quotation is published on p. 208 of MEL)

FURTHER DEBATE ON TITLE

The selection process for the elusive acceptable title continues. Churchill cables Scribner on 15 August: BUTTERWORTH FAVOURS AUTOBIOGRAPHY OF WINSTON CHURCHILL WITH SUBTITLE MY EARLY LIFE CABLE YOUR OPINION.[127]

Scribner replies the same day: WOULD DEPLORE AUTOBIOGRAPHY TITLE AS INEXACT AND MISLEADING CONSIDER A ROVING COMMISSION WITH SUBTITLE BOTH EFFECTIVE AND APT.[128]

Caught in the middle of these strongly held positions, Churchill writes to Butterworth on 16 August with a thoughtful review:

> I send you Scribner's cable: 'Would deplore autobiography title as inexact and misleading. Consider 'A Roving Commission' with subtitle both effective and apt.'
>
> There is no doubt from a literary point of view that 'A Roving Commission' with a subtitle 'Memoirs of My Early Life' is more descriptive and attractive. There is a force in what Scribner says in that it is not an autobiography nor anything like it, but only an account of my early years. I am impressed with his persistent opinion and I am sure you will give it all weight. Do you really think the difference between these two titles will make much difference to sales? 'A Roving Commission: Memoirs of My Early Life' by Winston S. Churchill, seems to me to be pretty good. Please give me your view.
>
> Let me know also whether it would be possible for Scribner to publish under one title and you under another: or whether this would lead to great confusion. I should be glad to know as soon as possible as I must let Scribner know. When I hear from you I will take the final decision. … Although we have got so much work on hand, there seems to be no harm in looking ahead. I think it would be a good thing if I collected the fifteen or twenty articles I have already written on eminent personages I have met and had them set up by Butler & Tanner as soon as the Memoirs proofs have been cleared.
>
> I hope to take out a net of ten thousand words thus reducing the Memoirs by one complete section.

Professor Lindemann thinks some account of my literary and religious or irreligious development should complete the picture, and that I must try to show the growth of my mental outlook, otherwise how can the Parliamentary and literary successes be explained. But I am finding other things to cut which can be spared.[129]

This is an impactful and insightful letter on many levels, as it reveals much about Churchill's thought processes in planning his time, making decisions, and how incredibly busy he felt he had to be at all times. He begins with a methodical and reasoned view on how to choose the title and ends it with 'I will take the final decision.' He then, with apparent inexhaustible energy (or need for money), suggests that he should get the printers to start printing an early version of what was to become his book *Great Contemporaries*. Remember: at this time, he is actively working on *The Eastern Front*, the abridged version of *The World Crisis*, *Marlborough*, these 'Memoirs' and numerous articles for magazines and newspapers. In addition, he promises to cut this book down by ten thousand words. Finally, at the instigation of his friend Lindemann, Churchill believes he needs to add something on his mental growth to the book, and he ends with the not so humble question, 'otherwise how can the Parliamentary and literary successes be explained[?]' This is truly a Churchillian letter.

At the same time that negotiations for a title were going on, there was also a concerted effort to negotiate the rights for serialisation of the book in the US. Curtis Brown, Churchill's London literary agent, sends a letter to Churchill on 11 August, stating, 'I am very sorry to say that we have now had a cable containing the information that Hearst's have finally declined the "Memoirs."'[130] He follows up ten days later with 'We hear this morning the *New York Times* has refused the Memoirs, but that the *Tribune* is sufficiently interested to ask for more time in which to consider the matter.'[131] No serialisation of the book would occur.

There is a note to an unknown reviewer on 17 August thanking them for comments which deal with specific points on Churchill's adventures in India and South Africa.[132]

On this same day, Churchill writes to David Beatty, former Admiral of the Fleet and First Sea Lord, who as a Lieutenant commanded a gunboat on the Nile while Churchill was with Kitchener in the Sudan. Beatty was thought by

Churchill to be in charge of the gunboat from which a bottle of champagne was thrown to him, as related in *My Early Life* (p. 195). Churchill asks,

> I wonder if you could clear up a small point for me which arises in connection with some Memoirs I am publishing shortly. Was it your gunboat on the eve of Omdurman from which Dick Molyneux and I were thrown a bottle of Champagne? I know that Prince Francis of Teck was on board the gunboat from which this welcome present came. But I am not sure whether it was your gunboat or another.
>
> Secondly, were you a Commander at this time or only a Lieutenant? I should be glad if you would drop me a line on these two points as soon as possible.[133]

This request must have been answered, though no record has been found. Churchill refers to Beatty on page 194 of *My Early Life*: 'The vessel was commanded by a junior naval Lieutenant named Beatty who had long served in the Nile flotillas and was destined to fame on blue water.'

By 18 August Churchill is sending sections of the book to Scribner:

> I send you herewith the first ten chapters of the Memoirs in a form to be put immediately into page proof. In the Cuba chapter I have left a passage about my journey to the States and meeting Bourke Cockran which I have cut from the English edition, as Butterworth is anxious to economize words as much as possible. Up to the end of this installment there is no other difference whatever between the two editions.
>
> We are still arguing about the title, and my last idea is 'My Early Life' by Winston Churchill. This perhaps is the best suggestion.
>
> I am also arranging that Butterworth shall send you a fine selection of illustrations and maps. I do not know how many you want to put in. He seems inclined to have a good lot of pictures.
>
> I shall never see the page proofs again in the American edition. Will you therefore kindly ask one of your trusted colleagues with a fresh eye, to read through from start to finish, and make sure it all goes straight.
>
> I do not expect more than a handful of verbal corrections in the page proofs, and certainly nothing that will alter the pagination. These will reach you in a week or ten days, but do not delay setting up the type.

Everyone who has seen these proofs seem to think we are going to have a very big sale over here, and I hope that we shall also have a good result in your country.[134]

The section on Bourke Cockran appears to have been eliminated in both the British and American editions.

The time had arrived when the three parties (Churchill, Scribner and Butterworth) had to reach a decision on what the title(s) would be. Another eleven days of haggling, however, were still in front of them. In the above letter, Churchill noted that they were still arguing about the title and that he currently favours 'My Early Life'. On this same day, Churchill cabled Butterworth: 'What do you think of My Early Life with no subtitle?'[135] Butterworth replies the next day in a cable: 'My Early Life in my opinion certainly good second best will adopt it if you prefer it.'[136] Any hope that the decision is near is dashed when Churchill receives this 19 August cable from Scribner, which ups the ante with a not-so-veiled threat: MY EARLY LIFE WEAK AND COLORLESS BUT PREFERABLE TO AUTOBIOGRAPHY LATTER CATCHPENNY SELECTION [i.e. cheap edition] STRONLY [sic] FAVOR ROVING COMMISSION AGREE POSTPONING PUBLICATION.[137]

Churchill, likely shocked by the cable, appears to agree with Scribner and cables back the next day: IMPRESSED BY YOUR SPIRITED VIEWS CONSIDER MEMORIES OF MY YOUTH STOP DO YOU OBJECT DIFFERENT TITLES ENGLAND AMERICA IF NOT COULD SETTLE ON ROVING COMMISSION AMERICA.[138] Here Churchill is offering to create two separate titles.

Churchill then offers another title to Butterworth in a 20 August cable: 'Another suggestion Memories of My Youth.'[139] Scribner's then accepts the concept of two titles in a cable the next day: REGRET DIFFERENT TITLES BUT SETTLE ON ROVING COMMISSION USING IN BRITISH AS SUBTITLE MEMORIES RATHER DEADLY.[140]

All parties finally agree, and Churchill sends this cable to Scribner on 29 August: TITLE HERE MY EARLY LIFE SUBTITLE ON THE TITLE PAGE ROVING COMMISSION STOP YOUR TITLE ROVING COMMISSION WITH SUBTITLE MY EARLY LIFE.[141]

The titles are now finally settled. The writing, editing and fact-checking can proceed full throttle. On 22 August, Churchill sends a letter to the editor of the *Oldham Chronicle* asking him to check on a myriad of facts from what will be Chapter XVII on his Oldham candidacy: people, dates, organisations and events from his unsuccessful campaign there.[142] On 26 August, Churchill receives from the *Oldham Chronicle* answers to his questions.[143]

Churchill continued to edit the chapters and was not just simply wordsmithing what he had written but was continuing to fact-check at a very detailed level, as indicated by the following letter to an unknown comrade from his early soldiering days:

> I should be very much obliged if you would add to your kindness by helping me to answer the following questions. They are all small points but one does not want to be wrong in them.
> 1. What was the forage allowance for horses in India at that time.
> 2. Was the Duke of Connaught the Colonel-in-chief of the 60th rifles?
> 3. Do you know whether Queen Victoria ever attended any reviews in Aldershot in the years 1895 or 1896? There were two big reviews but perhaps it was the Prince of Wales who came and stayed at the Pavilion.
> 4. Could you let me know what were the regulations in the army about beards and mustaches in 1895? My recollection is that beards were only to be worn by pioneers, but you could quote the regulation I should be much obliged.
> 5. What was Wingate's rank at the Battle of Omdurman?[144]

Churchill was not only fact-checking but also looking for ways to make the story more interesting by including facts such as whether or not Queen Victoria was present at his events.

Just when everything seemed to be settled concerning the titles, Scribner decides he wants one more kick at the can. He writes:

> With regard to the title, we have had such a rapid interchange of cables that there was little chance of writing. Without doubt Butterworth has

settled on his title by this time, so there is no sense in taking up the matter again. Naturally there is apt to be a certain amount of confusion in having two editions appear under different titles. We felt strongly, however, that the use of the word <u>autobiography</u> was misleading and that 'My Early Life' did not give a fair idea of the zest and liveliness of the text. I do not think that 'A Roving Commission' is perfect, but it has the advantages and we believe that we can continue to sell your book to boys long after the regular sale has ended.[145]

On 29 August, Pearman sends this note to the printer implementing the new title: 'In confirmation of my telephone call today, I am desired by Mr. Churchill to ask that you will be so good as to discontinue the words "Mr. Churchill's Reminiscences" on the left hand page throughout the book substituting for this the words "My Early Life," as this is the final decision for the title of the book.'[146]

On 30 August, the serialisation of *My Early Life* began in the *News Chronicle* and would consist of nineteen instalments printed almost daily until 20 September. The rights for this work had been bought for $7,500.[147] This series of articles was well received, provided good reimbursement for Churchill, and was excellent advertising for the upcoming publication of the book. This same day, 30 August, Churchill received a letter from Butterworth advising him that they had reached agreement for the Italian rights for the book and had almost finished the German rights.[148]

Maps and illustrations were still not set at this time. Churchill sends this letter to Butterworth on 2 September:

> I send you herewith the revised table of illustrations. If two have to be left out I recommend leaving out the two generals, Blood and Hamilton. The two contemporary sketches of my escape both go on one page and leaving out one would not be saving. You told me you would have the first one redrawn illustrating the position of the round house as shown by me in pencil in the sketch. You therefore [have] only to decide for yourself about leaving out the two generals, otherwise all is settled.[149]

The photographs of both generals were retained.

FOREIGN BOOK RIGHTS

In addition to writing, editing, negotiating for serialisation rights and attempting to create a title acceptable to all parties, negotiations with publishers in non–English speaking countries were underway for the rights to publish the book, along with what Churchill's revenue stream would be, including advances, and the rate per book he would be paid. The details of each are thought not necessary here, but suffice it to say that negotiations were in play in Italy, France, Germany, Sweden, Norway and Denmark, among others. Negotiations came largely under the purview of Churchill's literary agents at Curtis Brown, but at times his publisher, Thornton Butterworth, was working on a publisher-to-publisher deal, which led to interesting discussions among Churchill, Butterworth and Curtis Brown. One such example will be highlighted here as it again exemplifies Churchill's competitive and detailed approach to all he did. In this case, Churchill felt that Curtis Brown was proceeding with foreign rights negotiations at an unacceptably slow pace, and he had written to him raising the issue. Brown replies on 16 September:

> As to foreign rights, enclosed is a report from that department. I find that immediately on receipt of the [galley] proofs they were rushed off, and everything possibly done on this end. The foreign editors are very slow. We are now awaiting advance copies, even if unbound, of the book with which to negotiate the foreign book rights. All proofs received are in use for foreign serial purposes. The material makes a better impression with the foreign book publishers if it is received in book form, and is much more convenient for them.[150]

Churchill is not at all happy about this. He writes back on 20 September:

> I cannot understand why there is all this difficulty about you having proofs for the foreign editors. I sent you three complete copies of page proofs, with which you can set to work in Germany and France. These proofs are subject only to minor alterations. I also enclose you a set of illustrations. We went to press with Memoirs on the 15th September, and it is expected that advance copies will be available after the 30th September.[151]

Negotiations for the German rights appear to have gone nowhere for about a month. Then Butterworth writes Churchill on 17 October:

> I am pleased to say that I have at last succeeded in getting a definitive offer from Paul List Verlag of Leipzig for the German translation Rights to your book, 'My Early Life.' This would have been concluded some time before, but unfortunately Dr. List is lying ill in Austria. The terms they propose are as follows: – £100. Advance against a 12% Royalty on the net receipts for the book – for the first 10,000 copies; and 15% beyond.[152]

From what follows, it is clear that Curtis Brown did not know Butterworth was also negotiating with German publishers. Brown writes to Churchill on 21 October:

> It has happened before now that the manager of our office in Leipzig has gone to a German publisher with the offer of an English book at a good price, and has been told by the publisher that the answer must be delayed. It is subsequently found that the reason for the delay was that the publisher had telegraphed direct to the author or English publisher to see if he couldn't get the book direct for less than the amount specified by us. Accepting such offers direct, without giving us reasonable time to cover the ground, and leaving us with our labour for our pains, seems to me to be unfair to us.[153]

Two days later, Churchill writes to Brown, giving his direct opinion and perspective:

> Yours of the 21st. Mr. Butterworth is responsible for procuring the offer from List. It is a better offer than anything you have yet been able to procure me from Germany for all other books. Much of this material has been in your hands for two months, and complete copies have been available for the last three weeks. I have received no report from your agent in Germany as to progress, whereas quite quickly through this other channel, a good offer was forthcoming. I have delayed accepting this offer till a telegraphic answer arrives from your German agent, but

I cannot wait longer than Friday. Unless a better offer is forthcoming by then I shall authorise Butterworth to close with List.[154]

True to his word, Churchill writes to Brown on 25 October: 'I propose to accept List Verlag's offer which I have received from Mr. Butterworth.'[155]

The deal was signed, and it turns out that Germany, with the List Verlag edition *Weltabenteur im Dienst* ('My Early Life'), was one of the first two countries to publish non-English versions of the book in 1931. The other country was Sweden. This negotiation, and the manner in which it was carried out, again exemplifies how competitive Churchill was and that he did not tolerated tardiness in accomplishing a task.

BOOK ORDERS BEGIN

Churchill was pleased with this news in letter received from Butterworth on 4 September: 'You will, I feel sure, be pleased to learn that we have just received from our Agents in Canada, Messrs. Thos. Nelson & Sons, their initial order for 750 copies of your Memoirs.[156] This is, in fact, the first order for the book.

T.E. Shaw (the name that T.E. Lawrence – 'Lawrence of Arabia', author, soldier, diplomat and very close friend of Churchill's – used to enlist in the Royal Tank Corps in 1923 and legally assumed in 1927) sends a wonderful review of the book on 7 September:

> Your book is complete and rather wonderful. It is beautifully written, as to manner, and both style and contents form a picture of yourself more living than anything I thought possible. A hundred times as I read it I knocked my hands together saying, 'That is himself.' I wonder if those who do not know you (the unfortunate majority today, and all in the future) will see the whole Winston in the book or not? I rather fancy they will, and that you have cut away the roots of all biographers-to-be, in doing the thing yourself, perfectly and for all time.
>
> Another thing I felt as I read it, and that was how past is the epoch of your youth. Nothing of the world, or attitude or society you lived in remains. Not even yourself, for Winston of today is altogether another man. Part of your excellence lies in that flawless evocation of a *temporis acti*. It has gone, yet you can bring it to life, just in time. Your book will become a most precious social document.

The rife & merry wisdom, and the courage and flair and judgment I take rather for granted, having seen you so much in action: but as your current reputation is not at all made by your friends, the book will do you good amongst your readers. Not many people could have lived twenty-five years so without malice. On the other hand, you have succeeded overwhelmingly, so there are grounds for your finding life good. Think of your unfair advantages. You get as much out of today, and out of affairs, as any man alive among activists: and when you die you are going to pass over, without a word said, into the ranks of writers, and live again by your books. You will remain an indispensable part of the early 20th century.

You'll be rather sick of all this tommy-rot. I feel like going on hours, though. It is seldom that a reading man, who cares for personality & events, gets quite as sharp a pleasure as I have had from your book. It is head & shoulders better than all but the high chapters of your war-book: it is so perfect and balanced a whole. Really a work of art.

There is nothing to be done textually. Let no one but yourself change a line of it.[157]

Although some may read the review as far too adulatory from a younger man doting on an older man, I believe Shaw has captured the essence of the book and what makes it come alive, what makes it memorable. An important point he makes, one which will be brought to the fore over and over again in this book, is just how important Churchill's book is in bringing to light a bygone era and a way of life which shall never be seen again. Finally, Shaw notes that Churchill will be remembered as much for his writings as anything else he has accomplished. One must consider this was written before the Second World War.

Scribner's letter of 17 September updates Churchill on a number of items:

The charge for the set you had bound [it is unclear if this was a book or bound final page proofs] to give away will be deducted from the royalty; … we now have complete page-proofs as well as later proofs in which you have made a few additional corrections.… The only thing which causes me anxiety as to whether we can approximately meet the English publication date (which I understand is on or about October 20), is the question of illustrations.… I am sorry about the Canadian market, as Macmillan's had asked us for the book and were anxious to do their best with it. It was very kind of you, however, to have suggested modifying the advance because of this. I do not believe there is any chance of your losing anything in the long run and I will be glad to pay you any royalties earned by the book during the fall.[158]

It is unknown who received this special binding of the American edition of *My Early Life* or if the binding was different from the standard printing – which at this time was not yet being printed. All Churchill collectors would surely love to own it!

On this same day, Butterworth also updated Churchill:

We went to press yesterday with your book and hope to complete by the 30th September. If there are any further corrections which you may wish to make between now and then, please send them to us and we will immediately advise the printers, if the pages upon which they occur have not been printed they will be given effect to.[159]

What an incredible accommodation that Butterworth (printers, actually) would, on the fly, make corrections to any page not yet printed. At the present time at least three proof copies of the British first edition are known. Two are from the first impression and one is from the third impression. Descriptions of these copies are provided in Appendix 8 Chapter 6 Unrecorded Books and Other Media. It is not uncommon for there to be still-existing proof copies for most of Churchill's other books. As Churchill was receiving the above letter, he wrote to his long-time friend Lord Beaverbrook:

My dear Max,
Here are the proofs of my book. They may amuse an idle hour. We both had to try very hard when we were young.[160]

On 24 September, after Baldwin had returned from his holiday in Aix, Churchill wrote to him with a bit of tongue-in-cheek:

…I take this occasion to thank you for the most encouraging letter you have written me about my proofs. Everyone who has read these

Memoirs has been very favourable in their comments, and I am hopeful that the book will do more than it was originally written to do, namely, to pay the tax collector. There may even be a small surplus to nourish the author and his family.[161]

On 26 September, Churchill wrote to Marsh:

I enclose you a rather spikey article from the *Week-End Review*, which I thought would amuse you if you have not already seen it. The Printers contend that no apostrophe is needed after the word 'Boys.' I have adopted G. Gould's dealing that the sentences should read 'The only thing I would whip them for is not knowing English.' This does not express what I meant. What I said was exactly as the round about method I adopted. I was dealing with a high pathetical state of affairs and not what I would do in the present circumstances. However, I thought it was prudent to profit by the correction, as otherwise all the Reviewers would pounce upon it. Other mistakes noted by Gould had already been corrected by you.[162]

Astounding the attention to detail Churchill makes in creating his manuscripts and how much he loved grammar and word structure.
Marsh replies:

I shouldn't have called this 'spikey' – it is very good-humoured, complimentary, & well done. I think he is strictly speaking right about the apostrophe after 'boys,' also about the 'for' in 'for not knowing' – but you should stick to your guns about the 'would be' in what your typist delightfully calls the 'high pathetical state of affairs.' Maurice Baring makes an amusing contribution to the continuity in today's 'Week-end' which I meant to cut out for you in case you didn't take it in – I left it behind at luncheon. He quotes a similar exposure by a Frenchman of mistakes made by the best French writers. You have always been very prone to the construction 'I would have liked to have been,' & in the past I have often altered it in your MS – I may have left it in this time, because it doesn't really matter, and I am always very leery of altering page-proofs unless I can suggest something to take up the same space. I hope you will be at Chartwell when I come for Sunday week.[163]

The marketing plan for *My Early Life* is sent to Churchill by Butterworth on 26 September:

> It may interest you to know that we propose to advertise your book in advance of the publication, as follows:
>
> In 'The Times' *Literary Supplement* on the 9th & 16th October
>
> 'Sunday Times' & 'The Observer' on 12th and 19th October
>
> This is done with the object of creating a demand at the libraries and bookshops on the day of publication. But I feel sure it would greatly assist the end we have in view, if you would give an interview in one of the newspapers in regard to the book. This is a matter I know you could arrange, if you thought fit.
>
> Our first printing is for 5,000 and odd copies. The orders outside of London amount to date of 1,268, and we estimate that the London Subscription orders will amount to about 4,000 copies. If our surmise proves correct, we shall then be able to advertise that the first impression was sold out, or oversold, on the date of publication. [It is of interest that WSC put a comment here in his hand: 'This is a good advertising note.'] We have the paper ready at the printers for an immediate reprint.
>
> By Tuesday morning, I hope to get a set of the sheets paper bound, and I will send you a copy immediately, as I feel sure you would like to see it as soon as possible in its final form.
>
> We have arranged for the book rather an effective jacket. I shall be very interested to learn your opinion, when we are able to send it to you.[164]

Churchill replies the next day:

> I shall look forward to receiving a copy of the book in its final form. I am not very keen upon an interview. There has been an immense amount of publicity in the *Daily News* and I gave an interview to that paper some time ago. I expect you will have nearly 6,000 copies subscribed for before publication, and I have no doubt the reviews will be helpful.[165]

On 29 September, Churchill sends a letter to Charles Scribner:

> I send you herewith the contract as amended by our letters and telegrams. If you find it correct, will you have it recopied and send me a duplicate signed by you. [The contract is in the Churchill Archives (CHAR 8/277).]
>
> My son, who travels by the 'Majestic' on Wednesday next, will call upon you. He will give you an itinerary of lectures, and it may be that the sale of the Memoirs will be helped thereby in different towns in which he speaks and is advertised. You may supply him, at my expense, with twenty copies to give away to people who are kind to him on his journey.[166]

Churchill, always the promoter and thinking ahead, gets Randolph to advertise the new book.

Churchill receives his first preliminary copy of the book from Butterworth on 30 September and also an unusual comment about the Canadian public:

> I have the pleasure to send you under a separate cover a paper bound copy [perhaps a proof copy] of your book 'My Early Life.' I trust that you will approve of the general appearance. … [F]rom Nelson's we have heard as follows: 'We were sorry to learn that the *Star Newspaper* Syndicate had declined the book [that is, the serialisation thereof] but hope to get a good offer for it from a paper in Montreal. I have not had any opportunity myself of reading the proofs but am advised that the contents are much less interesting to the Canadian public than Mr. Churchill's former book. Nevertheless, we regard it as the most important item on our list this season and are looking forward to a large sale.[167]

The dust jacket arrives from Butterworth the next day:

> I am sending you a copy of the wrapper for your book. If you will fold it round 'Nero' you will get the effect and if you place it side by side with other books I think you will find, as we do, that, to use a Chevalier expression, it will 'knock them in the old Kent Road'! I hope you like it.[168]

One wonders whether the publishers (Butterworth) had any concept of how susceptible to fading both the dust jacket and binding were. Well known to bibliophiles, Churchill's first British edition, in particular, is almost always seen with severe bleaching of the deep reddish-purple colour, as the result of exposure to sunlight. A copy of the final printed book arrives on 3 October.[169]

Soon after the finished, jacketed copies were ready, Butterworth began sending out copies of those books for review. See Figure 1 for an image of the only known copy of the notice sent to media reviewers. The sheet provides the publication date of 20 October, the price of 21*s*., a request that the review should not be published prior to the date of release, and a note saying that Butterworth would appreciate a copy of the issue of the publication in which the review appears (newspaper or magazine). It is not known how many copies were sent for review.

An important diversion from the writing timeline is needed here to discuss an 'edition' of *My Early Life* that is infrequently mentioned and is not listed in the magnificent *Bibliography* by Cohen that is regularly referenced in this book. This is the so-called 'Times Book Club Edition', which is listed in the updated bibliography in Appendix 8 Chapter 6 Unrecorded Books and Other Media.

The Times Book Club, launched on 11 September 1905, was the brainchild of Charles Frederic Moberly Bell, the managing director of *The Times*, and Horace Everett Hooper, the advertising manager. The Book Club was designed to increase circulation for *The Times* by enticing subscribers with access to a wide selection of books that could be borrowed for free and then bought at a significant discount. There is an excellent, robust discussion in Cohen's *Bibliography* about the principles and practices of the Book Club and why it came to be a threat to authors and publishers – in particular, concerning what occurred with Churchill's book *Lord Randolph Churchill*.[170]

The Times Book Club bought copies of *Lord Randolph Churchill* from Macmillan in their original binding, and then some were rebound in a unique Times binding. In addition, many had a pasted-on Times Book Club label. The crux of the problem was the substantial discount at which the Book Club would sell the books to its members (*The Times* taking the loss to boost subscriptions), thus undercutting the publishers. A legal and advertising war ensued between the parties. Ultimately, the publishers won. The Book Club was redesigned and continued to function, albeit in a

Agencies Overseas:
EAST AFRICA
SOUTH AFRICA
AUSTRALASIA
CANADA
INDIA
JAPAN
WEST INDIES

THORNTON BUTTERWORTH L^{TD}
Publishers
15 BEDFORD STREET STRAND
LONDON · W · C · 2

Telephone:
TEMPLE BAR 4296-7
Telegrams:
COLYPHON WESTRAND
LONDON
Cables:
COLYPHON
H. T. BUTTERWORTH
SIR TRESHAM LEVER, BT.

Messrs. THORNTON BUTTERWORTH, LTD., have the pleasure to enclose a copy of

My Early Life

by Rt. Hon. Winston S. Churchill, C.H.

for the favour of review. A copy of the issue containing the notice would be much appreciated.

The published price is 21s. net.

The Publishing day is 20th October before which it is earnestly requested that your review will not appear.

In order to avoid confusion with Messrs. Butterworth & Co. kindly give our name as 'Thornton Butterworth.'

Figure 1. The only known copy of the request from the publisher for a review of *My Early Life*, with admonition concerning publication date (Author's collection).

different mode. Churchill himself had weighed in on the issue in a 6 June 1906, letter to his publisher of *Lord Randolph Churchill:*

> Mr. Macmillan,
> I am very sorry to see a cutting which reached me from *The Publisher and Bookseller* that *The Times* have played you a shabby trick. I do hope you will find it will not cause you any serious injury to the sale of the book. It certainly cannot in any way reflect upon your credit as a publisher. I do not see how you can stop people selling things they have bought below the cost price, but I can quite understand the annoyance and derangement which it causes.[171]

At least several of Churchill's books after *Lord Randolph Churchill* were offered in the Times Book Club selection, including *The World Crisis* and *Great Contemporaries* and, as shown below, *My Early Life*.[172]

The story of the *My Early Life* Times Book Edition begins with a somewhat contentious letter from the Times Book Club to Butterworth on 6 October:

> I have to acknowledge a proof copy of Mr. Winston Churchill's forthcoming book, and note that Mr. Clifford will call with a completed copy.
>
> I see that you speak of the published price, 21/-, as having been 'kept purposely low to secure a wide demand.' I am afraid, however, that 21/- can hardly be called low. It is so high that on every copy bought for this library we shall lose at least 2/6d. That is to say, if we set down the amount that we shall receive from subscribers for hire of each copy, and to that the amount that we shall eventually receive by the sale of that copy second hand, the two items will come to 2/6d. less than the amount we shall pay you per copy.
>
> If, therefore, your 'confident anticipation of a wide demand' is realised, as no doubt it will be, we stand to lose several hundred, perhaps a thousand or more, sums of 2/6d. That is to say, on an order for 800 copies we shall lose 100 pounds.
>
> The prospect is naturally less agreeable to a librarian than it is to a publisher.

I need only add that, of whatever number of this book we order, 90% at least will be bought for lending purposes and only some 10% for sale. That is to say, we shall lose money on 90% of what we order and make a profit – a small one – on only 10%.

Perhaps you will mention these points to Mr. Clifford before he calls.[173]

It is clear from this letter that the model for the Book Club has indeed changed; they now offer their books for a rental fee and only later sell them as used books. In their minds now, the club should make money, or at least not lose a great deal, and the club isn't seen as much as an enticement to newspaper sales as it was originally conceived. Butterworth informs Churchill of the Book Club's thoughts in a letter dated 8 October:

We have just received confirmation of the sale of Serial Rights of 'My Early Life' to the Associated Newspapers – of Ceylon Ltd. For 25 pounds.

I am also pleased to tell you that our first order in London, namely from Boots was for 1,000 copies, the number we estimated they would take, which is very satisfactory. Our total orders to date for Town, Country and Overseas amount to 2,457. I sincerely trust that the sales elsewhere in London will also come up to our estimate. I think I mentioned to you, when you called last week, that we put the second printing in hand for 2,500 copies.

I send for your private information copy of the letter our publicity dept. has received to-day from the Manager of 'The Times Book Club.' It is so extraordinary, that I think you would like to see it. If we were to accept Mr. Bute's statement, it would mean that The Times Book Club is working at a loss, which of course is not the case. We do not propose to take notice of this extraordinary effusion, but our Sales Manager will certainly see Mr. Bute about it.[174]

The Times Book Club did indeed order copies of *My Early Life*, but exactly how many were ordered is not known. They purchased copies of the first edition, first printing, second state, as indicated by the listing of *The World Crisis: 1911-1914* in the boxed list on the half-title verso. They either bought page sheets only or rebound the volumes. The volumes are bound in unornamented smooth burgundy cloth with plain gold spine lettering.

There is a small blue rectangular Times Book Club sticker on the rear fixed endpaper. The sticker also has the logo of *The Times* and the address '42 Wigmore Street, London, W1.'[175]

Churchill maintained his long-held belief that the Times Book Club edition cut into the sale of the trade edition. In 1908, he had addressed the Authors' Club in London on how writers are the most fortunate people in the world as their 'work is also their pleasure'. To the pleasure, laughter and cheers of his audience, he had commented, 'The pen is the great liberator of men and nations. No chains can bind, no poverty can choke, no tariff can restrict the free play of his mind. Even the Times Book Club can only exert a moderately depressing influence upon his rewards.'[176]

Churchill received good news from Butterworh on 10 October:

> Just a hurried line to say that we have to-day received confirmation from Milan of the sale of your memoirs for 75 pounds, in advance and on account of a ten percent royalty. …
>
> In the meantime I think we may say there is little doubt that in the course of the next day or two we shall have sold out the first Edition of your Memoirs.[177]

This was followed with another letter the next day: 'Thank you for your letter of the 9th instant received this morning. The sales to date amount to 4,020. We still have to fill orders from The Times Book Club, Mudies, Bumpus and various exporters. We should therefore reach a subscription order of 5,550.'[178]

Further sales information and advertising approaches come from Butterworth on the 14th:

> Sales of 'My Early Life' up to the time of writing amount to 4,830. And I hope to advise before our subscription closed that we have reached 5,500. It may be more, though we cannot tell: still, I trust it will not be less.
>
> It is a good start, and if the reviewers do full justice, repeat orders should be coming in within the next two or three weeks, and then we have Christmas sales to which to look forward. I shall be very disappointed if, in the long run, we do not sell 20,000 copies, – in fact you will recognise that I am optimistic, as well as enthusiastic.

> In addition to the foregoing sales, we have arranged with Harrods to make a special show in one of their shop windows of 150 copies, which we will supply to them for sale or return. I understand from Mr. Bourne that you suggested that we should supply them with the 'Reward for your Capture Alive or Dead.' This, I am glad to say, is only another instance where our ideas march side by side. We had already proposed that to them and we are now awaiting their decision.
>
> It may interest you to know that one of the Edinburgh Booksellers ordered six copies through our Northern Traveller; this our Sales Manager succeeded in getting increased to 24; but the Manager of that firm called to see me yesterday, and by a little personal persuasion, I got the order increased to fifty.[179]

As mentioned above, Churchill's son, Randolph, was to visit the US on a lecture tour. He stopped in to see Scribner in New York City. Scribner wrote to Winston on 15 October:

> Your son very kindly dropped at my office last week and left with me the proof of the new edition of *The World Crisis*. … Our formal publication date for *A Roving Commission* is October 24th. We shall have copies about 5 days in advance of this date. … I have told your son that he can draw on us for whatever copies he may need; and if the number is not too great, he can consider them as editorial copies. I am terribly anxious to have the book meet with success that we feel is its due, but this is a bad season and the last few days have been the most depressing since the panic.[180]

Over his writing lifetime, Churchill consistently sent inscribed copies of his newly published books (often sent pre-publication) to family, friends, colleagues who helped research and edit his manuscripts, as well as royals and people of prominence who could help promote his books. The full story of how he carried out this process and who received such copies in the case of *My Early Life* is detailed in Chapter 5. In that chapter are also excerpts from letters he received thanking him and providing the recipients' reactions to the book. Those letters –which began arriving on 16 October – are not replicated in this chapter. The following letter from Churchill's secretary (Mrs Pearman) to Butterworth concerns the shipping of the first of the inscribed copies:

Mr. Churchill desires me to send you herewith forty-six presentation copies which he has signed. Can you arrange to dispatch them not later than tomorrow night to their addresses. Will you telephone to me about this. I have also sent the photograph which you wanted for the 'Country Life,' to which Mr. Churchill is in full agreement.[181]

The photograph for *Country Life* is the image of Churchill in his full-dress uniform from the 4th Hussars that is shown facing page 80 in *My Early Life*. The image is embedded in an ecstatically positive book review published in the 25 October 1930 issue of *Country Life* on page 526 (see Chapter 5C, Fig. 7).

Churchill appears to have raised the idea (letter unlocated) that Butterworth should consider creating a special or limited edition of *My Early Life*. Butterworth responded,

In regard to the last paragraph in your letter concerning a Special and Limited Edition, I will discuss this with my Sales Department and write you later. We had thought of it, but did not feel at that time that the results would justify the special outlay. Still we will consider it further, and as I have said before, write you further later on.[182]

No follow-up correspondence has been found. The same day as the preceding letter, Churchill received Butterworth's final pre-publication sales estimate: '…I am able to give you what may be considered to be almost the final figures before publication: <u>6032.</u> As your estimate of sales was 6,000 copies, perhaps you will allow me to compliment you on your forecast.'[183]

Churchill's agreement with Butterworth specified a number of services and complimentary books. However, for services above and beyond those stipulated, Churchill was required to reimburse Butterworth. On 20 October, Churchill received invoices and notes indicating that he would receive his six complimentary copies of the book and that he owed them £45 for the creation of photographs and drawings for the book as well as £45 for corrections to the proofs and an additional £53 for shipping seventy-four books to Churchill's friends.[184]

When the day of publication arrived, 20 October, Butterworth sent both a letter and a telegram:

I confirm my wire to you this morning as follows: 'HEARTIEST CONGRATULATIONS ON INTERESTING, STIMULATING REVIEWS *OBSERVER* AND TODAY'S *TIMES*. STOP REMITTED IN FULL.'

They are most encouraging, especially that of *The Observer* and I have cabled the salient points of each to our agents in Canada, Australia, and South Africa, and I have also cabled them to Scribner's, as possibly they may be able to make use of them in their advertisements and wished them the best of luck.

In addition, I have sent copies of the reviews to Treves in Italy, List in Germany and Plon in France, and we shall send printed excerpts to all our customers.

We have now to wait and see how the demand sets in; but in the meantime we have sent forward paper to Butler & Tanners to be ready for a third printing at a moment's notice.

If the book meets with its deserts, we should sell 20,000 copies, and I shall not feel satisfied if we don't. We have done our damndest to stir up the booksellers, and we must hope that public recommendations will do the rest![185]

Churchill sent a letter to Butterworth on 23 October 1930 outlining his short-term plans for additional work and how he suggests he would calendar them:

Future Plans
It seems to me that the success of *My Early Life* would justify a further volume which might probably be called 'The Great Free Trade Split.' This volume would be a political history of England from the close of the Boer War to about the General election of 1910. It would incorporate some of the material already contained in my essays on Balfour, Rosebury, Chamberlain, Asquith, Morley, Lloyd George and others. It would be a story of the House of Commons and the violent convulsion. It would bridge the gap between *My Early Life* and the opening chapters of *World Crisis*. There would thus be a continuous record by me beginning with my father's active life, which began in 1874, down to the end of the war a period of almost fifty years. ...

Assuming we might do this, how should it be fit in with the abridged edition?

He then goes on to explain to Butterworth how he could fit it into the publishing schedule:

Our programme for the next year would therefore be:
End of January	Abridged edition
Beginning of March	'The Great Free Trade Split'
September	'The Eastern Front'[186]

Churchill certainly had no lack of energy or boldness. He then goes on to describe in detail what the financial arrangements should be. This same letter was sent to Scribner on 3 November.[187]

Churchill received his first royalty statement from Scribner's on 24 October:'For *A Roving Commission*: number sold 810, royalty 52 ½ Amount $425.78 from which was subtracted US Income tax at a rate of 5% Amount received $404.49.'[188]

The final letter in October, on the 29th, from Scribner updates Churchill on the sales and printing issues:

Enclosed is a report of the advance sales on *A Roving Commission*, together with the draft for royalty due, I am afraid that you will be disappointed in the number but it is next to impossible at the present time to secure a large advance sale on such a book. Fortunately it has nothing to do with the prospects of success of the volume and it is often more stimulating for a bookseller to have to keep reordering books because of demand rather than feeling he is having a difficult time in working off a large stock order. … Frankly I am a little mortified that the imposition of the type-page is not better. Our printer had instruction to drop a line and shift folios to the top of page but unfortunately he failed to carry them out.[189]

By the end of October 1930, the writing and editing is complete, and the book is launched by both publishers in the UK and the United States.

Notes

1. Frederick Woods, *Artillery of Words: The Writings of Sir Winston Churchill*, London, Leo Cooper, 1992, pp. 1–5.
2. Charles Eade, ed., *Churchill by His Contemporaries*, London, Hutchinson, 1953, p. 141.
3. David Lough, *No More Champagne: Churchill and His Money,* New York, Picador, 2015, p. 49.
4. A.J.P. Taylor, *Churchill: Four Faces and the Man,* London, Allan Lane, 1969, pp. 139–40.
5. Charles Eade, ed., *Churchill by His Contemporaries*, p. 62.
6. Woods, *Artillery of Words*, pp. 154–6.
7. Peter Clarke, *Mr. Churchill's Profession*, New York, Bloomsbury Press, 2012, pp. 190–91.
8. Martin Gilbert, *In Search of Churchill*, London, Harper Collins, 1994, p. 150.
9. David Reynolds, *In Command of History*, New York, Random House, 2005, pp. 501–2.
10. Reynolds, *In Command of History*, p. 434.
11. Woods, *Artillery of Words*, p. 156.
12. Maurice Ashley, *Churchill as Historian*, New York, Scribner's, 1969, Ch. 3.
13. Ashley, *Churchill as Historian*, p. 24.
14. Ashley, *Churchill as Historian*, p. 23.
15. Celia Sandys, 'The Young Churchill', speech to the Churchill Society, Calgary, Alberta, 23 September 1994, https://winstonchurchill.org/the-life-of-churchill/young-soldier/the-young-churchill/
16. Churchill, *My Early Life*, London, Thornton Butterworth, 1930, pp. 35–6.
17. Ashley, *Churchill as Historian*, p. 27.
18. Ashley, *Churchill as Historian*, p. 28.
19. Woods, *Artillery of Words*, p. 156.
20. Ashley, *Churchill as Historian*, p. 25.
21. Woods, *Artillery of Words*, p. 155.
22. Woods, *Artillery of Words*, pp. 155–6.
23. Woods, *Artillery of Words*, p. 156.
24. Ashley, *Churchill as Historian*, p. 25.
25. Mary Soames, *Speaking for Themselves: The Personal Letters of the Churchills*, London, Doubleday, 1998, p. 326.
26. Winston S. Churchill, *My Early Life,* London: Butterworth, 1930, p. 156.
27. Jacob Omnium, 'Under Cover', *The Bookseller and the Publishers Trades' Journal* (London, 16 July 1925), p. 73.
28. 'Agents' Income Tax', *The Scotsman* (Edinburgh, 18 June 1925), p. 6.

29. Churchill, *My Early Life*, p. 9.
30. William Manchester, *The Last Lion: Winston Spencer Churchill: Visions of Glory, 1874–1932*, Boston, Little, Brown and Company, 1983, p. 817.
31. Martin Gilbert, *The Prophet of Truth*, 1922-1929, Boston, Houghton Mifflin, 1977, p. 243.
32. Gilbert, *Prophet of Truth*, p. 245.
33. Martin Gilbert, *Companion Volume V, Part 1 The Exchequer Years*, Boston, Houghton Mifflin, 1981, p. 1326.
34. Winston S. Churchill, 'Boris Savinkov: The Story of a Man Who Was Not Without Honour Except in His Own Country', *Nash's Magazine*, vol. 82, no. 429 (February 1929), pp. 26–9.
35. Gilbert, CV, V, pt 1, p. 1333.
36. Diary of James Scrymgeour-Wedderburn, 21–23 September 1928, Dundee papers, 5C1:1340-47. (Quoted in David Lough, *No More Champagne*)
37. Curtis Brown letter to WSC, 25 October 1928 (CHAR 8/207/51.)
38. David Lough, *No More Champagne: Churchill and His Money*, New York: Picador, 2015.
39. Gilbert, *CV, V pt 1*, p. 1378.
40. Gilbert, *CV, V pt 1*, p. 1399.
41. Gilbert, *CV, V pt 1*, p. 1405.
42. Gilbert, *CV, V pt 1*, p. 1405.
43. Ronald I. Cohen, *Bibliography of the Writings of Sir Winston Churchill*, London, Thoemmes, 2006, pp. 1355–6.
44. Lough, *No More Champagne*, pp. 177–8.
45. Lough, *No More Champagne*, pp. 178–81.
46. Lough, *No More Champagne*, pp. 181–2.
47. Andrew Roberts, *Churchill: Walking with Destiny*, London, Allen Lane, 2018, pp. 336–41.
48. Gilbert, *Prophet of Truth*, pp. 338–51.
49. Lough, *No More Champagne*, pp. 182–95. (Excellent for financial details)
50. Gilbert, *CV, V, pt 2.*, p. 64.
51. Gilbert, *CV, V pt 2*, pp. 61–2.
52. Gilbert, *CV*, V, pt 2., pp. 132–3.
53. Gilbert, *CV, V pt 2.*, pp. 139–40.
54. Roy Jenkins, *Churchill: A Biography*, New York, Farrar, Straus and Giroux, 2001, p. 429.
55. Gilbert, *CV*, V, pt 2., p.141.

56. Churchill Archives, 6 March 1930 (CHAR 8/274). (The archives are available at ChurchillArchive.com and housed at Cambridge University.)
57. Churchill Archives, 12 March 1930 (CHAR 8/274).
58. Churchill Archives, 9 April 1930 (CHAR 8/274).
59. Churchill Archives, 16 April 1930 (CHAR 8/274).
60. Churchill Archives, 22 April 1930 (CHAR 8/274).
61. Churchill Archives, 24 April 1930 (CHAR 8/277).
62. Cohen, *Bibliography*, p. 334.
63. Churchill Archives, 8 May 1930 (CHAR 8/274).
64. Churchill Archives, 30 May 1930 (CHAR 8/276).
65. Cohen, *Bibliography,* p. 334.
66. Roberts, *Walking With Destiny*, p. 343.
67. Churchill Archives, 3 June 1930 (CHAR 8/277 image 51).
68. Churchill Archives, 5 June 1930 (CHAR 8/274).
69. Churchill Archives, 11 June 1930 (CHAR 8/274).
70. Churchill Archives, 13 June 1930 (CHAR 8/274).
71. Churchill Archives, 16 June 1930 CHAR 8/268).
72. Churchill Archives 17 June 1930 (CHAR 8/ 277).
73. Cohen, *Bibliography*, p. 327.
74. Cohen, *Bibliography*, p. 335.
75. Churchill Archives, 19 June 1930 (CHAR 8/296).
76. Churchill Archives, 20 June 1930 (CHAR 8/277).
77. Churchill Archives, 23 June 1930 (CHAR 8/277).
78. Churchill Archives, 26 June 1930 (CHAR 8/277)
79. Cohen, *Bibliography*, p. 336.
80. Cohen, *Bibliography*, p. 336.
81. Churchill Archives, 28 June 1930 (CHAR 8/274).
82. Churchill Archives, 1 July 1930 (CHAR 8/274).
83. Cohen, *Bibliography*, p. 336.
84. Churchill Archives, 2 July 1930 (CHAR 8/277).
85. Gilbert, *CV, V, pt 2.*, p. 169.
86. Churchill Archives, 10 July 1930 (CHAR 8/274).
87. Churchill Archives, 11 July 1930 (Char 8/274).
88. Churchill Archives, 14 July 1930 (CHAR 8/274).
89. Cohen, *Bibliography*, p. 336.
90. Cohen, *Bibliography*, p. 337.
91. Churchill Archives, 17 July 1930 (CHAR 8/268).
92. Churchill Archives, 23 July 1930 (CHAR 8/274).

93. Churchill Archives, 31 July 1930 (CHAR 8/274).
94. Bonhams, London, *The First World War Centenary Sale*, 1 October 2014, lot 194. ((https://www.bonhams.com)
95. Churchill Archives, 23 July 1930 (CHAR 8/268).
96. Churchill Archives, 25 July 1930 (CHAR 8/268).
97. Churchill Archives, 23 July 1930 (CHAR 8/268).
98. Churchill Archives, 25 July 1930 (CHAR 8/278).
99. Gilbert, *CV, V, part 2*, pp. 171–2.
100. Churchill Archives, 25 July 1930 (CHAR 8/268).
101. Churchill Archives, 25 July 1930 (CHAR 8/274).
102. Churchill Archives, 28 July 1930 (CHAR 8/268).
103. Churchill Archives, 29 July 1930 (CHAR8/268).
104. Gilbert, *CV, V, part 2*, p. 172.
105. Churchill Archives, 30 July 1930 (CHAR 8/277).
106. Cohen, *Bibliography*, p. 337.
107. Churchill Archives, 31 July 1930 (CHAR 8/268).
108. Gilbert, *CV, V, part 2*, p.179.
109. Churchill Archives, 4 September 1930 (CHAR (2/572).
110. Churchill Archives, 2 August 1930 (CHAR 8/269).
111. Churchill Archives, 2 August 1930 (CHAR 8/269).
112. Churchill Archives, 2 August 1930 (CHAR 8/274).
113. Churchill Archives, 5 August 1930 (CHAR 8/274).
114. Churchill Archives, 5 August 1930 (CHAR 8/269).
115. Churchill Archives, 6 August 1930 (CHAR 8/268).
116. Churchill Archives, 6 August 1930 (CHAR 8/274).
117. Churchill Archives, 9 August 1931 (CHAR 8/274).
118. Churchill Archives, 7 August 1930 (CHAR 8/276).
119. Churchill Archives, 9 August 1930 (CHAR 8/274).
120. Churchill Archives, 10 August 1930 (CHAR 8/274).
121. Gilbert, *CV, V, part 2*, p. p. 176.
122. Churchill Archives, 11August 1930 (CHAR 8/268).
123. Churchill Archives, 10 August 1930 (CHAR 8/268).
124. Churchill Archives, 13 August 1930 (CHAR 8/268).
125. Churchill Archives, 13 August 1930 (CHAR 8/268).
126. Churchill Archives, 14 August 1930 (CHAR 8/268).
127. Cohen, *Bibliography*, p. 337.
128. Churchill Archives, 15 August 1930 (CHAR 8/274).
129. Churchill Archives, 16 August 1930 (CHAR 8/274).

130. Churchill Archives, 11 August 1930 (CHAR 8/276).
131. Churchill Archives, 15 August 1930 (CHAR 8/276)
132. Churchill Archives, 17 August 1930 (CHAR 8/268).
133. Churchill Archives, 17 August 1930 (CHAR 8/268).
134. Churchill Archives, 18 August 1930 (CHAR 8/277).
135. Churchill Archives, 18 August 1930 (CHAR 8/274).
136. Churchill Archives, 19 August 1930 (CHAR 8/274).
137. Cohen, *Bibliography*, p. 337.
138. Churchill Archives, 20 August 1930 (CHAR 8/277).
139. Churchill Archives, 20 August 1930 (CHAR 8/274).
140. Cohen, *Bibliography*, p. 338.
141. Cohen, *Bibliography*, p. 338.
142. Churchill Archives, 22 August 1930 (CHAR 8/268).
143. Churchill Archives, 26 August 1930 (CHAR 8/ 268).
144. Churchill Archives, 23 August 1930 (CHAR 8/268).
145. Churchill Archives, 27 August 1930 (CHAR 8/277).
146. Churchill Archives, 28 August 1930 (CHAR 8/278).
147. Cohen, *Bibliography*, p. 1372.
148. Churchill Archives, 30 August 1930 (CHAR 8/274).
149. Churchill Archives, 2 September 1930 (CHAR 8/275).
150. Churchill Archives, 16 September 1930 (CHAR 8/276).
151. Churchill Archives, 20 September 1930 (CHAR 8/276).
152. Churchill Archives, 17 October 1930 (CHAR 8/276).
153. Churchill Archives, 21 October 1930 (CHAR 8/276).
154. Churchill Archives, 23 October 1930 (CHAR 8/276).
155. Churchill Archives, 25 October 1930 (CHAR 8/276).
156. Churchill Archives, 4 September 1930 (CHAR 8/275).
157. Churchill Archives, 7 September 1930 (CHAR 8/269).
158. Churchill Archives, 17 September 1930 (CHAR 8/277).
159. Churchill Archives, 17 September 1930 (CHAR 8/275).
160. Gilbert, *CV, V, part 2*, p. 183.
161. Gilbert, *CV, V, part 2*, p. 186.
162. Churchill Archives, 26 September 1930 (CHAR 8/268).
163. Churchill Archives, 28 September 1930 (CHAR 8/268)
164. Churchill Archives, 26 September 1930 (CHAR 8/275).
165. Churchill Archives, 27 September 1930 (CHAR 8/275).
166. Churchill Archives, 29 September 1930 (CHAR8/277).
167. Churchill Archives, 30 September 1930 (CHAR 8/275).

168. Churchill Archives, 1 October 1930 (CHAR 8/275).
169. Churchill Archives, 3 October 1930 (CHAR 8/275).
170. Cohen, *Bibliography*, pp. 134–40.
171. Gilbert, *CV, II, part 1*, pp.493–4.
172. Cohen, *Bibliography*, pp. 255, 477.
173. Churchill Archives, 6 October 1930 (CHAR 8/275).
174. Churchill Archives, 8 October 1930 (CHAR 8/275).
175. Author's Collection.
176. Winston S. Churchill, 'The Joys of Writing', Authors Club, London, 17 February 1908, in Robert Rhodes James, ed., *Winston S. Churchill: His Complete Speeches 1897-1963*, 8 vols., New York, Bowker, 1974, I: pp. 903–5.
177. Churchill Archives, 10 October 1930 (CHAR 8/275).
178. Churchill Archives, 11 October 1930 (CHAR 8/275).
179. Churchill Archives, 14 October 1930 (CHAR 8/275).
180. Churchill Archives, 15 October 1930 (CHAR 8/277).
181. Churchill Archives, 16 October 1930 (CHAR 8/275).
182. Churchill Archives, 16 October 1930 (CHAR 8/275).
183. Churchill Archives, 16 October 1930 (CHAR 8/275).
184. Churchill Archives, 20 October 1930 (CHAR 8/275).
185. Churchill Archives, 20 October 1930 (CHAR 8/275 image 62).
186. Churchill Archives, 23 October 1930 (CHAR 8/275).
187. Churchill Archives, 3 November 1930 (CHAR 8/275)
188. Churchill Archives, 24 October 1930 (CHAR 8/277).
189. Churchill Archives, 29 October 1930 (CHAR 8/277).

CHAPTER 4

Creation of *My Early Life* Using Churchill's Previous Publications

MANY CHARACTERISTICS OF *MY EARLY LIFE* DISTINGUISH IT FROM the rest of the Churchill canon. The book is his only autobiography, and it is written much more in the style of an oral story and commentary than any of his other books. One of the most fascinating distinctions is the fact that he wrote this book after many iterations of the stories he was highlighting had previously been published in newspapers or other books. He had written many books on his life (military) experiences which, themselves, were based on multiple earlier newspaper dispatches written contemporaneously with the events. These were published in the years from 1895 to 1900. Then in the early to mid-1920s, Churchill wrote a series of articles about his childhood, schooling and war experiences for popular periodicals in both the United States and England. (These were listed in Chapter 2 and will be described later in this chapter.) Thus, by the time he began writing *My Early Life* in the late 1920s, Churchill had three generations of text material that he had previously written and published. All of these were available to be used as the source material for this book. In some cases, to create the final product, he had as many as five different sources from which he could choose to weave excerpts. Elsewhere, he could choose to ignore some of the texts – or all of them, to start writing afresh.

Considering that each source was written at a single point in time, influenced by the various political, social and confidentiality concerns particular to that specific time, it should come as no surprise that changes in the tone and emphasis of a text and the inclusion or exclusion of certain facts and scenarios would be necessary. As mentioned previously, Churchill addresses this issue directly in his 1923 *Strand Magazine* article 'My Escape from the Boers':

> During the Boer War, in which I acted as a war correspondent for the *Morning Post* and later on served as a Lieutenant in the South African Light Horse, I gave some account of my escape from Pretoria. It was not, however, possible for me to tell the full story. To have done so would have been to compromise the liberty and perhaps the lives of those who helped me, and also to aggravate needlessly the difficulties of other British prisoners then still in captivity. For many years these reasons have disappeared, but I have not found the time or inclination to return to those exciting days, have since been plunged almost continuously in strife and stress. Now for the first time having recovered that leisure [he was out of Parliament at this time] and freedom from worry and anxiety to which we all look forward as the sequel to stirring times, I have found it possible again to turn over the records and memoranda of this vanished epoch in British affairs, and to complete an account which when it was written had necessarily to be mutilated and mysterious.[1]

Churchill would again rework the materials in the late 1920s into *My Early Life.*

This plethora of written material on his life, when combined with Churchill's encyclopedic memory and his proclivity to walk and dictate his material (which he did for much of the work on *My Early Life*), begs the question: just how did he pick and choose what materials to include from each source, and how much of his book did he edit or write completely anew? This is a fascinating topic. To approach it in a readable and rational manner, some of the most recognisable high points and episodes from *My Early Life* have been chosen for comparison with all of the pertinent available published sources, including his wartime dispatches, the books which grew out those dispatches, and the articles Churchill published in the 1920s. These publications have then been analysed chronologically to trace the evolution of the texts before he reached the final text for *My Early Life.*

Five episodes from the book have been chosen for this detailed analysis: his childhood; the war in Cuba; the cavalry charge at Omdurman; the armoured train episode in South Africa; and Churchill's escape from the Boers. For each comparison, the final text in *My Early Life* (*MEL*) will be displayed first; then, starting with the earliest written version, the reader will be taken chronologically through each version to view the additions, subtractions or edits contributing to the final product. These comparisons are lengthy and detailed and will be shown in Appendices 2–6 at the end of the book, in the acknowledgement that some readers may not want to study them in detail.

Notes
1. Winston Churchill, 'My Escape from the Boers', *Strand Magazine*, December 1923, p. 537.

CHAPTER 5

Launch of the Book

5A: GIFTED INSCRIBED COPIES OF *MY EARLY LIFE*

Churchill was well known for sending copies of his new books to friends, influential politicians, Royals, media moguls and anyone else who might now be known today as an 'influencer'. One group of friends, relatives, and colleagues (particularly those who helped research, review texts, or edit galley proofs) was given them as a true message of thanks and appreciation. The other group comprised those who he thought would help to promote the book via media, clubs and personal work interactions. This self-promotion was, of course, in addition to the large number of book reviews and advertisements sought and obtained through Thornton Butterworth in London and Charles Scribner's in New York. This media approach will be dealt with elsewhere.

My Early Life was no exception to the rule of gifting. Martin Gilbert states in *The Prophet of Truth*, Volume 5. from his multivolume biography of Churchill, that 'Churchill sent out more than a hundred personal copies of *My Early Life* to friends and colleagues.'[1] This section will provide information on who the recipients were and how they responded. It will also note where there is overlap among those who were sent early galley proofs to review and who subsequently received inscribed first editions. As will be seen, Churchill's decisions on to whom he would send the books and whether they would simply be signed or inscribed with specific comments were arrived at through a detailed process completely orchestrated and overseen by Churchill himself. Some insight on how this process worked can be gleaned from papers in the Churchill Archives at Cambridge.

In the Churchill Archives are several documents that list individuals who might receive *My Early Life*. The first is titled 'For Mr. Churchill's Information. List of books signed on the 14th and 15th Oct. [1930] with the names as written by you.' On this list are five handwritten names or names of entities and forty typed names. At the bottom of the list is handwritten 'Rough List'. [CHAR 8/812 (image 11 of 78)]

The second list is titled 'List of books *My Early Life* sent either by Butterworths or straight from Chartwell.' The list contains fifty-eight typed and three handwritten names. There is also a note 'Mr. Baruch & [?? Others] in America taken by Mrs. Churchill.' [CHAR 8/812 (image 10 of 78)]

A third list is also titled 'For Mr. Churchill's information. List of books signed on 14th and 15th Oct. with the names as written by him.' This list is similar to the first list above but adds new names. [CHAR 8/275 (image 57)]. Many names appear on more than one list.

This process was not unique to *My Early Life*, as similar lists for the first edition of *The Eastern Front* are also found in the archives. [CHAR 8/812]

This author has cross-referenced the names on the lists and searched the Churchill Archives for correspondence between WSC and the individuals concerning the books, as well as extensively searching for information on copies of the books themselves, where they might be, and what is known about the inscriptions. It should be noted that the publication date for the book was 20 October 1930. Many of the inscribed copies have been signed with earlier dates than this. It is likely that Churchill considered the recipients of such books a high-priority group, and, thus, any book inscribed with a date prior to 20 October is considered a special gift. Churchill often advised the recipients (via tipped-in notes) that they were receiving the books with the understanding that the contents were embargoed until the official release date (*vide infra*).

What follows is a comprehensive list of the recipients and the details on the books they received as could be ascertained through extensive research efforts. The first part of the list contains entries for which there is detailed information, while the second section lists individuals known to have received a book but for which no additional information is known. The third section lists individuals who received books after the end of October 1930, the launch month, up until the end of 1930.

On 16 October 1930, Churchill's secretary sent forty-six copies of signed books to Butterworth to distribute. [CHAR 8/275]

The list primarily takes the order from Churchill's most comprehensive list. [CHAR 8/812 (image 10 of 78)] The following information is provided when possible: salutation, inscription and signature, where known; any correspondence between Churchill and recipient related to the book; printing, state and binding of the book, where known; current location, condition of book, and if the book has been on the market or is held in a library. The names are listed as presented on Churchill's list. His immediate family, some of whom received books, were not on any of these lists. At present, it is believed that at least seventy-seven books were distributed in October 1930. The number distributed in November and December of 1930 is unknown.

The private letters, many of them very personal, written to Churchill in response to his gift provide a unique and special insider's glimpse into the non-public personality of Churchill, as well as the politics of the day; and, importantly, if they were to be compared to letters from another time, they would highlight just how different society in 1930 was from the Victorian era in terms of social norms and views. It is clear from some of the comments that the writers did not think, or worry, that their letters would be made public!

Known Recipients

H.M. King George V. The book, gifted to King George V on 14 October 1930, currently resides in the Royal Library, Windsor, as item RCIN 1020423. It was inscribed 'To the King / from Winston S. Churchill / Oct 14. 1930.' A letter from the King's private secretary (Lord Stamfordham) on Buckingham Palace stationery dated 22 October 1930 [CHAR 8/269] says:

> I forwarded to the King at Sandringham the copy of the book which you were good enough to send and His Majesty desires to thank you sincerely for what he looks forward to reading with special interest. … His Majesty and I read your postscript of two words [it is unknown at present what they were] as referring to the present times, and His Majesty thoroughly agrees with its sentiments! I confess to a feeling of pessimism and, whether one looks abroad at the whole Empire or at this Island alone, I fear we have bad times before us.

The postscript is not written on the inscription page of book but must have been in an accompanying note or letter which, thus far, has not been uncovered.

H.R.H. Edward Prince of Wales, future abdicated King; details of book and inscription unknown at present. Prince Edward wrote to WSC on 21 October 1930 [CHAR 8/269], 'Thank you again for sending me a signed copy of your latest book, which I shall read with especial interest and particularly the part about South Africa. I only wish I had even half the experiences you have, to write about if I could. ... I hope you will come and see me for a talk one day soon.' (Gilbert, *Companion Volume V*, part 2, p. 203)

General Byng of Vimy, (Field Marshal Julian Hedworth George Byng), general and friend from South Africa; details of book and inscription unknown at present. Lord Byng wrote on 28 October 1930 (CHAR 8/269), 'I found your book at Bryanson Square [his home] when I went to London yesterday. Thank you many times and again thank you. I read the part about the SALH [South African Light Horse] and enjoyed it, but, Heavens! How one has forgotten it all. But it is good for one's memory to have words like 'Inniskilling Hill' and 'Potgieters' brought back again.' (Gilbert, *Companion Volume V*, part 2, p. 213)

Rt. Hon. Sir Austen Chamberlain, Conservative PM, C of E, politician and friend; details of book and inscription at present unknown. Chamberlain wrote to WSC on 20 October 1930 [CHAR 8/269/23]: 'Many thanks indeed for sending me a copy of your book of which the *Times* writes so appreciatively this morning. It is a pleasure to have it as a gift from you, for our friendship is of long standing & old friendships become more precious as the years pass over them & more memories gather round them.' (Gilbert, *Companion Volume V*, part 2, p. 200)

Rt. Hon. Neville Chamberlain, PM (1937–1940). Inscribed on leaf following Lady Randolph's photograph: 'To/ Neville Chamberlin/ from/ Winston S. Churchill/ Oct 14, 1930.' WSC also included on Chartwell stationery a typed note laid in that states, 'This book is confidential until its publication on Monday next. / 14th October 1930.'

Chamberlain wrote to WSC on 21 October 1930 [CHAR 2/572/103]:

> I am much touched and gratified by your kindness in sending me
> your new book. I am told that it is one of your best and I am looking

forward to the pleasure of reading it, but at present I can't get it away from my wife to whom it is a Godsend as she is not very well and has been confined to her room for some days. Very many thanks.

(Gilbert, *Companion Volume* V, part 2, p. 203; part of Malcolm Forbes Jr. Collection, sold 2 June 2010, at Christie's, London, lot 97, £25,000)

General Sir Ian Hamilton, British general and friend; signed 'To Ian Hamilton from Winston S. Churchill Oct. 14, 1930'; For Churchill book collectors, this book would be listed in Cohen's bibliography as Cohen A91.1.b. Beneath the frontispiece photograph of Jennie Churchill (WSC's mother), Hamilton has noted, 'This dress [Lady Churchill's evening gown] was in its day considered one of Worth's masterpieces. The material was black silk with pale blue linings Ian Hamilton 16.10.30.'[3] (*Catalogue 26 Winston S. Churchill 1874-1965 Books Letters Manuscripts*, Glenn Horowitz Bookseller, 141 East 44th Street, NY, NY, n.d.)

Hamilton wrote to Churchill on 24 October 1930 [CHAR 8/269]:

As one whose affection for you always was, and still remains, quite independent of circumstance, your gift is doubly welcome— (1), because in a series of vivid pictures it reveals the Winston of the Victorian age; (2) because it ensures hundreds of years of life to that same young Winston and those fortunate to be his friends. Therefore, I am very pleased and also very grateful.

This book is not in the Hamilton Collection at King's College with other Hamilton books. It was recently sold by Peter Harrington Books in London (2024).

Lady Leslie, Leonie Blanche Jerome, Jennie's sister and Churchill's aunt; inscribed on the second front free endpaper: 'To, / Leonie / from/ Winston / Oct. 14. 1930.' Pictorial bookplate of Leonie Leslie to the front pastedown. Leonie, who called him 'Copper-top', often took care of young Winston during his childhood, and conspired with the nanny Mrs. Everest to keep Winston away from his grandmother the Duchess of Marlborough at Blenheim. Before a journey to Canada in 1943, Winston wrote his last letter to his aunt: 'You have sent me a lot of charming messages which have cheered me greatly on this long journey. They give me what no one else can give me, the link with my youth and with my mother.' Leslie writes to WSC on 22 October 1930 [CHAR 8/269[:

> What an angel you are to have sent me yr book — I am enjoying every line of it. How the early part carries me back to the Phoenix Park. I can see dear old Everest—so like Queen Victoria—waddling after you in the garden! The adventure and success of yr life is thrilling—& I appreciate all you say of yr mother—so glad you quoted Edgar d'Ab's [Edgar Vincent D'Abernon] description of her. (Gilbert, *Companion Volume* V, part 2, p. 206. Book sold at Magg Brothers, 'Inscribed', Catalogue London, item 218)

Churchill quoted the description of his mother on pp. 18–19 of *My Early Life* from Lord D'Abernon's memoirs:

> …I have the clearest recollection of seeing her for the first time. It was at the Vice-Regal Lodge at Dublin; She stood on one side to the left of the entrance. The Viceroy was on a dais at the farther end of the room surrounded by a brilliant staff, but eyes were not turned on him or on his consort, but on a dark, lithe figure, standing somewhat apart and appearing to be of another texture to those around her, radiant, translucent, intense. A diamond star in her hair, her favourite ornament—its lustre dimmed, by the flashing glory of her eyes. More of the panther than of the woman in her look, but with a cultivated intelligence unknown to the jungle. Her courage not less great than that of her husband—fit mother for descendants of the great Duke. With all these attributes of brilliancy, such kindliness and high spirits that she was universally popular. Her desire to please, her delight in life, and the genuine wish that all should share her joyous faith in it, made her the centre of a devoted circle.

General Sir Reginald Barnes, one of WSC's closest friends in the 4th Hussars in India; went to Cuba with Churchill; details of book and inscription presently unknown. Barnes wrote to WSC on 26 October 1930 [CHAR 8/269]:

Thanks to you a thousand times for the book. I have only so far just dipped into it, but it interests me enormously, & I am thrilled to read it. It will bring back to me, the many happy and interesting days that we have had together, which I always have, always shall, treasure in my inmost self. I loved your description of your entrance exam to Harrow, and the ablative absolute etc., you're feeling in which I so painfully share in common, and more than anything the absolute true note you strike in putting your mother's picture in the place of honor.

Dear old man, I am so glad you wrote it, as it shows the world the human and cherry Winston that I know, but which so many know nothing of. (Gilbert, *Companion Volume* V, part 2, pp. 210–11)

Sir Archibald Sinclair, WWI comrade and Private Secretary (1921–2); inscribed 'To Archie, from Winston, Oct. 14, 1930'; 1st ed. 2nd state. Sinclair wrote to WSC on 27 October 1930 [CHAR 8/269]:

I am indeed proud of and grateful for my author's copy of your thrilling and enchanting autobiography. It proves conclusively of what I had long suspected that of all the men I know you have the most enviably and enjoyably adventurous life.

We are all reading it with immense delight and real zeal—the children loved the description of Harrow and Robin [Sinclair's wife] rocked with laughter at the Amery story. (Gilbert, *Companion Volume* V, part 2, p. 212. Sold Christie's London, May 7, 1993, lot 28)

The Amery story, related on pp. 31–2 of *My Early Life*, is a funny tale from when Churchill was in his first term at Harrow:

One day when I had been no more than a month in the school, I saw a boy standing in a meditative posture wrapped in a towel on the very brink. He was no bigger than I was, so I thought him fair game. Coming stealthily behind, I pushed him in, holding on to his towel out of humanity, so that it should not get wet. I was startled to see a furious face emerge from the foam, and a being evidently of enormous strength making its way by fierce strokes to the shore. I fled; but in vain. Swift as the wind my pursuer overtook me, seized me in a ferocious grip and hurled me into the deepest part of the pool. I soon scrambled out on the other side and found myself surrounded by an agitated crowd of younger boys. 'You're in for it,' they said. 'Do you know what you have done? It's Amery; he's in the Sixth form. He is Head of his House; he is champion at Gym; he has got his football colours.' They continued to recount his many titles to fame and reverence, and to dilate upon the awful retribution that would fall upon me. I was convulsed not only with terror, but with the guilt of sacrilege. How could I tell his rank when he was in a bath-towel and so small? 1 determined to apologise immediately. I approached the potentate in lively trepidation. 'l am very sorry,' I said. 'I mistook you for a Fourth Form boy. You are so small.' He did not seem at all placated by this; so, I added in a most brilliant recovery, 'My father, who is a great man, is also small.' At this he laughed, and after some general remarks about my 'cheek' and how I had better be careful in the future, signified that the incident was closed.

The book was sold at PBA Galleries, London, in 2020 for $7,800. The book was sold in 2024 at Peter Harrington Rare Books in London; their catalogue stated: 'Housed in a blue half Morocco box. Half-tone frontispiece and 15 other plates, folding map, maps to text. Spine and extremities sunned, contents clean. A very good copy.'

Lord Beaverbrook, Max Aitken, friend, confidante, minister and businessman; signed 'To Max From Winston Oct 14, 1930.' The book was sold at Bloomsbury Auctions in London on 18 October 2012. It was subsequently rebound with the original Lord Beaverbrook book plate in dark plum full Morocco leather binding which features gilt decoration and print, raised spine bands, contrasting title and author panels, gilt top edge, and marbled paper end sheets. A matching half-leather clamshell case is executed in the same plum Morocco as the binding, with marbled paper sides matching the volume's end sheets. Churchill's inscription is in fine condition. Currently in private collection.

No note of thanks has thus far been found.

Lady Birkenhead, wife of the then recently deceased F.E. Smith, who had been a political ally and one of WSC's closest friends. She wrote to WSC on 21 October 1930 [CHAR 8/269]:

Thank you so much for your book which I became immersed(?) in when I went to bed last night—the only time I have to read! I think it is delightful—I was pleased to have it. I can't thank you dear Winston for all you are doing on my behalf—you are loved a true friend. Every day I miss him more—some decision arises that I want his advice on I feel so lost—this is terrible. One dreads waking up in the morning. It is much the worst time. Goodbye & thank you and bless you.

F.E. Smith had died the previous month on 30 September 1930, prematurely, at the age of fifty-eight.

Rt. Hon. Ramsey MacDonald, PM; copy inscribed: 'To / Ramsey MacDonald / from / Winston S. Churchill / Oct 14. 1930.' MacDonald wrote to WSC on 20 October 1930 [CHAR 8/269]: 'Thank you very much for your early days. I shall take the very first opportunity (e.g. when I have finished Trevelyan's "Blenheim" the end of which is only a hundred or so off) of going over them. … You are an interesting cuss — I, a dull dog. May yours bring you both credit and cash.' (Gilbert, *Companion Volume* V, part 2, p. 200, 1st Edition with dust jacket and with MacDonald's bookplate; sold at *The Political Sale,* Sotheby's, London, 15 July 1998, entry 155; Christie's, NY, 3 December 2010, lot 36, with dust jacket)

Sir James Hawkey, West Essex Unionist Association, Mayor of Wansted and Woodford (WSC's constituency); details of book and inscription unknown; Hawkey wrote to WSC on 20 October: 'It was extremely kind of you to send the autograph copy of your new book. It was quite a "Godsend" to me as I have been in bed during the weekend with a bad influenza cold. I am sure I need not tell you how very highly I shall always value the book.' It is unknown what, if any, inscription was written by WSC. [CHAR 8/269]

Rt. Rev. Dr. Welldon, Headmaster at Harrow; details of the book and inscription are at present unknown. Welldon wrote to WSC on 22 October 1930 [CHAR 8/269]:

I am grateful to you for sending a copy of your book. I am, I think, even more grateful for the kind references which you make in it to myself. It is a regret to me that you were not happier at Harrow; I wish I had done more to make you happy. But one chief difficulty of a Headmaster's life is the lack of time. There was, I think, hardly any boy whom I did not feel I could have helped, if I was given unlimited time. But when there are some hundreds of boys of whom it is necessary to think, one exceptional boy is apt to suffer loss. I think I did not fail to understand that you might have felt some pains at being surpassed by boys, who were so far intellectually your inferiors, in the commonly accepted lines, whether of work or play, in the School life. But I hope I may claim that I always believed in you. It seems to me that such troubles as may have occurred between us generally arose from relations with other masters and not to myself, and the distinction of your after life, as great as it has been, is not so great as is the pleasure which it has given me, and has not been to me in any sense a surprise.

You will let me add that the narrative of your escape from the Boers has caused me a thrilling sense of delight. (Gilbert, *Companion Volume V*, part 2, p. 205)

One of the kindnesses Churchill wrote about in *My Early Life* was on p. 36:

Mr. Welldon took a friendly interest in me, and knowing that I was weak in the Classics, determined to help me himself. His daily routine was heavy; but he added three times a week a quarter of an hour before evening prayers in which to give me personal attention. This was a great condescension for the Head-master, who of course never taught anyone but the monitors and the highest scholars. I was proud of the honour: I shrank from the ordeal.

Churchill further wrote on his departure from Harrow (p. 53): 'I had been surprised on taking leave of Mr. Welldon to hear him predict, with a confidence for which I could see no foundation, that I should be able to make my way all right. I have always been very grateful to him for this.'

Robert Boothby, MP, WSC's Parliamentary Secretary (1926–9); inscribed thus: 'Robert Boothby from Winston S. Churchill Oct. 14. 1930.' Boothby wrote on 3 November 1930 [CHAR 8/269], 'Just a line to thank you very much for the book. It is sheer joy from the first word to the last.'

Sold at Sotheby's London in 2015. Book rebound by the Chelsea Bindery in dark blue Morocco, spines with single-line gilt panel to compartments (gilt rampant lion device gilt to four of the six), single-line panel on sides, facsimile of Churchill's signature in gilt on front covers, two-line gilt turn-ins, burgundy endpapers, gilt edges. Housed in a custom-made leather-entry slipcase. (Gilbert, *Companion Volume* V, part 2, p. 217)

Colonel Lawrence, Lawrence of Arabia, Thomas Edward Lawrence CB DSO (1888–1935), British archaeologist, army officer, diplomat and writer who became renowned for his role in the Arab Revolt (1916–18) and the Sinai and Palestine Campaign (1915–18) against the Ottoman Empire during the First World War; a close friend of WSC; inscribed on second front fly-leaf: 'To Laurens, from Winston S. Churchill, Oct. 14, 1930'; As noted in the chapter on writing *My Early Life*, Lawrence reviewed the manuscript of the book and wrote substantial notes of his views. Book currently in Houghton Library, Harvard University, EC9 L4388 Zz930c.

Sir Samuel Hoare, Conservative politician; WSC signed, inscribed and dated 14 October 1930; exact wording unclear. Hoare wrote to WSC on 26 October 1930 [CHAR 8/269]:

> What a lovely book you have sent me. I have read every word of it, and I have loved it. But more than that I am jealous of it, as I also have written a book [*The Fourth Seal*, Heinemann, London, 1930], and in order that you should see how much better yours is than mine I am sending you an advance copy of it. But as mine is about Russia, you may like to throw an eye over it. (Gilbert, *Companion Volume* V, part 2, p. 210)

Book sold at Keys Fine Art Auctioneers, Norwich, UK on July 25, 2013.

Lady Desborough, Ettie Grenfell, Baroness Desborough, well-known socialite; WSC attended her parties. Details of book and inscription unknown. She writes to WSC in 1930 in an undated letter [CHAR 1/214/42-44]:

My dearest Winston, I cannot tell you how intoxicating I found that piece of writing—from the first word to the last—the 'attaque' is brilliant—sweeping one instantly into delight & intimate communion. It is fun—you have given us the best treat for years & years. … 'Examinations' one of the best. … Bless you for being all you are, & all that you are to us all.

Rt. Hon. Sir Laming Worthington-Evans, Conservative MP, Secretary of State for War (1924–9). Letter to WSC, 27 October 1930 [CHAR 2/169]: 'The more I read your "Early Life" the more I enjoy it, it makes a private story of action brilliantly written. I am enjoying every page of it!'

General Sir Bindon Blood, Army General (Malakand Field Force) and friend. Blood wrote to WSC on 20 October 1930 [CHAR 8/269]:

A thousand thanks for the copy of your new book that you have so kindly sent me. It will bring back all sorts of pleasant memories of old times! I get letters from India pretty regularly every mail, and of course sometimes I get stories of the doings … PS. I am filled with hope that the way to No 10 is clearing for you! (Gilbert, *Companion Volume* V, part 2, p. 201)

No details of book and inscription are presently known. Churchill would have to wait another decade before the path to No. 10 would be cleared!

E. Marsh, Edward (Eddie) Marsh, private secretary to WSC, close friend; WSC inscribed on flyleaf: 'To Eddie From Winston' (it likely was dated also, but this is not noted in catalogue). Marsh wrote to WSC on 20 October 1930 [CHAR 8/269]: 'Ever so many thanks for the Book—have told you so often how much I admire its contents that now I have nothing to do but congratulate you on its appearance & illustrations. I am delighted to see what an outstandingly good press it is getting—it will evidently bring you both fame & lucre.' Marsh was the most frequent and detailed reviewer of *My Early Life*, and he and WSC carried on a marvelous correspondence about the reviews, and the English language, as detailed in Chapter 3 on Churchill writing the book. Marsh's copy was sold at Sotheby's London in May 1953.

Brendan Bracken, 1st Viscount Bracken, PC (1901–1958), was an Irish-born businessman and politician. He was Minister of Information under WSC during WWII and a close friend and confidant of WSC's; He wrote a handwritten note to WSC on 8 North Street Westminster stationery on 18 November 1930 [CHAR 8/268]: 'My Dear Winston, Your book renews the delight one felt on reading most of the chapters in newspapers or magazines. I am so grateful to you. Yrs B.' Nothing is known of the inscription or the whereabouts of the book.

General Sir J. Edmonds, James Edmonds, WWI general and author. He wrote to WSC on 21 October 1930 [CHAR 8/269]: 'I was delighted to receive an inscribed copy of "My Early Life." A copy ought to be given to every English boy, he might then be able to compete with the Scotch and Irish!' (Gilbert, *Companion Volume* V, part 2, p. 202). Details of book and inscription unknown at present.

His Grace, The Duke of Westminster, Hugh Richard Arthur Grosvenor, 2nd Duke of Westminster, GCVO, DSO (1879–1953), was a British landowner and a friend of WSC. WSC inscribed on the fly-leaf: 'To Bendor from Winston. Oct 14, 1930.' Sold at Sotheby's, London, 19 June 1962. No reply found.

Rt. Hon. Stanley Baldwin, PM (1923–4, 1924–29, and 1935–7); inscribed 'To Stanley Baldwin / from / Winston S. Churchill / Oct. 14, 1930.' At present, unable to find any note thanking WSC. Book condition: spine faded, light damp staining on spine, foxing on preliminary leaves. Sold Christie's, NY, 22 June 2012, lot 177, $15,000.

P.J. Grigg, Sir Percy James Grigg, KCB, KCSI, PC (1890–1964), Secretary of State for War under WSC during WWII; had also worked with him during WWI. Grigg wrote to WSC on October 18, 1930 [CHAR 8/269]:

> I am delighted to have a copy of your new book for at least two reasons. First because you have given it and also because in reading it, I shall recall some of the magic of those long evenings at Chartwell when you were in a reminiscent mood, I acceptingly was content to listen in fascinated and happy silence.

How different it is now! But it is rather fascinating to see how events Baldwin are making certain the postponement, possibly indefinite of a radical fiscal change. And Snowden really is a bonny fighter. Oddly enough I have recently had an attack of optimism. Of course, we may have to live on a bump while democracy is learning sense, but it is an awfully big bump. And I don't think the country will really follow Sir Oswald Hitler. Perhaps there may be some consolation for you too in the situation. If you get beaten on protection at the next election you may drop it. And when you do you'll get back again & by then Baldwin will have returned to [?] or dust. But you don't want my reflections on what you probably consider a most gloomy political outlook. You must however have my gratitude for the book.

No details about the book are known.

Sir Harry McGowan, Chairman of Imperial Chemical Industries; on 22 October 1930 he wrote to WSC [CHAR 8/269]:

Thank you so much for the copy of your book which I am finding extraordinarily interesting. I must admit that I am amazed at the masterly way in which the language of the passages dealing with your earlier years reproduces the youthfulness of that time, while the gradual change of the idiom reflects the transition to mature years. I am quite sure that the book will have a good and ready sale and I may say that I am ordering a number of copies for some of my friends who will, I know, read it with as much interest as I am now doing.

No information on the book is available.

Earl of Derby, Edward Stanley, Lord Derby (17th), friend and Conservative politician. In a 23 October 1930 letter to WSC, he wrote [CHAR 2/169/84]: 'Thank you very much indeed for sending me a copy of your book, most kind of you & I really appreciate it.' No information on the book is known.

Major Hugo 'Mouche' Baring, soldier, businessman, very close friend; he, WSC and Reggie Barnes lived together in India. Baring wrote to WSC on 18 January 1931 [CHAR 8/269]:

> I cannot help saying—and not only to others, but boldly to myself how greater I've enjoyed 'My Early Life,' the very best autobiographical book I've ever read. I often do read and am interested in life stories—although the vast majority fail to be perfectly successful or satisfying as works of art—because scarcely anyone or so far as I am aware, nobody else can be in writing at once convincingly natural and unfailingly attractive—You have succeeded in this also! And your sense of humor never flags. Someday I hope to read it all over again; for it is exhilarating like a crisp spring day. You will never get 'old.' Yours is not a date, it is a quality; and nothing will take it from you.

No information is known about the book.

James L. Gavin, Editor, *Observer*, WSC friend of many years. Gavin wrote to WSC on 27 April 1931 [CHAR 8/269[: 'I was as delighted as surprised to get your magnus opus between one pair of covers. It makes me hope to read it all again before this year is out. It will always live. I thank you with uncommon thanks not only for it but for a thought like old times ever moved to memory.' No information is known about the book.

Donald Fergusson, Private Secretary to WSC as C of E. He wrote to WSC on 21 October 1930 [CHAR 8/ 269]:

> On returning home this morning after a weekend visit I found waiting for me the delightful surprise of your new book. It was extraordinarily kind of you to send it & to give me the very great pleasure of finding myself in the list of friends to whom you have sent presentation copies.
>
> I read the extracts that appeared in the *Daily News*, I didn't know whether more to envy the opportunities or to admire the way in which you prosper them all. I just saw the close of the glorious 25 years before 1914—& looking back it seems that then there were things worth doing in every branch of life—war and commerce, politics &

even administration & that since the war everything has disastrously changed. But after all it was only two cavalry subalterns who seized the chance of going to Cuba.

George (G.M.) Trevelyan, historian, Cambridge professor; details of inscription and book are unknown. Trevelyan wrote on 22 October 1930 [CHAR 8/269]:

> It was right kind of you to send me your book, and I am proud to have your name on the blank sheet. I have always been very fond of all your books—as my father was on the life of yours—; and I have always been particularly fond of autobiography, especially about a person's early years. ... I had doubly high expectations, and they have been surpassed. I think it is your best book, at least I am enjoying it most of all. So long as you are with us, it can't be said that the race of statesmen who are men of letters is extinct. You have a marvellous gift of writing—and it pleases me to learn that you were helped to it by dear old Somervell. Well now for the Great Duke. I can't tell you how much I am looking forward to it. I am almost ready to pay another year or two's Labour budget to make sure at getting it as soon as possible. (Gilbert, *Companion Volume* V, part 2, p. 207)

J.C. Smuts, General Jan Christian Smuts, South African statesman and military leader, friend of Churchill; he wrote to WSC on 23 January 1931 [CHAR 8/269]:

> My Dear Winston, Thank you ever so gratefully for saying that you will put your name in my copy of your book—of course I will value it all the more when I read it again with, if possible, more enjoyment. And this copy I am just now posting you is my very own; for the one I read before dawn. It is as thrilling a record of human adventure as has ever been written.

No information on the book is available.

Robert Somervell, history master at Harrow; No information on the book available. Somervell wrote to WSC on 20 October 1930 [CHAR 8/269]:

> A thousand thanks for the present of your book, with your name in it too, enhancing my pleasure in its possession. It reached us at Breakfast time, and I have but read a few pages as I have had a busy morning over my Hospital affairs. My wife seized upon it & could talk of nothing else at lunch. Now I have taken my first dip & find it so delightful that I shall have to ration myself to so many pages a day, to prolong the pleasure. It is most admirably done, and your kind mention of me touches me deeply. (Gilbert, *Companion Volume* V, part 2, p. 202)

Mrs. Oldbury, unknown connection. No information on the book available. She wrote a letter to WSC dated 20 October 1930 [CHAR 8/0269] : 'This morning I received your book "My Early Life." Autographed by your-self. I shall hold it as one of my treasured possessions & find much pleasure in reading the same. Please accept my best thanks.'

Sir Robert Horne, politician, minister, C of E (prior to Churchill in 1922). Horne wrote on 31 October 1930 [CHAR 8/269]:

> Your book has arrived and has proved a most alluring temptation to me to neglect everything else. I have been dipping into it at every possible interstice of time and found it fascinating. The way in which you have altered the style in giving the earliest part — by a method which suggests the evolving of a child's mind — is most subtle. Bless you for sending it to me. It will give me many happy hours; & what more can the most beneficent of your friends do for you than that? (Gilbert, *Companion Volume* V, part 2, p. 216)

Details of book and inscription are presently unknown.

Lord Darling, British Judge; Darling wrote to WSC on 3 November 1930 [CHAR 8/269]:

> I am delighted to receive a copy of your book sent to me by yourself. I was already reading your account of your 'Early Life' when your gift arrived, and I am certain that any interest & admiration will last till I reach the final line. … Of course you will continue to describe your

career—and I wish I could read your account of those days—nel mezzo del cammin di vita [from Dante ('In the middle of the journey of our life')] of criminal trials as I hope you found useful when you were Home Secretary. How I wish I could now write you to behold me do justice on some of the evil doers who now busy themselves with politics.

Details of book and inscription are presently unknown.

Lt. Col. Sir M. (Martin) Archer-Shee, CMG DSO (1873–1935), British army officer and Conservative politician. No note from Archer-Shee has been found. This book, with its presentation inscription from WSC to Martin Archer-Shee, is in Yale University Library, Beinecke Rare Book and Manuscript Library Reading Room with acquisition number: 1975 1534.

Westerham Library, London Road, Westerham, Kent, received a book from WSC; the librarian wrote to him [CHAR 8/269]:

> It is very good of you to have presented a copy of your latest book to the Westerham Library. I am writing to express very warm thanks for your generosity, which will be appreciated by all our readers. May I at the same time say with what interest & pleasure my two sons and I have been reading your book which we got as soon as it was released. I consider it a most amiable book to put into the hands of any young man & it is full of life & energy & appreciation of everything that makes life worth living, that I am sure it must do a great deal of good. Your accounts of the Boer war awoke many old memories for I was in New York in those days. My husband & I followed every phase of the war with deep interest. We went to hear you, when you gave an account at the Metropolitan Opera House in New York. I did not foresee then that we should eventually become neighbors in Westerham.

Lord Moynihan, noted British surgeon and friend of WSC, wrote to WSC on 20 October 1930 [CHAR 8/269]: 'You have given me great pleasure by the presentation of your book. I shall treasure it all my life as one of the most precious possessions and I am deeply grateful for your recollection of a promise.'

Lord Ashfield, Albert Stanley, President of the Board of Trade, Chairman and Managing Director of the London Underground. Although this book is on the Chartwell list as having been sent out in October 1930, the book (assumed to be the original and not a replacement) was sold at auction at Sotheby's, London, 12 December 2002, lot 71 (said to be first state, first edition). It was signed, 'To Ashfield from Winston S. Churchill. Nov. 25, 1930.'

Lord Reading, Rufus Daniel Isaacs, 1st Marquess of Reading, Viceroy of India, 1921–6, and Secretary of State of Foreign Affairs, 1931. This book is on the Chartwell list as having been sent out in October 1930. The book (assumed to be the original and not a replacement) was sold at auction at Sotheby's, London, 12 December 2002, lot 70 (said to be first state, first edition) and was signed, 'To Rufus from Winston S.C. Nov 1930.'

Sir Harry Goschen, Sir William Henry Neville Goschen, 1st Baronet, KBE, JP, DL (1865–1945), a British businessman and banker, wrote to WSC on stationery from 12 Austin Friars on 24 October 1930 [CHAR 8/269]: 'Your delightful present arrived this morning & I hasten to send you my most sincere thanks for your interesting book, which I am much looking forward to. The inscription [?] at the beginning much appreciated & makes it an always treasured possession & memento.' No additional information known.

Bernard Baruch, American politician and friend, wrote to WSC on 24 November 1930 [CHAR 1/214/38]: 'I can not tell you what joy I get from reading your book. You would be pleased to hear the many most favourable comments that are being made about it among the people with whom I come in contact.' No information on the book is known.

Sir Abe Bailey, friend of WSC, wrote to him on 20 October 1930 [CHAR 8/269]: 'Thank you so much for the book. I shall enjoy reading it as I do all your writings. I always think you are a second Gibbons. I only wish I could write like you. ….'

Diana Churchill, eldest daughter; inscription signed 'Diana From Papa Oct. 25, 1930.' Book was sold at Chartwell Booksellers in New York and was described thus:

This is a good copy of the less common First State/Second Binding (per Cohen) of the First English edition in rough pink cloth, with the variant five-line title block on the cover. The cloth is worn, the spine chipped and faded, the contents less than perfect but entirely intact. The book is preserved in a stunning, purpose-built, quarter-burgundy leather clamshell solander.

No thank-you note was found in the Churchill archives.

Sarah Churchill, WSC's daughter, wrote on 29 November 1930: 'This letter is to wish you many happy returns of the day [for WSC's birthday], and to thank you for giving me "My Early Life."' (Gilbert, *Companion Volume* V, part 2, p. 227). No information on the inscription or book are known. No information of books for Clementine, Randolph, or Mary (she would only have been eight years old at the time) has been found.

W. Mackenzie King, Canadian Prime Minister, wrote to WSC on 7 February 1931 [CHAR 2/177/90-91]:

> The New Year has brought me no more welcome gift or greeting than your book and your letter. It would be difficult for me to say how very much I prize this and how great this [?] the satisfaction which I have derived from the reading of this.
> 'My Early Life' is a charming biography. Had there remained nothing more to tell, the book would be an inspiration to old and young alike. Happily this story of middle life, is not as yet complete; when it is told, I, for one of many, shall hope for another volume which will [?] to your friends something on the lights and shadows of eventide of life.

Nothing is known of when and how this was signed. It is not listed on any of the Chartwell lists.

Edward Henry Carson, Lord Carson, Irish politician, First Lord of Admiralty, wrote to WSC on 5 Eaton Place stationery on 22 October 1930 [CHAR 8/269]: 'Thank you very much for sending me a copy of your book.

I read 50 pages yesterday and was most interested. I look forward to the remainder with great joy. It is certain that your characteristics developed at an early age, you were puckish always. ...'

Cyril Alington, Headmaster, Eton College, on stationery printed 'The Cloisters, Eton College, Windsor.' Alington wrote to WSC on 29 October 1930 [CHAR 8/269]: 'At the risk of boring you, I must tell you what a delightful afternoon I spent yesterday with your book. I didn't know whether just to envy you and your adventures or your sense of describing them... .' Much of the handwritten note is unreadable.

Brigadier-General Edward Spears, worked with WSC as when Churchill was First Lord of the Admiralty and during WWI, and they became friends. Spears wrote to WSC on 29 October 1930 [CHAR 8/269]:

> Thanks to your book a voyage which promised to be extremely dull has been delightful. I have enjoyed it enormously.—It is really you & many who will read it will realize your very loveable personality. It pulsates with life & will induce the pusillanimous to take courage. To me the book carries a special message for to my delight I found you had exactly the same educational difficulties I had had, for I was incapable of learning Latin, Greek or anything the purpose of which I could not understand—The coincidence goes further, I got the same marks as you did for mathematics at the Army entrance Exam. Your love of language I also shared, but alas it was for the French tongue. The story of your escape from Pretoria is extraordinarily exciting. It made me think of Casanova escaping from I Piombi at Venice but the shame of the S.A. Campaign.
>
> Bad Generals are a sad infliction but the just retribution of a people who treat their army as a toy, but when the troops fight badly that is shame indeed. Your book made me almost glad of the great war which was at least a vindication.
>
> I wonder if the last chapters will cause a slight tremor in the Conservative ranks!! I don't suppose so—this book will make you many friends & let me, as far as I am concerned, thank you for it & for the pleasure you have given me.

Lady Lytton, née Pamela Plowden, first love of Churchill, met in India, and a lifetime friend. Lytton wrote to WSC on 19 November 1930 [CHAR 8/269]:

> What a magician you are. Your book has charmed me out of myself into your life! This is so gay, so full, so courageous, so successful and so beautifully written. It is a book for every young man to read. It must be scattered about the universities & training colleges & it must be in everyone's home to make the old feel young again, & the youth feel wise. Indeed, it is a delightful, inspiring work. Is there any chance of you & Clemmie coming here for a Sunday before Christmas? Victor has been away in Palestine but returns on Saturday. <u>Do come</u>. It would be great pleasure & you shall have a small & glittering 'party' to amuse you. I long for some talks.

No additional information on the book is available.

Unknown, a person who lived at 48A Sloane Square, wrote to WSC on 30 October 1930 [CHAR 8/269]:

> I must thank you for having written 'My Early Life.' I have read it from start to finish & most of it twice over. I enjoyed it all & it is so vivid that all the scenes were easily pictured & I followed your adventures as if I had been sharing them with you. I am keeping my autographed copy—but have sent other copies to friends. You have made Christmas very easy for me. All will get your book as a present. Should you by chance come across 'a better book' please let me know. The best sentence & the truest is the very last sentence of all.

Admiral Sir Reginald Hugh Spencer Bacon, KCB, KCVO, DSO (Royal Navy), worked with WSC at Admiralty; he wrote to WSC on 31 October 1930 [CHAR 8/269]:

> This is the first time I have had the courage or the impudence to address you in this way, but your many kindnesses to me and the dedication of your book. I have not yet finished it but it has given me so much delight and what is for me more genuine inspiration and human assistance that

I want to write to you now about it while the impression is still vivid and while I have a rare 15 minute [?]. Of course I read Omdurman first, but then began at the beginning right through to the first Indian campaign. The Bangalore chapter is to me a great piece of work. The real Religio [?] a profound and manly philosophy without any bunk and no [?] either side. I was delighted with it seems to me what everyone ought think and feel. But then—so few do. Another reflection on the empire (Lei Square) incident. They were very reassuring to one who has rather 'spoken out of turn' at rather a critical time and likely to have to face the music for it sometime somewhere. Yours is the right philosophy 'we did our best.' I feel my unheroic—I didn't even loose off—to be beaten doesn't matter, to be betrayed however grossly is to be made to look a fool. I wish you were leading us now may be perfectly right about fool but I believe your leaderships worth the policy. Political life would really have some savour in following a man who can make one feel one wants to follow him. Old Asquith made me feel like that, George now did S.B. [Stanley Baldwin] couldn't. It is a rare gift to be able to lead but I seem to get the inspiration from men who do not ordinarily exercise it on the generality of mankind. These people out of this world say George was a more inspiring leader than Asquith anyway. I am interrupted now. Forgive this rambling communication. … But you dedicated your book to the next generation. To one of them at least it is a source of inspiration.

Evan Charteris, biographer, barrister, friend of WSC. Charteris wrote to WSC on 31 October 1930 [CHAR 8/269]: 'I have seldom read a book with so much enjoyment—as "My Early Life" for which an alternative title might have "Safety Last"—D'Artagnan, Cellerie, Monte Cristo & Casanova (re escape N.B.) are rolled into one & makes an entertaining story. I hope it is having the success it deserves.'

Mrs. Moreton Frewen, Clarita "Clara" Jerome (1851–1935), daughter of the New York City financier Leonard Jerome, and sister to Lord Randolph Churchill's wife Jennie, aunt of WSC; her husband, Moreton, was the disastrous editor of WSC's first book. WSC inscribed on the free front-end piece (ffep), 'To / Clara / from / Winston / Oct 14. 1930.' She wrote to WSC on 18 November 1930 [CHAR 8/269]:

Your charming and glorious gift—the beautiful Magenta book, with its Magenta jacket arrived safely here, forwarded from Brede! This most fascinating dear book, so fraught with many of my life's tender & happy memories, historic also for me, such as My many months work on the [?] Committee. I remember well, going with your mother to meet you at the station, upon your return from Egypt. What an excitement & what a welcome! The flags you brought home & your poor arm still bound up! Indeed, my life nowadays, to all memory—....

Viscount Hailsham, Douglas McGarel Hogg, 1st Viscount Hailsham, PC, KC (1872–1950), was a British lawyer and Conservative politician who twice served as Lord Chancellor. Hailsham wrote to WSC on 18 October 1930 [CHAR 8/269]:

I have this moment received your book. I should be able to thank you more adequately if I waited till I had read it, but I want to say at once how much I appreciate your giving me a copy with what interest I shall had a part of your life [*sic*] which from that time at least I am closely with [?]. My very warm thanks for the gift.

Captain Liddell Hart, Sir Basil Henry Liddell Hart (1895–1970), known most of his career as Captain B.H. Liddell Hart, was a British soldier, military historian and military theorist. WSC inscribed 'To Captain Liddell Hart from Winston S. Churchill Oct 28. 1930.' Book currently resides in the Maugham Library, Kings College, London; DA566.9 C5 CHU.

James Maxton, 1885–1946, was a British left-wing politician, and leader of the Independent Labour Party. He was a pacifist who opposed both world wars. WSC inscribed on the fly-leaf: 'To James Maxton from Winston S. Churchill Oct 14. 1930.' No thank you reply has been found. Book sold at Sotheby's London in 1984.

David Lloyd George, 1st Earl Lloyd-George of Dwyfor, OM, KStJ, PC (1863–1945) was PM from 1916 to 1922. A Liberal Party statesman and politician from Wales, he was known for leading the UK during the First World War, for social reform policies (including the National Insurance

Act 1911), his role in the Paris Peace Conference, and negotiating the establishment of the Irish Free State. He was a friend, ally and mentor to WSC. Inscriptions reads, 'David Lloyd George / From / Winston S. Churchill/ October 14, 1930' on fly-leaf, sold at Sotheby's NY, 26 June 2024, lot 1168, significant spine fade.

List of individuals who received an inscribed/signed copy according to lists in the Churchill Archives (or discovered by research elsewhere) but for whom no additional information is known:

His Grace, The Duke of Marlborough, Lieutenant-Colonel Charles Richard John Spencer-Churchill, 9th Duke of Marlborough, KG, TD, PC (1871–1934), British soldier and Conservative politician, and a close friend of Winston Churchill, who was his first cousin. He was often known as 'Sunny.'

Rt. Hon. Walter Guinness, 1st Baron Moyne, DSO & Bar, PC (1880–1944), was an Anglo-Irish politician and businessman. He served as the British Minister of State in the Middle East, he was financial secretary under WSC when he was C of E.

H.C. Vickers, Horace Cecil Vickers, Senior Partner, Vickers, da Costa; WSC's stockbroker.

Sir Philip Sassoon, Sir Philip Albert Gustave David Sassoon, 3rd Baronet, GBE, CMG (1888–1939) was a British politician, art collector, and socialite.

P. Buchan-Hepburn, Patrick George Thomas Buchan-Hepburn, 1st Baron Hailes, GBE, CH, PC (1901–1974), British Conservative politician, and personal secretary to WSC.

Major John and Lady Gwendoline Churchill, WSC's brother and sister-in-law ('Goonie'). Inscribed to Jack and Goonie, unknown if dated, currently in Churchill College Collection on loan from Randolph Churchill; leatherbound.

Lord Riddell, George Allardice Riddell, 1st Baron Riddell (1865–1934), was a British solicitor, newspaper proprietor and public servant. He was the owner of *News of the World.*

Wm. S. Stewart, Oldham Publishing.

Adam Curtis Brown, WSC's literary agent at the well-known Curtis Brown Company in London.

Madame Balsan, Consuelo Vanderbilt-Balsan (1877–1964); formerly Consuelo Spencer-Churchill, Duchess of Marlborough; born Consuelo Vanderbilt. She was a socialite and a member of the prominent American Vanderbilt family. A good friend of WSC.

Editor, *Oldham Chronicle*

Colonel Hordern. WSC employed him to do research for his books, including *The Eastern Front*.

Hon. Mrs. Greville.

Mrs. Lucy A. Fawcett sent a letter to WSC on 14 October requesting a signed book [CHAR 8/812]; this was followed by a letter from Sir James Hawkey, West Essex Unionist Association, from WSC's constituency [CHAR 8/812] asking WSC to send her a signed book, as she was one of the hardest workers for the party in their constituency – which he did.

General J.E.B. (Jack) Seely, great friend of WSC (from Harrow days); John Edward Bernard Seely (1868–1947), 1st Baron Mottistone CB, CMG, DSO, PC, TD, was Churchill's close friend, comrade in arms, and political ally for nearly half a century.

Lord Inchcape, James McKay, British businessman and administrator in India.

Mrs. Romilly (George).

Major Cyril Patterson (pilot)

CHAPTER 5 / LAUNCH OF THE BOOK

From the end of October until the end of December 1930, WSC continued to gift signed copies of My Early Life. *Where documentation has allowed, here is the list.*

Lord Southborough, a civil servant who worked with Churchill; he wrote a letter to WSC dated 8 November 1930 [CHAR 2/169/91]: 'To me this Early Life is like a picture gallery through which I walk scrutinizing the features & the dress of so many I have known from your father onward, it is so much more agreeable than any [?] we can attend with the living.'

H.W. Thompson, son of WSC's bodyguard (W.H. Thompson): inscription on title page reads, 'Inscribed for/ HW Thompson/ by / Winston S Churchill', second impression, 1st ed. *MEL.*

Alfred Duff-Cooper, friend and political ally of WSC; signed 'Inscribed by / Winston S. Churchill/ for the Dove/ November 22, 1930.' First Edition, London, Thornton Butterworth, 1930, spine faded, half-inch gouge on upper board, Duff-Copper bookplate. The book was sold at Christie's London, 22 June 2012.

Roger Frewen, WSC's godson. Signed 'To Roger Frewen from Winston S. Churchill Dec. 1, 1930.' First Ed, first printing, first state, in rebound full plum calf, evoking the original binding colour, with gilt decoration and print, raised spine bands, dark brown title and author panels gilt top edge, and marbled paper end sheets. Has Frewen bookplate. Clamshell case with similar design as book binding.

Hugo Hirst, Lord Hirst of Witton (1863–1943); signed 'Hugo Hirst / Inscribed by Winston S. Churchill / Dec. 9, 1930.' Book with sunned spine and containing Hirst's bookplate and 1st Ed., 2nd impression, sold at Christie's NY, 15 November 2011, lot 10, for $3,250.

Stanley James Webb, 1st Baron Passfield, President, Board of Trade (1924), Secretary of State for Dominion Affairs (1929–30), signed and inscribed on front free blank: 'To / Stanley James Webb / from / Winston S. Churchill/ Dec. 23. 1930.' First Edition Second Impression, London, 1930, covers bowed, faded, joints starting at head toning and foxing, Swann Auction Galleries, NY, 26 November 2013, lot 39.

Christopher Hobhouse, journalist, barrister, and author; killed in WWII; signed and inscribed second front free endpaper, 'To Christopher Hobhouse from Winston S. Churchill. Dec. 23, 1930.' 1st Ed., 2nd impression, spine faded, just rubbed at the head and tail, corners bumped, small paint fleck to the spine. Magg Brothers, London, 2019.

Tom Clarke, editor of the *Daily News* and *Westminster Gazette*. Signed and inscribed on front free endpaper: 'To Tom Clarke from Winston S. Churchill, Dec. 23, 1930, First Prize.' *My Early Life* had been serialised in the *Daily News* in August and September 1930, resulting in some correspondence between editor and author. The 'First Prize' comment refers jokingly to a competition held by the paper. Book has the usual faded spine, lots of foxing, including the area with the inscription.

Finally, there is a note in the Chartwell Archives as follows:

> 'November 20, 1930 note (unknown author) to WSC thanking him for having directed Thornton Butterworth to send two free copies to be used to transcribe the book into Braille.' [CHAR 8/269]

Shown below is a short list of people who it is quite likely would have received an inscribed copy of the book – however, there is no record of their having received one.

Names notable by their absence:
Frederick Lindemann (Lord Cherwell)
Clementine Churchill
Randolph Churchill (son)
Mary Churchill (however, only aged eight)
Lord Hugh Cecil ('Linky')

Notes

1. Martin Gilbert, *The Prophet of Truth 1922–1939*, Volume 5, Boston, Houghton Mifflin, 1977, p. 365.
2. Information on the book and inscription was reported with the permission of His Majesty The King, King Charles III.
3. Charles Frederick Worth (1825–1895) was a designer who dominated fashion trends at the end of the nineteenth century. He owned the House of Worth.

5B: BOOK REVIEWS OF *MY EARLY LIFE*

Every author, after she/he has written a book and received preliminary feedback from those chosen to evaluate and proofread the manuscript prior to publication, awaits with much anticipation the arrival of the first reviews of the published book. These reviews can make or break the success of the book and will significantly influence its commercial success. Churchill, who never left anything to chance if he could avoid it, was always deeply involved with the entire process of the commercialization of his books and certainly utilized every mechanism or pathway he could to influence individuals who might help him make a success of a project. Churchill was fully cognizant that his fame, reputation, and outspoken opinions would ensure that there would be many reviews written. As an optimist, he projected confidence to his publishers and friends that the book would be well received. He was not wrong!

Over the past 90-plus years, there have been literally hundreds of reviews of *My Early Life* published—the vast majority of which are positive. In this section I will present and discuss those reviews that are "classic book reviews" concerning the content, writing skills, story line and presentation of the material. In addition, there is another set of reviews that deal with the analysis of how Churchill wrote compared to other authors or the literary techniques he utilized in his writing. Finally, there is a group of writings that evaluate where his writing places him in the field of historic or autobiographical literature, etc. These later two sets of reviews will be dealt with in Chapter 7 on the analysis of Churchill's writing. The reviews chosen here were based on their insight into Churchill the man as well as the book and not on whether they were positive or negative. But, in fact, there were very few truly negative reviews.

There were a robust number of reviews beginning about a week before publication. These resulted from the books that the publishers sent to select entities such as newspapers, magazines, and library organizations. Both Butterworth and Scribner's sent copies to a worldwide audience. At the end of this chapter is a select bibliography that lists over 100 reviews arranged chronologically. In this section, select examples from that list will be provided (for reasons of space, most are excerpts from the review) and discussed as they provide much insight into how the book and the author were viewed. As one goes through the reviews, one is struck by the diversity of publications that printed reviews of this book, from standard international newspapers and periodicals to specialty publications such as the *International Sports and Dramatic News, The Cavalry Journal, Scientific American, Nature, The Education Outlook* and the *Infantry Journal*. Similarly, the people who provided the reviews are equally diverse and fascinating. The reviewers include noted historians (Foster Rhea Douglas), politicians (Duff Cooper), Pulitzer prizewinners (Bruce Catton), war correspondents (Henry Ward Woodd Nevison) and even a professor of chemistry (Henry E. Amstrong).

Arthur A. Baumann

One of the earliest and most often quoted reviews was published in the London *Observer*. It was written by Arthur A. Baumann, a British lawyer, author, editor (*Saturday Review*), businessman, and Conservative Party politician:

"After the dry husks of Lord Balfour's Autobiography, Mr. Churchill's book is like a beaker of champagne. Both men give an account of the first quarter of an illustrious public career. I doubt whether twenty years hence anyone will linger over the languid and parsimonious 'Chapters' of the elder statesman. I am sure that as long as there are young men and women they will thumb with delight the tale of adventures told by Mr. Churchill with the skill of Dumas and the spirit of a Peterborough. The incidents I find more exciting than any novel, and the revelation of character more absorbing than the postmortem analysis of the most industrious historian. This is the very stuff of autobiography. The author tells you everything he does, and why and how he did it, in the most natural way. There is no niggard shyness or self-suppression here. The young man's impecuniosity and sudden wealth, his successes and rebuffs, what a bumptious young ass he occasionally made of himself, how Kitchener, Roberts, and French tried to put him down, how he forced them all to like him, these things are told with humor and cynicism of middle age. For Mr. Churchill is old enough to chaff himself. … His infrequent relations with his father are a patch of pathos. … Mr. Churchill's story is a joyous scamper from one scene of adventure to another … The story of his escape from Pretoria prison, his journey in railway trucks, his concealment in a coalmine in the company with white rats, his arrival at Delagoa Bay in bales of wool, are the purest picaresque."[1]

The frequent quote "like a beaker of champagne" is a very well-known description of the *My Early Life* but rarely is it given in its full context. It is, in fact, being compared to Balfour's autobiography (*Chapters of Autobiography*) which had recently been published and is referred to as a "dry husk." [2] Ironically, Balfour had died in March 1930 before *My Early Life* was published, protecting Balfour from having to read this comparison to Churchill's book which he surely wouldn't have appreciated—nor would Churchill, for that matter. This review makes several salient points, which not only endears the book to the reader but sets a tone that is aped by many a reviewer. The first is the timelessness of the writing, which is described with the words "that as long as there are young men and women they will thumb with delight the tale of adventures." The second is that this represents a classic style of writing displaying "the skill of Dumas and the spirit of a Peterborough," "the very stuff of autobiography," and "more exciting than any novel, and the revelation of character more absorbing than the postmortem analysis of the most industrious historian." Lastly, he considers the book fun, representing "a joyous scamper from one scene of adventure to another." What a marvelous review to start the launch of a new book.

Robert Lynd

Robert Lynd, the writer and literary editor for the *News Chronicle* wrote:

> "Readers of the 'News Chronicle' have recently been fascinated by the story of how this ill-educated and incompetent boy laid the foundations of one of the most remarkable careers in the history of modern England, and today the full story is to be published in book form with the title, *My Early Life*. It is an extraordinarily exciting and high-spirited narrative, written in the exultant mood of Stalky's war-cry: 'I gloat. Hear me.' Mr. Churchill gloats even over his failures as preludes to his triumphs, and there is an air of genial boastfulness about the opening of the chapter called 'Examinations,' which runs: 'It took me three tries to pass into Sandhurst.' …
>
> "Opinions will differ as to whether Mr. Churchill owes more to luck or to pluck in his astonishing career. That he was lucky in being born into a great English family and into a world of powerful friends is obvious, but all the luck in the world does not make a Winston

Churchill. Mr. Churchill is what he is today first of all, not because he is the son of the Lord Randolph Churchill, but because of his fearlessness, his boyish adventurousness, and his indomitable willpower. Mr. Churchill entered upon life as though he were entering for an obstacle race in which life and limb must be risked, and his heart rose with the risks. …

"Mr. Churchill, however, has written something more than a story of adventure. He is also a philosopher and a humorist. For comedy, turn to his account of how he went up behind young Avery at Harrow and pushed him into the pool, or to the description of the schoolmaster's attempt to explain the meaning of the vocative case in Latin, when Winston was totally unable to grasp what was meant by 'O Table.' …

"'This naivete,' this candour of writing, will do much to disarm even the opponents of Mr. Churchill, and enable them to enjoy the spectacle of the progress of one whose real philosophy of life is a belief in energy and courage in their most dramatic forms. The cynical may see Mr. Churchill's autobiography merely the story of how a troublesome boy grew up to be a still more troublesome man. Most readers, however, will be unable to resist the spell of Mr. Churchill's genius and geniality and will enter—-aesthetically at least—into his own hearty enjoyment of his adventurous career."[3]

The *News Chronicle* had just published the 18-part series of excerpts from *My Early Life,* which was very well received as noted by Lynd. In this review he avows this "is an extraordinarily exciting and high-spirited narrative, written in the exultant mood of Stalky's war-cry: 'I gloat. Hear me.' This is a heady comparison as it refers to Rudyard Kipling's *Stalky & Co.*, published in 1897, and in similar manner Kipling describes his own school days, albeit in novel format. To be compared to Kipling is no small compliment. The 'War-Cry' refers to when the young lad girds his loins, lets out a war cry and plunges into military action.

Lynd notes that Churchill "has written something more than a story of adventure. He is also a philosopher and a humorist" and even a comedian. He concludes: "Most readers, however, will be unable to resist the spell of Mr. Churchill's genius and geniality and will enter-aesthetically at least-into his own hearty enjoyment of his adventurous career."

London Times *reviewer*
On October 20 a *London Times* reviewer wrote:

> "Mr. Churchill's reviewer would require to be almost as skilled a writer as he is himself, or at least to have unlimited space or quotation, in order to give an adequate notion of the charm and briskness of the book, published today. The material is, of course, splendid, as Mr. Churchill will agree. Anyone who could write at all would be able to make a good show of the events in which he was concerned up to the age of eight-and-twenty. But there would be few who could play on all the strings—humour, headlong excitement, quiet irony, melancholy regret for vanished customs and lore, love of sport, the pleasures of friendships—with so sure a hand. All the strings but one, perhaps, and that one which he also knows how to touch on occasion. There is no bitterness or invective, or none of a sort we are sorry to meet, such as the attack on the late Sir Charles Monro in 'The World Crisis'. ... We can only hope that this autobiography is but an instalment."[4]

This reviewer particularly highlights the breadth of Churchill's writing skills when he notes there are "few who could play on all the strings—humour, headlong excitement, quiet irony, melancholy regret for vanished customs and lore, love of sport, the pleasures of friendships—with so sure a hand." He also notes "We can only hope that this autobiography is but an instalment." There would be no follow-on autobiography.

A. Wyatt Tilby in The Yorkshire Post
Tilby on October 20 wrote:

> "To a man so constituted, revolutionary times have this compensation, that they are more interesting to live in, and to offer more opportunities, than periods of reaction; for the truth is that Mr. Churchill would be happier in hell full of action than a heaven of contemplation. The former has its bad moments, no doubt, when by-elections go wrong and Labour Governments that do not govern come in; but the latter would be merely boredom. Where Mr. Churchill is, the fight's the thing; and where unhappily there is no fight on, he does

the next best thing and write a first-class book about old fights and battles long ago.

"This is not, of course, a complete philosophy of life or the whole duty of man. But these sour reflections only occurred to me because Mr. Churchill's autobiography kept me out of bed most of the night, and, unlike him, I detest making up my sleep the next afternoon."[5]

This is a very different type of review wherein Trilby talks more about the foibles of the man rather than critique the book. The reviewer notes that when Churchill is out of office (though still in Parliament after the Conservatives lost control of the House in 1929) with no fight at hand (not quite true), he writes "a first-class book" about old fights. He comically notes that Churchill's book kept him "out of bed most of the night" and not getting enough sleep makes him tired and cranky.

The Aberdeen Press and Journal

The *Aberdeen Press and Journal* on October 20 prints a very positive review:

"The name Winston Churchill at once suggests First Lord of the Admiralty, Chancellor of the Exchequer, or author of *The World Crisis*, but those who remember the Sudan campaign and the Boer War will remember also another Winston Churchill, adventure-loving subaltern and brilliant war correspondent, whose writings brought him worldwide renown. Mr. Churchill describes those adventurous years which preceded his entry into politics in *My Early Life*, which Thornton Butterworth publish today at a guinea. It is a volume of sparkling delight, more entrancing than any novel, and told with that scintillating Churchillian humour and vitality which compels admiration. As autobiography it is a vivid, colourful panorama, exhilarating to the last paragraph, revealing the author man who, by his own unaided efforts, has carved himself a great career."[6]

This review highlights the exceptionally strong presentation of the episodes in Churchill's life with descriptions like: "sparkling delight," "scintillating Churchillian humour," "vitality which compels," and "vivid, colourful panorama." This is a very comprehensive and thoughtful review.

The Edinburgh Evening News

The *Edinburgh Evening News* on October 20 reported:

> "The author is always naïve and self-revealing; there is a real Churchillian flavour and frankness about the book, which shows the appeal of adventure to the young cavalry officer and the newspaper correspondent, and later statesman. The author deals much more with the military events than politics, although political personalities are introduced freely. Mr. Churchill does not conceal his opinion that the Tories of his time did not do well by his father, Lord Randolph Churchill, the vigorous exponent of Tory democracy." …
>
> "The story Mr. Churchill narrates of his escape from Pretoria constitutes some of the most thrilling pages in the book. …
>
> "Mr. Winston Churchill has always been outspoken, and the pages contain many critical sentences on generals and statesman. Such criticism was always part of Mr. Churchill. Consequently, the writer's path was not always easy, but characteristically he pushed on."[7]

This review points out that the book strongly reflects Churchill's personality—opinionated, pushy, outspoken and frank. In addition, the reviewer is much taken with how much Churchill provides critiques of generals, politicians, and political parties. The story of Churchill's escape from Pretoria is called "the most thrilling pages in the book."

The Winnipeg Tribune

The first reviews in Canada also occurred on October 20 and one of those was in *The Winnipeg Tribune*:

> "Churchill's chapters concerning the South African war are most vivid. His own escapades alone were most vivid, for when he was captured when driving an ambulance train [not quite true] and after a long spell [actually fairly short] of imprisonment escaped in the best melodramatic fashion."[8]

The Liverpool Echo

The Liverpool Echo published on October 20 a long and well-written review:

> "… There is not a dull page in *My Early Life*, the first volume of what promises to be one of the liveliest and most informative of modern biographies. …
>
> "He enlivens his already lively autobiography with human touches and revealing stories of the great men he met. His description of polo matches in India match those in 'Bengal Lancer.' He brings forgotten 'Characters' before our eyes with such anecdotes as about Colonel Brabazon of the Hussars who, arriving on Aldershot Station one day asked, 'Where is the twain for London?' 'Gone, sir,' said the stationmaster. 'Gone! Bwing another.' …
>
> "One looks forward with expectancy to the next volume of an autobiography as gripping and penetrating as the author's life of his father, Lord Randolph Churchill. His roving commission was not confined to the fields of war."[9]

This is a very comprehensive review full of insight and praise. Its author hopes this will just be the first of many volumes on Churchill's life, but it would not be. He provides many humorous anecdotes from the book and describes the book and its subjects with phrases such as: "He enlivens his already lively autobiography with human touches and revealing stories" and "as gripping and penetrating as the authors life." His comparison to "Bengal Lancers" is a reference to Francis Yeats-Brown's autobiography *The Lives of a Bengal Lancer*, an award-winning book (1930) that was turned into the 1935 movie *The Lives of a Bengal Lancer*.

The Liverpool Daily Post

The *Liverpool Daily Post* on October 20 wrote an insightful review and highlighted an important issue to Churchill: namely that the book was for future generations and was to be an inspiration to get them active and involved. The review thought the book would be highly successful in that mission.

> "…The chief attraction—and an irresistible attraction it is—of his book must lie not so much in any new facts it contains as in its frank personal

note and buoyancy of outlook. It is to be noticed indeed, that the volume is expressly dedicated to 'A New Generation.' 'I have thought,' Mr. Churchill states, 'that it might be of interest to the new generation to read a story of youthful endeavor, and I have set down candidly and with as much simplicity as possible my personal fortunes.'"[10]

The Sheffield Daily Telegraph
Their book reviewer wrote on October 20:

"This autobiography, as perfect an example of this very difficult form of literature that we have read for some considerable time, provides the key to the personality of the most brilliant figure in political life that this generation has known. Without it, the mental processes that have guided Mr. Churchill in his meteoric but somewhat erratic career would have been hidden from us. Now with emerging candour he tells us of his intellectual short comings and will no doubt be cited by those to whom school is still an ever present evil as another example, and a supreme one, of the small influence on one's future exerted by book learning and the facility to pass examinations."[11]

The *Sheffield Daily Telegraph* believes the book is a perfect example of what an autobiography should be and reveals "the personality of the most brilliant figure in political life." They agree with his analysis of the educational system.

The Times Literary Supplement
Certainly, one of the most impactful sources of book reviews is that of *The Times Literary Supplement* in London. They wrote on October 23:

"Mr. Churchill's record of his youth and young manhood is his finest literary achievement. This book is as regards style—or, one may say, styles—better than anything which has gone before. Its variation and development in this matter of style are the greatest of its charms. One fancies one hears the small boy, the youth at Sandhurst, the young soldier, the slightly older politician each telling his story in his own way. Of course no gentleman cadet, still less a small boy, could write like that; that Mr. Churchill should contrive to bewitch his readers into the momentary impression that they can is proof that he has at his command the art of the autobiographer. ...

"School days, sport, war, the world of fashion, politics, literature are among the phases of his first twenty-eight years which Mr. Churchill has to describe. In describing them he has some splendid purple patches, many touches of that pleasant form of humour based on the ironic understatement which is so fashionable today..."[12]

I don't believe there was ever an author who wouldn't relish having this book review. The authors aren't hesitant to flatly state this is a great book. They raise characteristics of the book that endear the book to them and to future readers. First, they state the book "is his finest literary achievement' and that his development in his style (s) of writing "are the greatest of its charms." An important and frequently discussed characteristic of the book is that Churchill's voice throughout the book changes with the passage of time. That is, you hear the young schoolboy speaking when he is describing his school day, and similarly you hear the adolescent voice of the new soldier in India when he is struggling with how to educate himself in history, philosophy and politics. This exemplary talent "contrive(s) to bewitch his readers" and proves "he has at his command the art of the autobiographer."

Duff Cooper

Duff Cooper was a well-known Conservative politician, C of E and friend of Churchill, particularly during Hitler's rise in the 1930s. He wrote a review in *The Spectator* on October 25 which provides some interesting insights:

> "For the task of writing autobiography Churchill is wonderfully well equipped. In the first place he is an artist in letters, in the second place he is an artist in life. Words are for him the precious material of a delicate craft, days are the still more precious, because more strictly limited, material out of which to construct a fabric of romance, adventure, and achievement. If he is sometimes prodigal of words, he has sufficient store of them to afford extravagance, while of days he has practiced so careful an economy that it is impossible to believe that he has ever wasted an hour. ...

"His artistry in Words was never more apparent than in the present volume. His admiration for Gibbons has not led him into committing Gibbon's error of describing his childhood in periods, better suited to chronicling the decline of Rome. He can assume the grand manner, not only better, when the occasion demands it, but in this record of his own early years he is not afraid to employ a prose that may be called conversational, and thus succeeds in one of the most difficult tasks in literature, *reproducing on paper the sound of the human voice.* (My emphasis)

"… A very magnificent canvas, and its magnificence is mainly due to the fact that the author has enjoyed writing it as much as he enjoyed living it, and that he is able to convey to the reader who shares it with him to the full. Into an age of introspection, Freudian complexes, doubt and despair, Mr. Churchill comes like a great wind into a musty, over furnished room. 'Elizabethan' is an epithet that is often used carelessly and usually wrongly, but certainly since Sir Walter Raleigh there has not appeared upon the English stage another character that has played so great and vivid a part there and has displayed so many and such various gifts, as has Mr. Churchill since he made his first speech in the promenade of the Empire Music Hall nigh forty years ago.

"Whatever was the business to hand, whether politics or polo, he threw himself passionately into it."[13]

This review is saturated with prose that demonstrates that Cooper knew Churchill well and much admired him. Like many reviewers he notes Churchill's superb writing skills with phrases like "he is an artist in letters"; "Words are for him the precious material of a delicate craft"; and "His artistry in Words was never more apparent." He also compares Churchill to Gibbons (an historian Churchill read and admired) and states that Churchill didn't fall into Gibbon's error of describing his own life in periods but rather Churchill creates his autobiography by telling stories of life in language and words that are almost conversational. This raises the issue that I believe Cooper was the first to describe in a review of the book and is highlighted in the above text. Cooper recognizes that Churchill is attempting to create a specific sound in his sentences that pleases the ear and focuses the mind on an image of the event. As Cooper states, Churchill "succeeds in one of the most difficult tasks in literature, reproducing on paper the sound of the human voice." This is a theme that is much more robustly developed in Chapter 7 on the analysis of Churchill's writing. Suffice it to say that Churchill was aware of this technique, and this is one of the reasons Churchill dictated the text for his book so as to hear the words and phrases as they were rolling off his tongue and going on to paper and to make the words sing and resonate much in the manner that Robert Frost did with his poems. Finally, as further proof of Cooper's understanding of Churchill the man, he states: "Whatever was the business to hand, whether politics or polo, he threw himself passionately into it." He recognized that Churchill thoroughly enjoyed writing this book.

Country Life

The iconic society magazine *Country Life* published a review on October 25 with a portrait photograph of the young Churchill in his full-dress Hussars uniform. [See Chapter 5C, fig. 7.] They were full of praise.

> "This book has at least two merits which place it entirely outside the ordinary run of biography. It is the work of a master of narrative whose comments on men and affairs are always apt and necessarily well informed, and it deals with a life of thrilling adventure, full of interest even to those who are too young to remember any of the events it describes, or the repercussions of the events on the lives of their elders. By those who remember the campaign of the 'nineties and lived through the period of the South African War, Mr. Churchill's story of those days will be found totally absorbing, and nobody who begins to read is likely to abandon the book without reading to the end. Of such a book it is manifestly impossible to give an adequate description in the compass of a short review. The crowded hours of glorious life which it describes are so crowded and so many as almost literally to take one's breath away, and all that one can say is that even more than in his previous contributions to the history of our times Mr. Churchill has used his gifts of humor and irony, of concise and lucid expression, and of vivid and illuminating phrase, with all the mastery which we have long known to be his. …."[14]

This review focuses on Churchill's storytelling ability and that it will be enjoyed by people of all ages. They describe Churchill as "a master of narrative" who "has used his gifts of humor and irony, of concise and lucid expression, and of vivid and illuminating phrase, with all the mastery which we have long known to be his." They conclude: "Nobody who begins to read is likely to abandon the book without reading to the end."

Henry Woodd Nevinson
Henry Woodd Nevinson was a war correspondent in the Second Boer War and WWI as well as an investigative reporter with strong antislavery and pro women's suffrage beliefs. He wrote a positive review in *The New Statesman* on October 25:

> "To those who only know Mr. Churchill's former books I need not say that this volume is written with extraordinary vivacity and power. Mr. Churchill may or may not be a model politician; he is certainly a model war-correspondent, and all read him with delight."[15]

Frank Forrester
Frank Forrester writes a long review in which he retells many of the incidents in *My Early Life* in *Reynold's Illustrated News* of October 26. His opinion is that whether or not you support Churchill's politics you will respect and like the book.

> "Whatever opinion you may have of Mr. Churchill as a Politician—and there is no man, except perhaps Lloyd George, who provokes such conflict of opinion—you are bound, if you have a spark of youth left in you, to envy the life of adventure he describes in *My Early Life*. And for those who think that opportunity makes the man the answer is plain that, in Winston Churchill's case at least, he made every one of his opportunities, usually against strong opposition. Nobody wanted him, not even Kitchener; but they all had to have him—he found somebody or other to 'wangle' it."[16]

The reviewer notes that the type of adventure enjoyed by Churchill is rather of a bygone era and not likely to be reproduced. He then quotes Churchill from *My Early Life*: "When I survey this work as a whole I find I have drawn a picture of a vanished age. The character of society, the foundations of politics, the methods of war, the outlook of youth, the scale of values, are all changed, and changed to an extent I should not have believed possible in so short a space without violent domestic revolution."[17]

Lewis Saul Benjamin

Lewis Melville, the pseudonym for Lewis Saul Benjamin, who was first known as an actor and then a well-published author wrote a review in *Saturday Review* on October 25 which speaks for itself:

> "Many men have done things, many others have written about things; but few have been given the gift to write well and vividly about their own achievements."[18]

Illustrated London News

The following review published in the *Illustrated London News* on November 8 provides a detailed synopsis of the book with a significant number of excerpts and an analysis of Churchill's personality and his growth in character and importance. The review is very positive. Several excerpts are presented here:

> "Few distinguished men can have been in their youth so precocious and so backward as Mr. Winston Churchill. *My Early Life*, the record of his career from his birth in 1874 to his marriage in 1908, makes no secret of either of the backwardness or the precocity."
>
> "Mr. Churchill devotes two of his best chapters to describing this battle [Omdurman]. 'In one aspect,' he says, 'a cavalry charge is very like ordinary life. So long as you are all right, firmly in your saddle, your horse in hand and well-armed, lots of enemies will give you a wide berth. But as soon as you have lost a stirrup, have a rein cut, have dropped your weapon, are wounded, or if your horse is wounded, then is the moment when from all quarters your enemies will rush upon you.'"
>
> "His escape from prison in Pretoria is the most exciting in the book; happily for his readers, Mr. Churchill relates it in the fullest detail. The comments of many of the English Newspapers on this exploit were most ungenerous. Mr. Churchill had been and continued after his escape to be loud in his criticism of the conduct of the war."

"His denunciation of the Governments behavior to the Boers at the end of the war was in no way mitigated by consideration of personal popularity. 'I must confess,' he says, 'that all through my life I have found myself in disagreement alternatively with both historic English parties.' A candid admission, this, and characteristic of the spirit of Mr. Churchill's fascinating book."[19]

George Currie

George Currie was a man with many talents and interests. He was Canadian born and educated at Harvard, fought in WWI and was a leading sportswriter of his day as well as an author and literary critic for the *Brooklyn Daily Eagle.* He wrote a very positive review on November 9:

"One of the amazing things about this book is Winston's ability to recapture the enthusiasm and zeal of his youth."

"… This fine facility for adorning a tale stands him in good stead…"

"The training this man underwent not only for a military career but public life makes him in many respects a political brother of our own President Roosevelt. … Like T.R. he has always been outspoken – a trait in the political world frequently called indiscreet—more's the pity— but some intimation of the opportunities to serve his country in a larger field in later life seems to have been in the back of his mind. He deliberately courted danger to acquire experience. In large measure his plan of action in youth accounts for his fearlessness in maturity which has too often been called reckless rashness."

"His chapter on 'the sensations of a cavalry charge' is a small military classic."

"As for this book, it reads with the fascination-poor, overworked but truthful word – of a rip-roaring story that loses nothing in the fact that it is the truth rather than fiction."[20]

Currie makes an interesting and apt comparison of Churchill to Teddy Roosevelt and seems to grasp the character of Churchill well.

The Scotsman

A comprehensive and very positive review was published in *The Scotsman* on November 17:

> "Not through the accidental advantages of birth and rank which helped him in the first stages of his career, but by native talent and sheer force of will and character, has Mr. Churchill pressed has way into the front rank of our public life.
>
> "These reminiscences of early days, up to the time when, still a young man, he was returned to Parliament as member for Oldham, and 'married and lived happily ever afterwards.' It will be read, less for any importance in the events they record than for the light they throw on the future politician and statesman. It is a characteristically frank and engaging narrative—one that reveals the boy as the father of the man, and also as the son of a father who succeeded, if in nothing else, in giving delighted surprises and disconcertments to his friends and to his adversaries. …
>
> "The story, for the most part related already by himself in books and magazines, is here retold consecutively, and with details … which it would not have been wise or safe to give at the time. Everything is, set down, not as it now appears, seen through the reflections and experiences of later years, but as witnessed and felt at the time, as 'a child, a schoolboy, a cadet subaltern, a war correspondent, and a youthful politician'; and to the reader, as well as to the author, it looks like 'a picture of a vanished age.'"[21]

From the first sentence on it is apparent that the reviewer understands the Churchill character and the components therein which drove Churchill to greatness. This is not important history in and of itself, but rather an engagingly and well-written description of the experiences themselves. This reviewer again recognizes the exquisite ability of Churchill to convey to the reader that the character speaking at each stage of the narrative in the voice of the individual at that age.

Otto F. Theis

Otto F. Theis was an American born writer who spent his career in London working as an editor for *Outlook* and as a literary agent. His papers and those of his wife, Louise Morgan, are archived in the Yale University Library. He wrote a scholarly in-depth review of the book and the man and provides substantial quotes from the book to bolster his arguments which are laudatory. The review was published in *Illustrated Sporting and Dramatic News* on November 22, 1930:

> " 'Adventures are to the adventurous,' Disraeli once wrote, and the phrase might serve as a motto for Mr. Winston Churchill's *My Early Life*. Read for pure adventure it is more enthralling than any piece of fiction. Mr. Churchill's description of a cavalry charge at Omdurman and the account of his escape from the Boers, for vividness and suspense and excitement deserve a place in every anthology of stirring deeds. [As will be seen there are a large number of anthologies that highlight these two events.] But this is only a superficial aspect of the book. It is besides a revealing self-portrait, a panorama of history, a picture of a vanished age, a gallery of portrait sketched, and, what is more important still, a philosophy and interpretation of life by one who has lived dangerously and held high and responsible positions. ...
>
> "He succeeds in recreating in realistic detail the points of view of himself as a schoolboy, cadet, subaltern, war correspondent, and youthful politician. There is no beating around the bush, no affected self-depreciation; he tells frankly of what he did and why; he admits successes and rebuffs with equal self-awareness. Whatever Mr. Churchill's limitations, he lived a rich and full life, built up by his own energy and will, for his initial advantages were no greater than thousands of others of his period.
>
> "As popularly Mr. Churchill is supposed to be inclined temperamentally towards military adventure and aggressiveness, it is worth quoting one of his general observations on war: 'Never, never, never believe any war will be smooth and easy, or that anyone who embarks on that strange voyage can measure the tides and hurricanes he will encounter. The Statesman who yields to war fever must realise that once the signal is given, he is no longer the master of policy but the slave of unforeseeable and uncontrollable events.'
>
> "He may have been wrong many times, but he has never lacked courage, conviction and enthusiasm. No statesmen has ever been freer

from hypocrisy and humbug, though he himself is perfectly aware how large a part they play in the 'social life of a great people dwelling in a state of democratic freedom.'

"In these days when the miasma of defeatism and the enervation of too much introspection is abroad in the land, a book like *My Early Life* is particularly timely in that it may stir others to action. [This could easily have been written in 2023 rather than 1930.] Any decision, even if wrong, is better than perpetual inaction.

"Mr. Churchill is an Imperialist. He and his kind, by sheer force of initiative, have made the Empire. They had the vision and took the risks. The significant thing, and the thing not to be lost sight of if we are to take more than a narrow view of Mr. Churchill and what he stands for is that the anti-Imperialist will shout at the top of his lungs in protest over conquest, but as soon as conquest is consolidated and made safe, he will not hesitate an instant to exploit it for his own profit."[22]

The first paragraph above absolutely captures the essence of the man and this book. It would be extremely difficult, if not impossible, to find a more succinct and apt description of why you would want to read this book. The highlighting of Churchill's true view of war rather than the perceived war monger characterization frequently promulgated on Churchill is spot on. Although this review would certainly not be seen in print today with all of its political incorrectness vis à vis imperialism and jingoism, we should and must view it in the context of its time and not in a present-day view. As both Churchill and Theis state, it is "a picture of a vanished age." A reading of the full review is worth the time.

The Times Recorder *(Zanesville, OH)*

Many small-town newspapers across the US and the UK published reviews of the book. Many are not captured in subsequent publications or cited in the literature. This is really a disservice because many of their reviews are first rate and worthy of being read. *The Times Recorder* (Zanesville, OH) published just one such review on November 28:

"This is a bewitching book from the first word to the last. … There is no figure in English political life more fascinating than that of

Winston Churchill, whose autobiography is here told from the year 1874 to 1908, when he married and 'lived happily ever afterward.'

"The amazing thing about this book is the swing and harmony of it. You hear the boy speaking to you in the early chapters, then it puts away the things of a child, and a young man stands up intent and daring, without swagger, to give way later to the grown man speaking and being listened to in the councils of his country. It is all simply done in the best tradition of an art that conceals art. There are whole passages that ought to be read aloud; the skirmish in the Mamund valley—the cavalry charge—and the best of all, the young subaltern of the Fourth Hussars at the bedside of his dying nurse. The heart of the man of fifty-six who writes so simply of human affections has not dried up with the years. Our common humanity rules strong within him. The is Churchill's best book."[23]

The review is not only thoughtful, but this last paragraph captures the essence of what Churchill was trying to create—his experiences in life through the eyes and mind of himself revealed in a voice and through words specifically chosen and woven together for the pleasure of the ear. As pointed out here, many of the sections should be read aloud to appreciate the fullness of the message.

Bruce Catton, Times Herald, *Orleans, NY*

Many smaller market newspapers contract with syndicated columnists to acquire news reports and book reviews. In this case Bruce Catton was the reviewer. He worked for the Newspaper Enterprise Association, a Scripps-Howard syndicate, and wrote editorials and book reviews. Catton is best known for his books on the American Civil War. He was the Pulitzer Prize winner (1954) for his *A Stillness at Appomattox*, his study of the final campaign of the war in Virginia.[24] This review appeared in the *Times Herald*, Orleans, NY on November 29:

"*A Roving Commission*, by Winston Churchill, is revealing and entertaining —for about 200 pages. Then it becomes just another who-I-am-and-how-I-did-it book. But its first half is worth reading.

"Mr. Churchill here tells the story of his early life; and it is an excellent picture of what you might call the close of the golden age for

England's upper class. We see how a young man born to the purple in imperial Britain grew up, entered the army, served his time in India and found life all to the good. There was no need to question providence about anything; it was ordered that some fortunate souls, being well-born, should rule the lesser breeds without the law, and everything was arranged nicely for them.

"This part of the tale is told with a good deal of wit. But later, as Mr. Churchill grew older and took to pushing himself forward with what must have been, to his contemporaries, an insufferable amount of crust—well, the book suffers; and, one loses a bit of the sympathy and admiration that the first part of the book aroused. However, the tale moves fast all the way through. This Englishman packed a good deal of excitement into his youth, and he gets much of it into the book."[25]

Catton appears to enjoy the book and recommends it. However, it is obvious to the reader that Catton is an anti-Imperialist, an anti-empire person and has no tolerance of an aristocracy or self-promoting people. One doesn't imagine Catton and Churchill would enjoy a conversation on politics, but then maybe Churchill would!

Thomas Russell (T.R) Ybarra

Thomas Russell (T.R) Ybarra, Venezuelan-born American journalist, wrote a book review for the *New York Times* on November 30 under the title "Adventure Filled the Years of Churchill's Youth' In *A Roving Commission*, the British Statesman Tells a Vivid, Stirring Story." This is a very positive review in a most influential publication.

"Brilliant and restless, enterprising and courageous, he sought adventures from his early youth and, what is more, he found them and liked them and went out in search of still others— the more dangerous the better. Thus it comes to pass that Winston Churchill, who might have spent his life like many another English aristocrat on exciting experiences such as fall to the lot of few aristocrats with a good mind and a gift for statecraft, can now—while yet in his fifties—look back not only on a series of constructive achievements in politics, but also on exciting experiences such as fall to the lot of few. And given his mentality, one is willing to wager that he gets more satisfaction out of remembering that he once actually participated in a cavalry charge and was actually a prisoner of war than out of anything connected with sittings of the British House of Commons or meetings of British Cabinet.

"In this latest book of his Mr. Churchill describes excellently his years of adventure. Besides being a playboy and a politician, he is a born writer. His book, though written recently, long after his period of adventuring, nevertheless preserves the zest of youth. Winston Churchill, the mature man, has played fair with Winston Churchill, the callow youth; the Winston Churchill now living in this post-war age of disillusionment and skepticism resuscitates for himself and his reader a Winston Churchill of a day that was brighter and happier, more real and more solid. … He has succeeded in what he set out to do.… His style is not alone vigorous. It is likewise vivid and modest, terse and lively, scintillating with wit and touched with a genuine charm. And what fun he had!"[26]

Ybarra captures the essence of Churchill with regards to his always needing action in his life when he states, "He gets more satisfaction out of remembering that he once actually participated in a cavalry charge and was actually a prisoner of war than out of anything connected with sittings of the British House of Commons or meetings of British Cabinet." Ybarra also appreciates the zest, liveliness and optimistic attitude which is so needed and appreciated in the post war (WWI) era which has been an "age of disillusionment and skepticism." This is a theme that has been recognized in a significant number of reviews.

J. W. T. (Joseph Warren Teets) Mason

J. W. T. (Joseph Warren Teets) Mason was an American writer and editor who devoted himself to the study of Eastern philosophy and religion. He worked both in London and the US. He worked for the *Daily Express* as the New York Editor (1908–1931) and wrote this positive review in the *Saturday Review* on December 12.

"Mr. Churchill has made a book that should thrill every normal boy and give a glow to old age as well. Youth can learn history from it and will be fascinated by its account of the way true adventure has led to fame.

Between the lines, the ghosts of Horatio Alger and George A. Henty intrude. No better boy's gift exists in the current literature. Nor does any better book for adulthood which imagines it was born in a prosaic age.

"Anyone reading Mr. Churchill's book will admit that times have changed; but the human spirit which reveals itself in Mr. Churchill's pages has not changed. That is the important thing and gives to this volume its major reason for study."

The author highlights Churchill's rise to success, the energy with which the book is written, and it is a book needed in this "prosaic age."[27]

Australasian *Review*
The following is a lengthy, thoughtful review full of quotes from the book and photographs of Churchill at Chartwell building brick walls. This is one of the earlier Australian reviews and was published in the *Australasian* on December 13.

"What politics may have in store for Mr. Churchill we cannot guess, but we are certain of this —that no achievement of statesmanship will equal his service to literature and history. His new book, *My Early Life*, will always be valuable as a history. At present it has that value with the added interest attaching to the record of an eminent and a picturesque living personality; but it must also take a high place in the realm of English letters as a fine piece of literature. That it is a romantic story is accidental, though fortunate. What makes it of value otherwise is the rare literary talent of the author and the candor of his character.

"His opinions and his comments are those he held not at the time of writing, but at the time the experience recorded. Consequently, we have here the naivete of the schoolboy, the brave flippancy of the young subaltern, and towards the end the gravity born of experience. Viewing the work as a whole, the effect of this is very charming. The author seems to be growing up under the reader's eyes."[28]

The reviewer sees Churchill's forte as writing rather than as a politician (this was pre-WWII), and he also found remarkable Churchill's ability to write as if he was at whatever age he was portraying himself at that time of his life.

Henry M. Hyde

Henry M. Hyde was a correspondent for the *Chicago Tribune* as well as the *Baltimore Sun* who was most known for his coverage of the "monkey trial" of John T. Scopes, schoolteacher in Tennessee. He wrote a whimsical book review, "The Early Life of Winston Churchill by Himself," in *The Evening Sun* on December 20.

> "The Rt. Hon Winston Churchill has achieved all but the very highest political distinction in the British Empire. He has never been Prime Minister. He has been a shining ornament of both the Liberal and Conservative Parties. His career has been something of a political sandwich, thick slices of Conservative bread enclosing a middle layer of liberal meat. … Somehow, though he now approaches 60 years, Winston Churchill has never grown up. He remains the infant prodigy, doing brilliant and astonishing things and applauding himself with quite unaffected and boyish pleasure. One is never quite sure what he will do next. But it is impossible not to sympathize with and feel a certain affection with a man who can end this story of his early life with these words:
>
> 'New struggles absorbed my thoughts and energies at least until September 1908, when I married and lived happily ever afterward.'"[29]

Foster Rhea Dulles

Foster Rhea Dulles was an American journalist, author, and professor of history with interests in political and cultural relations between the United States and East Asia. A short excerpt from his positive review in *The Bookman* in December 1930 is shown here.

> "It is a brilliant and vivid narrative packed with action, illuminated by graphic description, and enlivened by shrewd and often humorous comment. The youthful Churchill had a tremendous zest for life and he has managed to impart much of the spirit which made him so eager for experience and adventure to this unusual autobiography. … His story is told with such frankness and charm that its appeal, especially to those with any spirit of adventure, cannot be resisted."[30]

Henry E. Armstrong

What follows was, perhaps, one of the most unexpected and interesting reviews as it was published in one of the most prestigious scientific journals in the world. It was written by Henry E. Armstrong (1848–1937) the well-known British chemist and educator in *Nature,* December 27.

Armstrong has cogently used *My Early Life* to write a critique of education in England using Churchill's pithy descriptions of his education at all three of his pre-Sandhurst schools as examples of what needs to change, from removal of corporeal punishment to the importance of emphasizing the mastery of written, spoken, and read English literature. This monograph is worthy of being read in its entirety. As will be seen in the chapter describing the impact of Churchill's *My Early Life*, there have been many educators using Churchill's schooling as a jumping off place for critiques of all education processes. I will only present a few general comments from Armstrong's review.

> "Not only out of the mouth of babes but also public characters may come wisdom—even from a Winston Churchill. The autobiography he has recently published is full of meat for the would-be student of education. … He has written a most fascinating account of his irresponsible upbringing, which should shame the devil in all but one of his schoolmasters. The book is to be studied by every teacher who desires to play an honest hand, a warning to every parent.…
>
> "To me this book seems to be [one of] the most fascinating and important contributions to the study of educational practice of recent times, showing as it does the great need of an entire departure in method. On all grounds it is to be commended both to teachers and parents of sufficient intelligence to read between the lines and ponder the lessons it conveys; with sufficient courage to defy present day soul-killing school conventions."[31]

It is noteworthy that educators and child psychiatrists have been extremely receptive to what Churchill wrote in this book and employed Churchill as an example of all forms of learning disabilities and talents. Some apt, others completely off the mark!

"Paul Pry," Tasmanian Advocate *reviewer*

A Tasmanian reviewer gets right to the character of Churchill and certainly enjoyed the book. It was written by a reviewer using the pseudonym of "Paul Pry" in the *Advocate* on January 2, 1931.

> "Had Winston Churchill lived 200 years ago he would have been a pirate, or at least a privateer. Born in a less adventurous age, he has been something of a freebooter. Having very strong convictions and unlimited belief in them, he is always liable to commit his party against their better judgement; to dash in with brilliant daring while his more cautious fellows are deliberately making up their minds. *He has always been too important to leave out, and very dangerous to leave in.* [My emphasis] He has made more costly mistakes than any living Politician, only to offset them by some dashing coup which make their memory dim. But, right or wrong he is always busy, always where events are thickest, always plunging in where events are liable to happen. … His buoyant personality would make it as exciting story in any hands, but Mr. Churchill writes with the same brilliant verve he does everything else, and he is an ideal autobiographer."[32]

Richard E. Danielson

The *Atlantic Monthly* (known as *The Atlantic* since 2004) has been a major publication in the US for more than 150 years. It certainly has been highly influential in literary and book circles. Richard E. Danielson was editor of *The Sportsman* from 1927 to 1937, and then president of the Atlantic Monthly Company and associate editor of *The Atlantic Monthly*. He wrote a very thoughtful and insightful review in *The Atlantic Monthly* in January 1931. Here are some excerpts:

> "Versatile as a chameleon, energetic as the solar system, he goes round what he can't go through, never stopping, always on the jump. From one rung to another, up he goes, while all the world wonders. Boy and man, Churchill is himself. He may spin like a teetotum, yet he is no fixed weather cock, but goes whirling along the path he has set himself. How he learned to do it is told in the latest of his fascinating volume. … Winston Churchill never speaks or writes without distinction. In

the face of such a record it is of moment to study his formative years, especially when they are unfolded for us with such gusto by such a hero of his own adventures. Brilliant, bumptious, wayward, captivating, child of genius, he is the Alcibiades of the days we live in."

"Moreover he writes with humor, with the tolerance of experience, and the wisdom of one who has dealt with great affairs and lived with great men of his time. The result is a book intensely interesting as a story and a picture of a day that is passed, and as the expression of a most vivid and vigorous personality. You close the volume with a feeling of real respect for the author and a real liking for young Winston Churchill."[33]

This is another review that is worth reading in its entirety.

The Nation

A brief but positive review was recorded in *The Nation* on February 1, 1931.

"It is a racy narrative, vividly and at times brilliantly write, abounding in good stories, striking descriptions of personalities, and caustic comments on matters as primary and public-school education, military training, polo-playing in India and politics.… It would be hard to find a more entertaining book of reminiscence, or one from which, considering the rapidity of advance and the spectacular nature of some of the experiences, the tone of self-satisfaction is more conspicuously absent."[34]

The Cavalry Journal

One journal reviewing *My Early Life* was *The Cavalry Journal* published by The Royal United Service Institution, London. There are obvious reasons they would review it, but it is not a journal which quickly comes to top of mind when thinking about book reviews. It is not surprisingly written for the soldier-reader. *The Cavalry Journal*, Vol. 21, 1931, pp. 161-2.

"We know of no writer who can describe exciting events with more dramatic skill than Mr. Churchill, and his early life has provided plenty of scope for his talent. The story of his school days is a subject for study by the psychologist rather than the soldier, but once his military career has begun the interest never flags. Whatever opinions our fathers may have of his versatility as a politician or his reliability as a statesman, there is no denying that as a subaltern of fortune he takes a high place in our esteem."

"Perhaps the most striking feature of the story is the series of most remarkable coincidences which it reveals — the single-handed capture of Churchill the correspondent by Botha the burgher — the midnight visit of Churchill the refugee to the only Englishman in the land — the meeting of Churchill the candidate with his Oldham constituent at the bottom of a mine shaft. A modern novelist employing such devices would make himself a laughing-stock."

"We would not perhaps advise young officers to imitate Mr. Churchill to the letter, but we think they might do worse than by reading this book to assimilate a portion of his spirit."[35]

NEW EDITIONS, NEW REVIEWS

Ten years after its publication with the onset of WWII, a series of reviews appeared that introduced a new generation of people to the joys of reading *My Early Life*. These reviews were coincident with the publication of a new Scribner's printing. A few examples will be provided.

The first is another review targeted to the soldier. This time it is for the infantry and was published in the *Infantry Journal* in November 1941:

"…[MEL] only brings the life of its soldier-writer-statesman author to 1902. But it is a grand book for soldiers—witty, ironical and racy—not a bit like the usual British military memoir. And it has serious passages, of which this, perhaps, is the best: 'Never, never, never believe any war will be smooth and easy, or that anyone who embarks on the strange voyage can measure the tides and hurricanes he will encounter. … These words were written eleven years ago, They are the direct forebears in the language of 'blood, sweat and tears.'"[36]

Another rousing review from middle America was published to coincide with the release of the new printing of Scribner's American edition in 1941. *The Durand Gazette*, Durand, IL, published a review in September 1941:

"*A Roving Commission* turns a brilliantly revealing light on the outstanding Englishman of his day. Here is an autobiography which crackles and sparks like the very dynamo which Winston Churchill symbolizes in the power he is bringing to the defense of democracy and freedom. Originally published in 1930, *A Roving Commission* has been brought out again in a new 1941 edition because of the tremendous interest in this modern John Bull who promises blood, sweat and tears to his countrymen in their struggle against aggression."[37]

Reviews of *My Early Life* continue to be published up to the present. A few examples are worth mentioning. In 2016, Robert McCrum, the noted English writer and editor, published the article "The 100 Best Nonfiction Books: No. 43—*My Early Life: A Roving Commission* by Winston Churchill (1930) in *The Guardian*." The review provides a balanced and fully supportive story line. A few excerpts are provided:

"Churchill was one of the finest prose stylists of the last century, steeped in the works of Shakespeare, Gibbon and Macaulay. *My Early Life*, a precocious autobiography, is his masterpiece. ... As usual with Churchill, it's a zesty cocktail of mixed ingredients, including rehashed newspaper articles, scraps of speechmaking, and many hours of dictated material. The bulk of the book was compiled during the parliamentary holidays in the summer of 1928. The happy author told Stanley Baldwin, 'I have had a delightful month—building a cottage and dictating a book: 200 bricks and 2,000 words per day.'

"*My Early Life*, however, is more than just a ripping yarn. It is also a surprisingly direct and reflective, even intimate, self-portrait of an extraordinary character during his formative years, full of ironic wit and self-deprecating good humour. Churchill is also candid about his peculiar upbringing as the child of an Anglo-American marriage, his adored but distant mother (Jeanette Jerome), his doomed father (Lord Randolph Churchill), and his own miserable schooling at Harrow. In a famous passage, he confesses his enduring love for Mrs. Everest, his nanny. On her death, he wrote: 'She had been my dearest and most intimate friend during the whole of the 20 years I had lived.'"[38]

Michael Richards wrote a review in October 2008 in the *Finest Hour*:

"Senior editor Dalton Newfield says, 'Whenever anyone says they really want to understand Churchill, I invariably recommend *My Early Life* (published in USA as *A Roving Commission*.)' This reviewer would certainly second the motion, although I was predisposed to like it: I found Woods 37b [*My Early Life*] in a New England flea market for one dollar!"

"Churchill's account of his activities through his marriage in 1908 reads like a novel—perhaps unsurprisingly, since his early life was indeed a great adventure. There are some superb passages, many of which have become immortal, having been quoted and requoted in dozens of books about Sir Winston. My own favorite (having had the same experiences with mathematics as WSC), comes in Chapter III, and I can't better describe *My Early Life* than by quoting it:

'We arrived in an 'Alice-in-Wonderland' world, at the portals of which stood 'A Quadratic Equation.' This with a strange grimace pointed the way to the Theory of Indices, which again handed on the intruder to the full rigours of the Binomial Theorem. Further dim chambers lighted by sullen, sulfurous fires were reputed to contain a dragon called the 'Differential Calculus.' But this monster was beyond the bounds appointed by the Civil Service Commissioners who regulated this stage of Pilgrim's heavy journey. We turned aside, not indeed to the uplands of the Delectable Mountains, but into a strange corridor of things like anagrams and acrostics called Sines, Cosines and Tangents. Apparently they were very important, especially when multiplied by each other, or by themselves! They had also this merit—you could learn many of their evolutions off by heart. There was a question in my third and last Examination about these Cosines and Tangents in a highly square-rooted condition which must have been decisive upon the whole of my after life. It was a problem. But luckily I had seen its ugly face only a few days before and recognized it at first sight. I have never met any of these creatures since.'

But let us not give you any more of these rich mixtures than you may otherwise absorb quite happily and at length, in the book itself."[39]

As has been stated above there are many more reviews written concerning *My Early Life* and they are listed at the end of the chapter. Most are readily available.

Notes

1. Arthur A. Baumann, "Adventures to the Adventurous," *London Observer*, October 19, 1930, p. 6.
2. Arthur James Balfour, *Chapters of Autobiography*, London, Cassell and Company, 1930.
3. Robert Lynd, "Winston Churchill," *Daily News (News Chronicle)*, London, October 20, 1930, p. 8.
4. "Book of the Day, Mr. Churchill's Youth," *Times*, London, October 20, 1930, p. 8.
5. A. Wyatt Tilby, "The Book of the Day, Mr. Churchill Remembers His Youth," *Yorkshire Post*, Yorkshire, UK, October 20, 1930, p. 6.
6. "Thrills of a Roving Commission," *Aberdeen Press & Journal*, Scotland, October 20, 1930, p. 6.
7. "Mr. Churchill's Early Life," *Edinburgh Evening News*, Scotland, October 20, 1930, p. 6.
8. "Churchill Recalls Glory of Youth in New Book," *The Winnipeg Tribune*, Winnipeg, Canada, October 20, 1930, p. 3.
9. "Winston Churchill's Early Years," *The Liverpool Echo*, UK, October 20, 1930, p. 6.
10. "Mr. Churchill's Call to Youth," *Liverpool Daily Post*, UK, October 20, 1930, p. 4.
11. "The Adventure of Living," *The Sheffield Daily Telegraph*, UK, October 20, 1930, p. 3.
12. *The Times Literary Supplement*, London, October 23, 1930, p. 851.
13. Duff Cooper, "The Early Life of Winston Churchill," *The Spectator*, October 25, 1930, p. 599.
14. "My Early Life," *Country Life*, October 25, 1930, p. 526 (portrait).
15. H. W. Nevinson, *The New Statesman*, October 25, 1930, vol. 36, p. 85.
16. Frank Forrester, "A Book of the Week, Winston's Life of Adventure," *Reynold's Illustrated News*, London, October 26, 1930, p. 18.
17. Winston S. Churchill, *My Early Life*, London, Butterworth, 1930, p. 9.
18. Lewis Melville, "Mr. Churchill's Biography," *The Saturday Review*, October 25, 1930, p. 528.
19. "A Free-Lance with Pen and Sword, Being an Appreciation of 'My Early Life' By the Rt. Hon. Winston S. Churchill," *Illustrated London News*, London, November 8, 1930, p. 806.

20. George Currie, "Winston Churchill, Adventurer," *Brooklyn Daily Eagle*, Brooklyn, NY, November 9, 1930, p. 68.
21. "Winston Churchill," *The Scotsman*, Scotland, November 17, 1930, p. 2.
22. O. F. Theis, "A Great Autobiography," *The Illustrated Sports and Dramatic News*, London, November 22, 1930, p. 488.
23. "Roving Commission is Ably Reviewed," *The Times Recorder*, Zanesville, OH, November 28, 1930, p. 4.
24. Bruce Catton, *A Stillness at Appomattox*, New York, Doubleday, 1953.
25. "The Exciting Career of Mrs. [sic] Winston Churchill," *Times Herald*, Olean, NY, November 29, 1930, p. 8.
26. T.R. Ybarra, "Adventure Filled the Years of Churchill's Youth; In 'A Roving Commission,' the British Statesman Tells a Vivid, Stirring Story," *New York Times*, November 30, 1930, pp. 3 and 34.
27. J. W. T. Mason, "Churchill's Road to Fame," *Saturday Review of Literature*, December 20, 1930, p. 469.
28. "Books of the Day. Winston Churchill," *Australasian*, Melbourne, Australia, December 13, 1930, p. 7.
29. Henry M. Hyde, "The Early Life of Winston Churchill by Himself," *The Evening Sun*, Baltimore, MD, December 20, 1930, p. 8.
30. "Some Recent Biographies," *The Bookman*, December 1930, p. 193.
31. Henry E. Armstrong, "Mr. Winston Churchill on Miseducation," *Nature*, December 27, 1930, pp. 983–85.
32. "Life of Dash and Daring. Mr. W. Churchill's Career," *Advocate*, Burnie, Tasmania, January 2, 1931, p. 7.
33. Richard Danielson, "The Man of the Month, Winston Spencer Churchill," *Atlantic Monthly*, Vol. 17, January 1931, pp. 10-12.
34. "A Roving Commission," *The Nation*, Vol. 132, February 1, 1931, p. 194.
35. "Recent Publications," *The Cavalry Journal*, Vol. 21, 1931, pp. 161-2.
36. "Soldier, Writer, Statesman," *Infantry Journal*, Vol. 49, November 1941, pp. 90-1.
37. "Weekly Book Review" from *Omnibook Magazine*, in *The Durand Gazette*, Durand, Illinois, September 4, 1941, p. 6.
38. Robert McCrum, *The Guardian*, London, November 21, 2016, https://www.theguardian.com/books/2016/nov/21/100-best-nonfiction-books-my-early-life-winston-churchill
39. "My Early Life," *Finest Hour*, International Churchill Society, October 2008.

5C: LAUNCH, ADVERTISING, AND SALES

My Early Life (*MEL*) was launched in Great Britain on 20 October 1930 by Butterworth and in the US on 24 October 1930 by Scribner's. The promotion for the book was made via a multipronged approach by Churchill, Butterworth, Scribner's, and Thomas Nelson & Sons (Canada). The campaign included advertisements for the print media, for example, newspapers and magazines; advertising leaflets handed out to potential buyers such as bookshops and libraries; and dramatic window displays in large department stores such as Harrods. Both publishers had significant sales forces to call on bookshops and distributors. Churchill also created a serialised version of the book in instalments for the news media, as described in detail in this chapter and Chapter 3, and he sent inscribed copies of the book to many influential people, as described in Chapter 5A.

In August 1930, Churchill contracted with Mr Tom Clark, the editor of the *Daily News*, to publish a serialisation of *My Early Life* in *News Chronicle*.[1] The articles were timed to immediately precede the launch of the book to prepare the market and create public interest. These pre-launch publications were a powerful means of preparing the market for the book and creating a media buzz about Churchill. The newspaper published a high-impact statement giving the public a taste of what they could expect in the excerpts from *My Early Life*. On 26 August, the *Daily News* published the following notice under the heading 'Mr. Churchill's Youth':

> It is possible to disagree violently with Mr. Winston Churchill's politics. It is possible to criticize severely his whole attitude to life. We have often done both, and no doubt shall do so again. It is not possible to deny that among the public men of to-day there is no more interesting figure than Mr. Churchill. It is possible, indeed, to go very much further. It is extremely doubtful whether, in the whole history of the world, there has ever been a career so various, so many-sided and so uniformly brilliant. If adventure be the real zest of life, here is adventure with a vengeance. It is in the belief that in its secret heart this is what Youth believes that we are publishing from Saturday next Mr. Churchill's story of the adventures of his own youth, told by a writer whose bitterest opponents have never denied his incomparable brilliance and vividness. Many passages in these

reminiscences seem to us as brilliant and as vivid as anything that Mr. Churchill has ever written.²

The newspaper certainly didn't underplay the launch of their series of articles or the book, or even the talents or importance of Churchill. There were nineteen installments published, beginning 30 August, that ran almost daily until 20 September. Each instalment began with the statement: 'The following is the [xth] of a series of articles formed of extracts from Mr. Churchill's book, *My Early Life*.' It is of note that Churchill always wanted to keep his name in front of the reading public and so for the year following the launch of the book, November 1930 to December 1931, Churchill published a total of fifty-seven articles in newspapers, magazines and journals. For a complete listing see Cohen's *Bibliography of the Writings of Sir Winston Churchill*.³ These were not excerpts from *MEL* or retelling the stories in *MEL*, but, certainly, the impact of his name being out in the market would be additive to all the direct advertising, which will be described below.

Butterworth addressed the marketing plan for *My Early Life* with Churchill in a letter on 26 September:

> It may interest you to know that we propose to advertise your book in advance of the publication, as follows:
>
> In 'The Times' Literary Supplement on the 9th & 16th October
>
> 'Sunday Times' & 'The Observer' on 12th and 19th October
>
> This is done with the object of creating a demand at the libraries and bookshops on the day of publication.⁴

An additional full-page pre-launch advertisement was published in *The Publisher & Bookseller* on 10 October.⁵ As seen in Figure 1, it announces the book will be ready on 20 October and that customers should 'Order Now', as a second printing is already underway and the first edition is almost completely sold out.

CHAPTER 5 / LAUNCH OF THE BOOK

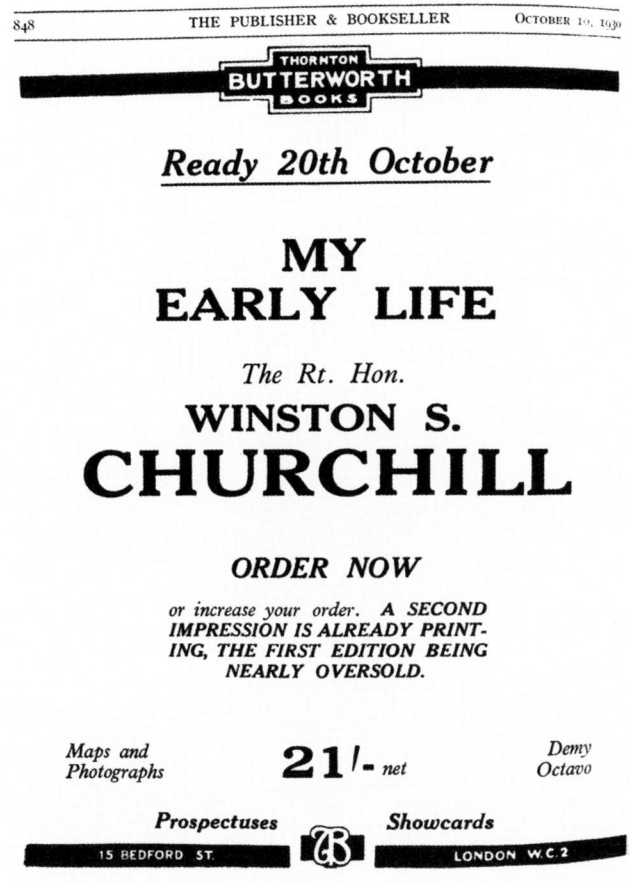

Figure 1. Pre-launch advertisement in *The Publisher & Bookseller*, London, 10 October 1930.

As might be anticipated from a publishing journal, the advertisement in *The Publisher & Bookseller* notes the size of the book as 'Demy Octavo' [8¾" x 5⅝" (22.1 cm x 14.2 cm)]. This is the only advertisement discovered that notes the book's size.

The pre-launch marketing pieces in the newspapers noted above were carried out as stated. The marketing pieces in the *Observer* will be used as examples. On 12 October, the following advertisement (Figure 2) was published on p. 5:

211

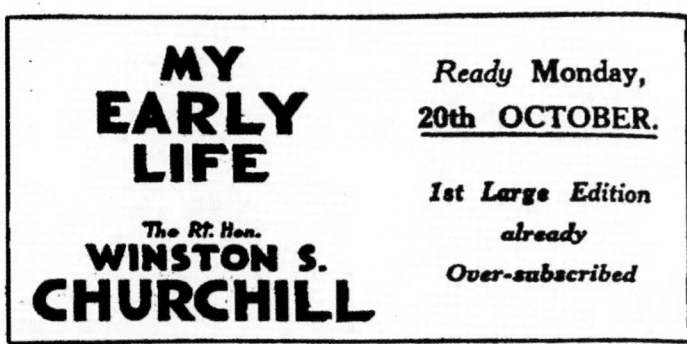

Figure 2. Pre-launch advertisement in the *Observer*, London, 12 October 1930.

It is a simple advertisement that shows the book will be ready on Monday the 20th and states that the 'large' first edition is already sold out. It has always seemed that an effective marketing approach for a book is to create a demand through advertising and then link it to the fact that the book is selling out fast so the consumer must move with alacrity to obtain a copy.

This is followed up on 17 October with another very similar advertisement (not mentioned in the above letter) but with the addition '2nd impression ready.' Then, on the 19th, they published a larger advertisement (Figure 3):

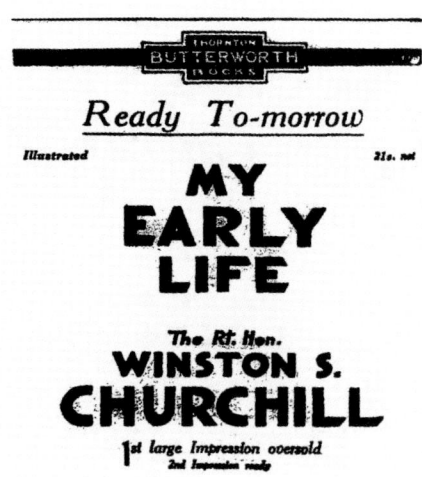

Figure 3. Pre-publication advertisement in the *Observer*, London, 19 October 1930.

The headline 'Ready To-morrow' signals imminent availability and notes that the '2nd Impression [is] ready'.

Following the launch, there is a widespread newspaper advertising campaign across all of Great Britain. Similarly, after the launch in the US and Canada there are advertising campaigns there, too. A list at the end of the chapter gives some examples worldwide of the advertising that was published. The list is not exhaustive in any sense, as there were hundreds, if not thousands, of advertisements. Some examples of the style and content of advertisements published in Great Britain, US, and Canada are given here.

In the week of publication, advertisements begin to quote from the early reviews to emphasise how good the book really is. The *Evening Standard* in London publishes the following on page 10 of the 23 October 1930 issue (Figure 4):

Figure 4. Advertisement in the *Evening Standard*, London, 23 October 1930.

This is the first advertisement to use what is probably the most iconic statement from a book review of *My Early Life*: that the book is 'Like a Beaker of Champagne.' (The reader is directed to the section on reviews to understand why the original author made that comparison.) The advertisement also announces that there is a '2nd large impression'.

Figure 5 shows the advertisement published by the *Graphic* in London on 25 October 1930 (p. 175):

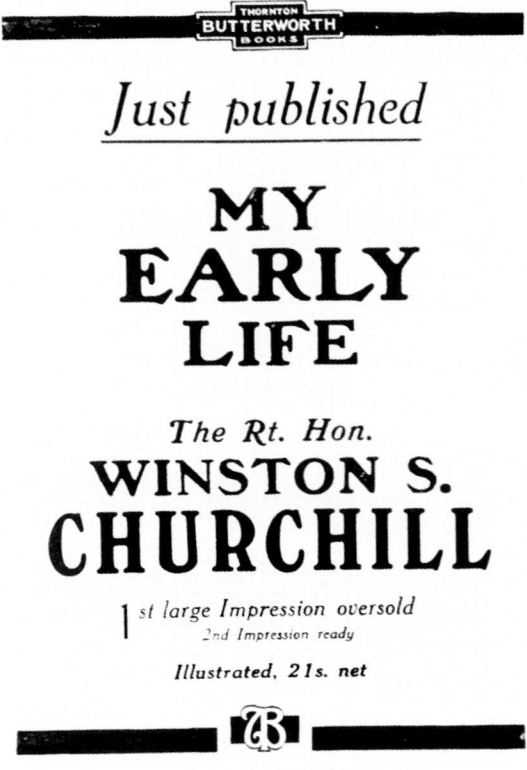

Figure 5. Advertisement in the *Graphic*, London, 26 October 1930.

This advertisement notes that the book is 'Just Published' and adds that 1st Impression is sold out and 2nd Impression is large and ready.

On 26 October, the *Observer* in London publishes on page 10 an advertisement replete with quotes from book reviews (see Figure 6). It notes that the book is illustrated and does not even mention the first edition, first printing:

Similar newspaper advertisements were published throughout Great Britain well into 1931. See examples in the list below.

In addition to standard newspaper advertisements, Churchill and the editor of the *Daily News* created an ingenious marketing tool when they agreed to

Figure 6. Advertisement in the *Observer*, London, 25 October 1930.

sponsor a writing competition to be run in the *News Chronicle* in parallel with Churchill's instalments of *My Early Life*. This would become a wildly popular contest and create a tremendous response in both the public and the press. On 30 August, the day the serialisation began, the *News Chronicle* ran a large-print front-page headline: 'Winston Churchill's Memoirs on Page Six.' Directly underneath, the lead story ('A Career on Offer') outlined the rules of the competition, which was for those aged seventeen to twenty-two:

> The first prize, offered for an article of not more than 1,000 words related to Mr. Churchill's articles is a probationary post, for one year certain, on the editorial staff of the *News-Chronicle*. There is ample evidence that this unique offer will result in an extremely heavy entrance list. ... Competitors must have read the complete series before writing their competition articles. For this reason, competition articles

will not be accepted until Sept. 20. ... A second prize of 50 guineas will be given, and there are ten other prizes of autographed copies of Mr. Churchill's book.

What a marketing coup! The planned competition was successful beyond their wildest dreams.

A news article on the competition and rules was also published in the *Daily News*, London, on 9 September (p. 1). Then, on 3 December 1930, the *Daily News* reported the following:

> From the *thousands* [emphasis added] of articles submitted, the judges have now selected the twelve which, in their opinion, show most evidence of journalistic talent on the part of the writers. These twelve will be submitted to the three final judges, Mr. Churchill, Mr. Tom Clarke [editor of the *News-Chronicle*] and Mr. Robert Lynd [the *News-Chronicle*'s literary editor}.

The news coverage of the competition was widespread and engendered much interest in the public.[6]

A front-page headline article in the *News Chronicle* on 23 December announced the winners of the competition. There had been nearly 3,000 entries. The winner was a twenty-year-old Oxford student, and he would take up his new position with the paper the following June when he would graduate from Oxford. The second prize went to a high school student. All the other finalists received autographed copies of *My Early Life*. The article states that 'Mr. Churchill especially called attention to the brilliance of his [the winner's] work.' The media coverage of the event was significant, and it was clearly a win for all; and, certainly, Churchill's new book received the publicity he, his publishers and the newspaper had desired.

As has been described in detail previously, there were hundreds of reviews of the book. Some of the reviews were what should be considered reviews/advertisements. Such reviews are always positive and also enlivened with images, for example, a striking picture of Churchill which not only catches the eye but also makes the book seem appealing and desirable to purchase. An example of this is shown in Figure 7, a layout published on p. 526 of the 25 October 1930 issue of the well-known British periodical *Country Life*:

My Early Life, by the Right Hon. Winston S. Churchill. (Thornton Butterworth, 21s. net.)

THIS book has at least two merits which place it entirely outside the ordinary run of biography. It is the work of a master of narrative whose comments on men and affairs are always apt and necessarily well informed, and it deals with a life of thrilling adventure, full of interest even to those who are too young to remember any of the events it describes, or the repercussions of those events on the lives of their elders. By those who remember the campaign of the 'nineties and who lived through the period of the South African War, Mr. Churchill's story of those days will be found entirely absorbing, and nobody who begins to read is likely to abandon the book without reading to the end. Of such a book it is manifestly impossible to give an adequate description in the compass of a short review. The crowded hours of glorious life which it describes are so crowded and so many as almost literally to take one's breath away, and all that one can say is that even more than Mr. Churchill in his previous contributions to the history of our times Mr. Churchill has used his gifts of humour and irony, of concise and lucid expression, of vivid and illuminating phrase, with all the mastery which we have long

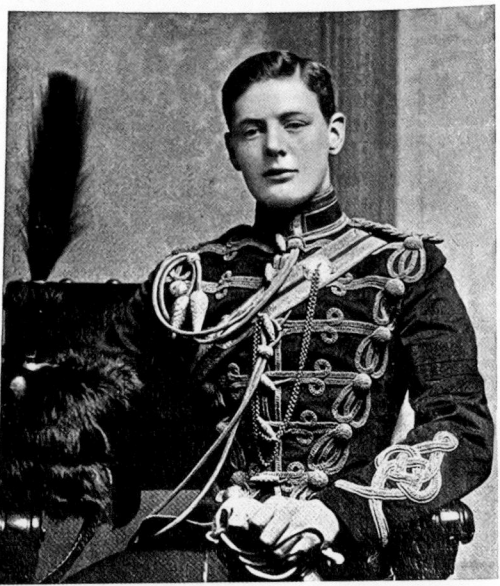

"MR. WINSTON CHURCHILL IN THE 4TH HUSSARS."
(From "My Early Life.")

known to be his. His story opens with his earliest recollections of Dublin and the Phœnix Park of long ago, when Lord Randolph was secretary to his father, the Duke of Marlborough, and it ends with a description of a dinner to Joseph Chamberlain in 1902, at which that statesman, as he paused at the door after dinner, turned and said: "You young gentlemen have entertained me royally, and in return I will give you a priceless secret. Tariffs! These are the politics of the future!" Between these two periods is packed a bewildering variety of adventure. Most people will probably read with great interest Mr. Churchill's description of the part he played during the South African War, and it is certainly an excellent thing that we should at last have his own careful narrative of his capture and imprisonment by the Boers and of his subsequent escape from captivity. His earlier campaigns were many. In 1895 he and a brother-officer obtained permission to follow the operations of a punitive expedition in Cuba. Then came the adventure of the Malakind Field Force, to be followed in quick succession by the Sudan Campaign and Kitchener's march to Omdurman. The story of Omdurman is told about as well as it is ever likely to be told, and the narrative falls little short in interest of the enthralling chapters which deal with South Africa. As for the earlier portions of this book, the passages which deal with Mr. Churchill's early youth and with his life at Harrow and Sandhurst are full of charm, and there are two chapters on India as a subaltern found it in the 'nineties, which nobody can afford to miss.

Figure 7. Advertisement in *Country Life*, October 1930.

The image included in the advertisement/review shows Churchill as a handsome soldier with much gravitas, albeit a youthful figure. It also highlights that the book is dominated by Churchill's military career.

To help promote worldwide coverage of the book, Butterworth cabled highlights from the published reviews to his agents in Canada, South Africa and Australia, and to Scribner in America, so they could use the material in their advertising campaigns.[7]

Butterworth, in conjunction with Churchill, also planned and created store-window displays following the launch of the book. One such display was created in the iconic store windows of Harrods in London. In a letter dated 14 October, Butterworth related the plan:

> …We have arranged with Harrods to make a special show in one of their shop windows of 150 copies, which we will supply to them for sale or return. I understand from Mr. Bourne that you suggested that we should supply them with the 'Reward for your Capture Alive or Dead.' This, I am glad to say is only another instance where our ideas march side by side.[8]

The poster/handbill for Churchill's recapture after his escape from the Boers was loaned by Churchill for the event. No images of the Harrods window display have thus far been uncovered.

A major source for advertising and sales was the 'Boots Booklovers Library' offered in Boots the Chemist shops across Great Britain. (See full description below.)

The Canadian advertising campaign was robust and countrywide, particularly in the major cities. There were two main types of advertisements: those published by Thomas Nelson & Sons, the publisher/agent for the sale of the book in Canada, and those published by major bookstores. Examples of each are shown. Figure 8 shows the advertisement published by the *Montreal Star* published on 25 October 1930 (p. 35):

Created by Thomas Nelson & Sons, it utilises the famous review quote at the top and provides a vignette of the contents of the book; it also notes that the book it is illustrated and costs $4.50 (Canadian). As will be seen below, the cost in the US is $3.50 (American).

The bookseller Burton's published an advertisement on page 15 of the 8 November 1930 issue of the *Gazette* of Montreal (Figure 9):

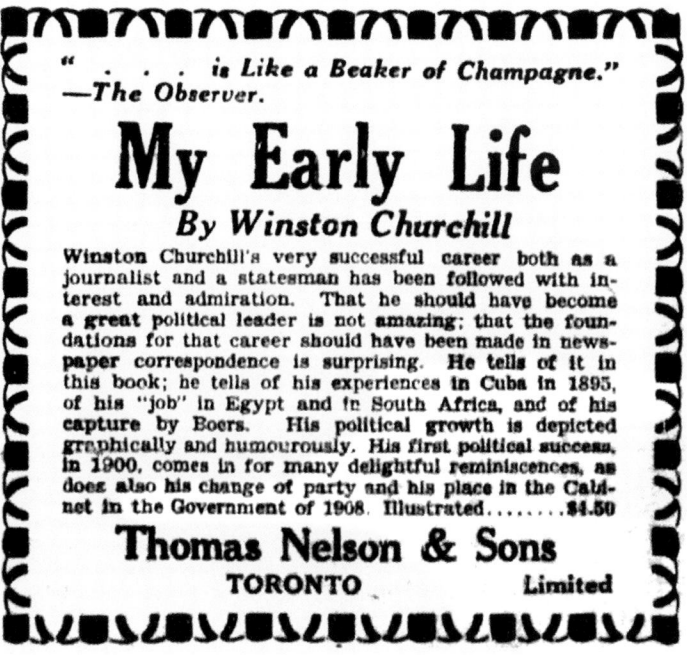

Figure 8. Advertisement in the *Montreal Star*, Montreal, 25 October 1930.

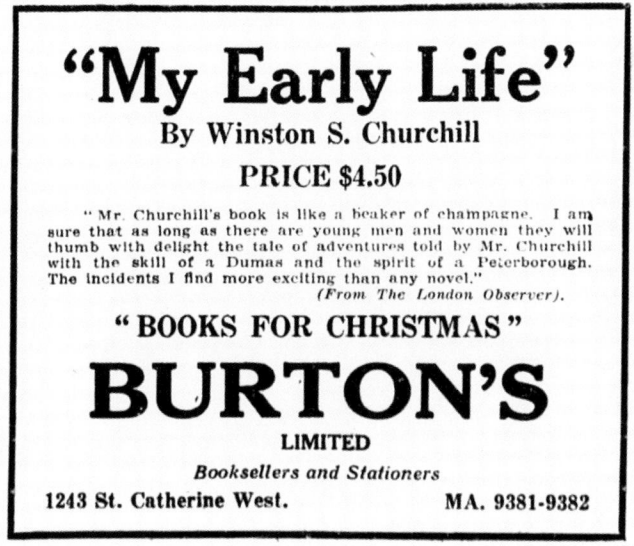

Figure 9. Advertisement in the *Gazette*, Montreal, 8 November 1930.

HENRY MORGAN & CO. LIMITED

BOOK ROOM NOTICE

"My Early Life: A Roving Commission"

by *The Right Hon. Winston Spencer Churchill*

Mr. Churchill's record of his youth and young manhood is his finest literary achievement. This book is not oratorical autobiography, and is, as regards style—or, one may say, styles—better than anything which has gone before. Its variation and development in this matter of style are the greatest of its charms. One fancies one hears the small boy, the youth at Sandhurst, the young soldier, the slightly older politician, each telling his story in his own way. Of course, no gentleman cadet, still less a small boy, could write like that; that Mr. Churchill should contrive to bewitch his readers into the momentary impression that they can is proof that he has at his command the art of the autobiographer.

4.50

HENRY MORGAN & CO. LIMITED

Figure 10. Advertisement in the *Montreal Star*, Montreal, 8 November 1930.

The advertisement features a long quote from a review in the *Observer* and notes that it would make a perfect Christmas present.

A much more formal and striking advertisement is published by the bookseller Henry Morgan. It refers to Churchill as 'the Right Hon. Winston Spencer Churchill'. They also provide their own review and call the book 'his finest literary achievement'. It was published in the *Montreal Star* on 8 November 1930, on page 29 (Figure 10).

Smaller, less expensive advertisements were printed in both major cities and smaller markets. Figure 11 shows an example below from Montreal's *Gazette* (20 December 1930, p. 18):

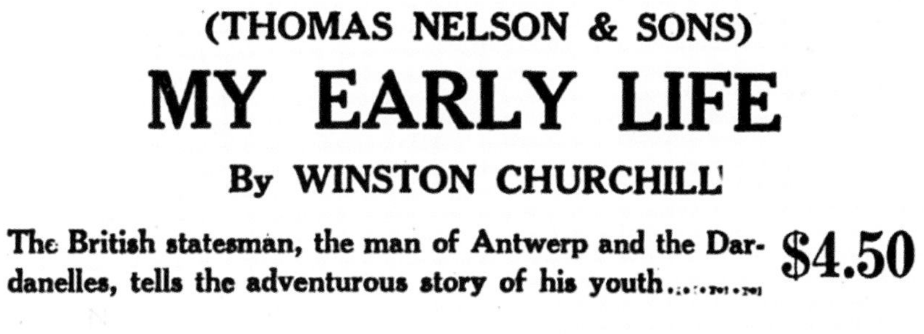

(THOMAS NELSON & SONS)
MY EARLY LIFE
By WINSTON CHURCHILL

The British statesman, the man of Antwerp and the Dardanelles, tells the adventurous story of his youth... **$4.50**

Figure 11. Advertisement in the *Gazette*, Montreal, 20 December 1930.

This advertisement would have seemed quite unusual and perhaps even an insult to Churchill, as they describe him as 'the man of Antwerp and the Dardanelles' – clearly not highlights in Churchill's life (Antwerp refers to an ill-fated land battle promoted by Churchill in the First World War. The Dardanelles refers to an ill-fated naval and land operation designed by Churchill. Both of these operations were carried out when he was First Lord of the Admiralty.)

Advertisements were created all across the US, most of them, and the largest of them, published in the larger cities. The *Chicago Tribune* printed numerous advertisements such as the one shown in Figure 12 which was published on 15 November 1930 on page 13:

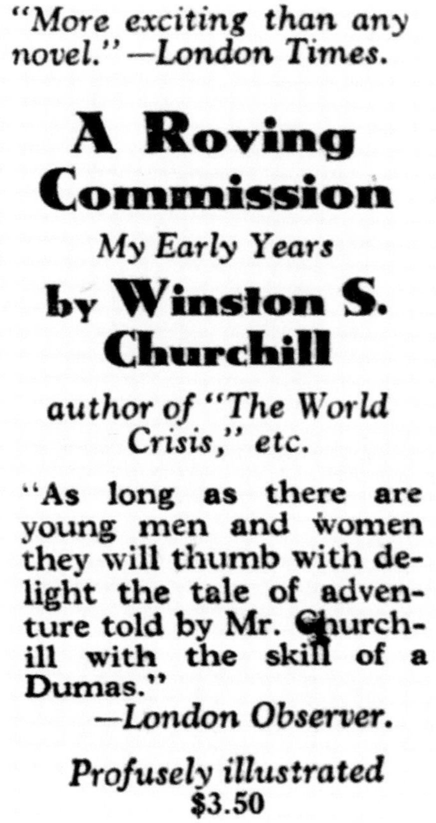

> "More exciting than any novel." —*London Times.*
>
> ## A Roving Commission
> My Early Years
> ### by Winston S. Churchill
> author of "The World Crisis," etc.
>
> "As long as there are young men and women they will thumb with delight the tale of adventure told by Mr. Churchill with the skill of a Dumas."
> —*London Observer.*
>
> Profusely illustrated
> $3.50

Figure 12. Advertisement in the *Chicago Tribune*, Chicago, 22 November 1930.

The advertisement contained two book review comments and noted a previous Churchill book (*World Crisis*) and the fact that the book was profusely illustrated.

National magazines (journals) such as the *Saturday Review of Literature* published comprehensive advertisements with images of Churchill and multiple quotations from published reviews. Figure 13 gives an example of one such advertisement (published on 29 November 1930 on page 398).

Smaller markets saw smaller advertisements published, for example, the one shown in Figure 14 which ran in the *Idaho Statesman* on 17 November (p. 18):

CHAPTER 5 / LAUNCH OF THE BOOK

"Like a beaker of champagne . . . as long as there are young men and women they will thumb with delight the tale of adventures told by Mr. Churchill with the skill of a Dumas."—London Observer.

A Roving Commission
My Early Life
by
Winston S. Churchill

Author of "The World Crisis," etc.

WINSTON CHURCHILL IN THE UNIFORM OF THE SOUTH AFRICAN LIGHT HORSE

"I do not believe a more delightful thing of its kind has been written in our day."—*John Buchan.*

"Mr. Churchill's record of his youth and young manhood is his finest literary achievement."
—*London Times Literary Supplement.*

"A very magnificent canvas, and its magnificence is mainly due to the fact that the author has enjoyed writing it as much as he enjoyed living it, and that he is able to convey his enjoyment to the reader who shares it with him to the full."
—*The Spectator (London).*

Profusely illustrated. $3.50   At your bookstore

Charles Scribner's Sons, New York

The first complete account of his spectacular escape from a Boer prison and flight across two hundred and fifty miles of hostile country to safety; his part in the charge of the 21st Lancers at Omdurman—the last great cavalry charge in military history; thrilling campaigns against the hill tribes in India; political campaigns in England and absorbing recollections of school days at Harrow and Sandhurst, all, as the London Times declares, "more exciting than any novel."

Figure 13. Advertisement in *Saturday Review*, New York, 29 November 1930.

> A ROVING COMMISSION. By Winston S. Churchill. New York. Charles Scribner's Sons. $3.50. English statesman tells of his early life.

Figure 14. Advertisement in the *Idaho Statesman*, Boise, 16 November 1930.

Finally, in some of the major US markets, such as Chicago and Philadelphia, advertisements were published with both quotes and an image of the book with its dust jacket. Figure 15 shows an example, published by the *Philadelphia Inquirer* on 6 December 1930 (p. 14):

> **A Roving Commission**
> My Early Life
> **by Winston S. Churchill**
> *author of "The World Crisis," etc.*
>
> "A bewitching book from the first word to the last.... Churchill's best book." —*New York Sun*.
>
> *Illustrated.* $3.50

Figure 15. Advertisement in the *Philadelphia Inquirer*, Philadelphia, 6 December 1930.

The following is a select list of publications with references that printed advertisements for *My Early Life*:

1. *Saturday Review*, London, 29 November 1930, Vol. 7, No. 19, p. 398.
2. *Nation*, 3 December 1930, New York, p. 623.
3. *Atlantic Monthly*, Boston, January 1931, p. 11.
4. *Atlantic Monthly*, Boston, February 1931, p. 11.

5. *Graphic*, London, 25 October 1930, p. 175.
6. *Christian Century*, Chicago, 10 December 1930, p. 1535.
7. *Ottawa Journal*, Ottawa, Canada, 1 November 1930, p. 19.
8. *Book Review Digest*, Books of 1930, New York, 1931, pp. 198–9.
9. *Chicago Tribune*, Chicago, 18 December 1930, p. 16.
10. *Saturday Review*, New York, 6 December 1930, p. 754.
11. *Scribner's Magazine*, New York, January 1931, p. 16.
12. *Birmingham Gazette*, Birmingham, UK, 30 April 1932, p. 4.
13. *Philadelphia Inquirer*, Philadelphia, 8 November 1930, p. 12.
14. *Princeton Alumni Magazine*, Vol. XXXI, No. 8, 14 November 1930, p. 194.
15. *Golden Book Magazine*, Vol. 30, 1930, p. 24.
16. *New York Times Book Review*, New York, 23 November 1930, p. 14.
17. *American Mercury*, Vol. 21, December 1930, p. xxvii.
18. *Chicago Tribune*, Chicago, 15 November 1930, p. 18.
19. *Atlantic Monthly*, November 1931, p. 19.
20. *Publishers Weekly*, 30 August 1930, p. 801.
21. *Saturday Review*, New York, 1 November 1930, p. 294.
22. *Saturday Review*, New York, 8 November 1930, p. 313.
23. *The Saturday Review*, New York, 29 November 1930, p. 398.
24. *Saturday Review*, New York, 6 December 1930, p. 436.
25. *Saturday Review*, New York, 3 January 1931, p. 507.
26. *Publishers Weekly*, 20 September 1930, p. 1233.
27. *Harper's Magazine*, February 1931, front advertising section.
28. *New Republic*, New York, 12 November 1930, p. 359.
29. *Nation*, New York, 3 December 1930, p. 623.
30. *The Bookman*, London, October 1930, p. 51.
31. *Chicago Daily Tribune*, 8 November 1930, p. 12.
32. *Christian Century*, Chicago, 3 December 1930, p. 1503.
33. *Intercollegian*, January 1931, vol. 48, p. 135.
34. *Times Literary Supplement*, London, 9 October 1930.
35. *Times Literary Supplement*, London, 16 October 1930.
36. *Sunday Times*, London, 12 October 1930.
37. *Sunday Times*, London, 19 October 1930.
38. *Observer*, London, 12 October 1930, p. 5.
39. *Observer*, London, 19 October 1930, p. 10.

40. *Observer*, London, 26 October 1930, p. 10.
41. *Observer*, London, 2 November 1930, p. 8.
42. *Guardian*, London, 23 October 1930, p. 7.
43. *Observer*, London, 23 November 1930, p. 34.
44. *Observer*, London, 4 October 1930, p. 9.
45. *Observer*, London, 23 October 1930, p. 34.
46. *Daily Telegraph*, London, 7 November 1930, p. 15.
47. *Birmingham Gazette*, Birmingham, 30 April 1931, p. 4.
48. *Evening Standard*, London, 23 October 1930, p. 10.
49. *Western Mail*, Cardiff, Wales, 23 October 1930, p. 11.
50. *Gazette,* Montreal, Canada, 8 November 1930, p. 15.
51. *Gazette,* Montreal, Canada, 20 December 1930, p. 18.
52. *Ottawa Gazette*, Ottawa, Canada, 1 November 1930, p. 19.
52. *Gazette*, Montreal, Canada, 6 December 1930, p. 13.
52. *Province*, Vancouver, Canada, 7 December 1930, p. 44.
53. *Montreal Star*, Montreal, Canada, 25 October 1930, p. 35.
54. *Vancouver Star*, Vancouver, Canada, 15 December 1930, p. 9.
55. *Victoria Times*, Victoria, B.C., Canada, 27 November 1930, p. 5.
56. *Montreal Star*, Montreal, Canada, 8 November 1930, p. 29.
57. *Birmingham Gazette*, Birmingham, 30 October 1930, p. 5.
58. *Chicago Tribune*, Chicago, 28 February 1931, p. 17.
59. *Chicago Tribune*, Chicago, 15 November 1930, p. 13.
60. *Philadelphia Inquirer*, Philadelphia, 6 December 1930, p. 14.
61. *Philadelphia Inquirer*, Philadelphia, 8 November 1930, p. 12.
62. *Chicago Tribune*, Chicago, 22 November 1930, p. 15.
63. *Vancouver Sun*, Vancouver, Canada, 15 December 1930, p. 9.
64. *Detroit Free Press*, Detroit, 6 February 1932, p. 10.
65. *Hartford Courant*, Hartford, 1 February 1932, p. 11. Signed copies.
66. *New York Times*, New York, 8 February 1931, p. 71.
67. *Daily Colonist*, Victoria, B.C, Canada, 16 November 1930, p. 16.
68. *Forum and Century*, Vol. LXXXIV, No. 6, December 1930, p. XIX.
69. *Scientific American*, Vol. CXLIV, February 1931, p. 147.
70. *Daily Observer*, London, 17 October 1930, p. 4.
71. *Los Angeles Times*, Los Angeles, 7 December 1930, p. 45.
72. *The Publisher & Bookseller*, London, 31 October 1930, p. 991.
73. *The Publisher & Bookseller*, London, 6 November 1931, p. 886.

74. *The Bookseller*, London, 6 February 1935, p. 103.
75. *The Bookseller*, London, 14 July 1972, p. 180.
76. *Scotsman*, Edinburgh, 11 December 1930, p. 2.
77. 'Portrait of a Patriot When Young', *Leicester Chronicle,* Leicester, UK, 18 August 1972, p. 22. (Movie and Book)
78. 'Cloke's / Book notes', *Hamilton Spectator*, Hamilton, Ontario, Canada, 6 December 1930, p. 20.
79. *The Publisher & Bookseller*, London, 10 October 1930, p. 848.

As can be appreciated, there was a significant and well-coordinated marketing plan, for which Churchill was a major contributor and driving force. The book received worldwide coverage in the press through both book reviews and advertisements. This resulted in significant sales, as will now be described below.

Sales Information

As noted in Chapter 3 on the writing of *My Early Life,* both the publishers and Churchill himself were optimistic about the sales potential of the book, while at the same time recognising that there was an ongoing worldwide depression and a battle among publishers to gain advantages over each other through price wars. The other major issue on Churchill's mind was his personal financial situation: he was deep in debt, he had a large cadre of unpaid bills, and he was at serious risk of defaulting on a number of loans.[9] This black cloud floated just above Churchill's head the entire time he was writing and editing the book, but as he did with most troublesome events or concerns, Churchill managed to compartmentalise the issues and rise above the situation to maintain a positive outlook.

Butterworth writes to Churchill on September 26 with first numbers on the book's printing and pre-sales:

> Our first printing is for 5,000 and odd copies. The orders outside of London amount to date of 1,268, and we estimate that the London Subscription orders will amount to about 4,000 copies. If our surmise proves correct, we shall then be able to advertise that the first impression was sold out, or oversold, on the date of publication. [It

is of interest that WSC put a comment here in his hand: 'This is a good advertising note.'] We have the paper ready at the printers for an immediate reprint.[10]

As was discussed in the section on advertising, Butterworth did advertise that the first run had sold out before its release.

Churchill replies the next day: 'I expect you will have nearly 6,000 copies subscribed for before publication, and I have no doubt the reviews will be helpful.'[11]

Butterworth updates Churchill on book orders in a letter dated 8 October:

> I am also pleased to tell you that our first order in London, namely from Boots was for 1,000 copies, the number we estimated they would take, which is very satisfactory. Our total orders to date for Town, Country and Overseas amount to 2,457. I sincerely trust that the sales elsewhere in London will also come up to our estimate. I think I mentioned to you, when you called last week, that we put the second printing in hand for 2,500 copies.[12]

A brief discussion of Boots referred to in Butterworth's letter is certainly warranted because Boots shops represented important venues for advertising and selling books. 'Boots' refers to 'Boots the Chemist', a national chain of shops across the UK selling pharmaceuticals and personal care items. From 1889 until 1966, they also ran the 'Boots Booklovers Library', a lending library contained within the individual shops nationwide. Boots employed professional library staff and displayed the books in an open library setting where customers could browse, borrow or buy books. These libraries were quite popular, as there were few true free lending libraries in the UK prior to the Public Libraries and Museum Act 1964.[13] From the number of books ordered by Boots (1,000), we know they were a significant force in the book market. In an article titled 'Books in Greatest Demand' in the *Evening Telegraph*, Dundee (24 October 1930, p. 9), Boots lists *My Early Life* as one of the top three books in demand in the nonfiction category.

Although there are no details of how *My Early Life* was handled financially, we do know how another of Churchill's books was. 'In 1939, one of the books listed for sale at four shillings was *Arms and the Covenant* by Winston Churchill. Originally published in 1938 and purchased by Boots for eighteen shillings, the book contained forty-one of the great man's passionate speeches, warning of the Nazi menace.'[14] This model was somewhat akin to the Times Book Club, where the book was made available for free by joining the club as a full member or was available for purchase by subscription, as noted above. Boots saw this offering as a public service and as a mechanism to drive customers into their store.

Butterworth follows up on 10 October: 'In the meantime I think we may say there is little doubt that in the course of the next day or two we shall have sold out the first Edition of your Memoirs.'[15] This was followed with another letter the next day: 'The sales to date amount to 4,020. We still have to fill orders from "The Times" Book Club, Mudies [another book club], Bumpus and various exporters. We should therefore reach a Subscription order of 5,550.'[16] Further sales information and advertising approaches come from Butterworth on the 14th: 'Sales of *My Early Life* up to the time of writing amount to 4,830. And I hope to advise before our subscription closed that we have reached 5,500. It may be more, though we cannot tell; still, I trust it will not be less.[17]

On 16 October, Churchill received Butterworth's final pre-publication sales estimate: '… I am able to give you what may be considered to be almost the final figures before publication: 6032. As your estimate of sales was 6,000 copies, perhaps you will allow me to compliment you on your forecast.'[18]

Interestingly, Butterworth was providing a day-by-day reporting of orders, and Churchill was rapidly responding. His financial concerns drove Churchill to be actively engaged in attempting to ensure the financial success of all of his writing endeavours.

Scribner's first edition press run was for 5,000 copies.[19] Churchill received his first royalty statement from Scribner's on 24 October 24, which stated: 'For *A Roving Commission*: number sold 810, royalty 52 ½. Amount $425.78 from which was subtracted US Income tax at a rate of 5% Amount received $404.49.'[20]

As noted in the letter, Churchill received 52½ cents per book sold, and the notes point out how far federal income tax has come, as the rate was only 5 percent in 1930. There was very good coordination and sharing of information on the book and its sales between the two publishers.

Butterworth sent a letter to Scribner on 7 November, updating him on the progress in the UK: 'The reviews of Churchill's book have been beyond our most optimistic hopes. While we are doing extremely well, I cannot help thinking that we are feeling somewhat the draught of trade depression. Nevertheless, we have ordered our third printing and I believe that it will go on selling for many months to come.[21]

As mentioned previously, Churchill always actively participated in the marketing of his books. He carefully followed the book sales on a daily basis and challenged his publishers to sell more, often questioning why the book wasn't performing better. Jonathan Rose, in a 2013 article titled 'Churchill at Scribner's: A Study in Failure', states his belief that Churchill's assumptions about American sales were quite out of sync with reality; but then he states that sales were actually pretty good considering the state of the economy at that time. He writes:

> Churchill seems not to have grasped that he was failing to reach the American common reader, in part because he had won a following among a much more select audience. During his trip to the United States in 1929 he was hosted lavishly by wealthy American Anglophiles, treated to five nights in a luxurious Los Angles hotel by the investment banker James R. Page, and then traveled to New York in Barnard Baruch's private railway car. These well-heeled gentlemen told him exactly what he wanted to hear: 'I met all the leading people & have heard on every side of my speech & talks (to circles of ten or twelve) have given much pleasure. I explained to them all about England & her affairs – showing how splendid & tolerant she was & and how we ought to work together. I gave a dinner & lunch to the leading men. I liked the best mostly British born, & all keenly pro-England.'

At San Simeon he talked with William Randolph Hurst, who 'seems very much set upon the idea of closer and more intimate relations between the English-speaking peoples.'… 'We are a power respected and considered to be revivified,' he exalted.

That conclusion was based on a self-selected and highly unrepresentative sample, though Churchill could point to the modest success of *My Early Life* (published October 1930). Butterworth sold 11,000 copies of the original twenty-one-shilling edition, but within a year Scribner's had sold out two printings, totaling almost 8,000 copies. In spite of (or perhaps because of) the deepening depression, readers wanted diverting and gripping stories set in a romantic past. Churchill won enthusiastic reviews from the *New York Times* ('Besides being a playboy and a politician, he is a born writer'), the *New York World* ('A brilliant book, with a notable style and a graphic tale to tell'), and the *Nation* ('a racy narrative, vividly and at times brilliantly written, abounding in good stories, striking descriptions of personalities, and caustic comments').[22]

Rose thus appears to come full circle in his thinking; his main issue with Churchill really seems to be that Churchill enjoyed spending his private time with affluent, educated, and successful people. Rose fails to mention that Churchill received much praise during his large lecture series during this same trip and certainly all of the audiences were not primarily millionaires.

About a month after launch, on 26 November, Butterworth informs Churchill:

> The sales of 'My Early Life' are:
>
> Home … … 6,207
> Overseas … 1,432
> Making a total of … 7,639
>
> For some time, the sales moved so slowly that we began to feel despondent; latterly, however, sales have improved remarkably, and we are now feeling much more hopeful as to the future. I should not be at all surprised if, during the Winter session, we did not put on another 1,000 or 1,500 copies.[23]

By 2 December, the book continues to sell and Butterworth reports total sales of 7,827.[24]

About six weeks after the US launch, Scribner reports to Churchill:

> … It may still be too early to predict, but for the first time since publication the reorders of the past week would seem to indicate that

the crisis has passed, and that even if the book did not fulfill all our expectations, at least it would not be in any sense a failure. Our records now show over 2,000 sold and the orders are coming in at around 100 copies per day.

There was a very fair review in *The New York Times* last Sunday which is our best book medium, and the next number of the *Atlantic Monthly* [see section on reviews] gives it quite a boost. We have ourselves spent an advertising appropriation several times over what the present sales justify. This is due, however, to our faith in the book and we believe that by carrying our campaign through the season, we shall reap our reward in the end.[25]

At this same time, Butterworth reports total sales of 8,062.[26] By 12 December Butterworth is upbeat and reports the following:

I am pleased to inform you that we have to-day received a second repeat order for 200 copies of *My Early Life* from our agents in Canada. The brings the Canadian figures up to 1,150, a quite remarkable sale for a comparatively small population. … The sales of *My Early Life* have now reached 8,521. Most encouraging! We have ordered a further reprint of 1,500 copies.[27]

This represents the fourth printing in 1930. In all, there would be six printings of the British first edition.

By the middle of December, Churchill is concerned about the sales of the book in the US and asks to be updated on the progress. Scribner replies in a letter on 19 December:

I have just received your cable inquiring about the sale of *A Roving Commission* and have replied 'Sales over five thousand' … We have exhausted our first printing of 5000 and have taken in over half of our second printing of 2000, so we will have to be printing again. … We have spent to date just over six thousand dollars in advertising the book, which shows our faith in it and the importance and the importance we feel its success will have on your forthcoming book.[28]

A small and often forgotten but extremely important market, particularly before the introduction of audiobooks, was the production of books in braille for the blind. Butterworth addresses this issue in a letter dated 22 December: 'We have received an application from the National Library for the Blind for permission to transcribe *My Early Life* into braille. We would be glad if you would inform us whether you are agreeable that they should do so?'[29] Churchill replies: 'I have no objections whatever to the transcription of *My Early Life* into Braille, indeed I should like it.'[30]

By 23 December, the orders for *My Early Life* were 9,202.[31]

Scribner closes out the year with a royalty statement reporting the following: 'Copies sold 4921, royalty 52 ½ amount $2594.03 advanced $425.78, US income tax $108.41 total $2059.84.'[32]

The first American edition would have three printings (two in 1930 and one in 1931) which totaled 8,960 copies.

Notes

1. Ronald I. Cohen, *Bibliography of the Writings of Sir Winston Churchill*, London, Thoemmes, 2006, p. 1372.
2. 'Mr. Churchill's Youth', *Daily News*, London, 26 August 1930, p. 6.
3. Cohen, *Bibliography*, p. 1372.
4. Churchill Archives, 26 September 1930 (CHAR 8/275).
5. *The Publisher & Bookseller*, London, 10 October 1930, p. 848.
6. 'A Career as a Prize', *News Chronicle*, London, 30 August 1930, p. 1; 'A Career as a Prize', *News Chronicle*, London, 17 September 1930, p. 9; 'A Career as a Prize', *News Chronicle*, London, 22 September 1930, p. 7; 'A Career as a Prize', *News Chronicle*, London, 2 September 1930, p. 1; *News Chronicle*, London, 24 September 1930, p. 9; 'Last Entry Form today', *News Chronicle*, London, 27 September 1930, p. 3; *Bedfordshire Times and Independent*, Bedford, UK, 26 December 1930, p. 7.
7. Churchill Archives, 20 October 1930 (CHAR 8/275).
8. Churchill Archives, 14 October 1930 (CHAR 8/275).
9. David Lough, *No More Champagne*, New York, Picador, 2015, Chapter 14.
10. Churchill Archives, 26 September 1930 (CHAR 8/275)
11. Churchill Archives, 27 September 1930 (CHAR 8/275)
12. Churchill Archives, 8 October 1930 (CHAR 8/275).
13. https://assets.publishing.service.gov.uk/government/uploads/system/uploads/attachment_data/file/594125/LibrariesAnnualReport2016Final.docx.pdf

14. Jackie Winter, *Lipsticks and Library Books: The Story of Boots Booklovers Library*, Dorset, Chantries Press, 2016, p. 89.
15. Churchill Archives, 10 October 1930 (CHAR 8/275).
16. Churchill Archives, 11 October 1930 (CHAR 8/275).
17. Churchill Archives, 14 October 1930 (CHAR 8/275).
18. Churchill Archives, 20 October 1930 (CHAR 8/275).
19. Cohen, *Bibliography*, p. 334.
20. Churchill Archives, 24 October 1930 (CHAR 8/277).
21. Cohen, *Bibliography*, p. 331.
22. Jonathan Rose, 'Churchill at Scribner's: A Study in Failure', *The Sewanee Review*, Vol. 121, No.1 (Winter) 2013). pp. 118–27.
23. Churchill Archives, 26 November 1930 (CHAR 8/275).
24. Churchill Archives, 2 December 1930 (CHAR 8/275).
25. Churchill Archives, 5 December 1930 (CHAR 8/277).
26. Churchill Archives, 8 December 1930 (CHAR 8/275).
27. Churchill Archives, 12 December 1930 (CHAR 8/275).
28. Churchill Archives, 19 December 1930 (CHAR 8/277).
29. Churchill Archives, 22 December 1930 (CHAR 8/275).
30. Churchill Archives, 27 December 1930 (CHAR 8/275).
31. Churchill Archives, 23 December 1930 (CHAT 8/275).
32. Churchill Archives, 31 December 1930 (CHAT 8/296).

CHAPTER 6

My Early Life: Previously Unrecorded English and Non-English Language Editions, Books, Recordings and Periodicals

The launch of *My Early Life* was well received, and several quick reprintings were carried out to meet demand. An interesting question that follows these early reprints is how have publishers subsequently dealt with the book over the last ninety-five years. One measure of a book's success and of the interest of any book collector is to note the number of editions, printings and variations that have been published in both English and non-English texts over time. The number of countries in which the book has been published is also of interest, as that is indicative of popularity. Thus, to provide a more complete understanding of Churchill as autobiographer and the impact of *My Early Life*, as well as to document how popular this book is, such information is provided here. A beginning source for this type of information on major authors is to consult a published bibliography. For Churchill, we are lucky to have a particularly useful and authoritative book.

The most comprehensive listing of editions, printings and variants of *My Early Life* is Ronald Cohen's *Bibliography of the Writings of Sir Winston Churchill*, which was published in 2006.[1] Cohen spent more than twenty years researching and writing this masterful work, and it is the benchmark against which all Churchill bibliographies must be compared. While accepting that it covers only books published before 2005, it remains the best source of information on Churchill's writings. It should be noted that Cohen focused primarily on English versions; he mentions non-English editions only briefly. Therefore, to address non-English versions, additional primary research is necessary.

In his bibliography, Cohen classifies Churchill's contributions to written materials into categories from 'A' to 'G'. The 'A' section includes books, pamphlets and leaflets wholly or substantially written by Churchill; 'B' includes works where Churchill contributed sections to books, pamphlets and leaflets; 'C' includes articles, reviews and news reports from war zones that appeared in serial publications; 'D' includes reports of speeches in publications such as books and pamphlets; 'E' includes reports of speeches in serial publications; 'F' includes communications such as letters and statements in books and pamphlets; and 'G' includes letters to editors.

This chapter contains information relating only to publications of or about *My Early Life*. This includes Cohen classification items A, B and C or items for which there is no Cohen classification such as DVDs. That is to say, they were not within the scope of his book or were published after Cohen's book went to press or not known to Cohen at the time of the publication of the book.

Cohen 'A items are 'works written wholly or substantially by Churchill'. This section contains all the books published by Churchill as the primary (single) author. *My Early Life* (*MEL*) is classified in the bibliography as 'Cohen A91', indicating that *MEL* was the ninety-first publication by Churchill that was wholly written by him. Each 'A' item represents a distinct written work. Within the A91 category, there are twenty-two major subcategories of English language titles, the last entry dated 2002. These subcategories indicate individual editions. Thus, there are twenty-two 'A' items. If reprints and variations of each primary edition are counted separately, the number of distinct books increases to ninety-six. In addition, there are forty-two non-English book entries mentioned in Cohen. Langworth (see below) adds seven more non-English books. In all, therefore, based on Cohen and Langworth, we now count 145 distinct versions of the book titled *My Early Life*.

For completeness, it is noted that there have been multiple bibliographies of Churchill's works, beginning in 1958 with Bernard J. Farmer's *A Bibliography of the Works of Sir Winston Churchill*.[2] It was privately published in London by the author and was mimeographed and stapled in dull green wrappers. There followed: Frederick Woods, *A Bibliography of the Works of Sir Winston Churchill, K.G. O.M. C.H. M.P.*[3]; Richard M. Langworth and H. Ashley Redburn, *Churchill Bibliographic Data*[4]; and Richard M. Langworth, *A Connoisseur's Guide to the Books of Sir Winston Churchill.*[5] A reference book by Curt J. Zoller, *Annotated Bibliography of Works About Sir Winston S. Churchill*, also contains books that include sections by Churchill, and it will be discussed later.[6] Cohen's *Bibliography* and Langworth's *Connoisseur's Guide* provide the most useful, detailed and authoritative information available. The two volumes also have the most information about Churchill's non-English editions, not just for *My Early Life* but across all Churchill volumes. Every serious Churchill collector should have a copy of each in their collection.

There are numerous publications that contain written words or speeches by Churchill. These publications may also contain works by other authors. These books are listed in Cohen as 'B' to 'G' items. Many of these categories contain material relevant to *My Early Life*. Appendix 8 Chapter 6 Unrecorded Books and Other Media at the end of the book lists previously unrecorded examples of printed and other media related to *My Early Life.*. The categories are:

i. English Language Editions (Books)
ii. Translated Editions (Books)
iii. Excerpts (Books)
iv. Anthologies and Selections (Books)
v. Readers Digest (Books & Magazines)
vi. Periodicals (Journals & Magazines)
vii. Movies, tapes, DVDs, etc. (Audio/Visual)

i. English Language Books

In the English Language section, there are fifteen entries not previously documented in the above reference books. The rarest of the entries is the Canadian first edition, which can only be identified as such if the book has the Canadian dust jacket with the Thomas Nelson imprint, as the book itself is a British first edition. As most people have not seen the dust jacket, a description is warranted. The colour, as for the first British edition, is printed in black on deep reddish-purple paper. (See Figure 1 for an image of front, spine, back of dust jacket, and front and rear dust jacket flaps.)

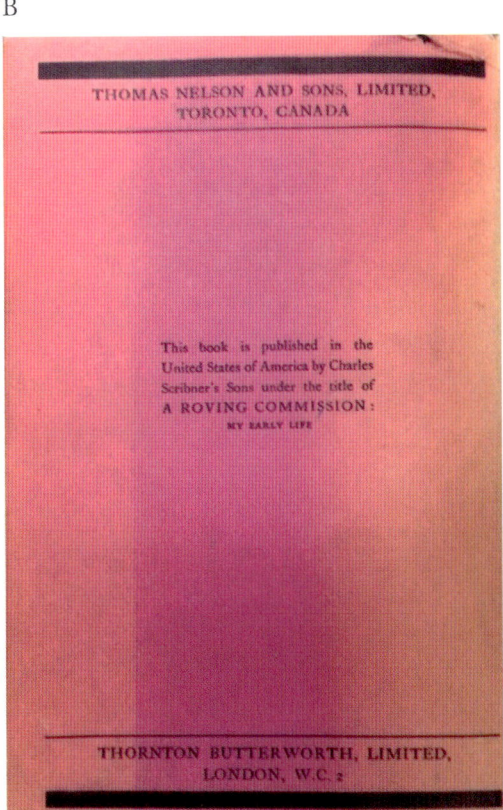

Figure 1. Canadian 1st edition 1930, dust jacket, front (A), back (B), spine (C), front flap (D) and back flap (E) As can be seen, there is mottled fading on the front and back of the dust jacket and severe fading on the spine.

CHAPTER 6 : *MY EARLY LIFE*: PREVIOUSLY UNRECORDED

C

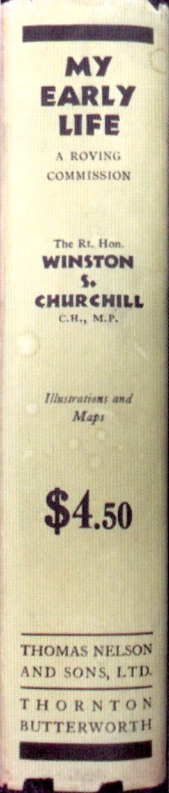

D

MY EARLY LIFE
A ROVING COMMISSION
By
The Rt. Hon.
WINSTON S. CHURCHILL
C.H., M.P.

THE name of Winston Churchill is well known to-day. He at once springs to mind as First Lord of the Admiralty, as Chancellor of the Exchequer, as author of 'The World Crisis.' But to those who remember the time of the Sudan and Boer Wars, another Winston Churchill is known—the brilliant officer and war correspondent whose high-spirited actions and writings brought him renown.

Mr. Churchill describes his life from his earliest recollections to his entry into politics ; from a private school to Harrow, to Sandhurst, and then as a subaltern in the 4th Hussars. From the moment of receiving his commission, Mr. Churchill was lured by war. He saw the Cuban rebellion, the Malakand and Tirah fighting, the Sudan and Boer Wars. These pages are alive with the thrill of cavalry charges and hand-to-hand conflict ; of escape from prison-camp and lonely days and nights on the veld. Great figures pass by—Kitchener, Buller, Roberts, Botha and many others—on a background that changes from the dust of the desert to the grassy plains ; to the Mahdi's fanatical army at Omdurman ; beleaguered Ladysmith. . . .

Then there are the years at home. Great names occur again in those of Salisbury, Rosebery, Chamberlain, Morley, Wolseley. The book closes with Mr. Churchill established in Parliament and rising to a new fame. It will reveal the author as a man who, by his own unaided efforts, has carved for himself a great career—a life of endeavour, of adventure, of achievement and brilliant success. *It will take its place among the great autobiographies of our day.*

E

AUTOBIOGRAPHIES & BIOGRAPHIES

THE WORLD I USED TO KNOW
1860–1912
By Marie von Bunsen
Illustrated   Demy 8vo   18s. net

THE LIFE OF FLORENCE NIGHTINGALE
By I. B. O'Malley
Illustrated   Demy 8vo   15s. net

RECOLLECTIONS OF A DEFECTIVE MEMORY
By Fred Kerr
Illustrated   Demy 8vo   15s. net

THE LIFE OF SIR WALTER SCOTT
By Stephen Gwynn
Portraits   Demy 8vo   15s. net

THE WAYS OF YESTERDAY
By A. M. W. Stirling
Illustrated   Demy 8vo   18s. net

THE LIFE OF BENITO MUSSOLINI
By Margherita G. Sarfatti
Illustrated   Demy 8vo   15s. net

SYBIL THORNDIKE
By Russell Thorndike
Illustrated   Demy 8vo   21s. net

NUDA VERITAS
By Clare Sheridan
Illustrated   Demy 8vo   21s. net

THE LIFE OF SIR CHARLES HANBURY-WILLIAMS
Ambassador at the Russian Court, 1756
By The Earl of Ilchester
Illustrated   Lge Demy 8vo   21s. net

LETTERS AND LEADERS OF MY DAY
By T. M. Healy, K.C.
Illustrated 2 vols   Lge Demy 8vo   £2. 2s. net

The Times Book Club edition is worth mentioning, as that book club supplied a large number of books to the public (see Figure 2) In fact, over the years, multiple books by Churchill were offered by the club. For a discussion of the book club and *My Early Life*, see Chapter 3.

ii. Translated Editions

The section on Translated Editions is, to the author's knowledge, the first in-depth study or listing of non-English versions of *MEL*. Therefore, a detailed study of the literature and libraries has been undertaken to find as many examples as possible. The results show that there are more than 110 non-English versions of *MEL* and that they span a wide geographic and linguistic range. They are printed in twenty-five languages and in thirty-one non-English-speaking countries. The Danish and Swedish languages account for the largest number, with sixteen and fifteen versions, respectively. There are eleven German, eight Italian, seven French, seven Portuguese and six Norwegian versions. Some interesting and uncommon non-English editions of *MEL* are shown in Figures 2 to 13.

iii. Excerpts

The section on Excerpts has expanded the most out of any of the sections. It now contains 263 entries, of which 243 are not recorded in Cohen's *Bibliography*. There are both English and non-English books containing excerpts from *MEL*. A full discussion of the topics which were excepted from *MEL*, as well as the impact that these excerpts have had on the literature, is covered in depth in Chapter 7.

iv. Anthologies

The Anthologies section in the appendix lists anthologies that contain excerpts solely from Churchill's works that contain an excerpt from *MEL*. Multi-author anthologies that include Churchill are listed in the section on 'B' items.

v. Reader's Digest

Reader's Digest is a well-known publisher of condensed versions of successful books worldwide. Their publications are targeted to audiences who desire a quick read or a summary-like approach. *Reader's Digest* has published many of Churchill's books in this format. *My Early Life* was no exception. There are least twenty examples known in both English and non-English versions, as listed in Appendix 8 Chapter 6 Unrecorded Books and Other Media.

vi. Periodicals
This section provides new materials related to *My Early Life* in journals and magazines.

vii. Movies, Tapes, DVDs, etc.
This section, which does not appear in Cohen's *Bibliography*, provides materials related to excerpts from *My Early Life*.

Notes
1. Ronald I. Cohen, *Bibliography of the Writings of Sir Winston Churchill*, New York, Thoemmes, 2006.
2. Bernard J. Farmer, *A Bibliography of the Works of Sir Winston Churchill*, London, privately published by the author, 1958.
3. Frederick Woods, *A Bibliography of the Works of Sir Winston Churchill, K.G. O.M. C.H. M.P*, London, Nicholas Vane, 1963, revised 1969, 1975, and an expanded reissue 1979.
4. Richard M. Langworth, and H. Ashley Redburn, *Churchill Bibliographic Data*, Hopkinton, NH, International Churchill Society, 1992.
5. Richard M. Langworth, *A Connoisseur's Guide to the Books of Sir Winston Churchill*, London, Brassey's, 1998, Second revised edition, 2000.
6. Curt J. Zoller, *Annotated Bibliography of Works About Sir Winston Churchill*, Armonk, NY, M.E. Sharpe, 2004.

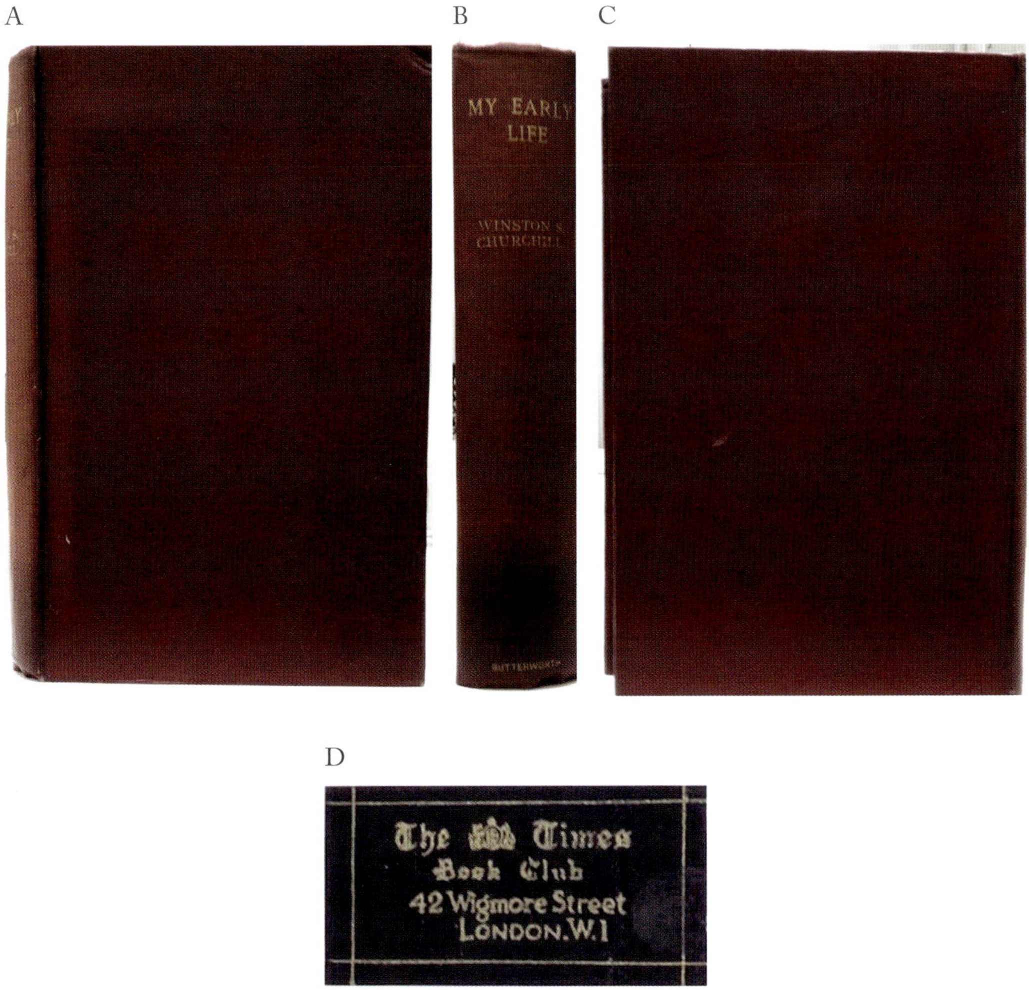

Figure 2. Times Book Club Edition, London, 1930, front (A) and back boards (B), spine (C) and label (D).

CHAPTER 6 : *MY EARLY LIFE*: PREVIOUSLY UNRECORDED

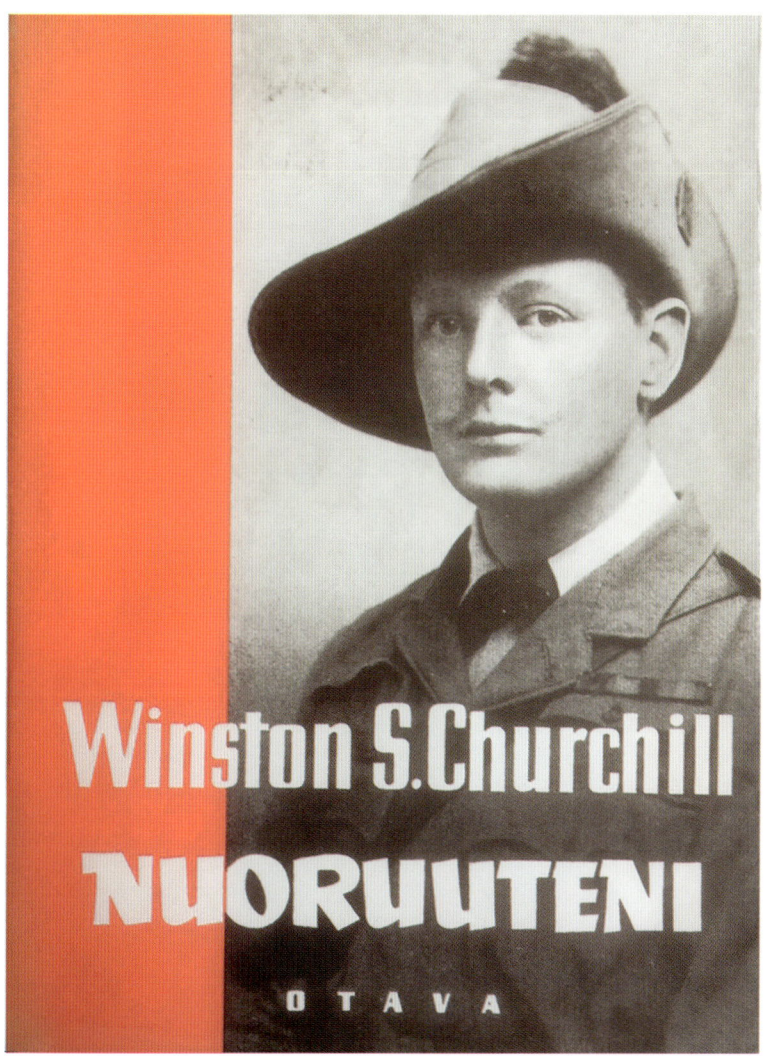

Figure 3. Finnish 1st Ed., 1954, card wrappers front cover.

Figure 4. Finnish 1938 Ed., abridgement of *MEL* known as *Sotavanki (Prisoner of War)*, front board.

CHAPTER 6 : *MY EARLY LIFE*: PREVIOUSLY UNRECORDED

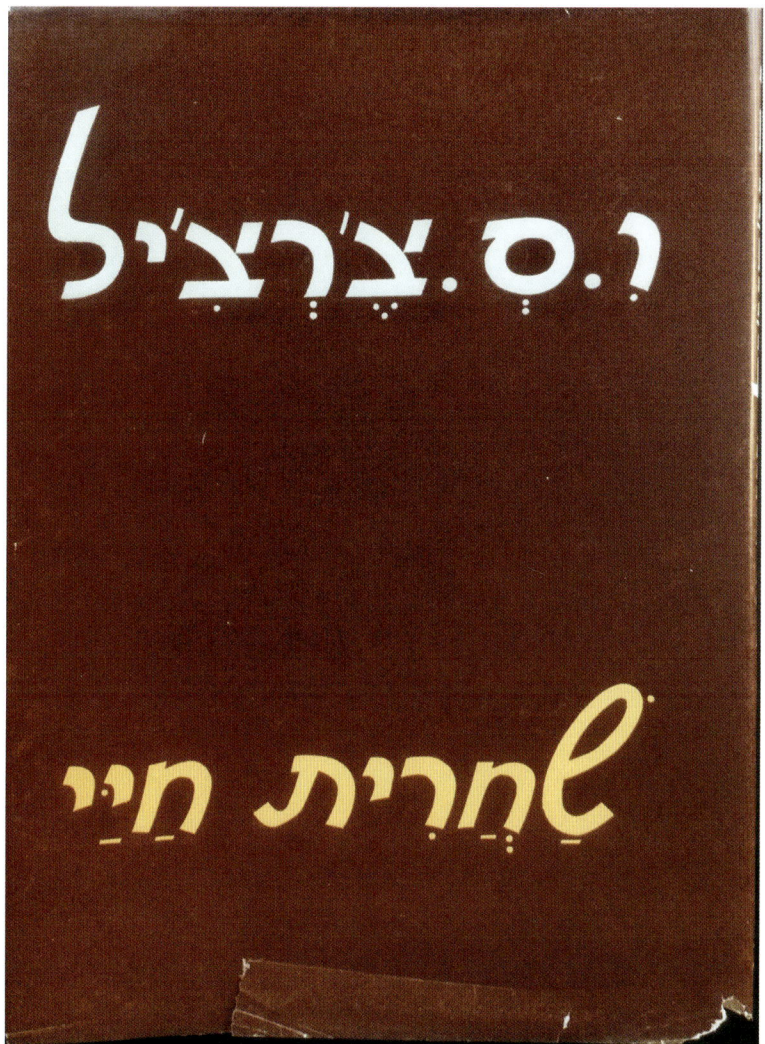

Figure 5. Hebrew 1st Ed., 1944, front dustjacket.

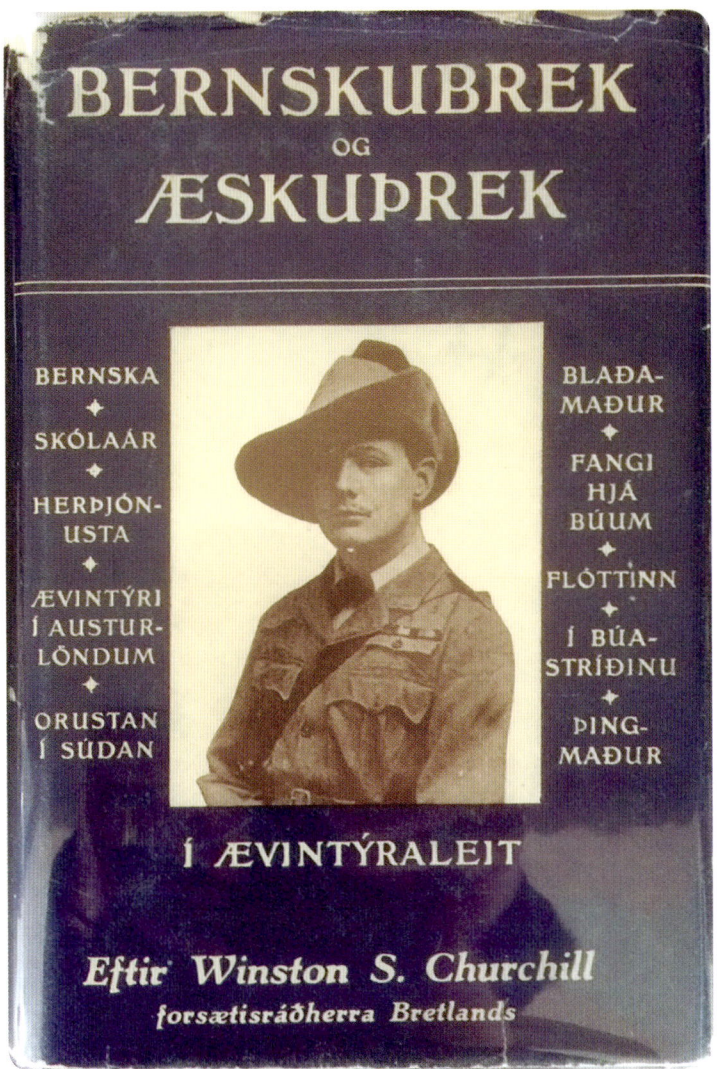

Figure 6. Icelandic 1st Ed., 1944, front dust jacket.

CHAPTER 6 : *MY EARLY LIFE*: PREVIOUSLY UNRECORDED

Figure 7. Italian 1st Ed., 1935, wrappers front.

Figure 8. Korean 2nd Ed., 1991, wrappers front.

CHAPTER 6 : *MY EARLY LIFE*: PREVIOUSLY UNRECORDED

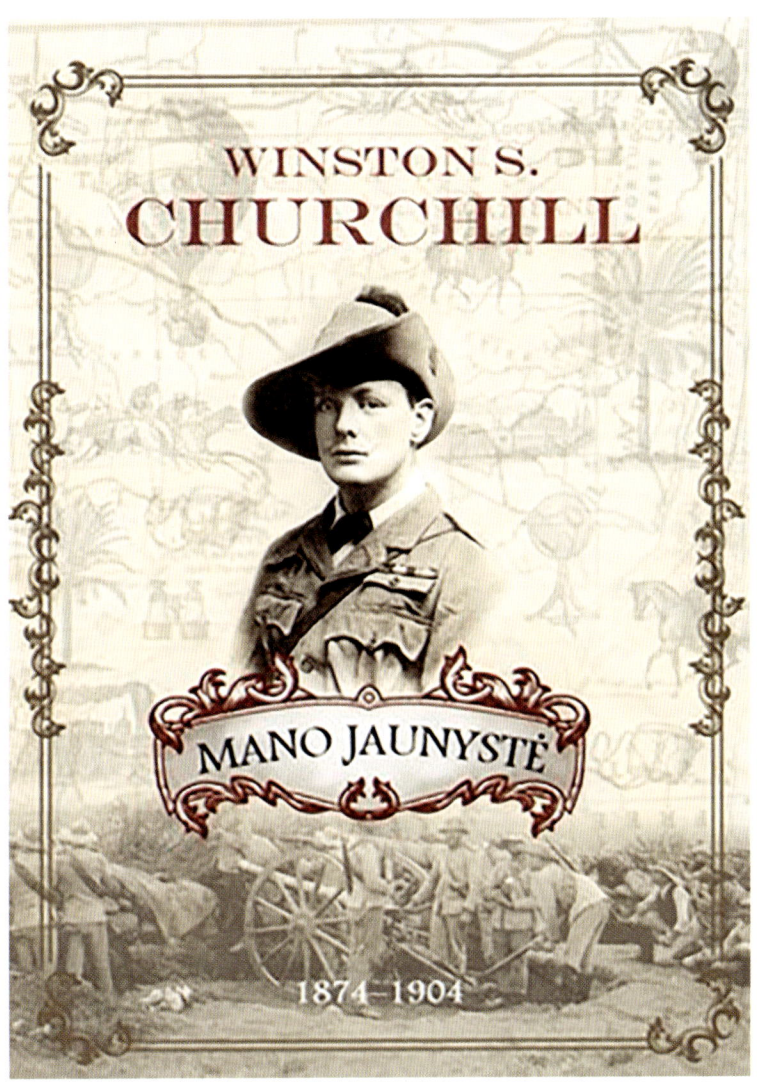

Figure 9. Lithuanian 1st Ed., 2019, hardback front.

Figure 10. Norwegian 1st Ed., 1935, wrappers front.

Figure 11. Norwegian 3rd Ed., 1956, hardback, dust jacket front.

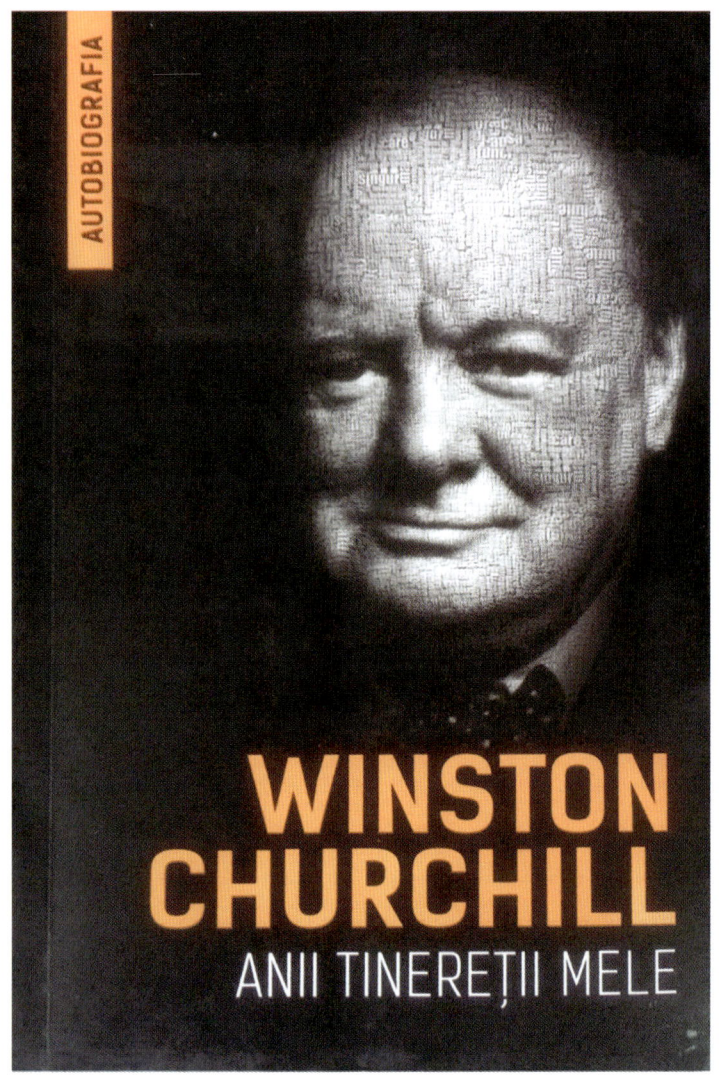

Figure 12. Romanian 1st Ed., 2019, wrappers front.

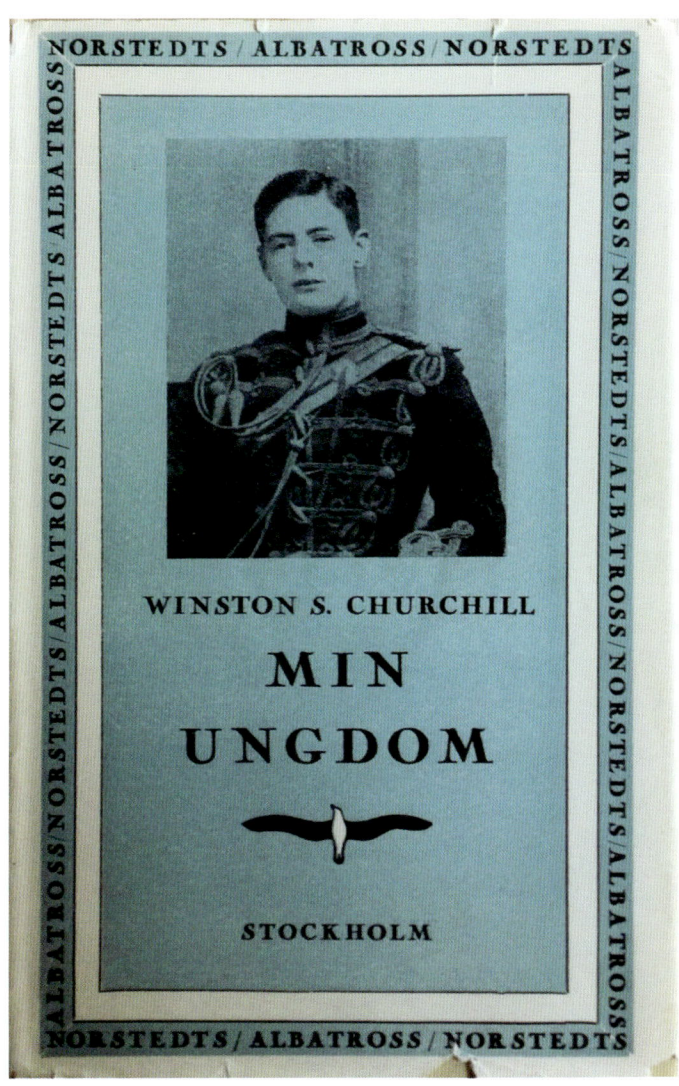

Figure 13. Swedish 1948 Ed., hardback, dust jacket front.

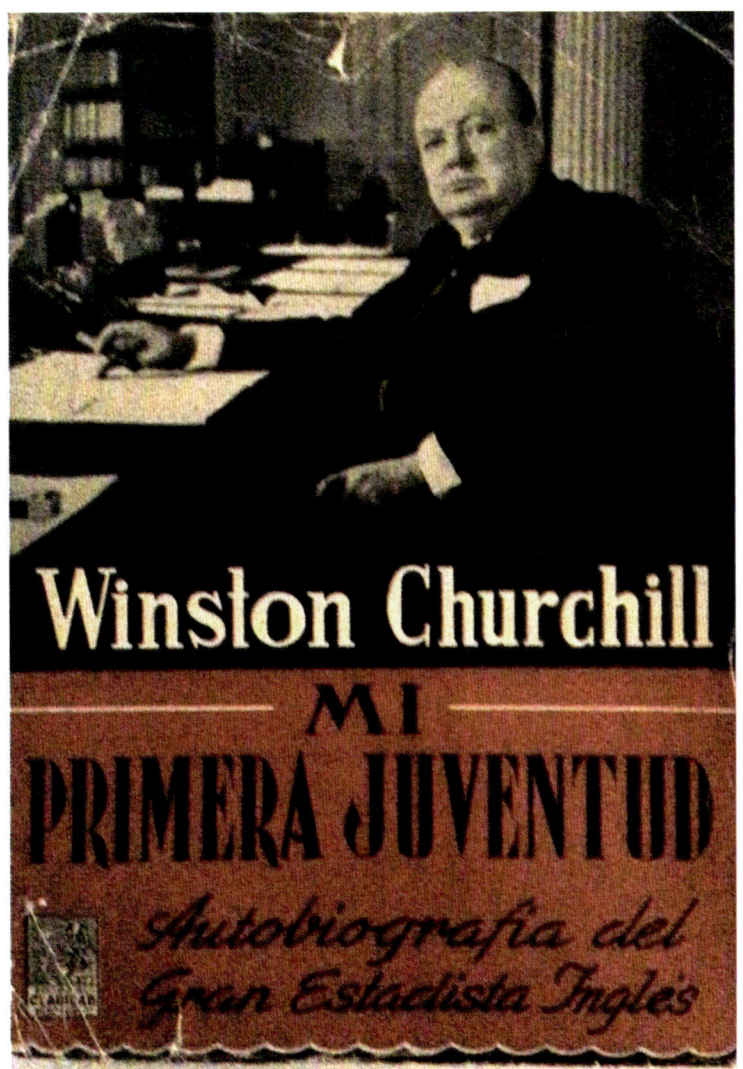

Figure 14. Uruguay 1st Ed., 1941, wrappers front.

CHAPTER 6 : *MY EARLY LIFE*: PREVIOUSLY UNRECORDED

Figure 15. Japanese 1st Ed., 1950, book spine (A), slip-case spine (B), and slip-case front (C).

CHAPTER 7

Global Impact of *My Early Life*

A DIVERSE RANGE OF PARAMETERS IS USED TO MEASURE BOTH THE short- and long-term impacts of a book. These metrics include number of books sold; number of editions and reprints; number of translations; the positivity, breadth and frequency of book reviews; the diversity of material cited; and the total number of citations of the book. Additional benchmarks may include whether or not the book has been converted into other media such as movies, audiobooks, or periodical excerpts, and if the book and its author has won recognised prizes or awards. The longevity of impact should also be considered. On the basis of measurement by such parameters, Churchill's *My Early Life* is a very impressive book.

Since *My Early Life/A Roving Commission*'s publication in 1930, the book has been continuously in print. There have been over 111 editions and printings in the US, the UK and Canada in both hardcover and paperback formats. Most of these have been well covered and described in great detail in Cohen's magnificent book, *Bibliography of the Writings of Sir Winston Churchill*.[1] *My Early Life* has also been published in thirty non-English-speaking countries in twenty-five languages, with over 110 editions and printings in various formats. Although Cohen and Langworth mention some of these foreign editions in their books (42 in Cohen and 7 not in Cohen are in Langworth), the lists are far from comprehensive.[2] Chapter 6 of this book provided information on these foreign (non-English) editions.

There are at least two editions in braille (English and French), and these are listed in Appendix 8 Chapter 6 Unrecorded Books and Other Media. There are at least seven audiobooks available.

The book or substantial sections of it have been published in eighteen *Reader's Digest* magazine issues or book anthologies including ones published in Swedish, German, Italian, Spanish and French. *My Early Life* has been published in part in seven Churchill anthologies. Excerpts have been published in twenty-two periodicals since 1930 – and this does not count the pre-1930 articles which contributed to the production of *My Early Life*, as was described in Chapter 4.

The 1972 epic British feature-length movie *Young Winston* was based directly on *My Early Life*. It was written and produced by Carl Foreman and directed by Richard Attenborough. It was nominated for three Academy Awards: Best Screenplay, Best Art Direction, and Best Costume Design. According to one of the movie brochures, Churchill had invited Foreman to visit him in 1961 after he had seen Foreman's movie the *Guns of Navarone*. At that meeting, Churchill had suggested that *My Early Life* would make an excellent film. Whether or not this is true is unknown; Foreman's name is not listed in the Chartwell visitors log. Churchill had been thinking about and exploring the possibility of a movie version of the book since at least 1940. He mentions this in a letter in 1956 that he wrote to his wife:

> What I have to tell you about is the downfall of my hopes about the film. Apparently, I sold it in 1941 to Warner Brothers for £7,500! They have done nothing about it all the time; and when we asked Nicholl Manisty if there was any record of any truck with them they said 'No.' However, yesterday afternoon they wrote a letter saying they had found a document which coupled with the American records make it quite clear that I have no possession. ... This seemed like such a good thing and so simple that I am sorry that it falls to the ground.[2]

This all changed in 1960 when Warner Brothers gave up the film rights and MGM decided not to go ahead with the project. Churchill's private secretary Anthony Montague Brown negotiated with Carl Foreman, who was at Columbia Pictures, for the rights to a film based on *My Early Life* for £100,000.[3] As noted, the film was eventually made in 1972, seven years after Churchill's death. There are extensive documents in the Churchill Archives concerning the film rights and negotiations. The film was shown worldwide and was critically acclaimed, winning numerous awards, and it resulted in the production of multiple soundtracks and videos/DVDs. (See Appendix 8 Chapter 6 Unrecorded Books and Other Media.)

One of the greatest measures of the book's impact is how often its ideas, events, concepts and writing style are cited by other authors when they incorporate direct text of *My Early Life* into their own publications. These authors cite Churchill's writing and thought processes as being emblematic or illustrative of a concept or style of writing that they are attempting to pursue or promote in their own publication. An extension of this concept is how often the materials are utilised directly for teaching purposes, for example, in textbooks or course syllabi or for the purpose of learning a new language. *My Early Life* performs highly in all these measures.

The first task in creating such a list of books is to decide what universe of publications should be analysed. For the purposes of this book, works have been selected in which significant tracts of text (more than just a few sentences) have quoted from *My Early Life*; the books chosen have not been written by Churchill himself, nor are they biographies of Churchill or predominantly about him. A book about the Boer War written by another author is included only if Churchill's role in the overall war is described with significant excerpts from *My Early Life*. Books such as encyclopedias, dictionaries, books of quotations or anecdotes and 'everything you need to know' books were excluded.

The closest analogous published list would be the Section B category in Cohen's *Bibliography of the Writings of Sir Winston Churchill*.[1] That list includes publications by an author other than Churchill in which a Churchill contribution from any source is present. There are 220 entries in Cohen related to all of Churchill's writings. Twenty of those items relate directly and only to *My Early Life*. A search for additional examples was undertaken via a detailed computer search of archives, libraries and other internet sources After careful screening, 263 books (including the 20 'Cohen B' items) were identified. These books would all now be classified as 'Cohen B' entries.

These 263 items have been analysed and then listed chronologically. In each case, the standard bibliographic information for the book is documented, along with the topic being discussed and the pages where the excerpted text can be found. This is followed by the location in *My Early Life* from which the text has been taken. This allows the reader to quickly scan which books relate to which incidents.

The diversity in the categories of books that incorporate and discuss sections of text from *My Early Life* is as broad as the qualities and traits of

Topic	Frequency
Harrow/School/Examinations	88
Great writing skills and command of English	36
Escape from the Boers	34
Cavalry Charge	34
India (includes self-education)	25
Ireland (childhood)	13
Large extract of book	11
Nanny Everest	11
Admonition to a new Generation ('Come on Now')	8
POW	7
Jump off bridge	7
Sandhurst	5
Toy soldiers	5
Fathers and sons	4
First Speech (Empire Theatre)	4
Flogging	4
Cuba	4
Fathers and sons	4
Armoured Train	3
Lake Lausanne (near-drowning)	3
C96 'Broomhandle' Mauser	2
Skin Graft (Sudan)	2
Horses (give to children)	1
Churchill to Churchill	1
Politics	1
Power of naps	1
Why I didn't go to university	1
Pushing Amery into pool	1
Bungalows (India)	1
General Botha	1
Guerilla warfare (SA)	1
Free will or predestination	1
First speech in Parliament	1
Quadratic equations	1

Table 1. Topics from *MEL* Reproduced and Quoted in Later Works (Cohen B items)

Churchill himself. The categories include textbooks; improvement books on writing and speaking which highlight Churchill's use of the English language, sentence structure and storytelling; adventure books; books on military life and prisoners of war; books on experiences in school and learning disabilities; lifestyle books, books on horses and polo; and even books on topics as unexpected as nannies or calculus.

Table 1 categorises the 'episodes', topics or sections from *My Early Life* that are cited in these works by their frequency of appearance. By far the most common topic is that of Churchill's experience as a young student and his proclaimed inability to conquer exams or learn the classics, his perceived isolation and unhappiness, and his viewing himself as a 'troublesome boy'. In this section is also included his perceived learning disabilities. Many authors 'diagnose' Churchill with a wide range of clinical conditions and learning disabilities – from most of which Churchill likely did not suffer. Such ill-formed notions will be noted in the descriptions that follow.

The second most common topic relates to his superlative skills in writing and the use of the English language. The importance and quality of his writings, in the minds of many people – including this author – is what Churchill will be remembered for, second only to his importance as a leader leading up to and through the Second World War.

The next three most common topics relate to episodes which occurred during his military service in the Sudan, South Africa and India. The common topic most unexpected at the start of this research was the frequency and depth of feeling with which authors of books related to nannies sensed and wrote about Churchill's interaction with and love for his nanny, Mrs Everest. The surprise was not that he had had such feelings for his nanny – of which anyone who knows about Churchill would be well aware – but that books concerning nannies cited Churchill as such a good example of the positive impact that a nanny could have on a child. The relationship between Winston and Mrs Everest was more that of a mother and child than a hired supervisor and her charge. Churchill's feelings for Mrs Everest were deep and long-lasting.

The remainder of the topics as listed in Table 1 are less-frequently cited but, nevertheless, still important.

Examples of how and why these authors chose sections from *My Early Life* are instructive for understanding the positive impact of Churchill's book. Each entry will show vignettes from the author's writing, or Churchill's writing in *My Early Life*, as simply foretastes of what might be expected if one chose to explore these books. The entries below are arranged chronologically as relates to Churchill's life and using the topics as listed in Table 1. This is only a small sample of the numerous topics and books.

LEARNING TO READ

As a very young child, Churchill lived in Ireland with his parents and his nanny Mrs Everett, who will be discussed in several entries in this section. It was she who taught Winston how to read. In the book *The Open Door: When Writers First Learned to Read*, Gilbar describes how twenty-nine well-known authors from Benjamin Franklin to Stephen King learned to read and the experiences they had as they learned. Churchill's story is told through Churchill's eyes as he described it in *My Early Life*. Churchill was taught to read as preparation for being taught by a governess. As Churchill relates, 'In order to prepare for this day Mrs. Everest produced a book called *Reading without Tears*. It certainly did not justify its title in my case. I was made aware that before the Governess arrived I must be able to read without tears. We toiled each day. My nurse pointed with a pen at different letters. I thought it all very tiresome.[4]

ENGLISH PROSE AND GRAMMAR

In the book *Portals: Reading, Writing and Critical Thinking*, Segall and Brown use examples from the literature to teach students how to understand and interpret literature so as to become better critical thinkers and write more impactfully.[5] The authors state:

> In this selection, Churchill demonstrates to educators that their lowliest students may some day be in a position to command profound respect for their criticism of the education they receive. ... In this unforgettable indictment of the British educational system from the perspective of a former student, he attacks the substitution of memorization for understanding, absorption in irrelevant subject matter, the meaninglessness of grades, and failure to facilitate students' interests and aspirations. ... [Churchill had] a dedication to English Style prose. Churchill did not hesitate to interrupt speakers in debates

in Parliament to correct their usage of the English language. … Even as a student at Harrow, he already wrote well.

Following a six-page excerpt of Churchill's educational experiences at a number of the schools he attended, the authors provide sections for the student on Reading Closely, Rhetorical Considerations, Class Discussions, Collaborative Activities, Writing Suggestions, and Related Reading. These sections highlight the techniques Churchill utilised to make his writing impactful, for example, understatement, self-deprecating humor, contextual clues for the reader, and the use of what has been called 'Churchillian prose'.

Segall and Brown note that Churchill frequently uses words such as 'invidious' and 'incongruous', which, though not simple words, convey precise information and are worthy of remembering and using. They also note that even though he frequently expresses humour and personal feeling, he maintains a certain tone of formality. Such use of Churchill's material for educating students is made frequently by other educators.

ENGLISH WRITING SKILLS

A Short Course in Writing Skills is just what it says: a course teaching secondary school students the skills needed to write impactful and interesting prose, with instruction on topics from punctuation, grammar and vocabulary to sentence and paragraph structure.[6] Twice in his book, Bruffee cites a section from *My Early Life* covering Churchill's Harrow experience. In this quoted section, Churchill describes himself as being considered too stupid for the classics, so he was forced to learn English for an extended period of time. Bruffee, in one case, is looking to teach grammar and, in the other, sentence structure. Another similar book is *Themes from Experience: A Manual of Literature for Writers*, which uses Churchill's section on his experience in school as a jumping-off point for students to hone their writing skills.[7]

LEARNING LATIN

In this episode in *My Early Life*, Churchill arrives at a new school and describes learning Latin declensions for the first time. He is befuddled when he learns that there is a form for nouns naming objects that is reserved for when one addresses said object – in his example, a table. He innocently asks the master why this is so, as he never addresses a table. His teacher tells him to stop being impertinent or he would be severely punished. This is a frequently quoted section that is at the same time funny, sad and quite surreal. In the textbook *Headway Advanced Student's Book*, the student is provided with this section of *My Early Life* and then asked a series of questions to check their comprehension of what Churchill was attempting to convey, and whether they thought teaching in this manner would be successful.[8]

LEARNING AND DISABILITIES

There is a group of books whose authors have used quotations from *My Early Life* of Churchill's description of how he viewed his early education to label him with a vast array of diagnoses from attention deficit disorder, hyperactivity, and hyper-aggressiveness to dyslexia. In my opinion, most appear to have been far off the mark. One such book is *Mommy, I Can't Sit Still: Coping With the Hyperactive and Hyperaggressive Child*.[9] In it, O'Leary quotes extensively from *My Early Life* on Churchill's stated problems in school and concludes that 'Churchill was a boy with academic and behavioral problems, and at the age of nine he was removed from school because of his problems. His childhood behavior was described by biographers as intractable, stubborn, spoiled, unpromising. Today, he would be called a "conduct problem."' Clearly, this psychology professor did not know or understand Churchill or the literature about him. Being beaten (the reason he was removed from his school) is not a learning or behavioural problem.

PUBLIC SCHOOL EDUCATION

The Old School Tie: The Phenomenon of the English Public School provides a comprehensive, in-depth and yet readable and enjoyable discussion of public schools from their historical evolution to their quirks, strengths and weaknesses.[10] Gathorne-Hardy describes Churchill's learning the classics, and the difficulty with the Latin declensions that was so humorously and painfully described in *My Early Life*. However, the author provides additional insight when he comments that 'Churchill is always represented as a complete dunce at school (a legend he cultivated). Indeed he is the archetypal comforter of all those bad at work. In fact, this isn't so. The truth is more interesting. Churchill was not in the least stupid nor bad at work; he was only bad at classics, a very different thing.'

EDUCATION

Unlike most books, which focus on a single episode from *My Early Life*, James W. Muller's interesting symposium compendium *Character & Identity: The Sociological Foundation of Literary and Historical Perspectives* contains a chapter that provides an insightful discussion of the whole of Churchill's educational process ('Winston Churchill at School').[11] The chapter spans his entire childhood and adolescence from early learning in Ireland through his time at St Georges, Brighton, Harrow and Sandhurst. Muller, a well-known scholar and Churchill expert, uses extensive quotations from *My Early Life* to make and support his suppositions concerning the impact that Churchill's education had had on him – and the impact that Churchill, in turn, had on education. It makes for interesting reading.

FATHERS AND SONS

Churchill was highly influenced by his father, even if the interactions between them were never of the quantity or quality that Churchill had desired. In Sulzberger's book *Fathers and Children: How Famous Leaders were Influenced by Their Fathers*, the chapter 'The Monument: Lord Randolph and Winston S. Churchill' addresses their complicated relationship. He uses extensive quotes from *My Early Life* to demonstrate that the long-term effects of these interactions persisted throughout Churchill's life.[12]

FIRST SPEECH (EMPIRE THEATRE), AND INDIA

Churchill's writings from *My Early Life* have often been quoted in books that describe what life was like during a specific era in British history. In *The Jubilee Years 1887-1897*, Hudson uses two excerpts. The first covers the time when Churchill was incensed by the members of the Temperance League who had attempted to close down the promenade with the accompanying bars adjacent to the Empire Theatre in Leicester Square, claiming that the activities taking place there were immoral. His first impromptu public speech outside the theatre was given to oppose their actions. In the second speech, Churchill describes life as a young soldier in India and how important polo was to him.[13]

CUBA

In London while on leave from the 4th Hussars in 1895, Churchill arranged for himself and a fellow officer to visit Cuba to obtain experience in one of the few active military confrontations in the world at that time: the Cuban insurrection against Spain. Churchill would be both an observer and a paid war correspondent. It was the first time Churchill came under hostile gunfire and his first time as a paid correspondent – on both counts, exactly what he had striven for. In *Uneasy Neighbors: Cuba and the United States*, Hoff and Regler employ extensive quotations from *My Early Life* to describe how Churchill rode with General Valdez and what the conditions were like.[14] In Cuba, Churchill obtained the experience and exposure he had desired.

SELF-EDUCATION (INDIA)

Contemporary writer Nicholas Basbanes has won many awards for his books on books, printing and bibliomania. In 2005, he published *Every Book Its Reader: The Power of the Printed Word to Stir the World*, which provides a fascinating tale of 'writings that have "made things happen" in the world, works that nudged the course of history and fired the imagination of countless influential people.'[15] Basbanes has chosen to include Churchill and his self-education while on duty in India, when Churchill began to voraciously read a vast array of literature including Gibbon and Macaulay. As Basbanes notes, 'Fittingly, Churchill began his course of self-instruction with Gibbon and was "immediately dominated" by both the story and the style.' Basbanes goes on to quote Churchill's description in *My Early Life* of this time in his life and how it inspired him to write.

INDIA: FRONTIER WAR

As it Happens: A Cascade Collection of Reportage collates stories of events that changed the world. It has been written for use in the classroom, specifically, to provide a wide range of literature that will appeal to students while also teaching them writing skills.[16] The editor has chosen to quote Churchill's description of his war experience in India.

INDIA: KHYBER

Churchill's descriptions of the battles in which he participated have been frequently cited in books written about those battles. One such book is *Khyber: British India's North West Frontier*. In it, Miller, describing the Malakand Force and Sir Bindon Blood as they attacked the Pathan swordsmen, notes, 'His [Churchill's] recollection of the episode is worth quoting at some length.'[17]

CAVALRY CHARGE AT OMDURMAN

Ernest Hemingway, the noted novelist, short story writer, journalist, and winner of the 1954 Nobel Prize in Literature, edited the book *Men at War*, a book on a topic he knew well.[18] He chose to include Churchill's description of his cavalry charge in the Sudan, a highly charged, impactful excerpt from *My Early Life*. Hemingway wrote in the introduction to *Men at War*,

> This collection of stories, accounts, and narratives is an attempt to give a true picture of men at war. It is not a propaganda book. It seeks to instruct and inform rather than to influence anyone's opinion. Its only and absolute standard for inclusion has been the soundness and truth of the material. I have seen much war in my lifetime and I hate it profoundly. But there are worse things than war; and all of them come with defeat. The more you hate war, the more you know that once you have been forced into it, for whatever reason it may be, you have to win it. You have to win it and get rid of the people that made it, and see that, this time, it never comes to us again.

How Churchillian! It seems rather obvious why Hemingway chose that section from *My Early Life*.

CAVALRY CHARGE AT OMDURMAN

The Faber Book of Reportage is a collection of the 'best' eye-witness accounts of world events from the plague in Athens in 430 BC to the fall of President Marco in the Philippines in 1986, as chosen by the editor, John Carey.[19] He has chosen Churchill's description of the cavalry charge from *My Early Life*.

CAVALRY CHARGE

The Great Horse Omnibus, from Homer to Hemingway is an anthology that describes famous horse stories throughout history.[20] The editor, Thurston Macauley, has chosen to include Churchill's description of the cavalry charge in 1898. (Of interest is that the noted singer and actor Bing Crosby wrote the introduction to the book.)

CAVALRY CHARGE

Another group of books in which Churchill is frequently cited are ones that address what it means to be a professional soldier. In *The Profession of Arms*, General Sir John Hackett 'attempts to uncover the forces that have shaped the professional men-at-arms of today and to find their lessons of relevance to today and the future.'[21] Certainly, this is a realm much occupied by Churchill, and the author has used Churchill's description in *My Early Life* of the cavalry charge to answer many questions.

C96 'BROOMHANDLE' MAUSER

Certainly, one of the most unique citations from *My Early Life* comes from two episodes, both relating to Churchill's choice of the C96 Mauser as his personal sidearm. In his book *The 'Broomhandle' Mauser*, Ferguson relates:

> Easily the most famous proponent of the C96 was future Prime Minister Winston Spencer Churchill, who purchased his first example in London on 25 July 1898, just prior to departing for the Sudan. ... Churchill sang the C96's praises as a sidearm superior in every way to both the revolver and other self-loading pistols. ... He apparently purchased another four examples on his return to Britain later in 1898.[22]

Fergusson quotes two episodes from *My Early Life*, one in the Sudan and the other in South Africa, to show how Churchill used the Mauser in battle.

SKIN GRAFT

During the war in Sudan, Churchill donates skin for a skin graft for a fellow soldier. Churchill 'wore' his scarred donation site as a badge of honour for the remainder of his life. Nuland, in his book *Doctors: The Biography of Medicine*, uses Churchill's description of the incident from *My Early Life* and then goes on to describe how unusual it was that, under the conditions in which the graft occurred, it should be successful.[23]

ESCAPE FROM THE BOERS

Traditions in Literature: America Reads utilises a section on Churchill's escape from the Boers in 1899 to teach comprehension of the written word.[24] Following a thirteen-page excerpt from *MEL*, students are provided a discussion session in which they must interpret Churchill's meaning of various passages, for example, 'No walls are so hard to pierce as living walls,' and are required to write about the tone of the writings and how Churchill portrays himself with both facts and feelings. A related textbook, *Insights: Themes in Literature,* uses the same Churchill excerpt to challenge students to better understand topics; for example, why Churchill is a man to remember, the writing techniques he used, and to learn about imaginative language.[25]

ESCAPE FROM THE BOERS

Escape stories presented in anthologies are extremely popular literature. One such example is *True Stories of Great Escapes,* which features Churchill's experiences taken from *My Early Life.*[26]

POLO

In *The World of Polo Past and Present*, P.N. Watson states that 'Winston Churchill, who played polo with the 4th Hussars, gave a very good idea, in *My Early Life*, of how much of the life of a cavalry officer serving in India was taken up with the game.' This is followed by a three-page excerpt from *My Early Life.*[27]

NANNIES

Gathorn-Hardy, in *The Unnatural History of the Nanny* devotes an entire chapter ('The Nanny Phenomenon and the Case of Winston Churchill') to a detailed description of the interaction between Mrs Everest and Winston.[28] Mrs Everest was engaged as Winston's nanny shortly after he was born in 1874. Churchill's son Randolph notes that 'From that time forward, until her death in 1895 when Winston was twenty, she was destined to be the principal confidant of his joys, his troubles, and his hopes.'[29] However, she was more than those things. As noted in the above book,

> The depth of Winston's love for Mrs. Everest, and hers for him, is shown by how long it continued. Its simple strength shines forth in their letters to each other. 'Winny dear, do try to keep the new suit expressly for visiting, the brown one will do for everyday wear, please do this to please me. I hope you will not take cold my darling take care not to get damp or wet.

The book goes on to quote extensively from *My Early Life*. A particularly poignant section is Churchill's describing how when later in his life – when he was twenty – Mrs Everest becomes seriously ill, and he rushes up to see her in London:

In *My Early Life*, he says, '… I returned to her bedside. She still knew me, but she gradually became unconscious. Death came very easily to her. She had lived such an innocent and loving life of service to others and held such a simple faith, that she had no fears at all, and did not seem to mind very much. She had been my dearest and most intimate friend during the whole of the twenty years I had lived.'

He would never forget her, and until his death he would refer to her and how much she meant to him. It is well worth reading this chapter on Churchill and Mrs Everest, as well as what he wrote about her in *My Early Life*. These sections provide an insight into Churchill which is not frequently recognised or discussed.

CHURCHILL TO CHURCHILL

A very humorous episode occurred when Churchill realised that he had a namesake in America (Winston Churchill, 1871–1940) who was also an author, a writer of historical fiction. Churchill wrote him a very pithy and funny letter on how they might manage any confusion that might arise. The book *A Letter Does Not Blush: A Collection of the Most Moving, Entertaining and Remarkable Letters in History* quotes this section of *My Early Life*.[30]

FIRST SPEECH TO PARLIAMENT

There are two 'first speeches' discussed by Churchill in *My Early Life*: the first, against temperance, at the Empire Theatre when he was a Sandhurst cadet; and the second, his first speech in Parliament (see below). In *The Literary Companion to Parliament*, a chapter titled 'Winny' describes many speeches and events in Parliament during Churchill's long and distinguished career using text and quotations from Churchill's writings, as well as from other authors.[31] Silvester sets the scene in Parliament:

Churchill delivered his maiden speech on February 18, 1901. Fortunately for him, he was preceded by Lloyd George, whose attack on the Conservative Government's conduct of the Boer War had, as the *Punch* correspondent put it, elicited the 'frantic cheers of Irish sympathisers' and had lured into the Chamber loungers from the lobby, students from the Library, and philosophers from the smoking room. A constant stream of diners-out flowed in. When young Winston rose from the corner seat of the bench behind Ministers … he faced and was surrounded by an audience that filled the chamber.

The author then quotes three pages from *My Early Life* on Churchill's description of the event as it happened. Although much has been written about the scene, Churchill's description remains the best.

'BEST BOOK' CITATION
William Deeds, columnist and former editor of the *Daily Telegraph*, wrote the following in an article about his seven favourite books (*The Week*, 22 June 2002): '…This is arguably the best of all his books. It's an attractive portrait of the age in which he grew up, written before the sheer pressure of writing for a living turned him into a literary co-operative.'

Notes

1. Ronald I. Cohen, *Bibliography: The Writings of Sir Winston Churchill*, London, Thoemmes, 2006.
2. Martin Gilbert and Larry P. Arnn, *Churchill Documents Volume 23*, Hillsdale, Hillsdale College Press, 2019, p. 2126.
3. Martin Gilbert, *Never Despair, 1945-1965*, Boston, Houghton Mifflin, 1988, pp. 1206–7.
4. Stephen Gilbar, *The Open Door: When Writers First Learned to Read*, Boston, David R. Godine, 1989, pp. 37–9.
5. Mary T. Segall and William R. Brown, *Portals: Reading, Writing and Critical Thinking*, Fort Worth, TX, Harcourt Brace, 1999, pp. 322–9.
6. Kenneth A. Bruffee, *A Short Course in Writing*, Boston, Little, Brown and Company, 1980, pp. 48–9 and 132–3.
7. William E. Buckler, *Themes from Experience: A Manual of Literature for Writers*, New York, W.W. Norton, 1962, pp. 210–18.
8. John and Liz Soars, *Headway Student's Book Advanced*, Oxford, Oxford University Press, 1990, pp. 14–5.
9. Daniel O'Leary, *Mommy, I Can't Sit Still*, New York, New Horizon Press, 1984, pp. 15–6.
10. Jonathan Gathorne-Hardy, *The Old School Tie*, New York, The Viking Press, 1978, pp. 140–2.
11. Morton A. Kaplan, ed., *Character & Identity: The Sociological Foundation of Literary and Historical Perspective*, St. Paul, MN, Paragon House, 2000: Chapter 6, 'Winston Churchill at School', by James W. Muller, pp. 83–111.
12. C.L. Sulzberger, *Fathers and Children: How Famous Leaders Were Influenced by Their Fathers*, New York, Arbor House, 1987, pp. 277–304.
13. Robert Hudson, *The Jubilee Years 1887-1898*, London, The Folio Society, 1996, pp. 145–6 and pp. 187–92.
14. Rhoda Hoff and Margaret Regler, *Uneasy Neighbors: Cuba and the United States*, New York, Franklin Watts, 1997, pp. 30–32.
15. Nicholas A. Basbanes, *Every Book its Reader: The Power of the Printed Word to Stir the World*, New York, Harper Collins, 2005, pp. 28–9.
16. Rosy Border, ed., *As It Happens: A Cascade Collection of Reportage*, London, Collins, 2001, pp. 46–9.
17. Charles Miller, *Khyber: British India's North West Frontier*, New York, Macmillan, 1977, pp. 268–9.
18. Ernest Hemingway, ed. and intro., *Men at War,* New York, Bramhall House, 1979; 'The Cavalry Charge at Omdurman', pp. 813–21.

19. John Carey, ed., *The Faber Book of Reportage*, London, Faber and Faber, 1988, pp. 401–7.
20. Thurston Macauley, *The Great Horse Omnibus, from Homer to Hemingway*, Chicago, Ziff-Davis Publishing Company, 1949, pp. 155–62.
21. General Sir John Hackett, *The Profession of Arms*, London, Sidgwick & Jackson, 1983, pp. 123–7.
22. Jonathan Ferguson, *The 'Broomhandle' Mauser*, Oxford, Osprey Publications, 2017, pp. 27–9.
23. Sherwin B. Nuland, *Doctors: The Biography of Medicine*, Birmingham, AL, Graphon Editions, 1988, p. 466.
24. James E. Miller, Helen McDonnell, and Russell J. Hogan, *Traditions in Literature: America Reads*, Glenview, IL, Scott, Foresman and Company, 1985, 7th Ed, pp. 471–83.
25. G. Robert Carlsen, ed., *Insights: Themes in Literature*, St. Louis, MO, McGraw-Hill Book Company, 1967, pp. 80–94.
26. Charles S. Verral, ed., *True Stories of Great Escapes*, Volume 2, London, Reader's Digest, 1995, pp. 7–22.
27. J.P.N. Watson, *The World of Polo Past and Present*, Topsfield, MA, Salem House, 1986, pp. 37–9.
28. Jonathan Gathorn-Hardy, *The Unnatural History of the Nanny*, New York, The Dial Press, 1973, pp. 17–32.
29. Randolph S. Churchill, *Winston S. Churchill, Volume I: Youth, 1974-1900*, London, Heinemann, pp. 33–4.
30. Nicholas Parsons, *A Letter Does Not Blush*, London, Buchan & Enright, 1984, p. 228–9.
31. Christopher Silvester, *The Literary Companion to Parliament*, London, Sinclair-Stephenson, 1996, pp. 417–9.

7A: ANALYSIS OF *MY EARLY LIFE* BY HISTORIANS

How post-publication historians and writers have viewed, analysed, and written about *My Early Life* provides an additional measure of the book's impact. As noted previously, professionals in a wide range of disciplines have employed excerpts from the book to embellish their writing and to strengthen their arguments. How have historians viewed *My Early Life*? The book has now been in print for over ninety years, so there is an abundance of thought to analyse.

Martin Gilbert, the well-known historian who has probably written more about Churchill than any other author, doesn't actually provide much critique of the book other than to say, 'It was a gentle, witty account of his school and Army days, with many reflections on life and politics.'[1]

He describes *My Early Life* in many of his books but mostly provides factual material and comments by others.

William Manchester, in his book *The Last Lion: Winston Spencer Churchill: Visions of Glory 1874–1932*, states:

> The liveliest biographer of Winston Churchill is Winston Churchill. He led a fascinating life, he knew it, and he exploited it. Like most journalists, he told his choicest stories over and over. He wrote no fewer than nine versions of his dramatic escape from the Boer prisoner-of-war camp in 1899. One, 'How I escaped from the Boers,' was published in the *Johannesburg Standard and Diggers' News* on December 23, 1899. Three others appeared in the *Morning Post*, on December 27 and 28, 1899, and January 24, 1900. Later came 'My Escape from Pretoria' (*War Pictures*, March 3, 1900), 'My Escape from Pretoria' (*News of the World*, February 10, 1935), 'How I escaped' (*Sunday Chronicle*, January 2, 1938), and the versions in chapters 21 and 22 of his book *A Roving Commission*. This last account appeared in several anthologies, and Churchill lectured on this feat innumerable times. There are no significant discrepancies among the many versions. He told this tale, and others, over and over simply because he had a family – and an expensive life-style – to support.[2]

As noted elsewhere in this book, Manchester missed several other publications of Churchill's story, including 'My Escape from the Boers' (*Cosmopolitan*, January 1924, pp. 30–34 and 161–6) and 'My Escape from the Boers' (*Strand Magazine*, December 1923, pp. 537–40, 542–4, and 546–7 and January 1924, pp. 14–8 and 20–23.

Robert Rhodes James, in *Churchill: A Study in Failure, 1900–1939*, wrote:

My Early Life (1930) is in so different a vein [compared to *Marlborough*] that it is difficult to believe that it came from the same mouth. Of all his books it is the most genial and, in a very real sense, warm. Churchill's memory – like that of all autobiographers – was conveniently selective. Like F.E. Smith, who dwelt so mournfully on the allegedly grinding poverty of his youth as he grew older until he firmly believed the harrowing fictions himself, Churchill subsequently exaggerated his early backwardness at school – thus providing countless wily schoolboys and troubled parents with exaggerated comfort. The narrowness by which he avoided the fate of 'social wastrel' drawn for him by his father is described in detail by Randolph Churchill and need not be emphasised here. The charm of the book lies in its warmth and wit; it contains, furthermore, some remarkable portraits of individuals, of which those of Mrs. Everest and Colonel Brabazon, commanding the 4th Hussars, may be particularly noted.

The most well-known parts of *My Early Life* are what might be called the 'adventure' parts, particularly the accounts of action on the North-West Frontier, in Cuba, and in South Africa, and other features of the book have tended to receive less consideration. [It is remarkable that he fails to mention the cavalry charge at Omdurman.] The outstanding feature of the work is the development of Churchill's self-portrait, often wittily drawn.

James then goes on to provide excerpts from the book as examples of Churchill's writing skills and then concludes with:

My Early Life is an authentic adventure story, full of night marches, cavalry charges, expeditions on the North-West Frontier, polo-matches, pitched battles against hordes of the Khalifa or the crack shots of the Boers, with an escape from a prisoner-of-war camp, and two parliamentary elections thrown in. The touch is light, and the pace vigorous and gay. It is deservedly, a classic of autobiography.[3]

Manfred Weidhorn has written several books on the literary Churchill and commented extensively on *My Early Life*. In *Sir Winston Churchill* he writes:

> Churchill is usually associated with a lush, even fustian, and windy rhetoric. This is an oversimplification. There are many Churchills – young, middle-aged, old, journalist, orator, administrator, memoirist, essayist, historian – and they do not write in the same way. There may be a multiplicity of styles in one work, as can be seen in the *A Roving Commission*, where the supple and varied narrative can suggest the viewpoint of a child, a Pathan tribesman, a gentleman cadet, a Victorian General or nobleman. The narrative can forge a lively apostrophe, anecdote, or essay, or he can paint brief moving scenes of the boy with father or his own last meeting with Botha.[4]
>
> A notable exception to the style of the middle period is *A Roving Commission*, the short, personable autobiography written after *The World Crisis* and before *Marlborough*. Resembling, like Beethoven's Fourth Symphony, a slender Grecian maiden, between two Norse giants, it took reviewers aback. Its informality, its cavalier tone, its retrospective, gay, gentle wise humor – often directed at himself, or at least the younger self – seemed hardly to be from the same pen which wrote the sulfuric, defensive, dour, political, formal *World Crisis*. To many, this unlikely and brief effusion dashed off with the left hand has become, no doubt against the hopes and expectations of its author, more satisfying and durable than any of his numerous ambitious tomes.[5]

In the book *Sword and Pen: A Survey of the Writings of Sir Winston Churchill*, Weidhorn notes the following:

> The structure and tone of the autobiography are shaped by the substance. It ends at 1900 because, as the story of Churchill finding himself and his vocations, it is, like all such books, a tale of education, an extramural education obtained in the nineties, when many things 'were in the

making.' With the creative writer's ability to evoke alien states of mind, Churchill recreates the 'point of view appropriate to my years, whether as a child, a schoolboy, a cadet, a subaltern, a war-correspondent or a youthful politician,' rather as in his other works he tries to convey through documents the authentic feeling of bygone days. This results in considerable irony and humor. But another dimension exists as well. Although the *Commission* in part handles the same material as is treated at length in his first four books, it is not a mere iteration. The events and beliefs presented earlier with enthusiasm and innocence are now colored by experience; the sad acknowledgement, the fall of man into the twentieth century, throws a grim irony over those now distant events. … The memoir is Churchill's somewhat patrician rendition of the 'lost generation' outlook, his attempt to put together the fragmented pieces of his intellectual world by harking back to a vanished Victorian Eden. It is, therefore, at once his sprightliest and saddest book.

For a terrible revelation has come upon the world. One of the major themes of his writings of the 1930s is the vast contrast between the elegant, innocent world he grew up in and the hectic, anxious age which overtook it. … The elegiac note, the nostalgia, the British love of tradition enters into everything which Churchill contemplates. … The pathos of the gulf between father and son is what the *Commission* adds to the detached picture painted by the dedicated but reticent young biographer. … The Commission seems slight next to Churchill's major works and is indeed superficial in some ways. Yet, perhaps precisely because of the absence of the prophetic stance, of literary or historical ambitions, because of the relief from compulsion to vindicate Churchill or prove Britain's mission, it is Churchill's most charming work. For once he does not worry over memos, official records, and appendices. Relying mainly on his memory, the narrator roves freely, and his style, not bound by the carefully connected minutiae which characterize most of his books, relaxes. Colloquialisms and warmth replace the magisterial tone. The author, here, as in the *Thoughts, en pantoufles*; despite his melancholy over the end of an era, the book radiates a playfulness and mellowness, a sense that all is jolly as a lark – to live, to recall, to record, and to read. In none of his works is a sense of humor so dominant or the style so lively.[6]

Keith Alldritt, in his book *Churchill The Writer: His Life as a Man of Letters,* writes:

> The book is about youth and throughout is a celebration of Youth. Churchill writes, 'the years 1895-1900 which are the staple of this story exceed in vividness, variety, and exertion anything I have known – except of course the opening months of the Great War.' Writing and publishing this autobiography when he is in his mid-fifties, Churchill is continually aware of a generation of readers younger than he. The book is dedicated 'To a New Generation.' And he ends his fourth chapter with a strong exhortation to its members: 'Come on now all you young men, all over the world. You are needed more than ever now to fill the gap of a generation shorn by the War. You have not an hour to lose. You must take your places in life's fighting line. Twenty to Twenty-five! These are the years! Don't be content with things as they are … Don't take no for an answer. Never submit to failure … You will make all kinds of mistakes; but as long as you are generous and true and also fierce, you cannot hurt the world or even seriously distress her. She is made to be wooed and won by youth.'
>
>   In these sentences Churchill speaks not only to his readers; he speaks also to himself. The principal emotion recalled in the book is youthful joy. Churchill evokes infectiously the joys of adventuring, of fighting, of danger and of seeing the landscape of the Indian frontier, of Egypt and South Africa. He also remembers the joy of becoming a writer and a successful one. … But if youthful happiness is a predominant theme in *My Early life*, Churchill also recalls the darker and more painful parts of growing up. For the autobiographer in late middle age certain miseries and humiliations are still keenly felt. … The prose in which this process is recorded also does justice to the mutation of a personality of great depth and intricacy. … The feature of Churchill's prose which most conspicuously assists his purpose is the very marked changes in tone. Take, for example, his propensity for sudden self-deprecation. … The gentle irony of this is a recurrent feature of the style of the book. Churchill in this autobiography records many occasions of solidarity with other people, occasions of fellowship and shared good feelings. There is the experience of combat, of playing

and winning in polo-matches, of intense discussions with a group of conservatives of his own generation when they all entered politics. But there is also the Churchill who knows himself to be resented and criticised by others, as must inevitably be the case with any such dynamic and assertive personality. If Churchill portrays himself as gregarious, he also portrays himself as the outsider. This sense of himself as someone apart and very much the object of criticism begins with the success of his first book. … The sense of himself as someone apart, which is expressed here in a tone that is partly injured, partly mocking and partly self-regarding, reveals itself in other passages. Churchill see himself as an outsider in more than one way. He is, for example, a historical and generational outsider. He is aware of a new generation knocking on the door, and wishes it well and encourages it. But he knows himself to be apart, and very distantly apart. He comes from a different time and an altogether social order. The contrasting of then and now is one of the most insistent themes in the autobiography. … Churchill the poet is there in the phrase 'a beautiful intricacy of archaic manoeuvre.' Just two nouns and two adjectives are put together to create a disproportionate density of meaning and feeling. It is a phrase that could easily have come from one of the greatest war poems of the century, David Jones's 'In Parenthesis.' Churchill writes poetic prose quite unselfconsciously. …

But despite the occasional wart this literary self-portrait is an impressive one. It is one of Churchill's best books and belongs with those other great autobiographies which are so important an element in the history of English prose, works such as the autobiography of John Stuart Mill and that of Ruskin in the nineteenth century, and in the twentieth that of Bertrand Russell and that of W.B. Yeats.[7]

Robert Payne, in his book, *The Great Man: A Portrait of Winston Churchill*, comments upon *My Early Life*:

But while in *The Story of the Malakand Field Force*, *The River War*, *London to Ladysm*ith and *Ian Hamilton's March* Churchill was concerned to tell the story like a good war correspondent without permitting himself to obtrude too much or too frequently, in *My Early Life* he unabashedly focuses on himself even to including at quite preposterous length the congratulatory letters he received from the Prince of Wales, Lord Salisbury, and other dignitaries. But this self-absorption has a quality of innocence. In middle age he was rejoicing in his lost youth: that youth of high adventures in many wars, the writing of many books and the friendship of many important people. He mentions the editors who paid him for the books and the book reviewers whose enthusiasm was sometimes tempered with words of caution. And so, he [Churchill, in *My Early Life*] quotes the book reviews.

My Early Life gives the impression of having been dictated rather than written: it is told conversationally, with warmth and good humor. He rarely consulted the books he had written in his youth, with the inevitable result that the student who compares for example the account of the battle of Omdurman in the *River War* with the account of the same battle in *My Early Life* and then again with the account given in the original dispatches, which have survived, finds curious discrepancies. No doubt the early versions are more accurate. But Churchill was perfectly justified in presenting himself as he saw himself more than thirty years later in the bright glare of a capacious and sometimes altering memory. Only when it comes to describing his escape from prison in Pretoria – an event which provoked much controversy – did he repeat what he had written earlier.

Churchill prided himself on his zest and exuberance, but these are not qualities often present in his books. They are present in *My Early Life*, which bubbles with excitement…[8]

Andrew Roberts, in his recent biography *Churchill: Walking with Destiny*, comments on *My Early Life* twice when he states:

Much of Churchill's well-documented naughtiness at the various schools to which he was sent seems to have stemmed from the desire to draw attention to himself, for unlike the archetypal child of the Victorian era he was determined to be both seen and heard. It is rare for anyone to depict themselves as less intelligent than they genuinely are, but Churchill did so in his autobiography *My Early Life* in 1930, which needs to be read in the context of his colourful self-mythologizing rather than as strictly accurate history. His school reports utterly belie his claims to have been an academic dunce. Those from St George's Preparatory School in Ascot, which he entered just before his eighth birthday in 1882, record him in six successive terms as having come in the top half or usually top third of the class.[9]

Pervading *My Early Life* was the assumption – mistaken as it turned out – that his story would primarily be interesting to future generations because of the glories of the British Empire. 'I was a child of the Victorian era,' Churchill writes, 'when the structure of our country seemed set, when its position in trade and on the seas was unrivalled, and when the realization of the greatness of our Empire and of our duty to preserve it was ever growing stronger.' No one reading *My Early Life* could have doubted how far Churchill would be willing to go to preserve the Empire from Ramsay MacDonald, Lord Simon, and 'Mahatma.'[10]

Henry Pelling, in his biography *Winston Churchill*, briefly comments:

> … *My Early Life*, which received a warm welcome when it appeared in October. It certainly showed his various literary skills at their best. As the *Times* commented, 'There be few who could play on all these strings – humour, headlong excitement, quiet irony, melancholy regret for vanished customs and glories, love of sport, the pleasures of friendship – with so sure a hand.' Later in life he [Churchill] agreed with Lady Bonham Carter that it was 'the best book I ever wrote,' and there will undoubtably be many who accept this judgement.[11]

Roy Jenkins comments in *Churchill: A Biography* that as Churchill's books got longer in later life, for example, *The Second World War* and *The History of the English-Speaking Peoples*, they were 'more bought than read'. He continues,

> That is one reason why his more taut and personal works, most notably *My Early Life* but also *Great Contemporaries* and *Painting as a Pastime* (1948) are like draughts of clear spring water. … *My Early Life* appeared on 20 October (1930) and sold around 10,000 copies by Christmas. It was received with considerable contemporary

acclaim as well as being the foundation of many subsequent editions and *the gradual achievement of a reputation as a minor classic* [emphasis added].[12]

Jonathan Rose, in his study of Churchill, *The Literary Churchill: Author, Reader, Actor*, describes various aspects of *My Early Life*. The first is how Churchill thought the market for his book would be very large based on the subset of people he met in the United States in 1929 when he was there on his lecture tour:

> That conclusion was based on a tiny, self-selected, and highly unrepresentative sample, but Churchill could point to the fair success of *My Early Life* (published in October 1930). Butterworth sold 11,000 copies of the original 21s. edition and 5,000 copies of a cheaper 1934 reprint. Within a year, Scribner's had sold out two printings totaling almost 8,000 copies, having invested more than $6,000 in advertising. In spite of (or perhaps because of) the deepening Depression, readers wanted diverting and gripping stories set in a romantic past era. Churchill won splendid reviews from the *New York Times*: 'Besides being a playboy and a politician, he is a born writer'; the *New York World* ('A brilliant book, with a notable style and a graphic tale to tell') and the *Nation* ('a racy narrative, vividly and at times brilliantly written, abounding in good stories, striking descriptions of personalities, and caustic comments.'[13]

Rose continues concerning why the book was a success:

> *My Early Life* won laudatory reviews on both side of the Atlantic, largely because its boyish enthusiasm and rosy Victorianism offered a relief from modern Stracheyite cynicism. 'The Winston Churchill now living in this post-war age of disillusionment and the skepticism resuscitates for himself and his reader a Winston Churchill of a day that was brighter and happier, more real and more solid,' wrote T. R. Ybarra in the *New York Times*. 'Into an age of introspection, Freudian complexes, doubt and despair, Mr. Churchill comes like a great wind blowing through a little window into musty, over-furnished room,' as Duff Cooper put in the *Spectator*.[14]

Rose reports a fascinating fact about the German translation of *My Early Life*:

> Given the determined and largely successful Nazi campaign to block Churchill's newspaper outlets, it is remarkable that a German translation of *My Early Life*, published in 1931 as *Weltabenteuer im Dienst* by Paul Verlag of Leipzig, remained in print long after Hitler's seizure of power. As late as July 1939 Churchill received a royalty statement, which showed that he had not earned back his advance of £100.[15]

Finally, Rose highlighted some little-known but important facts about the link between *My Early Life* and Churchill's winning of the Nobel Prize in 1953:

> There had been several Swedish editions of *My Early Life*, perhaps encouraged by a 1936 abridgment in the original language, published by Albert Bonniers Forlag for teaching English to schoolchildren. All that may have been a factor in the decision to award Churchill the Nobel Prize in Literature in 1953. It is often assumed that he won it for *The Second World War*, but in his presentation speech the eminent Swedish author Sigfrid Siwertz never mentioned that work. … Instead Siwertz extolled *My Early Life* as 'one of the world's most entertaining adventure stories, a fast moving tale that even a very youthful mind can follow with the keenest pleasure.'[16]

As will be seen elsewhere in this book, Siwertz prominently mentioned Churchill's wartime speeches as being honoured.

Peter de Mendelssohn, in *The Age of Churchill,* when discussing the source of information for the period of Churchill's life during schooling and army activities, states:

> This is his autobiography, *My Early Life*, on which we must rely increasingly for the next few chapters. This book, which covers the first quarter-century in Churchill's life, was written in 1930, and in the preface the author said: 'I have not only searched my memory but have

most carefully verified my facts from records which I possess. I have tried, in each part of the quarter-century in which the tale lies, to show the point of view appropriate to my years, whether a child, a school boy, a cadet, a subaltern, a war correspondent, or a youthful politician. If these opinions conflict with those now generally accepted, they must merely be taken as representing a phase in my early life, and not in any respect except where the context warrants, as modern pronouncements.'

If this was the aim, we must admit that the author has not everywhere achieved it; the 'point of view appropriate to my years' is not always clearly apparent, and in some cases it is obviously blurred. This can hardly surprise. It is always difficult to distill the genuine sense of youth when writing in later years; and Churchill must have found it particularly difficult at this time. More than once we come across passages of vital interest for our study, and essential for our understanding of the man, which clearly are neither the words nor thoughts of the young officer of twenty-one but those of a man of fifty-five, deeply at cross-purposes with the world and himself, and moreover not at that time at his best as a writer. It is necessary to make this qualification, and to remain aware of it. There is a slight cantankerous note in *My Early Life*, and an inclination towards cheap witticism and insipid sneering to which Churchill was prone in his less happy moments, relieved, it is true by his natural gift for clowning and polemical pranks. Memory is overshadowed by later experience and bitterness, and they could cloud our source and on occasion cause a sense of mild discomfort. Thus it is often hard to tell how much in these somewhat jaundiced ruminations is genuine youthful sentiment: how much subsequent matured thought; and how much, finally, no more serious, growling farewell to 'the good old days,' which perhaps were never quite as good as they seemed. The whole is, of course, unmistakably Churchillian and has its place of significant in a later phase of the story where the defects which bother us now will be seen to have their virtues.[17]

Notes

1. Martin Gilbert, *Churchill: A Life*, New York, Henry Holt and Company, 1991, p. 496.
2. William Manchester, *The Last Lion: Winston Spencer Churchill: Visions of Glory 1874–1932*, Boston, Little Brown and Company, 1983, p. 910.
3. Robert Rhodes James, *Churchill: A Study in Failure, 1900–1939*, London, Weidenfeld & Nicholson, 1970, pp. 313–5.
4. Manfred Weidhorn, *Sir Winston Churchill*, Boston, Twayne Publishers, 1979, p. 146.
5. Manfred Weidhorn, *Sir Winston Churchill*, p. 156.
6. Manfred Weidhorn, *Sword and Pen: A Survey of the Writings of Sir Winston Churchill*, Albuquerque, University of New Mexico Press, 1974, pp. 100–106.
7. Keith Alldritt, *Churchill The Writer: His Life as a Man of Letters*, London, Hutchinson, 1992, pp. 96–101.
8. Robert Payne, *The Great Man: A Portrait of Winston Churchill*, New York, Coward, McCann & Geoghegan, 1974, p. 192.
9. Andrew Roberts, *Churchill: Walking with Destiny*, London, Allen Lane, 2018, p. 14.
10. Andrew Roberts, *Churchill: Walking with Destiny*, p. 347.
11. Henry Pelling, *Winston Churchill*, London, Book Club Associates, 1974, pp. 403–4.
12. Roy Jenkins, *Churchill: A Biography*, New York, Farrar, Straus, and Giroux, 2001, p. 430.
13. Jonathan Rose, *The Literary Churchill: Author, Reader, Actor*, New Haven, Yale University Press, 2014, pp. 207–8.
14. Jonathan Rose, *The Literary Churchill: Author, Reader, Actor*, p. 220.
15. Jonathan Rose, *The Literary Churchill: Author, Reader, Actor*, p. 272.
16. Jonathan Rose, *The Literary Churchill: Author, Reader, Acto*r, p. 417.
17. Peter de Mendelssohn, *The Age of Churchill: Heritage and Adventure 1874-1911*, New York, Knopf, 1961, pp. 88–9.

7B: ANALYSIS OF THE WRITING STYLE

Thus far in this chapter, the impact of *My Early Life* (MEL) on subsequent publications and the view of modern historians on the book have been analysed. This section will evaluate how Churchill structured the book, the methods he utilized to create the "sound" and flow of the story, and why he chose to write (dictate) it in the manner he did.

The first important attribute of creating MEL to be recognized is that the vast preponderance of the book was dictated and not written by hand or by Churchill entering it in a typewriter (which to the best of knowledge he never did). Many have suggested this approach was related to the fact that he could get more text down on paper faster than by writing it out longhand. Although this may be true — it is faster, the overriding reason is that he wanted to hear the flow of words and how they fit together, not only to create the story but to hear the sound of the sentences to create a pleasing poetic or musical quality. He perceived that the sounds and flow of words would enhance the story and would engage the reader in the scene setting and atmosphere by creating a combined visual and auditory experience. He hoped that readers would read it aloud to themselves or someone else. As we shall see, he was quite successful in this endeavour to create an auditory experience.

Another important reason for dictation was that Churchill with his prodigious memory could integrate all the previous material (newspaper dispatches, books and published articles) he had written on each episode with new material in his head to create a coherent story without returning over and over again to each of the previous texts, which he certainly did on occasion. As described elsewhere in this book, MEL was not just a cut and paste of the material he had previously published but rather a very new piece with much new material and many new facts. It has a distinctly different tone and character compared to what he had previously published.

Robert Payne, in his book *The Great Man: A Portrait of Winston Churchill*, discusses these changes in *My Early Life* compared to Churchill's previous works when he notes: "But while in *The Story of the Malakand Field Force*, *The River War*, *London to Ladysmith,* and *Ian Hamilton's March* Churchill was concerned to tell the story like a good war correspondent without permitting himself to obtrude too much or too frequently, in *My Early Life* he unabashedly focuses on himself, even to including at quite preposterous length the congratulatory letters he received from the Prince of Wales, Lord

Salisbury, and other dignitaries. But this self-absorption has a quality of innocence. In middle age he was rejoicing in his lost youth: that youth of high adventures in many wars, the writing of many books, and the friendship of many important people. He mentions the editors who paid him for the books and the book reviewers whose enthusiasm was sometimes tempered with words of caution. And so he quotes the book reviews."[1]

Chapter 4 of this book details just how much he did and didn't excerpt from his earlier books and articles, which at times was significant. It must be mentioned that following the dictation of chapters in MEL, he would return later to the earlier material to fact check and to wordsmith the text where necessary.

A third reason he dictated the book was that he wanted to create each episode with an age-appropriate aura and tone for the event he was describing, and what better way to ensure that than to listen to the story and decide if that was how a ten-year-old or an 18-year-old would have said, thought, or described it. Churchill, himself, described this approach in MEL when he commented:

"I have tried, in each part of the quarter-century in which the tale lies, to show the point of view appropriate to my years, whether a child, a school boy, a cadet, a subaltern, a war correspondent, or a youthful politician. If these opinions conflict with those now generally accepted, they must merely be taken as representing a phase in my early life, and not in any respect except where the context warrants, as modern pronouncements."[2]

Each of the components cited above as to why the book was dictated will now be discussed at length, but first it will be noted that many reviewers did sense that the book was dictated and that it was more like the spoken word than the written word. Some examples of this insight are provided. Payne has stated: "*My Early Life* gives the impression of having been dictated rather than written: it is told conversationally, with warmth and good humor."[3]

One of the most insightful descriptions of this dictating process (albeit for a different Churchill book) and the results that it created is provided by Major-General Edmonds as described by Andrew Roberts: "Major-General Sir James Edmonds, the editor of the Government's Official War History, helped Churchill on *The World Crisis*, and recorded how he would brief Churchill at Chartwell on each chapter with the relevant documents and maps; Churchill would then dictate the story to his secretary, walking up and down his study. 'I heard what seemed to be a spirit voice whispering to him,' recalled Edmonds, 'but the whispers were his own; he murmured each sentence over to see how it sounded before he dictated it. He took infinite pains to polish up his prose; after two or three typewritten versions, he would have four or five galley-proofs — an expensive business for his publishers … He has the soul of an artist.'"[4]

What a marvellous description! It brings Churchill alive in this creative process. Martin Gilbert caught this sense of spontaneity and the free flow of words when he commented: "Churchill was an accomplished storyteller. He loved the ebb and flow of narrative, and in many of his books, and also in his speeches, portrayed the dramatic events that he had witnessed, and had often been a part of."[5]

Many a reviewer has captured not only the conversational nature of the writing in *My Early Life* and how pleasing it is to the ear but truly sensed the age-specific voice Churchill was employing to make the reader visualise him as he was at that time and not the middle-aged man who was composing the story. A reviewer in an Ohio newspaper succinctly captured the entire concept when he said:

"The amazing thing about this book is the swing and harmony of it. You hear the boy speaking to you in the early chapters, then it puts away the things of a child, and a young man stands up intent and daring, without swagger, to give way later to the grown man speaking and being listened to in the councils of his country. It is all simply done in the best tradition of an art that conceals art. There are whole passages that ought to be read aloud; the skirmish in the Mamund valley — the cavalry charge — and the best of all, the young subaltern of the Fourth Hussars at the bedside of his dying nurse. The heart of the man of fifty-six who writes so simply of human affections has not dried up with the years. Our common humanity rules strong within him."[6]

An *Australasian* review noted a similar theme and commented: "His opinions and his comments are those he held not at the time of writing, but at the time the experience recorded. Consequently, we have here the naivete of the school boy, the brave flippancy of the young subaltern, and towards the end the gravity born of experience. Viewing the work as a whole, the effect of this is very charming. The author seems to be growing up under the reader's eyes."[7]

The *Times Literary Supplement* echoed this important theme when they commented: "Its variation and development in this matter of style are the greatest of its charms. One fancies one hears the small boy, the youth at Sandhurst, the young soldier, the slightly older politician each telling his story in his own way. Of course no gentleman cadet, still less a small boy, could write like that; that Mr. Churchill should contrive to bewitch his readers into the momentary impression that they can is proof that he has at his command the art of the autobiographer."[8]

Two of Churchill's friends who received inscribed copies prior to publication of the book fully noticed this age-specific style and wrote to Churchill about it. Sir Harry McGowan, chairman, Imperial Chemical Industries wrote: "I must admit that I am amazed at the masterly way in which the language of the passages dealing with your earlier years reproduces the youthfulness of that time, while the gradual change of the idiom reflects the transition to mature years."[9] Sir Robert Horn, politician and C of E just prior to Churchill being C of E noted: "The way in which you have altered the style in giving the earliest part-by a method which suggests the evolving of a child's mind-is most subtle."[10]

The Scotsman notices this theme but adds to the conversation an important element that would be discussed by many reviewers as well as Churchill himself — that the descriptions are of a vanished age. The reviewer states: "Everything is, set down, not as it now appears, seen through the reflections and experiences of later years, but as witnessed and felt at the time, as 'a child, a schoolboy, a cadet subaltern, a war correspondent, and a youthful politician'; and to the reader, as well as to the author, it looks like "a picture of a vanished age."[11]

Although some of the descriptions are of a vanished age, they are not irrelevant to the present reader, as pointed out in a *Saturday Review* which offers: "Anyone reading Mr. Churchill's book will admit that times have changed; but the human spirit which reveals itself in Mr. Churchill's pages has not changed. That is the important thing and gives to this volume its major reason for study."[12]

Churchill knew he was writing of a vanish age and he so states in MEL: "I find I have drawn a picture of a vanished age. … I was a child of the Victorian era, when the structure of our country seemed firmly set, when its position in trade and on the seas was unrivalled, and when the realization of the greatness of our Empire and of our duty to preserve it was growing stronger."[13] However, this does not suggest that what Churchill is writing about is irrelevant today, as pointed out by the *Saturday Review* above. Keith Alldritt in his book *Churchill the Writer* touches on this theme of vanished age but does so with a slightly different approach. He sees this time difference more as a generational difference and notes "Churchill sees himself as an outsider in more ways than one. He is, for instance, a historical and generational outsider. He is aware of a new generation knocking on the door and wishes it well and encourages it. But he knows himself to be apart, and very distantly apart from it. He comes from a different time and an all together different social order. This contrasting of then and now in one of the most insistent themes in the autobiography."[14]

The style of Churchill's writing is in many ways a blend of prose and poetry. He writes with a lyrical flair that entices the reader to read aloud and almost sing the story being told. This lyrical and poetic voice has been recognised by literary and historical scholars. Alldritt develops this theme when he writes:

"At times, the prose style of *My Early Life* approaches poetry — and never more so than when Churchill evokes his experience, as a young cavalry officer in the 4th Hussars, of riding in squadron. There is a thrill and charm of its own in the glittering jingle of a cavalry squadron manoeuvring at the trot; and this deepens into joyous excitement when the same evolutions are performed at a gallop. The stir of the horses, the clank of their equipment, the thrill of motion, the tossing plumes, the sense of incorporation in a living machine, the suave dignity of the uniform – all combine to make cavalry drill a fine thing in itself. … Churchill the poet is there in the phrase 'a beautiful intricacy of archaic manoeuvre.' Just two nouns and two adjectives are put together to create a disproportionate density of meaning and feeling. It is a phrase that could easily have come from one of the greatest war poems of this century, David Jones's 'In Parenthesis.' Churchill *writes poetic prose quite unselfconsciously*."[15] [my emphasis]

Alldritt sums up his opinion of MEL by stating: "But despite the occasional wart this literary self-portrait is an impressive one. It is one of Churchill's best books and belongs with those other great autobiographies which are so important an element in the history of English prose, works such as the autobiography of John Stuart Mill and that of John Ruskin in the nineteenth [century] and in the twentieth that of Bertrand Russell and that of W.B. Yeats."[16]

Building on Alldritt's thoughts it is worthwhile to reference a few examples of this poetic and lyrical prose that Churchill uses to describe the cavalry at the battle of Omdurman in MEL. As one reads/speaks these passages it is important to listen to the sounds of the words and the interplay among the string of words and recognize how these sounds enhance the picture and make the action come alive and draw the reader into the scene much like an artist who will paint a path or road in the foreground of a painting to lead the viewer into the painting. Examples of Churchill's language, phrasing and specific word choices during the cavalry charge:

"Almost at the same moment the trumpet sounded 'Trot', and the whole long column of cavalry began to jingle and clatter across the front of these crouching figures. We were in the lull of the battle and there was perfect silence. Forthwith from every blue-black blob came a white puff of smoke, and a loud volley of musketry broke the odd stillness. Such a target at such a distance could scarcely be missed, and all along the column here and there horses bounded, and a few men fell."[17]

"Brought to an actual standstill in the enemy's mass, clutched at from every side, stabbed at and hacked at by spear and sword, they were dragged from their horses and cut to pieces by the infuriated foe."[18]

"I thought we were masters of the situation, riding the enemy down, scattering them and killing them. 1 pulled my horse up and looked about me. There was a mass of Dervishes about forty or fifty yards away on my left. They were huddling and clumping themselves together, rallying for mutual protection. They seemed wild with excitement, dancing about on their feet, shaking their spears up and down. The whole scene seemed to flicker. I have an impression, but it is too fleeting to define, of brown-clad Lancers mixed up here and there with this surging mob. The scattered individuals in my immediate neighbourhood made no attempt to molest me. Where was my troop? Where were the other troops of the squadron?"[19]

"But now from the direction of the enemy there came a succession of grisly apparitions; horses spouting blood, struggling on three legs, men staggering on foot, men bleeding from terrible wounds, fish-hook spears stuck right through them, arms and faces cut to pieces, bowels protruding, men gasping, crying, collapsing, expiring. Our first task was to succour these; and meanwhile the blood of our leaders cooled."[20]

Even a cursory analysis of these excerpts demonstrate that Churchill was knowledgeable and appreciative of poetic devices and used them frequently. He particularly enjoyed alliteration and you can visualise him standing in his study at Chartwell dictating and mulling over the sentence structure with phrases such as "**S**uccession of gri**S**ly apparitions; hor**S**es **S**pouting blood, **S**truggling on three legs, men **S**taggering on foot"; "Blue-Black Blob" and "**S**tabbed at and hacked at by **S**pear and **S**word." [Capitalization is mine.] It is quite beyond simple chance that he chose the words he did.

Onomatopoeia is the poetic device wherein words are employed to imitate sounds associated with what they describe. This device was frequently used by Churchill. Example above include: "cavalry began to jingle and clatter;" "scene seemed to flicker" and "horses spouting blood." Finally, a third example displayed in these excerpts is the use of caesura, which is a purposeful break or pause in the verse to allow one phrase to finish and another to begin and to create drama and tension. Churchill writes: "The scattered individuals in my immediate neighbourhood made no attempt to molest me. Where was my troop? Where were the other troops of the squadron?" The two pauses between the three sentences cause the reader to stop and fear that Churchill might get captured or that he is alone among a large number of the enemy. A powerful mechanism to engage the reader. I will not belabour a poetry analysis further, but these examples make clear Churchill thought much about his choice of words, sentence structure, and the use of poetic devices. He used them much more in *My Early Life* than in his other books, but certainly they are heavily represented in his speeches.

A final but significant quality of the writing displayed in *My Early Life* which needs exploring is how Churchill created the "sound of the human voice" on paper. This is a topic that has been much described and written about the poet Robert Frost both by academics and Frost himself. It was Duff Cooper, the well-known Conservative politician, C of E, and friend of Churchill who wrote about this in a review in *The Spectator* in 1930 and provided some interesting insights:

"His artistry in Words was never more apparent than in the present volume – His admiration for Gibbons has not led him into committing Gibbon's error of describing his childhood in periods, better suited to chronicling the decline of Rome. He can assume the grand manner, not only better, when the occasion demands it, but in this record of his own early years he is not afraid to employ a prose that may be called conversational, and thus succeeds in one of the most difficult tasks in literature, reproducing on paper the sound of the human voice."[21]

Some explanation of what this sound of the human voice or conversation means requires looking at what has been written by and concerning Robert Frost and his poetry. Frost, the iconic American poet and four-time Pulitzer Prize winner, developed an approach to his poetry which focused on the sound of the human voice and how people used words and sentences to create a kind of music. The concept for this began when Frost was an undergraduate student at Harvard. As noted by Elizabeth Isaacs, noted literary author: "He is said to have been drawn there [Harvard] by what he had heard of its great teachers: Irving Babbitt, George Santayana and William James. He has said that there he learned that 'all thinking was not something which had been done; it was something being done in immediate and continuous activity.' At Harvard he also found classical confirmation for his practice of metrics and diction, which he later called 'the sound of sense.' ('I first heard the voice of the printed word from a Virgilian *Eclogue*, from Homer's *Odyssey*, and from *Hamlet*.') He listened with keen ear to the Latin and Greek of Bobbitt and to the philosophical lectures of Santayana, 'whose golden speech impressed me with its deliberate speed and mental exposition of brilliance.'"[22]

Frost addressed this principle he termed "sound-posturing," or, more literally, getting the 'sound of sense' in an interview in 1915 using lines from Emerson's poem "Monadnock." His explanation does not require repeating the lines here as I believe the explanation is quite clear in and of itself. Frost explained:

"What we get in life and miss so often in literature is the sentence sounds that underlie the words. ... [L]et us take the example of two people who are talking to each other on the other side of a closed door, whose voices can be heard but whose words cannot be distinguished. Even though the words do not carry, the sound of them does, and the listener can catch the meaning of the conversation. This is because every meaning has a particular sound-posture, or, to put it in another way, the sense of every meaning has a particular sound which each individual is instinctively familiar with...."[23]

Frost clarifies his meaning when he comments: "This sound of which I speak has primarily to do with tone. It is what Mr. Bridges, the poet-laureate, characterized as speech-rhythm. Meter has to do with beat, and sound posture has a definite relation as an alternate tone between the beats. The two are one in creation but separate in analysis."[24] Frost further embellished this concept that the tone of a spoken sentence is independent of the sounds of the individual words that make up the sentence. "A Sentence," he said, "is a sound in itself on which other sounds called words may be strung." Frost variously refers to the pattern of sound made by a spoken sentence as a "sentence sound," a "sentence tone," and the "sound of sense," and he argues that a sentence sound can communicate an attitude or meaning apart from the meaning conveyed by the words. We can hear the sound of sense by itself, he says, if we listen to "voices behind a door that cuts off the words." This is particularly true if the people speaking are excited. In such cases we may be able to tell exactly what is meant without distinguishing a single word simply by listening to the tones of each sentence."[25]

The poet Amy Lowell, a contemporary of Frost's and a literary critic, notes Frost's clarity of presentation when she states he "tells you what he has seen *exactly* as he has seen it. And in the word *exactly* lies half his talent. The other half is a great simplicity of phrase." She states his words are "simple, straightforward and direct."[25]

My intention in drawing this comparison between the writings of Churchill and Frost is to highlight how Churchill the great orator (as well as writer) innately knew of the approach that poets utilized to make their poetry come alive. Although I have no evidence that Churchill read or studied Robert Frost, it is well known that Churchill loved poetry and read it often in his life. As described in *My Early Life*, Churchill won the headmaster's prize at Harrow for reciting from memory the 1,200-line *The Lays of Ancient Rome*, by Thomas Macaulay. He continued after Harrow to read, occasionally write, and frequently quote poetry. In an article "The Complete Poems of Sir Winston Churchill," Douglas J. Hall describes Churchill's poems and how poetry was an important part of Churchill's life.[26] In a newspaper interview Hall noted that despite the breadth of his literary interests, he is adamant that Churchill "was truly a poet at heart. Churchill spoke and wrote with a rhythm which made it almost poetical. He arranged his notes for his speeches in a format closely resembling blank verse. Although he was never a prolific poet himself, he greatly enjoyed poetry and had a remarkable capacity to commit to memory copious lines of verse which he loved to recall and recite at appropriate moments. In his writings and speeches, he regularly quoted lines from Macaulay and was still able to recite long passages from memory well into extreme old age."[27]

Churchill's oratorical brilliance has been established without question, and his use of the English language was unsurpassed. President John F. Kennedy aptly noted that Churchill "mobilized the English language and sent it into battle." This quote is often attributed to Kennedy but it was actually Edward R. Murrow who first said it.[28] Thus, when considering Churchill's highly honed skills in both writing and speaking and his love of the English language, it should come as no surprise that Churchill used the tone, choice of words, and the sounds of words, along with the flow of words to create a poetic style of storytelling in *My Early Life*. He knew much of poetry and used it in his best writings. Here follow some examples from *My Early Life* where the "verses" use all of the poetic devices and Frostian approaches described above.

Churchill is describing his escape from the Boers and needs to jump on a train:

"The train started slowly, but gathered speed sooner than I had expected. The flaring lights drew swiftly near. The rattle became a roar. The dark mass hung for a second above me. The engine-driver silhouetted against his furnace glow, the black profile of the engine, the clouds of steam rushed past. Then I hurled myself on the trucks, clutched at something, missed, clutched again, missed again, grasped some sort of hand-hold, was swung off my feet— my toes bumping on the line, and with a struggle seated myself on the couplings of the fifth truck from the front of the train. It was a goods train, and the trucks were full of sacks, soft sacks covered with coal-dust."[29]

The rhythm, word play with multiple alliterations, the intonation when reading aloud is so very striking. The staccato of the short lines and the mimicking of the train's motion and sounds with the cadence of the lines is striking. The description of trying to grab the train and missing and trying again and his toes bumping along the tracks creates the "sound of sense" described above. The lines are very powerful at creating a mood and a fearful and frightening tone.

Another example occurs when Churchill describes his arrival at Cuba to report on the insurrection:

"Here was a place where real things were going on. Here was a scene of vital action. Here was a place where anything might happen. Here was a place where something would certainly happen. Here I might leave my bones. These musings were dispersed by the advance of breakfast, and lost in the hurry of disembarkation."[30]

The repetition of "Here" over and over again with a strong emphasis on the word when reading this section aloud sets a tone of immediacy in time and place and an anticipation of action to come. He chooses words that evoke a mystery or unsettledness rather than state a simple conclusion. He does not state he might die but rather states, "Here I might leave my bones." This creates a more evocative tone.

This section has discussed Churchill's approach to writing his autobiography in terms of writing techniques and how he brought the story alive. In addition, it has recognized that Churchill dictated the vast majority of the book so as to be able to merge all his previously written works pertaining to his life and importantly to be able to hear the sound of the sentences and to create the tone and image that he desired. This is confirmed by the direct observations of a number of individuals who worked with Churchill, including Major-General Sir James Edmonds as noted above. Churchill has thus used his enormous skills in writing and speaking to put forth a nuanced literary masterpiece that warrants continued study and reading for generations to come.

Notes

1. Robert Payne, *The Great Man: A Portrait of Winston Churchill*, New York, Coward, McCann & Geoghegan, Inc., 1974, p. 192.
2. Winston S. Churchill, *My Early Life*, London, Butterworth, 1930, p. 9.
3. Payne, *The Great Man: A Portrait of Winston Churchill*, p. 192.
4. Andrew Roberts, *Churchill Walking with Destiny*, London, Allen Lane, 2018, p. 296.
5. Martin Gilbert, *Churchill: The Power of Words*, London, Bantam Press, 2014, p. 10.
6. "Roving Commission is Ably Reviewed," *The Times Recorder*, Zanesville, OH, November 28, 1930, p. 4.
7. *Australasian*, Melbourne, Australia, December 13, 1930, p. 7.

8. *The Times Literary Supplement*, London, October 23, 1930, p.851.
9. Sir Henry McGowen letter, Churchill Archives, October 22, 1930, (CHAR 8/269).
10. Sir Robert Horn letter, Churchill Archives, October 31, 1930, (CHAR 8/269).
11. *The Scotsman*, Edinburgh, November 17, 1930, p. 2.
12. J.W.T. Mason, *Saturday Review*, December 20, 1930, p. 469.
13. Churchill, *My Early Life*, p. 99.
14. Keith Alldritt, *Churchill the Writer: His Life as a Man of Letters*, London, Hutchinson, 1992, p. 98.
15. Keith Alldritt, *Churchill the Writer*, pp. 99–100.
16. Alldritt, *Churchill the Writer*, p. 101.
17. Churchill, *My Early Life*, pp. 203–204.
18. Churchill, *My Early Life*, p. 206.
19. Churchill, *My Early Life*, p. 207.
20. Churchill, *My Early Life*, p. 208.
21. Duff Cooper, *The Spectator*, London, October 25, 1930, p. 599.
22. Elizabeth Isaacs, *An Introduction to Robert Frost*, Denver: A. Swallow, 1962, p. 16.
23. Robert S. Newdick, "Robert Frost and the Sound of Sense" in *On Frost*, Edwin H. Cady and Louis J. Budd, ed., Durham, NC: Duke Univ. Press, 1991, p. 4.
24. Newdick, *On Frost*, p. 5.
25. John F. Sears, "Robert Frost and the Imagists: The Background of Frost's 'Sentence Sounds'," *The New England Quarterly*, Vol. 54, No. 4 (December, 1981), pp. 467–80.
26. Douglas J. Hall, "The Complete Poems of Sir Winston Churchill," *Finest Hour*, October 19, 2008, International Churchill Society.
27. Douglas J. Hall, in "Winston Churchill Manuscript Reveals his Poetic Side," *The Guardian*, February 6, 2013, https://www.theguardian.com/uk/2013/feb/06/winston-churchill-manuscript-poetic-side
28. Edward R. Murrow, broadcast November 30, 1954, in *Search of Light*, New York: Knopf, 1967, p. 276.
29. Churchill, *My Early Life*, p. 287.
30. Churchill, *My Early Life*, p. 91.

7C: CHURCHILL'S NOBEL PRIZE FOR LITERATURE

Winston Churchill won the Nobel Prize for Literature in 1953. This was certainly not the first time Churchill had been considered; in fact, he had been previously nominated twenty-two times in two different categories. He had been nominated for the Nobel Peace Prize by Halvdan in 1945 and by Vinding Kruse in 1950.[1] He was nominated for Literature in 1946; in 1948 by five individuals; in 1949 by two individuals; in 1950 by six individuals; in 1951 by two individuals; in 1952 by two individuals; and, finally, in 1953 by Birger Nerman – and it was this nomination that brought him the prize in literature. In 1953, thirty-four people were nominated for the Literature Prize, including Ernest Hemingway, Robert Frost, Carl Sandberg, Graham Greene and Walter de la Mare.[2]

Churchill and his writings had resonated with the citizens of Sweden long before the Second World War. Sweden was 'the only country to publish translations of *The River War* [1938], *Marlborough* [1934], *Thoughts and Adventures* [1933] before the outbreak of the War; the first country to translate *Great Contemporaries* [1937] and *While England Slept* [1938]; and the only country ever to translate *Lord Randolph Churchill* (in 1941).'[3] This information can now be updated to note that *The World Crisis* was also published before the war, in 1931. In addition, there are at least fifteen editions, reprints, and versions of *My Early Life* in Swedish, including a 1936 version published by Albert Bonniers Forlag for teaching English to Swedish schoolchildren. This familiarity of Churchill's work in Sweden may certainly have been an added factor in the decision to award him the Nobel Prize.

Churchill's original nomination for the Prize in Literature was not well received. As noted by Kjell Stromberg:

> The first report on the candidate, written by the aged Per Hallstrom, former permanent secretary of the Academy, was rather negative in its conclusions. He found no literary merit whatever in the little adventure novel entitled [*sic*] *Savrola*, which a youthful Lieutenant Churchill had written to relieve the boredom of garrison life in India when there was no enemy to fight. Although his first attempt at autobiography, a self-portrait based on childhood memories (*My Early Life*), is not entirely lacking in charm, or in artistic quality, in Hallstrom's opinion,

only the four-volume biography of his great ancestor Marlborough, the conqueror of Louis XIV, can serve as a basis for a judgment of Churchill as historian. He dismissed *The World Crisis*, Churchill's highly praised account of the First World War, as history.[4]

Over time, the reviews of Churchill's nominations improved, and it was recognised that a broader view of his contributions should be acknowledged and considered. When his oratory as well as his history books and autobiography were considered, then, surely, the totality would 'justify the award of the Nobel Prize, for Churchill was an orator without a peer in this century'.[5]

In 1953, the press widely reported that Hemingway and Churchill were the two most likely to be awarded the prize, and when Churchill won it, headlines often noted that Churchill beat Hemingway for the prize. The *Chicago Tribune* headline read 'Churchill Wins Nobel Award for Literature, Beats out Novelist Hemingway.'[6] There were several additional themes in the press reports about Churchill winning the prize, and many of these were briefly summarised in an article in the *Vancouver Sun*:

> In announcing the award, the Swedish Academy, which made the selection, said Churchill was chosen for 'his mastery in historic and biographic description as well as for the brilliant oratorical art with which he had defended human values.' It was an open secret that the 78-year-old Churchill, who has dedicated his remaining years to the cause of world peace, would have preferred the Nobel Peace Prize. Churchill's choice by the Swedish Academy of Literature, over such contenders as Ernest Hemingway of the U.S., is worth $33,840 in prize money.[7]

Many reports told the story of Churchill's Nobel Prize with a positive approach and some important facts but missed the mark on the body of work that was largely responsible for his success. One such example was the report in New York's *Brooklyn Daily Eagle*:

> Churchill, the first active statesman to be chosen for the award, received the prize for his war memoirs, 'The Second World War,'

whose five volumes bear such eloquent titles as 'The Gathering Storm' (Volume I); 'Their Finest Hour' (Volume II); 'The Grand Alliance' (Volume III); 'The Hinge of Fate,' (Volume IV); and 'Triumph and Tragedy' (Volume V). Churchill's fame in statesmanship craft tended to obscure his remarkable writing talents, but he was, even before the turn of the century, the highest-paid war correspondent of his time and author of several brilliant books on military campaigns. ... Churchill's wartime speeches rank among the greatest English writings of any era, and his eulogy of the late King George VI was a literary gem of such measured majesty it seemed almost to have been written in blank verse. In all, Churchill's name appears as author on the cover of 33 volumes of such diverse subjects as painting, biography, travel, politics, military tactics, autobiography and even fiction.[8]

This is a wonderfully positive and supportive review but, inappropriately, it states that he won the prize for his multi-volume *The Second World War*. This is a very common misconception, and the record can most easily be set right by providing insight into the Nobel Prize Committee's thinking by quoting from the presentation speech made by S. Siwertz. The major highlights of that speech are provided below, followed by additional information on how the award was viewed by the press and the public. The elegance of the speech is quite in keeping with the majesty of Churchill's writings. Emphasis is provided in bold to emphasize the author's points.

NOBEL PRIZE IN LITERATURE 1953

English Translation of Presentation Speech by S. Siwertz, Member of the Swedish Academy:

> Very seldom have great statesmen and warriors also been great writers. One thinks of Julius Caesar, Marcus Aurelius, and even Napoleon, whose letters to Josephine during the first Italian campaign certainly have passion and splendour. But the man who can most readily be compared with Sir Winston Churchill is Disraeli, who also was a versatile author... .

Churchill's John Bull profile stands out effectively against the elder statesman's chalk-white, exotic mask with the black lock of hair on the forehead. The conservative Disraeli revered the English way of life and tradition which Churchill, radical in many respects, has in his blood, including steadfastness in the midst of the storm and the resolute impetus which marks both word and deed. ... His prose is just as conscious of the goal and the glory as a runner in the stadium. His every word is half a deed. He is heart and soul a late Victorian who has been buffeted by the gale, or rather one who chose of his own accord to breast the storm. ...

Churchill's political and literary achievements are of such magnitude that one is tempted to resort to portray him as a Caesar who also has the gift of Cicero's pen. Never before has one of history's leading figures been so close to us by virtue of such an outstanding combination. In his great work about his ancestor, Marlborough, Churchill writes, 'Words are easy and many, while great deeds are difficult and rare.' Yes, but great, living, and persuasive words are also difficult and rare. And Churchill has shown that they too can take on the character of great deeds.

It is the exciting and colourful side of Churchill's writing which perhaps first strikes the reader. Besides much else, *My Early Life* (1930) is also one of the **world's most entertaining adventure stories**. Even a very youthful mind can follow with the keenest pleasure the hero's spirited start in life as a problem child in school, as a polo-playing lieutenant in the cavalry (he was considered too dense for the infantry), and as a war correspondent in Cuba, in the Indian border districts, in the Sudan, and in South Africa during the Boer War. Rapid movement, undaunted judgments, and a lively perception distinguish him even here. **As a word-painter the young Churchill has not only verve but visual acuteness**.

Trevelyan masterfully depicts Marlborough's campaigns, but in illusory power it is doubtful that Churchill's historic battle scenes can be surpassed.

In his historical works the personal and the factual elements have been intimately blended. He knows what he is talking about. In gauging the dynamics of events, his profound experience is unmistakable. He is the man who has himself been through the fire, taken risks, and withstood extreme pressure. **This gives his words a vibrating power.** ...

It is not easy to sum up briefly the greatness of Churchill's style. He says of his old friend, the Liberal statesman, John Morley, 'Though in conversation he paraded and manœuvred nimbly and elegantly around his own convictions, offering his salutations and the gay compliments of old-time war to the other side, [he] always returned to his fortified camp to sleep.' As a stylist Churchill himself, despite his mettlesome chivalry, is not prone to such amiable arabesques. He does not beat about the bush but is a man of plain speaking. His fervour is realistic, his striking – power is tempered only by broad-mindedness and humour. He knows that a good story tells itself. He scorns unnecessary frills, and his metaphors are rare but expressive.

Behind Churchill the writer is Churchill the orator – hence the resilience and pungency of his phrases. We often characterize ourselves unconsciously through the praise we give others. Churchill, for instance, says of another of his friends, Lord Birkenhead, 'As he warmed to his subject, there grew that glow of conviction and appeal, instinctive and priceless, which constitutes true eloquence.' The words might with greater justification have been said of Churchill himself. ...

Churchill's mature oratory is swift, unerring in its aim, and moving in its grandeur. There is the power which forges the links of history. Napoleon's proclamations were often effective in their lapidary style. But Churchill's eloquence in the fateful hours of freedom and human dignity was heart-stirring in quite another way. With his great speeches he has, perhaps, himself erected his most enduring monument. ... **A literary prize is intended to cast lustre over the author, but here it is the author who gives lustre to the prize.**[9]

[The Nobel Prize in Literature 1953 was awarded to Sir Winston Leonard Spencer Churchill 'for his mastery of historical and biographical description as well as for brilliant oratory in defending exalted human values.'][10]

The power of this last declaration could stand alone as a description of why it was appropriate to present the award to Churchill. Now it should be clearer to the reader why the award was made, and how both Churchill and the contemporary press responded to the award. The following are select excerpts from the popular press on the announcement of Churchill being awarded the prize.

The *Guardian* in London stated that:

> Sir Winston Churchill was offered and formally accepted in the Cabinet room at No. 10 Downing Street yesterday this year's Nobel Prize for Literature. It consists of an illuminated scroll, a gold medal weighing 10 oz and 175,292 Swedish crowns (about £10,000) payable in Sterling. The Swedish Academy's decision was conveyed to the Prime Minister by Mr. Gunnar Hagglot, the Swedish Ambassador. Sir Winston told him that he would regard it as a 'very great pleasure' to visit Stockholm to receive the prize. He described the Ambassador's news as 'very agreeable,' and said he thought it a very great honor 'to receive this distinction gained among all the other writers of the world.' He was particularly proud that it 'was a literary distinction. … I am very proud indeed to receive an honor which is international. I have received several awards that are national, but this is the first I have received which is international in character. I notice that the first Englishman to receive the Nobel prize for Literature was Rudyard Kipling and that another one equally awarded to Bernard Shaw. I cannot attempt to compete with either of those. I knew them both quite well and my thought was much more in accord with Mr. Rudyard Kipling than with Mr. Bernard Shaw. On the other hand, Mr. Rudyard Kipling never thought much of me whereas Mr. Bernard Shaw has often expressed himself in most flattering terms.' Sir Winston is the first statesman to receive the award. …
>
> No doubt the Swedish people is [*sic*] grateful that the academy did not confine itself to mention only Sir Winston's literary merits but also referred to his merits as a 'defender of high human values.'[11]

The *Daily Telegraph*, London, stated:

The official citation awarding the Nobel Prize for Literature for 1953 to Sir Winston Churchill was unanimously approved by members of the Swedish academy this afternoon. It created a precedent by specifically declaring that Sir Winston's use of the spoken as well as the written word had influenced the judges in their decision. The citation read: 'For his mastery in historical and biographical presentation and for the brilliant oratory in which he always stood forth as the defender of the eternal human values.'[12]

Not all in the lay press thought Churchill should qualify for the award. A report in the *Halifax Evening Courier* titled 'Sir Winston not writer in the real Nobel Prize sense' said, 'Two French newspapers to-day criticized the reported award of the Nobel Prize for Literature to the Prime Minister, Sir Winston Churchill because he was not a "real" writer.'

The left-wing *Franc Tireur*, while praising his memoirs, said:

Sir Winston is not a writer in the sense which the Nobel Prize seemed to imply up to now. The Swedish Academy has made it a custom to single out a strictly literary work by a novelist of world standing, a great thinker or a great poet. Winston Churchill is above all a statesman, who besides is also a gifted writer of memoirs. That is why it is a little surprising that, when the choice was between a famous professional writer such as Ernest Hemingway and others of the same class, and a statesman whose hobby is historical literature, the laurels should have gone to the later.[13]

The *Daily News* in London noted in an article headlined 'Churchill Award Starts Row' that 'Award of the Nobel Prize for Literature to Sir Winston Churchill has caused a row.' 'Alfred Nobel must look down from heaven and shake his head,' said the socialist newspaper *Morgen-Tidningen*, which reflected government views. 'The prize might as well have been given to Mao Tse-tung.'

Prince Wilhelm, brother of the king (Gustaf VI Adolf of Sweden) said he should have had it years ago, but the newspaper *Nyheter*, a great admirer of Sir Winston, said the wisdom of the committee in choosing him was 'doubtful'. The chairman of the Norwegian Authors Association, Mr Hans

Helberg, described the choice as 'depressing'.[14] Additional articles with such sentiments can be found. The main thrust of their disapproval appears to be that Churchill was neither a professional writer nor a trained historian. They deem him a politician or statesman and a dilettante who writes well but not the type of writer who should be considered for the Nobel Prize. The lay press were not the only group who were outspoken in their disapproval of Churchill.

CHURCHILL AS HISTORIAN

Academic historians have often debated or doubted whether Churchill should be considered a true historian, as he never obtained a history degree nor did he receive academic training in history. The noted American historian Samuel Eliot Morison, professor of history at Harvard University, wrote on this topic in 1953 following Churchill's being awarded the Nobel Prize. His widely syndicated essay very well addresses the academic concerns and puts Churchill's award in a positive and balanced historical perspective. Morison wrote:

> The entire historical profession is honored in the honor to Sir Winston; for it is the first time in half a century that an historian has won the Nobel Prize for literature; in 1902 it was bestowed on Theodor Mommsen. Restricted as this prize is to 'literature of – an idealist tendency,' few historians would even qualify, since few are able to apply 'idealist' tendencies to the past. Even if we define 'idealist' as synonymous with 'creative,' what historians might have won the prize – assuming, of course, that the prize had always existed? Herodotus certainly, and Thucydides, Gibbon would have rated, and Macaulay, and Lord Clarendon, the Winston Churchill of Charles the Second's day. Our own Parkman and Prescott, certainly. For Italy, Ferrero; for France, Henry Martin; possibly Sorel. And living historian George Macaulay Trevelyan. But I can not for the life of me think of another I would have voted for if I had been a judge.
>
> There is no question, but that Churchill is a great historian, He has verve, style, honesty, imagination, and above all, superb craftsmanship.
>
> How did he learn the craft? The young men and women today who are training to be historians wish to know. Well, my answer is,

background, innate capacity, experience, and a vigorous course of self-teaching; that each was essential, but no one would have worked without the others. Sir Winston is descendent of the great Marlborough; and the son of Lord Randolph Churchill, an important figure in Victorian politics; and, on the distaff side, he is a member of our oldest hereditary society, the Cincinnati. Thus, he absorbed history through the skin. History was in the air during his youth. People discussed it at his parents' table. He knew from childhood that he was heir to a great tradition. And right here is an important lesson for us. …

So we are back at the question, how did Winston become a great historian, the only one to win the Nobel Prize for Literature? First and foremost, this infiltration of history 'through the skin'. Second, a prodigious memory, which enables him to repeat verbatim a lecture that has interested him, or a whole Shakespeare play. Third, Harrow-on-the-Hill. He told us about that school in 'My Early Life.' He hated the classical education forced on him, but he had to go through with it. He had to translate Caesar, Ovid, Virgil, Horace, Martial, even with a trot. And he doubled his work in what we call English composition, because he swapped tasks with a good classicist who did his translations, while he wrote the other fellow's English compositions. Most of all, the encouragement of a wise headmaster and the English system of education, which requires every teacher, no matter what his subject, to each English. In the United States only the teachers in the English department teach English; the others let their students get by with any old gobbledygook; an aspiring historian has two strikes against him at the start. Winston hated Latin, but I will wager that when he read Caesar's 'Commentaries' the boy said to himself, 'I'll have something like that to write one day, and I'll do it better.' Which he did. …

Winston went through Sandhurst and obtained his commission. Then began his real literary education. It was in the winter of 1896-97, in his twenty-second year when, as an officer of the Fourth Hussars, he was stationed in Bangalore in India. He had already 'picked up a wide vocabulary …, and a liking for words, and for the feel of words fitting and falling into their places like pennies in the slot' – a gift that he never lost. Now he wished to find out about things, and concepts. *Ethics*. What did that mean? He had read Aristotle to find out. *History*.

What was that? He had read no history at school except a wretched abstract of Hume. So, he sent for sets of Gibbon and Macaulay and devoured them. … All that were vital for his literary future. He had critically read the two great stylists among modern English historians. He was too sensible to try to imitate their style. But the beauty, the muscular strength, the majestic cadence of their style did something to his mind, and there are distant echoes of Gibbon and Macaulay in his latest volume. Here is another lesson that our American historical students have never learned. Gibbon to them is 'old stuff', Macauley is 'old hat', Parkman is 'drum and trumpet history' and so on. They never read through an historian who is pre-eminent for his style. Without one inspiring example how can they become first rate historians themselves? …

Nobody, and certainly not Churchill, will claim that his *Second World War*, of which the sixth and final volume will shortly appear, is objective. He was too close to the events; too much a part of them. He had neither the time nor the staff to sift everything to the bottom; consequently, some assumptions of the time are accepted as facts, when the facts turn out to be different. But the general impression is correct. It is splendid history; magnanimous to our enemies, understanding and generous to England's allies, even to those who have sadly defected since 1945; vibrant with the passion and fervor of the time; written in muscular, virile prose.

So, here's a 'Hurrah!' for the Nobel Prize Committee, and a three-times-three for 'Winnie.' And if any historian, British or American, won't join in the cheer, let them be condemned to sit forever in a college library, reading Ph.D. dissertations![15]

Although this essay might be considered a bit too flowery in this age of cynicism and negativity, it is spot on in how it captures Churchill's life and writing style and why he was, indeed, an excellent choice for the Nobel Prize in Literature. One reason for electing to retell the story of the Nobel Prize is that the awarding speech by Siwertz strongly highlights the charm and power of *My Early Life* in his litany of reasons for awarding Churchill this award. This is just another indication of the impact *My Early Life* has had in literature.

Notes

1. The Nobel Prize, Nomination Archive, https://www.nobelprize.org/nomination/archive/show_people.php?id=1797
2. The Nobel Prize, Nomination Archive, https://www.nobelprize.org/nomination/archive/list.php?prize=4&year=1953
3. Jonathan Rose, *The Literary Churchill Author, Reader, Actor*, New Haven, Yale University Press, 2014, p. 417.
4. Kjell Stromberg, in *Nobel Prize Library: Albert Camus, Winston Churchill*, New York, Alexis Gregory, ed., 1971, pp. 407–8.
5. Stromberg, in *Nobel Prize Library: Albert Camus, Winston Churchill*, p. 408.
6. 'Churchill Wins Nobel Award for Literature', *Chicago Tribune*, Chicago, IL, 14 October 1953, p. 2.
7. 'Churchill Awarded Famed Nobel Prize', *Vancouver Sun*, Vancouver, BC, 13 October 1953, p. 1.
8. 'Statesman Churchill Awarded Nobel Prize—for Literature', *Brooklyn Daily Eagle*, New York, 15 October 1953, p. 1.
9. S. Siwertz, The Nobel Prize Award Ceremony Speech, https://www.nobelprize.org/prizes/literature/1953/ceremony-speech/
10. *Nobel Lectures, Literature 1901–1967*, Horst Frenz, ed., Elsevier Publishing Company, Amsterdam, 1969, pp. 487–95.
11. *Guardian*, London, 16 October 1953, p. 1.
12. *Daily Telegraph*, London, 16 October 1953, p. 1.
13. *Halifax Evening Courier*, Yorkshire, England, 14 October 1953, p. 6.
14. *Daily News*, London, 17 October 1953, p. 5.
15. 'Sir Winston Churchill: Nobel Prize Winner', in *Saturday Review*, Vol. 36, No. 44, 31 October 1953, pp. 22–3. https://www.enotes.com/topics/winston-churchill/criticism/criticism/samuel-eliot-morrison-essay-date-31-october-1953

CHAPTER 8

Conclusions

Churchill's autobiography deals with the first quarter-century of his life and, in many ways, lays the groundwork for how he wished to be perceived and how he would approach and create his political career. It has often been asked why he ended the story in about 1903, other than recording that he got married in 1908. The year 1903 was chosen because, in Churchill's mind, that was when, early in his political career, he had begun to question whether his views would continue to be consonant with the Conservative party. His political views and alignment had begun to change at that time. This dissonance would lead to his 'crossing the floor' to join the Liberal party in 1904, thus creating a clean break in his life's story.

As noted in Chapter 3, which covered the writing of *My Early Life*, Churchill had contemplated and actually proposed writing a follow-on piece to cover his life from 1903 up until the start of the First World War. Thus, in his mind, he would have written the complete story of his life, his father's life, and the British political scene from the 1870s up until the end of the First World War. That is to say, he had published all his major works, including his war correspondence books: *The River War*, *Lord Randolph Churchill*, *My African Journey*, *Liberalism and the Social Problem*, *The World Crisis* and *My Early Life*. Having published these, there would have been available a comprehensive view of Churchill and politics from his vantage point covering about fifty years of British history. Sadly, such a book to complete the sequence would never occur.

When it was published in 1930, *My Early Life* was immediately recognised as one of his best books and hailed as a literary masterpiece. Many reviewers noted that it was not only extremely well-written but also a joy to read. Such an opinion has not faded over the last ninety years.

As pointed out by Alldritt, *My Early Life* is a prototypical *Bildungsroman*, that is, a book that focuses on the psychological and moral growth of the subject from childhood to adulthood, a story in which character change is significant and compelling.[1] In the case of *My Early Life*, author and protagonist are one and the same, and so the change in character and personality growth are those that Churchill wants you to know about.

What distinguishes Churchill, the consummate writer, in this book apart from all his other works is the multitude of distinct literary styles, tones and compositional structures that he employs to tell his story. Unlike all of his other historical and biographical books, he discards all citation of documents, footnotes and references to concurrent or past publications and literature. He utilises the personal narrative, often in an exuberant, joyous, celebratory voice that is appropriate to the age at the time of the lead character. He is joyous in his descriptions of his youth and all he has accomplished, from his worldwide travels to military battles to his self-education and his writing experiences. His writing brings these episodes alive to the reader in an engaging and captivating manner. Although the personal 'I' narrative predominates, at times, he steps back to speak of himself in the third person.

As Weidhorn notes,

[T]he structure and the tone of the autobiography are shaped by the substance. ... With the creative writer's ability to evoke alien states of mind, Churchill recreates the 'point of view appropriate to my years, whether as a child, a school boy, a cadet, a subaltern, a war-correspondent or a youthful politician,' rather as in his other works he tries to convey through documents the authentic feeling of bygone days. This results in considerable irony and humor.[2]

Churchill often develops a narrative with two audiences. First, he speaks to the reader but then also to himself with the purpose of reminding himself and the reader of the personal characteristics needed to be successful and to have an impact on the world. For in Churchill's mind, unless one is on the leading edge of change and of being impactful for the greater good of society, life would not seem to be worthwhile. If one is not making a difference, then what difference does a person make? For example, while he is writing to a 'new generation', as he calls the youth of Britain, and is exhorting them – 'Come on all you young men, all over the world. You are needed more than ever now to fill the gap of a generation shorn by the War. You have not an hour to lose. You must take your places in life's fighting line. ... Don't be content with things the way they are. ... Don't take no for an answer. Never submit to failure' – he is also addressing himself.[3] How Churchillian! And how inspirational to a new generation – and himself, as he reminds himself how he got to where he is. This is also prefigures what Churchill would absolutely need to do in the next fifteen years vis-à-vis Hitler and the Second World War.

All is not joyful, however. Churchill is superb in portraying irony, isolation and failure throughout the book when retelling the dreadful and isolating experience in his early education (at least from his perspective) and life, including his being caned at school; his inability (or lack of desire) to learn the classics; the multiple attempts that would be required before he was admitted to Sandhurst; reports from his school masters to his parents mentioning his laziness and slovenly character; and his perceptions of isolation from and the disinterest of his parents. These are some of the most compelling and heart-wrenching passages in the book.

Churchill frequently comments on another type of isolation: generational separation. He recognises that his youth was lived in a Victorian era that was long gone, with its unique social, political and moral standards. It was an era that could not ever be reproduced. This theme is repeated over and over again in the text. He likely uses this storyline to encourage the new generation to realise that they have many more opportunities and the ability to be impactful and move upwards socioeconomically. Although he laments some of the changes, he recognises that the opportunities of the new world far outweigh the losses from the old. Weidhorn describes this generational isolation as 'his attempt to put together the fragmented pieces of his intellectual world by harking back to a vanished Victorian Eden. It is, therefore, at once his sprightliest and saddest book.'[4]

Another persistent theme is that of the heroic. As mentioned earlier, Churchill always saw himself as Saint George fighting the dragon. To that end, everything he does in life – whether as a soldier, learning English, escaping from being a POW, or attempting to get his parents' attention – is done in a grand, heroic and theatrical manner. The style of writing displays this heroism not only to characterise his behaviour and how he desires to be perceived but also to provide an example for the next generation to emulate. These passages were quite intended to produce this effect, and in so doing, they enhance the literary quality of the book.

Two of the most distinctive and captivating qualities of Churchill's writing are his use of poetic prose and the use of the sounds of words and the sounds of well-structured sentences. These qualities can best be appreciated by reading the passages – indeed, the whole book – out loud. If this is done, a whole new appreciation for the book will become quite evident. Both of these topics are discussed at some length within the chapter on analysis of the book and won't be repeated here other than to quote the words of Alldritt: 'Churchill the poet is there in the phrase "a beautiful intricacy of archaic manoeuvre." Just two nouns and two adjectives are put together to create a disproportionate density of meaning and feeling. … Churchill writes poetic prose quite unselfconsciously.'[5]

My Early Life provides essential insights and comprehension into Churchill the adolescent, the soldier, the man, the writer, the thinker, the politician, the orator and the self-promoter that to not read and understand it fully does not allow one to fully understand Churchill. The good news is that it is so beautifully written and such a joy to read that no excuses can be found to not read or reread it. In addition, an appreciation of the impact the book has had on subsequent literature (as described in Chapter 7) compel one to want to understand why it has been so impactful, and that requires one to read it. The fact that the book has been continuously in print for more than ninety years and has been translated into twenty-five languages speaks volumes.

Finally, perhaps the best way to characterise *My Early Life*, and Churchill the writer, is to quote the Nobel Prize Committee:

> A literary prize is intended to cast lustre over the author, but here it is the author who gives lustre to the prize.
>
> The Nobel Prize in Literature 1953 was awarded to Sir Winston Leonard Spencer Churchill 'for his mastery of historical and biographical description as well as for brilliant oratory in defending exalted human values.'[6]

Notes

1. Keith Alldritt, *Churchill the Writer: His Life as a Man of Letters*, London, Hutchinson, 1992, p. 96.
2. Manfred Weidhorn, *Sword and Pen*, Albuquerque, University of New Mexico Press, 1974, p. 100.
3. Winston S. Churchill, *My Early Life*, Butterworth, London, 1930, p. 74.
4. Weidhorn, *Sword and Pen*, p. 101
5. Alldritt, *Churchill the Writer*, p. 100.
6. *Nobel Lectures, Literature 1901-1967*, Editor Horst Frenz, Elsevier Publishing Company, Amsterdam, 1969, pp. 487–95.

APPENDIX 1

Brief Biographies

Asquith, Herbert (1852–1928), also the Earl of Oxford and Asquith, Liberal Prime Minister 1908–16, leader of opposition 1916–18 and 1920–22, leader of the Liberal Party 1908–22, Chancellor of the Exchequer 1905–1908, early supporter of Churchill when he joined the Liberal Party; later sacrificed Churchill when he formed coalition government in 1915.

Bacon, Admiral Sir Reginald Hugh Spencer (1863–1947), worked with Churchill when he was First Lord of the Admiralty, known for his great technical skills; became friends with Churchill.

Baldwin, Stanley (1867–1947), Earl Baldwin of Bewdley, Conservative Prime Minister 1923–24, 1924–9 and 1935–7, Chancellor of the Exchequer 1922–23, early supporter of Churchill, named him Chancellor of the Exchequer in 1924; later at odds with Churchill.

Balfour, Arthur (1848–1931), 1st Earl of Balfour, Conservative Prime Minister 1902–1905, fought frequently with Churchill over tariff issue; Churchill moved to Liberals during his Premiership.

Barnes, General Sir Reginald (1871–1946), member of 4th Hussars and close friend of Churchill in India and Cuba; they remained in contact throughout Barnes's lifetime.

Baruch, Bernard (1870–1965), American financier and statesman, friend of Churchill; they wrote and visited each other frequently; Churchill asked him frequently for financial advice.

Beaverbrook (Aiken), Max (1879–1964), also Lord Beaverbrook, newspaper owner, Minister of Aircraft Production 1940–41, Minister of Supply 1941–42, Minister of War Production, 1942; close friend and confidant of Churchill.

Benn, William Wedgwood (1877–1960) 1st Viscount Stansgate, Liberal politician who later joined the Labour Party; Secretary of State for India 1929–31 and Secretary of State for Air 1945–6.

Birkenhead, Lady (1913–92), Sheila (née Beery) Smith, wife of Lord Birkenhead; good friend of Churchill.

Birkenhead, Lord (1872–1930), F.E. Smith and 1st Lord of Birkenhead, Conservative Secretary of State for India 1924–8; close friend and confidante of Churchill.

Blood, Sir Bindon (1842–1940), British General with service in Afghanistan, India, Egypt and South Africa; interacted with Churchill; Churchill dedicated his first book, *The Story of the Malakand Field Force*, to him.

Boothby, Robert (1900–1986), Baron Boothby, Conservative MP, Parliamentary Private Secretary to Chancellor of the Exchequer Winston Churchill (1926–9).

Bracken, Brendan (1901–1958), Irish-born businessman (founder of modern *Financial Times*) and a minister in the British Conservative cabinet; a close friend and advisor of Churchill.

Brown, A. Curtis (1868–1945), American-born British literary agent, founded Curtis Brown Agency in London; one of Churchill's literary agents.

Buchan, John (1875–1940), Scottish novelist, historian, Unionist politician and Governor General of Canada (1935–40); served in the Second Boer War and the Western trenches in the Second World War.

APPENDIX 1 / BRIEF BIOGRAPHIES

Butterworth, Thornton (1864–1942), publisher and founder of publishing company of same name, published Churchill's *The World Crisis*, *My Early Life*, *India*, *Thoughts and Adventures*, *Great Contemporaries* and *Step By Step*.

Carson, Sir Edward (1854–1935), Baron Carson, Irish Unionist MP, barrister and judge; First Lord of the Admiralty (1916–17).

Cecil, Hugh (1869–1956), Lord Cecil, Conservative MP 1895–1906, 1910–37, member of the Hughligans with Churchill; friend and ally of Churchill.

Chamberlain, Austen (1863–1937), Conservative, Chancellor of the Exchequer 1903–1905 and 1919–21, Secretary of State for Foreign Affairs 1924–9, First Lord of the Admiralty 1931.

Chamberlain, Neville (1869–1940), Conservative politician, Prime Minister 1937–40, promulgated appeasement; under duress, brought Churchill into Cabinet in 1939; resigned Premiership in 1940.

Churchill, Clementine (1885–1977), wife of Winston, life peer, indispensable to Churchill's success in life and career.

Churchill, Diana (1909–1963), eldest daughter of Winston and Clementine.

Churchill, Lady Randolph (1854–1921), Jeanette Jerome, American-born British socialite, mother of Winston.

Churchill, Lord Randolph (1849–1895) Conservative MP and Chancellor of the Exchequer, father of Winston.

Churchill, John (Jack) (1880–1947), younger brother and only sibling of Winston, fought in Boer War and First World War, stockbroker, close to Winston.

Churchill, Randolph (1911–1968), Conservative MP, son and biographer of Winston.

Churchill, Sarah (1914–1982), daughter of Winston and Clementine, actress and dancer.

Cooper, Duff (1890–1954), 1st Viscount Norwich, Conservative MP, Secretary of State for War (1935–37) and Ambassador to France (1944–48).

Deakin, Sir Frederick William (1913–2005), known as F.W. Deakin, British historian, literary assistant to Churchill, leader of Churchill's writing 'syndicate'.

Eden, Anthony (1897–1977) Earl of Avon, Conservative, Foreign Secretary 1935 –1938, resigned over appeasement, strong ally of Churchill, succeeded Churchill as PM in 1955

Edward, Prince of Wales (1894 –1972), abdicated as Edward VIII, then known as the Duke of Windsor; a friend of Churchill, who initially defended him and sought to obtain time for him to consider whether to abdicate or not.

Everest, Elizabeth (1832–1895), known as 'Woom' or 'Woomany', Winston's nurse or nanny; was extremely close to Winston throughout her life and highly influential on his development as a child and young man.

Fergusson, John (1891–1963), Sir John Donald Balfour Fergusson, civil servant, Private Secretary to Churchill during his time as Chancellor of the Exchequer.

Fisher, John (Jackie) (1841–1920), Lord Fisher, Admiral of the Fleet, known for his naval reform, associate and advisor to Churchill; at times, a colleague and supporter, but his behavior would lead to Churchill resigning from Admiralty.

George V, H.R.H. King (1865–1936), reigned 1910–36, father of George VI and Edward VIII (abdicated).

Grenfell, Ettie, Baroness Desborough (1867–1952), socialite hostess and friend of Churchill; Churchill frequented her social events.

Grey, Edward (1862–1933), 1st Viscount Grey of Fallodon, Liberal, Secretary of State for Foreign Affairs 1905–16.

Grigg, Sir Percy James (PJ) (1890–1964), friend of Churchill and British civil servant; he was moved at Churchill's request from being Permanent Under-Secretary of State at the War Office to Secretary of state for War during the Second World War.

Haldane, Aylmer (1862–1950), British Army General, colleague of Churchill in Boer War; captured together and held as POWs; later complained that Churchill had escaped with his plan and had left him and his colleagues behind.

Hamilton, Sir Ian (1853–1947), British General, Second Boer War, Churchill first met him in 1897, they interacted over many years from the Boer War through the Second World War;, friends who corresponded frequently over the years; Churchill titled one of his books *Ian Hamilton's March*.

Harcourt, Lewis Vernon (1863–1922), 1st Viscount Harcourt PC Liberal MP, Secretary of State for the Colonies 1910–1915.

Hoare, Samuel (1880–1959), 1st Viscount Templewood, Conservative MP, held multiple senior posts including Secretary of State for Air, Secretary of State for India, Foreign Secretary, and First Lord of the Admiralty.

Hore-Belisha, Leslie (1893 –1957), 1st Baron Hore-Belisha, switched parties over time from Liberal to National Liberal and then Conservative, MP, Minister of Transport (1934–7), Secretary of State for War (1937–40).

Horne, Robert (1871–1940), 1st Viscount Horne of Slamannan, Scottish businessman, advocate and Unionist politician, preceded Churchill as Chancellor of the Exchequer.

Horsbrugh, Florence (1889–1969), Baroness Horsbrugh, Conservative MP, Minister of Education (1951–4).

Jerome, Leonie Blanche (1859–1943), Lady Leslie, Jennie's sister and Winston's aunt, very close to Winston and helped bring him up.

Jerome, Clarita (Clara) (1851–1935), Mrs Moreton Frewen, Jennie's sister and Winston's aunt, close to Winston; her husband was the disastrous proofreader for Churchill's first book while Churchill was in India.

Joynson-Hicks, William (1865–1932), 1st Viscount Brentford, Conservative MP and solicitor.

King, W. Mackenzie (1874–1950), Canadian statesman, PM of Canada, colleague, but not close friend of Churchill.

Kitchener, Horatio Herbert (1850–1916), Field Marshal, Sirdar at Battle of Omdurman and leader in Second Boer War, attempted to block Churchill from being added to cavalry in Sudan, interacted with Churchill in Sudan, South Africa and in First World War.

Lawrence, Thomas Edward (1888–1935), known as T.E. Shaw and Lawrence of Arabia, British archeologist, soldier, writer and close friend and confidant of Churchill and advisor on the Middle East.

Lindemann, Frederik (1886–1957), 1st Viscount Cherwell, known as 'The Prof', Oxford Professor of Physics and scientific advisor to Churchill and close friend.

Lloyd George, David (1863–1945), Liberal, Chancellor of the Exchequer 1908–15, Minister of Munitions 1915–16, Secretary of State for War 1916, Prime Minister 1916–22, very close ally during Churchill's Liberal years.

Lloyd, Selwyn (1904–1978), Baron Selwyn-Lloyd, Conservative MP, Minister of Supply (1954–5). Minister of Defence (1955), Secretary of State for Foreign affairs (1955–60).

Lyttelton, Oliver (1893–1972) 1st Viscount Chandos, Conservative MP, President of the Board of Trade (1940–1941 and 1945), Secretary of state for the Colonies (1951–1954).

MacDonald, Ramsey (1866–1937), Labour Party leader and PM (1924, 1929–35).

Marquis, Frederick James (1883–1964), 1st Earl of Woolton, Conservative MP, Minister of Food (1940–43), Minister of Reconstruction; Lord President of the Council (1951–2).

Marsh, Sir Edward (1872–1953), British polymath, arts patron, translator, friend and Private Secretary to Churchill; edited Churchill books including *My Early Life*.

McKenna, Reginald (1863 –1943), Liberal, First Lord of the Admiralty 1908–11, Home Secretary 1911–15, Chancellor of the Exchequer 1911–15.

McNeill, Ronald (1861–1934), 1st Baron Cushendun, Unionist MP, Financial Secretary to the Treasury (1925–7).

Moynihan, Berkeley (1865–1936), 1st Baron Moynihan, British surgeon and friend of Churchill, he was a Major-General in the British Army in the Forst World War.

Palmer, Roundall (1887–1971), Viscount Wolmer, Conservative MP, Parliamentary Secretary to the Board of Trade and Assistant Postmaster-General (1924–9).

Plowden, Pamela (1874–1971), Lady Lytton, first true love of Churchill; refused marriage but they were very close and life-long friends; she also became friends with Clementine.

Sandys, Duncan (1908–1987), Baron Duncan-Sandys, Conservative MP, Minister of Supply (1951–4), Minister of Housing and Local

Government (1954–7), Minister of Defence (1957–79, son-in-law of Winston Churchill.

Scribner, Charles III (1890–1952), known as Charles, Jr.; became President of Scribner's Publishers in New York in 1932, dealt with Churchill on *My Early Life*.

Scurr, John (1876–1932), Labour Party MP and trade union official.

Sinclair, Archibald (1890–1970), 1st Viscount Thurso, Liberal MP, Churchill's second in command during active service in First World War, Private Military Secretary to Churchill (1919–21); remained close friends.

Smuts, Jan Christian (1870–1950), South African statesman, Field Marshal, Prime Minister of South Africa (1919–24 and 1939–48), close friend of Churchill; it was he who interrogated Churchill in South Africa after his capture in the Boer War.

Somervell, Robert (1851–1933), history master at Harrow; by Churchill's acknowledgement in *My Early Life*, he was the master responsible for Churchill's learning to write proper English; they corresponded throughout Somervell's life.

Snowden, Philip (1864–1937), 1st Viscount Snowden, Labour/National Party, Chancellor of the Exchequer 1924, 1929–31, epic verbal battles with Churchill over budgets; held strong socialist views.

Spears, Major-General Sir Edward Louis (1886–1974), British Army and MP, became close friends with Churchill when Churchill was First Lord of Admiralty (prior to First World War) and when Churchill was in France during First World War; acted as liaison to French Government and Churchill's advisor prior to and during Second World War.

Spencer-Churchill, Lieutenant-Colonel Charles Richard John (1871–1934), 9th Duke of Marlborough, British soldier and Conservative politician, a close friend of his first cousin Winston Churchill; he was often known as 'Sunny'.

Spencer-Churchill, Lily (1854–1909), Duchess of Marlborough, aunt of Winston, strong supporter both personally and financially.

Trevelyan, George (1876–1962), British historian and academic, Churchill very much admired his works.

Welldon, James, Rt. Rev. Dr. (1854–1937), English clergyman and scholar, headmaster at Harrow when Churchill was there as student; corresponded regularly with Churchill thereafter.

Winterton, Lord (1883–1962), Edward Turnour, 6th Earl Winterton Irish peer and MP for 47 years, Under-Secretary of State for India (1922–9).

Wood, Sir Kinsley (1881–1943), Conservative MP, Minister of Health (1935–8), Secretary of State for Air (1938–40) and Chancellor of the Exchequer (1940–3).

APPENDIX 2

Chapter 4: Childhood

In these Appendices, a detailed comparison of five episodes from *My Early Life* (*MEL*) will be analysed (Childhood, War in Cuba, Omdurman [cavalry charge], Armoured train episode in South Africa, and Churchill's escape from the Boers). For each comparison, the final text of the episode, as present in *My Early Life*, will be displayed first. Then, beginning with the earliest written version published and proceeding chronologically through each subsequent published version, the reader will be afforded a means of viewing and comparing the additions, subtractions or edits made on the way to the final product. This will allow an assessment of how the telling of these critical episodes in his life evolved in his own mind over more than a quarter of a century – or how he altered the stories to better convey the messages he wished to send to his readers.

This author's comments on the changes made, where they would be clarifying, will be provided in **bold** after the *MEL* text. The use of the bolded text makes it easier for the reader to differentiate such comments from Churchill's text. In each case, all the references for the studied materials will be cited. The text from the First British Edition, Second Printing, 1930, of *MEL* is used throughout this analysis.

The text will be broken down into digestible sections for the analysis. Edits (additions or exclusions) will be denoted by blue (added) or red (removed or absent) from previous text, respectively.

APPENDIX 2 / CHAPTER 4: CHILDHOOD

Texts compared:
MEL, Chapter I, 'Childhood', pp. 15–29 and part of Chapter II, 'Harrow', pp. 30–32.
'When I was Young', *Strand Magazine*, December 1924, Vol. LXVII, pp. 604–12.

MEL, p. 15.
When does one first begin to remember? When do the waving lights and shadows of dawning consciousness cast their print upon the mind of a child? My earliest memories are Ireland. I can recall scenes and events in Ireland quite well, and sometimes dimly, **even** people. Yet I was born on November 30, 1874, and I left Ireland early in the year 1879. My father had gone to Ireland as secretary to his father, the Duke of Marlborough, appointed Lord-Lieutenant by Mr. Disraeli in 1876. We lived in a house called 'The Little Lodge,' about a stone's throw from the Viceregal. Here I spent nearly three years of childhood. I have clear and vivid impressions of some events. I remember my grandfather, the Viceroy, unveiling the Lord Gough statue in 1878. A great black crowd, scarlet soldiers on horseback, strings pulling away a brown shiny sheet, the old Duke, the formidable grandpapa, talking loudly to the crowd. I recall even a phrase he used: 'and with a withering volley he shattered the enemy's line.' I quite understood that he was speaking about war and fighting and that a 'volley' meant what the black-coated soldiers (Riflemen) used to do with loud bangs so often in the Phoenix Park where I was taken for my morning walks. This, I think, is my first coherent memory.

Only one word added from the *Strand* text.

Strand, December 1924, p. 604.
When does one first begin to remember? When do the waving lights and shadows of dawning consciousness cast their print upon the mind of a child? My earliest memories are Ireland. I can recall scenes and events in Ireland quite well, and sometimes dimly, **[even]** people. Yet I was born on November 30, 1874, and I left Ireland early in the year 1879. My father had gone to Ireland as secretary to his father, the Duke of Marlborough, appointed Lord-Lieutenant by Mr. Disraeli in 1876. We lived in a house called "The Little Lodge,' about a stone's throw from the Viceregal. Here I

spent nearly three years of childhood. I have clear and vivid impressions of some events. I remember my grandfather, the Viceroy, unveiling the Lord Gough statue in 1878. A great black crowd, scarlet soldiers on horseback, strings pulling away a brown shiny sheet, the old Duke, the formidable grandpapa, talking loudly to the crowd. I recall even a phrase he used: 'and with a withering volley he shattered the enemy's line.' I quite understood that he was speaking about war and fighting and that a 'volley' meant what the black-coated soldiers (Riflemen) used to do with loud bangs so often in the Phoenix Park where I was taken for my morning walks. This, I think, is my first coherent memory.

MEL, pp. 15–16.
Other events stand out more distinctly. We were to go to a pantomime. There was great excitement about it. The long-looked-for afternoon arrived. We started from the Viceregal and drove to the Castle where other children were no doubt to be picked up. Inside the Castle was a great square space paved with small oblong stones. It rained. It nearly always rained—just as it does now. People came out of the doors of the Castle, and there seemed to be much stir. Then we were told we could not go to the pantomime because the theatre had been burned down. All that was found of the manager **was** **[were]** the keys that had been in his pocket. We were promised as a consolation for not going to the pantomime to go next day and see the ruins of the building. I wanted very much to see the keys, but this request does not seem to have been well received,

In one of these years we paid a visit to Emo Park, the seat of Lord Portarlington, who was explained: to me as a sort of uncle. **Of** **[About]** this place I can give very clear descriptions, though I have never been there since I was four or four and a half, The central point in my memory is a tall white stone tower which we reached after a considerable drive. I was told it had been blown up by Oliver Cromwell, I understood definitely that he had blown up all sorts of things and was therefore a very great man.

Only two words changed between the two versions.

Strand, December 1924, p. 604.
Other events stand out more distinctly. We were to go to a pantomime. There was great excitement about it. The long-looked-for afternoon arrived. We started from the Viceregal and drove to the Castle where other children were no doubt to be picked up. Inside the Castle was a great square space paved with small oblong stones. It rained. It nearly always rained—just as it does now. People came out of the doors of the Castle, and there seemed to be much stir. Then we were told we could not go to the pantomime because the theatre had been burned down. All that was found of the manager **were** the keys that had been in his pocket. We were promised as a consolation for not going to the pantomime to go next day and see the ruins of the building. I wanted very much to see the keys, but this request does not seem to have been well received,

In one of these years we paid a visit to Emo Park, the seat of Lord Portarlington, who was explained: to me as a sort of uncle. **About** this place I can give very clear descriptions, though I have never been there since I was four or four and a half, The central point in my memory is a tall white stone tower which we reached after a considerable drive. I was told it had been blown up by Oliver Cromwell, I understood definitely that he had blown up all sorts of things and was therefore a very great man.

MEL, pp. 16–17.
My nurse, Mrs. Everest, was nervous about the Fenians. I gathered these were wicked people and there was no end to what they would do if they had their way. On one occasion when I was out riding on my donkey, we thought we saw a long dark procession of Fenians approaching. I am sure now it must have been the Rifle Brigade out for a route march, But we were all very much alarmed, particularly the donkey, who expressed his anxiety by kicking. I was thrown off and had concussion of the brain. This was my first introduction to Irish politics!

In the Phoenix Park there was a great round clump of trees with a house inside it. In this house there lived a personage styled the Chief Secretary or the Under Secretary, I am not clear which. But at any rate from this house there came a man called Mr. Burke. He gave me a drum. I cannot remember what he looked like, but I remember the drum. Two years afterwards when we were back in England, they told me he had been murdered by the Fenians in this same Phoenix Park we used to walk about in every day. Everyone round me seemed much upset about it, and I thought how lucky it was the Fenians had not got me when I fell off the donkey.

Strand, December 1924, p. 605.
Exactly the same text used for *MEL*. Therefore, the above text not repeated here.

MEL, p. 17.
It was at 'The Little Lodge' I was first menaced with Education. The approach of a sinister figure described as 'the Governess' was announced. Her arrival was fixed for a certain day. In order to prepare for this day Mrs. Everest produced a book called *Reading without Tears*. It certainly did not justify its title in my case. I was made aware that before the Governess arrived I must be able to read without tears. We toiled each day. My nurse pointed with a pen at the different letters. I thought it all very tiresome. Our preparations were by no means completed when the fateful hour struck and the Governess was due to arrive. I did what so many oppressed peoples have done in similar circumstances: I took to the woods. I hid in the extensive shrubberies—forests they seemed— which surrounded 'The Little Lodge.' Hours passed before I was retrieved and handed over to 'the Governess.' We continued to toil every day, not only at letters but at words, and also at what was much worse, figures, Letters after all had only got to be known [recognised], and when they stood together in a certain way one recognised their formation [got to know their pattern] and that it meant a certain sound or word which one uttered when pressed sufficiently. But the figures were tied into all sorts of tangles and did things to one another which it was extremely difficult to forecast with complete accuracy. You had to say what they did each time they were tied up together, and the Governess apparently attached enormous importance to the answer being exact. If it was not right, it was wrong. It was not any use being 'nearly right.' In some cases these figures got into debt with one another: you had to borrow one or carry one, and afterwards you had to pay back the one you had borrowed. These complications cast a steadily gathering shadow over my daily life.

Slight rephrasing with words in blue added for *MEL*.

Strand, December 1924, pp. 605–6
It was at 'The Little Lodge' I was first menaced with education. The approach of a sinister figure described as 'the Governess' was announced. Her arrival was fixed for a certain day. In order to prepare for this day Mrs. Everest produced a book called "Reading without Tears". It certainly did not justify its title in my case. I was made aware that before the Governess arrived I must be able to read without tears. We toiled each day. My nurse pointed with a pen at the different letters. I thought it all very tiresome. Our preparations were by no means completed when the fateful hour struck and the Governess was due to arrive. I did what so many oppressed peoples have done in similar circumstances: I took to the woods. I hid in the extensive shrubberies—forests they seemed— which surrounded 'The Little Lodge.' Hours passed before I was retrieved and handed over to 'the Governess.' We continued to toil every day, not only at letters but at words, and also at what was much worse, figures, Letters after all had only got to be recognised, and when they stood together in a certain way one got to know their pattern and that it meant a certain sound or word which one uttered when pressed sufficiently. But the figures were tied into all sorts of tangles and did things to one another which it was extremely difficult to forecast with complete accuracy. You had to say what they did each time they were tied up together, and the Governess apparently attached enormous importance to the answer being exact. If it was not right, it was wrong. It was not any use being 'nearly right.' In some cases these figures got into debt with one another: you had to borrow one or carry one, and afterwards you had to pay back the one you had borrowed. These complications cast a steadily gathering shadow over my daily life.

MEL, p. 18.
They took one away from all the interesting things one wanted to do in the nursery or in the garden. They made increasing inroads upon one's leisure. One could hardly get time to do any of the things one wanted to do. They became a general worry and preoccupation. More especially was this true when we descended into a dismal bog called 'sums.' There appeared to be no limit to these. When one sum was done, there was always another. Just as soon as 1 managed to tackle a particular class of these afflictions, some other much more variegated type was thrust upon me.

My mother took no part in these impositions, but she gave me to understand that she approved of them and she sided with the Governess almost always. My picture of her in Ireland is in a riding habit, fitting like a skin and often beautifully spotted with mud. She and my father hunted continually on their large horses; and sometimes there were great scares because one or the other did not come back for many hours after they were expected.

My mother always seemed to me a fairy princess: a radiant being possessed of limitless riches and power. Lord D'Abernon has described her as she was in these Irish days in words for which I am grateful.

New sentences in blue further describing his mother were added which were not in *Strand*. Churchill liked d'Aberon's description of his mother. The quote by Lord d'Abernon is 'More of the panther than of the woman in her look.'[1]

Strand, December 1924, p. 606.
They took one away from all the interesting things one wanted to do in the nursery or in the garden. They made increasing inroads upon one's leisure. One could hardly get time to do any of the things one wanted to do, They became a general worry and preoccupation. More especially was this true when we descended into a dismal bog called 'sums.' There appeared to be no limit to these. When one sum was done, there was always another. Just as soon as 1 managed to tackle a particular class of these afflictions, some other much more variegated type was thrust upon me.

My mother took no part in these impositions, but she gave me to understand that she approved of them and she sided with the Governess almost always. My picture of her in Ireland is in a riding habit, fitting like a skin and often beautifully spotted with mud. She and my father hunted continually on their large horses; and sometimes there were great scares because one or the other did not come back for many hours after they were expected.

[My mother always seemed to me a fairy princess: a radiant being possessed of limitless riches and power. Lord D'Abernon has described her as she was in these Irish days in words for which I am grateful.]

Break here for several pages where new material appears in *MEL* that has no counterpart in *Strand*. The new material relates to further descriptions of what he remembers about his mother as well as his mother's appointing of Mrs. Everett as his nanny. Churchill was always enamoured of his nanny and wrote lovingly of her.

MEL, pp. 19–20.
I revisited 'The Little Lodge' when lecturing on the Boer War in Dublin in the winter of 1900. I remembered well that it was a long low white building with green shutters and verandahs, and that there was a lawn around it about as big as Trafalgar Square and surrounded by forests. I thought it must have been at least a mile from the Viceregal. When I saw it again, I was astonished to find that the lawn was only about sixty [thirty] yards across, that the forests were little more than bushes [hedges], and that it only took a minute to ride to it from the Viceregal where I was staying.

My next foothold of memory is Ventnor. I loved Ventnor. Mrs. Everest had a sister who lived at Ventnor. Her husband had been nearly thirty years a prison warder. Both then and in later years he used to take me for long walks over the Downs or through the Landslip. He told me many stories of mutinies in the prisons and how he had been attacked and injured on several occasions by the convicts. When I first stayed at Ventnor we were fighting a war with the Zulus. There were pictures in the papers of these Zulus. They were black and naked, with spears called 'assegais' which they threw very cleverly. [I used to practice myself with the stems of bracken, which made splendid 'assegais.' The Zulus] They killed a great many of our soldiers, but judging from the pictures, not nearly so many as our soldiers killed of them. I was very angry with the Zulus, and glad to hear they were being killed; and so was my friend, the old prison warder. After a while it seemed that they were all killed, because this particular war came to an end and there were no more pictures of Zulus in the papers and nobody worried any more about them.

A few new words added for MEL are shown in blue above to replace the words in red. They relate to the size of the lawn and the type of shrubbery. Several sentences were removed from the *Strand* article for *MEL* and are shown below in red.

Strand, December 1924, p. 606.
I revisited 'The Little Lodge' when lecturing on the Boer War in Dublin in the winter of 1900. I remembered well that it was a long low white building with green shutters and verandahs, and that there was a lawn around it about as big as Trafalgar Square and entirely surrounded by forests. I thought it must have been at least a mile from the Viceregal. When I saw it again, I was astonished to find that the lawn was only about thirty yards across, that the forests were little more than hedges, and that it only took a minute to ride to it from the Viceregal where I was staying.

We left Ireland at the end of 1879. Ireland fades in consequence from my recollection.

My next foothold of memory is Ventnor. I loved Ventnor. Mrs. Everest had a sister who lived at Ventnor. Her husband had been nearly thirty years a prison warder. Both then and in later years he used to take me for long walks over the Downs or through the Landslip. He told me many stories of mutinies in the prisons and how he had been attacked and injured on several occasions by the convicts. When I first stayed at Ventnor we were fighting a war with the Zulus. There were pictures in the papers of these Zulus. They were black and naked, with spears called 'assegais' which they threw very cleverly. I used to practice myself with the stems of bracken, which made splendid 'assegais.' The Zulus killed a great many of our soldiers, but judging from the pictures, not nearly so many as our soldiers killed of them. I was very angry with the Zulus, and glad to hear they were being killed; and so was my friend, the old prison warder. After a while it seemed that they were all killed, because this particular war came to an end and there were no more pictures of Zulus in the papers, and nobody worried any more about them.

MEL, pp. 20–21.
One day when we were out on the cliffs near Ventnor, 'we saw a great splendid ship with all her sails set, passing the shore only a mile or two away. 'That is a troopship,' they said, 'bringing the men back from the war.' But it may have been from India, I cannot remember. Then all of a sudden there were black clouds and wind and the first drops of a storm, and we just scrambled home without getting wet through. The next time I went out on those cliffs there was no splendid ship in full sail, but three black masts were pointed

out to me, sticking up out of the water in a stark way. She was the *Eurydice*. She had capsized. Just about this time also there happened the 'Tay Bridge Disaster.' A whole bridge tumbled down while a train was running on it in a great storm, and all the passengers were drowned. I supposed they could not get out of the carriage windows in time. It would be very hard to open one of those windows where you have to pull up a long strap before you can let it down. No wonder they were all drowned. All my world was very angry that the Government should have allowed a bridge like this to tumble down. It seemed to me they had been very careless, and I did not wonder at all that the people said they would vote against them for being so lazy and neglectful as to let such a shocking thing happen.

Churchill removed all the text shown in red below from the *Strand* which described in detail the death of the sailors in the capsized boat. This made for a less gruesome text.

Strand, December 1924, p. 607.
One day when we were out on the cliffs near Ventnor, 'we saw a great splendid ship with all her sails set, passing the shore only a mile or two away. 'That is a troopship,' they said, 'bringing the men back from the war.' But it may have been from India, I cannot remember. Then all of a sudden there were black clouds and wind and the first drops of a storm, and we just scrambled home without getting wet through. The next time I went out on those cliffs there was no splendid ship in full sail, but three black masts were pointed out to me, sticking up out of the water in a stark way. She was the Eurydice. She had capsized in this very squall and gone to the bottom with eight hundred sailors on board. The divers went down to bring up the corpses. I was told, and it made a scar on my mind, that some of the divers had fainted with terror at seeing the fish eating the corpses of the poor soldiers who had been drowned just as they were coming back home after all their hard work and danger in fighting savages. I seem to have seen some of these corpses towed very slowly by boats one sunny day. There were many people on the cliffs to watch, and we all took off our hats in sorrow.

Just about this time also there happened the 'Tay Bridge Disaster.' A whole bridge tumbled down while a train was running on it in a great storm, and all the passengers were drowned. I supposed they could not get out of the carriage windows in time. It would be very hard to open one of those windows where you have to pull up a long strap before you can let it down, No wonder they were all drowned. All my world was very angry that the Government should have allowed a bridge like this to tumble down. It seemed to me they had been very careless, and I did not wonder at all that the people said they would vote against them for being so lazy and neglectful as to let such a shocking thing happen.

MEL, pp. 21–2.
In 1880 we were all thrown out of office by Mr. Gladstone. Mr. Gladstone was a very dangerous man who went about rousing people up, lashing them into fury so that they voted against the Conservatives and turned my grandfather out of his place as Lord-Lieutenant of Ireland. He liked this place much less than his old office of Lord President of the Council, which he had held in Lord Beaconsfield's previous Government [1867]. When he was Lord-Lieutenant he had to spend all his money on giving entertainments to the Irish in Dublin; and my grandmother had also got up a great subscription called 'The Famine Fund.' However, it was borne in upon me that the Irish were a very ungrateful people: they did not say so much as 'Thank you' for the entertainments, nor even for 'The Famine Fund.' **The Duke would much rather have stayed in England where he could live in his own home at Blenheim and regularly attend the Cabinet. But he always did whatever Lord Beaconsfield told him to do.** Lord Beaconsfield was the great enemy of Mr. Gladstone, and everybody called him 'Dizzy.' However, this time 'Dizzy' had been thoroughly beaten by Mr. Gladstone, so we were all flung out into Opposition and the country began to be ruined very rapidly. Everyone said it was 'going to the dogs.' And then on top of all this Lord Beaconsfield got very ill. He had a long illness; and as he was also very old, it killed him. I followed his illness from day to day with great anxiety, because everyone said what a loss he would be to his country and how no one else could stop Mr. Gladstone from working his wicked will upon us all. 1 was always sure Lord Beaconsfield was going to die, and at last the day came when all the people I saw went about with very sad faces because, as they said, a great and splendid Statesman, who loved our country and defied the Russians, had died of a broken heart because of the ingratitude with which he had been treated by the Radicals.

The text shown in blue above was added and did not appear in the *Strand* version. Churchill now emphasizes that events were beyond the Duke's control and that the Duke always obeyed Beaconsfield. The text in red below is how the original article was written.

Strand, December 1924, p. 607.
In 1880 we were all thrown out of office by Mr. Gladstone. Mr. Gladstone was a very dangerous man who went about rousing people up, lashing them into fury so that they voted against the Conservatives and turned my grandfather out of his place as Lord-Lieutenant of Ireland. He liked this place much less than his old office of Lord President of the Council, which he had held in 1867. When he was Lord-Lieutenant he had to spend all his money on giving entertainments to the Irish in Dublin; and my grandmother had also got up a great subscription called 'The Famine Fund.' However, it was borne in upon me that the Irish were a very ungrateful people: they did not say so much as 'Thank you' for the entertainments, nor even for 'The Famine Fund.' The Duke was very glad to come back to England, where he could live in his own home at Blenheim; but he was sorry to sit no longer in the Cabinet with Lord Beaconsfield. Lord Beaconsfield was the great enemy of Mr. Gladstone, and everybody called him 'Dizzy.' However, this time 'Dizzy' had been thoroughly beaten by Mr. Gladstone, so we were all flung out into Opposition and the country began to be ruined very rapidly. Everyone said it was 'going to the dogs.' And then on top of all this Lord Beaconsfield got very ill. He had a long illness; and as he was also very old, it killed him. I followed his illness from day to day with great anxiety, because everyone said what a loss he would be to his country and how no one else could stop Mr. Gladstone from working his wicked will upon us all. 1 was always sure Lord Beaconsfield was going to die, and at last the day came when all the people I saw went about with very sad faces because, as they said, a great and splendid Statesman, who loved our country and defied the Russians, had died of a broken heart because of the ingratitude with which he had been treated by the Radicals."

MEL, pp. 22–3
I have already described the dreaded apparition in my world of 'The Governess.' But now a much worse peril began to threaten. I was to go to school. I was now seven years old, and I was what grown-up people in their offhand way called 'a troublesome boy.' It appeared that I was to go away from home for many weeks at a stretch in order to do lessons under masters. The term had already begun, but still I should have to stay seven weeks before I could come home for Christmas. Although much that I had heard about school had made a distinctly disagreeable impression on my mind, an impression, I may add, thoroughly borne out by the actual experience, I was also excited and agitated by this great change in my life. I thought in spite of the lessons, it would be fun living with so many other boys, and that we should make friends together and have great adventures. Also I was told that 'school days were the happiest time in one's life'. **Several grown-up people [They]** added that in their day, when they were young, schools were very rough: there was bullying, they didn't get enough to eat, they had 'to break the ice in their pitchers' each morning (a thing I have never seen done **in my life [before or since]**). But now it was all changed. School life nowadays was one long treat. All the boys enjoyed it. Some of my cousins who were a little older had been quite sorry—I was told— to come home for the holidays. Cross-examined, the cousins did not confirm this; they only grinned. Anyhow I was perfectly helpless. Irresistible tides drew me swiftly forward. I was no more consulted about leaving home than I had been about coming into the world.

The text in blue above is new for *MEL*. shown below in red is what was originally written in the Strand.

Strand, December 1924, p. 608.
I have already described the dreaded apparition in my world of 'The Governess.' But now a much worse peril began to threaten. I was to go to school. I was now seven years old, and I was what grown-up people in their offhand way called 'a troublesome boy.' It appeared that I was to go away from home for many weeks at a stretch in order to do lessons under masters. The term had already begun, but still I should have to stay seven weeks before I could come home for Christmas.

Although much that I had heard about school had made a distinctly disagreeable impression on my mind, an impression, I may add, thoroughly borne out by the actual experience, I was also excited and agitated by this great change in my life. I thought in spite of the lessons, it would be fun living with so many other boys, and that we should make friends together and have great adventures. Also I was told that 'school days were the happiest time in one's life.' They added that in their day, when they were young, schools were very rough: there was bullying, they didn't get enough to eat, they had 'to break the ice in their pitchers' each morning (a thing I have never seen done before or since). But now it was all changed. School life nowadays was one long treat. All the boys enjoyed it. Some of my cousins who were a little older had been quite sorry—I was told— to come home for the holidays. Cross-examined, the cousins did not confirm this; they only grinned. Anyhow I was perfectly helpless. Irresistible tides drew me swiftly forward. I was no more consulted about leaving home than I had been about coming into the world.

MEL, p. 23.
It was very interesting buying all the things one had to have for going to school. No less than fourteen pairs of socks were on the list. Mrs. Everest thought this was very extravagant. She said that with care ten pairs would do quite well. Still it was a good thing to have some to spare, as one could then make sure of avoiding the very great dangers inseparable from 'sitting in wet feet.'

The fateful day arrived. My mother took me to the station in a hansom cab. She gave me three half-crowns, which I dropped on to the floor of the cab, and we had to scramble about in the straw to find them again. We only just caught the train. If we had missed it, it would have been the end of the world. However, we didn't, and the world went on.

The school my parents had selected for my education was one of the most fashionable and expensive in the country. It modelled itself upon Eton and aimed at being preparatory for that Public School above all others. It was supposed to be the very last thing in schools. Only ten boys in a class; electric light (then a wonder); a swimming pond, spacious football and cricket grounds; two or three school treats, or 'expeditions' as they were called, every term; the masters all M.A.'s in gowns and mortar-boards; a chapel of its own; no hampers allowed; everything provided by the authorities. It was a dark

November afternoon when we arrived at this establishment. We had tea with the Headmaster, with whom my mother conversed in the most easy manner. I was preoccupied with the fear of spilling my cup and so making 'a bad start.' I was also miserable at the idea of being left alone among all these strangers in this great, fierce, formidable place. After all I was only seven, and I had been so happy in my nursery with all my toys, I had such wonderful toys: a real steam engine, a magic lantern, and a collection of soldiers already nearly 2 thousand strong. Now it was to be all lessons, Seven or eight hours of lessons every day except half-holidays, and football or cricket in addition.

Strand, December 1924, p. 608.
Text in *MEL* exactly the same as that in the *Strand* article.

MEL, p. 24.
When the last sound of my mother's departing wheels had died away, the Headmaster invited me to hand over any money I had in my possession. I produced my three half-crowns, which were duly entered in a book, and I was told that from time to time there would be a 'shop' at the school with all sorts of things which one would like to have, and that I could choose what I liked up to the limit of the seven and sixpence. Then we quitted the Headmaster's parlour and the comfortable private side of the house, and entered the more bleak apartments reserved for the instruction and accommodation of the pupils. I was taken into a Form Room and told to sit at a desk. All the other boys were out of doors, and I was alone with the Form Master. He produced a thin greeny-brown, covered book filled with words in different types of print.

'You have never done any Latin before, have you?' he said.

'No, sir.'

'This is a Latin grammar.' He opened it at a well-thumbed page. 'You must learn this,' he said, pointing to a number of words in a frame of lines. 'I will come back in half an hour and see what you know.'

Behold me then on a gloomy evening, with an aching heart, seated in front of the First Declension.

Strand, December 1924, p. 609.
Text exactly the same as used for *MEL*.

MEL, pp. 24–5.

Mensa	a table
Mensa	O table
Mensam	a table
Mensae	of a table
Mensae	to or for a table
Mensa	by, with or from a table

What on earth did it mean? Where was the sense in it? It seemed absolute rigmarole to me. However, there was one thing I could always do: I could learn by heart. And I thereupon proceeded, as far as my private sorrows would allow, to memorise the acrostic-looking task which had been set me.

In due course the Master returned.

'Have you learnt it?' he asked.

'I think I can say it, sir,' I replied, and I gabbled it off.

He seemed so satisfied with this that I was emboldened to ask a question.

'What does it mean, sir?'

'It means what it says, Mensa, a table. Mensa is a noun of the First Declension. There are five declensions. You have learnt the singular of the First Declension.'

'But,' I repeated, 'what does it mean?'

'Mensa means a table,' he answered.

'Then why does mensa also mean O table,' I enquired, 'and what does O table mean?'

'Mensa, O table, is the vocative case,' he replied.

'But why O table?' I persisted in genuine curiosity.

'O table, —you would use that in addressing a table, in invoking a table.' And then seeing he was not carrying me with him, 'You would use it in speaking to a table.'

'But I never do,' I blurted out in honest amazement.

'If you are impertinent, you will be punished, and punished, let me tell you, very severely,' was his conclusive rejoinder.

Such was my first introduction to the classics from which I have been told, many of our cleverest men have derived so much solace and profit.

Strand, December 1924, p. 609–10.

Text here is exactly the same as that used for *MEL*.

MEL, p. 26.
The Form Master's observations about punishment were by no means without their warrant at St. James's School. Flogging with the birch in accordance with the Eton fashion was a great feature in its curriculum. But I am sure no Eton boy, and certainly no Harrow boy of my day, ever received such a cruel flogging as this Head-master was accustomed to inflict upon the little boys who were in his care and power. They exceeded in severity anything that would be tolerated in any of the Reformatories under the Home Office. My reading in later life has supplied me with some possible explanations of his temperament. Two or three times a month the whole school was marshalled in the Library, and one or more delinquents were hauled off to an adjoining apartment by the two head boys, and there flogged until they bled freely, while the rest sat quaking, listening to their screams. This form of correction was strongly reinforced by frequent religious services of a somewhat High Church character in the chapel. Mrs. Everest was very much against the Pope. If the truth were known, she said, he was behind the Fenians. She was herself Low Church, and her dislike of ornaments and ritual, and generally her extremely unfavourable opinion of the Supreme Pontiff, had prejudiced me strongly against that personage and all religious practices supposed to be associated with him. I therefore did not derive much comfort from the spiritual side of my education at this juncture. On the other hand, I experienced the fullest applications of the secular arm.

How I hated this school, and what a life of anxiety I lived there for more than two years. I made very little progress at my lessons, and none at all at games. I counted the days and the hours to the end of every term, when I should return home from this hateful servitude and arrange my soldiers in line of battle on the nursery floor. The greatest pleasure I had in those days was reading.

The sentence below in red was added for the *MEL* version and was not in the *Strand* article.

Strand, December 1924, p. 610.

The Form Master's observations about punishment were by no means without their warrant at St. James's School. Flogging with the birch in accordance with the Eton fashion was a great feature in its curriculum. But I am sure no Eton boy, and certainly no Harrow boy of my day, ever received such a cruel flogging as this Head-master was accustomed to inflict upon the little boys who were in his care and power. They exceeded in severity anything that would be tolerated in any of the Reformatories under the Home Office. [My reading in later life has supplied me with some possible explanations of his temperament.] Two or three times a month the whole school was marshalled in the library, and one or more delinquents were hauled off to an adjoining apartment by the two head boys, and there flogged until they bled freely, while the rest sat quaking, listening to their screams. This form of correction was strongly reinforced by frequent religious services of a somewhat High Church character in the chapel. Mrs. Everest was very much against the Pope. If the truth were known, she said, he was behind the Fenians. She was herself Low Church, and her dislike of ornaments and ritual, and generally her extremely unfavourable opinion of the Supreme Pontiff, had prejudiced me strongly against that personage and all religious practices supposed to be associated with him. I therefore did not derive much comfort from the spiritual side of my education at this juncture. On the other hand, I experienced the fullest applications of the secular arm.

How I hated this school, and what a life of anxiety I lived there for more than two years. I made very little progress at my lessons, and none at all at games. I counted the days and the hours to the end of every term, when I should return home from this hateful servitude and range my soldiers in line of battle on the nursery floor. The greatest pleasure I had in those days was reading.

MEL, pp. 26–7.
When I was nine and one half my father gave me *Treasure Island*, and I remember the delight with which I devoured it. My teachers saw me at once backward and precocious, reading books beyond my years and yet at the bottom of the Form. They were offended. They had large resources of compulsion at their disposal, but I was stubborn. Where my reason, imagination or interest were not engaged, I would not or I could not learn. In all the twelve years I was at school no one ever succeeded in making

me write a Latin verse or learn any Greek except the alphabet. I do not at all excuse myself for this foolish neglect of opportunities procured at so much expense by my parents and brought so forcibly to my attention by my Preceptors. Perhaps if I had been introduced to the ancients through their history and customs, instead of through their grammar and syntax, I might have had a better record.

1 fell into a low state of health at St. James's School, and finally after a serious illness my parents took me away, Our family doctor, the celebrated Robson Roose, then practised at Brighton; and as I was now supposed to be very delicate, it was thought desirable that I should be under his constant care. 1 was accordingly, in 1883, transferred to a school at Brighton kept by two ladies. This was a smaller school than the one I had left. It was also cheaper and less pretentious. But there was an element of kindness and of sympathy which I had found conspicuously lacking in my first experiences. Here I remained for three years; and though I very nearly died from an attack of double pneumonia, I got gradually much stronger in that bracing air and gentle surroundings. At this school I was allowed to learn things which interested me: French, History, lots of Poetry by heart, and above all Riding and Swimming. The impression of those years makes a pleasant picture in my mind, in strong contrast to my earlier school day memories.

Strand, December 1924, pp. 610–11.
Text here exactly the same as that to be used in MEL.

MEL, pp. 27–8
The remainder of Chapter I in *MEL* has no counterpart in the *Strand* article. This material tells the story of Churchill and his going to chapel and what he thought about Mrs. Everest's view of Church. The story picks up in *MEL* Chapter II with his entry to Harrow.

MEL, Chapter II *Harrow*, p. 29.

I had scarcely passed my twelfth birthday when I entered the inhospitable regions of examinations, through which for the next seven years I was destined to journey. These examinations were a great trial to me. The subjects which were dearest to the examiners were almost invariably those I fancied least. I would have liked to have been examined in history, poetry and writing essays. The examiners, on the other hand, were partial to Latin and mathematics. And their will prevailed. Moreover, the questions which they asked on both these subjects were almost invariably those to which I was unable to suggest a satisfactory answer, I should have liked to be asked to say what I knew. They always tried to ask what I did not know. When I would have willingly displayed my knowledge, they sought to expose my ignorance. This sort of treatment had only one result: I did not do well in examinations.

This was especially true of my Entrance Examination to Harrow. The Head-master, Mr. Welldon, however, took a broad-minded view of my Latin prose: he showed discernment in judging my general ability. **This was the more remarkable, because I was found unable to answer a single question in the Latin paper. I wrote my name at the top of the page. I wrote down the number of the question 'I'. After much reflection I put a bracket round it thus '(I)'. But thereafter I could not think of anything connected with it that was either relevant or true. Incidentally there arrived from nowhere in particular a blot and several smudges.**

Churchill added the sentences in blue to the *MEL* text; they did not appear in the *Strand*. These sentences clearly embellish the frustration and pain that Churchill experienced.

Strand, December 1924, p. 611.

"I had scarcely passed my twelfth birthday when I entered the inhospitable regions of examinations, through which for the next seven years I was destined to journey. These examinations were a great trial to me. The subjects which were dearest to the examiners were almost invariably those I fancied least. I would have liked to have been examined in history, poetry and writing essays. The examiners, on the other hand, were partial to Latin and mathematics. And their will prevailed. Moreover, the questions which they asked on both these subjects were almost invariably those to which I was unable to suggest a satisfactory answer, I should have liked to be asked to say what I knew. They always tried to ask what I did not know. When I would have willingly displayed my knowledge, they sought to expose my ignorance. This sort of treatment had only one result: I did not do well in examinations.

This was especially true of my Entrance Examination to Harrow. The head-master, Dr. Welldon, however, took a broad-minded view of my Latin prose: he showed discernment in judging my general ability.

MEL, p. 30.

In consequence of his decision, I was in due course placed in the third, or lowest, division of the Fourth, or bottom, Form. The names of the new boys were printed in the School List in alphabetical order; and as my correct name, Spencer-Churchill, began with an 'S', I gained no more advantage from the alphabet than from the wider sphere of letters. 1 was in fact only two from the bottom of the whole school; and these two, I regret to say, disappeared almost immediately through illness or some other cause.

The Harrow custom of calling the roll is different from that of Eton. At Eton the boys stand in a cluster and lift their hats when their names are called, At Harrow they file past a Master in the school yard and answer one by one, My position was therefore revealed in its somewhat invidious humility. It was the year 1887. Lord Randolph Churchill had only just resigned his position as Leader of the House of Commons and Chancellor of the Exchequer, and he still towered in the forefront of politics. In consequence large numbers of visitors of both sexes used to wait on the school steps, in order to see me march by; and I frequently heard the irreverent comment, 'Why, he's last of all!'

I continued in this unpretentious situation for nearly a year. However, by being so long in the lowest form I gained an immense advantage over the cleverer boys. They all went on to learn Latin and Greek and splendid things like that. But I was taught English.

Here, Churchill has added the last three sentences of this section, as well as a new introductory phrase, as shown in blue above. The three sentences are pivotally important words, for he would use them over and over again when discussing his writing skills. In addition, they would be quoted quite

frequently by later publications, as described in Chapter 7 of this book covering the impact of *MEL*, as the genesis of Churchill's love of and skill in writing.

Strand, December 1924, p. 611–2.
I was in due course placed in the third, or lowest, division of the Fourth, or bottom, Form. The names of the new boys were printed in the School List in alphabetical order; and as my correct name, Spencer-Churchill, began with an 'S', I gained no more advantage from the alphabet than from the wider sphere of letters. I, was, in fact only two from the bottom of the whole school; and these two, I regret to say, disappeared almost immediately through illness or some other cause.

The Harrow custom of calling the roll is different from that of Eton. At Eton the boys stand in a cluster and lift their hats when their names are called, At Harrow they file past a Master in the school yard and answer one by one. My position was therefore revealed in its somewhat invidious humility. It was the year 1887. Lord Randolph Churchill had only just resigned his position as Leader of the House of Commons and Chancellor of the Exchequer, and he still towered in the forefront of politics. In consequence large numbers of visitors of both sexes used to wait on the school steps, in order to see me march by; and I frequently heard the irreverent comment, 'Why, he's last of all!'

I continued in this unpretentious situation for nearly a year.

There follows a page and a half of text in *MEL* (pp. 30–32) which is not based on the *Strand* article. This section highlights the theme of learning English and being grounded in grammar and composition and includes the words:

> *Thus I got into my bones the essential structure of the ordinary British sentence—which is a noble thing.* And when in after years my schoolfellows who had won prizes and distinction for writing such beautiful Latin poetry and pithy Greek epigrams had to come down again to common English, to earn their living or make their way, I did not feel myself at any disadvantage. *Naturally I am biased in favour of boys learning English. I would make them all learn English: and then I would let the clever ones learn Latin as an honor, and Greek as a treat.*

But the only thing I would whip them for is not knowing English. I would whip them hard for that. [emphasis added]

This section would be quoted again and again in the years that follow and is essential to know and understand if one is to appreciate how Churchill felt about the English language and writing.

The text in *MEL* relating to the *Strand* article begins again on p. 32.

MEL, p. 32.
It was thought incongruous that while I apparently stagnated in the lowest form, I should gain a prize open to the whole school for reciting to the Headmaster twelve hundred lines of Macaulay's 'Lays of Ancient Rome' without making a single mistake. 1 also succeeded in passing the preliminary examination for the Army while still almost at the bottom of the school. This examination seemed to have called forth a very special effort on my part, for many boys far above me in the school failed in it. I also had a piece of good luck. We knew that among other questions we should be asked to draw from memory a map of some country or other. The night before by way of final preparation I put the names of all the maps in the atlas into a hat and drew out New Zealand. I applied my good memory to the geography of that Dominion. Sure enough the first question in the paper was: 'Draw a map of New Zealand.' This was what is called at Monte Carlo an *en plein*, and I ought to have been paid thirty-five times my stake. However, I certainly got paid very high marks for my paper.

The text in blue was added for *MEL* and did not exist in the *Strand*. It embellishes and clarifies the sentence.

Strand, December 1924, pp. 611–12.
It was thought incongruous that [while I apparently stagnated in the lowest form,] I should gain a prize open to the whole school for reciting to the Headmaster twelve hundred lines of Macaulay['s 'Lays of Ancient Rome'] without making a single mistake. 1 also succeeded in passing the preliminary examination for the Army while still almost at the bottom of the school. This examination seemed to have called forth a very special effort on my part, for many boys far above me in the school failed in it.

I also had a piece of good luck. We knew that among other questions we should be asked to draw from memory a map of some country or other. The night before by way of final preparation I put the names of all the maps in the atlas into a hat and drew out New Zealand. I applied my good memory to the geography of that Dominion. Sure enough the first question in the paper was: 'Draw a map of New Zealand.' This was what is called at Monte Carlo an *en plein*, and I ought to have been paid thirty-five times my stake. However, I certainly got paid very high marks for my paper.

MEL, p. 33.
I was now embarked on a military career. This orientation was entirely due to my collection of soldiers. I had ultimately nearly fifteen hundred. They were all of one size, all British, and organised as an infantry division with a cavalry brigade. **My brother Jack commanded the hostile army. But by a Treaty for the Limitation of Armaments he was only allowed to have coloured troops; and they were not allowed to have artillery.** Very important! I could muster myself only eighteen field-guns—besides fortress pieces. But all the other services were complete—except one. It is what every army is always short of—transport. My father's old friend, Sir Henry Drummond Wolff, admiring my array, noticed this deficiency and provided a fund from which it was to some extent supplied.

The text in blue above is new and does not appear in the *Strand*. It is unclear why Churchill wanted to admit the disadvantage Jack had in not having artillery.

Strand, December 1924, p. 612.
I was now embarked on a military career. This orientation was entirely due to my collection of soldiers. I had ultimately nearly fifteen hundred. They were all of one size, all British, and organised as an infantry division with a cavalry brigade. Very important! I could muster myself only eighteen field-guns—besides fortress pieces. But all the other services were complete—except one. It is what every army is always short of—transport. My father's old friend, Sir Henry Drummond Wolff, admiring my array, noticed this deficiency and provided a fund from which it was to some extent supplied.

MEL, p. 33–4.

The day came when my father himself paid a formal visit of inspection. All the troops were arranged in the correct formation of attack. He spent twenty minutes studying the scene—which was really impressive—with a keen eye and captivating smile. At the end he asked me if I would like to go into the Army. I thought it would be splendid to command an Army, so I said 'Yes' at once; and immediately I was taken at my word. For years I thought my father with his experience and flair had discerned in me the qualities of military genius. But I was told later that he had only come to the conclusion that I was not clever enough to go to the Bar. However that may be, the toy soldiers turned the current of my life. Henceforward all my education was directed to passing into Sandhurst, and afterwards to the technical details of the profession of arms. Anything else I had to pick up for myself.

Strand, December 1924, p. 612.
Text here is the exactly the same as that used in *MEL*.

This is the end of the text in the article. The text in *MEL* continues on.

In summary, for pages 15–34 of *MEL* (except for about three pages of new text added) the *Strand* article provides the vast majority of the text in used in *MEL*. Most of the new materials relate to his schooling and his learning of the beauty of the English language.

Notes

1. Mary Lovell, *The Churchills in Love And War*, New York, W.W. Norton & Company, 2011, p. 65.

APPENDIX 3

Chapter 4: War in Cuba

Texts compared:
MEL, pp. 88–102.
Michael Wolff, *The Collected Essays of Sir Winston Churchill*, London, Library of Imperial History, 1976, Vol. I, 'Churchill and War', pp. 3–25.
'When I Risked Court Martial in Search of War', *Cosmopolitan*, 24 October 1924, vol 77, pp. 80–81, 112–3.

All of Chapter VI of *My Early Life* (*MEL*) concerns setting the stage for Churchill's plan to visit Cuba, as well as his military experience there. Much of the writing, as will be seen, is new and not adapted from previous work. What is analysed here are those places where previously published material is woven into the story. The same format as described in the section on 'Childhood' will be used here. The *Collected Essays* book mentioned above contains the wartime dispatches Churchill wrote during his Cuban experience. I have not included in any of the text comparisons the serialisation of *My Early Life* as *Memories of My Youth*, published in the *News Chronicle* in August–September 1930, because the text is taken directly from the book. Below are the direct comparisons using the same format as the previous comparisons. The text from the story in *My Early Life* is presented first, then followed by texts in the other publications which are listed chronologically. Comments as thought useful on the similarities and difference are provided in **bold** after the text from *My Early Life*. Comments are **bolded** to make it easy to differentiate the authors comments from the Churchill text.

MEL, p. 88.
In the closing decade of the Victorian era the Empire had enjoyed so long a spell of almost unbroken peace, that medals and all they represented in experience and adventure were becoming extremely scarce in the British Army. The veterans of the Crimea and the Indian Mutiny were gone from the active list. The Afghan and Egyptian warriors of the early eighties had reached the senior ranks. Scarcely a shot had been fired in anger since then, and when I joined the 4th Hussars in January 1895 scarcely a captain, hardly even a subaltern, could be found throughout Her Majesty's forces who had seen even the smallest kind of war. Rarity in a desirable commodity is usually the cause of enhanced value; and there has never been a time when war service was held in so much esteem by the military authorities or more ardently sought by officers of every rank. It was the swift road to promotion and advancement in every arm. It was the glittering gateway to distinction. It cast a glamour upon the fortunate possessor alike in the eyes of elderly gentlemen and young ladies. How we young officers envied the senior Major for his adventures at Abu Klea!

The opening of Chapter VI is exactly the same as the opening paragraph in the *Cosmopolitan* article. There was new material added to *MEL* as shown in blue above. Shown in red below is where the new text was inserted into the original text in the article. The new text provides insight into how important Churchill believes medals, awards and personal recognition is in advancing a person's career.

Cosmopolitan, October 1924, p. 80.
In the closing decade of the Victorian era the Empire had enjoyed so long a spell of almost unbroken peace, that medals and all they represented in experience and adventure were becoming extremely scarce in the British Army. The veterans of the Crimea and the Indian Mutiny were gone from the active list. The Afghan and Egyptian warriors of the early eighties had reached the senior ranks. Scarcely a shot had been fired in anger since then, and when I joined the 4th Hussars in January 1895 scarcely a captain, hardly ever a subaltern, could be found throughout Her Majesty's forces who had seen even the smallest kind of war. [Rarity in a desirable commodity is usually the cause of enhanced value; and there has never been a time when

war service was held in so much esteem by the military authorities or more ardently sought by officers of every rank. It was the swift road to promotion and advancement in every arm. It was the glittering gateway to distinction. It cast a glamour upon the fortunate possessor alike in the eyes of elderly gentlemen and young ladies.] How we young officers envied the senior Major for his adventures at Abu Klea!

MEL, pp. 88–9.
How we admired the Colonel with his long row of decorations! We listened with almost insatiable interest to the accounts which they were good enough to give us on more than one occasion of stirring deeds and episodes already melting into the mist of time. How we longed to have a similar store of memories to unpack and display, if necessary repeatedly, to a sympathetic audience! How we wondered whether our chance would ever come—whether we too in our turn would have battles to fight over again and again in the agreeable atmosphere of the after-dinner mess table? Prowess at polo, in the hunting-field, or between the flags, might count for something, But the young soldier who had been 'on active service' and 'under fire' had an aura about him to which the Generals he served under, the troopers he led, and the girls he courted, accorded a unanimous, sincere, and spontaneous recognition.

The text in blue above, newly added to *MEL*, further glorifies the acquisition of battle experience and how important to a person's career it is. The text in red below shows where the text was added to the article.

Cosmopolitan, October 1924, p. 80.
How we admired the Colonel with his long row of decorations! [We listened with almost insatiable interest to the accounts which they were good enough to give us on more than one occasion of stirring deeds and episodes already melting into the mist of time. How we longed to have a similar store of memories to unpack and display, if necessary repeatedly, to a sympathetic audience!] How we wondered whether our chance would ever come—whether we too in our turn would have battles to fight over again and again in the agreeable atmosphere of the after-dinner mess table? Prowess at polo, in the hunting-field, or between the flags, might count for something. But

the young soldier who had been 'on active service' and 'under fire' had an aura about him to which the Generals he served under, the troopers he led, and the girls he courted, accorded a unanimous, sincere, and spontaneous recognition.

MEL, p. 99.
We pulled on our clothes anyhow, **and retired along the river as gracefully as might be and returned to the General's headquarters. When we arrived, there was a regular skirmish going on half a mile away, and the bullets were falling all over the camp**. The rebels **were armed mainly with [who use]** Remingtons, **and the** deep note of their pieces contrasted strangely with the shrill rattle of the magazine rifles of the Spaniards. After about half an hour the insurgents had had enough, and went off carrying away with them the wounded and dead, with which it was hoped they were not unprovided.

The text in blue above was newly added to the text in *MEL*. Below are the fragments extracted from the text in the original dispatch. The new text highlights that there was an active skirmish underway and that all were at risk.

Collected, December 2, 1895, p. 12.
We pulled on our clothes anyhow, …The rebels **who use** Remingtons, … deep note of their pieces contrasted strangely with the shrill rattle of the magazine rifles of the Spaniards. After about half an hour the insurgents had had enough and went off carrying … the**ir** wounded and dead away them.

MEL, p. 100.
The General and his staff rode forward until the smoke-crested crackling fence was only four or five hundred yards away. Here we halted, and sitting mounted, without the slightest cover or concealment, watched the assault of the infantry. During this period the air was full of whizzings, and the palm trees smitten by the bullets yielded resounding smacks and thuds. The Spaniards were on their mettle; and we had to do our best to keep up appearances. It really seemed very dangerous indeed, and I was astonished to see how few people were hit amid all this clatter. In our group of about twenty, only three or four horses and men were wounded, and not one

killed. **Presently, to my relief, the sound of the Mauser volleys began to predominate, and the rebel fire to slacken till it finally ceased altogether.**

The text shown in blue above was newly added to *MEL* from the *Cosmopolitan* and the text in red below was removed from the text as published in *MEL*.

Cosmopolitan, October 1924, p. 81.
…the General and his staff **and two British visitors** rode **solemnly** forward **on their horses** until the smoke-crested crackling fence was only four or five hundred yards away. Here we halted, and sitting mounted, without the slightest cover or concealment, watched the assault of the infantry. During this period the air was full of whizzings, and the palm trees smitten by the bullets yielded resounding smacks and thuds. The Spaniards were on their mettle; and we had to do our best to keep up appearances. It really seemed very dangerous indeed, and I was astonished to see how few people were hit amid all this clatter. In our group of about twenty, only three or four horses and men were wounded, and not one killed.

MEL, pp. 100, 102.
For a moment I could see figures scurrying to the shelter of the woods, and then came silence. The infantry advanced and occupied the enemy's position. Pursuit was impossible owing to the impenetrable **jungle** [**nature of the Woods in the rear and, as the force**].
As our column had **now** only one day's rations left, we withdrew across the plain to La Jicotea. **Spanish honour and our own curiosity alike being satisfied, the column returned to the coast, and we to England. We did not think the Spaniards were likely to bring their war in Cuba to a speedy end.**

The text in blue above was newly added and the text in red below was removed for the *MEL* text. The new text provides a closing to the episode and Churchill's conclusion about the longevity of the insurrection.

Collected, December 2, 1895, p. 13.
For a moment I could see figures scurrying to the shelter of the woods, and then came silence. The infantry advanced and occupied the enemy's position. Pursuit was impossible owing to the impenetrable **nature of the**

Woods in the rear and, as the force had now only one day's rations left, we withdrew across the plain to La Jicotea.

This section highlights for the first time that Churchill had all the previously published materials at hand when he wrote or dictated sections of *MEL*, as evidenced by picking and choosing select sentences and even individual words or phrases from those sources and weaving them with new sentences to create the text for *MEL*. Most of the text for the Cuba chapter is new and is a much more robust description of events than that found in any of the other texts. He has also glorified the importance of military experience and bravery more fully then previously.

APPENDIX 4

Chapter 4: Cavalry Charge

Text Comparisons:
My Early Life (*MEL*), Chapter XIV 'The Eve Of Omdurman', pp. 186–96.
My Early Life (*MEL*), Chapter XV 'The Sensations Of A Cavalry Charge', pp. 197–211.
Cosmopolitan, 'A Hand to Hand Fight with Desert Fanatics', December 1924, pp. 94–5, and 152–5.
The River War, London, Longmans, Green and Company, 1899. The texts of *MEL* and *The River War* are completely different. Many of the same descriptive words are used; however, the sentences are quite different.[1]
Morning Post, London, 31 August–13 October, 1898. This series of fifteen newspaper reports of Churchill's experiences cover this same topic, but no text is excerpted for *MEL*.

The story of the cavalry charge was published in at least four separate publications by Churchill, as noted above. The *Cosmopolitan* article was the only source from which Churchill drew direct text for *MEL*. The serialization of *MEL* as *Memories of My Youth*, published in the *News Chronicle* in August/September 1930, has not been included, as the text is taken directly from the book. Below are the direct comparisons presented using the same format as the comparisons in the previous appendices. The text from the story in *MEL* is presented first, followed by text from the *Cosmopolitan*. Comments as thought useful by the author on the similarities and difference are provided in **bold** after the text from *My Early Life*.

MEL, p. 186.
Nothing like the Battle of Omdurman will ever be seen again. It was the last link in the long chain of those spectacular conflicts whose vivid and majestic splendour has done so much to invest war with glamour. Everything was visible to the naked eye. The armies marched and manoeuvred on the crisp surface of the desert plain through which the Nile wandered in broad reaches, now steel, now brass. **[British]** Cavalry charged at full gallop in close order, and infantry or spearmen stood upright ranged in lines or masses to resist them. From the rocky hills which here and there flanked the great river the whole scene lay revealed in minute detail, curiously twisted, blurred and interspersed with phantom waters by the mirage. **The finite and concrete presented itself in the most keenly-chiselled forms, and then dissolved in a shimmer of unreality and illusion.** Long streaks of gleaming water, where we knew there was only desert, cut across the knees or the waists of marching troops. Batteries of artillery or long columns of cavalry emerged from a filmy world of uneven crystal on to the hard yellow-ochre sand, and took up their positions amid jagged red-black rocks with violet shadows. Over all the immense dome of the sky, dun to turquoise, turquoise to deepest blue, pierced by the flaming sun, weighed hard and heavy on marching necks and shoulders.

Text in blue above was added new and does not appear in the *Cosmopolitan* article. Where it was placed is shown in red below. The text in blue below appeared in the article but was removed in the *MEL* text. The new text highlights the ephemeral nature of vision on the hot desert sand.

Cosmopolitan, December 1924, p. 94.
Nothing like the Battle of Omdurman will ever be seen again. It was the last link in the long chain of those spectacular conflicts whose vivid and majestic splendour has done so much to invest war with glamour.

 Everything was visible to the naked eye. The armies marched and manoeuvred on the crisp surface of the desert plain through which the Nile wandered in broad reaches, now steel, now brass. **British** cavalry charged at full gallop in close order, and **the** infantry or spearmen stood upright ranged in lines or masses to resist them.

 From the rocky hills which here and there flanked the great river the whole scene lay revealed in minute detail, curiously twisted, blurred and interspersed with phantom waters by the mir- age. [The finite and concrete presented itself in the most keenly-chiselled forms, and then dissolved in a shimmer of unreality and illusion.] Long streaks of gleaming water, where we knew there was only desert, cut across the knees or the waists of marching troops. Batteries of artillery or long columns of cavalry emerged from a filmy world of uneven crystal on to the hard yellow-ochre sand, and took up their positions amid jagged red-black rocks with violet shadows. Over all the immense dome of the sky, dun to turquoise, turquoise to deepest blue, pierced by the flaming sun, weighed hard and heavy on marching necks and shoulders.

MEL, p. 186–7.
The 21st [Twenty-First] Lancers, having crossed to the left bank of the Nile at its confluence with the Atbara in the evening of August 15, [1898 and] journeyed forward by nine days' march to the advanced concentration camp just north of the Shabluka Cataract. This feature is peculiar. Across the 4,000-mile course of the Nile to the Mediterranean, Nature has here flung a high wall of rock. The river, instead of making a ten-mile detour round its western extremity, has preferred a frontal attack, and has pierced or discovered a way through the very centre of the obstructing mass, The Shabluka position was considered to be formidable. It was impossible to ascend the cataract in boats and steamers in any force that would be effective, unless the whole range of hills had first been turned from the desert flank, Such an operation would have presented a fine tactical opportunity to a Dervish army crouched behind the Shabluka hills ready to strike at the flank of any army making the indispensable turning movement. It was therefore no doubt with great relief that Sir Herbert Kitchener received from his cavalry, his scouts and his spies, the assurance that this strong position was left undefended by the enemy.

The text in blue above are new text additions and are not in the *Cosmopolitan* article. Where the new text was inserted into the article is shown in red below. The words in blue below were deleted in the *MEL* version. The added text provides a much more robust description of the scene and setting, and the level of anxiety associated with a potential attack.

Cosmopolitan, December 1924, p. 94.

The Twenty-First Lancers, having crossed to the left bank of the Nile at its confluence with the Atbara in the evening of August 15, 1898 and journeyed forward by nine days' march to the advanced concentration camp just north of the Shabluka Cataract. [This feature is peculiar. Across the 4,000-mile course of the Nile to the Mediterranean, Nature has here flung a high wall of rock. The river, instead of making a ten-mile detour round its western extremity, has preferred a frontal attack, and has pierced or discovered a way through the very centre of the obstructing mass, The Shabluka position was considered to be formidable. It was impossible to ascend the cataract in boats and steamers in any force that would be effective, unless the whole range of hills had first been turned from the desert flank, Such an operation would have presented a fine tactical opportunity to a Dervish army crouched behind the Shabluka hills ready to strike at the flank of any army making the indispensable turning movement. It was therefore no doubt with great relief that Sir Herbert Kitchener received from his cavalry, his scouts and his spies, the assurance that this strong position was left undefended by the enemy.]

MEL, pp. 187–8.

But, except, for a few fleeting horsemen, no hostile sight or sound disturbed or even diversified our march, and when the vast plain reddened in the sunset, we followed our lengthening shadows peacefully but thirstily again to the sweet waters of the river. Meanwhile the flat-bottomed gunboats and stern-wheel steamers, drawing endless tows of sailing boats carrying our supplies, had safely negotiated the cataract, and by the 27th [twenty-seventh] all our forces, desert and river, were concentrated south of the Shabluka hills with only five clear marches over open plain to the city of our quest.

On the 28th [twenty-eighth] the army set forth on its final advance. We moved in full order of battle and by stages of only eight or ten miles a day so as to save all our strength for the collision at any moment. We carried nothing with us but what we and our horses stood up in. We drew our water and food each night from the Nile and its armada. The heat in this part of Africa and at this time of the year was intense. In spite of thick clothes, spine-pads, broad-brimmed pith helmets, one felt the sun leaning down upon one and piercing our bodies with his burning rays. The canvas waterbags which hung from our saddles, agreeably cool from their own evaporation, were drained long before the afternoons had worn away. How delicious it was in the evenings when, the infantry having reached and ordered their bivouac, the cavalry screen was withdrawn, and we filed down in gold and purple twilight to drink and drink and drink again from the swift abundant Nile.

The text in blue above are new text additions and are not in the *Cosmopolitan* article, and where the new text was inserted into the article is shown in red below. The few words in blue below were changed for the *MEL* version. The added text provides a much more robust description of the situation and thus engages the reader to a greater extent.

Cosmopolitan, December 1924, pp. 94–5.
But, except, for a few fleeting horsemen, no hostile sight or sound disturbed or even diversified our march, and when the vast plain reddened in the sunset, we followed our lengthening shadows peacefully but thirstily again to the sweet waters of the river. Meanwhile the flat-bottomed gunboats and stern-wheel steamers, drawing endless tows of sailing boats carrying our supplies, had safely negotiated the cataract, and by the twenty-seventh all our forces, desert and river, were concentrated south of the Shabluka hills with only five clear marches over open plain to the city of our quest.

On the twenty-eighth [28th] the army set forth on its final advance. We moved in full order of battle and by stages of only eight or ten miles a day so as to save all our strength for the collision [at any moment]. We carried nothing with us but what we and our horses stood up in. [We drew our water and food each night from the Nile and its armada. The heat in this part of Africa and at this time of the year was intense. In spite of thick clothes, spine-pads, broad-brimmed pith helmets, one felt the sun leaning down upon one and piercing our bodies with his burning rays. The canvas waterbags which hung from our saddles, agreeably cool from their own evaporation, were drained long before the afternoons had worn away. How delicious it was in the evenings when, the infantry having reached and ordered their bivouac, the cavalry screen was withdrawn, and we filed down in gold and purple twilight to drink and drink and drink again from the swift abundant Nile.]

MEL, p. 189.

At about half-past ten **[on September first]** we topped a broad swell of sand and saw before us, scarcely a mile away, all our advanced patrols and parties halted in a long line, observing something which lay apparently immediately across their path **[like a forest of thorn bushes]**. Soon we also were ordered to halt, and presently a friendly subaltern who had been on patrol came along with what to us was momentous **and decisive** news. 'Enemy in sight,' he said, beaming. 'Where?' we asked. 'There, can't you see? Look at that long brown smear. That's them. They haven't bolted,' and he went on his way. **We had all noticed this dark discoloration of the distant horizon, but had taken it to be a forest of thornbushes. The best field-glasses failed to disclose any other impression from the point where we were halted. Then came the regimental-sergeant-major, also coming back from the outpost line.**

The text in blue above are new text additions and are not in the *Cosmopolitan* article. Where the new text was inserted into the article is shown in red below. The few words in blue below were changed for the *MEL* version. The added text provides a much more robust description of the situation and illustrates how difficult it was to see the enemy. This creates an uncertainty and sudden jarring of the nerves when the enemy is seen.

Cosmopolitan, December 1924, p. 95.

At about half-past ten **on September first** we topped a broad swell of sand and saw before us, scarcely a mile away, all our advanced patrols and parties halted in a long line, observing something which lay apparently immediately across their path **like a forest of thorn bushes**. Soon we also were ordered to halt, and presently a friendly subaltern who had been on patrol came along with what to us was momentous **[and decisive]** news.
'Enemy in sight,' he said, beaming. 'Where?' we asked. 'There, can't you see? Look at that long brown smear. That's them. They haven't bolted,' and he went on his way.

[We had all noticed this dark discoloration of the distant horizon, but had taken it to be a forest of thornbushes. The best field-glasses failed to disclose any other impression from the point where we were halted. Then came the regimental-sergeant-major, also coming back from the outpost line.]

APPENDIX 4 / CHAPTER 4: CAVALRY CHARGE

MEL, p. 189–90.
Next came an order for [from] the support to send a subaltern whose horse was not exhausted up to the Colonel in the out-post line.

'Mr. Churchill,' said my squadron leader, and off I trotted.

There was a shallow dip followed by another rise of ground before I found Colonel Martin in the outpost line near some sandhills.

'Good morning,' he said. 'The enemy has just begun to advance; They are coming on pretty fast. I want you to see the situation for yourself, and then go back as quickly as you can without knocking up your horse, and report personally to the Sirdar. You will find him marching with the infantry.'

So, I was to meet Kitchener after all! Would he be surprised to see me? Would he be angry? Would he say 'What the devil are you doing here? I thought I told you not to come.' Would he be disdainfully indifferent? Or would he merely receive the report without troubling to inquire the name of the officer who brought it? Anyhow, one could not have a better reason of service for accosting the great man than the news that a hostile army was advancing against him. The prospect interested and excited me as much as the approaching battle, and the possibilities in the rear seemed in no way less interesting, and in some respects not less formidable, than the enemy on our front.

The text in blue above are new text additions and are not in the *Cosmopolitan* article; where the new text was inserted into the article is shown in red below. The added text provides new excitement and anticipation of meeting Kitchener, who had previously refused Churchill permission to join this expedition. Kitchener was unaware that Churchill had gone around him to gain access. Now they would meet face to face.

Cosmopolitan, December 1924, p. 95.
Next came an order from the support to send a subaltern whose horse was not exhausted up to the Colonel in the outpost line.

'Mr. Churchill,' said my squadron leader, and off I trotted.

There was a shallow dip followed by another rise of ground before I found Colonel Martin in the outpost line [near some sandhills].

'Good morning,' he said. 'The enemy has just begun to advance. They are coming on pretty fast. I want you to see the situation for yourself, and then go back as quickly as you can without knocking up your horse, and report personally to the Sirdar. You will find him marching with the infantry.

So I was to meet Kitchener after all! Would he be surprised to see me? Would he be angry? Would he say 'What the devil are you doing here? I thought I told you not to come.'

Would he be disdainfully indifferent? Or would he merely receive the report without troubling to inquire the name of the officer who brought it? [Anyhow, one could not have a better reason of service for accosting the great man than the news that a hostile army was advancing against him.] The prospect interested and excited me as much as the approaching battle [and the possibilities in the rear seemed in no way less interesting, and in some respects not less formidable, than the enemy on our front].

MEL, pp. 190–91.
Having thoroughly observed the enemy and been told all that there was to tell in the outpost line, I started to trot and canter across the six miles of desert which separated the advanced cavalry from the main body of the army. The heat was scorching, and as I thought it almost certain we should be fighting on horseback all the afternoon, I took as much care of my horse as the urgency of my orders allowed. In consequence nearly forty minutes had passed before 1 began to approach the mass of the infantry. I paused for a moment to rest my horse and survey the scene from the spur of a black rocky hill which gave a general view. The sight was truly magnificent. The British and Egyptian army was advancing in battle array. Five solid brigades of three or four infantry battalions each, marching in open columns, echeloned back from the Nile. Behind these great blocks of men followed long rows of artillery, and beyond these there trailed out interminable strings of camels carrying supplies. On the river abreast of the leading brigade moved masses of heavily-laden sailing-boats towed by a score of stern-wheel steamers, and from this mass there emerged gleaming grimly seven or eight large white gunboats ready for action. On the desert flank and towards the enemy a dozen squadrons of Egyptian cavalry at wide intervals could be seen supporting the outpost line, and still further inland the grey and chocolate columns of the Camel Corps completed the spacious panorama.

Having breathed my horse, for I did not wish to arrive in a flurry, I rode towards the centre of the infantry masses. Soon I saw at their head a considerable cavalcade following a bright red banner. Drawing nearer I saw the Union Jack by the side of the Egyptian flag. **[Here, evidently was the personage I sought.]** Kitchener was riding alone two or three horses' lengths in front of his Headquarters Staff. **His two standard-bearers marched immediately behind him, and the principal officers of the Anglo-Egyptian army staff followed in his train exactly as one would expect from the picture-books.**

The text in blue above are new text additions and are not in the *Cosmopolitan* article; where the new text was inserted into the article is shown in red below. The text in blue below was omitted in the *MEL* version. The new text makes Kitchener's procession even more regal.

Cosmopolitan, December 1924, p. 95.
Having thoroughly observed the enemy and been told all that there was to tell in the outpost line, I started to trot and canter across the six miles of desert which separated the advanced cavalry from the main body of the army. The heat was scorching, and as I thought it almost certain we should be fighting on horseback all the afternoon, I took as much care of my horse as the urgency of my orders allowed. In consequence nearly forty minutes had passed before 1 began to approach the mass of the infantry.

I paused for a moment to rest my horse and survey the scene from the spur of a black rocky hill which gave a general view. The sight was truly magnificent. The British and Egyptian army was advancing in battle array. Five solid brigades of three or four infantry battalions each, marching in open columns, echeloned back from the Nile. Behind these great blocks of men followed long rows of artillery, and beyond these there trailed out interminable strings of camels carrying supplies. On the river abreast of the leading brigade moved masses of heavily laden sailing-boats towed by a score of stern-wheel steamers, and from this mass there emerged gleaming grimly seven or eight large white gunboats ready for action. On the desert flank and towards the enemy a dozen squadrons of Egyptian cavalry at wide intervals could be seen supporting the outpost line, and still further inland the grey and chocolate columns of the Camel Corps completed the spacious panorama.

Having breathed my horse, for I did not wish to arrive in a flurry, I rode towards the centre of the infantry masses. Soon I saw at their head a considerable cavalcade following a bright red banner. Drawing nearer I saw the Union Jack by the side of the Egyptian flag. Here, evidently was the personage I sought. Kitchener was riding alone two or three horses' lengths in front of his Headquarters Staff. [His two standard-bearers marched immediately behind him, and the principal officers of the Anglo-Egyptian army staff followed in his train exactly as one would expect from the picture-books.]

MEL, pp. 191–2.
I approached at an angle, made a half circle, drew my horse alongside and slightly in rear of him, and saluted. It was the first time I had ever looked upon that remarkable countenance, already well known, afterwards and probably for generations to be familiar to the whole world. He turned his grave face upon me. The heavy moustaches, the queer rolling look of the eyes, the sunburnt and almost purple cheeks and jowl made a vivid manifestation upon the senses,

'Sir,' I said, 'I have come from the 21st Lancers with a report.' He made a slight nod as a signal for me to continue [nodded slightly]. I described the situation in terms which I had studied on my ride to make as compendious as possible. The enemy were in sight, apparently in large numbers; their main body lay about seven miles away and almost directly between our present position and the city of Omdurman. Up to 11 o'clock they had remained stationary, but at five minutes past eleven they were seen to be in motion, and when I left forty minutes before they were still advancing rapidly.

The text in blue above are new text additions and are not in the *Cosmopolitan* article; where the new text was inserted into the article is shown in red below. New text adds details about the enemy.

APPENDIX 4 / CHAPTER 4: CAVALRY CHARGE

Cosmopolitan, December 1924, pp. 152–3.
I approached at an angle, made a half circle, drew my horse alongside and slightly in rear of him, and saluted. It was the first time I had ever looked upon that remarkable countenance, already well known, afterwards and probably for generations to be familiar to the whole world. He turned his grave face upon me. The heavy moustaches, the queer rolling look of the eyes, the sunburnt and almost purple cheeks and jowl made a vivid manifestation upon the senses.

'Sir,' I said, 'I have come from the 21st Lancers with a report.' He nodded slightly. I described the situation in terms [which I had studied on my ride to make] as compendious as possible. [The enemy were in sight, apparently in large numbers; their main body lay about seven miles away and almost directly between our present position and the city of Omdurman. Up to 11 o'clock they had remained stationary, but at five minutes past eleven they were seen to be in motion, and when I left forty minutes before they were still advancing rapidly.]

MEL, p. 192.
He listened in absolute silence to every word, our horses crunching the sand as we rode forward side by side. Then, after a considerable pause, he said, 'You say the Dervish Army is advancing. How long do you think I have got?' My answer came out in a flash: 'You have got at least an hour—probably an hour and a half, sir, even if they come on at their present rate.' He tossed his head in a way that left me in doubt whether he accepted or rejected this estimate, and then with a slight bow signified that my mission was discharged. I saluted, reined my horse in, and let his retinue flow past.

I began to calculate speeds and distances rather anxiously in order to see whether my precipitate answer conformed to reason. In the result I was pretty sure I was not far out. Taking 4 miles an hour as the maximum rate at which the Dervish jog-trot could cover what I judged to be seven miles, an hour and a half was a safe and sure margin.

The text in blue above are new text additions and are not in the *Cosmopolitan* article; where the new text was inserted into the article is shown in red below. The new text now shows Churchill was worried he might have spoken too hastily but, in the end, he felt he was correct.

Cosmopolitan, December 1924, p. 153.
He listened in absolute silence [to every word], our horses crunching the sand as we rode forward side by side. Then, after a considerable pause, he said, 'You say the Dervish Army is advancing. How long do you think I have got?'

My answer came out in a flash: 'You have got at least an hour—probably an hour and a half, sir, even if they come on at their present rate.'

He tossed his head in a way that left me in doubt whether he accepted or rejected this estimate, and then with a slight bow signified that my mission was discharged. I saluted, reined my horse in, and let his retinue flow past.

[I began to calculate speeds and distances rather anxiously in order to see whether my precipitate answer conformed to reason. In the result I was pretty sure I was not far out. Taking 4 miles an hour as the maximum rate at which the Dervish jog-trot could cover what I judged to be seven miles, an hour and a half was a safe and sure margin.]

MEL, p. 194.
However, there was to be no battle on September 1 [that day]. I had scarcely rejoined my squadron in the outpost line when the Dervish army came to a standstill, and after giving a tremendous *feu de joie* seemed to settle down for the night. We watched them all the afternoon and evening, and our patrols skirmished and scampered about with theirs, It was not until the light faded that we returned to the Nile and were ordered to tuck away our men and horses within the zeriba under the steep bank of the river [or thorn stockade].

In this sheltered but helpless posture we were informed that trustworthy news had been received that the enemy would attack by night. The most severe penalties were denounced [declared] against anyone who under any circumstances whatever—even to save his life—fired a shot from pistol or carbine inside the perimeter of the thorn fence. If the Dervishes broke the line and penetrated the camp, we were to defend ourselves by fighting on foot with our lances or swords.

The text in blue above are new text additions and are not in the *Cosmopolitan* article; where the new text was inserted into the article is shown in red below. New text simply provides additional colour.

Cosmopolitan, December 1924, p. 153.
However, there was to be no battle that day. I had scarcely rejoined my squadron in the outpost line when the Dervish army came to a standstill, and [after giving a tremendous *feu de joie*] seemed to settle down for the night. [We watched them] all the afternoon and evening, and our patrols skirmished and scampered about with theirs, It was not until the light faded that we returned to the Nile and were ordered to tuck away our men and horses within the zeriba or thorn stockade.

In this sheltered but helpless posture we were informed [that trustworthy news had been received] that the enemy would attack by night. The most severe penalties were declared against anyone who under any circumstances whatever—even to save his life—fired a shot from pistol or carbine inside the perimeter of the thorn fence. If the Dervishes broke the line and penetrated the camp, we were to defend ourselves by fighting on foot with our lances or swords.

The story continues in *MEL*, from p. 197 to 200, which represents the beginning of Chapter XV. Churchill is providing information on the morning of the battle and describing what the army and he were doing and feeling with very colourful language. This is all new material that is not in the *Cosmopolitan* article. Below the story continues both in *MEL* and *Cosmopolitan*.

MEL, p. 201.
The whole of the Khalifa's army, nearly 60,000 strong [over 50,000], advanced in battle order [array to attack us. Great masses of men, bright with thousands of flags and sparkling with steel points, march forward] from their encampment of the night before, topped the swell of ground which hid the two armies from one another, and then rolled down the gently-sloping amphitheatre in the arena of which, backed upon the Nile, Kitchener's 20,000 troops were drawn up shoulder to shoulder to receive them. Ancient and modern confronted one another. The weapons, the methods and the fanaticism of the Middle Ages [Crusading times] were brought by an extraordinary anachronism into dire collision with the organisation and inventions of the nineteenth century. The result was not surprising. As the successors of the Saracens descended the long smooth slopes which led to

the river and their enemy, they encountered the rifle fire of two and a half divisions of trained infantry, drawn up two deep and in close order and supported by at least 70 guns on the river bank and in the gunboats, all firing with undisturbed efficiency. Under this fire [blast of death] the whole attack withered and came to a standstill, with a loss of perhaps six or seven thousand men, at least 700 yards away from the British-Egyptian line [our lines]. The Dervish army, however, possessed nearly 20,000 rifles of various kinds, from the most antiquated to the most modern, and when the spearmen could get no farther, these riflemen lay down on the plain and began a ragged, unaimed but considerable fusillade at the dark line of the thorn-fence zeriba. Now for the first time they began to inflict losses on their antagonists, and in the short space that this lasted perhaps two hundred casualties occurred among the British and Egyptian troops.

The text in blue above are new or changed words or phrases not in the *Cosmopolitan* article. The words in blue below are the original text in the article and the text in red shows where the new text in *MEL* would be placed. Most changes represent style changes except for rewording to inflate the number of the enemy.

Cosmopolitan, December 1924, p. 153.
Early on the night of September second, the whole of the Khalifa's army, over 50,000 [nearly 60,000] strong, advanced in battle array to attack us. Great masses of men, bright with thousands of flags and sparkling with steel points, march forward from their encampment of the night before, topped the swell of ground which hid the two armies from one another, and then rolled down the gently-sloping amphitheatre in the arena of which, backed upon the Nile, Kitchener's 20,000 troops were drawn up shoulder to shoulder to receive them.

Ancient and modern confronted one another. The weapons, the methods and the fanaticism of Crusading times were brought by an extraordinary anachronism into dire collision with the organisation and inventions of the nineteenth century. [The result was not surprising.]

As the successors of the Saracens descended the long smooth slopes which led to the river and their enemy, they encountered the rifle fire of two and a half divisions of trained infantry, drawn up two deep and in close order and supported by at least 70 guns on the river bank and in the gunboats, all firing with undisturbed efficiency. Under this **blast of death** the whole attack withered and came to a standstill, with a loss of perhaps six or seven thousand men, at least 700 yards away from **our lines**.

The Dervish army, however, possessed nearly 20,000 rifles of various kinds, from the most antiquated to the most modern, and when the spearmen could get no farther, these riflemen lay down on the plain and began a ragged, unaimed but considerable fusillade at the dark line of the thorn-fence zariba. Now for the first time they began to inflict losses **[on their antagonists]**, and in the short space that this lasted perhaps two hundred casualties occurred among the British and Egyptian troops.

MEL, p. 202.
Seeing that the attack had been repulsed with great slaughter and that he was nearer to the city of Omdurman than the Dervish army, Kitchener immediately wheeled his five brigades into his usual echelon formation, and with his left flank on the river proceeded to march south towards the city, intending thereby to cut **off** what he considered to be the remnants of the Dervish army from their capital, their base, their food, their water, their home, and to drive them out into the vast deserts which stared on every side. But the Dervishes were by no means defeated. The whole of their left, **having overshot the mark,** had not even been under fire. The Khalifa's reserve of perhaps 15,000 men was still intact. All these swarms now advanced with undaunted courage to attack the British and Egyptian forces, which were no longer drawn up in a prepared position, but marching freely over the desert. This second shock was far more critical than the first. The charging Dervishes succeeded everywhere in coming to within **a hundred or** two hundred yards of the troops, and the rear brigade of Soudanese, attacked from two directions, was only saved from destruction by the skill and firmness of its commander, General Hector Macdonald. However, discipline and machinery triumphed over the most desperate valour, and after an enormous carnage, certainly exceeding 20,000 men, who strewed the ground in heaps and swathes 'like snowdrifts,' the whole mass of the Dervishes dissolved into fragments and into particles and streamed away into the fantastic mirages of the desert.

Very minor changes only. The text in blue above are new or modified words or phrases. The text in red below are where the new text would have been placed.

Cosmopolitan, December 1924, p. 153.
Seeing that the attack had been repulsed with great slaughter and that he was nearer to the city of Omdurman than the Dervish army, Kitchener immediately wheeled his five brigades into his usual echelon formation, and with his left flank on the river proceeded to march south towards the city, intending thereby to cut [off] what he considered to be the remnants of the Dervish army from their capital, their base, their food, their water, their home, and to drive them out into the vast deserts which stared on every side.

But the Dervishes were by no means defeated. The whole of their left [, having overshot the mark,] had not even been under fire. The Khalifa's reserve of perhaps 15,000 men was still intact. All these swarms now advanced with undaunted courage to attack the British and Egyptian forces, which were no longer drawn up in a prepared position, but marching freely over the desert.

This second shock was far more critical than the first. The charging Dervishes succeeded everywhere in coming to within [a hundred or] two hundred yards of the troops, and the rear brigade of Soudanese, attacked from two directions, was only saved from destruction by the skill and firmness of its commander, General Hector Macdonald. However, discipline and machinery triumphed over the most desperate valour, and after an enormous carnage, certainly exceeding 20,000 men, who strewed the ground in heaps and swathes 'like snowdrifts,' the whole mass of the Dervishes dissolved into fragments and into particles and streamed away into the fantastic mirages of the desert.

MEL, pp. 202–3.
The Egyptian cavalry and the camel corps had been protecting the right flank of the zeriba when it was attacked, and the 21st Lancers were the only horsemen on the left flank **nearest to Omdurman**. Immediately after the first attack had been repulsed, we were ordered to leave the zeriba, ascertain what enemy forces, if any, stood between Kitchener and the city, and if possible drive these forces back and clear the way for the advancing army.

Of course as a regimental officer one knows very little of what is taking place over the whole field of battle. We waited by our horses during the first attack close down by the river's edge, sheltered by the steep Nile bank from the bullets which whistled overhead. As soon as the fire began to slacken and it was said on all sides that the attack had been repulsed, a General arrived with his staff at a gallop with instant orders to mount and advance. In two minutes the four squadrons were mounted and trotting out of the zeriba in a southerly direction. We ascended again the slopes of Jebel Surgham which had played its part in the first stages of the action, and from its ridges soon saw before us the whole plain of Omdurman with the vast mud city, its minarets and domes, spread before us six or seven miles away. After various halts and reconnoitring we found ourselves walking forward in what is called 'column of troops.' There are four troops in a squadron and four squadrons in a regiment. Each of these troops now followed the other, I commanded the second [third] troop from the rear, comprising between twenty and twenty-five Lancers.

In this section, Churchill adds more detail about what he knew and didn't know about the impeding battle and focuses the story even more on what he experienced and felt. He also changed which troop (from third to second) he was leading. It is unknown whether this was simply a mistake in the article or if there was another motive in making this change. The text in blue above is the new text and the text in red below is where that text has been added to the original article.

Cosmopolitan December 1924, p. 154.
The Egyptian cavalry and the camel corps had been protecting the right flank of the zeriba when it was attacked, and the 21st Lancers were the only horsemen on the left flank [nearest to Omdurman]. Immediately after the first attack had been repulsed we were ordered to leave the zeriba, ascertain what enemy forces, if any, stood between Kitchener and the city, and if possible drive these forces back and clear the way for the advancing army. [Of course as a regimental officer one knows very little of what is taking place over the whole field of battle. We waited by our horses during the first attack close down by the river's edge, sheltered by the steep Nile bank from the bullets which whistled overhead. As soon as the fire began to slacken

and it was said on all sides that the attack had been repulsed, a General arrived with his staff at a gallop with instant orders to mount and advance.]

In two minutes the four squadrons were mounted and trotting out of the zeriba in a southerly direction. We ascended again the slopes of Jebel Surgham which had played its part in the first stages of the action, and from its ridges soon saw before us the whole plain of Omdurman with the vast mud city, its minarets and domes, spread before us six or seven miles away. After various halts and reconnoitring we found ourselves walking forward in what is called 'column of troops.' There are four troops in a squadron and four squadrons in a regiment. Each of these troops now followed the other. I commanded the third troop from the rear, comprising between twenty and twenty-five Lancers.

MEL, pp. 203-4.
Everyone expected that we were going to make a charge. That was the one idea that had been in all minds since we had started from Cairo. Of course there would be a charge. In those days, before the Boer War, British cavalry had been taught little else. Here was clearly the occasion for a charge. But against what body of enemy, over what ground, in which direction or with what purpose, were matters hidden from the rank and file. We continued to pace forward over the hard sand, peering into the mirage-twisted plain in a high state of suppressed excitement. Presently I noticed, 300 [four hundred] yards away on our flank and parallel to the line on which we were advancing, a long row of blue-black objects, two or three yards apart. I thought there were about a hundred and fifty. Then I became sure that these were men—enemy men—squatting on the ground. Almost at the same moment the trumpet sounded 'Trot', and the whole long column of cavalry began to jingle and clatter across the front of these crouching figures. We were in the lull of the battle and there was perfect silence. Forthwith from every blue-black blob came a white puff of smoke, and a loud volley of musketry broke the odd stillness. Such a target at such a distance could scarcely be missed, and all along the column here and there horses bounded and a few men fell.

The intentions of our Colonel had no doubt been [intended] to move round the flank of the body of Dervishes he had now located, and who, concealed in a fold of the ground behind their riflemen, were invisible to us, and then to attack them from a more advantageous quarter; but once the fire was opened and losses began to grow, he must have judged it inexpedient to prolong his procession across the open plain. The trumpet sounded 'Right wheel into line', and all the sixteen troops swung round towards the blue-black riflemen. Almost immediately the regiment broke into a gallop, and the 21st Lancers were committed to their first charge in war!

Churchill has added significant text, which brings the enemy closer and with larger numbers and raises the tension in the scene by highlighting all the unknowns of the battle to be. The text in blue above are the new sections and the text in red below is where he placed them.

Cosmopolitan, December 1924, p. 154.
[Everyone expected that we were going to make a charge. That was the one idea that had been in all minds since we had started from Cairo. Of course there would be a charge. In those days, before the Boer War, British cavalry had been taught little else. Here was clearly the occasion for a charge. But against what body of enemy, over what ground, in which direction or with what purpose, were matters hidden from the rank and file. We continued to pace forward over the hard sand, peering into the mirage- twisted plain in a high state of suppressed excitement.] Presently I noticed, four hundred yards away [on our flank] and parallel to the line on which we were advancing, a long row of blue-black objects, two or three yards apart. I thought there were about a hundred [and fifty]. Then I became sure that these were men—enemy men—squatting on the ground. Almost at the same moment the trumpet sounded 'Trot', and the whole long column of cavalry began to jingle and clatter across the front of these crouching figures. We were in the lull of the battle and there was perfect silence. Forthwith from every blue-black blob came a white puff of smoke, and a loud volley of musketry broke the odd stillness. Such a target at such a distance could scarcely be missed, and all along the column here and there horses bounded and a few men fell.

[The intentions of] Our Colonel had no doubt intended [been] to move round the flank of the body of Dervishes he had now located, and who, concealed in a fold of the ground behind their riflemen, were invisible to us, and then to attack them from.a more advantageous quarter: but once the fire was opened and losses began to grow, he must have judged it inexpedient to prolong his procession across the open plain. The trumpet sounded 'Right wheel into line', and all the sixteen troops swung round towards the blue-black riflemen. Almost immediately the regiment broke into a gallop, and the 21st Lancers were committed to their first charge in war!

MEL, pp. 204–5.
I propose to describe exactly what happened to me: what I saw and what I felt. I recalled it to my mind so frequently after the event that the impression is as clear and vivid as it was a quarter of a century ago. The troop I commanded was, when we wheeled into line, the second [third] from the right of the regiment. I was riding a handy, surefooted, grey Arab polo pony. Before we wheeled and began to gallop, the officers had been marching with drawn swords. On account of my shoulder, I had always decided that if I were involved in hand-to-hand fighting, I must use a pistol and not a sword. I had purchased in London a Mauser automatic pistol, then the newest and the latest design. I had practised carefully with this during our march and journey up the river. This then was the weapon with which I determined to fight. I had first of all to return my sword into its scabbard, which is not the easiest thing to do at a gallop. I had then to draw my pistol from its wooden holster and bring it to full cock. This dual operation took an appreciable time, and until it was finished, apart from a few glances to my left to see what effect the fire was producing, I did not look up at the general scene. Then I saw immediately before me, and now only half the length of a polo ground away, the row of crouching blue figures firing frantically, wreathed in white smoke. On my right and left my neighbouring troop leaders made a good line. Immediately behind was a long dancing row of lances couched for the charge. We were going at a fast but steady gallop. There was too much trampling and rifle fire to hear any bullets. After this glance to the right and left and at my troop, I looked again towards the enemy. The scene appeared to be suddenly transformed. The blue-black men were still firing, but behind them there now came into view a depression like a shallow sunken road. This was crowded and crammed with men rising up from the ground where they had hidden. Bright flags appeared as if by magic, and I saw arriving from nowhere Emirs on horseback among and around the mass of the enemy. The Dervishes appeared to be ten or twelve [seven or eight] deep at the thickest,

a great grey mass gleaming with steel, filling the dry watercourse. In the same twinkling of an eye I saw also that our right overlapped their left, that my troop would just strike the edge of their array, and that the troop on my right would charge into air. My subaltern comrade [Both my subaltern comrades] on the right, Wormald of the 7th Hussars, could see the situation too; and we both increased our speed to the very fastest gallop and curved inwards like the horns of the moon. One really had not time to be frightened or to think of anything else but these particular necessary actions which I have described. They completely occupied mind and senses.

Churchill again adds significant text to the original article, making the enemy larger and closer. He starts this section stating how clear and accurate his memory of this event is – so, presumably, we should believe it word for word. In addition, he talks about buying his Mauser pistol with which he plans to fight with rather than use his sword. He adds the name of one of his colleagues, presumably to make it more personal. He removes how he had hurt his shoulder in India and what his shoulder disability is. The text in blue above is the newly added text, and the text below in red is where in the article it would be placed. The wording of his injury, in blue below, was removed from the *MEL* text.

Cosmopolitan, December 1924, p. 154.
[I propose to describe exactly what happened to me: what 1 saw and what I felt. I recalled it to my mind so frequently after the event that the impression is as clear and vivid as it was a quarter of a century ago.] The troop I commanded was, [when we wheeled into line], the third from the right of the regiment. I was riding a handy, surefooted, grey Arab polo pony. Before we wheeled and began to gallop, the officers had been marching with drawn swords. [On account of] My shoulder, as the result of an accident some years before, is liable to become dislocated on the slightest provocation. I had therefore always decided that if I were involved in hand-to-hand fighting, I must use a pistol and not a sword. [I had purchased in London a Mauser automatic pistol, then the newest and the latest design. I had practised carefully with this during our march and journey up the river. This then was the weapon with which I determined to fight.] I had first of all to return my sword into its scabbard, which is not the easiest thing to do

at a gallop. I had then to draw my pistol from its wooden holster and bring it to full cock. This dual operation took an appreciable time, and until it was finished, apart from a few glances to my left to see what effect the fire was producing, I did not look up at the general scene.

Then I saw immediately before me, and now only half the length of a polo ground away, the row of crouching blue figures firing frantically, wreathed in white smoke. On my right and left my neighbouring troop leaders made a good line. Immediately behind was a long dancing row of lances couched for the charge. We were going at a fast but steady gallop. There was too much trampling and rifle fire to hear any bullets.

After this glance to the right and left and at my troop, I looked again towards the enemy. The scene appeared to be suddenly transformed. The blue[-black] men were still firing, but behind them there now came into view a depression like a shallow sunken road. This was crowded and crammed with men rising up from the ground where they had hidden. Bright flags appeared as if by magic, and I saw arriving from nowhere Emirs on horseback among and around the mass of the enemy. The Dervishes appeared to be seven or eight deep [at the thickest], a great grey mass gleaming with steel [filling the dry watercourse].

In the same twinkling of an eye I saw also that our right overlapped their left, that my troop would just strike the edge of their array, and that the troop on my right would charge into air, Both my subaltern comrades on the right[, Wormald of the 7th Hussars, could see] the situation too; and we both increased our speed to the very fastest gallop and curved inwards like the horns of the moon. One really had not time to be frightened or to think of anything else but these particular necessary actions which I have described. They completely occupied mind and senses.

MEL, pp. 205–6.
The collision was now very near. I saw immediately before [behind] me, not ten yards away, the two blue men who lay [particularly] in my path. They were perhaps [–] a couple of yards apart. [As] I rode at the interval between them. They both fired. I passed through the smoke conscious that I was unhurt. The trooper immediately behind me was killed at this place and at this moment, whether by these shots or not I do not know. I checked my pony as the ground began to fall away beneath his feet. The clever animal dropped

like a cat four or five feet down on to the sandy bed of the watercourse, **and in this sandy** bed I found myself surrounded by what seemed to be dozens of men. They were not thickly-**packed** enough [packed] at this point for me to experience any actual collision with them. Whereas **Grenfell's** [the] troop next but one on my left was brought to a complete standstill and suffered very heavy losses, we seemed to push our way through as one has sometimes seen **mounted** policemen **break up** [regulate] a crowd. In less time than it takes to relate, my pony had scrambled up the other side of the ditch. I looked round.

Once again, I was on the hard, crisp desert, my horse at **a trot** [the slowest of canters]. I had the impression of scattered Dervishes running to and fro in all directions. Straight before me a man threw himself on the ground. The reader must remember that I had been trained as a cavalry soldier to believe that if ever cavalry broke into a mass of infantry, the latter would be at their mercy. My first idea therefore was that the man was terrified. But simultaneously I saw the gleam of his curved sword as he drew it back for a ham-stringing cut. I had room and time enough to turn my pony out of his reach, and leaning over on the off side I fired two shots into him at about three yards. As I straightened myself in the saddle, I saw before me another figure with uplifted sword. I raised my pistol and fired. So close were we that the pistol itself actually struck him. Man and sword disappeared below and behind me.

Churchill again has added more action to the *MEL* text compared to the *Cosmopolitan* article and in the first sentence reverses the position of the enemy to in front of him, not behind him – which actually makes more sense. He also adds the name of a fellow officer to make it more personal. The blue text above are the new words or phrases. The words in blue below are the original words and in red what has been substituted.

Cosmopolitan, December 1924, p. 154.
The collision was now very near. I saw immediately **behind** me, not ten yards away, the two blue men who lay **particularly** in my path – a couple of yards apart. **As** I rode at the interval between them, **they** both fired. I passed through the smoke conscious that I was unhurt. The trooper immediately behind me was killed, [at this place and at this moment,] whether by these

shots or not I do not know. I checked my pony as the ground began to fall away beneath his feet. The clever animal dropped like a cat four or five feet down on to the sandy bed of the watercourse. **[, and in this sandy bed]** I found myself surrounded by what seemed to be dozens of men. They were not thickly**[-packed]** enough **packed** at this point for me to experience any actual collision with them. Whereas **the** troop next but one on my left was brought to a complete standstill and suffered very heavy losses, we seemed to push our way through as one has sometimes seen **[mounted]** policemen **regulate** a crowd. In less time than it takes to relate, my pony had scrambled up the other side of the ditch. I looked round.

Once again I was on the hard, crisp desert, my horse at **the slowest of canters**. I had the impression of scattered Dervishes running to and fro in all directions, Straight before me a man threw himself on the ground. The reader must remember that I had been trained as a cavalry soldier to believe that if ever cavalry broke into a mass of infantry, the latter would be at their mercy. My first idea therefore was that the man was terrified. But simultaneously I saw the gleam of his curved sword as he drew it back for a ham-stringing cut. I had room and time enough to turn my pony out of his reach, and leaning over on the offside I fired two shots into him at about three yards.

As I straightened myself in the saddle, I saw before me another figure with uplifted sword. I raised my pistol and fired. So close were we that the pistol itself actually struck him. Man and sword disappeared below and behind me.

MEL, pp. 206–7.
On my left, ten yards away, was an Arab horseman in a bright-coloured tunic and steel helmet, with chain-mail hangings. I fired at him. He turned aside. I pulled my horse into a walk and looked around again.

In one respect a cavalry charge is very like ordinary life. So long as you are all right, firmly in your saddle, your horse in hand, and well-armed, lots of enemies will give you a wide berth. But as soon as you have lost a stirrup, have a rein cut, have dropped your weapon, are wounded, or your horse is wounded, then is the moment when from all **quarters** **[sides]** enemies rush upon you. Such was the fate of not a few of my comrades in the troops immediately on my left. Brought to an actual standstill in the enemy's mass, clutched at from every side, stabbed at and hacked at by spear and sword, they were dragged from their horses and cut to pieces by the infuriated foe. But this I did not at the time see or understand. My impressions continued to be sanguine, I thought we were masters of the situation, riding the enemy down, scattering them and killing them. 1 pulled my horse up and looked about me. There was a mass of Dervishes about forty or fifty yards away on my left. They were huddling and clumping themselves together, rallying for mutual protection. They seemed wild with excitement, dancing about on their feet, shaking their spears up and down. The whole scene seemed to flicker. I have an impression, but it is too fleeting to define, of brown-clad Lancers mixed up here and there with this surging mob. The scattered individuals in my immediate neighbourhood made no attempt to molest me. Where was my troop? Where were the other troops of the squadron? Within a hundred yards of me I could not see a single officer or man. I looked back at the Dervish mass. I saw two or three riflemen crouching and aiming their rifles at me from the fringe of it. Then for the first time that morning I experienced a sudden sensation of fear. I felt myself absolutely alone. I thought these riflemen would hit me and the rest devour me like wolves. What a fool I was to loiter like this in the midst of the enemy! I crouched over the saddle, spurred my horse into a gallop and drew clear of the mêlée. Two or three hundred yards away I found my troop already faced about and partly formed up. The other three troops of the squadron were re-forming close by.

One major paragraph (shown in blue above) is added to the *MEL* text that is not in the article. It provides Churchill's impression that is like a dream or vision. Below in red is where it was inserted.

Cosmopolitan, December 1924, pp. 154–5.
On my left, ten yards away, was an Arab horseman in a bright-coloured tunic and steel helmet, with chain-mail hangings. I fired at him. He turned aside. I pulled my horse into a walk and looked around again.

In one respect a cavalry charge is very like ordinary life. So long as you are all right, firmly in your saddle, your horse in hand, and well-armed, lots of enemies will give you a wide berth. But as soon as you have lost a stirrup, have a rein cut, have dropped your weapon, are wounded, or your horse is wounded, then is the moment when from all quarters enemies rush upon you. Such was the fate of not a few of my comrades in the troops immediately on my left. Brought to an actual standstill in the enemy's mass, clutched at from every side, stabbed at and hacked at by spear and sword, they were dragged from their horses and cut to pieces by the infuriated foe. But this I did not at the time see or understand. My impressions continued to be sanguine, I thought we were masters of the situation, riding the enemy down, scattering them and killing them.

I pulled my horse up and looked about me. **[There was]** A mass of Dervishes about forty or fifty yards away on my left. They were huddling and clumping themselves together, rallying for mutual protection. They seemed wild with excitement, dancing about on their feet, shaking their spears up and down.

[The whole scene seemed to flicker. I have an impression, but it is too fleeting to define, of brown-clad Lancers mixed up here and there with this surging mob. The scattered individuals in my immediate neighbourhood made no attempt to molest me.]

Where was my troop? Where were the other troops of the squadron? Within a hundred yards of me I could not see a single officer or man. I looked back at the Dervish mass. I saw two or three riflemen crouching and aiming their rifles at me from the fringe of it. Then for the first time that morning I experienced a sudden sensation of fear. I felt myself absolutely alone. I thought these riflemen would hit me and the rest devour me like wolves. What a fool I was to loiter like this in the midst of the enemy! I crouched over the saddle, spurred my horse into a gallop and drew clear of the mêlée. Two or three hundred yards away I found my troop all ready faced about and partly formed up. The other three troops of the squadron were re-forming close by.

MEL, pp. 207–8.
Suddenly in the midst of the troop up sprung a Dervish. How he got there I do not know. He must have leaped out of some scrub or hole. All the troopers turned upon him thrusting with their lances: but he darted to and fro causing for the moment a frantic commotion. Wounded several times, he staggered towards me raising his spear. 1 shot him at less than a yard. He fell on the sand, and lay there dead. How easy to kill a man! But I did not

worry about it. I found I had fired the whole magazine of my Mauser pistol, so I put in a new clip of ten cartridges before thinking of anything else.

I was still prepossessed with the idea that we had inflicted great slaughter on the enemy and had scarcely suffered at all ourselves. Three or four men were missing from my troop. Six men and nine or ten horses were bleeding from spear thrusts or sword cuts. We all expected to be ordered immediately to charge back again. The men were ready, though they all looked serious. Several asked to be allowed to throw away their lances and draw their swords. 1 asked my second sergeant if he had enjoyed himself. His answer was 'Well, I don't exactly say I enjoyed it, Sir; but I think I'll get more used to it next time.' At this the whole troop laughed.

The entire section above is new and was added to the *MEL* text. This is by far the most personal and violent description of what Churchill, himself, did in action as he killed a man at point blank range. As best as I can discern, this is the first time Churchill ever published this story. It is chilling to juxtapose the gruesome killing with the humour at the end of the paragraph. However, this type of release of nervous energy in a battle situation is not unknown.

MEL, p. 208.
But now from the direction of the enemy there came a succession of grisly apparitions; horses spouting blood, struggling on three legs, men staggering on foot, men bleeding from terrible wounds, fish-hook spears stuck right through them, arms and faces cut to pieces, bowels protruding, men gasping, crying, collapsing, expiring. Our first task was to succour these; and meanwhile the blood of our leaders cooled. They remembered for the first time that we had carbines. Everything was still in great confusion. But trumpets were sounded and orders shouted, and we all moved off at a trot towards the flank of the enemy. Arrived at a position from which we could enfilade and rake the watercourse, two squadrons were dismounted and in a few minutes with their fire at three hundred yards compelled the Dervishes to retreat. We therefore remained in possession of the field. Within twenty minutes of the time when we had first wheeled into line and begun our charge, we were halted and breakfasting in the very watercourse that had so nearly proved our undoing. There one could see the futility of the much

vaunted *Arme Blanche*. The Dervishes had carried off their wounded, and the corpses of thirty or forty enemy were all that could be counted on the ground. Among these lay the bodies of over twenty Lancers, so hacked and mutilated as to be mostly unrecognisable. In all out of 310 officers and men the regiment had lost in the space of about two or three minutes five [six] officers and sixty-five [seventy-three] men killed and wounded, and 120 horses— nearly a quarter of its strength.

Churchill primarily decreases the number of casualties of both officers and men shown in blue above.

Cosmopolitan, December 1924, p. 155.
But now from the direction of the enemy there came a succession of grisly apparitions; horses spouting blood, struggling on three legs, men staggering on foot, men bleeding from terrible wounds, fish-hook spears stuck right through them, arms and faces cut to pieces, bowels protruding, men gasping, crying, collapsing, expiring. Our first task was to succour these; and meanwhile the blood of our leaders cooled. They remembered for the first time that we had carbines.

Everything was still in great confusion. But trumpets were sounded and orders shouted, and we all moved off at a trot towards the flank of the enemy. Arrived at a position from which we could enfilade and rake the watercourse, two squadrons were dismounted and in a few minutes with their fire at three hundred yards compelled the Dervishes to retreat. We therefore remained in possession of the field.

Within twenty minutes of the time when we had first wheeled into line and begun our charge, we were halted and breakfasting in the very watercourse that had so nearly proved our undoing. [There one could see the futility of the much vaunted *Arme Blanche*.] The Dervishes had carried off their wounded, and the corpses of thirty or forty enemy were all that could be counted on the ground. Among these lay the bodies of over twenty Lancers, so hacked and mutilated as to be mostly unrecognisable. In all [out of 310 officers and men] the regiment had lost in the space of about two or three minutes six officers and seventy-three men killed and wounded, and 120 horses— nearly a quarter of its strength.

MEL, p. 210.
Such were my fortunes in this celebrated episode. It is very rarely that cavalry and infantry, while still both unshaken, are intermingled as the result of an actual collision. Either the infantry keep their heads and shoot the cavalry down, or they break into confusion and are cut down or speared as they run, But the two or three thousand Dervishes who faced the 21st Lancers in the watercourse at Omdurman were not in the least shaken by the stress of battle or afraid of cavalry. Their fire was not good enough to stop the charge, but they had no doubt faced horsemen many a time in the wars with Abyssinia. They were familiar with the ordeal of the charge. It was the kind of fighting they thoroughly understood. Moreover, the fight was with equal weapons, for the British too fought with sword and lance as in the days of old.

This text above is all new in *MEL* and not in the article. Here Churchill gives credit to the Dervishes for their fighting ability.

MEL, p. 210.
A white gunboat seeing our first advance had hurried up the river in the hopes of being of assistance. From the crow's nest, its commander, Beatty, watched the whole event with breathless interest. Many years passed before I met this officer or knew that he had witnessed our gallop. When we met, I was First Lord of the Admiralty and he the youngest Admiral in the Royal Navy. 'What did it look like? I asked him. 'What was your prevailing impression?' 'It looked,' said Admiral Beatty, 'like plum duff: brown currants scattered about in a great deal of suet.' **With this striking, if somewhat homely, description my account of this adventure may fittingly close.**

New final sentence.

Cosmopolitan December 1924, p. 155.
A white gunboat seeing our first advance had hurried up the river in the hopes of being of assistance. From the crow's nest, its commander, Beatty, watched the whole event with breathless interest. Many years passed before I met this officer or knew that he had witnessed our gallop. When we met, I was First Lord of the Admiralty and he the youngest Admiral in the Royal Navy.

'What did it look like? I asked him. 'What was your prevailing impression?'

'It looked,' said Admiral Beatty, 'like plum duff: brown currants scattered about in a great deal of suet.'

[With this striking, if somewhat homely, description my account of this adventure may fittingly close.]

With this text both the chapter and the article end.

Notes

1. Cohen has described *The River War* as 'a remarkable work because of its author, length, content and audacity. It was based on 15 articles Churchill wrote for the *Morning Post* in 1898, when he was not 24 years old. Yet he was already a rising political star, having run and lost for Parliament four months earlier. At 962 pages, it (*The River War*) analysed the Anglo-Egyptian reconquest of the Sudan, a conflict largely forgotten today – except for its dramatic concluding event, one of history's last great cavalry charges, in which Churchill himself participated.' *The River War* covers this same information provided in Chapters XIV 'The Operation of the First of September', pp. 257–68 and Chapter XV 'The Battle of Omdurman', pp. 269–300. See Ronald I. Cohen, '"The River War" Returns in a Masterful and Scholarly New Edition' in *The Churchill Project Hillsdale College*, 12 July 2021, https://winstonchurchill.hillsdale.edu/river-war-new-edition/.

APPENDIX 5

Chapter 4: Armoured Train

Text comparisons:
MEL, Chapter XIX, *The Armoured Train*, pp, 253–73.
Dispatches to *The Morning Post*, 'Young Winston's Wars', pp. 164–72.[1]
London to Ladysmith, Chapter VIII, Fate of the Armoured Train, pp. 74–94.[2]
   (**Same story told but in different words from those used in** *MEL*)
Cosmopolitan, January 1925, Vol. 78, pp. 70–72. (**Strikingly similar**)

The story of the wreck of the armoured train and Churchill's subsequent capture by the Boers was described by Churchill in at least four separate publications as noted above. The serialisation of *My Early Life* as *Memories of My Youth*, published in the *News Chronicle* in August/September 1930, has not been included for comparison, as the text is taken directly from the book. As will be seen, although the story told in Churchill's newspaper dispatches in the *Morning Post* in 1899 is the same as that in *MEL*, very little exact text has been copied from those dispatches included in *MEL*. A similar situation occurs with *London to Ladysmith*. For the *Cosmopolitan* article 'A Trapped Armored Train', the text from the article is adopted almost word for word, as will be seen. Below are the direct comparisons using the same format as for the comparisons in earlier appendices. The text from the story in *MEL* is presented first, followed by texts in the other publications, which are listed chronologically. Comments as thought useful by the author on the similarities and differences are provided after the text from *My Early Life* in **bold**.

Train attacked
MEL, pp. 257–8

Cavalry reconnaissances were pushed out every morning for ten or fifteen miles towards the enemy to give us timely notice of their expected advance; and in an unlucky moment it occurred to the General in [temporary] command on the spot to send his armoured train along the sixteen miles of intact railway line to supplement the efforts of the cavalry.

Nothing looks more formidable and impressive than an armoured train; but nothing is in fact more vulnerable and helpless. It was only necessary to blow up a bridge or culvert to leave the [poor] monster stranded, far from home and help, at the mercy of the enemy. This situation [consideration] did not seem to have occurred to our commander. He decided to put a company of the Dublin Fusiliers and a company of the Durban Light Infantry into an [the] armoured train of six trucks, and [to] add a small six-pounder naval gun with some sailors landed from H.M.S. Terrible, together with a breakdown gang [of plate-layers], and to send this considerable portion of his force out to reconnoitre towards Colenso [upon a reconnaissance 'into the blue']. [The officer he elected for the duty of commanding this operation was my friend Captain Haldane.] Captain Haldane was the officer he selected for the duty of commanding this operation. Haldane told me on the night of November 14 [fourteenth] of the task which had been set him for the next day and on which he was to start at dawn. He did not conceal his misgivings on the imprudence of the enterprise, but he was of course, like everyone else at the beginning of a war, very keen upon adventure and a brush with the enemy. 'Would I come with him?' He would like it if I did! Out of comradeship, and because I thought it was my duty to gather as much information as I could for the *Morning Post*, also because I was eager for trouble, I accepted the invitation without demur.

The first four and a half pages (pp. 253–7) of chapter XIX (The Armoured Train) are new text not previously published. Therefore, the text noted above begins at p. 257 where there is analogous text in the *Cosmopolitan* article. The text in blue below was only in the *Cosmopolitan* article and was removed from the text for *MEL*. The most interesting section removed is the line stating that Captain Haldane was Churchill's friend. Over the years, Haldane had accused Churchill of abandoning his colleagues, including Haldane, following his escape from the Boers and of going off by himself for selfish reasons, leaving in prison Haldane and the others who had helped to craft the escape. In addition, after the *Cosmopolitan* article was published in 1925, Haldane resumed his accusations against Churchill. Thus, it is not surprising Churchill dropped the text about Haldane being a friend. The text in red below is where the new phrases were added to the article text. The text in blue below was removed from the *MEL* text.

Cosmopolitan, January 1925, pp. 70–71.
Cavalry reconnaissances were pushed out every morning for ten or fifteen miles towards the enemy to give us timely notice of their expected advance; and in an unlucky moment it occurred to the General in temporary command on the spot to send his armoured train along the sixteen miles of intact railway line to supplement the efforts of the cavalry,

Nothing looks more formidable and impressive than an armoured train; but nothing is in fact more vulnerable and helpless. It was only necessary to blow up a bridge or culvert to leave the poor monster stranded, far from home and help, at the mercy of the enemy. This consideration did not seem to have occurred to our commander. He decided to put a company of the Dublin Fusiliers and a company of the Durban Light Infantry into the armoured [train of six] trucks, to add a small six-pounder naval gun with some sailors landed from H.M.S. Terrible, together with a break-down gang of plate-layers, and to send this considerable portion of his forces upon a reconnaissance 'into the blue.' The officer he elected for the duty of commanding this operation was my friend Captain Haldane. Captain Haldane told me on the night of November fourteenth of the task which had been set him for the next day and on which he was to start at dawn. He did not conceal his misgivings on the imprudence of the enterprise, but he was of course, like everyone else at the beginning of a war, very keen upon adventure and a brush with the enemy. 'Would I come with him?' He would like it if I did! Out of comradeship, and because I thought it was my duty to gather as much information as I could, I accepted [the invitation without demur].

MEL, pp. 258–9.

The military events which followed are well known and have often been discussed [described]. The armoured train proceeded about fourteen [fifteen] miles towards the enemy and got as far as Chieveley station without a sign of opposition or indeed of life or movement on the broad [vast] undulations of the Natal landscape. We stopped for a few moments at Chieveley to report our arrival at this point by telegraph to the General. No sooner had we done this than we saw, on a hill between us and home which overlooked the line at about 600 [five hundred] yards distance, a number of small figures moving about and hurrying forward. Certainly they were Boers [the enemy]. Certainly they were behind us. What would [were] they be doing with the railway line? There was not an instant to lose. We started immediately on our return journey. As we approached the hill, I was standing on a box with my head and shoulders above the steel plating of the rear armoured truck [the silence of the countryside was broken by the rifle and cannon fire]. I saw a cluster of [thirty or forty] Boers [and a field gun] on the crest [of the hill. The shell of this gun burst; it seemed only a few feet above my head]. It was shrapnel. Suddenly three wheeled things appeared among them [on the crest], and instantly bright flashes of light opened and shut ten or twelve times. A huge white ball of smoke sprang into being and tore out into a cone, only as it seemed a few feet above my head. It was shrapnel—the first I had ever seen in war, and very nearly the last! The steel sides of the truck tanged with a patter of bullets.

The words in blue above are new words or sentences found in *MEL* and changed from the text in the *Cosmopolitan* article which formed the basis for much of the text in *MEL*. The last few sentences added to *MEL* certainly add colour and excitement to the story. The blue text in the *Cosmopolitan* section are the original text in that article and the red is where the last few new sentences were added in *MEL*.

Only five words (in black below) come directly from the book *London to Ladysmith*.

L to L, p. 166.
Suddenly three wheeled things appeared on the crest…

Cosmopolitan, 1925, pp. 70–71.
The military events which followed are well known and have often been described. The armoured train proceeded about fifteen miles towards the enemy and got as far as Chieveley station without a sign of opposition or indeed of life or movement on the vast undulations of the Natal landscape. We stopped for a few moments at Chieveley to report our arrival at this point by telegraph to the General. No sooner had we done this than we saw behind us, on a hill between us and home which overlooked the line at about five hundred yards distance, a number of small figures moving about and hurrying forward. Certainly they were the enemy. Certainly they were behind us. What were they [be] doing with the railway line? There was not an instant to lose. We started immediately on our return journey. As we approached the hill, the silence of the countryside was broken by the rifle and cannon fire. I was standing on a box with my head and shoulders above the steel plating of the rear armoured truck. I saw thirty or forty Boers and a field gun on the crest of the hill. The shell of this gun burst; it seemed only a few feet above my head. It was shrapnel. [Suddenly three wheeled things appeared among them, and instantly bright flashes of light opened and shut ten or twelve times. A huge white ball of smoke sprang into being and tore out into a cone, only as it seemed a few feet above my head. It was shrapnel—the first I had ever seen in war, and very nearly the last! The steel sides of the truck tanged with a patter of bullets.]

MEL, p. 259.
It had flashed across my mind that there must be some trap farther on. I was just turning to Haldane to suggest that someone should scramble along the train and make the engine-driver reduce speed, when suddenly there was a tremendous shock [crash], and he and I and all the soldiers in the truck were pitched head over heels on to its floor. The armoured train travelling at not less than forty miles an hour had been thrown off the metals by some obstruction, or by some injury to the line. [The first three vehicles were all derailed; the engine remain on the line and so did the three trucks remaining, in one of which we were.]

In our truck no one was seriously hurt, and it took but a few seconds for me to scramble to my feet and look over the top of the armour. The train lay in a valley about 1,200 [a thousand] yards on the homeward [other] side of the enemy's hill. On the top of this hill were scores of figures running forward and throwing themselves down in the grass, from which there came almost immediately an accurate and heavy rifle fire. **The bullets whistled overhead and rang and splattered on the steel plates like a hailstorm.** I got down from my perch, and Haldane and I debated what to do. It was agreed that he with the little naval gun and his Dublin Fusiliers in the rear truck should endeavour to keep down the enemy's firing, and that I should go and see what had happened to the train, what was the damage to the line, and whether there was any chance of repairing it **or clearing the wreckage out of the way**.

I nipped out of the truck accordingly and ran along the line to the head of the train. The engine **[, as I have said,]** was still on the rails. The first truck, an ordinary bogey, had turned completely head over heels, killing and terribly injuring some of the plate-layers who were upon it; **but it [. It]** lay quite clear of the track. The next two armoured trucks, which contained the Durban Light Infantry, were both derailed, one still upright and the other on its side. They lay jammed against each other **in disorder**, **[a V-shaped position, quite]** blocking the homeward path of the rest. Behind the over- turned trucks the Durban Light Infantry men, bruised, shaken and some severely injured, had found a temporary shelter. The enemy's fire was continuous, and soon there mingled with the rifles the bang of the field guns and the near explosion of their shells. We were in the toils **of the enemy**.

Shown in blue above are the new words or phrases Churchill added to the text of the *Cosmopolitan* article to create the *MEL* text. The text in blue below are the original text of the article and in red where the new text was added.

Cosmopolitan, January 1925, p. 71.
It had flashed across my mind that there must be some trap farther on. I was just turning to Haldane to suggest that someone should scramble along the train and make the engine-driver reduce speed, when suddenly there was a tremendous **crash**, and he and I and all the soldiers in the truck were pitched head over heels on to its floor. The armoured train travelling at not less than forty miles an hour had been thrown off the metals by some obstruction, or by some injury to the line. **The first three vehicles were all derailed; the**

engine remain on the line and so did the three trucks remaining, in one of which we were.

In our truck no one was seriously hurt, and it took but a few seconds for me to scramble to my feet and look over the top of the armour. The train lay in a valley about a thousand yards on the other side of the enemy's hill. On the top of this hill were scores of figures running forward and throwing themselves down in the grass, from it there came almost immediately an accurate and heavy rifle fire. [The bullets whistled overhead and rang and splattered on the steel plates like a hailstorm.] I got down from my perch, and Haldane and I debated what to do. It was agreed that he with the little naval gun and his Dublin Fusiliers in the rear truck should endeavour to keep down the enemy's firing, and that I should go and see what had happened to the train, what was the damage to the line, and whether there was any chance of repairing it [or clearing the wreckage out of the way].

I nipped out of the truck accordingly and ran along the line to the head of the train. The engine, as I have said, was still on the rails; the first truck, an ordinary bogey, had turned completely head over heels, killing and terribly injuring some of the plate-layers who were upon it. [; but it] It lay quite clear of the track. The next two armoured trucks, which contained the Durban Light Infantry, were both derailed, one still upright and the other on its side. They lay jammed against each other in [disorder,] a V-shaped position, quite blocking the homeward path of the rest. Behind the overturned trucks the Durban Light Infantry men, bruised, shaken and some severely injured, had found a temporary shelter. The enemy's fire was continuous, and soon there mingled with the rifles the bang of the field guns and the near explosion of their shells. We were in the toils [of the enemy].

MEL, p. 261.
I formed the opinion that it would be possible to use the engine as a ram to pull and push the two wrecked trucks clear of the line, and consequently that escape for the whole force was possible. The line appeared to be uninjured, no rail had been removed. I returned along the line to Captain Haldane's truck and told him through a loophole what was the position and what I proposed we should do. He agreed to all I said and undertook to keep the enemy hotly engaged meanwhile.

I was very lucky in the hour that followed not to be hit. It was necessary for me to be almost continuously moving up and down the train or standing in the open, telling the engine-driver what to do. [This man a civilian, wounded in the head by a shell splinter and distracted with pain, would obey my order and no one else's.]

Shown below in blue is the text that Churchill removed from the article to create the text in *MEL*. It is unclear why he chose to remove this passage. Churchill also reversed the order of the first two sentences.

Cosmopolitan, January 1925, p. 72.
The line appeared to be uninjured, no rail had been removed. I formed the opinion that it would be possible to use the engine as a ram to butt and push the two wrecked trucks clear of the line and thereby open up a way of escape for the whole force. I returned along the line to Captain Haldane's truck and told him through a loophole what was the position and what I proposed we should do. He agreed to all I said and undertook to keep the enemy hotly engaged meanwhile.

I was very lucky in the hour that followed not to be hit. It was necessary for me to be almost continuously moving up and down the train or standing in the open, telling the engine-driver what to do. This man a civilian, wounded in the head by a shell splinter and distracted with pain, would obey my order and no one else's.

MEL, p. 262.
The heat [hope] and excitement of the work were such as to absorb me completely. I remember [, however,] thinking that it was [just] like working in front of an iron target at a rifle range at which men were continually firing. We struggled for seventy minutes among these clanging, rending iron boxes, amid the repeated explosions of shells and the ceaseless hammering of bullets, and with only five or six inches of twisted ironwork to make the difference between danger, captivity and shame on the one hand, and safety, freedom and triumph on the other.

Shown in blue above is a sentence added to the article which provides much more specificity to the scene, thus making it much more filled with action

and life-threatening action. The text in blue below is the original wording in the article.

Cosmopolitan, January 1925, p. 72.
The hope and excitement of the work were such as to absorb me completely. I remember, however, thinking that it was just like working in front of an iron target at a rifle range at which men were continually firing.

MEL, p. 264.
Above all things we had to be careful not to throw the engine off the line. But at last, as the artillery firing steadily increased and the second gun came into action from the opposite flank, I decided to run a great risk. The engine was backed to its fullest extent and driven full tilt at the obstruction. There was a harsh crunching tear, the engine reeled on the rails, and as the obstructing truck reared upwards, ground its way past and gained [on to] the homeward side, free and, as it turned out, safe. But our three remaining trucks were fifty yards away, still the wrong side of the obstruction, which [that had derailed the train and] had fallen back into its original place after the engine had passed [position]. What were we to do? Certainly we could not take the engine [go] back. Could we then drag the trucks by hand up to the engine? They were narrower than the engine and there would be just room for them to slip past."

The text in blue above are new or altered text from that in the *Cosmopolitan* article. The red text below is the original wording in the article or where the new text was placed in MEL. Most changes are simply clarifying.

Cosmopolitan, January 1925, p. 72.
Above all things we had to be careful not to throw the engine off the line. But at last, as the artillery firing steadily increased and the second gun came into action, [from the opposite flank,] I decided to run a great risk. The engine was backed [to its fullest extent] and driven full tilt at the obstruction. There was a harsh crunching tear, the engine reeled on the rails, and as the obstructing truck reared upwards, ground its way past on to the homeward side, free and, as it turned out, safe. But our three remaining

trucks were fifty yards away, still the wrong side of the obstruction, that had derailed the train and had fallen back into its original position.

What were we to do? Certainly we could not go back. Could we then drag the trucks by hand up to the engine? They were narrower than the engine and there would be just room for them to slip past.

MEL, pp. 264–5.
I went back again to Captain Haldane. He accepted the plan. He ordered his men to climb out of their steel pen and try to push it towards the engine. The plan was sound enough, but it broke down under the force of circumstances, The truck was so heavy that it required all hands to move it; the fire was so hot and the [increasing] confusion so great and increasing that the men drifted away from the exposed side. The enemy, relieved of our counter-fire, were now plainly visible in large numbers on the face of the hill, firing furiously. We then agreed that the engine should go slowly back along the line with all the wounded, who were now numerous, and that the Dublin and the Durban men should retreat on foot, sheltering themselves [as much as possible] behind the engine which would go at a foot's pace. Upwards of forty [fifty] persons, of whom the greater part were streaming with blood, were crowded on the engine and its tender, and we began to move slowly forward. I was in the cab of the engine directing the engine-driver. It was crammed so full of wounded men that one could scarcely move. The shells burst all around, some striking the engine, others dashing the gravel of the track upon it and its unhappy human freight. The pace increased, the infantry outside began to lag [to double, to struggle] and then to be left behind. [When] At last I forced [got] the engine-driver to stop altogether, but before I could get the engine stopped we were already 300 yards away from our infantry. Close at hand was the bridge across the Blue Krantz River, a considerable span. I told the engine-driver to cross the bridge and wait on the other side, and forcing my way out of the cab I got down on to the line and went back along it to find Captain Haldane, and to bring him and his Dublin Fusiliers along.

Shown in blue above is the new or amended text in the *MEL* version. Below in red is where that new text was added to the article; the blue text

below is the original text in the article. Changes are mostly for colour or clarification.

Cosmopolitan, January 1925, p. 72.
I went back again to Captain Haldane. [He accepted the plan.] He ordered his men to climb out of their steel pen and try to push it towards the engine. The plan was sound enough, but it broke down under the force of circumstances. The truck was so heavy that it required all hands to move it. The fire was so hot and the increasing confusion so great and increasing that the men drifted away from the exposed side.

The enemy, relieved of our counter-fire, were now plainly visible in large numbers on the face of the hill, firing furiously. We then agreed that the engine should go slowly back along the line with all the wounded, who were now numerous, and that the Dublin and the Durban men should retreat on foot, sheltering themselves as much as possible behind the engine which would go at a foot's pace. Upwards of fifty persons, [of whom the greater part were streaming with blood,] were crowded on the engine and its tender, and we began to move slowly forward.

I was in the cab of the engine directing the engine-driver. It was crammed so full of wounded men that one could scarcely move. The shells burst all around, some striking the engine, others dashing the gravel of the track upon it and its unhappy human freight. The pace increased, the infantry outside began to double, to struggle and then to be left behind. When at last I got the engine-driver to stop altogether, [but before I could get the engine stopped] we were already 300 yards away from our infantry. Close at hand was the bridge across the Blue Krantz River, a considerable span. I told the engine-driver to cross the bridge and wait on the other side. [, and] Forcing my way out of the cab I got down on to the line and went back along it to find Captain Haldane, [and] to bring him and his Dublin Fusiliers along.

MEL, p. 265.
But while these events had been taking place everything else had been in movement. I had not retraced my steps 200 [one hundred] yards when, instead of Haldane and his company, two figures in plain clothes appeared upon the line. 'Plate-layers!' I said to myself, and then with a surge of

realization, 'Boers!' My mind retains its impression of these tall figures, full of energy, clad in dark, flapping clothes, with slouch, storm-driven hats, poising on their levelled rifles hardly a hundred yards away. I turned again and ran back towards the engine, the two Boers firing as I ran between the metals. Their bullets, sucking to right and left, seemed to miss only by inches. We were in a small cutting with banks about six feet high on either side. I flung myself against the bank of the cutting. It gave no cover. Another glance at the two figures; one was now kneeling to aim. Movement seemed the only chance. Again I darted forward: again two soft kisses sucked in the air; but nothing struck me. This could not endure. I must get out of the cutting—that damnable corridor! I jigged to the left, and scrambled up the bank. The earth sprang up beside me. I got through the wire fence unhurt. Outside the cutting was a tiny depression. I crouched in this, struggling to get my breath again.

Above in blue is the text added to or edited from the original article. The text was highly edited as can be seen. Below is the original text. The new text adds excitement and an aura of danger.

Cosmopolitan, January 1925, p. 72.
But while these events had been taking place everything else had been in movement. I had not retraced my steps one hundred yards when, instead of Haldane and his Company, two dark figures in plain clothes, with slouched hats, sprang up and levelled their rifles at me. I turned again and ran back towards the now distant engine. The two Boers fired again and again as I ran between the metals. They were not one hundred yards away when I started and their bullets seemed to miss only by inches. We were in a small cutting with banks about six feet high on either side, and there was absolutely no cover. I determined to get out of the blasted corridor. I darted to the left, scrambled up the bank, got through a wire fence untouched, but so completely winded that I threw myself on the ground to get my breath.

MEL, pp. 265–6.
Fifty yards away was a small [masonry] platelayer's cabin of masonry; there was cover there. About 200 yards away was the rocky gorge of the Blue Krantz River; there was plenty of cover there. I [rose,] determined to make

a dash for the river. I rose to my feet. Suddenly on the other side of the railway, separated from me by the rails and two uncut wire fences, I saw a horseman galloping furiously, a tall, dark figure, holding his rifle in his right hand. He pulled up his horse almost in its own length and shaking the rifle at me shouted a loud command. We were forty yards apart. That morning I had taken with me, Correspondent-status notwithstanding, [– despite the fact that I was a war correspondent –] my Mauser pistol. I thought I could kill this man, and after the treatment I had received I earnestly desired to do so, I put my hand to my belt, the pistol was not there. When engaged in clearing the line, getting in and out of the engine, etc., I had taken it off. It came safely home on the engine. I have it now!

The text in blue above is new or edited text. Below in blue is the original text, and the red is where the new text was changed, or new text added.

Cosmopolitan, January 1925, p. 72.
Fifty yards away was a small masonry plate-layer's cabin [of masonry]; there was cover there. About 200 yards away was the rocky gorge of the Blue Krantz River; there was [plenty of] cover there. I rose, determined to [make a] dash for the river. [I rose to my feet.]

Suddenly on the other side of the railway, separated from me by the rails and two uncut wire fences, I saw a horseman galloping furiously – a tall, dark figure, holding his rifle in his right hand. He pulled up his horse almost in its own length and shaking the rifle at me shouted a [loud] command. We were forty yards apart.

That morning I had taken with me – despite the fact that I was a war correspondent – my Mauser pistol. I thought I could kill this man, and after the treatment I had received. I earnestly desired to do so. I put my hand to my belt; the pistol was not there. When engaged in clearing the line, getting in and out of the engine. [etc.,] I had taken it off. [It came safely home on the engine. I have it now!]

MEL, p. 266.
But at this moment I was quite unarmed. Meanwhile, I suppose in about the time this takes to tell, the Boer horseman, still seated on his horse, had covered me with his rifle. The animal stood stock still, so did he, and so did

I. I looked towards the river, I looked towards the platelayer's hut. The Boer continued to look along his sights. I thought there was absolutely no chance of escape, if he fired he would surely hit me, so I held up my hands and surrendered myself a prisoner of war.

The text in blue above are newly added text; red text below indicates where they were added to the article.

Cosmopolitan, January 1925, p. 2.
[But at this moment I was quite unarmed. Meanwhile, I suppose in about the time this takes to tell, the Boer horseman, still seated on his horse had covered me with his rifle.] The animal stood stock still, [so did he,] and so did I. I looked towards the river, I looked towards the plate-layer's hut. The Boer continued to look along his sights. I thought there was absolutely no chance of escape. If he fired, he would surely hit me, so I held up my hands and surrendered [myself a prisoner of war].

MEL, p. 266–7.
'When one is alone and unarmed,' said the great Napoleon, in words which flowed into my mind in the poignant minutes that followed, 'a surrender may be pardoned.' Still he might have missed; and the Blue Krantz ravine was very near and the two wire fences were still uncut. However, the deed was done. Thereupon my captor lowered his rifle and beckoned to me to come across to him. I obeyed. I walked [climbed] through the wire fences and across [crossed] the line and stood by his side. He sprang off his horse and began firing in the direction of the bridge upon the retreating engine and a few straggling British figures. Then when the last had disappeared he re-mounted and at his side I tramped back towards the spot where I had left Captain Haldane and his company. I saw none of them.

They were already prisoners. I noticed that it was raining hard. As I plodded through the high grass [sopping field] by the side of my captor a disquieting and timely reflection came into my mind. I had two clips of Mauser ammunition, each holding ten rounds, in two little breast pockets one on each side of my khaki coat. These cartridges were the same as I had used at Omdurman, and were the only kind supplied for the Mauser pistol. They were [contain] what are called 'soft-nosed bullets.' I had never given them a thought until now**; and** it was borne in upon me that they might be a very dangerous possession. I dropped the right-hand clip on the ground without being seen. I had got the left-hand clip in my hand and was about to drop it, when my captor looked down sharply and said in English, 'What have you got there?'

Minor textual changes in blue noted above. Text in red below show the original wording.

Cosmopolitan, January 1925, p. 72.
'When one is alone and unarmed,' said the great Napoleon, in words which flowed into my mind in the poignant minutes that followed, 'a surrender may be pardoned.' Still he might have missed; and the Blue Krantz ravine was very near and the two wire fences were still uncut. However, the deed was done. Thereupon my captor lowered his rifle and beckoned to me to come across to him, I obeyed. I **climbed** through the wire fences, **crossed** the line and stood by his side. He sprang off his horse and began firing in the direction of the bridge upon the retreating engine and a few straggling British figures. Then when the last had disappeared he re-mounted and at his side I tramped back towards the spot where I had left Captain Haldane and his company. I saw none of them. They were already prisoners. **[I noticed that it was raining hard.]**

As I plodded through the **sopping field** by the side of my captor a disquieting and timely reflection came into my mind. I had two clips of Mauser ammunition, each holding ten rounds, in two little breast pockets one on each side of my khaki coat. These cartridges were the same as I had used at Omdurman, and were the only kind supplied for the Mauser pistol. They **contain** what are called 'soft-nosed bullets.' I had never given them a thought until now. **[; and]** It was borne in upon me that they might be a very dangerous possession. I dropped the right-hand clip on the ground without being seen. I had got the left-hand clip in my hand and was about to drop it, when my captor looked down sharply and said in English, 'What have you got there?

MEL, p. 267.
'What is it?' I said, opening the palm of my hand, 'I picked it up.'

He took it, looked at it and [to my relief,] threw it away. We continued to plod on until we reached the general gang [group] of prisoners and found ourselves speedily in the midst of many hundreds of mounted Boers who streamed into view, in long columns of twos and threes, many holding umbrellas over their heads in the pouring rain.

Minor new changes shown in blue above.

Cosmopolitan, January 1925, p. 72.
'What is it?' I said, opening the palm of my hand, 'I picked it up.'

He took it, looked at it, and to my relief, threw it away. We continued to plod on until we reached the general group of prisoners and found ourselves speedily in the midst of many hundreds of mounted Boers who streamed into view, in long columns of twos and threes, many holding umbrellas over their heads in the pouring rain.

MEL, p. 267–8.
Such is the episode of the armoured train and the story of my capture on November 15, 1899. It was not until three years later, when the Boer Generals visited England to ask for some loan or assistance on behalf of their devastated country, that I was introduced at a private luncheon to their leader, General Botha. We talked of the war and I briefly told the story of my capture. Botha listened in silence; then he said, 'Don't you recognise me? I was that man. It was I who took you prisoner. I, myself,' and his bright eyes twinkled with pleasure. Botha in white shirt and frock coat looked very different in all save size and darkness of complexion from the wild wartime figure I had seen that rough day in Natal. But about the extraordinary fact there can be no doubt, He had entered upon the invasion of Natal as a burgher; his own disapproval of the war had excluded him from any high command at its outset. This was his first action. But as a simple private burgher serving in the ranks he had galloped on ahead and in front of the whole Boer forces in the ardour of pursuit. Thus we met.

Churchill adds a new ending to this paragraph in *MEL* as shown in blue above. Below is shown the original ending in red. This is the end of the article.

Cosmopolitan January 1925, p. 72.

Such is the episode of the armoured train and the story of my capture on November 15, 1899. It was not until three years later, when the Boer Generals visited England to ask for some loan or assistance on behalf of their devastated country, that I was introduced at a private luncheon to their leader, General Botha. We talked of the war and I briefly told the story of my capture. Botha listened in silence; then he said, 'Don't you recognise me? I was that man. It was I who took you prisoner. I, myself,' and his bright eyes twinkled with pleasure.

Botha in white shirt and frock coat looked very different in all save size and darkness of complexion from the wild war-time figure I had seen that rough day in Natal. But about the extraordinary fact there can be no doubt. He had entered upon the invasion of Natal as a burgher. His own disapproval of the war had excluded him from any high command at its outset. **But in a month he was Commander-in-Chief of the Boer Armies. But on this occasion, as a private serving in the ranks, he galloped on ahead of the whole Boer forces in the ardour of pursuit, and thus it was that we first became acquainted.**

MEL, pp. 268–72.
The chapter continues on for more than four pages with a discussion of Botha and Churchill's transport to the prisoner of war camp, but this is all new material not present in the *Cosmopolitan* **article.**

Notes
1. Frederick Woods, ed., *Young Winston's Wars: The Original Dispatches of Winston S. Churchill, War Correspondent, 1897-1900*, New York, Viking Press, 1973.
2. Winston S. Churchill, *London to Ladysmith Via Pretoria*, London, Longmans, Green and Company, 1900.

APPENDIX 6

Chapter 4: Escape

As is well known, Churchill was captured by the Boers while he was a war correspondent. He was incarcerated as a prisoner of war and treated as a hostile combatant. He escaped the prison and, only later, joined the military as a cavalry officer.

The story of Churchill's escape and the subsequent newspaper coverage around the world thrust him into the limelight as a truly international figure for the first time. His reputation in the United Kingdom also soared and he became an even more prominent figure who was highly sought-after as a speaker and as a candidate for Parliament. Therefore, it is not surprising that Churchill published the story concerning his escape in five separate publications over a thirty-one-year span. He would continue to publish serialised versions long after the publication of *My Early Life*. As mentioned in Chapter 2 ('Becoming a Writer'), Haldane accused Churchill of dishonourable behaviour concerning his escape from prison. He contended that Churchill had left alone, without waiting for Haldane. However, Churchill always maintained he had acted with honour and that Haldane had not jumped the fence because guards had appeared and made it too risky. Churchill was already over the fence, and he had had no option but to go it alone. Churchill, since the first accusation by Haldane, would fiercely defend himself whenever anyone even suggested that he had acted dishonourably. There is an abundance of material concerning this issue, including detailed descriptions by Haldane of the event in the chapter titled 'Escape 1899' in the Companion Volume 1, Part 2 of the official Churchill biography.[1] The reader is referred there for further study.

Another incident related to this controversy arose in 1912 when *Blackwell's Magazine* published a parody on Churchill titled 'A Lost Letter of Ancient Rome' in which, among other statements, the author writes,

> When captured by our Asian foes,
> How cleverly he homeward stole,
> And broke his prison and parole![2]

This was interpreted by Churchill and others to imply that Churchill had acted illegally in his escape. Churchill immediately threatened and then instituted a libel lawsuit against *Blackwell's* and the author – a lawsuit which ended in a hearing at which Churchill testified. In the end, the magazine and the author both issued apologies and printed a retraction in the magazine.[3] This incident has specific importance in the context of this book because, in preparation, Churchill submitted to the court a fourteen-page account of his escape, written on Admiralty stationery.[4] This document provides another comparator for the final text in *My Early Life*.

As described in Chapter 7 of this book ('Impact of *My Early Life*'), the escape episode is one of the most highly referenced sections of *My Early Life*.

In this chapter, comparisons will be made of the texts from the following publications:

MEL, Chapter XXI, 'I Escape From the Boers – I', pp. 282–99 and Chapter XXII, 'I Escape From the Boers – II', pp. 300–312.[5]
Dispatches to the *Morning Post*, December 21–23, 1899, in *Young Winston's Wars*, pp. 178–89.[6]
L to L, Chapter XI, 'I Escape From the Boers', pp. 177–204.[7]
Strand Magazine, 'My Escape From the Boers', December 1923, pp. 537–47.[8]
Strand Magazine, 'My Escape From the Boers, Part II', January 1924, pp. 14–23.[9]
Cosmopolitan, 'I Escape From the Boers', January 1924, pp. 30–34 and 161–66.[10]

Where appropriate the April 1912 'legal' document as described above will be compared.

The text from *My Early Life* will be broken down into digestible sections for the analysis. Below are the direct comparisons using the same format as has been used in the previous appendices. The text from the story in *MEL* is presented first. This is followed by analogous texts from the earlier publications, which are listed chronologically. Material highlighted in yellow are the texts from the other publications where the exact text is found in *MEL*. Comments on the similarities and difference are provided in **bold** after the text from *MEL* and elsewhere. Where there are large sections in *MEL* that are new and unique and not derived from early publications, those will be so noted. The reader will also be able to visualise the chronological progression of the text where there are multiple sources.

Of all the textural comparisons made in this book on the five episodes chosen from *MEL*, this section on Churchill's escape is by far the most robust, as there were so many early variations published. In the opening of Chapter XXI of *MEL*, Churchill notes that he has written previously about this topic: 'I shall transcribe what I wrote at the time where I cannot improve upon it.' He also notes in the *Strand* article below that much new material is added that could not be published in his dispatches or subsequent book for fear of reprisals, as to do so would have compromised soldiers and civilians still in the war or those who were helpful to him in his escape. Finally, again, to help the reader, the author's comments will be **bolded**.

Opening of section of 'Escape'
MEL, p. 282.

During the first three weeks of my captivity, although I was a party to all plans of revolt or escape, I was engaged in arguing with the Boer Authorities that they should release me as a Press Correspondent. 'They replied that I had forfeited my non-combatant status by the part I had taken in the armoured train fight. I contended that I had not fired a shot and had been taken unarmed. This was strictly true. But the Natal newspapers had been captured by the Boers. These contained glowing accounts of my activities, and attributed the escape of the engine and the wounded entirely to me. General Joubert therefore intimated that even if I had not fired a shot myself, I had injured the Boer operations by freeing the engine, and that I must therefore be treated as a prisoner-of-war. As soon as I learned of this decision, in the first week of December, I resolved to escape.

I shall transcribe what I wrote at the time where I cannot improve upon it.

As will be seen below, none of the earlier versions contain similar text to that above. In each case, what is shown is the opening section of each version.

Dispatches, 21–23 December 1899
How unhappy is that poor man who loses his liberty! No degree of material comfort, no consciousness of good behaviour, can balance the hateful degradation of imprisonment. Before I had been an hour in captivity I resolved to escape. Many plans suggested themselves, were examined and rejected. For a month I thought of nothing else. But the peril and difficulty restrained action. I think that it was the news of the British defeat at Stormberg that clinched the matter. All the news we heard in Pretoria was derived from Boer sources, and was hideously exaggerated and distorted.

L to L, p. 17. (**Same as Dispatches with added words in blue**)
How unhappy is that poor man who loses his liberty? What can the wide world give him in exchange! No degree of material comfort, no consciousness of correct behaviour, can balance the hateful degradation of imprisonment. Before I had been an hour in captivity, as the previous pages evidence, I resolved to escape. Many plans suggested themselves, were examined, and rejected. For a month I thought of nothing else. But the peril and difficulty restrained action. I think that it was the report of the British defeat at Stormberg that clinched the matter. All the news we heard in Pretoria was derived from Boer sources, and was hideously exaggerated and distorted.

Strand Magazine, December 1923, p. 537. (**New text for this article**)
Churchill offers a bit of background when he informs the readers that he was a War Correspondent for the *Morning Post* and sent back reports on his capture; however, because of the risk to those still engaged in the conflict, he did not reveal the entire story – which he now plans to do.

I was taken prisoner on the 15th November, 1899, when the British armoured train was cut off, derailed and pounded to pieces by artillery at Chieveley Station, near Natal. I was taken with other prisoners to Pretoria by march, and rail, and on November 19th was confined in the States Model Schools, then occupied by about fifty other British officer prisoners-of-war. I shall transcribe what I have already where I cannot improve on it.

He then goes on using similar descriptions, as seen below (e.g. 'The States Model Schools…').

Cosmopolitan, January 1924, p. 30. (**Same as the *Strand*, except for two words**) I was taken prisoner on the fifteenth of November, 1899, when the British armored train was cut off, derailed and pounded to pieces by artillery at Chieveley Station near Natal. I was taken with other prisoners to Pretoria by march and rail, and on November 19th was confined in the States Model Schools, then occupied by about fifty other British officer prisoners of war.

Description of State Model School Prison
MEL, p. 282.
The State Model Schools stood in the midst of a quadrangle, and were surrounded on two sides by an iron grille and on two by a corrugated-iron fence about ten feet high. These boundaries offered little obstacle to anyone who possessed the activity of youth, but the fact that they were guarded on the inside by sentries, fifty yards apart, armed with rifle and revolver, made them a well-nigh insuperable barrier. No walls are so hard to pierce as living walls.

After anxious reflection and continual watching, it was discovered by several of the prisoners that when the sentries along the eastern side walked about on their beats they were sat certain moments unable to see the top of a few yards of the wall near the small circular lavatory office which can be seen on the plan.

As will be seen below, a significant part of the text is derived from each of the publications; and as one moves chronologically closer to *MEL*, the text becomes identical. It is interesting that Churchill dropped the sentences in the dispatch below concerning the idea of bribing the sentries. In *L to L*, he even expands on the concept and mentions he can't afford it. What he wrote about the episode for the *Strand* article became the text he would use for *MEL*.

Dispatches, 21–23 December 1899 (**Yellow highlighted text used for *MEL***) The State Model Schools, the building in which we were confined, is a brick structure standing in the midst of a gravel quadrangle and surrounded on two sides by an iron grille and on two by a corrugated iron fence about 10 feet high. These boundaries offered little obstacle to anyone who possessed the activity of youth, but the fact that they were guarded on the inside by sentries armed with rifle and revolver fifty yards apart made them a well-nigh insuperable barrier. No walls are so hard to pierce as living walls. I thought of the penetrating power of gold, and the sentries were sounded. They were incorruptible. I seek not to deprive them of the credit, but the truth is that the bribery market in this country has been spoilt by the millionaires.

L to L, p. 79. (**Text in yellow highlight used for *MEL*)**
The States Model Schools stand in the midst of a quadrangle, and are surrounded on two sides by an iron grille and on two by a corrugated iron fence about 10 feet high. These boundaries offered little obstacle to anyone who possessed the activity of youth, but the fact that they were guarded on the inside by sentries, fifty yards apart, armed with rifle and revolver, made them a well-nigh insuperable barrier. No walls are so hard to pierce as living walls. I thought of the penetrating power of gold, and the sentries were sounded. They were incorruptible. I seek not to deprive them of the credit, but the truth is that the bribery market in the Transvaal has been spoiled by the millionaires. I could not afford with my slender resources to insult them heavily enough.

Strand, December 1923, p. 537. (**This exact text used for *MEL*)**
The States Model Schools stand in the midst of a quadrangle, and were surrounded on two sides by an iron grille and on two by a corrugated iron fence about ten feet high. These boundaries offered little obstacle to anyone who possessed the activity of youth, but the fact that they were guarded on the inside by sentries, fifty yards apart, armed with rifle and revolver, made them a well-nigh insuperable barrier. No walls are so hard to pierce as living walls.

After anxious reflection and continual watching, it was discovered by several of the prisoners that when the sentries along the eastern side walked about on their beats they were at certain moments unable to see the top of a few yards of the wall near the small circular lavatory office which can be seen on the plan.

Cosmopolitan, January 1924, p. 30. (**Same as the *Strand* except for one word**)
The States Model Schools stand in the midst of a quadrangle, and are surrounded on two sides by an iron grille and on two by a corrugated iron

fence about ten feet high. These boundaries offered little obstacle to anyone who possessed the activity of youth, but the fact that they were guarded on the inside by sentries, fifty yards apart, armed with rifle and revolver, made them a well-nigh insuperable barrier. No walls are so hard to pierce as living walls. After anxious reflection and continual watching, it was discovered by several of the prisoners that when the sentries along the eastern side walked about on their beats they were at certain moments unable to see the top of a few yards of the wall near the small circular lavatory office which can be seen on the plan.

MEL, p. 283.
The electric lights in the middle of the quadrangle brilliantly lighted the whole place, but the eastern wall was in shadow. The first thing was therefore to pass the two sentries near the office. It was necessary to hit off the exact moment when both their backs should be turned together. After the wall was scaled we should be in the garden of the villa next door. There the plan came to an end. Everything after this was vague and uncertain. How to get out of the garden, how to pass unnoticed through the streets, how to evade the patrols that surrounded the town, and above all how to cover the two hundred and eighty miles to the Portuguese frontier, were questions which would arise at a later stage.

Dispatches, p. 180. (**Highlighted text in yellow used in** *MEL*; **non-highlighted text deleted**)
The electric lights in the middle of the quadrangle brilliantly lighted the whole place, but cut off the sentries beyond them from looking at the eastern wall. For behind the light all seemed by contrast darkness. The first thing was therefore to pass the two sentries near the offices. It was necessary to hit off the exact moment when both their backs should be turned together. After the wall was scaled we should be in the garden of the villa next door. There the plan came to an end. Everything after this was vague and uncertain. How to get out of the garden, how to pass unnoticed through the streets, how to evade the patrols that surrounded the town, and above all how to cover the two hundred and eighty miles to the Portuguese frontier, were questions which would arise at a later stage.

L to L, p. 181. (**Highlighted text is in *MEL* and is the same as Dispatches**)
The electric lights in the middle of the quadrangle brilliantly lighted the whole place but cut off the sentries beyond them from looking at the eastern wall, for from behind the lights all seemed darkness by contrast. The first thing was therefore to pass the two sentries near the offices. It was necessary to hit off the exact moment when both their backs should be turned together. After the wall was scaled we should be in the garden of the villa next door. There our plan came to an end. Everything after this was vague and uncertain. How to get out of the garden, how to pass unnoticed through the streets, how to evade the patrols that surrounded the town, and above all how to cover the two hundred and eighty miles to the Portuguese frontiers, were questions which would arise at a later stage.

Strand, December 1923, p. 537. (**This exact text was used for *MEL* and *Cosmopolitan*)
Cosmopolitan, January 1924, p. 30.
The electric lights in the middle of the quadrangle brilliantly lighted the whole place, but the eastern wall was in shadow. The first thing was therefore to pass the two sentries near the office. It was necessary to hit off the exact moment when both their backs should be turned together. After the wall was scaled we should be in the garden of the villa next door. There the plan came to an end. Everything after this was vague and uncertain. How to get out of the garden, how to pass unnoticed through the streets, how to evade the patrols that surrounded the town, and above all how to cover the two hundred and eighty miles to the Portuguese frontier, were questions which would arise at a later stage.

Aborted Escape Attempt
MEL, p. 283.
Together with Captain Haldane and Lieutenant Brockie I made an abortive attempt, not pushed with any decision, on December 11. There was no difficulty in getting into the circular office. But to climb out of it over the wall was a hazard of the sharpest character. Anyone doing so must at the moment he was on the top of the wall be plainly visible to the sentries fifteen yards away, if they were in the right place and happened to look! Whether the sentries would challenge, or fire depended entirely upon their individual

dispositions, and no one could tell what they would do. Nevertheless I was determined that nothing should stop my taking the plunge the next day. As the 12th wore away my fears crystallized more and more into desperation. In the evening, after my two friends had made an attempt, but had not found the moment propitious, I strolled across the quadrangle and secreted myself in the circular office. Through an aperture in the metal casing of which it was built I watched the sentries. For some time they remained stolid and obstructive. Then all of a sudden one turned and walked up to his comrade, and they began to talk. Their backs were turned.

As seen below, the first major excerpt to be used for *MEL* is from the *Strand* and the *Cosmopolitan* versions in *MEL*. Only the MEL version contains the other officers' names.

Dispatches, 21–23 December 1899, p. 181. (**The highlighted phrases are used in *MEL*)**
Choosing my opportunity ==I strolled across the quadrangle and secreted myself in== one of the offices. Through a chink I watched the sentries. For half an hour they remained stolid and obstructive. ==Then all of a sudden one== and walked up to his comrade and they began to talk.

L to L
No direct reporting of this section in this book.

Legal Document, 1912, p. 3. The entire text is red as there is no direct word for word insertion into *MEL*.
We [WSC, Haldane, Brockie] resolved, therefore to make an attempt on the night of the 11th December about 7 PM. We all went across the yard at different times into the roundhouse, and waited a long time in the hope of being able to climb over the back wall. But the sentry stood in such an unfavourable position, and the danger appeared to be so great, that very reluctantly we all came back and gave up the attempt for the night. The next day more bad news came in, and I was insistent that at whatever risk, we should force the thing through that night. As soon as it got dark, and before the moon rose, Haldane and I both got into the roundhouse and waited for a chance of climbing over; but after much hesitation we

could not make up our minds to it, again thought it too dangerous; and came back to the veranda. Brockie then came up and asked us why we had not got over. Haldane explained the difficulty of the sentry's position, and Brockie said: 'You're afraid.' Haldane replied: 'You can go and see yourself'. Brockie then went across the yard, got into the roundhouse and remained there some time. Then I said to Haldane: 'I will go back again'. I went across the yard, and at the entrance to the roundhouse I met Brockie coming out, but we dare not speak to each other in the presence of the sentry. [**I had come to the conclusion that we should waste the whole night in hesitations unless the matter were clinched once and for all; and as the sentry turned to light his pipe, I jumped on to the ledge of the wall and in a few seconds had dropped into the garden safely on the other side. Here I crouched and waited for the others to come. I expected them to come every minute. My position in the garden was a very anxious one because I had only a few small and leafless bushes to hide behind, and people kept passing to and fro, and the lights of the houses were burning. Altogether I waited more than an hour and a half in the garden for the others to join me. Twice a man from the house walked along a path within 7 or 8 yards of me.**] Meanwhile Brockie had rejoined Haldane, had agreed with him that the sentry's position made the attempt too dangerous, and both of them went into the dining room where the evening meal had already begun. They had not abandoned the attempt for the night, and meant to have another try after dinner.

After I had waited about a quarter of an hour, I managed to attract the attention, by tapping gently, of an officer who had come to the roundhouse for a private purpose, and told him to tell Haldane that I had succeeded in getting over, and that he must come and make the attempt to join me as soon as he could. Both he and Brockie then came back, and I suppose about half an hour after I got over, Haldane attempted to climb the wall. Whether he made a slight noise, or just through bad luck, the sentry turned round at the moment and he was seen as his shoulders were about level with the top of the wall by the sentry. The sentry immediately challenged him, leveled his rifle at him, and ordered him to come back, which of course he was forced to do. It was very lucky for him that the sentry was a humane man who gave him a chance to come back instead of firing at once, which at that very close range – 5 or 6 yards – would probably have been fatal.

This is a fascinating account, far more detailed than any other version of the story, and it is significantly different in terms of the facts claimed and the interactions between the three comrades. The bolded and bracketed text above was in the typed manuscript, but it has pen strike marks across the entire section. The description suggests there were many more, and more detailed, discussions between the parties before Churchill went over the wall. This text was written with the intent of providing a more legal justification. No other versions contain the story of Haldane almost being shot.

Strand Magazine, December 1923, p. 537. (**New text and highlighted sections used in *MEL*)**
Together with two other officers I made an aborted attempt, not pushed with any decision, on the 11th of December. There was no difficulty in getting into the circular office. But to climb out of it over the wall was a hazard of the sharpest character. Anyone doing so must at the moment he was on the top of the wall be plainly visible to the sentries fifteen yards away, if they were in the right place and happened to look! Whether the sentries would challenge or fire depended entirely upon their individual dispositions, and no one could tell what they would do. Nevertheless I was determined that nothing should stop my taking the plunge the next day. As the 12th wore away my fears crystallized more and more into desperation. In the evening, after my two friends had made an attempt but had not found the moment propitious, I strolled across the quadrangle and secreted myself in the circular office. Through an aperture in the metal casing of which it was built I watched the sentries. For some time, they remained stolid and obstructive. Then all of a sudden one turned and walked up to his comrade, and they began to talk. Their backs were turned.

Cosmopolitan, January 1924, p. 30. (**Exactly the same as *Strand*)**
Together with two other officers I made an abortive attempt, not pushed with any decision, on the eleventh of December. There was no difficulty in getting into the circular office. But to climb out of it over the wall was a hazard of the sharpest character. Anyone doing so must at the moment he was on the top of the wall be plainly visible to the sentries fifteen yards away, if only they happened to look! Whether the sentries would challenge or fire

depended entirely upon their individual dispositions. Nevertheless, I was determined that nothing should stop my taking the plunge the next day. As the twelfth wore away my fears crystallized more and more into desperation. In the evening after my two friends had made an attempt but had not found the moment propitious, I strolled across the quadrangle and secreted myself in the circular office. Through an aperture in the metal casing of which it was built I watched the sentries. For some time they remained stolid and obstructive. Then all of a sudden one turned and walked up to his comrade, and they began to talk. Their backs were turned.

Escape
MEL, p, 284.
Now or never! I stood on a ledge, seized the top of the wall with my hands, and drew myself up. Twice I let myself down again in sickly hesitation, and then with a third resolve scrambled up and over. My waistcoat got entangled with the ornamental metal-work on the top. I had to pause for an appreciable moment to extricate myself. In this posture I had one parting glimpse of the sentries still talking with their backs turned fifteen yards away. One of them was lighting his cigarette, and I remember the glow on the inside of his hands as a distinct impression which my mind recorded. Then I lowered myself lightly down into the adjoining garden and crouched among the shrubs. I was free! The first step had been taken, and it was irrevocable. It now remained to await the arrival of my comrades. The bushes in the garden gave a good deal of cover, and in the moonlight their shadows **fell dark** **[lay black]** on the ground. I lay here for an hour in great impatience and anxiety.

Dispatches, 21–23 December 1899, p. 181. (**Text in yellow highlight used for *MEL* except the two words in red**)
Now or never. I darted out of my hiding place and ran to the wall, seized the top with my hands and drew myself up. Twice I let myself down again in sickly hesitation, and then with a third resolve scrambled up. The top was flat. Lying on it I had one parting glimpse of the sentries, still talking, still with their backs turned; but, I repeat fifteen yards away. Then I lowered myself silently down into an adjoining garden and crouched among the scrubs. I was free. The first step had been taken and it was irrevocable.

It now remained to await the arrival of my comrades. The bushes of the garden gave a good deal of cover, and in the moonlight their shadows lay black on the ground.

L to L, p. 183. (**Exactly the same as Dispatches**)
Now or never. I darted out of my hiding place and ran to the wall, seized the top with my hands and drew myself up. Twice I let myself down again in sickly hesitation, and then with a third resolve scrambled up. The top was flat. Lying on it I had one parting glimpse of the sentries, still talking, still with their backs turned; but, I repeat, fifteen yards away. Then I lowered myself silently down into the adjoining garden and crouched among the shrubs. I was free. The first step had been taken, and it was irrevocable.

It now remained to await the arrival of my comrade. The bushes of the garden gave a good deal of cover, and in the moon- light their shadows lay black on the ground.

Strand, December 1923, p. 53. (**Substantial changes from *L to L* (the underlined words were retained from *L to L*) and this complete text used exactly for both *MEL* and *Cosmopolitan*)**

Cosmopolitan, January 1924, p. 30.
Now or never! I stood on a ledge, seized the top of the wall with my hands, and drew myself up. Twice I let myself down again in sickly hesitation, and then with a third resolve scrambled up and over. My waistcoat got entangled with the ornamental metal-work on the top. I had to pause for an appreciable moment to extricate myself. In this posture I had one parting glimpse of the sentries still talking with their backs turned fifteen yards away. One of them was lighting his cigarette, and I remember the glow on the inside of his hands as a distinct impression which my mind recorded. Then I lowered myself lightly down into the adjoining garden and crouched among the shrubs. I was free! The first step had been taken, and it was irrevocable. It now remained to await the arrival of my comrades. The bushes in the garden gave a good deal of cover, and in the moonlight their shadows fell dark on the ground. I lay here for an hour in great impatience and anxiety.

Waiting for Other Officers Outside the Wall
MEL, p. 285.
Suddenly I heard a voice from within the quadrangle say, quite loud, 'All up.' I crawled back to the wall. Two officers were walking up and down inside, jabbering Latin words, laughing and talking all manner of nonsense—amid which I caught my name. I risked a cough. One of the officers immediately began to chatter alone. The other said, slowly and clearly, 'They cannot get out.' The sentry suspects. It's all up. Can you get back again? But now all my fears fell from me at once. To go back was impossible. I could not hope to climb the wall unnoticed. There was no helpful ledge on the outside. Fate pointed onwards. Besides, I said to myself, 'Of course, I shall be recaptured, but I will at least have a run for my money.' I said to the officers, 'I shall go on alone.'

Dispatches, 21–23 December 1899, p. 182. (**Exact text used for all subsequent publications including** *MEL*)
L to L, pp. 186–7.
Strand, December 1923, p. 538.
Cosmopolitan, January 1924, pp. 30–31.
Suddenly I heard a voice from within the quadrangle say, quite loud, 'All up.' I crawled back to the wall. Two officers were walking up and down inside, jabbering Latin words, laughing and talking all manner of nonsense—amid which I caught my name. I risked a cough. One of the officers immediately began to chatter alone. The other said, slowly and clearly, 'They cannot get out.' The sentry suspects. It's all up. Can you get back again? But now all my fears fell from me at once. To go back was impossible. I could not hope to climb the wall unnoticed. There was no helpful ledge on the outside. Fate pointed onwards. Besides, I said to myself, 'Of course, I shall be recaptured, but I will at least have a run for my money.' I said to the officers, 'I shall go on alone.'

Legal Document, 1912. (**Again, the description here is much more detailed and not aligned with the other publications or** *MEL* **directly**)

Meanwhile, I was waiting in the greatest anxiety in the garden on the other side, and of course knew nothing of this. At length I heard someone in the round house trying to communicate with me by tapping, and going close to the wall I had a conversation with Haldane who had come to tell me that he had made his attempt and had been stopped by the sentry; that the position of the sentry now made it quite impossible for him or Brockie to follow that night. This was of course a tremendous blow to me and seemed to make my position absolutely hopeless. I could not climb back because the wall was higher on the outside than on the in, and there was no ledge to help me. Had I attempted to come back, I should have made a tremendous noise and been detected instantly. If I had walked round to the front of the building and given myself up to the sentry, an instant enquiry would have been made and our loophole of escape would have been effectively closed in the future. On the other hand, to go on alone seemed quite hopeless; Brockie with his knowledge of Kaffir and Dutch had been our only chance of buying food without being detected. How was I alone, without any local knowledge, without even a compass or a map, or any fixed plan of what to do except walk by night and hide by day, to cover 500 miles of wild and hostile country to the frontier? So hopeless did this appear that I would gladly have climbed back again had this been possible. Haldane and I discussed the situation in whispers through the chinks in the corrugated iron fence; he quite agreed with me that it was impossible to come back, and that I must go on alone. It was a great disappointment to him to be left behind, but he bade me good-bye and wished me well.

The text is much more detailed and it involves Haldane, by name, much more than any of the other versions. It explicitly states that Haldane agreed with Churchill's decision to go alone and even wished him well. Churchill then goes on to describe that, on his return to England, 'I have since learned that people have said that I ought not to have climbed over the wall alone without Haldane, and that we had agreed to climb over together, Brockie following a few minutes later. I can solemnly testify that I was never a party to any agreement of this kind.' He then goes on to defend his actions. The escape itself is the focus of the document, not the longer journey to freedom. To this author's knowledge this document was never made public at the time. There is no commentary available concerning its veracity. Haldane's reaction would have been most interesting to hear.

The document contains no further material that is germane to the remaining parts of the 'Escape' chapter.

On the Run
MEL, p. 285.

Now I was in the right mood for these undertakings—failure being almost certain, no odds against success affected me. All risks were less than the certainty. A glance at the plan will show that the gate which led into the road was only a few yards from another sentry. I said to myself, 'Toujours de l'audace,' put my hat on my head, strode into the middle of the garden, walked past the windows of the house without any attempt at concealment, and so went through the gate and turned to the left. I passed the sentry at less than five yards. Most of them knew me by sight. Whether he looked at me or not I do not know, for I never turned my head. I restrained with the utmost difficulty an impulse to run. But after walking a hundred yards and hearing no challenge, I knew that the second obstacle had been surmounted. I was at large in Pretoria.

Dispatches, p. 282. (**Text used exactly for *MEL* except the non-highlighted words, which are removed**)

Now I was in the right mood for these undertakings—that is to say that, thinking failure almost certain, no odds against success affected me. All risks were less than the certainty. A glance at the plan will show that the gate which led into the road was only a few yards from another sentry. I said to myself, 'Toujours de l'audace,' put my hat on my head, strode into the middle of the garden, walked past the windows of the house without any attempt at concealment, and so went through the gate and turned to the left. I passed the sentry at less than five yards. Most of them knew me by sight. Whether he looked at me or not I do not know, for I never turned my head. I restrained with the utmost difficulty an impulse to run. But after walking a hundred yards and hearing no challenge, I knew that the second obstacle had been surmounted. I was at large in Pretoria.

L to L, p. 187. (**Same as Dispatches, except sentence in red here is removed**)

Now I was in the right mood for these undertakings—that is to say that, thinking failure almost certain, no odds against success affected me. All risks were less than the certainty. A glance at the plan will show that the gate which led into the road was only a few yards from another sentry. I said to myself, 'Toujours de l'audace' put my hat on my head, strode into the middle of the garden, walked past the windows of the house without any attempt at concealment, and so went through the gate and turned to the left I passed the sentry at less than five yards. Most of them knew me by sight. Whether he looked at me or not I do not know, for I never turned my head. [I restrained with the utmost difficulty an impulse to run.] But after walking a hundred yards and hearing no challenge, I knew that the second obstacle had been surmounted. I was at large in Pretoria.

Strand, December 1923, p. 538. (**Exact text used in *MEL* and the sentence above in red added back; this text used also for *Cosmopolitan*)**
Cosmopolitan, January 1924, p. 32.
Now I was in the right mood for these undertakings—failure being almost certain, no odds against success affected me. All risks were less than the certainty. A glance at the plan will show that the gate which led into the road was only a few yards from another sentry. I said to myself, 'Toujours de l'audace,' put my hat on my head, strode into the middle of the garden, walked past the windows of the house without any attempt at concealment, and so went through the gate and turned to the left. I passed the sentry at less than five yards. Most of them knew me by sight. Whether he looked at me or not I do not know, for I never turned my head. I restrained with the utmost difficulty an impulse to run. But after walking a hundred yards and hearing no challenge, I knew that the second obstacle had been surmounted. I was at large in Pretoria.

Begins Trek to Freedom
MEL, pp. 285–6.
I walked on leisurely through the night, humming a tune and choosing the middle of the road. The streets were full of burghers, but they paid no attention to me. Gradually I reached the suburbs, and on a little bridge I sat down to reflect and consider. I was in the heart of the enemy's country. I knew no one to whom I could apply for succour. Nearly three hundred miles stretched between me and Delagoa Bay. My escape must be known at dawn. Pursuit would be immediate. Yet all exits were barred. The town was picketed, the country was patrolled, the trains were searched, the line was guarded. I wore a civilian brown flannel suit. I had seventy-five pounds in my pocket and four slabs of chocolate, but the compass and the map which

might have guided me, the opium tablets and meat lozenges which should have sustained me, were in my friends' pockets in the State Model Schools. Worst of all, I could not speak a word of Dutch or Kaffir, and how was I to get food or direction?

For reasons unknown, Churchill included the sentence about civilian clothes only in *MEL* and the original Dispatches but not in the intervening three versions.

Dispatches, 21–23 December 1899, p. 183. **(These exact words were used for *MEL*)**
I walked on leisurely through the night, humming a tune and choosing the middle of the road. The streets were full of burghers, but they paid no attention to me. Gradually I reached the suburbs, and on a little bridge I sat down to reflect and consider. I was in the heart of the enemy's country. I knew no one to whom I could apply for succour. Nearly three hundred miles stretched between me and Delagoa Bay. My escape must be known at dawn. Pursuit would be immediate. Yet all exits were barred. The town was picketed, the country was patrolled, the trains were searched, the line was guarded. I wore a civilian brown flannel suit. I had seventy-five pounds in my pocket and four slabs of chocolate, but the compass and the map which might have guided me, the opium tablets and meat lozenges which should have sustained me, were in my friends' pockets in the State Model Schools. Worst of all, I could not speak a word of Dutch or Kaffir, and how was I to get food or direction?

L to L, p. 188. **(Very similar but not exact text from Dispatches)**
I walked on leisurely through the night, humming a tune and choosing the middle of the road. The streets were full of burghers, but they paid no attention to me. Gradually I reached the suburbs, and on a little bridge I sat down to reflect and consider. I was in the heart of the enemy's country. I knew no one to whom I could apply for succor. Nearly three hundred miles stretched between me and Delagoa Bay. My escape must be known at dawn. Pursuit would be immediate. Yet all exits were barred. The town was picketed, the country was patrolled, the trains were searched, the line was guarded. [I wore a civilian brown flannel suit.] I had seventy-five pounds in

my pocket and four slabs of chocolate, but the compass and the map which might have guided me, the opium tablets and meat lozenges which should have sustained me, were in my friends' pockets in the State Model Schools. Worst of all, I could not speak a word of Dutch or Kaffir, and how was I to get food or direction?

Strand, December 1923, pp. 537–8. (**Same text as *L to L* and used exactly for *Cosmopolitan*)**
Cosmopolitan, January 1924, p. 32.
I walked on leisurely through the night, humming a tune and choosing the middle of the road. The streets were full of burghers, but they paid no attention to me. Gradually I reached the suburbs, and on a little bridge I sat down to reflect and consider. I was in the heart of the enemy's country. I knew no one to whom I could apply for succour. Nearly three hundred miles stretched between me and Delagoa Bay. My escape must be known at dawn. Pursuit would be immediate. Yet all exits were barred. The town was picketed, the country was patrolled, the trains were searched, the line was guarded. I had seventy-five pounds in my pocket and four slabs of chocolate, but the compass and the map which might have guided me, the opium tablets and meat lozenges which should have sustained me, were in my friends' pockets in the State Model Schools. Worst of all, I could not speak a word of Dutch or Kaffir, and how was I to get food or direction?

Looking for the Railway
MEL, p. 286.
But when hope had departed, fear had gone as well. I formed a plan. I would find the Delegoa Bay Railway. Without map or compass, I must follow that in spite of the pickets. I looked at the stars. Orion shone brightly. Scarcely a year before he had guided me when lost in the desert to the banks of the Nile. He had given me water. Now he should lead to freedom. I could not endure the want of either.

Dispatches, p. 183. (**Exact text from Dispatches used for *L to L*, *Strand*, *Cosmopolitan* and *MEL*)**
L to L, pp. 188–9.
Strand, December 1923, p. 539.
Cosmopolitan, January 1924, p. 32.

But when hope had departed, fear had gone as well. I formed a plan. I would find the Delegoa Bay Railway. Without map or compass, I must follow that in spite of the pickets. I looked at the stars. Orion shone brightly. Scarcely a year before he had guided me when lost in the desert to the banks of the Nile. He had given me water. Now he should lead to freedom. I could not endure the want of either.

Trekking On
MEL, p. 286. **(Text same as Dispatches, but additional new last sentence added)**
After walking south for half a mile I struck the railway. Was it the line to Delagoa Bay or the Pietersburg branch? If it were the former, it should run east. But, so far as I could see, this line ran northwards. Still, it might be only winding its way out among the hills. 1 resolved to follow it. The night was delicious. A cool breeze fanned my face, and a wild feeling of exhilaration took hold of me. At any rate, I was free, if only for an hour. That was something. The fascination of the adventure grew. Unless the stars in their courses fought for me, I could not escape. Where, then, was the need of caution? I marched briskly along the line. Here and there the lights of a picket fire gleamed. Every bridge had its watchers. But I passed them all, making very short detours at the dangerous places, and really taking scarcely any precautions. **Perhaps that was the reason I succeeded**.

Dispatches, 21–23 December 1899, p. 183. **(text used directly in MEL with one added sentence)**
After walking south for half a mile I struck the railway. Was it the line to Delagoa Bay or the Pietersburg branch? If it were the former, it should run east. But, so far as I could see, this line ran northwards. Still, it might be only winding its way out among the hills. 1 resolved to follow it. The night was delicious. A cool breeze fanned my face, and a wild feeling of exhilaration took hold of me. At any rate, I was free, if only for an hour. That was some- thing. The fascination of the adventure grew. Unless the stars in their courses fought for me, I could not escape. Where, then, was the need of caution? I marched briskly along the line. Here and there the lights of a picket fire gleamed. Every bridge had its watchers. But I passed them all,

making very short detours at the dangerous places, and really taking scarcely any precautions. [Perhaps that was the reason I succeeded.]

L to L, pp. 189–90. (**Text same as Dispatches, with the new sentence added**)
After walking south for half a mile, I struck the railroad. Was it the line to Delagoa Bay or the Pietersburg branch? If it were the former, it should run east. But so far as I could see this line ran northwards. Still, it might be only winding its way out among the hills. I resolved to follow it. The night was delicious. A cool breeze fanned my face, and a wild feeling of exhilaration took hold of me. At any rate, I was free, if only for an hour. That was something. The fascination of the adventure grew. Unless the stars in their courses fought for me, I could not escape. Where, then, was the need of caution? I marched briskly along the line. Here and there the lights of a picket fire gleamed. Every bridge had its watchers. But I passed them all, making very short detours at the dangerous places, and really taking scarcely any precautions. Perhaps that was the reason I succeeded.

Strand, December 1923, p. 539. (**Text used directly for MEL**)
After walking south for half a mile, I struck the railroad. Was it the line to Delagoa Bay or the Pietersburg branch? If it were the former it should run east. But so far as I could see this line ran northwards. Still, it might be only winding its way out among the hills. I resolved to follow it. The night was delicious. A cool breeze fanned my face and a wild feeling of exhilaration took hold of me. At any rate, I was free, if only for an hour. That was something. The fascination of the adventure grew. Unless the stars in their courses fought for me, I could not escape. Where, then, was the need of caution? I marched briskly along the line. Here and there the lights of a picket fire gleamed. Every bridge had its watchers. But I passed them all, making very short detours at the dangerous places, and really taking scarcely any precautions. Perhaps that was the reason I succeeded.

Cosmopolitan, January 1924, p. 32. (**Shortened from *Strand***)
After walking south for half a mile, I struck the railroad. Was it the line to Delagoa Bay or the Pietersburg branch? [If it were the former it should run east. But so far as I could see this line ran northwards. Still, it might be only winding its way out among the hills.] I resolved to follow it. The night was

delicious. A cool breeze fanned my face and a wild feeling of exhilaration took hold of me. At any rate, I was free, if only for an hour. [That was something. The fascination of the adventure grew. Unless the stars in their courses fought for me I could not escape. Where, then, was the need of caution?] I marched briskly along the line. Here and there the lights of a picket fire gleamed. Every bridge had its watchers. But I passed them all, making very short detours at the dangerous places, and really taking scarcely any precautions. Perhaps that was the reason I succeeded.

New Strategies
MEL, p. 287. (**Similar to Dispatches, except added sentences in blue and minor text changes in red**)
As I walked I extended my plan. I could not march three hundred miles to the frontier. I would board a train in motion and hide under the seats, on the roof, on the couplings—anywhere. I thought of Paul Bultitude's escape from school in *Vice Versa*. 1 saw myself emerging from under the seat and bribing or persuading some fat first-class passenger to help me. What train should I take? The first, of course. After walking for two hours I perceived the signal lights of a station. I left the line, and circling round it, hid in the ditch by the track about two hundred [200] yards beyond the platform [it]. I argued that the train would stop at the station and that it would not have got up too much speed by the time it reached me. An hour passed. I began to grow impatient. Suddenly 1 heard the whistle and the approaching rattle. Then the great yellow head-lights of the engine flashed into view. The train waited five minutes at the station, and started again with much noise and steaming. I crouched by the track. I rehearsed the act in my mind. I must wait until the engine had passed, otherwise I should be seen. Then I must make a dash for the carriages.

Dispatches, p. 183–4. (**Noted in text below where new sentence was added**)
As I walked I extended my plan. I could not march three hundred miles to the frontier. I would board a train in motion and hide under the seats, on the roof, on the couplings—anywhere. [I thought of Paul Bultitude's escape from school in *Vice Versa*. 1 saw myself emerging from under the seat and bribing or persuading some fat first-class passenger to help me.] What train should I take? The first, of course. After walking for two hours I perceived the signal lights of a station. I left the line, and circling round it, hid in the

ditch by the track about 200 yards beyond it. I argued that the train would stop at the station and that it would not have got up too much speed by the time it reached me. An hour passed. I began to grow impatient. Suddenly 1 heard the whistle and the approaching rattle. Then the great yellow head-lights of the engine flashed into view. The train waited five minutes at the station, and started again with much noise and steaming. I crouched by the track. I rehearsed the act in my mind. I must wait until the engine had passed, otherwise I should be seen. Then I must make a dash for the carriages.

L to L, p. 190. (**Exactly the same as Dispatches**)
As I walked I extended my plan. I could not march three hundred miles to the frontier. I would board a train in motion and hide under the seats, on the roof, on the couplings—anywhere. What train should I take? The first, of course. After walking for two hours I perceived the signal lights of a station. I left the line, and circling round it, hid in the ditch by the track about 200 yards beyond it. I argued that the train would stop at the station and that it would not have got up too much speed by the time it reached me. An hour passed. I began to grow impatient. Suddenly 1 heard the whistle and the approaching rattle. Then the great yellow head-lights of the engine flashed into view. The train waited five minutes at the station, and started again with much noise and steaming. I crouched by the track. I rehearsed the act in my mind. I must wait until the engine had passed, otherwise I should be seen. Then I must make a dash for the carriages."

Strand, December 1923, p. 540. (**Same as *L to L* except for blue text**)
As I walked I extended my plan. I could not march three hundred miles to the frontier. I would board a train in motion and hide under the seats, on the roof, on the couplings—anywhere. What train should I take? The first, of course. After walking for two hours I perceived the signal lights of a station. I left the line, and circling round it, hid in the ditch by the track about two hundred yards beyond it. I argued that the train would stop at the station and that it would not have got up too much speed by the time it reached me. An hour passed. I began to grow impatient. Suddenly 1 heard the whistle and the approaching rattle. Then the great yellow head-lights of the engine flashed into view. The train waited five minutes at the station, and started again with much noise and steaming. I crouched by the track. I rehearsed

==the act in my mind. I must wait until the engine had passed, otherwise I should be seen. Then I must make a dash for the carriages.==

Cosmopolitan, January 1924, p. 32–3. **(Exactly the same as the *Strand* except sentences in red deleted here)**
As I walked I extended my plan. I could not march three hundred miles to the frontier. I would board a train in motion and hide under the seats, on the roof, on the couplings—anywhere. What train should I take? The first, of course. After walking for two hours I perceived the signal lights of a station. I left the line, and circling round it, hid in the ditch by the track about two hundred yards beyond it. I argued that the train would stop at the station and that it would not have got up too much speed by the time it reached me. An hour passed. I began to grow impatient. Suddenly 1 heard the whistle and the approaching rattle. Then the great yellow head-lights of the engine flashed into view. The train waited five minutes at the station, and started again with much noise and steaming. I crouched by the track. [I rehearsed the act in my mind. I must wait until the engine had passed, otherwise I should be seen. Then I must make a dash for the carriages.]

Begins Train Trip
MEL, p. 287 **(All texts exactly the same)**
The train started slowly, but gathered speed sooner than I had expected. The flaring lights drew swiftly near. The rattle became a roar. The dark mass hung for a second above me. The engine-driver silhouetted against his furnace glow, the black profile of the engine, the clouds of steam rushed past. Then I hurled myself on the trucks, clutched at something, missed, clutched again, missed again, grasped some sort of hand-hold, was swung off my feet—my toes bumping on the line, and with a struggle seated myself on the couplings of the fifth truck from the front of the train. It was a goods train, and the trucks were full of sacks, soft sacks covered with coal-dust. They were in fact bags filled with empty coal bags going back to their colliery. I crawled on top and burrowed in among them. In five minutes I was completely buried. The sacks were warm and comfortable.

Since all texts are exactly the same in each rendition of this section, the text is shown below only once.

Dispatches, 21–23 December 1899, p. 184.
L to L, p. 191.
Strand, December 1923, p. 340.
Cosmopolitan, January 1924, p. 33.

The train started slowly, but gathered speed sooner than I had expected. The flaring lights drew swiftly near. The rattle became a roar. The dark mass hung for a second above me. The engine-driver silhouetted against his furnace glow, the black profile of the engine, the clouds of steam rushed past. Then I hurled myself on the trucks, clutched at something, missed, clutched again, missed again, grasped some sort of hand-hold, was swung off my feet—my toes bumping on the line, and with a struggle seated myself on the couplings of the fifth truck from the front of the train. It was a goods train, and the trucks were full of sacks, soft sacks covered with coal-dust. They were in fact bags filled with empty coal bags going back to their colliery. I crawled on top and burrowed in among them, In five minutes I was completely buried. The sacks were warm and comfortable.

Worries on Train
MEL, p. 287–8.
Perhaps the engine-driver had seen me rush up to the train and would give the alarm at the next station; on the other hand, perhaps not. Where was the train going to? Where would it be unloaded? Would it be searched? Was it on the Delagoa Bay line? What should I do in the morning? Ah, never mind that. Sufficient for the night was the luck thereof. Fresh plans for fresh contingencies. 1 resolved to sleep, nor can I imagine a more pleasing lullaby than the clatter of the train that carries an escaping prisoner at twenty miles an hour away from the enemy's capital.

The text from Dispatches is used directly in *MEL*. Two of the next three versions are the same and, thus, will only be shown once. The differences in the *Cosmopolitan* article will be shown.

Dispatches, p. 184. (**All the exact text used for *MEL*)**
L to L, p. 191–2.
Strand, December 1923, p. 540.

Perhaps the engine-driver had seen me rush up to the train and would give the alarm at the next station; on the other hand, perhaps not. Where was the train going to? Where would it be unloaded? Would it be searched? Was it on the Delagoa Bay line? What should I do in the morning? Ah, never mind that. Sufficient for the night was the luck thereof. Fresh plans for fresh contingencies. 1 resolved to sleep, nor can I imagine a more pleasing lullaby than the clatter of the train that carries an escaping prisoner at twenty miles an hour away from the enemy's capital.

Cosmopolitan, January 1924, p. 33. **(Shortened version of *Strand*; first sentence from *Strand* deleted here)**
[Perhaps the engine-driver had seen me rush up to the train and would give the alarm at the next station; on the other hand, perhaps not.] Where was the train going to? Where would it be unloaded? Would it be searched? Was it on the Delagoa Bay line? What should I do in the morning? Ah, never mind that. Sufficient for the night was the luck thereof. Fresh plans for fresh contingencies. 1 resolved to sleep, nor can I imagine a more pleasing lullaby than the clatter of the train that carries an escaping prisoner at twenty miles an hour away from the enemy's capital.

Jumping Off First Train
MEL, p. 288.
How long I slept I do not know, but I woke up suddenly with all feelings of exhilaration gone, and only the consciousness of oppressive difficulties heavy on me. I must leave the train before daybreak, so that I could drink at a pool and find some hiding-place while it was still dark. I would not run the risk of being unloaded with the coal bags. Another night I would board another train, I crawled from my cosy hiding-place among the sacks and sat again on the couplings. The train was running at a fair speed, but I felt it was time to leave it, I took hold of the iron handle at the back of the truck, pulled strongly with my left hand, and sprang. My feet struck the ground in two gigantic strides, and the next instant I was sprawling in the ditch considerably shaken but unhurt. The train, my faithful ally of the night, hurried on its journey.

The texts in each version are exactly the same, so they will be shown below only once.

Dispatches, pp.184–5.
L to L, pp. 192–3.
Strand, December 1923, p. 540.
Cosmopolitan, January 1924, p. 33.

How long I slept I do not know, but I woke up suddenly with all feelings of exhilaration gone, and only the consciousness of oppressive difficulties heavy on me. I must leave the train before daybreak, so that I could drink at a pool and find some hiding-place while it was still dark. I would not run the risk of being unloaded with the coal bags. Another night I would board another train, I crawled from my cosy hiding-place among the sacks and sat again on the couplings. The train was running at a fair speed, but I felt it was time to leave it, I took hold of the iron handle at the back of the truck, pulled strongly with my left hand, and sprang. My feet struck the ground in two gigantic strides, and the next instant I was sprawling in the ditch considerably shaken but unhurt. The train, my faithful ally of the night, hurried on its journey.

Finding Water
MEL, p. 288.
It was still dark. I was in the middle of a wide valley, surrounded by low hills, and carpeted with high grass drenched in dew. I searched for water in the nearest gully, and soon found a clear pool. I was very thirsty, but long after I had quenched my thirst I continued to drink, that I might have sufficient for the whole day.

   Presently the dawn began to break, and the sky to the east grew yellow and red, slashed across with heavy black clouds. I saw with relief that the railway ran steadily towards the sunrise. I had taken the right line, after all.

The texts in each publication below are exactly the same, so they will be shown only once.

Dispatches, p. 185.
L to L, p. 185.
Strand, December 1923, p. 40.
Cosmopolitan, January 1924, p. 33.

It was still dark. I was in the middle of a wide valley, surrounded by low hills, and carpeted with high grass drenched in dew. I searched for water in the nearest gully, and soon found a clear pool. I was very thirsty, but long after I had quenched my thirst I continued to drink, that I might have sufficient for the whole day.

Presently the dawn began to break, and the sky to the east grew yellow and red, slashed across with heavy black clouds. I saw with relief that the railway ran steadily towards the sunrise. I had taken the right line, after all.

Finding a Hiding Place
MEL, pp. 288–9.

Having drunk my fill, I set out for the hills, among which I hoped to find some hiding-place, and as it became broad daylight I entered a small grove of trees which grew on the side of a deep ravine. Here I resolved to wait till dusk. I had one consolation: no one in the world knew where I was—I did not know myself. It was now four o'clock. Fourteen hours lay between me and the night. My impatience to proceed while I was still strong doubled their length. At first it was terribly cold, but by degrees the sun gained power, and by ten o'clock the heat was oppressive. My sole companion was a gigantic vulture, who manifested an extravagant interest in my condition, and made hideous and ominous gurglings from time to time. From my lofty position I commanded a view of the whole valley. A little tin-roofed town lay three miles to the westward, scattered farmsteads, each with a clump of trees, relieved the mono- tony of the undulating ground. At the foot of the hill stood a Kaffir kraal, and the figures of its inhabitants dotted the patches of cultivation or surrounded the droves of goats and cows which fed on the pasture.... During the day I ate one slab of chocolate, which, with the heat, produced a violent thirst. The pool was hardly half a mile away, but I dared not leave the shelter of the little wood, for I could see the figures of white men riding or walking occasionally across the valley, and once a Boer came and fired two shots at birds close to my hiding-place. But no one discovered me.

All the texts in each version below are exactly identical and will be shown only once.
Dispatches, p. 185.
L to L, pp. 193–5.
Strand, December 1923, p. 540.
Cosmopolitan, January 1924, p. 33.

Having drunk my fill, I set out for the hills, among which I hoped to find some hiding-place, and as it became broad daylight I entered a small grove of trees which grew on the side of a deep ravine. Here I resolved to wait till dusk. I had one consolation: no one in the world knew where I was—I did not know myself. It was now four o'clock. Fourteen hours lay between me and the night. My impatience to proceed while I was still strong doubled their length. At first it was terribly cold, but by degrees the sun gained power, and by ten o'clock the heat was oppressive. My sole companion was a gigantic vulture, who manifested an extravagant interest in my condition, and made hideous and ominous gurglings from time to time. From my lofty position I commanded a view of the whole valley. A little tin- roofed town lay three miles to the westward, scattered farmsteads, each with a clump of trees, relieved the mono- tony of the undulating ground. At the foot of the hill stood a Kaffir kraal, and the figures of its inhabitants dotted the patches of cultivation or surrounded the droves of goats and cows which fed on the pasture…. During the day I ate one slab of chocolate, which, with the heat, produced a violent thirst. The pool was hardly half a mile away, but I dared not leave the shelter of the little wood, for I could see the figures of white men riding or walking occasionally across the valley, and once a Boer came and fired two shots at birds close to my hiding-place. But no one discovered me.

Hiding Scared
MEL, pp. 289–90.
The elation and the excitement of the previous night had burnt away, and a chilling reaction followed. I was very hungry, for I had had no dinner before starting, and chocolate, though it sustains, does not satisfy. I had scarcely slept, but yet my heart beat so fiercely and I was so nervous and perplexed about the future that I could not rest. I thought of all the chances that

lay against me; I dreaded and detested more than words can express the prospect of being caught and dragged back to Pretoria. I found no comfort in any of the philosophical ideas which some men parade in their hours of ease and strength and safety. They seemed only fair-weather friends. I realised with awful force that no exercise of my own feeble wit and strength could save me from my enemies, and that without the assistance of that High Power which interferes in the eternal sequence of causes and effects more often than we are always prone to admit, I could never succeed. I prayed long and earnestly for help and guidance. My prayer, as it seems to me, was swiftly and wonderfully answered.

Each earlier version is slightly different.

Dispatches, p 186. (**text in red removed in *MEL*)**
The elation and the excitement of the previous night had burnt away, and a chilling reaction followed. I was very hungry, for I had had no dinner before starting, and chocolate, though it sustains, does not satisfy. I had scarcely slept, but yet my heart beat so fiercely and I was so nervous and perplexed about the future that I could not rest. I thought of all the chances that lay against me; I dreaded and detested more than words can express the prospect of being caught and dragged back to Pretoria. [I do not mean that I would rather have died than have been retaken, but I have often feared death for much less.] I found no comfort in any of the philosophical ideas [that] some men parade in their hours of ease and strength and safety. They seemed only fair-weather friends. I realised with awful force that no exercise of my own feeble wit and strength could save me from my enemies, and that without the assistance of that High Power which interferes in the eternal sequence of causes and effects more often than we are always prone to admit, I could never succeed. 1 prayed long and earnestly for help and guidance. My prayer, as it seems to me, was swiftly and wonderfully answered.

L to L, pp. 195–6. (**Text same as in Dispatches**)
The elation and the excitement of the previous night had burnt away, and a chilling reaction followed. I was very hungry, for I had had no dinner before starting, and chocolate, though it sustains, does not satisfy. I had scarcely slept, but yet my heart beat so fiercely and I was so nervous and

perplexed about the future that I could not rest. I thought of all the chances that lay against me; I dreaded and detested more than words can express the prospect of being caught and dragged back to Pretoria. [I do not mean that I would rather have died than have been retaken, but I have often feared death for much less.] I found no comfort in any of the philosophical ideas [that] some men parade in their hours of ease and strength and safety. They seemed only fair-weather friends. I realised with awful force that no exercise of my own feeble wit and strength could save me from my enemies, and that without the assistance of that High Power which interferes in the eternal sequence of causes and effects more often than we are always prone to admit, I could never succeed. 1 prayed long and earnestly for help and guidance. My prayer, as it seems to me, was swiftly and wonderfully answered.

Strand, December 1923, pp. 540, 542. (This text is used directly for *MEL*; the sentence in red above deleted here; the sentences in blue removed in *Cosmopolitan* version)
The elation and the excitement of the previous night had burnt away, and a chilling reaction followed. I was very hungry, for I had had no dinner before starting, and chocolate, though it sustains, does not satisfy. I had scarcely slept, but yet my heart beat so fiercely and I was so nervous and perplexed about the future that I could not rest. I thought of all the chances that lay against me; I dreaded and detested more than words can express the prospect of being caught and dragged back to Pretoria. I found no comfort in any of the philosophical ideas which some men parade in their hours of ease and strength and safety. They seemed only fair-weather friends. I realised with awful force that no exercise of my own feeble wit and strength could save me from my enemies, and that without the assistance of that High Power which interferes in the eternal sequence of causes and effects more often than we are always prone to admit, I could never succeed. I prayed long and earnestly for help and guidance. My prayer, as it seems to me, was swiftly and wonderfully answered.

Cosmopolitan, January 1924, p. 34. (The most abbreviated discussion)
The elation and the excitement of the previous night had burned away, and a chilling reaction followed. I was very hungry, for I had had no dinner before

starting, and chocolate, though it sustains, does not satisfy. I had scarcely slept, but yet my heart beat so fiercely and I was so nervous and perplexed about the future that I could not rest. I thought of all the chances that lay against me; I dreaded and detested more than words can express the prospect of being caught and dragged back to Pretoria. [I found no comfort in any of the philosophical ideas which some men parade in their hours of ease and strength and safety. They seemed only fair-weather friends. I realized realised with awful force that no exercise of my own feeble wit and strength could save me from my enemies, and that without the assistance of that High Power which interferes in the eternal sequence of causes and effects more often than we are always prone to admit, I could never succeed.] I prayed long and earnestly for help and guidance. My prayer, as it seems to me, was swiftly and wonderfully answered.

Churchill describes that he added new text in *MEL* and why he did so.

MEL, p. 290. **(Text in blue added to text in *Strand*)**
I wrote these lines many years ago while the impression of the adventure was strong upon me. Then I could tell no more. To have done so would have compromised the liberty and perhaps the lives of those who had helped me. For many years these reasons have disappeared. The time has come when I can relate the events which followed, and which changed my nearly hopeless position into one of superior advantage.

Dispatches, p. 187. **(Completely different)**
I cannot now relate the strange circumstances which followed, and changed my nearly hopeless position into one of superior advantage. But after the war is over I shall hope to lengthen this account, so remarkable will the addition be that I cannot believe the reader will complain.

L to L, p. 196. **(Text same as Dispatches)**
I cannot now relate the strange circumstances which followed, and changed my nearly hopeless position into one of superior advantage. But after the war is over I shall hope to lengthen this account, so remarkable will the addition be that I cannot believe the reader will complain.

Strand, December 1923, p. 542. (**With new text added, as noted in red, this is the text that would be used for** *MEL*)
I wrote these lines many years ago while the impression of the adventure was strong upon me. Then I could tell no more. [**To have done so would have compromised the liberty and perhaps the lives of those who had helped me. For many years these reasons have disappeared.**] The time has come when I can relate the events which followed, and which changed my nearly hopeless position into one of superior advantage.

Cosmopolitan, January 1924
No similar statement.

Planning to Catch Another Train
MEL, p. 290.
During the day I had watched the railway with attention. I saw two or three trains pass along it each way. I argued that the same number would pass at night. I resolved to board one of these. I thought I could improve on my procedure of the previous evening. I had observed how slowly the trains, particularly long goods-trains, climbed some of the steep gradients. Sometimes they were hardly going at a foot's pace. It would probably be easy to choose a point where the line was not only on an up grade but also on a curve. Thus I could board some truck on the convex side of the train when both the engine and the guard's van were bent away, and when consequently neither the engine-driver nor the guard would see me. This plan seemed to me in every respect sound. 1 saw myself leaving the train again before dawn, having been carried forward another sixty or seventy miles during the night. That would be scarcely one hundred and fifty miles from the frontier. And why should not the process be repeated? Where was the flaw? I could not see it. With three long bounds on three successive nights I could be in Portuguese territory.

Strand, December 1923, p. 542. (**Same text as** *MEL*; **first appeared here**)
During the day I had watched the railway with attention. I saw two or three trains pass along it each way. I argued that the same number would pass at night. I resolved to board one of these. I thought I could improve on my procedure of the previous evening. I had observed how slowly the

trains, particularly long goods-trains, climbed some of the steep gradients. Sometimes they were hardly going at a foot's pace. It would probably be easy to choose a point where the line was not only on an up grade but also on a curve. Thus I could board some truck on the convex side of the train when both the engine and the guard's van were bent away, and when consequently neither the engine-driver nor the guard would see me. This plan seemed to me in every respect sound. 1 saw myself leaving the train again before dawn, having been carried forward another sixty or seventy miles during the night. That would be scarcely one hundred and fifty miles from the frontier. And why should not the process be repeated? Where was the flaw? I could not see it. With three long bounds on three successive nights I could be in Portuguese territory.

Cosmopolitan, January 1924, p. 34 (**Shortened version of the *Strand***)
During the day I had watched the railway with attention. I saw two or three trains pass along it each way. I argued that the same number would pass at night. I resolved to board one of these. [I thought I could improve on my procedure of the previous evening. I had observed how slowly the trains, particularly long goods-trains, climbed some of the steep gradients. Sometimes they were hardly going at a foot's pace. It would probably be easy to choose a point where the line was not only on an up grade but also on a curve. Thus I could board some truck on the convex side of the train when both the engine and the guard's van were bent away, and when consequently neither the engine-driver nor the guard would see me. This plan seemed to me in every respect sound.] I saw myself leaving the train again before dawn, having been carried forward another sixty or seventy miles during the night. That would be scarcely one hundred and fifty miles from the frontier. And why should not the process be repeated? Where was the flaw? I could not see it. With three long bounds on three successive nights I could be in Portuguese territory.

Waiting for the Train
MEL, pp. 290–91.
Meanwhile I still had two or three slabs of chocolate and a pocketful of crumbled biscuit—enough, that is to say, to keep body and soul together at a pinch without running the awful risk of recapture entailed by accosting a

single human being. In this mood I watched with increasing impatience the arrival of darkness.

The long day reached its close at last. The western clouds flushed into fire; the shadows of the hills stretched out across the valley; a ponderous Boer wagon with its long team crawled slowly along the track towards the township, the Kaffirs collected their herds and drew them round their kraal; the daylight died, and soon it was quite dark. Then, and not until then, I set forth. I hurried to the railway line, scrambling along through the boulders and high grass and pausing on my way to drink at a stream of sweet cold water. I made my way to the place where I had seen the trains crawling so slowly up the slope, and soon found a point where the curve of the track fulfilled all the conditions of my plan. Here, behind a little bush, I sat down and waited hopefully. An hour passed; two hours passed; three hours—and yet no train. Six hours had now elapsed since the last, whose time I had carefully noted, had gone by. Surely one was due. Another hour slipped away. Still no train! My plan began to crumble and my hopes to ooze out of me. After all, was it not quite possible that no trains ran on this part of the line during the dark hours? This was in fact the case, and I might well have continued to wait in vain till daylight.

Dispatches, p. 186.
None of the first paragraph found in *MEL* is in Dispatches. The last two sentences in blue did not make it to the text in *MEL*.

The long day reached its close at last. The western clouds flushed into fire; the shadows of the hills stretched out across the valley; a ponderous Boer wagon with its long team crawled slowly along the track towards the town. The Kaffirs collected their herds and drew them round their kraal. The daylight died, and soon it was quite dark. Then, and not until then, I set forth. I hurried to the railway line, scrambling along through the boulders and high grass and pausing on my way to drink at a stream of sweet cold water. I waited for some time at the top of a steep gradient in the hope of catching a train. But none came, and I gradually guessed, and have since found out I guessed right, that the train I had already traveled in was the only one that ran at night.

L to L, pp. 196–7 (**Same as Dispatches**)
The long day reached its close at last. The western clouds flushed into fire; the shadows of the hills stretched out across the valley. A ponderous Boer wagon, with its long team, crawled slowly along the track towards the town. The Kaffirs collected their herds and drew around their kraal. The daylight died, and soon it was quite dark. Then, and not till then, I set forth. I hurried to the railway line, pausing on my way to drink at a stream of sweet, cold water. I waited for some time at the top of the steep gradient in the hope of catching a train. But none came, and I gradually guessed, and I have since found that I guessed right, that the train I had already travelled in was the only one that ran at night.

Strand, December 1923, p. 542. (**Exact text to be used for *MEL***)
The long day reached its close at last. The western clouds flushed into fire; the shadows of the hills stretched out across the valley; a ponderous Boer wagon with its long team crawled slowly along the track towards the township, the Kaffirs collected their herds and drew them round their kraal; the daylight died, and soon it was quite dark. Then, and not until then, I set forth. I hurried to the railway line, scrambling along through the boulders and high grass and pausing on my way to drink at a stream of sweet cold water. I made my way to the place where I had seen the trains crawling so slowly up the slope, and soon found a point where the curve of the track fulfilled all the conditions of my plan. Here, behind a little bush, I sat down and waited hopefully. An hour passed; two hours passed; three hours—and yet no train. Six hours had now elapsed since the last, whose time I had carefully noted, had gone by. Surely one was due. Another hour slipped away. Still no train! My plan began to crumble and my hopes to ooze out of me. After all, was it not quite possible that no trains ran on this part of the line during the dark hours? This was in fact the case, and I might well have continued to wait in vain till daylight.

Cosmopolitan, January 1924, p. 34. (**Shortened version of the *Strand* text**)
The long day reached its close at last. The western clouds flushed into fire; the shadows of the hills stretched out across the valley; a ponderous Boer wagon with its long team crawled slowly along the track towards the township, the Kaffirs collected their herds and drew them round their kraal;

the daylight died, and soon it was quite dark. Then, and not until then, I set forth. I hurried to the railway line, scrambling along through the boulders and high grass and pausing on my way to drink at a stream of sweet cold water. I made my way to the place where I had seen the trains crawling so slowly up the slope. [, and soon found a point where the curve of the track fulfilled all the conditions of my plan.] Here, behind a little bush, I sat down and waited hopefully. An hour passed; two hours passed; three hours—and yet no train. Six hours had now elapsed since the last, whose time I had carefully noted, had gone by. Surely one was due. Another hour slipped away. Still no train! My plan began to crumble and my hopes to ooze out of me. After all, was it not quite possible that no trains ran on this part of the line during the dark hours?

This was in fact the case, and I might well have continued to wait in vain till daylight.

Frustration With No Train
MEL, p. 291.
However, between twelve and one in the morning I lost patience and started along the track, resolved to cover at any rate ten or fifteen miles of my journey. I did not make much progress. Every bridge was guarded by armed men; every few miles were huts. At intervals there were stations with tin-roofed villages clustering around them. All the veldt was bathed in the bright rays of the full moon, and to avoid these dangerous places I had to make wide circuits and even [often] to creep along the ground. Leaving the railroad I fell into bogs and swamps, brushed through high grass dripping with dew, and waded across the streams over which the bridges carried the railway. I was soon drenched to the waist. I had been able to take very little exercise during my month's imprisonment, and I was quickly tired with walking and with want of food and sleep. Presently I approached a station. It was a mere platform in the veldt, with two or three buildings and huts around it. But laid up on the sidings, obviously for the night, were three long goods-trains. Evidently the flow of traffic over the railway was uneven. These three trains, motionless in the moonlight, confirmed my fears that traffic was not maintained by night on this part of the line. Where, then, was my plan which in the afternoon had looked so fine and sure?

Dispatches, p. 186. (**Only the section in blue would be used for** *MEL*)
At last I resolved to walk on and make, at any rate, twenty miles of my journey. I walked for about six hours. How far I travelled I do not know, but I do not expect it was very many miles in the direct line. Every bridge was guarded by armed men; every few miles were huts. At intervals there were stations with tin-roofed villages clustering around them. All the veldt was bathed in the bright rays of the full moon, and to avoid these dangerous places I had to make wide circuits and often to creep along the ground. Leaving the railroad I fell into bogs and swamps, brushed through high grass dripping with dew, and so I was drenched to the waist. I had been able to take little exercise during my month's imprisonment, and I was soon tired out with walking, as well as from want of food and sleep. I felt very miserable when I looked around and saw here and there the light of houses, and thought of the warmth and comfort within them, but knew that they only meant danger to me.

L to L, pp. 197–8 (**Very similar to Dispatches**)
At last I resolved to walk on, and make, at any rate, twenty miles of my journey. I walked for about six hours. How far I travelled I do not know, but I do not think that it was very many miles in the direct line. Every bridge was guarded by armed men; every few miles were gangers' huts; at intervals there were stations with villages clustering round them. All the veldt was bathed in the bright rays of the full moon, and to avoid these dangerous places I had to make wide circuits and often to creep along the ground. Leaving the railroad I fell into bogs and swamps, and brushed through high grass dripping with dew, so that I was drenched to the waist. I had been able to take little exercise during my month's imprisonment, and I was soon tired out with walking, as well as from want of food and sleep. I felt very miserable when I looked around and saw here and there the lights of houses, and thought of the warmth and comfort within them, but knew that they only meant danger to me.

Strand, December 1923, pp. 542–3 (**Exact text is used for both** *Cosmopolitan* **and** *MEL*)
Cosmopolitan, January 1924, p. 34.

However, between twelve and one in the morning I lost patience and started along the track, resolved to cover at any rate ten or fifteen miles of my journey. I did not make much progress. Every bridge was guarded by armed men; every few miles were huts. At intervals there were stations with tin-roofed villages clustering around them. All the veldt was bathed in the bright rays of the full moon, and to avoid these dangerous places I had to make wide circuits and even to creep along the ground. Leaving the railroad I fell into bogs and swamps, brushed through high grass dripping with dew, and waded across the streams over which the bridges carried the railway. I was soon drenched to the waist. I had been able to take very little exercise during my month's imprisonment, and I was quickly tired with walking and with want of food and sleep. Presently I approached a station. It was a mere platform in the veldt, with two or three buildings and huts around it. But laid up on the sidings, obviously for the night, were three long goods-trains. Evidently the flow of traffic over the railway was uneven. These three trains, motionless in the moonlight, confirmed my fears that traffic was not maintained by night on this part of the line. Where, then, was my plan which in the afternoon had looked so fine and sure?

Checking Out Trains
MEL, p. 292.
It now occurred to me that I might board one of these stationary trains immediately, and hiding amid its freight be carried forward during the next day—and night too if all were well. On the other hand, where were they going to? Where would they stop? Where would they be unloaded? Once I entered a wagon my lot would be cast. I might find myself ignominiously unloaded and recaptured at Witbank or Middelburg, or at any station in the long two hundred miles which separated me from the frontier. It was necessary at all costs before taking such a step to find out where these trains were going. To do this I must penetrate the station, examine the labels on the trucks or on the merchandise, and see if I could extract any certain guidance from them. I crept up to the platform and got between two of the long trains on the siding. I was proceeding to examine the markings on the trucks when loud voices rapidly approaching on the outside of the trains filled me with fear. Several Kaffirs were laughing and shouting in their unmodulated tones, and I heard, as I thought, a European voice arguing

or ordering. At any rate, it was enough for me. I retreated between the two trains to the extreme end of the siding, and slipped stealthily but rapidly into the grass of the illimitable plain.

Dispatches, p. 187 (**Nothing like the above paragraph here**)
After six or seven hours of walking I thought it unwise to go further lest I should exhaust myself, so I lay down in a ditch to sleep. I was nearly at the end of my tether. Nevertheless, by the will of God, I was enabled to sustain myself during the next few days, obtaining food at great risk here and there, resting in concealment by day and walking only at night. On the fifth day I was beyond Middleburg, as far as I could tell, for I dared not inquire nor as yet approach stations near enough to read the names.

L to L, p. 198 (**Exactly the same as Dispatches**)
After six or seven hours of walking I thought it unwise to go further lest I should exhaust myself, so I lay down in a ditch to sleep. I was nearly at the end of my tether. Nevertheless, by the will of God, I was enabled to sustain myself during the next few days, obtaining food at great risk here and there, resting in concealment by day and walking only at night. On the fifth day I was beyond Middelburg, so far as I could tell, for I dared not inquire nor as yet approach the stations near enough to read the names.

Strand, December 1923, p. 543. (**New text exactly as it would appear in *MEL***)
It now occurred to me that I might board one of these stationary trains immediately, and hiding amid its freight be carried forward during the next day—and night too if all were well. On the other hand, where were they going to? Where would they stop? Where would they be unloaded? Once I entered a wagon my lot would be cast. I might find myself ignominiously unloaded and recaptured at Witbank or Middelburg, or at any station in the long two hundred miles which separated me from the frontier. It was necessary at all costs before taking such a step to find out where these trains were going. To do this I must penetrate the station, examine the labels on the trucks or on the merchandise, and see if I could extract any certain guidance from them. I crept up to the platform and got between two of the long trains on the siding. I was proceeding to examine the markings on the trucks when loud voices rapidly approaching on the outside of the trains filled me with fear. Several

Kaffirs were laughing and shouting in their unmodulated tones, and I heard, as I thought, a European voice arguing or ordering. At any rate, it was enough for me. I retreated between the two trains to the extreme end of the siding, and slipped stealthily but rapidly into the grass of the illimitable plain.

Cosmopolitan, January 1924, p. 34. (**Text in red deleted from *Strand* version; blue 'two hundred' changed to '250'**)

It now occurred to me that I might board one of these stationary trains immediately, and hiding amid its freight be carried forward during the next day—and night too if all were well. On the other hand, where were they going to? Where would they stop? Where would they be unloaded? Once I entered a wagon my lot would be cast. I might find myself ignominiously unloaded and recaptured at Witbank or Middelburg, or at any station in the long 250 [two hundred] miles which separated me from the frontier. It was necessary at all costs before taking such a step to find out where these trains were going. To do this I must penetrate the station, examine the labels on the trucks or on the merchandise, and see if I could extract any certain guidance from them. I crept up to the platform and got between two of the long trains on the siding. I was proceeding to examine the markings on the trucks when loud voices rapidly approaching on the outside of the trains filled me with fear. [Several Kaffirs were laughing and shouting in their unmodulated tones, and I heard, as I thought, a European voice arguing or ordering. At any rate,] It was enough for me. I retreated between the two trains to the extreme end of the siding, and slipped stealthily but rapidly into the grass of the illimitable plain.

Continues on Foot

MEL, pp. 292–3.

There was nothing for it but to plod on—but in an increasingly purposeless and hopeless manner. I felt very miserable when I looked around and saw here and there the lights of houses and thought of the warmth and comfort within them, but knew that they meant only danger to me. Far off on the moonlit horizon there presently began to shine the row of six or eight big lights which marked either Witbank or Middelburg station. Out in the darkness to my left gleamed two or three fires. I was sure they were not the lights of houses, but how far off they were or what they were I could not be certain. The idea formed in my mind that they were the fires of a Kaffir kraal. Then I began to think that the best use I could make of my remaining strength would be to go to these Kaffirs, 1 had heard that they hated the Boers and were friendly to the British. At any rate, they would probably not arrest me. They might give me food and a dry corner to sleep in. Although I could not speak a word of their language, yet I thought perhaps they might understand the value of a British bank-note. They might even be induced to help me. A guide, a pony—but, above all, rest, warmth, and food—such were the promptings which dominated my mind. So I set out towards the fires.

Dispatches, p. 186 **(Has the following sentence used in *MEL*)**
I felt very miserable when I looked around and saw here and there the lights of houses and thought of the warmth and comfort within them, but knew that they meant only danger to me.

L to L, pp. 197–8 **(Has the same sentence as Dispatches and in *MEL*)**
I felt very miserable when I looked around and saw here and there the lights of houses and thought of the warmth and comfort within them, but knew that they meant only danger to me.

Strand, December 1923, pp. 543–4. **(New text that would be used exactly in *MEL*)**
There was nothing for it but to plod on—but in an increasingly purposeless and hopeless manner. I felt very miserable when I looked around and saw here and there the lights of houses and thought of the warmth and comfort within them, but knew that they meant only danger to me. Far off on the moonlit horizon there presently began to shine the row of six or eight big lights which marked either Witbank or Middelburg station. Out in the darkness to my left gleamed two or three fires. I was sure they were not the lights of houses, but how far off they were or what they were I could not be certain. The idea formed in my mind that they were the fires of a Kaffir kraal. Then I began to think that the best use I could make of my remaining strength would be to go to these Kaffirs, 1 had heard that they hated the Boers and were friendly to the British. At any rate, they would probably not arrest me. They might give me food and a dry corner to sleep in. Although I could not speak a word of their language, yet I thought perhaps they might understand the value of a British bank-note. They might even be induced to help me. A guide,

a pony—but, above all, rest, warmth, and food—such were the promptings which dominated my mind. So I set out towards the fires.

Cosmopolitan, January 1924, p. 34. **(Text in red below has been deleted from the *Strand* version)**

There was nothing for it but to plod on—but in an increasingly purposeless and hopeless manner. I felt very miserable when I looked around and saw here and there the lights of houses and thought of the warmth and comfort within them, but knew that they meant only danger to me. Far off on the moonlit horizon there presently began to shine the row of six or eight big lights which marked either Witbank or Middelburg station. Out in the darkness to my left gleamed two or three fires. I was sure they were not the lights of houses, but how far off they were or what they were I could not be certain. The idea formed in my mind that they were the fires of a Kaffir kraal. Then I began to think that the best use I could make of my remaining strength would be to go to these Kaffirs, 1 had heard that they hated the Boers and were friendly to the British. At any rate, they would probably not arrest me. **[They might give me food and a dry corner to sleep in. Although I could not speak a word of their language, yet I thought perhaps they might understand the value of a British bank-note.]** They might even be induced to help me. A guide, a pony—but, above all, rest, warmth, and food—such were the promptings which dominated my mind. So I set out towards the fires.

Confusion
MEL, p. 293.

I must have walked a mile or so in this resolve before a realisation of its weakness and imprudence took possession of me. Then I turned back again to the railway line and retraced my steps perhaps half the distance. Then I stopped and sat down, completely baffled, destitute of any idea what to do or where to turn. Suddenly without the slightest reason all my doubts disappeared. It was certainly by no process of logic that they were dispelled. I just felt quite clear that I would go to the Kaffir kraal. I had sometimes in former years held a 'Planchette' pencil and written while others had touched my wrist or hand. I acted in exactly the same unconscious or subconscious manner now.

Dispatches
No equivalent text here.

L to L
No equivalent text here.

Strand, December 1923, p. 544. **(New text, used exactly for *Cosmopolitan* and *MEL*)**
Cosmopolitan, January 1924, p. 34.
I must have walked a mile or so in this resolve before a realisation of its weakness and imprudence took possession of me. Then I turned back again to the railway line and retraced my steps perhaps half the distance. Then I stopped and sat down, completely baffled, destitute of any idea what to do or where to turn. Suddenly without the slightest reason all my doubts disappeared. It was certainly by no process of logic that they were dispelled. I just felt quite clear that 1 would go to the Kaffir kraal. I had sometimes in former years held a 'Planchette' pencil and written while others had touched my wrist or hand. I acted in exactly the same unconscious or subconscious manner now.

Resolve
MEL, p 293–4.
I walked on rapidly towards the fires, which I had in the first instance thought were not more than a couple of miles from the railway line. I soon found they were much farther away than that. After about an hour or an hour and a half they still seemed almost as far off as ever. But I persevered, and presently between two and three o'clock in the morning I perceived that they were not the fires of a Kaffir kraal. The angular outline [silhouette] of buildings began to draw out against them, and soon I saw that I was approaching a group of houses around the mouth of a coal-mine. The wheel which worked the winding gear was plainly visible, and I could see that the fires which had led me so far were from the furnaces of the engines. Hard by, surrounded by one or two slighter structures, stood a small but substantial stone house two storeys high.

Dispatches
No equivalent text.

L to L
No equivalent text.

Strand, December 1923, p. 544. (**New text; same as** *MEL* **with one word change**)
"I walked on rapidly towards the fires, which I had in the first instance thought were not more than a couple of miles from the railway line. I soon found they were much farther away than that. After about an hour or an hour and a half they still seemed almost as far off as ever. But I persevered, and presently between two and three o'clock in the morning I perceived that they were not the fires of a Kaffir kraal. The angular silhouette of buildings began to draw out against them, and soon I saw that I was approaching a group of houses around the mouth of a coal-mine. The wheel which worked the winding gear was plainly visible, and I could see that the fires which had led me so far were from the furnaces of the engines. Hard by, surrounded by one or two slighter structures, stood a small but substantial stone house two storeys high.

Cosmopolitan, January 1924, pp. 34, 161. (**Now exactly as in** *MEL*)
I walked on rapidly towards the fires, which I had in the first instance thought were not more than a couple of miles from the railway line. I soon found they were much farther away than that. After about an hour or an hour and a half they still seemed almost as far off as ever. But I persevered, and presently between two and three o'clock in the morning I perceived that they were not the fires of a Kaffir kraal. The angular outline of buildings began to draw out against them, and soon Isaw that I was approaching a group of houses around the mouth of a coal-mine. The wheel which worked the winding gear was plainly visible, and I could see that the fires which had led me so far were from the furnaces of the engines. Hard by, surrounded by one or two slighter structures, stood a small but substantial stone house two storeys high.

Seeking Shelter
MEL, p. 294.

I halted in the wilderness to survey this scene and to revolve [consider] my action. It was still possible to turn back. But in that direction I saw nothing but the prospect of further futile wanderings terminated by hunger, fever, discovery, or surrender. On the other hand, here in front was a chance. I had heard it said before I escaped that in the mining district of Witbank and Middelburg there were a certain number of English residents who had been suffered to remain in the country in order to keep the mines working. Had I been led to one of these? What did this house which frowned dark and inscrutable upon me contain? A Briton or a Boer; a friend or a foe? Nor did this exhaust the possibilities. I had my seventy-five pounds in English notes in my pocket. If I revealed my identity, I thought that I could give reasonable assurance of a thousand. I might find some indifferent neutral-minded person who out of good nature or for a large sum of money would aid me in my bitter and desperate need. Certainly I would try to make what bargain I could now—now while I still had the strength to plead my cause and perhaps to extricate myself if the results were adverse. Still the odds were heavy against me, and it was with faltering and reluctant steps that I walked out of the shimmering gloom of the veldt into the light of the furnace fires, advanced towards the silent house, and struck with my fist upon the door.

Dispatches
No equivalent text.

L to L
No equivalent text.

Strand, December 1923, p. 544. **(New text here that would be used exactly for *MEL*)**

I halted in the wilderness to survey this scene and to revolve my action. It was still possible to turn back. But in that direction I saw nothing but the prospect of further futile wanderings terminated by hunger, fever, discovery, or surrender, On the other hand, here in front was a chance. I had heard it said before I escaped that in the mining district of Witbank and Middelburg there were a certain number of English residents who had been suffered to remain in the country in order to keep the mines working. Had I been led to one of these? What did this house which frowned dark and inscrutable upon me contain? A Briton or a Boer; a friend or a foe? Nor did this exhaust the possibilities. I had my seventy-five pounds in English notes in my pocket. If I revealed my identity, I thought that I could give reasonable assurance of a thousand. I might find some indifferent neutral-minded person who out of good nature or for a large sum of money would aid me in my bitter and desperate need. Certainly I would try to make what bargain I could now—now while I still had the strength to plead my cause and perhaps to extricate myself if the results were adverse. Still the odds were heavy against me, and it was with faltering and reluctant steps that I walked out of the shimmering gloom of the veldt into the light of the furnace fires, advanced towards the silent house, and struck with my fist upon the door.

Cosmopolitan, January 1924, p. 161. **(Red text in brackets removed in this version; red text not in brackets changed in this version)**

I halted in the wilderness to survey this scene and to revolve my action. It was still possible to turn back. But in that direction I saw nothing but the prospect of further futile wanderings terminated by hunger, fever, discovery, or surrender, On the other hand, here in front was a chance. I had heard it said before I escaped that in the mining district of Witbank and Middelburg there were a certain number of English residents who had been suffered to remain in the country in order to keep the mines working. Had I been led to one of these? [What did this house which frowned dark and inscrutable upon me contain? A Briton or a Boer; a friend or a foe? Nor did this exhaust the possibilities.] I had my 75 pounds in English notes in my pocket. If I revealed my identity, I thought that I could give reasonable assurance of a thousand. I might find some indifferent neutral-minded person who out of good nature or for a large sum of money would aid me in my bitter and desperate need. Certainly I would try to make what bargain I could now— now while I still had the strength to plead my cause and perhaps to extricate myself if the results were adverse.

Still the odds were heavy against me, and it was with faltering and reluctant steps that I walked out of the shimmering gloom of the veldt into the light of the furnace fires, advanced towards the silent house, and struck with my fist upon the door.

Knocks on Unknown Door
MEL, p. 295.

There was a pause. Then I knocked again. And almost immediately a light sprang up above and an upper window opened.

'Wer ist da?' cried a man's voice.

I felt the shock of disappointment and consternation to my fingers.

'I want help; I have had an accident,' I replied.

Some muttering followed. Then I heard steps descending the stairs, the bolt of the door was drawn, the lock was turned. It was opened abruptly, and in the darkness of the passage a tall man hastily attired, with a pale face and dark moustache, stood before me.

'What do you want?' he said, this time in English.

I had now to think of something to say. I wanted above all to get into parley with this man, to get matters in such a state that instead of raising an alarm and summoning others he would discuss things quietly.

'I am a burgher,' I began. 'I have had an accident. I was going to join my commando at Komati Poort, I have fallen off the train. We were skylarking. I have been unconscious for hours. I think I have dislocated my shoulder.'

It is astonishing how one thinks of these things. This story leapt out as if I had learnt it by heart. Yet I had not the slightest idea what I was going to say or what the next sentence would be.

Dispatches
No similar text.

L to L
No similar text.

Strand, December 1923, p. 544. **(New text, used exactly for *Cosmopolitan* and *MEL*)**
Cosmopolitan, January 1924, p. 161.

There was a pause. Then I knocked again. And almost immediately a light sprang up above and an upper window opened.

'Wer ist da?' cried a man's voice.

I felt the shock of disappointment and consternation to my fingers.

'I want help; I have had an accident,' I replied.

Some muttering followed. Then I heard steps descending the stairs, the bolt of the door was drawn, the lock was turned. It was opened abruptly, and in the darkness of the passage a tall man hastily attired, with a pale face and dark moustache, stood before me.

'What do you want?' he said, this time in English.

I had now to think of something to say. I wanted above all to get into parley with this man, to get matters in such a state that instead of raising an alarm and summoning others he would discuss things quietly.

'I am a burgher,' I began. 'I have had an accident. I was going to join my commando at Komati Poort, I have fallen off the train. We were skylarking. I have been unconscious for hours. I think I have dislocated my shoulder.'

It is astonishing how one thinks of these things. This story leapt out as if I had learnt it by heart. Yet I had not the slightest idea what I was going to say or what the next sentence would be.

Potential Safe Haven
MEL, p. 295–6.

The stranger regarded me intently, and after some hesitation said at length, 'Well, come in.' He retreated a little into the darkness of the passage, threw open a door on one side of it, and pointed with his left hand into a dark room, I walked past him and entered, wondering if it was to be my prison. He followed, struck a light, lit a lamp, and set it on the table at the far side of which I stood. I was in a small room, evidently a dining-room and office in one. I noticed besides the large table, a roll desk, two or three chairs, and one of those machines for making soda-water, consisting of two glass globes set one above the other and encased in thin wire-netting. On his end of the table my host had laid a revolver, which he had hitherto presumably been holding in his right hand.

'I think I'd like to know a little more about this railway accident of yours,' he said, after a considerable pause.

'I think,' I replied, 'I had better tell you the truth.'

'I think you had,' he said, slowly.

So I took the plunge and threw all I had upon the board.

'I am Winston Churchill, War Correspondent of the *Morning Post*. I escaped last night from Pretoria. I am making my way to the frontier.' (Making my way!) 'I have plenty of money. Will you help me?'

There was another long pause. My companion rose from the table slowly and locked the door. After this act, which struck me as unpromising, and was certainly ambiguous, he advanced upon me and suddenly held out his hand.

'Thank God you have come here! It is the only house for twenty miles where you would not have been handed over. But we are all British here, and we will see you through.'

Dispatches
No similar text.

L to L
No similar text.

Strand, December 1923, pp. 544, 546. (**New text; except for the one word deleted, used exactly in for *Cosmopolitan* and *MEL*)**
Cosmopolitan, January 1924, p. 161.
The stranger regarded me intently, and after some hesitation said at length, 'Well, come in.' He retreated a little into the darkness of the passage, threw open a door on one side of it, and pointed with his left hand into a dark room, I walked past him and entered, wondering if it was to be my prison. He followed, struck a light, lit a lamp, and set it on the table at the far side of which I stood. I was in a small room, evidently a dining-room and office in one. I noticed besides the large table, a roll desk, two or three chairs, and one of those machines for making soda-water, consisting of two glass globes set one above the other and encased in thin **[wire-]**netting. On his end of the table my host had laid a revolver, which he had hitherto presumably been holding in his right hand.

'I think I'd like to know a little more about this railway accident of yours,' he said, after a considerable pause.

'I think,' I replied, 'I had better tell you the truth.'

'I think you had,' he said, slowly.

So I took the plunge and threw all I had upon the board.

'I am Winston Churchill, War Correspondent of the *Morning Post*. 1 escaped last night from Pretoria. I am making my way to the frontier.' (Making my way!) 'I have plenty of money. Will you help me?'

There was another long pause. My companion rose from the table slowly and locked the door. After this act, which struck me as unpromising, and was certainly ambiguous, he advanced upon me and suddenly held out his hand.

'Thank God you have come here! It is the only house for twenty miles where you would not have been handed over. But we are all British here, and we will see you through.'

Meets John Howard
MEL, p. 296–7.

It is easier to recall across the gulf of years the spasm of relief which swept over me, than it is to describe it. A moment before I had thought myself trapped; and now friends, food, resources, aid, were all at my disposal. I felt like a drowning man pulled out of the water and informed he has won the Derby!

My host now introduced himself as Mr. John Howard, manager of the Transvaal Collieries. He had become a naturalised burgher of the Transvaal some years before the war. But out of consideration for his British race and some inducements which he had offered to the local Field Cornet, he had not been called up to fight against the British. Instead he had been allowed to remain with one or two others on the mine, keeping it pumped out and in good order until coal-cutting could be resumed. He had with him at the mine-head, besides his secretary, who was British, an engine-man from Lancashire and two Scottish miners. All these four were British subjects and had been allowed to remain only upon giving their parole to observe strict neutrality. He himself as burgher of the Transvaal Republic would be guilty of treason in harbouring me, and liable to be shot if caught at the time or found out later on.

'Never mind,' he said, 'we will fix it up somehow.' And added, 'The Field Cornet was round here this afternoon asking about you. They have got the hue and cry out all along the line and all over the district.'

I said that I did not wish to compromise him.

Let him give me food, a pistol, a guide, and if possible a pony, and I would make my own way to the sea, marching by night across country far away from the railway line or any habitation.'

Dispatches
No similar text.

APPENDIX 6 / CHAPTER 4: ESCAPE

L to L
No similar text.

Strand, December 1923, p. 546. (**New text, used exactly for** *Cosmopolitan* **and** *MEL*)
Cosmopolitan, January 1924, pp. 161–2.
It is easier to recall across the gulf of years the spasm of relief which swept over me, than it is to describe it. A moment before I had thought myself trapped; and now friends, food, resources, aid, were all at my disposal. I felt like a drowning man pulled out of the water and informed he has won the Derby!

My host now introduced himself as Mr. John Howard, manager of the Transvaal Collieries. He had become a naturalised burgher of the Transvaal some years before the war. But out of consideration for his British race and some inducements which he had offered to the local Field Cornet, he had not been called up to fight against the British. Instead he had been allowed to remain with one or two others on the mine, keeping it pumped out and in good order until coal-cutting could be resumed. He had with him at the mine-head, besides his secretary, who was British, an engine-man from Lancashire and two Scottish miners. All these four were British subjects and had been allowed to remain only upon giving their parole to observe strict neutrality. He himself as burgher of the Transvaal Republic would be guilty of treason in harbouring me, and liable to be shot if caught at the time or found out later on.

'Never mind,' he said, 'we will fix it up somehow.' And added, 'The Field Cornet was round here this afternoon asking about you. They have got the hue and cry out all along the line and all over the district.'

I said that I did not wish to compromise him.

Let him give me food, a pistol, a guide, and if possible a pony, and I would make my own way to the sea, marching by night across country far away from the railway line or any habitation.

Howard Agrees to Help
MEL, p. 297.
He would not hear of it. He would fix up something. But he enjoined the utmost caution. Spies were everywhere. He had two Dutch servant-maids actually sleeping in the house. There were many Kaffirs employed about

the mine premises and on the pumping-machinery of the mine. Surveying these dangers, he became very thoughtful.

Then: 'But you are famishing.'

I did not contradict him. In a moment he had bustled off into the kitchen, telling me meanwhile to help myself from a whisky bottle and the soda-water machine which 1 have already mentioned. He returned after an interval with the best part of a cold leg of mutton and various other delectable commodities, and, leaving me to do full justice to these, quitted the room and let himself out of the house by a back door.

Nearly an hour passed before Mr. Howard returned. In this period my physical well-being had been brought into harmony with the improvement in my prospects. I felt confident of success and equal to anything.

'It's all right,' said Mr. Howard. 'I have seen the men, and they are all for it. We must put you down the pit to-night, and there you will have to stay till we can see how to get you out of the country. One difficulty,' he said, 'will be the skoff (food). The Dutch girl sees every mouthful I eat. The cook will want to know what has happened to her leg of mutton. I shall have to think it all out during the night. You must get down the pit at once. We'll make you comfortable enough.'

Dispatches
No similar text.

L to L
No similar text.

Strand, December 1923, pp. 546–7. (**New text, used exactly in both the** *Cosmopolitan* **article and** *MEL*)
Cosmopolitan , January 1924, p. 162.
He would not hear of it. He would fix up something. But he enjoined the utmost caution. Spies were everywhere. He had two Dutch servant-maids actually sleeping in the house. There were many Kaffirs employed about the mine premises and on the pumping-machinery of the mine. Surveying these dangers, he became very thoughtful.

Then: 'But you are famishing.'

I did not contradict him. In a moment he had bustled off into the kitchen, telling me meanwhile to help myself from a whisky bottle and the soda-water machine which 1 have already mentioned. He returned after an interval with the best part of a cold leg of mutton and various other delectable commodities, and, leaving me to do full justice to these, quitted the room and let himself out of the house by a back door.

Nearly an hour passed before Mr. Howard returned. In this period my physical well-being had been brought into harmony with the improvement in my prospects. I felt confident of success and equal to anything.

'It's all right,' said Mr. Howard. 'I have seen the men, and they are all for it. We must put you down the pit to-night, and there you will have to stay till we can see how to get you out of the country. One difficulty,' he said, 'will be the skoff (food). The Dutch girl sees every mouthful I eat. The cook will want to know what has happened to her leg of mutton. I shall have to think it all out during the night. You must get down the pit at once. We'll make you comfortable enough.'

Directed to the Mine
MEL, p. 298.
Accordingly, just as the dawn was breaking, I followed my host across a little yard into the enclosure in which stood the winding-wheel of the mine. Here a stout man, introduced as Mr. Dewsnap, of Oldham, locked my hand in a grip of crushing vigour.

'They'll all vote for you next time,' he whispered. **[I had just contested Oldham unsuccessfully in June of that year.]**

A door was opened and I entered the cage. Down we shot into the bowels of the earth. At the bottom of the mine were the two Scottish miners with lanterns and a big bundle which afterwards proved to be a mattress and blankets. We walked for some time through the pitchy labyrinth, with frequent turns, twists, and alterations of level, and finally stopped in a sort of chamber where the air was cool and fresh. Here my guide set down his bundle, and Mr. Howard handed me a couple of candles, a bottle of whisky, and a box of cigars.

'There's no difficulty about these,' he said. 'I keep them under lock and key. Now we must plan how to feed you to-morrow.'

'Don't you move from here, whatever happens,' was the parting injunction. 'There will be Kaffirs about the mine after daylight, but we shall be on the look-out that none of them wanders this way. None of them has seen anything so far.'

Dispatches
No similar text.

L to L
No similar text.

Strand, December 1923, p. 547. **(New text, used exactly for *Cosmopolitan* and *MEL* except the sentence in blue – deleted in both)**
Cosmopolitan, January 1924, p. 162.
Accordingly, just as the dawn was breaking, I followed my host across a little yard into the enclosure in which stood the winding-wheel of the mine. Here a stout man, introduced as Mr. Dewsnap, of Oldham, locked my hand in a grip of crushing vigour.

'They'll all vote for you next time,' he whispered. I had just contested Oldham unsuccessfully in June of that year. A door was opened and I entered the cage. Down we shot into the bowels of the earth. At the bottom of the mine were the two Scottish miners with lanterns and a big bundle which afterwards proved to be a mattress and blankets. We walked for some time through the pitchy labyrinth, with frequent turns, twists, and alterations of level, and finally stopped in a sort of chamber where the air was cool and fresh. Here my guide set down his bundle, and Mr. Howard handed me a couple of candles, a bottle of whisky, and a box of cigars.

'There's no difficulty about these,' he said. 'I keep them under lock and key. Now we must plan how to feed you to-morrow.'

'Don't you move from here, whatever happens,' was the parting injunction. 'There will be Kaffirs about the mine after daylight, but we shall be on the look-out that none of them wanders this way. None of them has seen anything so far.'

In the Coal Mine

MEL, pp. 298.

My four friends trooped off with their lanterns, and I was left alone. Viewed from the velvety darkness of the pit, life seemed bathed in rosy light. After the perplexity and even despair through which I had passed I counted upon freedom as certain. Instead of a humiliating recapture and long months of monotonous imprisonment, probably in the common jail, I saw myself once more rejoining the Army with a real exploit to my credit, and in that full enjoyment of freedom and keen pursuit of adventure dear to the heart of youth. In this comfortable mood, and speeded by intense fatigue, I soon slept the sleep of the weary—but [just—and] of the triumphant.

Dispatches
No similar text.

L to L
No similar text.

Strand, December 1923, p. 547. **(New text, used exactly for *Cosmopolitan* and *MEL* except for two words)**
Cosmopolitan, January 1924, p. 162.

My four friends trooped off with their lanterns, and I was left alone. Viewed from the velvety darkness of the pit, life seemed bathed in rosy light. After the perplexity and even despair through which I had passed I counted upon freedom as certain. Instead of a humiliating recapture and long months of monotonous imprisonment, probably in the common jail, I saw myself once more rejoining the Army with a real exploit to my credit, and in that full enjoyment of freedom and keen pursuit of adventure dear to the heart of youth. In this comfortable mood, and speeded by intense fatigue, I soon slept the sleep of the just—and of the triumphant.

Chapter XXIII 'I Escape From the Boers – II'

Rats

MEL, p. 300.

I do not know how many hours I slept, but the following afternoon must have been far advanced when I found myself thoroughly awake. I put out my hand for the candle, but could feel it nowhere. I did not know what pitfalls these mining galleries might contain, so I thought it better to lie quiet on my mattress and await developments. Several hours passed before the faint gleam of a lantern showed that someone was coming. It proved to be Mr. Howard himself, armed with a chicken and other good things. He also brought several books. He asked me why I had not lighted my candle. I said I could not find it. 'Didn't you put it under the mattress?', he asked.

'No.'

'Then the rats must have got it.'

Dispatches
No similar text.

L to L
No similar text.

Strand, January 1924, p. 14. (**New text, used exactly for** *Cosmopolitan* **and** *MEL*)
Cosmopolitan, January 1924, p. 162

I do not know how many hours I slept, but the following afternoon must have been far advanced when I found myself thoroughly awake. I put out my hand for the candle, but could feel it nowhere. I did not know what pitfalls these mining galleries might contain, so I thought it better to lie quiet on my mattress and await developments. Several hours passed before the faint gleam of a lantern showed that someone was coming. It proved to be Mr. Howard himself, armed with a chicken and other good things. He also brought several books. He asked me why I had not lighted my candle. I said I could not find it. 'Didn't you put it under the mattress?', he asked.

'No.'

'Then the rats must have got it.'

Sequestered in Mine
MEL, p. 300.
He told me there were swarms of rats in the mine, that some years ago he had introduced a particular kind of white rat which was an excellent scavenger, and that these had multiplied and thriven exceedingly. He told me he had been to the house of an English doctor twenty miles away to get the chicken. He was worried at the attitude of the two Dutch servants, who were very inquisitive about the depredations upon the leg of mutton for which I had been responsible. If he could not get another chicken cooked for the next day, he would have to take double helpings on his own plate and slip the surplus into a parcel for me while the servant was out of the room. He said that inquiries were being made for me all over the district by the Boers, and that the Pretoria Government was making a tremendous fuss about my escape. The fact that there were a number of English remaining in the Middelburg mining region indicated it as a likely place for me to have turned to, and all persons of English origin were more or less suspect.

Dispatches
No similar text.

L to L
No similar text.

Strand, January 1924, pp. 14–5. (**New text, used exactly in** *MEL*)
He told me there were swarms of rats in the mine, that some years ago he had introduced a particular kind of white rat which was an excellent scavenger, and that these had multiplied and thriven exceedingly. He told me he had been to the house of an English doctor twenty miles away to get the chicken. He was worried at the attitude of the two Dutch servants, who were very inquisitive about the depredations upon the leg of mutton for which I had been responsible. If he could not get another chicken cooked for the next day, he would have to take double helpings on his own plate and slip the surplus into a parcel for me while the servant was out of the room. He said that inquiries were being made for me all over the district by the Boers, and that the Pretoria Government was making a tremendous fuss about my escape. The fact that there were a number of English remaining in

the Middelburg mining region indicated it as a likely place for me to have turned to, and all persons of English origin were more or less suspect.

Cosmopolitan, January 1924, p. 162. **(One word changed, and red sentence deleted here from** *Strand*)
He told me there were swarms of rats in the mine, that some years ago they had introduced a particular kind of white rat which was an excellent scavenger, and that these had multiplied and thriven exceedingly. He told me he had been to the house of an English doctor twenty miles away to get the chicken. He was worried at the attitude of the two Dutch servants, who were very inquisitive about the depredations upon the leg of mutton for which I had been responsible. [If he could not get another chicken cooked for the next day, he would have to take double helpings on his own plate and slip the surplus into a parcel for me while the servant was out of the room.] He said that inquiries were being made for me all over the district by the Boers, and that the Pretoria Government was making a tremendous fuss about my escape. The fact that there were a number of English remaining in the Middelburg mining region indicated it as a likely place for me to have turned to, and all persons of English origin were more or less suspect.

Living in the Mine
MEL, p. 300.
I again expressed my willingness to go on alone with a Kaffir guide and a pony, but this he utterly refused to entertain. It would take a lot of planning, he said, to get me out of the country, and I might have to stay in the mine for quite a long time.

'Here,' he said, 'you are absolutely safe. Mac' (by which he meant one of the Scottish miners) 'knows all the disused workings and places that no one else would dream of. There is one place here where the water actually touches the roof for a foot or two. If they searched the mine, Mac would dive under that with you into the workings cut off beyond the water. No one would ever think of looking there. We have frightened the Kaffirs with tales of ghosts, and, anyhow, we are watching their movements continually.'

He stayed with me while I dined, and then departed, leaving me, among other things, half-a-dozen candles, which, duly warned, I tucked under my pillow and mattress.

I slept again for a long time, and woke suddenly with a feeling of movement about me. Something seemed to be pulling at my pillow. I put out my hand quickly. There was a perfect scurry. The rats were at the candles. I rescued the candles in time, and lighted one. Luckily for me, I have no horror of rats as such, and being reassured by their evident timidity, I was not particularly uneasy. All the same, the three days I passed in the mine were not among the most pleasant which my memory re-illumines. The patter of little feet and a perceptible sense of stir and scurry was continuous. Once I was waked up from a doze by one actually galloping across me. On the candle being lighted these beings became invisible.

Dispatches
No similar text.

L to L
No similar text.

Strand, January 1924, pp. 15–6. (**New text, used exactly in** *Cosmopolitan* **and** *MEL*)
Cosmopolitan, January 1924, pp. 162–3.

I again expressed my willingness to go on alone with a Kaffir guide and a pony, but this he utterly refused to entertain. It would take a lot of planning, he said, to get me out of the country, and I might have to stay in the mine for quite a long time.

'Here,' he said, 'you are absolutely safe. Mac' (by which he meant one of the Scottish miners) 'knows all the disused workings and places that no one else would dream of. There is one place here where the water actually touches the roof for a foot or two. If they searched the mine, Mac would dive under that with you into the workings cut off beyond the water. No one would ever think of looking there. We have frightened the Kaffirs with tales of ghosts, and, anyhow, we are watching their movements continually.'

He stayed with me while I dined, and then departed, leaving me, among other things, half-a-dozen candles, which, duly warned, I tucked under my pillow and mattress.

I slept again for a long time, and woke suddenly with a feeling of movement about me. Something seemed to be pulling at my pillow. I put out my hand quickly. There was a perfect scurry. The rats were at the candles. I rescued the candles in time, and lighted one. Luckily for me, I have no horror of rats as such, and being reassured by their evident timidity, I was not particularly uneasy. All the same, the three days I passed in the mine were not among the most pleasant which my memory re-illumines. The patter of little feet and a perceptible sense of stir and scurry was continuous. Once I was waked up from a doze by one actually galloping across me. On the candle being lighted these beings became invisible.

Tours the Mine
MEL, p. 301–2.
The next day—if you can call it day— arrived in due course. This was the 14th December, and the third day since I had escaped from the States Model Schools. It was relieved by a visit from the two Scottish miners, with whom I had a long confabulation. I then learned, to my surprise, that the mine was only about two hundred feet deep.

There were parts of it, said Mac, where one could see the daylight up a disused shaft. Would I like to take a turn around the old workings and have a glimmer? We passed an hour or two wandering round and up and down these subterranean galleries, and spent a quarter of an hour near the bottom of the shaft, where, grey and faint, the light of the sun and of the upper world was discerned. On this promenade I saw numbers of rats. They seemed rather nice little beasts, quite white, with dark eyes which I was assured in the daylight were a bright pink. Three years afterwards a British officer on duty in the district wrote to me that he had heard my statement at a lecture about the white rats and their pink eyes, and thought it was the limit of mendacity. He had taken the trouble to visit the mine and see for himself, and he proceeded to apologise for having doubted my truthfulness.

Dispatches
No similar text.

L to L
No similar text.

Strand, January 1924, p. 16. (**New text, and exactly as used for *MEL*)**
The next day—if you can call it day— arrived in due course. This was the 14th December, and the third day since I had escaped from the States Model Schools. It was relieved by a visit from the two Scottish miners, with whom I had a long confabulation. I then learned, to my surprise, that the mine was only about two hundred feet deep.

There were parts of it, said Mac, where one could see the daylight up a disused shaft. Would I like to take a turn around the old workings and have a glimmer? We passed an hour or two wandering round and up and down these subterranean galleries, and spent a quarter of an hour near the bottom of the shaft, where, grey and faint, the light of the sun and of the upper world was discerned. On this promenade I saw numbers of rats. They seemed rather nice little beasts, quite white, with dark eyes which I was assured in the daylight were a bright pink. Three years afterwards a British officer on duty in the district wrote to me that he had heard my statement at a lecture about the white rats and their pink eyes, and thought it was the limit of mendacity. He had taken the trouble to visit the mine and see for himself, and he proceeded to apologise for having doubted my truthfulness.

Cosmopolitan, January 1924, p. 163. (**Word changes in red and sentences in red removed from *Strand*)**
The next day—if you can call it day— arrived in due course. This was the **fourteenth of** December, and the third day since I had escaped from the States Model Schools. It was relieved by a visit from the two Scottish miners, with whom I had a long confabulation. I then learned, to my surprise, that the mine was only about **200** feet deep.

There were parts of it, said Mac, where one could see the daylight up a disused shaft. Would I like to take a turn around the old workings and have a glimmer? We passed an hour or two wandering round and up and down these subterranean galleries, and spent a quarter of an hour near the bottom of the shaft, where, grey and faint, the light of the sun and of the upper world was discerned, On this promenade I saw numbers of rats. They seemed rather nice little beasts, quite white, with dark eyes which I was assured in the daylight were a bright pink. **[Three years afterwards a British officer on duty in the district wrote to me that he had heard my statement at a lecture about the white rats and their pink eyes, and thought it was the limit of** mendacity. He had taken the trouble to visit the mine and see for himself, and he proceeded to apologise for having doubted my truthfulness.]

Visit to the Surface
MEL, p. 302.
On the 15th Mr. Howard announced that the hue and cry seemed to be dying away. No trace of the fugitive had been discovered throughout the mining district. The talk among the Boer officials was now that I must be hiding at the house of some British sympathiser in Pretoria. They did not believe that it was possible I could have got out of the town. In these circumstances he thought that I might come up and have a walk on the veldt that night, and that if all was quiet the next morning I might shift my quarters to the back room of the office. On the one hand he seemed reassured, and on the other increasingly excited by the adventure. Accordingly, I had a fine stroll in the glorious fresh air and moonlight, and thereafter, anticipating slightly our programme, I took up my quarters behind packing-cases in the inner room of the office. Here I remained for three more days, walking each night on the endless plain with Mr. Howard or his assistant.

Dispatches
No similar text.
L to L
No similar text.

Strand, January 1924, p. 16. **(New text, used exactly in *MEL*)**
On the 15th Mr. Howard announced that the hue and cry seemed to be dying away. No trace of the fugitive had been discovered throughout the mining district. The talk among the Boer officials was now that I must be hiding at the house of some British sympathiser in Pretoria. They did not believe that it was possible I could have got out of the town. In these circumstances he thought that I might come up and have a walk on the veldt that night, and that if all was quiet the next morning I might shift my quarters to the back room of the office. On the one hand he seemed reassured, and on the other increasingly excited by the adventure. Accordingly, I had a fine stroll in the glorious fresh air and moonlight, and thereafter, anticipating slightly our programme, I took up my quarters behind packing-cases in the inner room

of the office. Here I remained for three more days, walking each night on the endless plain with Mr. Howard or his assistant.

Cosmopolitan, January 1924, p. 163. (**Text in red removed in this version; one word changed – in red**)
On the fifteenth Mr. Howard announced that the hue and cry seemed to be dying away. No trace of the fugitive had been discovered throughout the mining district. The talk among the Boer officials was now that 1 must be hiding at the house of some British sympathiser in Pretoria. They did not believe that it was possible I could have got out of the town. In these circumstances he thought that I might come up and have a walk on the veldt that night, and that if all was quiet the next morning I might shift my quarters to the back room of the office. [On the one hand he seemed reassured, and on the other increasingly excited by the adventure.] Accordingly, I had a fine stroll in the glorious fresh air and moonlight, and thereafter, anticipating slightly our programme, I took up my quarters behind packing-cases in the inner room of the office. Here I remained for three more days, walking each night on the endless plain with Mr. Howard or his assistant.

Plan to Reboard a Train
MEL, p. 303.
On the 16th, the fifth [fourth] day of escape, Mr. Howard informed me he had made a plan to get me out of the country. The mine was connected with the railway by a branch line. In the neighbourhood of the mine there lived a Dutchman, Burgener by name, who was sending a consignment of wool to Delagoa Bay on the 19th. This gentleman was well disposed to the British. He had been approached by Mr. Howard, had been made a party to our secret, and was willing to assist. Mr. Burgener's wool was packed in great bales and would fill two or three large trucks. These trucks were to be loaded at the mine's siding. The bales could be so packed as to leave a small place in the centre of the truck in which I could be concealed. A tarpaulin would be fastened over each truck after it had been loaded, and it was very unlikely indeed that, if the fastenings were found intact, it would be removed at the frontier. Did 1 agree to take this chance?

Dispatches
No similar text.

L to L
No similar text.

Strand, January 1924, p. 16. **(New text; except for the change from 'fourth' to 'fifth', the exact text is used for *MEL*)**
On the 16th, the <mark>fourth</mark> day of escape, Mr. Howard informed me he had made a plan to get me out of the country. The mine was connected with the railway by a branch line. In the neighbourhood of the mine there lived a Dutchman, Burgener by name, who was sending a consignment of wool to Delagoa Bay on the 19th. This gentleman was well disposed to the British, He had been approached by Mr. Howard, had been made a party to our secret, and was willing to assist. Mr. Burgener's wool was packed in great bales and would fill two or three large trucks. These trucks were to be loaded at the mine's siding. The bales could be so packed as to leave a small place in the centre of the truck in which I could be concealed. A tarpaulin would be fastened over each truck after it had been loaded, and it was very unlikely indeed that, if the fastenings were found intact, it would be removed at the frontier. Did 1 agree to take this chance?

Cosmopolitan, January 1924, pp. 163–4. **(Minor changes from *Strand* in red)**
On the <mark>sixteenth</mark>, the fourth day of <mark>freedom</mark>, Mr. Howard informed me he had made a plan to get me out of the country. The mine was connected with the railway by a branch line. In the neighbourhood of the mine there lived a Dutchman, Burgener by name, who was sending a consignment of wool to Delagoa Bay on the <mark>nineteenth</mark>. This gentleman was well disposed to the British, He had been approached by Mr. Howard, had been made a party to our secret, and was willing to assist. Mr. Burgener's wool was packed in great bales and would fill two or three large trucks. These trucks were to be loaded at the mine's siding. The bales could be so packed as to leave a small place in the centre of the truck in which I could be concealed. A tarpaulin would be fastened over each truck after it had been loaded, and it was very unlikely indeed that, if the fastenings were found intact, it would be removed at the frontier. Did 1 agree to take this chance?

Anxieties About New Train Trip
MEL, pp. 303–4.

I was more worried about this than almost anything that had happened to me so far in my adventure. When by extraordinary chance one has gained some great advantage or prize and actually had it in one's possession and been enjoying it for several days, the idea of losing it becomes almost insupportable. I had really come to count upon freedom as a certainty, and the idea of having to put myself in a position in which I should be perfectly helpless, with- out a move of any kind, absolutely at the caprice of a searching party at the frontier, was profoundly harassing. Rather than face this ordeal I would much have preferred to start off on the veldt with a pony and a guide, and far from the haunts of man to make my way march by march beyond the wide territories of the Boer Republic. However, in the end I accepted the proposal of my generous rescuer, and arrangements were made accordingly.

I should have been still more anxious if I could have read some of the telegrams which were reaching English newspapers. For instance:

Pretoria, December 13. —Though Mr. Churchill's escape was cleverly executed there is little chance of his being able to cross the border.

Pretoria, December 14. —It is reported that Mr. Winston Churchill has been captured at the border railway station of Komati Poort.

Lourenço Marques, December 16. —It is reported that Mr. Churchill has been captured at Waterval Boven.

London, December 16. —With reference to the escape from Pretoria of Mr. Winston Churchill, fears are expressed that he may be captured again before long and if so may probably be shot;

or if I had read the description of myself and the reward for my recapture which were now widely distributed or posted along the railway line (a facsimile of which is given on the opposite page).

I am glad I knew nothing of all this.

As will be seen below, the last section of this text starting with 'I should have been still more anxious…' was added to the *Strand* text to produce the final *MEL* text. The added text clearly embellishes the story and indicates what a big story his escape had been and how much the Boers had wanted him captured.

Dispatches
No similar text.

L to L
No similar text.

Strand, January 1924, p. 16. (**First paragraph new and replicated exactly in** *MEL*; **all the text in red is not in the** *Strand* **article – it was added for** *MEL*)
I was more worried about this than almost anything that had happened to me so far in my adventure. When by extraordinary chance one has gained some great advantage or prize and actually had it in one's possession and been enjoying it for several days, the idea of losing it becomes almost insupportable. I had really come to count upon freedom as a certainty, and the idea of having to put myself in a position in which I should be perfectly helpless, with out a move of any kind, absolutely at the caprice of a searching party at the frontier, was profoundly harassing. Rather than face this ordeal I would much have preferred to start off on the veldt with a pony and a guide, and far from the haunts of man to make my way march by march beyond the wide territories of the Boer Republic. However, in the end I accepted the proposal of my generous rescuer, and arrangements were made accordingly.

[I should have been still more anxious if I could have read some of the telegrams which were reaching English newspapers. For instance:

Pretoria, December 13. —Though Mr. Churchill's escape was cleverly executed there is little chance of his being able to cross the border.

Pretoria, December 14. —It is reported that Mr. Winston Churchill has been captured at the border railway station of Komati Poort.

Lourenço Marques, December 16. —It is reported that Mr. Churchill has been captured at Waterval Boven.

London, December 16. —With reference to the escape from Pretoria of Mr. Winston Churchill, fears are expressed that he may be captured again before long and if so may probably be shot;

or if I had read the description of myself and the reward for my recapture which were now widely distributed or posted along the railway line (a facsimile of which is given on the opposite page).

I am glad I knew nothing of all this.]

Cosmopolitan, January 1924, p. 194. **(Shortest version, with all red text shown below not in the *Cosmopolitan* article)**
I was more worried about this than almost anything that had happened to me so far in my adventure. [When by extraordinary chance one has gained some great advantage or prize and actually had it in one's possession and been enjoying it for several days, the idea of losing it becomes almost insupportable.] I had really come to count upon freedom as a certainty, and the idea of having to put myself in a position in which I should be perfectly helpless, without a move of any kind, absolutely at the caprice of a searching party at the frontier, was profoundly harassing. [Rather than face this ordeal I would much have preferred to start off on the veldt with a pony and a guide, and far from the haunts of man to make my way march by march beyond the wide territories of the Boer Republic.] However, in the end I accepted the proposal of my generous rescuer, and arrangements were made accordingly.

Anxiety Continues
MEL, pp. 304, 306.
The afternoon of the 18th dragged slowly away. I remember that I spent the greater part of it reading Stevenson's *Kidnapped*. Those thrilling pages which describe the escape of David Balfour and Alan Breck in the glens awakened sensations with which I was only too familiar. To be a fugitive, to be a hunted man, to be 'wanted', is a mental experience by itself. The risks of the battlefield, the hazards of the bullet or the shell are one thing. Having the police after you is another. The need for concealment and deception breeds an actual sense of guilt very undermining to morale. Feeling that at any moment the officers of the law may present themselves or any stranger may ask the questions, 'Who are you?' 'Where do you come from?' 'Where are you going?'—to which questions no satisfactory answer could be given—gnawed the structure of self-confidence. I dreaded in every fibre the ordeal which awaited me at Komati Poort and which I must impotently and passively endure if I was to make good my escape from the enemy.

In this mood I was startled by the sound of rifle-shots close at hand, one after another at irregular intervals. A [dozen] sinister explanation [hypotheses] flashed through my mind. The Boers had come! Howard and his handful of Englishmen were in open rebellion in the heart of the enemy's country! I had been strictly enjoined upon no account to leave my hiding-place behind the packing-cases in any circumstances whatever, and I accordingly remained there in great anxiety. Presently it became clear that the worst had not happened. The sounds of voices and presently of laughter came from the office. Evidently a conversation amicable, sociable in its character was in progress. I resumed my companionship with Alan Breck. At last the voices died away, and then after an interval my door was opened and Mr. Howard's pale, sombre face appeared, suffused by a broad grin. He relocked the door behind him and walked delicately towards me, evidently in high glee.

Dispatches
No similar text.

L to L
No similar text.

Strand, January 1924, p. 16–7. (**New text with only the two words noted in blue and red to be deleted or changed, respectively; this becomes the text used for** *MEL*)
The afternoon of the 18th dragged slowly away. I remember that I spent the greater part of it reading Stevenson's 'Kidnapped'. Those thrilling pages which describe the escape of David Balfour and Alan Breck in the glens awakened sensations with which I was only too familiar. To be a fugitive, to be a hunted man, to be 'wanted', is a mental experience by itself. The risks of the battlefield, the hazards of the bullet or the shell are one thing. Having the police after you is another. The need for concealment and deception breeds an actual sense of guilt very undermining to morale. Feeling that at any moment the officers of the law may present themselves or any stranger may ask the questions, 'Who are you!' 'Where do you come from?' 'Where are you going?'—to which questions no satisfactory answer could be given—gnawed the structure of self-confidence. I dreaded in every fibre the ordeal which awaited me at Komati Poort and which I must impotently and passively endure if I was to make good my escape from the enemy.

In this mood I was startled by the sound of rifle-shots close at hand, one after another at irregular intervals. A dozen sinister hypotheses flashed through my mind. The Boers had come! Howard and his handful of Englishmen were in open rebellion in the heart of the enemy's country! I had been strictly enjoined upon no account to leave my hiding-place behind the packing-cases in any circumstances whatever, and I accordingly remained there in great anxiety. Presently it became clear that the worst had not happened. The sounds of voices and presently of laughter came from the office. Evidently a conversation amicable, sociable in its character was in progress. I resumed my companionship with Alan Breck. At last the voices died away, and then after an interval my door was opened and Mr. Howard's pale, sombre face appeared, suffused by a broad grin. He re-locked the door behind him and walked delicately towards me, evidently in high glee.

Cosmopolitan, January 1924, p. 164. (**Similar to text in** *Strand*, **except for one word changed, in red, and three sentences removed, in red**)

The afternoon of the eighteenth dragged slowly away. I remember that I spent the greater part of it reading Stevenson's 'Kidnapped'. Those thrilling pages which describe the escape of David Balfour and Alan Breck in the glens awakened sensations with which I was only too familiar. To be a fugitive, to be a hunted man, to be 'wanted', is a mental experience by itself. [The risks of the battlefield, the hazards of the bullet or the shell are one thing. Having the police after you is another. The need for concealment and deception breeds an actual sense of guilt very undermining to morale.] Feeling that at any moment the officers of the law may present themselves or any stranger may ask the questions, 'Who are you?' 'Where do you come from?' 'Where are you going?'—to which questions no satisfactory answer could be given—gnawed the structure of self-confidence. I dreaded in every fibre the ordeal which awaited me at Komati Poort and which I must impotently and passively endure if I was to make good my escape from the enemy.

In this mood I was startled by the sound of rifle-shots close at hand, one after another at irregular intervals. A dozen sinister hypotheses flashed through my mind. The Boers had come! Howard and his handful of Englishmen were in open rebellion in the heart of the enemy's country! I had been strictly enjoined upon no account to leave my hiding-place behind the packing cases in any circumstances whatever, and I accordingly remained there in great anxiety. Presently it became clear that the worst had not happened. The sounds of voices and presently of laughter came from the office. Evidently a conversation amicable, sociable in its character was in progress. I resumed my companionship with Alan Breck. At last the voices died away, and then after an interval my door was opened and Mr. Howard's pale, sombre face appeared, suffused by a broad grin. **[He re-locked the door behind him and walked delicately towards me, evidently in high glee.]**

MEL, p. 305.
Full-page image of the 'Wanted Dead or Alive' poster (handbill) is shown. This is not shown in any of the other publications.

Reboards Train
MEL, pp. 306–7.
'The Field Cornet has been here,' he said. 'No, he was not looking for you. He says they caught you at Waterval Boven yesterday. But I didn't want him messing about, so I challenged him to a rifle match at bottles. He won two pounds off me and has gone away delighted.'

'It is all fixed up for to-night,' he added.

'What do I do?' I asked.

'Nothing. You simply follow me when I come for you.'

At two o'clock on the morning of the 19th I awaited, fully dressed, the signal. The door opened. My host appeared. He beckoned. Not a word was spoken on either side. He led the way through the front office to the siding where three large bogie trucks stood. Three figures, evidently Dewsnap and the miners, were strolling about in different directions in the moonlight. A gang of Kaffirs were busy lifting an enormous bale into the rearmost truck.

Howard strolled along to the first truck and walked across the line past the end of it. As he did so he pointed with his *left* **[right]** hand. I nipped on to the buffers and saw before me a hole between the wool bales and the end of the truck, just wide enough to squeeze into. From this there led a narrow tunnel formed of wool bales into the centre of the truck. Here was a space wide enough to lie in, high enough to sit up in. In this I took up my abode.

Three or four hours later, when gleams of daylight had reached me through the interstices of my shelter and through chinks in the boards of the flooring of the truck, the noise of an approaching engine was heard. Then came the bumping and banging of coupling-up. And again, after a further pause, we started rumbling off on our journey into the unknown.

APPENDIX 6 / CHAPTER 4: ESCAPE

Dispatches
No similar text.

L to L
No similar text.

Strand, January 1924, pp. 17–8. (**New text, used exactly for** *MEL*, **except 'left' was replaced by 'right'; the same text in** *Cosmopolitan*)
Cosmopolitan, January 1924, p. 164.
'The Field Cornet has been here,' he said. 'No, he was not looking for you. He says they caught you at Waterval Boven yesterday. But I didn't want him messing about, so I challenged him to a rifle match at bottles. He won two pounds off me and has gone away delighted.'

'It is all fixed up for to-night,' he added.

'What do I do?' I asked.

'Nothing. You simply follow me when I come for you.'

At two o'clock on the morning of the 19th I awaited, fully dressed, the signal. The door opened. My host appeared. He beckoned. Not a word was spoken on either side. He led the way through the front office to the siding where three large bogie trucks stood. Three figures, evidently Dewsnap and the miners, were strolling about in different directions in the moonlight. A gang of Kaffirs were busy lifting an enormous bale into the rearmost truck.

Howard strolled along to the first truck and walked across the line past the end of it. As he did so he pointed with his right hand. I nipped on to the buffers and saw before me a hole between the wool bales and the end of the truck, just wide enough to squeeze into. From this there led a narrow tunnel formed of wool bales into the centre of the truck. Here was a space wide enough to lie in, high enough to sit up in. In this I took up my abode.

Three or four hours later, when gleams of daylight had reached me through the interstices of my shelter and through chinks in the boards of the flooring of the truck, the noise of an approaching engine was heard. Then came the bumping and banging of coupling up. And again, after a further pause, we started rumbling off on our journey into the unknown."

Hidden on Train
MEL, pp. 307–8.

I now took stock of my new abode and of the resources in munitions and supplies with which it was furnished. First there was a revolver. This was a moral support, though it was not easy to see in what way it could helpfully be applied to any problem I was likely to have to solve. Secondly, there were two roast chickens, some slices of meat, a loaf of bread, a melon, and three bottles of cold tea. The journey to the sea was not expected to take more than sixteen hours, but no one could tell what delay might occur to ordinary commercial traffic in time of war.

There was plenty of light now in the recess in which I was confined. There were many crevices in the boards composing the sides and floor of the truck, and through these the light found its way between the wool bales. Working along the tunnel to the end of the truck, I found a chink which must have been nearly an eighth of an inch in width, and through which it was possible to gain a partial view of the outer world. To check the progress of the journey I had learnt by heart beforehand the names of all the stations on the route. I can remember many of them to-day: Witbank, Middelburg, Bergendal, Belfast, Dalmanutha, Machadodorp, Waterval Boven, Waterval Onder, Elands, Nooidgedacht, and so on to Komati Poort. We had by now reached the first of these. At this point the branch line from the mine joined the railway. Here, after two or three hours' delay and shunting, we were evidently coupled up to a regular train, and soon started off at a superior and very satisfactory pace.

Dispatches
No similar text.

L to L
No similar text.

Strand, January 1924, p. 18. **(New text, used exactly for the *Cosmopolitan* and *MEL*)**
Cosmopolitan, January 1924, p. 164.
I now took stock of my new abode and of the resources in munitions and supplies with which it was furnished. First there was a revolver. This was a

moral support, though it was not easy to see in what way it could helpfully be applied to any problem I was likely to have to solve. Secondly, there were two roast chickens, some slices of meat, a loaf of bread, a melon, and three bottles of cold tea. The journey to the sea was not expected to take more than sixteen hours, but no one could tell what delay might occur to ordinary commercial traffic in time of war.

There was plenty of light now in the recess in which I was confined. There were many crevices in the boards composing the sides and floor of the truck, and through these the light found its way between the wool bales. Working along the tunnel to the end of the truck, I found a chink which must have been nearly an eighth of an inch in width, and through which it was possible to gain a partial view of the outer world. To check the progress of the journey I had learnt by heart beforehand the names of all the stations on the route. I can remember many of them to-day: Witbank, Middelburg, Bergendal, Belfast, Dalmanutha, Machadodorp, Waterval Boven, Waterval Onder, Elands, Nooidgedacht, and so on to Komati Poort. We had by now reached the first of these. At this point the branch line from the mine joined the railway. Here, after two or three hours' delay and shunting, we were evidently coupled up to a regular train, and soon started off at a superior and very satisfactory pace.

Traveling on the Train
MEL, p. 308.
All day long we travelled eastward through the Transvaal; [and] when darkness fell we were laid up for the night at a station which, according to my reckoning, was Waterval Boven. We had accomplished nearly half of our journey. But how long should we wait on this siding? It might be for days; it would certainly be until the next morning. During all the dragging hours of the day I had lain on the floor of the truck occupying my mind as best I could, painting bright pictures of the pleasures of freedom, of the excitement of rejoining the army, of the triumph of a successful escape—but haunted also perpetually by anxieties about the search at the frontier, an ordeal inevitable and constantly approaching. Now another apprehension laid hold upon me. I wanted to go to sleep. Indeed, I did not think I could possibly keep awake. But if I slept I might snore! And if I snored while the train was at rest in the silent siding, I might be heard. And if I were heard! I decided in principle that

it was only prudent to abstain from sleep, and shortly afterwards fell into a blissful slumber from which I was awakened the next morning by the banging and jerking of the train as the engine was again coupled to it.

Between Waterval Boven and Waterval Onder there is a very steep descent which the locomotive accomplishes by means of a rack and pinion. We ground our way down this at three or four miles an hour, and this feature made my reckoning certain that the next station was, in fact, Waterval Onder. All this day, too, we rattled through the enemy's country, and late in the afternoon we reached the dreaded Komati Poort. Peeping through my chink, I could see this was a considerable place, with numerous tracks of rails and several trains standing on them. Numbers of people were moving about. There were many voices and much shouting and whistling. After a preliminary inspection of the scene I retreated, as the train pulled up, into the very centre of my fastness, and covering myself up with a piece of sacking lay flat on the floor of the truck and awaited developments with a beating heart.

Dispatches
No similar text.

L to L
No similar text.
Strand, January 1924, p. 18. (**New text, used exactly in *MEL* except for the removal of the word 'and'**)
All day long we travelled eastward through the Transvaal; and when darkness fell we were laid up for the night at a station which, according to my reckoning, was Waterval Boven. We had accomplished nearly half of our journey. But how long should we wait on this siding? It might be for days; it would certainly be until the next morning. During all the dragging hours of the day I had lain on the floor of the truck occupying my mind as best I could, painting bright pictures of the pleasures of freedom, of the excitement of rejoining the army, of the triumph of a successful escape—but haunted also perpetually by anxieties about the search at the frontier, an ordeal inevitable and constantly approaching. Now another apprehension laid hold upon me. I wanted to go to sleep. Indeed, I did not think I could possibly keep awake. But if I slept I might snore! And if I snored while the train was at rest in the silent siding, I might be heard. And if I were heard! I decided in principle that

it was only prudent to abstain from sleep, and shortly afterwards fell into a blissful slumber from which I was awakened the next morning by the banging and jerking of the train as the engine was again coupled to it.

Between Waterval Boven and Waterval Onder there is a very steep descent which the locomotive accomplishes by means of a rack and pinion. We ground our way down this at three or four miles an hour, and this feature made my reckoning certain that the next station was, in fact, Waterval Onder. All this day, too, we rattled through the enemy's country, and late in the afternoon we reached the dreaded Komati Poort. Peeping through my chink, I could see this was a considerable place, with numerous tracks of rails and several trains standing on them. Numbers of people were moving about. There were many voices and much shouting and whistling. After a preliminary inspection of the scene I retreated, as the train pulled up, into the very centre of my fastness, and covering myself up with a piece of sacking lay flat on the floor of the truck and awaited developments with a beating heart.

Cosmopolitan, January 1924, p. 164. **(One word changed, in blue, and sentences removed, in red, compared to the *Strand*)**
All day long we travelled eastward through the Transvaal; and when darkness fell we were laid up for the night at a station which, according to my reckoning was Waterval Boven. We had accomplished nearly half of our journey. But how long should we wait on this siding? It might be for days; it would certainly be until the next morning. [During all the dragging hours of the day I had lain on the floor of the truck occupying my mind as best I could, painting bright pictures of the pleasures of freedom, of the excitement of rejoining the army, of the triumph of a successful escape—but haunted also perpetually by anxieties about the search at the frontier, an ordeal inevitable and constantly approaching. Now another apprehension laid hold upon me.]

I wanted to go to sleep. Indeed, I did not think I could possibly keep awake. But if I slept I might snore! And if I snored while the train was at rest in the silent siding, I might be heard. And if I were heard! I decided in principle that it was only prudent to abstain from sleep, and shortly afterwards fell into a blissful slumber from which I was awakened the next morning by the banging and jerking of the train as the engine was again coupled to it.

Between Waterval Boven and Waterval Onder there is a very steep descent which the locomotive accomplishes by means of a rack and pinion. We ground our way down this at three or four miles an hour, and this feature made my reasoning certain that the next station was, in fact, Waterval Onder. All this day, too, we rattled through the enemy's country, and late in the afternoon we reached the dreaded Komati Poort. Peeping through my chink, I could see this was a considerable place, with numerous tracks of rails and several trains standing on them. Numbers of people were moving about. There were many voices and much shouting and whistling. After a preliminary inspection of the scene I retreated, as the train pulled up, into the very centre of my fastness, and covering myself up with a piece of sacking lay flat on the floor of the truck and awaited developments with a beating heart.

Train Stops in Rail Yard
MEL, pp. 309–10.

Three or four hours passed, and I did not know whether we had been searched or not. Several times people had passed up and down the train talking in Dutch. But the tarpaulins had not been removed, and no special examination seemed to have been made of the truck. Meanwhile darkness had come on, and I had to resign myself to an indefinite continuance of my uncertainties. It was tantalizing to be held so long in jeopardy after all these hundreds of miles had been accomplished, and I was now within a few hundred yards of the frontier. Again 1 wondered about the dangers of snoring. But in the end I slept without mishap.

We were still stationary when I awoke. Perhaps they were searching the train so thoroughly that there was consequently a great delay! Alternatively, perhaps we were forgotten on the siding and would be left there for days or weeks, I was greatly tempted to peer out, but I resisted. At last, at eleven o'clock, we were coupled up, and almost immediately started. If I had been right in thinking that the station in which we had passed the night was Komati Poort, I was already in Portuguese territory. But perhaps I had made a mistake. Perhaps I had miscounted. Perhaps there was still another station before the frontier. Perhaps the search still impended. But all these doubts were dispelled when the train arrived at the next station. I peered through my chink and saw the uniform caps of the Portuguese officials on the platform and the name Resana Garcia painted on a board. I restrained all expression of my joy until we moved on again. Then, as we rumbled and banged along, I pushed my head out of the tarpaulin and sang and shouted and crowed at the top of my voice. Indeed, I was so carried away by thankfulness and delight that I fired my revolver two or three times in the air as a *feu de joie*. None of these follies led to any evil results.

Dispatches
No similar text.

L to L
No similar text.

Strand, January 1924, pp. 18, 20. **(New text, used exactly in *MEL*)**
Three or four hours passed, and I did not know whether we had been searched or not. Several times people had passed up and down the train talking in Dutch. But the tarpaulins had not been removed, and no special examination seemed to have been made of the truck. Meanwhile darkness had come on, and I had to resign myself to an indefinite continuance of my uncertainties. It was tantalizing to be held so long in jeopardy after all these hundreds of miles had been accomplished, and I was now within a few hundred yards of the frontier. Again I wondered about the dangers of snoring. But in the end I slept without mishap.

We were still stationary when I awoke. Perhaps they were searching the train so thoroughly that there was consequently a great delay! Alternatively, perhaps we were forgotten on the siding and would be left there for days or weeks, I was greatly tempted to peer out, but I resisted. At last, at eleven o'clock, we were coupled up, and almost immediately started. If I had been right in thinking that the station in which we had passed the night was Komati Poort, I was already in Portuguese territory. But perhaps I had made a mistake. Perhaps I had miscounted. Perhaps there was still another station before the frontier. Perhaps the search still impended. But all these doubts were dispelled when the train arrived at the next station. I peered through my chink and saw the uniform caps of the Portuguese officials on the platform and the name Resana Garcia painted on a board. I restrained all expression of my joy until we moved on again. Then, as we rumbled and banged along, I pushed my head out of the tarpaulin and sang and shouted and crowed at the top of my voice. Indeed, I was so carried away by thankfulness and delight that I fired my revolver two or three times in the air as a *feu de joie*. None of these follies led to any evil results.

Cosmopolitan, January 1924, p. 165. **(Similar to *Strand*, except sentences in red removed)**

Three or four hours passed, and I did not know whether we had been searched or not. Several times people had passed up and down the train talking in Dutch. But the tarpaulins had not been removed, and no special examination seemed to have been made of the truck. Meanwhile darkness had come on, and I had to resign myself to an indefinite continuance of my uncertainties. It was tantalizing to be held so long in jeopardy after all these hundreds of miles had been accomplished, and I was now within a few hundred yards of the frontier. Again I wondered about the dangers of snoring. But in the end I slept without mishap.

We were still stationary when I awoke. Perhaps they were searching the train so thoroughly that there was consequently a great delay! Alternatively, perhaps we were forgotten on the siding and would be left there for days or weeks! I was greatly tempted to peer out, but | resisted. At last, at eleven o'clock, we were coupled up, and almost immediately started. If I had been right in thinking that the station in which we had passed the night was Komati Poort, I was already in Portuguese territory. But perhaps I had made a mistake. [Perhaps I had miscounted. Perhaps there was still another station before the frontier.] Perhaps the search still impended. But all these doubts were dispelled when the train arrived at the next station. I peered through my chink and saw the uniform caps of the Portuguese officials on the platform and the name Resana Garcia painted on a board.

I restrained all expression of my joy until we moved on again. Then, as we rumbled and banged along, I pushed my head out of the tarpaulin and sang and shouted and crowed at the top of my voice. Indeed, I was so carried away by thankfulness and delight that I fired my revolver two or three times in the air as a *feu de joie*. None of these follies led to any evil results.

Train Continues On
MEL, p. 310.

It was late in the afternoon when we reached Lourenço Marques. My train ran into a goods yard, and a crowd of Kaffirs advanced to unload it. I thought the moment had now come for me to quit my hiding-place, in which I had passed nearly three anxious and uncomfortable days. I had already thrown out every vestige of food and had removed all traces of my occupation. I now slipped out at the end of the truck between the couplings, and mingling unnoticed with the Kaffirs and loafers in the yard—which my slovenly and unkempt appearance well fitted me to do—I strolled my way towards the gates and found myself in the streets of Lourenço Marques.

Burgener was waiting outside the gates. We exchanged glances. He turned and walked off into the town, and I followed twenty yards behind. We walked through several streets and turned a number of corners. Presently he stopped and stood for a moment gazing up at the roof of the opposite house. I looked in the same direction, and there—blest vision! —I saw floating the gay colours of the Union Jack. It was the British Consulate.

The secretary of the British Consul evidently did not expect my arrival.

'Be off,' he said. 'The Consul cannot see you to-day. Come to his office at nine to-morrow, if you want anything.'

At this I became so angry, and repeated so loudly that I insisted on seeing the Consul personally at once, that that gentleman himself looked out of the window and finally came down to the door and asked me my name. From that moment every resource of hospitality and welcome was at my disposal. A hot bath, clean clothing, an excellent dinner, means of telegraphing—all I could want.

Dispatches
No similar text.

L to L
No similar text.

Strand, January 1924, p. 20. **(New text, used exactly for *MEL*)**
It was late in the afternoon when we reached Lourenço Marques. My train ran into a goods yard, and a crowd of Kaffirs advanced to unload it. I thought the moment had now come for me to quit my hiding-place, in which I had passed nearly three anxious and uncomfortable days. I had already thrown out every vestige of food and had removed all traces of my occupation. I now slipped out at the end of the truck between the couplings, and mingling unnoticed with the Kaffirs and loafers in the yard—which my slovenly and unkempt appearance well fitted me to do—I strolled my way towards the gates and found myself in the streets of Lourenço Marques.

Burgener was waiting outside the gates. We exchanged glances. He turned and walked off into the town, and I followed twenty yards behind. We walked through several streets and turned a number of corners. Presently he stopped and stood for a moment gazing up at the roof of the opposite house. I looked in the same direction, and there—blest vision! —I saw floating the gay colours of the Union Jack. It was the British Consulate.

The secretary of the British Consul evidently did not expect my arrival.

'Be off,' he said. 'The Consul cannot see you to-day. Come to his office at nine to-morrow, if you want anything.'

At this I became so angry, and repeated so loudly that I insisted on seeing the Consul personally at once, that that gentleman himself looked out of the window and finally came down to the door and asked me my name. From that moment every resource of hospitality and welcome was at my disposal. A hot bath, clean clothing, an excellent dinner, means of telegraphing—all I could want.

Cosmopolitan, January 1924, p. 165. (**Similar to** *Strand*, **with some word changes – in blue**)

It was late in the afternoon when we reached Lourenço Marques. My train ran into a goods yard, and a crowd of Kaffirs advanced to unload it. I thought the moment had now come for me to quit my hiding-place, in which I had passed nearly three anxious and uncomfortable days. I had already thrown out every vestige of food and had removed all traces of my occupation. I now slipped out at the end of the truck between the couplings, and mingling unnoticed with the Kaffirs and loafers in the yard—which my slovenly and unkempt appearance well fitted me to do—I strolled my way towards the gates and found myself in the streets of Lourenço Marques.

Burgener was waiting outside the gates. We exchanged glances. He turned and walked off into the town, and I followed twenty yards behind. We walked through several streets and turned a number of corners. Presently he stopped and stood for a moment gazing up at the roof of the opposite house. I looked in the same direction, and there—blest vision! —I saw floating the gleaming colours of the Union Jack. It was the British Consulate.

The secretary of the British Consul evidently did not expect my arrival.

'Be off,' he said. 'The Consul cannot see you to-day. Come to his office at nine to-morrow, if you want anything.'

At this I became so angry, and repeated so loudly that I insisted on seeing the Consul personally at once, that that gentleman himself looked out of the window and finally came down to the door and asked me my name. From that moment every resource of hospitality and welcome was at my disposal. A hot bath, clean clothing, an excellent dinner, means of telegraphing—all, in fact that one could need was accorded me.

Freedom
MEL, p. 311.
I devoured the file of newspapers which was placed before me. Great events had taken place since I had climbed the wall of the States Model Schools. The Black Week of the Boer War had descended on the British Army. General Gatacre at Stormberg, Lord Methuen at Magersfontein, and Sir Redvers Buller at Colenso, had all suffered staggering defeats, and casualties on a scale unknown to England since the Crimean War. All this made me eager to rejoin the army, and the Consul himself was no less anxious to get me out of Lourenço Marques, which was full of Boers and Boer sympathizers. Happily the weekly steamer was leaving for Durban that very evening; in fact, it might almost be said it ran in connection with my train. On this steamer I decided to embark.

The news of my arrival had spread like wildfire through the town, and while we were at dinner the Consul was at first disturbed to see a group of strange figures in the garden, These, however, turned out to be Englishmen fully armed who had hurried up to the Consulate determined to resist any attempt at my recapture. Under the escort of these patriotic gentlemen I marched safely through the streets to the quay, and at about ten o'clock was on salt water in the steamship *Induna*.

Dispatches
No similar text.

L to L
No similar text.

Strand, January 1924, p. 20. (**New text, used exactly for** *Cosmopolitan* **and** *MEL*)

Cosmopolitan, January 1924, p. 165.

I devoured the file of newspapers which was placed before me. Great events had taken place since I had climbed the wall of the States Model Schools. The Black Week of the Boer War had descended on the British Army. General Gatacre at Stormberg, Lord Methuen at Magersfontein, and Sir Redvers Buller at Colenso, had all suffered staggering defeats, and casualties on a scale unknown to England since the Crimean War. All this made me eager to rejoin the army, and the Consul himself was no less anxious to get me out of Lourenço Marques, which was full of Boers and Boer sympathizers. Happily the weekly steamer was leaving for Durban that very evening; in fact, it might almost be said it ran in connection with my train. On this steamer I decided to embark.

The news of my arrival had spread like wildfire through the town, and while we were at dinner the Consul was at first disturbed to see a group of strange figures in the garden, These, however, turned out to be Englishmen fully armed who had hurried up to the Consulate determined to resist any attempt at my recapture. Under the escort of these patriotic gentlemen I marched safely through the streets to the quay, and at about ten o'clock was on salt water in the steamship *Induna*.

Arrives Durban

MEL, pp. 511–2.

I reached Durban to find myself a popular hero. I was received as if I had won a great victory. The harbour was decorated with flags. Bands and crowds thronged the quays. The Admiral, the General, the Mayor pressed on board to grasp my hand. I was nearly torn to pieces by enthusiastic kindness. Whirled along on the shoulders of the crowd, I was carried to the steps of the town hall, where nothing would content them but a speech, which after a becoming reluctance I was induced to deliver. Sheaves of telegrams from all parts of the world poured in upon me, and I started that night for the Army in a blaze of triumph.

Here, too, I was received with the greatest goodwill. I took up my quarters in the very platelayer's hut within one hundred yards of which I had a little more than a month before been taken prisoner, and there with the rude plenty of the Natal campaign celebrated by a dinner to many friends my good fortune and Christmas Eve.

This is the end of the two chapters of *MEL* on Churchill's escape. Both *Strand* and *Cosmopolitan* continue on with additional text. Both of these articles have many illustrations not in *MEL*.

Dispatches
No similar text.

L to L
No similar text.

Strand, January 1924, pp. 21–2. (New text, used directly for *Cosmopolitan* and *MEL*)
Cosmopolitan, January 1924, pp. 165–6.
I reached Durban to find myself a popular hero. I was received as if I had won a great victory. The harbour was decorated with flags. Bands and crowds thronged the quays. The Admiral, the General, the Mayor pressed on board to grasp my hand. I was nearly torn to pieces by enthusiastic kindness. Whirled along on the shoulders of the crowd, I was carried to the steps of the town hall, where nothing would content them but a speech, which after a becoming reluctance I was induced to deliver. Sheaves of telegrams from all parts of the world poured in upon me, and I started that night for the Army in a blaze of triumph.

Here, too, I was received with the greatest goodwill. I took up my quarters in the very platelayer's hut within one hundred yards of which I had a little more than a month before been taken prisoner, and there with the rude plenty of the Natal campaign celebrated by a dinner to many friends my good fortune and Christmas Eve.

Churchill has certainly woven an impressive story of his escape by selectively drawing upon his previous publications. It is clear that Churchill took substantial care to pick and choose not only sentences and paragraphs but individual words from among the various versions or altogether newly chosen words to include in *My Early Life*. Churchill was carefully creating not only the story he wished to convey but also the sound and imagery that would most embellish the impact and mood to capture the imagination and empathy of the reader. Churchill is attempting to invite the reader into the story with him so they may more fully experience what Churchill felt. He seems to be quite successful in this endeavour. The original dispatches and their reprinting in a nearly contemporaneous book form provide a background of facts and incidents. They were primarily written as newspaper accounts and therefore do not provide much in the manner of colourful descriptions or personal opinions and certainly not much on the impact of the events on Churchill or how Churchill might be perceived. In contrast, the *Strand* article was directly written from Churchill's perspective, and it is all about Churchill, his adventures and how he wants the world to see and recognise him. Therefore, it is not surprising that large tracts of the *Strand* article are directly inserted into his autobiography. His goals in writing the book were to further enhance his reputation as both a person and writer, as well as to challenge the youth of Britain at the time of the book's publication to grab life by the throat and make a difference in the world. He is saying that the era of his youth (late Victorian England) is long gone and will never return but the drives to survive and succeed are eternal and vitally important to the youth of the day. Change is not brought about by being passive, and risks are worth taking to make the world a better place. This spirit of survival and risk-taking is fully displayed in this story of Churchill's escape.

The *Cosmopolitan* article is by and large a shortened version of the *Strand* article, presumably contracted to meet word limits imposed by the magazine's editor. From a storytelling perspective, the shortened version does not differ significantly from the *Strand* article. However, in some places, Churchill may have removed information that he thought would not be as interesting to American audiences as British ones. At the time of the article, 1924, *Cosmopolitan* was an American literary magazine.

Notes

1. Churchill, Randolph S., *Winston S. Churchill*, Companion Volume I Part 2, 1896-1900, Boston, Houghton Mifflin, 1967, pp. 1087–136.
2. 'A Lost Letter of Ancient Rome', *Blackwood's Magazine*, Vol CXCI, February 1912, pp. 270–76.

3. 'Mr. Churchill's Libel Case', *Derby Daily Telegraph*, Derbyshire, UK, May 20, 1912, p. 3; 'First Lord Libelled, Apology from Blackwood's', Warning to Critics, and Record Withdrawn', *The Daily Herald*, London, May 21, 1912, p. 6.
4. Churchill Archives, March 7, 1912, (CHAR 1/30/18-32).
5. Churchill, Winston S., *My Early Life: A Roving Commission*, London, Thornton Butterworth, 1930, 1st ed., second printing.
6. Woods, Frederick, *Young Winston's Wars: The Original Dispatches of Winston S. Churchill War Correspondent, 1897-1900*, New York, The Viking Press, 1973, 1st US edition.
7. Churchill, Winston S., *London to Ladysmith Via Pretoria*, New York, Longmans, Green, and Co., 1900, 1st US edition.
8. Churchill, Winston S., 'My Escape From the Boers, Now Told in Full for the First Time', *Strand Magazine*, December 1923, Vol. LXVI, pp. 537–40, 542–4, 546–7.
9. Churchill, Winston S., 'My Escape From the Boers, Now Told in Full for the First Time, Part II', *Strand Magazine*, January 1924, Vol. LXVII, pp. 14–8, 20–3.
10. Churchill, Winston S., 'My Escape From the Boers', *Cosmopolitan*, January 1924, Vol. LXXVI, No. 1, pp. 3–34, 161–6

APPENDIX 7

Chapter 5: Bibliography

The following is a comprehensive, chronological list of book reviews with references for readers who wish to read a more complete set of reviews.

1. 'Forthcoming Books: Winston', *Yorkshire Post*, UK, 8 October 1930, p. 6.
2. Arthur A. Baumann, 'Adventures to the Adventurous', *Observer*, London, 19 October 1930, p. 6.
3. 'Churchill Recalls Glory of Youth in New Book', *Winnipeg Tribune*, Winnipeg, Manitoba, Canada, 20 October 1930, p. 3.
4. Thomas T. Champion, 'Rt. Hon. Churchill Dealt with His Career in Book', *Ottawa Journal*, Ottawa, Ontario, Canada, 20 October 1930, p. 1.
5. 'Thrills of a Roving Commission', *Aberdeen Press & Journal*, Scotland, 20 October 1930, p. 6.
6. Robert Lynd, 'Winston Churchill', *Daily News* (News Chronicle), London, 20 October 1930, p. 8.
7. '*Book* of the Day: Mr. Churchill's Youth', *The Times*, London, 20 October 1930, p. 8.
8. A. Wyatt Tilby, 'The Book of the Day: Mr. Churchill Remembers His Youth', *Yorkshire Post*, Yorkshire, UK, 20 October 1930, p. 6.
9. 'Churchill Protested When Told How to Speak to a Table, by Latin Master', *Sun Times*, Owen Sound, Ontario, Canada, 20 October 1930, p 1.
10. 'Winston – By Himself', *Daily Herald*, London, 20 October 1930, p. 2.
11. 'Mr. Churchill's Early Life', *Edinburgh Evening News*, Scotland, 20 October 1930, p. 6.

12. 'Mr. Churchill's Call to Youth', *Liverpool Daily Post*, UK, 20 October 1930, p. 4.
13. 'Winston Churchill's Early Years', *Liverpool Echo*, UK, 20 October 1930, p. 6.
14. 'The Adventure of Living', *Sheffield Daily Telegraph*, UK, 20 October 1930, p. 3.
15. *Daily Sketch*, London, 20 October 1930.
16. 'My Career Is What I Made It', *Manchester Evening News*, UK, 20 October 1930, p. 6.
17. 'Churchill's Autobiography is Published', *Victoria Daily Times*, Victoria, BC, Canada, 20 October 1930, p. 2.
18. *Windsor Star*, Windsor, Ontario, Canada, 20 October 1930, p. 16.
19. 'The Adventure of Living', *Glasgow Herald*, Glasgow, 20 October 1930, p. 12.
20. Thomas T. Champion, 'Churchill Tells Story of His Early Days', *Kingston Whig-Standard*, Kinston, Ontario, Canada, 21 October 1930, p. 4.
21. 'Churchill's Book is Lively Story of Youth', *Province*, Vancouver, BC, Canada, 21 October 1930, p. 26.
22. 'Winston Churchill Looks Back Upon His Early Years', *Gazette*, Montreal, Quebec, Canada, 21 October 1930, p. 11.
23. 'Autobiography of Winston Churchill Tells Vivid Story', *Expositor*, Brantford, Ontario, Canada, 21 October 1930, p. 5.
24. 'Winston Churchill Tells Lively Story of Younger Period', *Calgary Daily Herald*, Calgary, Alberta, Canada, 21 October 1930, p. 2.
25. *Evening Standard*, London, 23 October 1930, p. 10.
26. 'Winston Churchill Sketches Wittily His Early Years', *Edmonton Journal*, Edmonton, Alberta, Canada, 23 October 1930, p. 9.
27. 'My Early Life', *Country Life*, 25 October 1930, p. 526. (portrait)
28. Duff Cooper, 'The Early Life of Winston Churchill', *Spectator*, 25 October 1930, p. 599.
29. H.W. Nevinson, *New Statesman*, 25 October 1930, Vol. 36, p. 85.
30. Frank Forrester, 'A Book of the Week: Winston's Life of Adventure', *Reynold's Illustrated News*, London, 26 October 1930.
31. *Times Literary Supplement*, London, 23 October 1930, p. 851.
32. *New York Sun*, New York, October 1930.

33. Lewis Melville, 'Mr. Churchill's Biography', Saturday Review, 30 October 1930, p. 528.
34. Thomas T. Champion, 'Winston Churchill on Himself', *Star-Phoenix*, Saskatoon, Saskatchewan, Canada, 30 October 1930, p. 13.
35. H.C. Lodge, *Books*, 23 November 1930, p. 4.
36. John Buchan, *Week-End Review Illustrated*, 1930.
37. 'My Early Life', *Ottawa Journal*, Ottawa, Ontario, Canada, 1 November 1930, p. 19.
38. Michael J. Walsh, 'Churchill, Adventurer', *Border Cities Star*, Windsor, Ontario, Canada, 3 November 1930, p. 4.
39. 'Churchill's Story is Full of Thrills', *Toronto Star*, Toronto, Ontario, Canada, 8 November 1930, p. 4.
40. 'A Free-Lance with Pen and Sword, Being an Appreciation of "My Early Life" by the Rt. Hon. Winston S. Churchill', *Illustrated London News*, London, 8 November 1930, p. 806.
41. Robert Munford, 'Churchill's Autobiography', *Richmond News Leader*, Richmond, VA, USA, 8 November 1930, p. 8.
42. *Nation and Atheneum*, London, 8 November 1930, p. 197.
43. 'Churchill's Youth', *Gazette*, Montreal, Quebec, Canada, 8 November 1930, p. 12.
44. George Currie, 'Winston Churchill, Adventurer', *Brooklyn Daily Eagle*, Brooklyn, NY, USA, 9 November 1930, p. 68.
45. *Ottawa Library Journal*, Volume XV, November 1930, p. 69.
46. 'Of Making Many Books', *St. Louis Post-Dispatch*, 13 November 1930, p. 3B.
47. W. Everard Edmonds, 'A Roving Commission', *Edmonton Journal*, Edmonton, Alberta, Canada, 15 November 1930, p. 4.
48. 'Winston Churchill', *Scotsman*, Scotland, 17 November 1930, p. 2.
49. 'A Roving Commission', *Detroit Free Press*, Detroit, MI, USA, 17 November 1930, p. 11.
50. John O'London, 'Balfour and Churchill', *Calgary Herald*, Calgary, Alberta, Canada, 21 November 1930, p. 4.
51. O.F. Theis, 'A Great Autobiography', *Illustrated Sports and Dramatic News*, London, 22 November 1930, p. 488.
52. *New York Times Book Review*, New York, 23 November 1930, p. 14.

53. 'Roving Commission is Ably Reviewed', *Times Recorder*, Zanesville, OH, USA, 28 November 1930, p. 4.
54. *Burlington Daily News*, Burlington, VT, USA, 28 November 1930, p. 4.
55. 'Balfour and Churchill', *Calgary Daily Herald*, Calgary, Alberta, Canada, 21 November 1930, p. 4.
56. 'The Exciting Career of Mrs. [sic] Winston Churchill', *Times Herald*, Olean, NY, USA 29 November 1930, p. 8.
57. 'Churchill, Father and Son', *Stockton Evening Record*, Stockton, CA, USA, 29 November 1930, p. 22.
58. 'The Exciting Career of Mr. Winston Churchill', *Sunday Times Democrat*, Okmulgee, OK, USA, 30 November 1930, p. 19.
59. 'The Early Reminiscences of Winston Churchill', *Hartford Courant*, Hartford, CT, USA, 30 November 1930, p. 64.
60. Exciting Career of Mr. Churchill', *Sunday Record*, Columbia, SC, USA, 30 November 1930, p. 6.
61. 'Exciting Career of Mr. Churchill', *Evansville Press*, Evansville, IL, 30 November 1930, p. 24.
62. T.R. Ybarra, 'Adventure Filled the Years of Churchill's Youth; in "A Roving Commission", the British Statesman Tells A Vivid, Stirring Story', *New York Times*, 30 November 1930, pp. 3, 34.
62. 'My Early Life', *London Observer*, 2 November 1930, p. 8.
63. 'Some Recent Biographies', *The Intercollegian*, December 1930, p. 193.
64. 'Mr. Churchill's Career', *Sydney Morning Herald*, Australia, 6 December 1930, p. 10.
65. Bruce Catton, 'Mr. Winston Churchill', *Press of Atlantic City*, New Jersey, 6 December 1930, p. 17.
66. *New York World*, New York, 7 December 1930.
67. 'Books of the Day. Winston Churchill', *Australasian*, Melbourne, Australia, 13 December 1930, p. 7.
68. 'A Roving Commission', *Indianapolis News*, 13 December 1930, p. 5.
69. 'Mr. Churchill's Memories', *Poverty Bay Herald*, New Zealand, 13 December 1930, p. 12.
70. 'Winston Churchill Adventures to the Adventurous', *Evening Star*, New Zealand, 16 December 1930, p. 13.

71. Josephine Boylan, 'Churchill Recounts the Adventures of 'A Roving Commission', *St. Louis Globe-Democrat*, St. Louis Missouri, 20 December 1930, p. 20.
72. *Age*, Melbourne, Australia, 20 December 1930, p. 6.
73. Henry M. Hyde, 'The Early Life of Winston Churchill By Himself', *Evening Sun*, Baltimore, MD, 20 December 1930, p. 8.
74. J. W. T. Mason, 'Churchill's Road to Fame', *Saturday Review of Literature*, 20 December 1930, p. 469.
75. Josephine Boylan, 'Churchill Recounts the Adventures of "A Roving Commission"', St. *Louis Globe-Democrat*, St. Louis, MO, USA, 20 December 1930, p. 20.
76. Henry E. Armstrong, 'Mr. Winston Churchill on Miseducation', *Nature*, 27 December 1930, pp. 983–5.
77. 'Some Recent Biographies', *The Bookman*, December 1930, p. 193.
78. *The Book Review Digest*, Books of 1930, New York, 1931, pp. 198–9.
79. *The Booklist*, Vol. 27, No. 3, January 1931, pp. 203–4.
80. 'Mr. Churchill. Early life Narrated', *Queensland Times*, Ipswich, Australia, 1 January 1931, p. 6.
81. 'Life of Dash and Daring. Mr. W. Churchill's Career', *Advocate*, Burnie, Tasmania, 2 January 1931, p. 7.
82. 'Winston Churchill A Romantic Personality', *Kalgoorlie Miner*, Western Australia, 7 January 1931, p. 1.
84. A.M. Pooley, 'Winston's Early Life', *Evening News*, London, 8 January 1931, p. 2.
85. *The National Review*, London, January 1931, Vol. 95, p. 145.
86. 'The Age of International Innocence', *The Outlook*, 14 January 1931, p. 69.
87. 'The Man of the Month, Winston Spencer Churchill', *Atlantic*, Vol. 17, January 1931, pp. 10–12.
88. 'Recent Publications', *The Cavalry Journal*, Vol. 21, 1931, pp. 161–2.
89. 'Adventures of Winston Churchill', *Catholic Advocate*, Brisbane, Australia, 8 January 1931, p. 10.
90. 'Three Cheers For Churchill. The Story of a Statesman Who Has Had a Hand in Everything', *Pittsburgh Press*, Pittsburgh, 18 January 1931, p. 86.
91. 'A Roving Commission', *Arizona Daily Star*, 25 January 1931, p. 17.

92. *Wisconsin Library Bulletin*, Vol. 27, issue 2, February 1931, p. 59.
93. 'A Roving Commission', *The Nation*, Vol. 132, 1 February 1931, p. 194.
94. 'The Library Corner', *Ontario Intelligencer*, Canada, 3 February 1931, p. 3.
95. 'The Exciting Career of Mr. Winston Churchill', *Long Beach Sun*, California, 16 February 1931, p. 12.
96. 'For your Consideration', *Scientific American*, Vol. CXLIV, February 1931, p. 147.
97. *Book Review Digest*, Books of 1930, New York, The H. W. Wilson Company, 1931, pp. 198–9.
98. *Wilson Library Bulletin*, March 1931, Vol. 5, p. 277.
99. Charles H. Barker, 'Mr. Churchill at School', *Education Outlook*, Vol. VIII, March 1931, p. 80.
100. Wickham Steed, 'Winston Churchill: "Gentleman Adventurer"', *Current History*, Vol. 33, March 1931, pp. 848–53.
101. L.H. Watson, 'Churchill, Winston S. – A Roving Commission; My Early life. 1930', *Military Review*, Vol. 10, 31 March 1931, pp. 43–4.
102. *Pittsburgh Sun-Telegraph*, Pittsburgh, PA, 15 March 1931, p. 50.
103. *Ames Daily Tribune*, Ames, Iowa, 21 March 1931, p. 6.
104. 'Memory of Omdurman', *Boston Guardian*, Boston, MA, USA, 28 March 1931, p. 12.
105. 'Winston Spencer Churchill: My Early Life: A Roving Commission', *Nation*, Vol. 132, 1931, p. 194.
106. Witt Bowdan, *The Annals of the American Academy of Political and Social Science*, Vol. 154, March 1931, pp. 189–90.
107. 'A Roving Commission', *Daily Californian*, Friday, 19 June 1931, p. 8.
108. T.H. Thomas, 'Review', *Journal of Modern History*, Vol. 3 No. 3, September 1931, pp. 511–12.
109. *Enid Morning News*, Enid, CA, USA, 27 September 1931, p. 4.
110. 'Mr. Churchill's Advice to Young Authors', *Traralgon Record*, Victoria, Australia, 19 May 1932, p. 4.
111. 'Winston Churchill's Literary Fame—Statesman Turned Historian', *Advertiser*, Adelaide, Australia, 11 March 1933, p. 9.
112. 'A Reader's List', *New Republic*, 27 December 1939, p. 296.
113. 'Mr. Churchill's Story of His Early Life', *New York Times*, New York, 1 August 1941, p. 2.

114. 'Weekly Book Review' from *Omnibook Magazine*, in *Durand Gazette*, Durand, IL, USA, 4 September 1941, p. 6.
115. 'Soldier, Writer, Statesman', *Infantry Journal*, Vol. 49, November 1941, pp. 90–91.
116. Siriol Hugh-Jones, 'Sir Winston is Irresistible', *Tatler*, London, February 3, 1960, p. 212.
117. Austin M. Fox, 'Maggie and Winston', *Courier Express*, Buffalo, 9 June 1982, p. 10.
118. Max Hasting, 'Moved to Tears', *Sunday Telegraph*, 8 June 2003, p. 45.
119. Michael Richards, 'Book Review', *The Finest Hour*, 1 October 2008, p. x.
120. Martyn Drakard, 'BOOK REVIEW: Churchill's Early Years', *Observer*, Uganda, 2 December 2009.
121. *Wilson Quarterly*, Vol. 18, Winter 1994, p. 45.
122. *Week-End Review of Politics, Books, the Theatre, Art and Music*, 1930.
123. *New Statesman and Nation*, 1958, Vol. 55, p. 838.
124. D. W. Brogan, *Spectator*, 4 July 1958, Vol. 201, p. 38.
125. Charles R. Sullivan, 'The Disenchanted Whiggism of Winston Churchill's "My Early Life"', *Journal of Historical Biography*, Vol. 7, Spring 2010, pp. 1–29.
126. Robert McCrum, *Guardian*, London, 21 November 2016.
127. Richard M. Langworth and Henry Fearon, '"A Sun that Never Sets": Churchill's Wonderful Autobiography, "My Early Life"', Churchill Project, 15 June 2018
    Churchill project https://winstonchurchill.hillsdale.edu/churchills-autobiography-my-early-life/.
128. 'My Early Life', *Sunday Telegraph*, London, 27 August 2000, p. 49.

APPENDIX 8

Chapter 6: Unrecorded Books and Other Media

This appendix is designed to provide a listing of those Churchill books, excerpts and other material related to *My Early Life* that are not listed in Cohen's *Bibliography*. This is not a full bibliography but, rather, a list that can be used by collectors or those interested in *My Early Life* to identify previously unrecorded issues. The entries are listed chronologically. Where there is an applicable Cohen category, a book is assigned a Cohen number with an asterisk (*). Where there is no applicable Cohen number, the item is assigned a sequential designation with the format 'Stiles B.x or Stiles C.x,' where 'Stiles' represents the author's designation' and the capital letter represents the category from Cohen's Bibliography.

Three proof copies of *My Early Life* have been found and examined. The first is a proof of the first edition, first printing; it is bound in plain grey-brown paper wrappers with no external printing on the front, back, or spine of the wrapper. It appears to be printed on thicker paper, as it bulks 1½" rather than the 1 1/8" for the published book. The text seems exactly as finally published, but the photograph of Sir Ian Hamilton is not present. The volume is signed 'Winston S. Churchill' in black ink on the half-title. A tipped-in note states that it was signed in London on 28 November 1955. The second proof is the same as the one described above but is not signed.

The third proof is very unusual in that it contains sheets of the first edition, third impression, printed in November 1930, not October 1930. This proof is printed on thick paper just as the first proof described. These pages are uncut and sewn into very rudimentary wrappers. The wrappers are light tan (distinct from the two described above) and have no printing on front, back, or spine. None of the illustrations from the printed book have been inserted. It is unclear why this proof was generated. By the time of the printing of this proof copy, both earlier printings of the book were widely available in bookshops and libraries.

i. English Language Editions

As noted previously, there are twenty-two categories of *My Early Life* editions in Cohen Section A, and when reprints and other versions are included, the number rises to ninety-six. Therefore, only new editions or versions are listed here.

A91.1.c* *My Early Life*, London, Thornton Butterworth, 1930, 1st Ed., 1st printing, second state variant. First states were bound in both a coarse and a smooth plum-coloured cloth; they have the title stamped on the front cover in either three or five lines; and they contain a list of eleven Churchill titles in the boxed list of 'Works by the same Author' on the half-title verso. Second state copies are distinguished by the addition of 'THE WORLD CRISIS: 1911–1914' to the boxed list of works on the half-title verso, making twelve titles. In his excellent bibliography of Churchill's works, Ronald Cohen states: '… most, perhaps even all, copies of the second state will be found in binding cases in which the front cover is stamped in 5, rather than 3, lines…' This unrecorded variant is a first printing, second state copy in the coarse cloth binding with three lines on the front cover.

A91.s.1 *My Early Life*, London, The Times Book Club and Thornton Butterworth, 1930, bound in unornamented smooth burgundy cloth with plain gold spine lettering. (The cloth material has similarities to the cloth binding of The Times Book Club's *Lord Randolph Churchill*.) There is a small blue rectangular Times Book Club sticker on the rear fixed endpaper. The sticker also has the logo of *The Times* and the address 42 Wigmore Street, London, W1. This book is mentioned in Langworth (p. 132). See Figure 2 Chapter 6.

A91.s.2 <u>My Early Life</u>, London and Toronto, Thornton Butterworth Ltd, British first state with eleven titles on half-title verso and five-line Title, 1930, Canadian first, Jacket imprinted 'Thomas Nelson and Sons, LTD', stamped price $4.50, Canadian firsts can only be distinguished by the presence of the Thomas Nelson dust jacket. The Canadian dust jackets are mentioned by Langworth (p. 133). See Figure 1 Chapter 6.

A91.s.3 <u>My Early Life</u>, London, Royal National Institute for the Blind, 1933, five volumes of interpoint braille, no additional information known.

Cohen lists A91.4 as the sole printing of the Swedish School Edition; however, three more have been located, as listed below:

    A91.4.b* <u>My Early Life</u> (Swedish School Edition), Förkortad Skolupplaga, Stockholm, Albert Bonniers Forlag, 1944, 2nd printing (tan cover), softcover (the first edition (A91.4) was red softcover.

    A91.4.c* <u>My Early Life</u> (Swedish School Edition), Förkortad Skolupplaga, Stockholm, Albert Bonniers Forlag, 1946, 3rd printing, in English, tan softcover.

    A91.4.d* <u>My Early Life </u>(Swedish School Edition), Förkortad Skolupplaga, Stockholm, Albert Bonniers Forlag, 1950, 4th printing (light tan cover), softcover.

A91.6.c* <u>My Early Life</u>, London, Macmillan & Co. Ltd., 1943, with dustjacket. Affixed to the front pastedown is an elaborate printed grey plate noting that the book is a gift from British industrialist Alexander Duckham to customers in 1943. The presentation reads 'Written when he certainly had no conception of becoming 'Pater Patrice' I feel that Mr. Churchill's biography up to 1901 will be an appropriate and acceptable token of goodwill to our customers on our 44th birthday anniversary, November 1943.' The plate is facsimile signed 'Alexander Duckham.' Duckham's was the second-largest independent UK blenders of oil after Castrol. This is technically not a separate printing by the publisher, but many copies were created, as distinguishable by the unique book plate. The item would seem to be of interest to collectors so is included here.

A91.s.4 <u>A Roving Commission/My Early Life</u>, unknown, pirated ed., very cheaply made, 1940, this appears to be a pirated edition of the Dorothy

Thompson Introduction 2nd American Scribner edition, Cohen A91.5. The book dimensions are 8' x 5¼' x 7/8', which are much smaller than any of the variants of this impression. The pages are equally small at 7¾' x 5'. There is no half-title or mention of WSC's other books as mentioned on the verso of the half-title in Scribner's MEL. The title page is smaller than Scribner's and similar in design except no mention is made of Scribner or New York, but it has the date (1940). The verso of the title page is completely different and appears to be typewriter-printed rather than created by the usual press run printing.

The pagination is different, and, of interest, the last page of the Thompson *Introduction* does not have the date – which is present in the Scribner publication. The hardback binding is blue cloth. The spine has linear decorations top and bottom, not seen in the Scribner printings. The title and author on the spine are debossed, unlike that on the Scribner's printings. The paper is extremely cheap and is well toned. There are no other distinguishing markings anywhere in the book. None of the photographs are present.

A91.s.5 My Early Life, Centenary First Edition, London, The Diner's Club, London, 1974, 1st Ed. thus.

Cohen lists A91.16.a and A91.16.b, 1977 and 1979, respectively. Printings of the Hudson River editions. There are two more:

    A91.16.c* My Early Life, Hudson River Editions, New York, Scribner's, 1980, third printing.
    A91.16.d* My Early Life, Hudson River Edition, New York, Scribner's/McMillan, 1988, 4th printing.

A91.s.6 My Early Life, London, The Folio Society, 1st Printing, 2007, in slipcase.

A91.s.7 My Early Life, London, The Folio Society, 2nd Printing, 2008, in slipcase.

A91.s.8 A Roving Commission: My Early Life, Scholar Select, Sacramento, CA, Andesite Press, 2015, softcover.

A91.s.9 <u>A Roving Commission: My Early Life</u>, Scholar Select, Sacramento, CA., Franklin Classics, 2018, hardcover.

A91.s.10 <u>My Early Life: A Roving Commission</u>, South Bend, Indiana, St. Augustine's Press, 2024, James W. Muller, editor; two issues published, a 100-copy limited hand-bound leather edition by Felton Bookbinding Ltd. In full goatskin with the spine featuring raised, gilt decorated bands framed by gilt rules, twin spine labels, the boards featuring beveled edges, gilt ruled borders and Churchill's gilt-stamped facsimile signature on the front cover. A limitation page is hand-numbered and signed by the editor. Each copy housed in a matching cloth slipcase with Churchill's gilt-stamped facsimile signature on the front cover. There is also a standard cloth hardback edition in dust jacket. Neither issue has been seen at the time of this writing. Both issues also contain Churchill's *The Dream*.

ii. Translated Editions

This section provides a list of non–English language versions of *My Early Life*. Previously, there were noted to be forty-two non-English entries in Cohen[1], and Langworth[2] added seven more versions. This updated list provides a total of 111 versions. Entries are listed in chronological order, and the language of each book is noted within each description. Descriptive information on each book deemed by the author to be significant has been provided.

De Unge Aar (*My Early Life*), Copenhagen, Steen Hasselbalchs, 1931, 1st Danish ed., brown leather or leatherette binding, with pattern in brown and black and tan floral-like pattern on front and rear boards; spine has, starting at top, a rib with black line under it followed by six additional ribs and terminating at the bottom with two black lines; under the second rib in gold lettering is 'WINSTON S. / CHURCHILL', between ribs 5 and 6 in gold lettering is 'DE / UNGE AAR'; top edge brown patterned colour; book is in green card slip-case.

De Unge Aar (*My Early Life*), Copenhagen, Steen Hasselbalchs, 1931, 1st Danish ed., cream coloured wrappers; front cover in brown ink top to bottom: Churchill Coat of Arms, 'Winston S. Churchill' in script, title in bold block letters, 3 'wavy' lines, publisher's name, spine top to bottom in brown ink Churchill coat of arms, 'Winston S. Churchill' in script, 1 'wavy' line, bold letters 'DE / UNGE / AR', and publisher's logo.

Weltabenteur Im Dienst (*My Early Life*), Leipzig, Paul List Verlag, 1931, 1st German ed., 1st imp., light brown boards, front cover in large gold lettering 'CHURCHILL', under that in much smaller letters 'Weltabenteur Im Dienst'; spine light tan and brown pattern with 2 black boxes separated by gold bar, upper box with gold on black 'WINSTON S. / CHURCHILL'; lower box, title in gold on black, at bottom publisher's emblem.

Min Ungdom (*My Early Life*), Stockholm, P.A. Norstedt, 1931, 1st ed. Swedish, hardcover, tan-orange spine with small brown box near top with title and author in gold letters, grey brownish green mottled pattern front and rear boards, front board with publisher's imprint in gold, top edge of pages with tan-orange colour similar to spine.

Min Ungdom (*My Early Life*), Stockholm, P.A. Norstedt, 1931, 1st ed. Swedish, hardcover, bound in green half leather with paisley in green, red, dark green and black colours front and back boards. (Known that publisher offered leather options; Unknown whether this is one of the options or was privately bound).

Min Ungdom (*My Early Life*), Stockholm, P.A. Norstedt, 1931, 1st ed. Swedish, hardcover, bound in half tan leather (patterned) with front and back boards with swirling patterned cloth in tan, orange, blue and brown, with all page edges in same coloured pattern as is the front and rear free and fixed end papers. (Known that publisher offered leather options; unknown whether this is one of the options or was privately bound).

Min Ungdom (*My Early Life*), P.A. Norstedt & Soners Forlag, Stockholm. 1931, 1st Swedish ed., translator, Beatrice Constredt, cream card wrappers, front cover top to bottom, in red ink 'Winston / Churchill, Min / Ungdom'; in black ink a single wavy line under which is 'P. A. Norstedt & / Soners Forlag / Stockholm'; spine tan in black ink top to bottom doublet lines / 'Winston' / 'Churchill' / doublet line; back cover in red and black ink advertising for non-Churchill books.

Memorie 1874-1903 (*My Early Life*), Milan, Italy, Fratelli Treves, 1935, 1st Italian ed., card wraps, front cover with large photograph of WSC in full dress as Lt. in 4th Hussars, above image in black ink 'WINSTON CHURCHILL', and under that in red ink 'MEMORIE', bottom left in white ink 'TREVES', spine off-white, top to bottom all in black ink, single line, CHURCHILL / MEMORIE, publisher's imprint, single line; back cover off-white with code, LL L. 20 –.

Memorie 1874-1903 (*My Early Life*), Milan, Italy, Fratelli Treves, Milan, 1935, 1st Italian ed., blue hardback, front board large gold box near all four edges with gold flying bird in centre, top edge blue, side and bottom edges uncut, spine blue with top to bottom all in gold, single line, 'CHURCHILL, MEMORIE', bottom 'Fratelli / TREVES / Editori' / single line; back board all blue.

Ungdom (*My Early Life*), Oslo, Gyldendal Norsk Forlag, 1935, 1st Norwegian ed., hardback, cloth light blue, front debossed rectangle around edges, gold publisher's imprint, upper centre; spine top to bottom, 3 gold horizontal lines, blue box surrounded by gold lines, within box in gold 'WINSTON / S. CHURCHILL', small gold line, 'UNGDOM', at bottom 4 gold lines; unknown if issued with dust jacket.

Ungdom (*My Early Life*), Norway, Gyldendal, 1935, 1st Norwegian ed., E. Krohn-Hansen, translator, wrappers, front white border on two sides and top, large image of young WSC (1900, J. E. Purdy, Boston, 3, photographed while on lecture tour in America) upper 2/3 of front, below which is a black box containing in white letters 'WINSTON S. CHURCHILL / UNGDOM / GYLDENDAL NORSK FORLAG'; spine white with black lettering top to bottom, 'WINSTON S. / CHURCHILL, UNGDOM, GYLDENDAL'.

Mes Aventures De Jeunesse (*My Early Life*), Paris, Payot, 1937, 1st French ed., bound in bright red cloth with printed picture of WSC in South African bush hat attached on front board in debossed rectangle; spine red cloth with gold lettering top to bottom 'Churchill, Mes aventures / de Jeunesse'. This hardbound issue may have been privately bound and no documentation is available that it was routinely offered by the publisher.

Mes Aventures De Jeunesse (*My Early Life*), Paris, Payot, 1937, 1st French ed. with pale green illustrated wrappers; front board, large thin line rectangle surrounding most of text, in black ink top to bottom, in small letters the following: 'COLLECTION D'ÉTUDES, DE DOCUMENTS ET DE TÉMOIGNAGES / POUR SERVIR A / L'HISTOIR DE NOTRE TEMPS', long thin line / 'WINSTON S. CHURCHILL', small thin line, 'MES AVENTURES / DE JEUNESSE', image of WSC in South African bush hat, under the image, 'Avec huit cartes et deux croquis dans le texte', under that 'Payot, Paris'; spine, top to bottom, in black lettering, long thin line 'WINSTON / S. CHURCHILL', long thin line, 'MES AVENTURES / DE JEUNESSE', long thin line, brown and gold sticker with '45 fr. / PAYOT / PARIS', long thin line, 'PAYOT / PARIS', at bottom '1937'; rear cover multiple written advertisements.

Sotavanki Winston Churchill in Muistelmein Mukaan, (Prisoner of War Winston Churchill in Memories), Helsinki, Kustannusosakeyhtio Otava, 1938, large excerpt from *MEL* of Boer War events, 1st Finnish ed. hardback, 106 pp., front cover with colour drawing of Churchill behind wire fence with armed guard watching over him, title in orange, subtitle in white and publisher in orange; spine, white background with blue decorative panel within which is 'Betty Rauanhwimo: Sotavanki' in blue; back list of all books in this series in blue with publisher's information at bottom.

Minha Mocidade (*My Early Life*), Rio de Janeiro, Editora Nord-Sul, 1941, 1st Brazilian ed. (Portuguese), wrappers, front cover top ¼ orange background with white lettering 'Winston S. Churchill / MINHA MOCIDADE'; lower two-thirds with image of WSC with bow tie and hat *c*. 1940; spine white background top in orange lettering 'Winston / Churchill', vertical lettering in black 'MINHA MOCIDADE', at bottom, in brown lettering 'EDIRA NORD-SUL', in black lettering '20$000'; back cover in orange and black lettering multiple advertisements.

Mi Primera Juventud (*My Early Life*), Buenos Aries, +Editorial Claridad, 1941, 1st Argentinian ed. (Spanish), white card wrappers, front page top to bottom, in black letters 'Winston Churchill', in rust letters 'MI

/ PRIMERA / JUVENTUD', printer's logo, bottom in black letters 'EDITORIAL / CLARIDAD / BUENOS AIRES'; spine, rust background, top to bottom, two white lines (upper larger), in black lettering 'WINSTON / CHURCHILL', white curved design, in black letters 'MI / PRIMERA / JUVENTUD', white line across black box, within black box a rust coloured publisher's logo, white line across box, under box on rust background in black letters 'EDITORIAL/ CLARIDAD / BUENOS AIRES', two white lines under that; back wrappers white with publisher's logo; dust jacket pale blue, top to bottom, in rust lettering 'MI / PRIMERA / JUVENTUD', under that black, red and white lines then a dark blue box within it in white lettering 'WINSTON / CHURCHILL' then white, red and black lines; dust jacket spine pale blue background, top to bottom, two red lines (upper thicker) then in black letters 'WINSTON / CHURCHILL', then in red letters 'MI / PRIMA JUVENTUD', then blue, red and white line above a dark blue box containing the publisher's logo, then a white, red and blue line terminating the dark blue box, then in black lettering 'EDITORIAL / CLARIDAD / BUENOS AIRES' and then two red lines (lower thicker).

Mi Primera Juventud (*My Early Life*), Montevideo, +Editorial Claridad, 1941, 1st Uruguay ed. (Spanish), front wrappers top 2/3 B/W photograph of WSC sitting at desk with cigar in right hand and looking to the left directly at viewer, at bottom of photograph in white lettering 'Winston Churchill', under that on red background a small white horizontal line broken in centre in black lettering 'MI' (start of title), under that in black lettering 'PRIMERA JUVENTUD', under that in black script 'Autobiografia del / gran Estadista Ingle's', to the left the publisher's boxed logo, bottom wavy white line above black base; spine, white background, thick then thin line near top, under that in black 'WINSTON / CHURCHILL', then in black 'MI / Primera / Juventud', then ¾ down the spine the publisher's logo, and at the bottom, 'Editorial / Claridad / Montevideo' then a thin, then thick black lines; back wrappers white background with orange/brown boxed publisher's logo; at bottom right is '$' and then a sticker with the number '15'.

SHACHARIT CHAYAI (*My Early Life*), Tel Aviv, Omanuith Co. Ltd., 1944, 1st Hebrew ed., hard back darkish mauve coloured (front and back); spine background same colour with vertical gold lettering in Hebrew 'Winston Churchill / My Early Life'; reddish-brown dust jacket with white and yellow lettering on front; jacket spine same reddish-brown background with white and yellow lettering 'Winston Churchill' and 'My Early Life' in Hebrew, back of dust jacket paragraph in Hebrew.

Bernskubrek og Æskuþrek (*My Early Life*), Reykjavik, Snaelandsútgáfan, 1944 (December 1), 1st Icelandic ed., Benedikt Tómasson, translator, hard cover dark red, front cover top to bottom 'WINSTON CHURCHILL' BERNSKUBREK / OG ÆSKUÞREK', spine top to bottom 'WINSTON / CHURCHILL', 'BERNSKUBREK / OG / ÆSKUÞREK, SNAELAND / 1944'; dust jacket, front dark blue background top to bottom, in white letters 'BERNSKUBREK / OG / ÆSKUÞREK', double white line, image of WSC in South Africa bush hat, on left of image top to bottom, 'BERNSKA', star device, 'SKÓLAAR', star device, 'HERÞJÓN – / USTA', star device, 'ÆVINTYRI / I AUSTUR- / LÖNDUM', star device, 'ORUSTAN I SÚDAN'; right side of image, top to bottom, in white lettering 'BLAÐA- / MAÐUR', star device, 'FANGI / HJÁ / BÚUM', star device, 'FLÓTTINN', star device, 'I BÚA- / STRÍÐINU', star device, 'ÞING- / MAÐUR; under image in white lettering 'I ÆVINTÝRALEIT', bottom of front jacket in white lettering 'Eftir Winston S. Churchill / forsætisrádherra Bretlands'; spine dust jacket, blue background in orange lettering top to bottom, 'WINSTON / CHURCHILL, BERNSKU- / BREK OG / ÆSKUÞREK, SNAELAND, 1944'; back of dust jacket, white background double-line box, inside top to bottom, picture of Churchill medallion from 1941, in black lettering Winston Churchill, 1874 – 30. Nov – 1944, paragraph in Icelandic about Churchill.

Bernskubrek og Æskuþrek (*My Early Life*), Reykjavik, Snaelandsútgáfan, 1944 (December 1), 1st Icelandic ed., Benedikt Tómasson, translator, hard cover medium brown, front board top to bottom 'WINSTON CHURCHILL, BERNSKUBREK / OG ÆSKUÞREK', spine top to bottom 'WINSTON / CHURCHILL, BERNSKUBREK / OG / ÆSKUÞREK, SNAELAND / 1944'; dust jacket, front dark blue background top to bottom, in white letters 'BERNSKUBREK / OG / ÆSKUÞREK', double white line image of WSC in South Africa bush hat, on left of image top to bottom, 'BERNSKA', star device, 'SKÓLAAR, STAR DEVICE, HERÞJON – / USTA', star device, 'ÆVINTYRI / I AUSTUR- / LÖNDUM', star device, 'ORUSTAN I SÚDAN'; right side of image, top to bottom, in white lettering 'BLAÐA- / MAÐUR', star device, 'FANGI / HJÁ / BÚUM', star device, 'FLÓTTINN', star device, 'I BÚA- / STRÍÐINU', star device, 'ÞING – / MAÐUR'; under image in white lettering 'I ÆVINTÝRALEIT', bottom of front jacket in white lettering 'Eftir Winston S. Churchill/ ÆVINTÝRALEIT Bretlands'; spine dust jacket blue background in orange lettering top to bottom, 'WINSTON / CHURCHILL, BERNSKU- / BREK OG / ÆSKUÞREK, SNAELAND, 1944'; back of dust jacket, white background double-line box, inside top to bottom, picture of Churchill medallion from 1941, in black lettering 'Winston Churchill, 1874 – 30. Nov – 1944', paragraph in Icelandic about Churchill; distinct binding colour from above. Unknown which binding was printed first.

Bernskubrek Og Æskuþrek (*My Early Life*), Reykjavik, Snaelandsútgáfan, 1944, 1st Icelandic ed., softcover, unknown design, no copies examined.

De Unge Aar (*My Early Life*), Copenhagen, Steen Hasselbalchs, 1945, 2nd Danish ed., bound in half brown leather with colourful patterned swirl design in brown, red, blue, and tan boards front and back, spine brown leather with seven ribs. Between the second and third rib in gold lettering 'WINSTON / S. CHURCHIL / DE UNGE AAR'.

De Unge Aar (*My Early Life*), Copenhagen, Steen Hasselbalchs, 1945, 2nd Danish ed., cream-coloured wrappers; front cover, top to bottom: in gold ink Churchill Coat of Arms, in brown ink 'Winston S. Churchill' in script, in bold brown block letters 'DE UNGE AAR', 3 'wavy' lines, in brown ink 'HASSELBALCH'; spine, top to bottom in gold ink Churchill coat of arms, in brown ink 'Winston S. Churchill' in script, 1 'wavy' line, bold brown letters 'DE / UNGE / AAR', publisher's logo; back cover in small brown letters at bottom 'FR BAGGESKGL, HOFBOGTRYKKRI, KOBENHAVN'.

Mine Unge År (*My Early Life*), Oslo, Gyldendal Norsk Forlag, 1945, 2nd Norwegian ed., bluish-green cloth hard cover, front board in gold publisher's imprint logo (debossed), spine top to bottom two gold lines, blue box with gold perimeter lines, inside box with gold lettering 'WINSTON S. / CHURCHILL', small gold line, 'MINE UNGE AR', 4 gold lines at the bottom.

Mine Unge År (*My Early Life*), Oslo, Gyldendal Norsk Forlag, 1945, 2nd Norwegian ed., one quarter red leather with tabs, marbled white, light blue and medium blue paper front and back; spine, 4 ribs, top and bottom with gilt decorative filigree, 4 fancy curved line decorations in gilt, between rib 1 and 2, gold lines top and bottom and between lines author and title in gilt. This binding thought to be offered by publisher.

Weltabenteur Im Dienst (*My Early Life*), Munich, Paul List Verlag, 1946, 2nd German ed., green cloth spine with debossed black and green angled pattern, dark cream boards, front cover printed in black top to bottom 'CHURCHILL., in smaller letters 'WELTABENTEURER IM DIENST'; spine two dark green boxes separated by off-white bar, upper box in gold lettering 'WINSTON S. / CHURCHILL', in lower box in gold lettering 'WELTABENTEUR / IM DIENST', unknown which binding is earlier (*infra vide*), both printed one year after the war and noted on verso of title page 'Published under Military Government information Control License No. US-E-139.'

Weltabenteur Im Dienst (*My Early Life*), Leipzig/Munich, Paul List Verlag, 1946, 2nd German ed., brown/tan pebbled leatherette binding (hardcover), front top to bottom in gold lettering 'CHURCHILL', smaller gold lettering 'WELTABENTEUER / IM DIENST'; spine debossed angled pattern in brown/black, brown box with gold lettering top to bottom 'WINSTON S. / CHURCHILL', thick yellow line, smaller gold lettering 'WELTABENTEUER / IM DIENST', at bottom publisher's imprint logo.

Memorie (*My Early Life*), Italy, Garzanti, 1946, 2nd Italian ed., tan card wrappers, front, top to bottom, in black lettering 'WINSTON CHURCHILL', in red lettering 'MEMORIE', in black lettering '(1874–1903)', in small lettering 'Con 3 carte, e 12 illustrazioni', publisher's logo in black, in red 'GARZANTI', spine top to bottom, black thin line, 'CHURCHILL', thin line, in red 'MEMORIE', at bottom thin black line, back cover LL in black Lire 300.—.

Qiu ji er zi zhuan- wo de zao nian sheng huo (*My Early Life*), Shanghai, Hua mei chu ban she, 1946, Chinese 1st ed., no copy examined.

Memorie 1874-1903 (*My Early Life*), Milan, Garzanti, 1947, 2nd Italian ed., 2nd printing, termed 6th edition on verso of title page, tan card wraps, front, top to bottom, in black lettering 'WINSTON CHURCHILL', in red lettering 'MEMORIE', in black lettering '(1874–1903)', in small black lettering 'Con 3 carte, e 12 illustrazioni', publisher's logo in black, in red, 'GARZANTI'; spine, top to bottom, black thin line, 'CHURCHILL', thin line, in red 'MEMORIE', at bottom thin black line, in red 'MEMORIE', thin black line; back cover LL is paste on label 'Prezzo Lire 500'.

Mijn Jonge Jaren (*My Early Life*), Amsterdam, Albert de Lang, Amsterdam, 1947, 1st Dutch ed., cream boards, front, title in black letters 'MIJN / JONGE- / JAREN'; spine, brick red cloth with black lettering top to bottom, 'Churchill' (italics font), 'MIN / JONGE / JAREN', at bottom script initials of publisher 'AdL'.

Memórias De Minha Juventude (*My Early Life*), Lisbon, Portugal, Editorial Século, 1947, 1st Portuguese ed., green wrappers, front, top to bottom in light green letters 'WINSTON S. CHURCHLL', top left cartoon image of Churchill with cigar, light red image of a book with title of this book in white letters 'MEMÓRIAS / DA MINHA / JUVENTUDE', left side near bottom of book the word 'STAR' followed by a star symbol, at bottom, in a lighter green box in pale green letters 'Editorial Século' in script; spine, top to bottom in pale green letters 'WINSTON / S. CHURCHILL, MEMÓRIAS DA MINHA JUVENTUDE', bottom, publisher's logo; back, long list of books advertised in a light green box with a white border centered in green background.

Min Ungdom (*My Early Life*), Stockholm, Albatross/Norstedts, 1948, 2nd Swedish ed., translator, Beatrice Cronstedt, smaller, cheaper series than 1st ed., hardcover with light tan boards, front cover debossed publisher's logo centered; spine tan with black box with gold line above and below, within box in gold letter 'WINSTON S. / CHURCHILL' small gold line, in gold lettering 'MIN / UNGDOM'; dust jacket buff, front large narrow box with light blue filler in black letters inside narrow box 'NORSTEDTS ALBATROSS' repeated around entire box, a slightly smaller white box just inside the large box, then a pale blue box inside that box, within this box at the top is an image of Churchill in 4th Hussars dress uniform, under that in black letters 'WINSTON S. CHURCHILL', under that 'MIN / UNGDOM', under that an albatross with white body and black wings, under that in black letters 'STOCKHOLM'; dust jacket, spine, top to bottom two pale blue bars upper larger than the lower, vertically arranged in black letters 'Winston S. Churchill' in italics font, in block font, 'MIN UNGDOM', 'Norstedts Albatross-Serie' in black letters followed by same two pale blue bars bottom larger than top, dust jacket back same concentric boxes, in large centre box is a description of the Albatross series.

De Unge Aar (*My Early Life*), Copenhagen, Steen Hasselbachs, 1948, 3rd Danish ed., binding half dark brown smooth leather with boards of paisley-line design in brown, cream and grey; spine 5 ribs, thin gold line at top between rib 1 and 2 in gold lettering 'Winston / S. Churchill, DE UNGE / AAR', thin gold line at bottom; marked as edition of 20,000; see following books with distinct binding; unknown if each of these were offered by Steen Hasselbachs or if they were privately bound; it is known that at least some half leather brown bindings were offered by publisher.

De Unge Aar (*My Early Life*), Copenhagen, Steen Hasselbalch, 1948, 3rd Danish ed., half dark brown pebbled leather with horizontal striped cloth front and back with various shades of brown alternated light tan; spine 3 thin gold lines under which in gold lettering is 'WINSTON / S. CHURCHILL, DE / UNGE AAR' with 4 gold lines at bottom; marked as an edition of 20,000; see book above; unknown if publisher offered this specific leather binding or if it was privately bound.

De Unge Aar(*My Early Life*), Copenhagen, Steen Hasselbalch, 1948, 3rd Danish ed., half dark green textured leather with vertically striped cloth front and back with wavy lines of white alternated light green; spine, 1 thin gold line near top under which are 4 prominent ribs each with solid gold line above and below, under top rib in gold lettering 'WINSTON S. / CHURCHILL', under the third rib in gold lettering, 'DE UNGE / AAR', 1 thin gold line at bottom; marked as an edition of 20,000; see books above, unknown if publisher offered this specific binding or if it was privately bound.

Mijn Jonge Jaren (*My Early Life*), Utrecht, Uitgeverij Het Spectrum, 1948, 2nd Dutch ed., card wrappers, front, black and grey striped background, front, image of Churchill smoking cigar ~1940s in a brownish gold oval frame with bulldog at top, attached to the bottom 2 sides of the frame are Union Jacks, under that a ribbon design in gold within which in black lettering is 'Winston S. Churchill' and under that 'Mijn jonge Jaren'; spine, gold background in white lettering vertically down 'Winston S. Churchill / Mijn Jonge Jaren', at very bottom in a black box publisher's logo in gold; back, within a buff box with blue inner rectangle near periphery, within box in black lettering several paragraphs in Dutch about Churchill, at bottom is publisher's logo in blue.

De Unge Aar (*My Early Life*), Copenhagen, Steen Hasselbalch, 1949, 4th Danish ed., fine half black pebbled leather with black, blue, cream and red paisley boards front and back, spine with 4 ribs, between 1st and 2nd rib in gold lettering 'WINSTON / S. CHURCHILL, DE UNGE / AAR'; cream dust jacket, on front top to bottom: Churchill crest in gold, 'Winston S. Churchill' in cursive, in bold brown block printing 'DE UNGE AAR', 3 wavy brown lines, in brown letters 'HASSELBALCH' at bottom; spine dust jacket, top to bottom Churchill crest in gold, in brown cursive lettering 'Winston S. Churchill', one wavy brown line, in brown block lettering 'DE / UNGE / AAR', at bottom in brown lettering, initial 'SH' for publisher; back, advertising for other books of the publisher.

Waga Hansei (*My Half Life*), Osaka, Seikosha, 1950, 1st Japanese ed., cloth hardback, dark black, blue solid front and back with no markings, spine same colour with top to bottom in gold printing, two solid horizontal lines, under that, 'MY EARLY / LIFE', under that a single horizontal line, under that 'W. CHURCHILL', under that two horizontal lines and at the bottom, 'SEIKOSIA'. Pale green cardboard slip-case, spine green with black box near the top with Japanese characters in off-white, under the box vertically aligned Japanese characters in two vertical rows, front of slip-case all green background with letters in white, spelling 'MY / EARLY / LIFE' covering entire page, superimposed is a script facsimile Churchill signature 'Winston S. Churchill' running horizontally but angling upwards, back of slip-case with same green and 'MY / EARLY / LIFE' covering entire page and at the bottom of page in a box made of black printing 'HOIKUSIA'.

Mijn Jonge Jaren (*My Early Life*), Utrecht, Het Spectrum, 1950, 2nd Dutch ed., no copy examined.

Weltabenteur Im Dienst (*My Early Life*), Homburg, Rowohlt, (No. 36 in a series of biographies), 1951, 3rd German ed., 1st printing of 50,000, yellow card front and back with orangish cloth spine, front top to bottom: on bright yellow background in black lettering 'WINSTON S. / CHURCHILL', a double map of Africa (blue and black) with a pencil lying point up on the map, above the map in red script 'Weltabenteur / im dienst', on left of map, 3 vertical sets of letters 'ro / ro / ro', bottom right initials 'SP'; spine, on orange cloth top to bottom in black lettering 36, then author and title vertically placed 'WINSTON S. CHURCHILL, WELTABENTEUR', at bottom vertical 'ro / ro / ro'; back, compass symbol.

Maisha YA Winston S. Churchill, Hajinah B. Mohamed, translator, London, Macmillan and Co., 1952, 1st ed., text in Swahili. This is a biography using sections from *My Early Life*, buff-coloured wrappers, front buff background with blue design border, top to bottom in blue lettering 'MAISHA YA, WINSTON S. CHURCHILL', drawing of Churchill with bow tie, H. B. Mohamed; back at bottom 'Mohamed: Winston S. Churchill' (Swahili) / thin line / 'TOUGH MANILA COVER'.

Meine Frühen Jahre (*My Early Life*), Hamburg, Hanseatische Druckanstalt GmbH, 1953, from a series 'Nobel-Preis Fur Literatur' in German, only known edition, green hardback, front borders with gold linear and swirl design, centred is top to bottom, gold crown, in gold lettering 'NOBEL PREIS, 1951–1953, LAGERKVIST, MAURIAC, CHURCHILL'; spine, same linear and curved gold design on borders of spine, top to bottom, 'NOBEL, PREIS FUR, LITERATUR', gold crown, LAGERKVIEST, Barabbas, MAURIAC, Einode der Liebe, CHURCHILL, Meine frühen jahre', at bottom publisher logo, '1951–1953'; in unmarked buff slip-case. (Although this could be a Cohen B item, because of the completeness of the *My Early Life*, the decision was made to place it here.)

Min Ungdom (*My Early Life*), Stockholm, Norstedts, 1953, marked 5th Swedish ed., 18,000 printed, translator, Beatrice Cronstedt, tan smooth boards, front board with black small horse and rider; spine, black box with gold border, inside box in gold lettering 'Winston S. / Churchill', small gold line, in gold lettering 'MIN / UNGDOM'; light green grey dust jacket, front, from top to bottom, in white lettering 'Winston S. Churchill' in italics font, in black ink, 'MIN / UNGDOM', black horse and rider, in black lettering, 'Norstedts'; spine top to bottom, three black lines, white background box, in box in black lettering 'Winston S. / Churchill', small black line, 'MIN, UNG- / DOM', 15 black lines to bottom; dust jacket, back contains informative paragraph on Churchill, *My Early Life* and the Nobel Prize.

Min Ungdom (*My Early Life*), Stockholm, Norstedts, 1953, 6th Swedish ed., 23,000 printed, translator, Beatrice Cronstedt, tan smooth boards, front board with black small horse and rider; spine, black box with gold border, inside box in gold lettering 'Winston S. / Churchill', small gold line, in gold lettering 'MIN / UNGDOM'; presumed to have had the same dust jacket as above, but none examined.

Min Ungdom (*My Early Life*), Stockholm, Norstedts, 1953, marked 6th Swedish ed., 23,000 (printed) translator, Beatrice Cronstedt, greenish grey wrappers, front, from top to bottom, in white lettering 'Winston S. Churchill' in italics font, in black ink, 'MIN / UNGDOM', black horse and rider, in black lettering, 'Norstedts'; spine top to bottom, 3 black lines, white background box, in box in black lettering 'Winston S. / Churchill', small black line, 'MIN, UNG- / DOM', 15 black lines to bottom; dust jacket, back contains informative paragraph on Churchill, *My Early Life* and the Nobel Prize.

Min Ungdom (*My Early Life*), Stockholm, Norstedts, 1953, marked 7th Swedish ed., 26,000 (printed), translator, Beatrice Cronstedt, pale blue boards, front and back boards plain; spine, top with green box with gold lines top and bottom, in gold lettering 'W.S. CHURCHILL', short gold line, 'MIN UNGDOM', bottom long gold line; no dust jacket, if one exists, has been examined.

Weltabenteur Im Dienst (*My Early Life*), Hamburg, Rowohlt, May 1954, 3rd German ed. 3rd printing of 25,000, yellow card front and back with orangish cloth spine, front top to bottom on bright yellow background in black lettering 'WINSTON S. / CHURCHILL', a double map of Africa (blue and black) with a pencil lying point up on the map, above the map in red script 'Weltabenteur / im dienst', on left of map 3 vertical sets of letters 'ro / ro / ro', bottom right initials 'SP'; spine on orange cloth top to bottom in black lettering '36', then author and title vertically placed 'WINSTON S. CHURCHILL, WELTABENTEUR', at bottom vertical 'ro / ro / ro'; back, compass symbol.

Nuoruuteni (My Early Life), Helsinki, Kustannuosakeyhtio Otava, 1954, 1st Finnish ed., 1st imp., red cloth boards, front and back boards plain; spine, black box near top with upper and lower gold lines, in box in gold lettering 'WINSTON S. / CHURCHILL', small gold dot, in gold lettering 'NUORUUTENI'; dust jacket, front left side 1.5' red background, right side photograph of Churchill in South African bush hat, ¾ down the front in white lettering 'Winston A. Churchill', 'NUORUUTENI, OTAVA'; spine, all red with black lettering vertically placed 'Winston S. Churchill', small black dot, 'NUORUUTENI'; back, in black lettering description of Churchill, *My Early Life* and the Nobel Prize.

Nuoruuteni (*My Early Life*), Helsinki, Kustannuosakeyhtio Otava, 1954, 1st Finnish wrappers ed., 1st imp., card wrapper, front left side 1.5' red background, right side photograph of Churchill in South African bush hat, ¾ down the front in white lettering 'Winston A. Churchill', 'NUORUUTENI, OTAVA'; spine, all red with black lettering vertically placed 'Winston S. Churchill', small black dot, 'NUORUUTENI'; back, in black lettering description of Churchill, *My Early Life* and the Nobel Prize.

Min Ungdom (*My Early Life*), Stockholm, Vingforlaget, 1955, Swedish, paperback ed., cover black background, front top to bottom, in white lettering 'Winston S. / Churchill', in red lettering 'Min/ ungdom', at bottom left in white lettering 'Vingforlaget'; spine on black background top to bottom in white lettering 'Winston / S. Churchill', 'MIN / UNGDOM'; large buff vertical box, within box top to bottom in red lettering 'Winston S. Churchill', in red lettering 'MIN UNGDOM', large paragraphs on Churchill and the Nobel Prize.

Min Ungdom (*My Early Life*), Stockholm, Vingforlaget, 1955, 5th Swedish ed., translator, Beatrice Cronstedt, blue/white boards with white geometric designs front and back, white buff spine, top to bottom all in blue print, wavy line, 'WINSTON / S. CHURCHILL', 'MIN / UNGDOM', 4 wavy lines equally spaced down the spine; dark blue dust jacket, front top to bottom, in white lettering 'Winston S. / Churchill', in red lettering 'Min / ungdom', lower left, in white lettering 'Vingforlaget'; spine, top to bottom, in white lettering 'Winston / S. Churchill', 'MIN / UNGDOM'; back of dust jacket, large vertical white buff vertical rectangle with large paragraphs about Churchill and the Nobel Prize.

Min Ungdom (*My Early Life*), Stockholm, Vingforlaget, 1955, 5th Swedish ed., pale blue boards front and back plain, white buff spine, top to bottom all in blue print, wavy line, 'WINSTON / S. CHURCHILL', 'MIN / UNGDOM', 4 wavy lines equally spaced down the spine, distinct from above; likely had the same dust jacket as above, but none examined.

Ungdom (*My Early Life*), Oslo, Gyldenal Norsk Forlog, 1956, 3rd Norwegian ed., hardback tan, buff and white cloth and paper, front and back with multiple concentric geometric designs and large diamond in the middle; spine buff and top to bottom small black box bordered top and bottom with gold wreathing, in box in gold lettering 'WINSTON S. / CHURCHILL', 3 gold boxes with black line through the middle, lower black box similar to one above with 'UNGDOM' in gold lettering; dust jacket, front top ¾ with Union Jack background with image of a young Churchill, a blue line separates the Union Jack from a buff box enclosing in black lettering 'WINSTON S. CHURCHILL', in red lettering 'UNGDOM', wavy dark grey line above pale blue background and in white lettering 'GYLDENDAL NORSE FORLAG'; spine, top and bottom pale blue bars, on white background top to bottom in black ink 'WINSTON S. / CHURCHILL', in red lettering 'UNGDOM', at bottom publisher's logo; back dust jacket, full page of publisher's other books.

De Unge Aar (*My Early Life*), Copenhagen, Steen Hasselbalchs Forlag, 1956, 5th Danish ed., brown leatherette boards, front board gold geometric design, spine, top to bottom, gold line, in gold lettering 'WINSTON S. / CHURCHILL', 'DE UNGE / AAR', gold line at bottom, in red card slipcase.

De Unge Aar (*My Early Life*), Copenhagen, Steen Hasselbalch Forlag, 1956, 5th Danish ed., 30,000 printed, yellow wrappers, front top to bottom, large photograph of Churchill on horseback in India ,with white border, in black lettering beneath 'Winston S. Churchill', in red lettering 'DE UNGE AAR', at bottom in black lettering 'HASSELBALCH'; spine, top to bottom in black ink 'Winston S. / Churchill', in red lettering 'DE / UNGE/ AAR', at bottom publisher's logo; back, at bottom in small black lettering 'DYVA & JEPPSENS BOGTRYKKEH! A/3, KGL. HOFLEVERANDOR KOBENHAVN K'.

Mes Jeunes Années (*My Early Life*), France, Club Français du Livre, 1960, 2nd French ed., 12,750 issued, plain red boards front and back; spine black leatherette with 6 debossed bars between bar 1 and 2 in gold lettering 'Sir Winston / Churchill', between bar 2 and 3 in gold lettering 'Mes jeunes / années', between bar 5 and 6 is a debossed circle with a gold logo of publisher, red ribbon marker; no dust jacket issued.

Gli Anni Della Mia Giovinezza (*My Early Life*), Italy, Garzanti, 1961, 3rd Italian ed., medium blue cloth hardback, front board with gold facsimile Churchill signature, spine, top to bottom in gold lettering Winston / Churchill, in gold box in blue lettering 'Gli Anni / Dela Mia / Giovinezza', under box decorative gold small squares in linear pattern, near bottom gold publisher's logo, in gold lettering 'GARZANTI'; dust jacket, brownish rust background, top to bottom, in white lettering 'Winston / Churchill', large image of a young Churchill with bow tie and wing collar, to the left of his head in black lettering 'glia anni / dell amia / giovinezza', at bottom right in white lettering 'GARZANNI'; spine, top to bottom, in black lettering 'Winston / CHURCHILL', vertically up the spine 'GLIA ANNI DELLA

MIA GIOVINEZZA', at bottom in black logo of publisher; back of dust jacket, a listing of publisher's other books in the Memorie series.

Gli Anni Della Mia Giovinezza (*My Early Life*), Italy, Garzanti, 1961, 3rd Italian ed., impression of January 1971, softcover yellow front background, from top to bottom, in blue lettering 'gli anni dell amia / giovinezza', in red lettering Churchill, in blue lettering 'La formazione di un grande leader, / nell 'Inghilierra degli anni gloriosi', right lower dust jacket image of Churchill in South African bush hat, bottom left in white lettering 'Garzanti'; spine with white background, top in black ink logo, in black lettering vertically 'Churchill', in black '276' in diamond-shaped enclosure, in black ink vertically 'glia anni dell amia giovinezza'; back cover in black lettering paragraph about Churchill's life.

De Unge Ar (*My Early Life*), Copenhagen, Steen Hasselbalchs Forlag, 1963, 6th Danish ed., 43,000 copies issued, paperback, front cover grey background, top to bottom, photograph of Churchill on horseback wearing uniform of Queen's Own Oxfordshire Hussars, *c*. 1914, upper left in black lettering 'WINSTON CHURCHILL', bottom in red orange lettering 'DE UNGE AR', under that in red orange 'HASSELBALCH'; spine buff background, vertically in black ink 'WINSTON CHURCHILL', in orange red 'de / unge / ar', in black logo of publisher; back cover title in black 'WINSTON CHURCHILL', in orange red 'de / unge / ar', photograph of Churchill with hat, cane and cigar *c*. 1940, to the left in black lettering brief synopsis of Churchill's life, at bottom left 'Kr. 7.75' enclosed in two black lines above and below, at very bottom left in red lettering 'HASSELBALCH'.

Min Ungdom (*My Early Life*), Stockholm, Vingforlaget, 1963, 6th Swedish ed., translator, Beatrice Cronstedt, blue cloth boards, front and rear boards plain; spine with debossed white background box with gold design at top and bottom of box, within the box in gold lettering 'Winston S. / Churchill', thick gold bar, 'Min / ungdom'; dust jacket, front and spine with top white background and red lower background, on front top to bottom in black lettering 'WINSTON S. / Churchill' in white background, in red background 'MIN / UNG / DOM'; spine in white background in black lettering 'Winston S. / Churchill', 'MIN

/ UNGDOM'; back of dust jacket, titled with 'Winston S. Churchill', 'MIN UNGDOM', paragraph about Churchill and Nobel Prize, bottom left in black box in white lettering Pris inb. 12: –'.

Sekai no Ningenzou (World's Personalities), Tokyo, Kadokawa Shoten, 1964, Japanese ed., volume 15 of 26, no copy examined.

Mes Jeunes Années (*My Early Life*), London, Odhams Press Limited, 1965, Le Club Français du Livre, 2nd French ed., 2nd printing, plain red boards front and back, spine black leatherette with 6 debossed bars between bar 1 and 2 in gold lettering 'Sir Winston / Churchill', between bar 2 and 3 in gold lettering 'Mes jeunes / années', between bar 5 and 6 is a debossed circle with a gold logo of publisher, red ribbon marker; no dust jacket was issued.

Meine Frühen Jahre (*My Early Life*), in Nobelpreis fur Literatur 1953, Zurich, P List, Coron Verlag, 1965, German ed., plain white boards, front board, top to bottom, in gold lettering 'Winston S. Churchill', in black lettering 'Meine frühen Jahre', embossed in large white letters 'NOBELPREIS / FUR / LITERATUR', arranged within the embossed letters is a debossed gold crown; spine, top to bottom, in gold lettering 'Winston S. / Churchill', in black lettering 'Meine / frühen Jahre', at bottom in gold lettering 'Nobelpreis / fur / Literatur / 1953'.

Mein Frühen Jahre (*My Early Life*), Munich, Paul List Verlag, 1965, German 4th ed., softcover, front, top of page white with black lettering 'List Taschenbucher ……. LIST' (on one line), under that a black background, left side, in yellow lettering 'WINSTON / CHURCHILL', to the right in white 'Meine / frühen / Jahre', under that a large photograph of Churchill speaking on a microphone *c*. WWII; spine, white background, top to bottom, in all black lettering, 'LIST', black line, '293/4', vertically upward, 'Winston S. Churchill / Mein frühen Jahre'; back cover, in black lettering 'LIST', long black line, paragraph summary of book.

La Juventude De Winston Churchill (*My Early Life*) in 'Vida Illustres', Mexico, Editorial Novaro, 1965, 34 pp., Mexican softcover, comic format, issue 112, front cover image of Churchill at scene of train he used to escape Boers (Churchill dressed in clothes of 1960s, blue jeans etc., shown with box cars – not the type of car he hid in); at top left is the logo of the publisher, centred below in green lettering 'Vidas Ilustres', bottom in orange lettering 'LA JUVENTUDE DE, WINSTON CHURCHILL'; back, advertisements.

Ungdom (*My Early Life*), Oslo, Gyldendal Norsk Forlag, 1965, Norwegian ed.; no copy examined.

Minha Mocidade (*My Early Life*), Rio de Janeiro, Brazil, Nova Fronteira, 1967, 2nd Brazilian ed., text in Portuguese, brown leatherette boards and spine, front board, top to bottom, in gold lettering 'TRABALHOS LITTERARIOS / DE /CARLOS LACERDA', near bottom, in gold lettering 'Winston S. Churchill', 'MINHA MOCIDADE', 'Traduçao'; spine, top to bottom, thin gold line, large vertical grey box with gold line on top and bottom, inside box in gold script the signature of the writer of the preface Carlos Lacerda, volume number '4', in gold the logo of the publisher, long thin gold line at the bottom.

Minha Mocidade (*My Early Life*), Rio de Janeiro, Brazil, Editora Nova Fronteira, 1967, 2nd Brazilian ed., text in Portuguese, white card wrappers, front cover, top to bottom, in black lettering 'MINHA / MOCIDADE', in black lettering 'WINSTON CHURCHILL', oval photograph of Churchill in his 4th Hussars dress uniform, 'TRADUCAO E PREFACIO, DE, CARLOS LACERDA', at bottom publisher's triangular logo; spine top to bottom, vertically down 'WINSTON, CHURCHILL, MINHA MOCIDADE', publisher's triangular logo; back cover advertisement for this book.

Sekai no Jinseirou (*Philosophy of Life in the World*), Tokyo, Kadokawa Shoten, 1968, volume 5, Japanese ed.; no copy examined.

Min Ungdom (*My Early Life*), Stockholm, Borforlaget Norstedts, 1972, 7th Swedish ed., translator, Beatrice Cronstedt, buff white softcover, front cover top to bottom in black lettering 'Winston / Churchill', image of Churchill on horse in India with pith helmet and 4th Hussars uniform, in black lettering 'Min ungdom', bottom right in black lettering, 'Pan / NORSTEDTS'; spine, in black lettering vertically down 'Winston Churchill/ Min ungdom'; at bottom, in black, publisher's logo.

My Early Life (チャーチル自伝), Tokyo, Student Company, 1972, Japanese ed., translated by Shinichi Kobayashi, 119 pp.; no copy examined.

Memoires d'un Jeune Homme (*My Early Life*), Edition Speciale, Paris, 1972, 5th French ed., solid red softcover, front top to bottom, small black lettering 'SIR', same line in large lettering 'winston / churchill', in black 'MEMOIRES / D'UN / JEUNE HOMME', image of Churchill on horse in India with pith helmet and 4th Hussars uniform, to left of horse, in black lettering 'quand / de charges / en évasions / le jeune lion / faisait ses griffes', bottom left in black lettering 'édition speciale'; spine vertically up Sir Winston / CHURCHILL, memoires d'un jeune homme, at very bottom 'e.s.'; back cover, descriptive paragraph about book.

De Unge Ar (*My Early Life*), Copenhagen, Schonberg, 1973, Danish ed., paperback, front cover, top orange bar 1½" thick with 'Winston Churchill' in black lettering, remainder of front with B/W photograph on horseback in Fourth Hussars uniform in India superimposed in orange lettering 'DE UNGE AR', right lower vertical black and white bar with publisher's name and logo; white spine with lettering vertically down in black 'Winston Churchill DE UNGE AR', bottom with orange background publisher's logo in black; back, orange, white and black background starting top to bottom, in black 'Winston Churchill' under that in orange 'DE UNGE AR', under that, in black, paragraph about the book, logo in white to the left of the paragraph, near bottom in black in Danish: 'The English have now under Karl Foremann, made a big film from the book.'

Ungdom (*My Early Life*), Oslo, Gyldendal Norsk Forlag, 1973, Norwegian ed.; no copy examined.

Ta neanika mou hronia (*My Early Life*), Athens, Papyros Graphic Arts, 1974, Greek ed., paperback, front cover, background photograph of Churchill in top hat as a boy, top left red round circle with white lettering 'BINEP' surrounded by white square, under that in Greek 'Winston Churchill', and under that, 'My Early Life' in Greek, top right in pale blue crenellated circle the price; spine running vertically up 'Winston Churchill' and title in Greek on white background, printer's logo at bottom and number 487 in black at top; back cover, 2 paragraphs in Greek about Churchill and the book.

Moja mlada leta (*My Early Life*), V Ljubljani, Cankarjeva, 1976, Slovenian ed., bright red hardback, front top right in white lettering 'winston / spencer / churchill', under that, centred in gold lettering, a facsimile signature of Churchill; under that an inverted triangle in gold with symbol in the centre; to the right, a curved gold linear arch going up from the bottom to the right edge; no copy examined.

De Unge Ar (*My Early Life*), Copenhagen, Schonberg, 1977, Danish ed., paperback; no copy examined.

Τα νεανικά μου χρόνια (*My Early Life*), Athens, Πάπυρος, 1977, Greek ed., hardback, 314 pp.; no copy examined.

Waga Seishunki (*My Young Years*), Tokyo, Shufu-no-Tomo Sha, 1978, Japanese ed., Volume 22 in series titled 'Nobel Sho Bungaku Zenshu' (Nobel Prize Literature); no copy examined.

Nae Jolmun Nal Eui Chuuk (*My Early Life*), Seoul, Pum Jo Sa, 1987, 1st Korean ed., softcover, front glossy white background with pink outlining, top left 'My Early Life', under that and centered in pink is Korean title; under that in black additional words and them in small letters additional Korean words to the right; under that in pink outline a 5" x 4 ½" colour photograph positioned on the left lower page and to the right at the bottom, in Korean, the publisher; spine, white background with 'W. S. Churchill' in black running vertically down with Korean lettering in black under Churchill's name below both of those in black and then red lettering in Korean is title and at bottom of spine publisher in black Korean lettering; back, white and grey background with pink borders and full paragraph in black Korean lettering.

Min Ungdom (*My Early Life*), Stockholm, Norstedts, 1989, 8th Swedish ed., translator, Beatrice Cronstedt, glossy black hardcover front and spine, front board, top to bottom, in white lettering 'Winston, CHURCH (on horizontal then vertically down) ILL', set within that right angle of words is an image of Churchill from about 1914, under image in white lettering 'Min Ungdom', thin white line under that, 'Norstedts'; spine vertically down in white lettering 'Winston Churchill, Min ungdom'; back board with white background, description of book and 2 brief reviews; at bottom, bar codes.

Nae Jolmun Nal Eui Chuuk (*My Early Life*), Seoul, Korea, Cheong-Mok, 1991, 2nd Korean ed., speckled tan wrappers, front cover top image of Churchill in 4th Hussars dress uniform surrounded by a white and pale blue border; under that, words in purple lettering in Korean, and under that an image of Churchill in the 1910s; to the left of the image is a light blue box containing Korean words and the number 57; at very bottom is publisher's logo; spine title and 'Churchill' in Korean in purple lettering; bottom, publisher's logo; back cover, image of Churchill in about 1914; paragraph description of book in Korean and at right bottom, bar codes.

チャーチル自伝 (直読直解アトム英文双書 (74)) (*My Early Life*), Japan, Gakuseisha, 1992, Wrappers, 119 pp., Atom Books by Ready Vocabulary Method, Japanese ed. This book was printed in Japanese with notes and vocabulary (English to Japanese) and was written to allow Japanese readers to read world classics without an additional dictionary. The book contains the first three chapters of *My Early Life*. Wrappers bright pink, front with title and author (Winston L.S. Churchill) in English, remainder of text in Japanese, also with image of tree and someone standing under it – presumably the tree of knowledge. Spine and back wrapper all in black lettering in Japanese.

Mein Frühen Jahre (*My Early Life*), in *Nobelpreis Fur Literatur, 1951–1953*, Zurich, Coron Verlag, 1993, German ed., bright red leatherette boards, front board with borders in gold linear and swirl design, centered is gold crown; spine, same linear and curved gold design on borders of spine as front board, top to bottom, in gold lettering, 'NOBELPREIS, FUR, LITERATUR', gold crown, 'LAGERKVIEST', 'Barabbas', 'MAURIAC', 'Einode der Liebe', 'CHURCHILL', 'Meine frühen jahre', at bottom publisher's logo, '1951–1953'; all edges bright gilt, with tan sewn-in book marker, in unmarked bright red cardboard slip-case, This is from a luxury edition series begun in 1985 limited to 998 copies and highlighting each of the winners of the Nobel Prize for Literature including Churchill in 1953.

(Although this could be a Cohen B item, because of the completeness of the *My Early Life*, the decision was made to place it here.)

Meine Frühen Jahre (*My Early Life*), in 'Nobelpreis Fur Literatur, Mauriac, Die Einode der Liebe/ Churchill Meine Frühen Jahre/ Hemingway Wem die Stundeschlagt', 1952–1954, Zurich, Coron Verlag, Lachen am Zurichese, 1993, German language ed., Century Edition, limited to 1,999 copies, full red leather binding, front, at periphery of all four sides is a gold linear design made up of small gold circle, centred top ¼ of front is a gold 'N' in gold circle made up of small circles; spine, top to bottom all in gold lettering horizontal line made up of small gold circles, 'NOBELPREIS / FUR / LITERATUR', 2 horizontal lines made up of circles bordering an embossed ridge, image of a crown, 2 horizontal gold lines bordering an embossed ridge, 'MAURISC, Die Einode / Liebe', short solid thin line, 'CHURCHILL, Meine frühen Jahre', small horizontal sold line, 'HEMINGWAY', 'Wem die Stunde / schlagt', 2 horizontal lines made up of circles bordering an embossed ridge, a second set of 2 horizontal lines made up of circles bordering an embossed ridge, the 'N' logo of publisher, '1952–1954', a single horizontal line made up of circles, red ribbon bookmarker sewn in. (Although this could be a Cohen B item, because of the completeness of the *My Early Life*, the decision was made to place it here.)

Mes Aventures De Jeunesse (*My Early Life*), Paris, T. Mage, 1994, French, ISBN: 9782878912210; no copy examined.

Mé Životni Začátky (*My Early Life*), Prague, NLN, Nakladelstvi Lidové noviny, 1996, Czech ed., hard cover with dust jacket; front cover (unknown if dust jacket or front hard cover is the image examined), image of Churchill in South Africa *c.* 1899 in army fatigues, upper left long quotation in Czech, diagonally upward near the bottom, in yellow lettering 'WINSTON S. / CHURCHILL', under that in red lettering 'Me Zivotni / Zacatky'; ISBN: 80-7106-150-6; no copy examined.

Gli Anni Dell' Aventura, (*My Early Life*), Milan, Bompiani, 1997, Italian ed., paperback, front cover in white, black line across the top, under that a blue-grey panel with author in black, under that a maroon panel with title in white, under that a photograph of Churchill in South African uniform and bush hat; at bottom, in white, publisher.

*Qiuji'er wen ji: wo de zao nian sheng hu*o (Churchill anthology, *My Early Life*), Nanjing Shi, Jiangsu People's Publishing House, 1998, Chinese edition; no copy examined.

Moja Mlodosc (*My Early Life*), Poland, Zysk I S-ka, 2000, 1st Polish ed., black cloth hardback, front board, in white lettering, 'WINSTON CHURCHILL, MOJA MLEODOSC'; spine vertically down, 'WINSTON CHURCHILL, MOJA MLODOSC'; dust jacket, front, brownish purple with sepia photograph of Churchill with his dress calvary uniform from India, under the photograph in white is 'WINSTON CHURCHILL, MOJA MLODSC; spine brownish purple background, vertically down in white lettering 'WINSTON CHURCHILL, MOJA MLODOSC'; back of dj, in white lettering, a paragraph describing the book; at bottom left, in white lettering, 'ZYSK I S-KA, WYDAWNICTWO, ISBN 83-7150-842-7, Cena 45 zl';, on right, bar code.

Dall' Avana a Durban (*My Early Life*), Italy, CDA Vivalda, 2005, Ugo Tolomei, translator, 4th Italian ed., 1st impression, new trade card wrappers, front, light tan background from top to bottom, in red lettering on left, 'WINSTON', under that a thin black horizontal line, a map South Africa around Pretoria, in red lettering 'CHURCHILL', overlaying the map is an image of Churchill from *c.*1899 in a suit, to the left in gold lettering, 'VIAGGI, E AVENTUR, DI GIOVENTU'; at bottom, in gold lettering, 'DALL'AVANA, A DURBAN'; spine black background, top small image of Churchill (head shot), vertically upward in white lettering 'Winston CHURCHILL', 'Dall Avana a Durban', at bottom red square with red line under it, in green number '41'. In green lettering horizontally, 'CDA& / Vivalda / Editore'; back cover, in white lettering, a paragraph about the book; upper left, in yellow, 'le trace'; at bottom right, bar code information.

Os Meus Primeiros Anos (*My Early Life*), Lisbon, Portugal, Guerra & Paz, 2007, Portuguese ed., card wrappers, front, on black glossy background at top in white capitals centred, 'WINSTON', under that 'CHURCHILL', under that, blue line, under that, centered, 'OS MEUS PRIMEIROS

ANOS', under that a black and white photograph, portrait taken at the time he left the Conservatives in 1904, standing with waistcoat and bold watch chain (Picture Post Library), left side blue vertical blue stripe with publisher's imprint at bottom, and over the lower left image is publisher's name in white, 'Guerra &Paz' ('&' in red), spine blue with publisher's imprint in red at bottom and white letter running up vertically 'WINSTON CHURCHILL – OS MEUS PRIMEIROS ANOS'; back, white background with vertical blue stripe on right and printed in blue a long summary of the book, and at bottom, publisher's imprint, and in black text 'COLECCAO O PASSADO E O PRESENTE', and to the right, a barcode.

Mes Jeunes Années (*My Early Life*), Paris, Tallandier, 2007, French ed., softcover, front, top 1/3 red background, bottom 2/3 grey, from top to bottom in white lettering 'WINSTON CHURCHILL', 'Mes jeunes années', in red lettering 'TEXTO, Collection dirigée par Jean-Claude Zylberstein', photograph of Churchill in 4th Hussars dress uniform; spine, same red upper background and white lower background, top to bottom, vertically upward 'WINSTON CHURCHILL', 'mes jeunes années', at bottom horizontally in red, 'TEXTO', publisher's logo in red; back cover, paragraph about book in black lettering, publisher's name in enclosed box, bar code.

Mine Unge Ar (*My Early Life*), Copenhagen, Denmark, Rosenkilde, 2008, Danish ed., card wrappers, front top, image of Churchill as a young MP at bottom of image in white lettering 'Winson S. Churchill', under that an image of Churchill as POW in South Africa, at top of this image in red lettering 'MINE UNGE AR', at bottom of image in red lettering 'ROSENKILDE'; spine, red background, top to bottom in white lettering 'Winston S. Churchill', in black lettering 'MINE UNGE AR', in white lettering 'ROSENKILDE'; back, background image of Churchill as young MP, three paragraphs about the book in red and black lettering, and at bottom right, bar code.

Mes Jeunes Années (*My Early Life*), Longueuil, Institut Nazareth et Louis-Braille, 2009, 8 volumes en braille abrégé complet., French braille edition; no copy examined.

De Unge Ar (*My Early Life*), Copenhagen, Rosenkilde, 2009, Danish edition, hardback; no copy examined.

Mi Juventud (*My Early Life*), Granda, Spain, EDITORIAL ALMED, 2010, Spanish ed., hardback, black boards, spine, in gilt author, title, and publisher; spine, front starting at top, left side in red 'MI / JUVENTUD', to the right 'Winston' in white; under that, 'Churchill' in white; under that, 'Autobiografia' in blue; under that, photograph of Churchill in dress 4th Hussars Uniform 1890s; lower left bottom, publisher in white.

My Early Life (Cyrillic), Moscow, Kolibri, 2011, Russian ed., hard cover, front, photograph of Churchill in 4th Hussars dress uniform, top in white lettering 'Winston Churchill' in Cyrillic; under that, on left, 'My Early Life' in Cyrillic; under that, in white lettering, '1874–1904'; near bottom at left, in large brackets, publisher's information in Cyrillic; spine, white background, in black lettering vertically upwards 'WINSTON CHURCHILL' in Cyrillic, between Winston and Churchill is the title in black lettering in Cyrillic and the date '1874–1904'; back, white background, in black lettering in English 'Winston / Churchill, MY EARLY LIFE / 1874–1904', paragraph on Churchill's life in Cyrillic black lettering; and at bottom, bar code.

Minha Mocidade (*My Early Life*), Rio de Janeiro, Brazil, Nova Fronteira, 2011, 2nd Brazilian ed. (Portuguese), black card wrappers, front background is image of Churchill in his dress uniform of the 4th Hussars, top right in yellow lettering 'Winston / Churchill'; under that, in white lettering, 'Minha / Mocidade', under that, a short thin horizontal line; under that, in grey lettering, 'Tradçao e Prefacio de', under that, in white lettering, 'Carlos Lacerda'; at bottom right, in white, a triangle with line under it (logo of publisher), under that in white lettering 'EDITORA / NOVE / FROTNEIRA'; spine, top to bottom, vertically down in yellow lettering 'Winston Churchill', then in white 'Minha Mocidade'; then, in white, the publisher's logo; back, black background, top in yellow lettering 'Minha Mocidade', then in white lettering a paragraph about the book; bottom right in white the publisher's logo and name, and then bar codes.

Waga hansei (*My Early Life*), Tokyo, Chuko Kronshinsha, 2014, Japanese ed., white (top) and grey wrappers, top to bottom in Japanese black lettering

'Winston Churchill', in grey in white lettering 'CHUKOCLASSICS', at bottom publisher's logo and 'W78'; spine same white and grey background, then the title and author in Japanese, at bottom the publisher in Japanese; back, same white and grey background in the grey panel in white letters 'CHUKOCLASSICS'; dust jacket with red (top) and grey background, same lettering as on card wrappers; the only difference is back bottom dust jacket has multiple bar codes.

My Early Life (Chinese), city unknown, Huawen Publishing House, 2015, Chinese ed. (? third), yellow wrappers, front top, photograph of Churchill with cigar in his mouth *c.* 1940; under that, title and author in Chinese with black and red lettering; at bottom, publisher's logo and name in black (Chinese lettering); spine, yellow background, title, author and publisher's information all in Chinese; back, paragraph about the book in Chinese black lettering, at bottom 2 QR codes and 1 bar code.

Mine unge ar (*My Early Life*), Copenhagen, Lindhardt and Ringhof, 2016, Danish ed., black hardback, plain front and rear boards; spine in white lettering vertically down 'WINSTON SPENCER / CHURCHILL', 'Mine unge Ar', at bottom publisher's logo; dust jacket, front, background photo of Churchill about 1900 with John Bull hat, in red lettering across his chest 'Winston SPENCER / CHURCHILL', 'Mine unge ar', under that in white lettering 'Forord af Uffe Ellemann-Jensen', 'Lindhardt og Ringhof'; spine, grey background, top to bottom vertically down in red lettering 'WINSTON SPENCER / CHURCHILL', 'Mine unge ar', publisher's logo; back, grey background, top a quote about the book in Danish in black lettering, 2 small photographs of Churchill as a young boy in sailor suit and in dress uniform of the 4th Hussars, 2 brief paragraphs about Churchill, at bottom left publisher's logo and bottom right bar code.

Ifjusagom 1874-1904 (*My Youth*), Budapest, Hungry, Saxum, 2017, 1st Hungarian ed., hardback, front background is image of Churchill in his dress uniform of 4th Hussars, above picture in red lettering 'WINSTON / CHURCHILL', under that in black lettering, 'IFJUSAGOM', at bottom left in white lettering is 'SAXUM'; no copy examined.

丘吉尔传：我的青春 (*My Early Life*), China (unknown city), Zhejiang Literature, 2017, Chinese ed., pale lilac card wrappers, front, top 2/3 image of Churchill by Karsh, top left Chinese characters in gold, at bottom left of photograph in gold lettering 'MY EARLY LIFE / Winston Churchill', at bottom with lilac background in gold lettering title, author, publisher information and review quote, all in Chinese; spine, lilac background in gold lettering title, author and publisher information; back, all lilac background, a paragraph, in gold lettering, about the book in Chinese, six small photographs of Churchill: young boy in sailor suit, 4th Hussars dress uniform, young MP, giving 'V' sign in WWII, smoking cigar at Chartwell, elder statesman, bottom, 1 QR code and a bar code.

My Early Life, China, China Translation and Publishing company, 2017, Chinese ed., paperback, front cover with photograph of Churchill in 4th Hussars dress uniform, author in white, title in yellow and red, publisher and logo in white.

Anii Tinertii Mele (*My Early Life*), Bucharest, Romania, Editura Herald, 2019, 1st Romanian ed., translated by Anca Irina Ionescu, black card wrappers, front image of Churchill in later life, top left vertically in small orange box in black lettering 'AUTOBIOGRAFIA', bottom right in orange lettering 'WINSTON / CHURHILL', under that in white lettering 'ANII TINERETII MELE'; spine, black background with vertical lettering upward in orange 'WINSTON CHURCHILL', in white lettering 'ANII TINERTII MELE', at very bottom publisher's logo; back, top left in orange box in black lettering 'AUTOBIOGRAFIA', 3 small paragraphs in white lettering about Churchill, at bottom left publisher's logo and right bar code.

My Early Life, Armenia, 2019, hardcover; only information known.

Mano Jaunyste, 1874-1904, Lithuania, Briedis, 2019, Lithuanian ed., hardcover, cover with image of Churchill in South African uniform and bush hat; no copy examined.

윈스턴 처칠, 나의 청춘: 가장 위대한 영국인, 청년 처칠의 자서전 /, Winston Churchill, My Youth: The Autobiography of the Greatest Englishman, Young Churchill, Haengbuk, Goyang, 2020, 3rd Korean edition, no copy examined.

Minha Mocidade (*My Early Life*), Rio de Janeiro, Harper Collins, 2021, Winner of Nobel Prize in Literature Series, 1st ed. this series, Brazilian Portuguese, wrappers, front B/W photograph of WSC as a young man *c*. 1901, printed over the photograph top right laurel wreath bracketing the words 'VENCEDO DO PREMIO NOBEL DE LITERATURA' under that 'TRADUCAO E PREFACIO DE CARLOS LACERDA', bottom right 'WINSTON/ CHURCHILL' under that 'MINHA MOCIDADE' (blue lettering) under that 'Harper/Collins' with flame logo; spine dark background vertically down, 'WINSTON' (then larger font) 'CHURCHILL', under that 'MINHA/MOCIDADE' (blue lettering), under that 'Harper Collins' and logo. Back, dark continuation of photograph with WSC's right hand and desk visible; top large paragraph about the book and bottom barcode and 'HarperCollins Brasil / www.harpercollins.com.br'.

Meine Fruhen Jahre (*My Early Life*), Zurich, Switzerland, Kampa Verlag, 2023, new edition, light blue green hardcover, front, top silhouette of Churchill formed by smoke from a lit cigar 2/3 down the front, within the silhouette in white lettering 'WINSTON CHURCHILL', under that, in orange lettering, 'MEINE / FRUHEN / JAHRE', under that the lit cigar in an ashtray, under that 3 photographs, Churchill as a child in sailor's suit, standing with Kaiser reviewing German troops before WWI and Churchill in dress uniform of 4th Hussars, under the first photograph in white lettering 'GATSBY'; spine, vertically upward in white lettering 'WINSTON / CHURCHILL', then in orange lettering 'MEINE FRUHEN JAHRE', at very bottom in white lettering 'GATSBY'; back, long paragraph in white lettering about Churchill, all in German, a quote about the book in German from *The Guardian*, London, and, at the very bottom, bar code.

iii. Excerpts from My Early Life

Cohen 'B' items or would-be Cohen 'B' items. In this section, all the 'B' items are shown chronologically, including the twenty items from Cohen's 'B' list with the Cohen identification numbers. In addition, 244 previously unrecognized 'B' items have been identified and added to the list. They are labelled 'Stiles Bx', where 'x' is a sequential number denoting chronological order; 'B1' is the oldest such item. An 'F' at the end of the label (e.g., 'Stiles BxF') denotes a non–English language book. For each entry, the standard bibliographic information of the book excerpting the material is included, as well as the topic of the excerpted material, the page(s) in the book where the Churchill material is found, and the pages in *MEL* from which the material has been excerpted. For a fulsome discussion of the topics excerpted and the tremendous impact that *MEL* had on the literature, see Chapter 7.

Cohen B59 Fifty True Stories Stranger than Fiction, London, Odhams, 1936 and 1948. Churchill contribution: 'My Escape from the Boers', pp. 26–38, excerpt from *MEL* starting on p. 282.

B59/1 Adventures and Encounters, London, Longmans, Green and Co., 1958, 11th impression, (1936 original edition). Churchill contribution: 'My Escape from the Boers', pp. 46–62, excerpt from *MEL* starting on p. 282.

B60. Quest and Conquest: An Anthology of Personal Adventures, Compiled by E.V. Odle, London, MacMillan & Co., 1936, 1st ed. Churchill contribution: 'The Armoured Train', pp. 67–77, excerpt from *MEL* starting on p. 256.

Stiles B1F Sotavanki (Prisoner of War), Betty Rauanheimo, Helsingissa, Finland, Kustaannusosakeyhtio, 1938, 1st Finnish ed., 104 pp., hardcover, primarily covers WSC exploits in South Africa, states in introduction: 'This book has been taken with the permission of Mr. Winston Churchill from his memoirs of My Early Life.' Also listed in non-English versions above.

Stiles B2 Inside Europe, John Gunther, London, Hamish Hamilton, 1940. Churchill contribution: 'calvary charge', p. 323–4, excerpt from *MEL* starting on p. 206.

B74 High Road to Adventure, Earl P. Hanson, Ed., New York, National Travel Club, 1941, 1st ed., with dj. Churchill contribution: 'Escape from the Boers', pp. 5–29, excerpt from *MEL* starting on p. 282.

B81.1 Men at War, Ernest Hemingway, Ed., New York, Crown Publishers, 1942. Churchill contribution: 'The Cavalry Charge at Omdurman', pp. 813–21, excerpt from *MEL* starting on p. 197.

Cohen A170 I Escape, London, Macmillan & Co., Ltd., 1942?, 1st ed., only printing, The first chapter of this booklet, pp. 3–19, is Chapter XXI ('I Escape from the Boers'), excerpt from MEL pp. 282–99, and the second chapter, pp. 20–31, is Chapter XXII ('I Escape from the Boers – II') excerpt from *MEL* pp. 300–312. (Although Cohen terms this an 'A' item, it has been included here, as it is excerpted from *MEL*.)

Stiles B3 Britain at War: An Anthology, Arthur Stanley, London, Eyre, and Spottiswood, 1943. Churchill contribution: 'A Cavalry Charge at Omdurman', pp. 232–3, excerpt from *MEL* starting on p. 205.

B97 Time To Be Young, Great Stories of the Growing Years, Whit Burnett, Ed., 1st ed., Philadelphia, Lippincott, 1945. Churchill contribution: 'Examinations at Harrow', pp. 293–301 excerpt from *MEL* beginning p. 29.

Stiles B4 Adventure & Discovery for Boys & Girls, Kenneth Lindsay, London, Jonathan Cape, 1946, with dj. Churchill contribution: 'My Early Life' (Harrow), pp. 20–26, excerpt from *MEL* starting on p. 29.

Stiles B5 The Hard Way Home, William C. Braly, Washington, Infantry Journal Press, 1947, 1st ed. Churchill contribution: description of being a prisoner of war, p. 169, excerpt from *MEL* starting on p. 273.

Stiles B6 These Wonderful People, Noel Ames, Ed., Chicago, Peoples Book Club, 1947. Churchill contribution: 'I Escape from the Boers', pp. 34–57, excerpt from *MEL* starting on p. 282.

Stiles B7 How the English Live, Joseph S. Bentwich and A.A. Mendilow, London, Longmans, 1949. Churchill contribution: 'Indian campaign', p. 277, excerpt from *MEL* starting on p. 151.

Stiles B8 The Great Horse Omnibus from Homer to Hemingway, Thurston Macauley, Chicago, Ziff–Davis Publishing Company, 1949, 1st ed., with dj. Churchill contribution: 'Sensations of a Cavalry Charge', pp. 155–162, excerpt from *MEL* starting on p. 201.

Stiles B9 Modern Autobiography An Anthology, Frederick T. Wood, London, Macmillan & Co. Ltd, 1954, 1st ed., 4th printing. Churchill contribution: 'An Escape From the Boers', pp. 22–51, excerpt from *MEL* starting on p. 282.

Stiles B10 The English at School, G. F. Lamb, London, George Allen and Uwin Ltd, 1950, 1st ed., with dj. Churchill contribution: 'Mr. Churchill Enters Harrow', p. 182, excerpt from *MEL* starting on p. 29.

B129/1 Proud Heritage: A Portrait of Greatness, London, John Dron, 1951, in slipcase. Churchill contribution: 'epilogue', p. 105 excerpt from *MEL*, p. 82.

Stiles B11 Interpretative Speech, Lionel B. Crocker, New York, Prentice-Hall, 1952. Churchill contribution: 'The Study of English', Harrow, p. 288, excerpt from *MEL* starting on p. 30.

B142 The Escapers, Eric Ernest Williams, Ed., London, Collins and Eyre & Spottiswoode, 1953, 1st ed. with dj. Churchill contribution: 'Escape From the Boers', pp 150–62, excerpt from *MEL* starting on p. 265.

Stiles B12 Essays and Studies, Guy Boas, London, J. Murray, 1954. Churchill contribution: 'Harrow', pp. 23–4, excerpt from *MEL* starting on p. 29.

Stiles B13 Essays Old and New, Robert U. Jameson, New York, Harcourt, Brace and Jovanovich, 1954, 3rd ed. Churchill contribution: 'Harrow', pp. 182–92, excerpt from *MEL* starting on p. 29.

Stiles B14 The Types of Literature: Short Story, Novel, Poetry, Drama, Essay, Criticism, Francis Connolly, Ed., New York, Harcourt, Brace and Company, 1955. Churchill contribution: 'Early Schooling', pp. 416–9, excerpt from *MEL* starting on p. 22.

B152 The New Hilton Bedside Book, Chicago, Hilton Hotels, 1955, 1st ed., Softcover. Churchill contribution: 'Escape from Pretoria', pp. 13–31, excerpt from *MEL* starting on p. 282.

Stiles B15 Adult Education in the Canadian University, J.R. Kidd, Toronto, Canadian Association for Adult Education, 1956. Churchill contribution: 'Why I didn't go to University', p. 26, excerpt from *MEL* starting on p. 21.

Stiles B16 <u>The Writer's Book</u>, Helen Hull, Ed., New York, Barnes and Noble, 1956. Churchill contribution: 'The Origin of Style', Harrow, learning English, p. 313, excerpt from *MEL* starting on p. 30.

Stiles B17 <u>His Kingdom for a Horse</u>, Wyatt Blassingame, New York, Franklin Watts, 1957. Churchill contribution: a chapter paraphrasing WSC's experience at Omdurman with multiple quotes from *MEL*, pp. 143–57, and a quote from *MEL* on parents giving horse to children (p. xii).

Stiles B18F <u>Weltabenteuer Im Dienst (My Early Life)</u> in Reader's Digest Auswahlbucher, Vol IV, 1957, Verlag Das Beste, Stuttgart, German, two distinct bindings noted (green cloth and orange leather spine with grey striped cloth), pp. 153–250, large excerpt from *MEL*.

Stiles B19 <u>An American Rhetoric</u>, William Whyte Watt, New York, Rhinehart, 1957, 1st ed.. Churchill contribution: 'Learning English in School', p. 332, excerpt from *MEL* starting on p. 30.

Stiles B20 <u>My Early Life</u>, excerpts including chapters I, II, XXI and XXII of *MEL*, in <u>Student's Series 17</u>, Dr. Hans Zehrer, Ed., Wiesbaden, Germany, Brandstetter Verlag, 1958, teaching aid for students with extensive German notes at the end.

Stiles B21 <u>The Nature of Belief</u>, Martin Cyril D'Arcy, St. Louis, MO, Herder, 1958. Churchill contribution: 'India self–education', pp. 197–8, excerpt from *MEL* starting on p. 144.

Stiles B22 <u>Creative Living … Five</u>, E.W. Buxton, Ed., Toronto, W.J. Gage and Company Limited, 1958?, 1st ed., Churchill contribution: 'My Early Life', School days prior to and including Harrow, pp. 128–33 excerpt from *MEL* starting on p. 22.

Stiles B23 <u>Reader's Digest Condensed Books</u>, The Reader's Digest Association, 1958, London, 'My Early Life', pp. 231–318, extensive excerpt from *MEL*.

Stiles B24F Le Mie Prime Guerre: Condensato del Libro, My Early Life (A Roving Commission), Winston Churchill, William Faulkner, Milano: Selezione Reader's Digest, Italian, 1958.

B163 4th Hussar The Story of the 4th Queens Own Hussars 1865–1958, David Scott Daniell, 1959, Gale and Polden, Aldershot, 1st ed., Churchill contribution: 'Foreword', signed in facsimile and dated 30 September 1957: p. vii; dinner with Brabazon, p. 221, excerpt from *MEL*, p. 282; joining the regiment, pp. 221–3, excerpt from *MEL* starting on p. 84; India, pp. 226–33 excerpt from *MEL* starting on p. 117.

Stiles B25F Min Ungdom (My Early Life) in Det Bastas Bokval, Reader's Digest, Stockholm, Aktiebolag, 1959, red dj, Swedish, pp. 313–404, extensive excerpt from *MEL*.

Stiles B26 Winston S. Churchill My Early Life, Norman T. Carrington, London. James Brodie, 1960, wraps, tan, this is Zoller A209 but certainly should be a Cohen B with all the extensive quotes from *MEL* on all topics of birth, youth, schooling, Sandhurst, Hussars, India, knowledge through reading, Sudan, Boer War and Escape, Khaki election and early Parliament.

Stiles B27 Great True Escape Stories, Fred Urquhart, London, Arco Publications, 1960, 1st reprint, with dj. Churchill contribution: 'Escape from the Boers', pp. 7–20 excerpt from *MEL* starting on p. 284.

Stiles B28 A Choice of Ornaments, Nicolas Bentley, London, Readers Union, 1961. Churchill contribution: 'Cavalry charge', pp. 95–8, excerpt from *MEL* starting on p. 197.

Stiles B29 The Story of Sandhurst, Hugh Thomas, London, Hutchinson, 1961, with dj. Churchill contributions: Sandhurst, pp. 154–7, excerpt from *MEL*, pp. 43, 57–9 and 73, and Admonition, pp. 237–8, excerpt from *MEL*, p. 74.

Stiles B30 Ten Master Historians, L.M. Angus–Butterworth, Aberdeen, University Press, 1961. Churchill contribution: India (Self–education), pp. 157–9, excerpt from *MEL* starting on p. 124.

Stiles B31 Sandhurst – The Story of the Royal Military College Sandhurst, and the Royal Military Academy Sandhurst 1741–1961, John V.C. Smyth, London, Weidenfeld and Nicolson, 1961, with dj. Churchill contribution: three sections on Sandhurst, p. 105–6, excerpts from *MEL* on pp. 37, 49, and 57.

Stiles B32 Precis Practice for Overseas Students, J.A. Bright and K.F. Nicholson, Hong Kong, Longmans, 1962. Churchill contribution: 'Harrow School', pp. 26–7, excerpted from *MEL* starting on p. 31.

Stiles B33 Themes from Experience: A Manual of Literature for Writers, William Buckler, New York, W.W. Norton, 1962. Churchill contribution: 'Harrow', pp. 210–18, excerpt from *MEL* starting on p. 29.

B178 Modern English Prose and Poetry, Nelda B. Kubat and James G. Magill, New York, Macmillan, 1963, 1st Am. Ed., paperback. Churchill contribution: 'Harrow' pp. 223–32, excerpt from *MEL* starting on p. 29.

Stiles B34 Morning Faces A Miscellany on Childhood and Learning, John and Adeline Hartcup, London, Heinemann, 1963. Churchill contribution: 'Harrow', learning English, pp. 191–4, excerpt from *MEL* starting on p. 29.

Stiles B35F En Busca De Aventuras (My Early Life) in Biblioteca De Selecciones, Selecciones Del Reader's Digest, Madrid, Spain, 1963, Spanish, pp. 7–110, extensive excerpt from *MEL*.

Stiles B36F En Busca De Aventuras (My Early Life) in Biblioteca De Selecciones, Selecciones Del Reader's Digest, Mexico, 1963, Spanish, pp. 275–374, extensive excerpt from *MEL*.

Stiles B37 A Reader for Parents A Selection of Creative Literature About Children, Child Study Association of America, New York, W.W. Norton, 1963, 1st ed., with dj. Churchill contribution: Harrows days, pp. 112–7 excerpt from *MEL*, starting on p. 29.

Stiles B38 Modern English Readings, Roger Sherman Loomis, New York, Holt, Rhinehart and Winston, 1963. Churchill contribution: jump off the bridge, 'Examinations' (Harrow), Switzerland, Sandhurst, politics, pp. 106–16, excerpts from *MEL* starting on p. 39.

Stiles B39 <u>With Fire and Sword Great War Adventures</u>, Quentin Reynolds and Robert Leckie, New York, The Dial Press, 1963, 1st ed., Churchill contribution: 'The Cavalry Charge at Omdurman', pp.175–87, excerpt from *MEL* starting on p. 197.

Stiles B40 <u>A Second Book of Nonfiction</u>, Alice C. Baum and Brother Anthony Cyril, eds., New York, Macmillan, 1964. Churchill contribution: 'Boarding School Days', pp. 121–30 excerpt from *MEL* starting on p. 22.

Stiles B41 <u>Readings in Exposition</u>, Roger Sherman Loomis, Donald Lemen Clark, and John Harlan Middendorf, New York, Holt, Rhinehart and Winston, 1963, 'Examinations', Harrow, pp. 106–9, excerpt from *MEL* starting on p. 39.

Stiles B42 <u>English Today and Tomorrow: A Guide for Teachers of English</u>, Hans Paul Guth, Englewood Cliffs, NJ, Prentice–Hall, 1964. Churchill contribution: learning Latin at Harrow, pp. 308–9, excerpt from *MEL* starting on p. 24.

Stiles B43 <u>The Teaching of English</u>, Randolph Quirk and A.H. Smith, Eds., Oxford, Oxford University Press, 1964. Churchill contribution: Harrow and learning English, pp. 6–7, excerpt from *MEL* starting on p. 30.

Stiles B44 <u>The Socratic Enigma: a Collection of Testimonies Through Twenty–Four Centuries</u>, Herbert Spiegelberg, Indianapolis, 1964. Churchill contribution: India (education), pp. 115–6, excerpt from *MEL* starting on p. 124.

Stiles B45 <u>The Comprehensive School</u>, Robin Pedley, London, Penguin Books, 1964. Churchill contribution: 'examinations', p. 13, excerpts from *MEL* starting on p. 29.

Stiles B46 <u>Writers Guide and Index to English</u>, Porter G. Perrin, Chicago, Scott, Foresman & Company, 1965, 4th Ed., Churchill contribution: description of his jumping off the bridge in a game and being severely injured, pp. 129–131, excerpt from *MEL* starting on p. 43.

Stiles B47 <u>Footprints in Time</u>, Edwin A. Richardson, Ed., Toronto, The House of Grant, 1965, 1st ed., Churchill contribution: 'Omdurman', p. 168 excerpt from *MEL* starting on p. 205.

Stiles B48 <u>Procession</u>, John Gunther, New York, Harper & Row, 1965, hardcover with dj. Churchill contribution: 'cavalry charge', pp. 123–4, excerpt from *MEL* starting on p. 206.

Stiles B49 <u>Writer's Guide and Index to English</u>, Porter G. Perrin, Atlanta, Scott, Foresman and Company, 1965. Churchill contribution: 'jump off the bridge', pp. 129–30, excerpt from *MEL* starting on p. 43.

Stiles B50 <u>A Man of Destiny Winston S. Churchill</u>, Editors of Country Beautiful, Waukesha, WI, Country Beautiful Foundation, 1965, Binding blue cloth with attached paper colour photo of WSC. Churchill contribution: At 'Little Lodge', pp. 17–18, excerpt from *MEL* starting at p. 17; 'Gaining a Prize', pp. 18–19, excerpt from *MEL* starting on p. 32; 'Death of His Nurse', p. 19, excerpt from *MEL* starting on p. 86; The 'Well–to–Do', p. 19, excerpt from *MEL* starting on p. 144.

Stiles B51 <u>A Man of Destiny Winston S. Churchill</u>, Editors of Country Beautiful, Waukesha, WI, Country Beautiful Foundation, 1965, Binding back all white, front yellowish with printed head shot of WSC (different image than the preceding entry). Churchill contribution: 'At "Little Lodge"', pp. 17–18, excerpt from *MEL* starting at p 17. ; 'Gaining a Prize', pp. 18–19, excerpt from *MEL* starting on p. 32; 'Death of His Nurse', p. 19, excerpt from *MEL* starting on p. 86; The 'Well-to-Do', p. 19, excerpt from *MEL* starting on p. 144.

Stiles B52 <u>Churchill: The Life Triumphant: The Historical Record of Ninety Years</u>, Editors of American Heritage Magazine, New York, American Heritage Magazine, 1965. Churchill contribution: 'First Memories', p. 65, excerpt from *MEL* starting on p. 15; 'The Specter of Education', p. 65–6, excerpt from *MEL* starting on p. 17; 'The Heritage of Lord Randolph', p. 66, excerpt from *MEL* starting on p. 84; 'The English Sentence – A Noble thing', p. 66, excerpt from *MEL* starting on p. 30; 'A Quieter Pastime', p. 68, excerpt from *MEL* starting on p. 226; 'In Victory: Magnanimity', p. 70, excerpt from *MEL* starting on p. 346.

Stiles B53 <u>Epic Stories of Adventure</u>, Patrick Pringle, London, Evans Brothers, 1965. Churchill contribution: 'Wanted – Dead or Alive',

'Escape from the Boers', pp. 54–70, excerpt from *MEL* starting on p. 258.

Stiles B54 Essay, Hans P. Guth, Ed., Belmont, CA, Wadsworth Publishing Company, 1966, Second Edition, paperback. Churchill contribution: 'My Early Life' (Harrow), pp. 84–92, excerpt from *MEL* starting on p. 23.

Stiles B55 Salute The Soldier, Captain Eric Bush, London, George Allen & Unwin Ltd, 1966, 1st ed., with dj. Churchill contribution: 'The Eve of Omdurman', pp. 152–3 except from *MEL* starting on p. 189; 'The Souvenir' (description of Churchill's giving a skin graft), p. 157, excerpt from *MEL* starting on p. 211.

Stiles B56 Insights Themes in Literature, G. Robert Carlsen, Ed., St. Louis, MO, McGraw-Hill Book Company, 1967. Churchill contribution: 'I Escape From the Boers', pp. 80–94, excerpt from *MEL* beginning p. 282.

Stiles B57 Readings in English History, Arvel B. Erickson, New York, Scribner, 1967. Churchill contribution: 'examinations', p. 412, excerpt from *MEL* starting on p. 29.

Stiles B58 Think, Talk and Write, Jean Giles, London, Longmans, 1967. Churchill contribution: 'Courage Under Fire', Indian campaign, pp. 61–3, excerpt from *MEL* starting on p. 155.

Stiles B59 Journey into Night: An Anthology, H.J. Deverson, New York, W.W. Norton, 1967. Churchill contribution: 'How I Escaped from the Boers', pp. 79–88, excerpt from *MEL* staring on p. 282.

Stiles B60 Just English-3, Merron Chorny, Toronto, Dent, 1968. Churchill contribution: 'Harrow School', pp. 179–80, excerpt from *MEL* starting on p. 32.

Stiles B61 The Bitter Heritage: Vietnam and American Democracy, 1941-1968, Arthur M. Schlesinger, Greenwich, CT, Fawcett Publication, 1968. Churchill contribution: South Africa guerilla warfare, p. vii, excerpt from *MEL* starting on p. 368.

Stiles B62 <u>American Composition and Rhetoric</u>, Donald Davidson, New York, Scribner's, 1968. Churchill contribution: 'Examinations', pp. 12–15, excerpt from *MEL* starting on p. 39.

Stiles B63 <u>Values in Literature</u>, Mary Ellen Chase, Arno Jewett, and William Evans, New York, Houghton Mifflin, 1968. Churchill contribution: 'My Escape from the Boers', pp. 17–26, excerpt from *MEL* starting on p. 282.

Stiles B64 <u>A Selection From Scrutiny</u>, Volume 2, F.R. Leavis, Cambridge, Cambridge University Press, 1968, 'politics', p. 276, excerpt from *MEL* starting on p. 47.

Stiles B65 <u>Doctors: The Biography of Medicine</u>, Sherwin B. Nuland, Birmingham, AL, Graphon Editions, 1968. Churchill contribution: 'skin graft', Sudan, p. 466, excerpt from *MEL* starting on p. 211.

Stiles B66 <u>Great Escapes</u>, David Howarth, Ed., New York, David White Publishers, 1969, 1st Am. ed., with dj. Churchill contribution: 'I Escape from the Boers', pp. 94–124, excerpt from *MEL* starting on p. 282.

Stiles B67 <u>Advanced Comprehension and Comment</u>, John Bevis Pendlebury, London, Nelson, 1969. Churchill contribution: 'The Mamund Valley' (teaching the use of irony), p. 85–6, excerpt from *MEL* starting on p. 149.

Stiles B68 <u>Speaking into Writing: A Guidebook for English Composition</u>, John Nist, New York, St. Martin's Press, 1969. Churchill contribution: 'Harrow' (learning English writing), p. 64–5, excerpt from *MEL* starting on p. 30.

Stiles B69 <u>Gentlemen at Arms</u>, Peter Ling, London, Peter Owen, 1969, 1st ed., with dj. Churchill contribution: 'The Young Subaltern', p. 201–206, excerpt from *MEL* starting on p. 39.

Stiles B70 <u>Readings in the History of Education</u>, Margaret Gillett, Toronto, McGraw-Hill, 1969. Churchill contribution: 'The Education of a 'Troublesome Boy'', pp. 168–175, excerpt from *MEL* starting on p. 22.

Stiles B71 <u>Adventures in Values</u>, Isabel M. Kincheloe and Lester H. Cook, New York, Harcourt Brace Javanovich, 1969. Churchill contribution:

'My Escape from the Boers', pp. 10–19, excerpt from *MEL* starting on p. 285.

Stiles B72 English and Continental Literature, Russell Sharp, Ed., Freeport, NY, Books for Libraries Press, 1970, hardback. Churchill contribution: 'A Roving Commission' (Harrow School), pp. 570–575, excerpt from *MEL* pp. 40, 53.

Stiles B73 English Literature, G. Armour Craig and Frank M. Rice, Boston, Ginn and Company, 1970. Churchill contribution: 'Journey to Freedom', pp. 720–722, excerpt from *MEL* starting on p. 307.

Stiles B74 The Roberts English Series: A Linguistics Program (Teacher's Edition), Paul Roberts, Charles S. Ross, and Julian Boyd, New York, Harcourt, Brace and World, 1970. Churchill contribution: 'Days at Harrow', pp. 155–64, excerpt from *MEL* starting on p. 29.

Stiles B75 Readings for the Senior Assembly, D.M. Prescott, London, Blandford Press, 1970. Churchill contribution: 'The Faith of an Escaper', pp. 11–20, excerpt from *MEL* starting on p. 284.

Stiles B76 Aims of Education, Leslie Melville Brown, New York, Teachers College Press, 1970. Churchill contribution: 'self-education', 'examinations', 'Harrow', pp. 125–30, excerpt from *MEL* starting on p. 52.

Stiles B77 Fifty Voices of the Twentieth Century, Emery Kelen, New York, Lothrop, Lee & Shepard, 1970, with dj. Churchill contribution: 'admonition' (Come on all), p. 28, excerpt from *MEL* p. 74.

Stiles B78 Learning about Politics: A Reader in Political Socialization, Roberta S. Sigel, New York, Random House, 1970. Churchill contribution: 'jumping off the bridge', p. 249, excerpt from *MEL* starting on p. 44.

Stiles B79 Rhetoric, Albert E. DiPippo, New York, Glencoe Press, 1971. Churchill contribution: 'Harrow', learning English, p. 281, excerpt from *MEL* starting on p. 30.

Stiles B80 New English Language Test Papers, Edward Loring Black, London, J. Murry, 1971. Churchill contribution: 'India' (used to teach language skills), pp. 61–3, excerpt from *MEL* starting on p. 149.

Stiles B81F Mis Anos Mozos (My Early Life) in Grandes Biografias, Selecciones Del Reader's Digest, Madrid, Spain, 1971, dark blue boards, pp. 7–104, extensive excerpt from *MEL*, Spanish.

B194 Albert Camus, Winston Churchill, Nobel Prize Library, New York, Helvetica Press, Inc., 1971. Churchill contribution: 'I Escape from the Boers', pp. 185–200, excerpt from *MEL* starting on p. 282.

Stiles B82 Tales in School, Jacynth Hope-Simpson, London, Hamish Hamilton, 1971, 1st ed., with dj. Churchill contribution: 'The Entrance Exam', p. 17, excerpt from *MEL* starting on p. 29.

Stiles B83 They Saw It Happen: An Anthology of Eye-Witnesses' Accounts of Events in British History 1897–1940, Asa Briggs, Oxford, Basil Blackwell, 1972, fourth impression, with dj. Churchill contribution: 'Churchill's Escape From the Boers', pp. 5–10, excerpt from *MEL* starting on p. 306.

Stiles B84 'Some Technical Aspects of Applied Psychoanalysis, E. Victor Wolfenstein, in *The Psychoanalytic Study of Society: Founded as Psychoanalysis and the Social Sciences, Volume 5*, New York, International Universities Press, 1972. Churchill contribution: 'father's death', p. 180, excerpt from *MEL* starting on p. 76.

B196 Reader's Digest 50th Anniversary Treasury, Pleasantville, NY, Reader's Digest, 1972, 1st ed., with dj, Churchill's contribution: 'A Troublesome Boy' (Harrow), pp. 448–52, excerpt from *MEL* starting on p. 53, taken from *Reader's Digest* August 1949.

Stiles B85 The Dominant Man, George Maclay and Humphry Knipe, New York, Delacorte, 1972. Churchill contribution: 'Harrow', pushing Amery in pool, pp. 126–7, excerpt from *MEL* starting on p. 31.

Stiles B86 Educational Psychology: A Contemporary View, Del Mar, CA, CRM, 1973. Churchill contributions: 'Harrow' (Latin), p. 39 and

'Harrow' (memorising poems), p. 336, excerpt from *MEL* starting on p. 24 and p. 32, respectively.

Stiles B87 <u>The Unnatural History of the Nanny</u>, Jonathan Gathorn-Hardy, New York, The Dial Press, 1973, 1st Am. ed., with dj. Churchill contribution: 'nanny Everest', pp. 17–32, excerpt from *MEL* starting on p. 86.

Stiles B88 <u>British Winners of the Nobel Literary Prize</u>, Walter E. Kidd, Norman, OK, University of Nebraska Press, 1973, with dj. Churchill contribution: 'nanny Everest', p. 220, excerpt from *MEL* starting on p. 86; there are multiple excerpts from many of Churchill's books.

Stiles B89 <u>Insights: A Selection of Creative Literature About Children</u>, Anna M.W. Wolf, NY, Jason Aronson, 1973, 1st ed., with dj. Churchill contribution: 'Early School Days', pp. 112–7, excerpt from *MEL* starting on p. 29.

Stiles B90 <u>Great Europeans: Builders of Civilization</u>, John Canning, London, Souvenir Press, 1973. Churchill contribution: 'Harrow' (learning English), pp. 436–7, excerpt from *MEL* starting on p. 30.

Stiles B91 <u>Syntax & Style</u>, Clarence E. Schneider, San Francisco, Chandler & Sharp, 1974. Churchill contribution: trip to Switzerland, pp. 150–51, 'Harrow', pp. 210–12, excerpts from *MEL* starting on p. 50 and p. 29, respectively.

Stiles B92 <u>The Child at School: A Pediatrician's Manual for Teachers</u>, Ronald S. Illingworth, New York, Wiley, 1974. Churchill contribution: 'examinations', p. 132, excerpt from *MEL* starting on p. 29.

Stiles B93 <u>The Rise and Fall of the British Nanny</u>, Jonathan Gathorne-Hardy, London, Arrow Books, 1974. Churchill contribution: 'nanny Everest', p. 29–30, excerpt from *MEL* starting on p. 86.

Stiles B94 <u>Dervish: The Rise and Fall of an African Empire</u>, Philip Warner, New York, Taplinger Company, 1975, with dj. Churchill contribution: charge of the 21st Lancers at Omdurman, pp. 216–22, excerpt from *MEL* starting on p. 204.

Stiles B95 <u>The Escape of 'The Goeben': Prelude to Gallipoli</u>, Redmond McLaughlin, New York, Charles Scribner's Sons, 1974, 1st ed., with dj. Churchill contribution: quote from 'Omdurman battle', p. 20, excerpt from *MEL* starting on p. 208.

Stiles B96 <u>The Annual of Psychoanalysis</u>, J.E. Gedo, New York, Charles E. Thomas, 1975. Churchill contribution: jumping off the bridge, p. 224, excerpt from *MEL* starting on p. 43.

Stiles B97 <u>Political Leadership in Industrialized Societies: Studies in Comparative Analysis</u>, Lewis J. Edinger, Huntington, NY, 1976. Churchill contribution: jumping off the bridge, pp. 167–8, excerpted from *MEL* starting on p. 43.

Stiles B98 <u>Family Treasuries of Great Biographies</u>, Vol. VII, Reader's Digest Association, 1976, Pleasantville, NY, with dj. Churchill contribution: 'My Early Life', pp. 7–110, extensive excerpt from *MEL*.

Stiles B99 <u>Contemporary Speech</u>, Mary Francis Hopkins, Skokie, IL, National Textbook Company, 1976. Churchill contribution: 'Harrow examinations', p. 150, excerpt from *MEL* starting on p. 29.

Stiles B100 <u>Swords and Covenants</u>, Adrian Preston and Peter Dennis, Eds., Totowa, NJ, Croom Helm, 1976, std., with dj. Churchill contribution: description of Political Officers with the Malakand Field Force, pp. 125–6, excerpt from *MEL* starting on p. 145.

Stiles B101 <u>The Cultural Context of Childhood</u>, Ronald W. Henderson and John R. Bergan, Columbus, OH, Merrill, 1976. Churchill contribution: 'learning to read', Ireland, p. 396, excerpt from *MEL* starting on p. 17.

Stiles B102 <u>From Paragraph to Essay: Readings for Progress in Writing</u>, Woodrow Ohlsen, Ed., New York, Scribner's, 1977, paperback starting. Churchill contribution: 'A Roving Commission', 'Escape forms the Boers', pp. 7–9, excerpt from *MEL* p. 273.

B200 <u>True Stories of Great Escapes</u>, Charles S. Verral, Ed., Pleasantville, NY, *The Reader's Digest*, 1977. Churchill contribution: 'My Escape', pp. 347–62, excerpt from *MEL* starting on p. 256.

Stiles B103 Learning Language, P.G. Penner and R.E. McConnell, Toronto, Macmillan Company, 1977. Churchill contribution: 'taking exams', pp. 173–4, excerpt from *MEL* starting on p. 29.

Stiles B104 Old Bungalows in Bangalore, Janett Pott, London, W.H. Houldershaw, 1977. Churchill contribution: 'India' (Bungalow), p. 48, excerpt from *MEL* starting on p. 120.

Stiles B105 The Public School Phenomenon: 597–1977, Jonathan Gathorne-Hardy, London, Hodder and Stoughton, 1977. Churchill contribution: 'Learning Latin' (mensa), pp. 140–41, extract from *MEL* starting on p. 24.

Stiles B106 Khyber: British India's North West Frontier, Charles Miller, New York, Macmillan, 1977, 1st ed., with dj. Churchill contribution: description of Pathan swordsmen and Sir Bindon Blood, pp. 268–9, excerpt from *MEL* starting on p. 155.

Stiles B107 Schools and Schooling in England and Wales, Michael Hyndman, London, Harper & Row, 1978, 1st ed., paperback, Churchill contribution: School and 'learning Latin' (mensa), pp. 135–7, excerpt from *MEL* starting on p. 22.

Stiles B108 The Old School Tie, Jonathan Gathorne-Hardy, New York, The Viking Press, 1978, 1st Am. ed., with dj. Churchill contribution: school, 'learning Latin', pp. 140–142, excerpt from *MEL* starting on p. 24.

Stiles B109 Reading and Learning in the Content Classroom: Diagnostic and Instructional Strategies, Thomas H. Estes, Boston, Allyn and Bacon, 1978. Churchill contribution: School, 'mensa', pp. 96–8, excerpt from *MEL* starting on p. 24.

Stiles B110 First Glance Childhood Creations of the Famous, Tuli Kuperberg and Sylvia Topp, Maplewood, NJ, Hammond Incorporated, 1978, with dj. Churchill contribution: 'Headmaster Welldon and learning at Harrow', pp. 28–9, excerpt from *MEL* starting on p. 29.

Stiles B111 Personnel Management in Government: Politics and Process, Jay M. Shafritz, New York, Dekker, 1978. Churchill contribution: Examinations, p. 26, excerpt from *MEL* starting on p. 29.

Stiles B112 <u>Pollock's History of English Dolls & Toys</u>, Kenneth Fawdry, London, Benn, 1979. Churchill contribution: 'toy soldiers', p. 139, excerpt from *MEL* starting on p. 33.

B202 <u>The World's Greatest Horse Stories</u>, J.N.P. Watson, Ed., New York, Paddington Press, 1979, 1st ed. with dj. Churchill contribution: 'Officer riding school', pp. 132–3, excerpt from *MEL* starting on p. 84; 'cavalry charge', pp. 135–38, excerpt from *MEL* starting on p. 203; 'Polo and India', pp. 257–8, excerpt from *MEL* starting on p. 120.

B81.6 <u>Men at War</u>, Ernest Hemingway, Intro., New York, Bramhall House, 1979, 2nd ed., with dj. Churchill contribution: 'The Cavalry Charge at Omdurman', pp. 813–21, excerpt from *MEL* starting on p. 197.

Stiles B113 <u>Going to School: An Anthology of Prose About Teachers and Students</u>, Abraham H. Lass and Norma L. Tasman, Eds, New York, Mentor Books, 1980, paperback. Churchill contribution: 'Danger! School Ahead!' pp. 114–9, excerpt from *MEL* starting on p. 17.

Stiles B114 <u>Understanding Standard Costing</u>, T.M. Walker, London, Gee, 1980. Churchill contribution: confusing mathematics, p. 24, excerpt from *MEL* starting on p. 17.

Stiles B115F <u>Je m'evade de chez les Boers (I Escape from the Boers)</u>, in Grandes Evasions Du XXe Siecle, Volume II, Selection Du Reader's Digest, Paris, 1980, French. Churchill contribution: 'I Escape from the Boers', pp. 75–92, excerpt from *MEL* starting on p. 243.

Stiles B116 <u>A Short Course in Writing</u>, Kenneth A. Bruffee, Boston, Little, Brown and Company, 1980, paperback. Churchill contribution: 'Harrow School Experience', pp. 48–9 excerpt from *MEL* starting on p. 30; 'Harrow School Experience', pp. 132–3 excerpt from *MEL* starting on p. 30.

Stiles B117 <u>40 Comprehensive Exercises in English</u>, R.E. Houseman, Amersham, Hulton Educational Publications, 1981. Churchill contribution: 'Escape from Boers', p. 119, excerpt from *MEL* starting p. 265.

Stiles B118 <u>Almanac of Adventure</u>, Richard Whitingham, Ed., Chicago, Rand McNally, 1982, 1st ed., with dj. Churchill contribution: 'Escaping the Boers', pp. 91–4, excerpt from *MEL* starting on p. 265.

Stiles B119 <u>Children of the Great Country Houses</u>, Adeline Hartcup, London, Sidgwick & Jackson, 1982. Churchill contribution: 'rather a bricklayer's son', p. 22, excerpt from *MEL* starting on p. 52.

Stiles B120 <u>On the Contrary Essays by Men and Women</u>, Martha Rainbolt and Janet Fleetwood, eds., Albany, State University of New York Press, 1983, 1st ed., Churchill contribution: 'School Days' pp. 131–3, excerpt from *MEL* starting on p. 23.

Stiles B121 <u>The Profession of Arms</u>, General Sir John Hackett, London, Sidgwick & Jackson, 1983, 1st ed., with dj. Churchill contribution: 'Charge of the 21st Lancers', pp. 123–7, excerpt from *MEL* starting on p. 203.

Stiles B122 <u>British Literature for Christian Schools: The Modern Tradition: 1688 to the Present</u>, Ronald Arthur Horton, Greenville, SC, Bob Jones University Press, 1982. Churchill contribution: 'St. James and Harrow School', pp. 378–83, excerpt from *MEL* starting on p. 23.

Stiles B123 <u>Education for Continuity & Change: A New Model for Christian Religious Education</u>, Mary Elizabeth Moore, Nashville, Abington, 1983, paperback. Churchill contribution: description of self-education in India, p. 143, excerpt from *MEL* starting on p. 138.

Stiles B124 <u>The British Cavalry</u>, Philip Warner, London, J.M. Dent & Son Ltd., 1984, 1st ed., with dj. Churchill contribution: 'Charge at Omdurman', pp. 159–63 excerpt from *MEL* starting on p. 204.

Stiles B125F <u>Viktor Hugo, Yulius Keysar, Stendal, T.E. Lorens, Vergilius, Vinston Ts'erts'il</u>, Tel–Aviv, Miśrad ha-biṭaḥon, ha-Hotsa'ah la-'or, 1984, Hebrew Edition. Churchill contribution: 'The Cavalry Charge at Omdurman', excerpt from *MEL*.

Stiles B126 <u>Mommy, I Can't Sit Still</u>, K. Daniel O'Leary, New York, New Horizon Press, 1984, 1st ed., with dj. Churchill contribution: 'Troublesome Boy', pp. 15–6 excerpt from *MEL* starting on p. 22.

Stiles B127 <u>A Letter Does Not Blush</u>, Nicholas Parsons, London, Buchan & Enright, 1984, 1st ed., with dj. Churchill contribution: letter from WSC to Mr. Winston Churchill (USA), p. 228–9, excerpt from *MEL* starting on p. 231.

Stiles B128 <u>The Oxford Book of Military Anecdotes</u>, Max Hastings, ed., London, Oxford University Press, 1985, with dj. Churchill contribution: 'Description of Colonel Brabazon', pp. 295–8 excerpt from *MEL* starting on p. 81; 'description of charge of the 21st Lancers at Omdurman', pp. 304–8, excerpt from *MEL* starting on p. 203.

Stiles B129 <u>Models for Expository Writing: Model Paragraphs and Essays</u>, Anthony C. Walker, ed., New York, Science Research Associates, 1985. Churchill contribution: 'Incident on Lake Lausanne', pp. 7–8, excerpt from *MEL* starting on p. 50.

Stiles B130 <u>Traditions in Literature</u>, James E. Miller, Helen McDonnell and Russell J. Hogan, Glenview, IL, Scott, Foresman and Company, 1985, 7th Ed., Churchill contribution: 'I Escape from the Boers', pp. 471–83, excerpt from *MEL* starting at p. 282.

Stiles B131 <u>Stories Out of School</u>, Alvin Stardust, London, Quiller Press, 1986, 1st ed., with dj. Churchill contribution: 'learning Latin' (Mensa O Mensa) on pp. 77–8, excerpt from *MEL* starting on p. 24, Foreword by Princess Anne.

Stiles B132 <u>Insight</u>, Peter Chilver, Cheltenham, Thornes, 1986. Churchill contribution: 'Churchill's Youth', a description of his first speech at Empire Music Hall, pp. 143–5 excerpt from *MEL* starting on p. 70.

Stiles B133 <u>Child of My Love</u>, Sue Ryder, London, Collins Harvill, 1986. Churchill contribution: 'POW', p. 224, excerpt from *MEL* starting on p. 273.

Stiles B134 <u>The World of Polo Past and Present</u>, J.N.P. Watson, Topsfield, MA, Salem House, 1986, 1st ed., with dj. Churchill contribution: playing polo in India, pp. 37–9, excerpt from *MEL* starting on p. 120. Also, a *Punch* cartoon of Churchill from 1931 ('The Self–Chukker', p. 38).

Stiles B135 <u>Afghanistan: Agony of a Nation</u>, Sandy Gall, London, The Bodley Head, 1986, 1st ed, with dj. Churchill contribution: description of battle at Malakand Pass, pp. 31–2, excerpted from *MEL* starting on p. 155.

Stiles B136 <u>Living in Victorian Times</u>, Sydney Wood, London, John Murray, 1986, softcover, 1st ed., Churchill contribution: 'Childhood' (Mother and Mrs. Everest), p. 11; school and flogging, p. 85, excerpts from *MEL*, pp. 18 and 25, respectively.

Stiles B137 <u>Thoughts Among the Ruins: Collected Essays on Europe and Beyond</u>, George Lichtheim, New Brunswick, Transaction Books, 1986. Churchill contribution: his father, p. 9, excerpt from *MEL* starting on p. 60.

Stiles B138 <u>Prose Models</u>, Gerald Henry Levin, San Diego, Harcourt Brace Jovanovich, 1987. Churchill contribution: 'First Introduction to Classics' (Mensa O Mensa), pp. 41–3, excerpt from *MEL* starting on p. 23.

Stiles B139 <u>Fathers and Children: How Famous Leaders Were Influenced By Their Fathers</u>, C.L. Sulzberger, New York, Arbor House, 1987, 1st ed., with dj. Churchill contributions: mother and Mrs. Everest, p. 280; Father, pp. 281–2; desire to be born in earlier times, p. 281; serving in India, p. 283; calvary charge, p. 284, excerpts from *MEL*, pp. 19, 52, 60, 141 and 201, respectively.

Stiles B140 <u>Nannies, Au Pairs, Mothers' Helpers – Caregivers</u>, Lin Yeiser, New York, Vintage Books, 1987, paperback. Churchill contribution: two separate entries, description of his mother ('She shone for me … like the Evening Star'), p. 139, excerpted from *MEL*, p. 19, and description of Mrs. Everest's death, pp. 155–6, excerpted from *MEL*, p. 86.

Stiles B141 <u>Sandhurst: A Documentary</u>, Michael Yardley, London, Harrap, 1987. Churchill contribution: Sandhurst, pp. 44–7, excerpt from *MEL* starting on p. 57.

Stiles B142 <u>The Faber Book of Reportage</u>, John Carey, Ed., London, Faber and Faber, 1988 (reprint), with dj. Churchill contribution: 'The Battle of Omdurman, 2 September 1898', pp. 401–7 excerpt from *MEL* starting on p. 197.

Stiles B143 <u>Return to Mathematics Circles: A Fifth Collection of Mathematical Stories and Anecdotes</u>, Howard Whitley Eves, Boston, PWS-Kent, 1988. Churchill contributions: view of mathematics, p. 105, excerpt from *MEL* starting on p. 41.

Stiles B144 <u>Reef of Time: Johannesburg in Writing</u>, Digby Ricci, Graighall, South Africa, Ad. Donker, 1988. Churchill contribution: 'Johannesburg and Pretoria', pp. 65–7, extract from *MEL* starting on p. 359.

Stiles B145 <u>Aging and Political Leadership</u>, Angus McIntyre, Ed., Albany, State University of New York Press, 1988. Churchill contribution: jump off bridge, pp. 232–3, excerpt from *MEL* starting on p. 43; 'Escape from the Boers', p. 234, excerpt from *MEL* starting on p. 280.

Stiles B146 <u>Doctors: The Biography of Medicine</u>, Sherwin B. Nuland, New York, Knopf, 1988. Churchill contribution: skin graft in Sudan, p. 466, excerpt from *MEL* starting on p. 211.

Stiles B147 <u>Eye-Witness to History</u>, John Carey, Ed., Cambridge, Harvard University Press, 1988, 1st ed., with dj (brown, green and buff). Churchill contribution: 'The Battle of Omdurman, 2 September 1899', pp. 401–406, excerpt from *MEL* starting on p. 197.

Stiles B148 <u>Eye–Witness to History</u>, John Carey, Ed., Cambridge, Harvard University Press, 1988, 1st ed., with dj (all green and buff). Churchill contribution: 'The Battle of Omdurman, 2 September 1898', pp. 401–406, excerpt from *MEL* starting on p. 197.

Stiles B149 <u>To Change an Army: General Sir John Burnett-Stuart and British Armored Doctrine, 1927-1928</u>, Harold R. Winton, Lawrence, KS, University Press of Kansas, 1988. Churchill contribution: entrance exams for Sandhurst, p. 46, excerpt from *MEL* starting on p. 57.

Stiles B150 <u>The Open Door: When Writers First Learned to Read</u>, Steven Gilbar, Ed., Boston, David R. Godine, 1989, 1st ed., with dj. Churchill contribution: learning to read (at 'The Little Lodge'), pp. 37–9, excerpt from MEL starting on p. 17.

Stiles B151 <u>Acres and Heirlooms: The Survival of Britain's Historical Estates</u>, Madeleine Beard, New York, Routledge, 1989, 'cavalry drills' (Sandhurst), pp. 3–4, excerpt from *MEL* starting on p. 78.

Stiles B152 <u>Prose Models: Canadian, American, and British Essays for Composition</u>, Toronto, Harcourt Brace Janovich, 1989. Churchill contribution: 'My First Introduction to the Classics', Harrow, pp. 63–5, excerpt from *MEL* starting on p. 23.

Stiles B153 <u>Firefight! The History of Personal Firepower</u>, Peter Newark, London, Guild Publishing, 1989, 1st ed., with dj. Churchill contribution: Story of WSC and his Mauser pistol, model 1896, with ten–round box magazine and excerpts on the 'Battle of Omdurman' and the use of his pistol, pp. 158–159, excerpt from *MEL* starting on p. 205.

Stiles B154 <u>Reader's Digest Great Biographies</u>, *Reader's Digest*, 1990, Pleasantville, NY, green boards, image of WSC as young soldier on front board. Churchill contribution: 'My Early Life', pp. 505–606, excerpt from *MEL* starting on p. 15.

Stiles B155 <u>Who's Calling the Shots?</u> Nancy Carlsson-Paige, New Society Publishers, 1990. Churchill contribution: 'toy soldiers', p. 107, excerpt from *MEL* starting on p. 33.

Stiles B156 <u>Headway Student's Book Advanced</u>, John & Liz Soars, Oxford, Oxford University Press, 1990, softcover. Churchill contribution: 'First day at school' (Mensa O Mensa), pp. 14–5, excerpt from *MEL* starting on p. 23.

Stiles B157 <u>Who's Calling the Shots? How to Respond Effectively to Children's Fascination with War Play and War Toys</u>, Nancy Carlsson-Paige and Diane E. Levin, Philadelphia, PA, 1990. Churchill contribution: 'toy soldiers', p. 107, excerpt from *MEL* starting on p. 33.

Stiles B158 <u>Telltale 4: Victorian Britain</u>, John West, Huntingdon, UK, Elm Publications, 1991, paperback. Churchill contribution: 'Harrow School and Latin', pp. 149–153, excerpt from *MEL* starting on p. 23.

Stiles B159 <u>Traditions in Literature: America Reads</u>, Helen McDonnell, James E. Miller, Jr., and Russell J. Hogan, Eds., Glenview, IL, Scott

Foresman, 1991, textbook, with questions and study materials. Churchill contribution: 'I Escape from the Boers', pp. 611–26, excerpt from *MEL* starting on p. 282.

Stiles B160 The Foundations of Students' Learning, Kevin Marjoribanks, London, Oxford Press, 1991. Churchill contribution: Harrow, 'learning English', p. 4, excerpt from *MEL* starting on p. 31.

Stiles B161 Telltale 4, John West, Huntingdon, West, 1991. Churchill contribution: 'Harrow experience', pp. 149–53, excerpt from *MEL* starting on p. 23.

Stiles B162 A Guide to Better Punctuation, A.M. Burt, Cheltenham, Stanley Thorne, 1991. Churchill contribution: 'learning Latin' (mensa), pp. 78–9, excerpt from *MEL* starting on p. 24.

Stiles B163 Apple Pie 3, Francoise Lemarchand and Kathleen Julie, Paris, Hatchette, 1991. Churchill contribution: 'learning Latin', pp. 128–9, excerpt from *MEL* starting on p. 24.

Stiles B164 Practical English Handbook, Floyd C. Watkins and William B. Dillingham, Eds., Boston, Houghton Mifflin Company, 1992, 9th Ed., paperback. Churchill contribution: 'Escape from the Boers', pp. 156–8, excerpt from *MEL* starting on p. 296. Used as an example to teach sentence structure and grammar.

Stiles B165 True Tales of British India and the Princely States, Michael Wise, Brighton, In Print Publishing, 1993. Churchill contribution: 'Bullets Everywhere' (India), pp. 174–7, excerpt from *MEL* starting on p. 154.

Stiles B166 Radical Joe: A Life of Joseph Chamberlain, Dennis Judd, Cardiff, University of Wales Press, 1993. Churchill contribution: 'khaki election', p. 225, excerpt from *MEL* starting on p. 372.

Stiles B167 A Dublin Anthology, Douglas Bennett, Ed., Dublin, Gill & Macmillan, 1994, 1st ed., paperback. Churchill contribution: 'My Early Life' (early childhood memories of Dublin), pp. 139–141, excerpt from *MEL* starting on p. 15.

Stiles B168 <u>Seven Pathways of Learning</u>, David G. Lazear, Tucson, AZ, Zephyr Press, 1994. Churchill contribution: 'examinations', p. ix, excerpt from *MEL* starting on p. 29.

Stiles B169 <u>Reader's Digest Great Biographies in Large Type: Charlotte Bronte Winston Churchill</u>, Reader's Digest Fund for the Blind, Pleasantville, NY, 1994, paperback. Churchill contribution: 'My Early Life', pp. 285–480, excerpt from *MEL* starting on p. 15.

Stiles B170 <u>Before And After</u>, Gaylon E. McCollough, Birmingham, AL, Booksmith, 1994. Churchill contribution: Churchill admonition 'Come on all …', p. 210, excerpt from *MEL* starting on p. 74.

Stiles B171 <u>Waterfield's School: A Preparatory School in its Victorian Heyday</u>, Simon Wright, East Sussex, Herons Ghyll Press, 1994. Churchill contribution: 'School' (flogging), p. 81, excerpt from *MEL* starting on p. 26.

Stiles B172 <u>How to Multiply Your Baby's Intelligence</u>, Glenn J. Doman and Janet Doman, Garden City Park, NY, Avery Publication Group, 1994. Churchill contribution: 'examinations', pp. 113–4, excerpt from *MEL* starting on p. 29.

Stiles B173 <u>The Stamp of the School: Reminiscences of the Thatcher School</u>, John S. Huyler, Seattle, WA, Special Child Publications, 1994. Churchill contribution: give your son horses, p. 15, excerpt from *MEL* starting on p. 59.

Stiles B174 <u>A Wartime Log</u>, Art and Lee Beltrone, Charlottesville, VA, Howell Press, 1995, 1st ed., with dj. Churchill contribution: 'The Prisoner' discussed what it is like to be POW in South Africa, p. 77, excerpt from *MEL* starting on p. 177.

Stiles B175 <u>True Stories of Great Escapes</u>, Volume 2, Charles S. Verral, ed., London, *Reader's Digest*, 1995, 1st ed., Churchill contribution: 'My Escape', pp. 7–22 excerpt from *MEL* starting p. 256.

Stiles B176 <u>The Oxford Book of Schooldays</u>, Patricia Craig, Oxford, Oxford Press, 1995. Churchill contribution: 'Schooldays', pp. 145–6 and

'A Little Learning', pp. 385–6 excerpt from *MEL* starting on p. 26 and 29, respectively.

Stiles B177 The Jubilee Years 1887-1898, Robert Hudson, London, The Folio Society, 1996, with slipcase. Churchill contribution: Churchill's first public speech (at Empire Theatre, 1894), pp. 145–6, excerpt from *MEL* starting on p. 64; description of his time in India, pp. 187–92, excerpt from *MEL* starting on p. 118.

Stiles B178 From Dorset with Love, Bob Croxford, Cornwall, Atmosphere Publishing, 1996. Churchill contribution: jumping off bridge, p. 64, excerpt from *MEL* starting on p. 64.

Stiles B179 The Literary Companion to Parliament, Christopher Silvester, Ed., London, Sinclair–Stevenson, 1996. Churchill contribution: 'First Speech in Parliament', pp. 417–9, excerpt from *MEL* starting on p. 377.

Stiles B180 Challenges for Living: Fifty Assemblies for Secondary Schools, Ian Stuart, Norwich, Religious and Moral Education Press, 1996. Churchill contribution: 'Admonition', p. 33, excerpt from *MEL* starting on p. 74.

Stiles B181 Experimental Psychology, Anne Myers and Christine H. Hansen, Pacific Grove, CA, 1997. Churchill contribution: school, examinations, p. 160, excerpt from *MEL* starting on p. 29.

Stiles B182 Uneasy Neighbors: Cuba and the United States, Rhoda Hoff and Margaret Regler, New York, Franklin Watts, 1997. Churchill contribution: 'Winston Churchill Joins the Army', pp. 30–32, excerpt from *MEL* starting on p. 97.

Stiles B183 An Underground Education: The Unauthorized and Outrageous Supplement to Everything You Thought You Knew About Art, Sex, Business, Crime, Science, Medicine, and Other Fields of Human Knowledge, Richard Zacks, New York, Bantam Doubleday Dell, 1997. Churchill contribution: School (flogging), pp. 166–7, excerpted from *MEL* starting on p. 26.

Stiles B184 Literary Theory: An Anthology, Julie Rivkin and Michael Ryan, Malden, MA, Blackwell, 1998. Churchill contribution: 'Sandhurst' and wanting military action, pp. 864–5, excerpt from *MEL* starting on p. 58.

Stiles B185 Play from Birth to Twelve and Beyond: Contexts, Perspectives, and Meaning, Doris Pronin Fromberg and Doris Begen, New York, Garland, 1998. Churchill contribution: 'toy soldiers and career', p. 513, excerpt from *MEL* starting on p. 33.

Stiles B186 Empire by Default: the Spanish-American War and the Dawn of the American Century, Ivan Musicant, New York, H. Holt, 1998 Churchill contribution: 'Cuba', pp, 60–61, excerpt from *MEL* starting on p. 89.

Stiles B187 Portals: Reading, Writing and Critical Thinking, Mary T. Segall and William R. Brown, Fort Worth, TX, Harcourt Brace, 1999, 1st ed., soft cover. Churchill contribution: 'school experiences' at St. James, Harrow and Sandhurst, pp. 322–9, excerpt from *MEL* starting on pp. 23, 26, 29, and 52.

Stiles B188 The Isles: A History, Norman Davies, London, Macmillan, 1999. Churchill contribution: 'Cavalry charge', p. 862–4, excerpt from *MEL* starting on p. 201.

Stiles B189 Classical Rhetoric for the Modern Student, Edward P.J. Corbett, New York, Oxford Press, 1999. Churchill contribution: 'Learning English at Harrow', pp. 414–5, excerpt from *MEL* starting on p. 30.

Stiles B190 Seasons of Our Lives: Spring, the Path to Discovery; Summer, to Love or Let Go; Autumn, the Changing Moods; Winter, the Pleasure and the Parting, Martyn Lewis, Harpenden, Lennard, 1999. Churchill contribution: 'Toy soldiers and father', p. 39, excerpt from *MEL* starting on p. 33.

Stiles B191 Style and Statement, Edward P.J. Corbett, New York, Oxford Press, 1999. Churchill contribution: 'Harrow Experience', pp. 78–89, excerpt from *MEL* starting on p. 30.

Stiles B192 <u>The Learning Game</u>, Jonathan Smith, London, Little, Brown and Company, 2000, with dj. Churchill contribution: 'Winston Churchill Learns Latin', pp. 61–3, excerpt from *MEL* starting on p. 24.

Stiles B193 <u>The Best of the Raconteurs</u>, Mary Morley and Tim Heald, London, The Folio Society, 2000, Churchill's contribution: 'Mensa, A Table', pp. 13–4 excerpt from MEL starting on p. 24.

Stiles B194 <u>Character & Identity: The Sociological Foundation of Literary and Historical Perspective</u>, Morton A Kaplan, Ed., St. Paul, MN, Paragon House, 2000, 1st ed., Churchill's contribution: Chapter 6 'Winston Churchill at School', by James W. Muller, pp. 83–111, extensive quotes from *MEL* including pp. 25, 36, 31, 40, 41, 47, 52, 59 and 66.

Stiles B195 <u>American Generalship: Character is Everything: The Art of Command</u>, Edgar F. Puryear, Novata, CA, Presidio, 2000. Churchill contribution: Sandhurst, p. 163, excerpt from *MEL* starting on p. 58; India (self–education), p. 163, excerpt from *MEL* staring p. 125; India (self–education), pp. 163–4, excerpt from *MEL* starting on p. 126.

Stiles B196 <u>Latin, or the Empire of a Sign: From the Sixteenth to the Twentieth Centuries</u>, Françoise Waquet, London, Verso, 2001. Churchill contribution: 'learning Latin' (mensa), p. 140–41, excerpt from *MEL* starting on p. 25.

Stiles B197 <u>As It Happens: A Cascade Collection of Reportage</u>, Rosy Border, Ed., London, Collins, 2001, 1st ed. 2nd printing. Churchill contribution: 'The North–West Frontier', pp. 46–9, excerpt from *MEL* starting on p. 154.

Stiles B198 <u>World's Greatest Biographies: Abraham Lincoln, Winston Churchill, Thomas Edison</u>, Readers Digest Association, Pleasantville, NY, 2001, with dj. Churchill contribution: 'My Early Life', pp. 242–345, extensive excerpt from *MEL* starting on p. 15.

Stiles B199 <u>Classic Horse Stories: Fourteen Timeless Horse Tales</u>, Steven D. Price, Ed., Guilford, CT, Lyons Press, 2002. Churchill contribution: 'Sensations of a Calvary Charge', pp. 153–66, excerpt from *MEL* starting on p. 201.

Stiles B200 The Mammoth Book of Heroes, Jon E. Lewis, Ed., New York, Carroll & Graf, 2002, 1st ed., paperback (only format), Churchill contribution: 'Omdurman', pp. 465–671, excerpt from *MEL* starting on p. 197.

Stiles B201 The Good Grammar Guide, Richard Palmer, London, Routledge, 2003. Churchill contribution: 'learning Latin', pp. xii–xiii, excerpt from *MEL* starting on p. 25.

Stiles B202 Gamma: Exploring Euler's Constant, Julian Havil, Princeton, Princeton University Press, 2003. Churchill contribution: view of mathematics, p. 12, excerpt from *MEL* starting on p. 41.

Stiles B203 When We Were Young: A Compendium of Childhood, John Burningham, Ed., London, Bloomsbury, 2004, 1st ed., with dj. Churchill contributions: 'First Memories', p. 5, excerpt from *MEL* starting on p. 15; 'First Day' (at School), p. 20, excerpt from *MEL* starting on p. 24.

Stiles B204 The Book of Life: A Compendium of the Best Autobiographical and Memoir Writing, Eve Claxton, Ed., London, Ebury Press, 2005, with dj. Churchill contribution: 'Entering Sandhurst', pp. 186–8, excerpt from *MEL* starting on p. 39.

Stiles B205 The Mammoth Book of True War Stories, Jon E. Lewis, Ed., New York, Carroll & Graf Publishers, 2005, paperback. Churchill contribution: 'The 21st Lancers at Omdurman', pp. 40–47, excerpt from *MEL* starting on p. 197.

Stiles B206 England: The Autobiography, John Lewis-Stempel, London, Viking, 2005, 1st ed., with dj. Churchill contribution: 'Omdurman, 2 September 1898', pp. 289–91, excerpt from *MEL* starting on p. 204.

Stiles B207 Dyscalculia: Action Plans for Successful Learning in Mathematics, Glynis Hannell, London, David Fulton, 2005. Churchill contribution: 'learning mathematics', p. 83, excerpt from *MEL* starting on p. 17.

Stiles B208 British Music Hall: An Illustrated History, Richard A. Baker, Stroud, Sutton, 2005. Churchill contribution: 'first speech at Empire Theatre', p. 44, excerpt from *MEL* starting on p. 71.

Stiles B209 Every Book its Reader, Nicholas A. Basbanes, New York, Harper Collins, 2005, 1st ed. with dj. Churchill contribution: 'self-learning India', pp. 28–9, excerpt from *MEL* starting on p. 125.

Stiles B210 Fantasies of Empire: The Empire Theatre of Varieties and the Licensing Controversy of 1894, Joseph W. Donahue, Iowa City, University of Iowa Press, 2005. Churchill contribution: 'first speech at Empire Theatre', p. 173, excerpt from *MEL* starting on p. 173.

Stiles B211 Sources of the Western Tradition, Volume II: From the Renaissance to the Present, Marvin Perry, Joseph R. Peden and Theodore H. Von Laue, Boston, Houghton Mifflin Company, 2006. Churchill contribution: 'The Battle of Omdurman', pp. 255–9, excerpt from *MEL* starting on p. 198.

Stiles B212 Eyewitness to War, Anthony and Nicholas Bird, Chichester, Summersdale, 2006, 1st ed., with dj. Churchill contribution: 'The Charge of the 21st Lancers at Omdurman', pp. 82–7, excerpt from *MEL* starting on p. 204.

Stiles B213 Reader's Digest True Lives: Stories of Hope, Honor & Humor, Steve Gelman, Ed., Pleasantville, NY, The Reader's Digest Association, 2006, with dj. Churchill contribution: 'A Troublesome Boy', story of Churchill's early schooling, pp. 144–7, excerpted from *MEL* starting on p. 53.

Stiles B214 Change and Motion: Calculus Made Clear, Michael Starbird, Chantilly, VA, The Great Courses, 2006. Churchill contribution: 'School' (quadratic equations), pp. 15–6, excerpt from *MEL* starting on p. 39.

Stiles B215 The Autobiography of the British Soldier, John Lewis-Stemple, Ed., London, Headline Publishing Group, 2007, with dj. Churchill contribution: 'Omdurman: The 21st Lancers Charge the Dervishes, 2 September 1898', pp. 222–4, excerpt from *MEL* starting on p. 204.

Stiles B216 The Mathematics of Oz: Mental Gymnastics from Beyond the Edge, Clifford A. Pickover, New York, Cambridge University Press, 2007. Churchill contribution: view of mathematics, p. 198, excerpt from *MEL* starting on p. 41.

Stiles B217 The Practice of Writing, Valerie Ross, Boston, Pearson Custom Publishers, 2007. Churchill contribution: 'Harrow School', p. 125, excerpt from *MEL* starting on p. 30.

Stiles B218 The World's Best Memoir Writing: The Literature of Life from St. Augustine to Gandhi, and from Pablo Picasso to Nelson Mandela, Eve Claxton, Naperville, IL, Sourcebooks, 2007. Churchill contribution: 'My Early Life/ Roving Commission' (examinations), pp. 199–201, excerpt from *MEL* staring on p.39.

Stiles B219 England, Our England, Alan Titchmarsh, London, Hodder & Stoughton, 2007, with dj. Churchill contribution: 'School, Mensa, O Mensa', pp. 74–6, excerpt from *MEL* starting on p. 23.

Stiles B220 Carpe Diem: Put a Little Latin in Your Life, Harry Mount, New York, Hyperion, 2007. Churchill contribution: 'learning Latin', pp. 27–8, excerpt from *MEL* starting on p. 25.

Stiles B221 Prisoner of War, Charles Rollings, London, Ebury Press, 2007, with dj. Churchill contribution: 'On being a POW', p. 3, excerpt from *MEL* starting on p. 273.

Stiles B222 Voices From the Front Line, Anthony & Nicholas Bird, Eds., West Sussex, Summersdale, 2008, paperback. Churchill contribution: 'The Charge of the 21st Lancers at Omdurman', pp. 82–7, excerpt from *MEL* starting on p.204.

Stiles B223 Amo, Amos, Amat – and All That: How to Become a Latin Lover, Harry Mount, London, Short, 2008. Churchill contribution: 'learning Latin', pp. 34–5, excerpt from *MEL* starting on p. 25.

Stiles B224 Victorian Literature, Steven Croft, Ed., Oxford Student Texts, Oxford, Oxford University Press, 2009, paperback. Churchill contributions: 'Harrow examinations', pp. 33–35, excerpt from *MEL* starting on p. 29; 'charge at Omdurman', pp. 92–94, excerpt from *MEL* starting on p. 205.

Stiles B225 Tort Law: Cases and Materials, Ernest J. Weinrib, Toronto, Emond Montgomery Publications, 2009. Churchill contribution: view of mathematics, p. 220, excerpt from *MEL* starting on p. 41.

Stiles B226 Nobel Winds and Breezes, Alexander L. Mohr, Amsterdam, A.L. Mohr, 2009. Churchill contribution: 'Polo', pp. 103–9, excerpt from *MEL* starting on p. 221.

Stiles B227 Captured in Time: Five Centuries of South African Writing, John Clare, Johannesburg, Jonathan Bell, 2010. Churchill contribution: 'Armoured Train' and 'General Botha', pp. 263–5 and 265–6, excerpt from *MEL* starting on p. 264.

Stiles B228 Vanished Kingdoms: The History of Half-Forgotten Europe, Norman Davies, London, Allen Lane, 2011, 1st ed., with dj. Churchill contribution: 'Childhood in Ireland', p. 647, excerpt from *MEL* starting on p. 15.

Stiles B229 Performances of Violence, Austin Sarat, Carleen R. Basler and Thomas L. Dumm, Amherst, University of Massachusetts, 2011. Churchill contribution: 'military action in Cuba', p. 22, excerpt from, starting on p. 91.

Stiles B230 The Collective Imagination: The Creative Spirit of Free Societies, Peter Murphy, Surrey, Ashgate, 2012, Churchill's contribution: free will or predestination, p. 58, excerpted from *MEL* starting on p. 42.

Stiles B231 Damn Few: Making the Model SEAL Warrior, Rorke Denver, Hyperion, New York, 2013, with dj. Churchill contribution: 'admonition' (Come on all), p. 97, excerpted from *MEL* starting on p. 74.

Stiles B232 Dyscalculia: Action Plans for Successful Learning in Mathematics, Glynis Hannell, New York, Routledge, 2013. Churchill contribution: learning mathematics, p. 76, excerpt from *MEL* starting on p. 17.

Stiles B233 World Order: Reflections on the Character of Nations and the Course of History, Henry Kissinger, London, Allen Lane, 2014. Churchill contribution: 'India' (Pathans), p. 319–20, excerpt from *MEL* starting on p. 149.

Stiles B234 The Mathematics Devotional: Celebrating the Wisdom and Beauty of Mathematics, Clifford A. Pickover, New York, Stirling, 2014. Churchill contribution: mathematics, p. 68, excerpt from *MEL* starting on p. 41.

Stiles B235 <u>Secrets of Productive People: 50 Techniques to Get Things Done</u>, Mark Forster, London, John Murray Learning, 2015. Churchill contribution: 'power of naps', pp. 205–6, excerpt from MEL starting on p. 95.

Stiles B236 <u>Reading Latin: Text and Vocabulary</u>, Peter V. Jones, Cambridge, Cambridge University Press, 2016. Churchill contribution: learning Latin, pp. ix–x, excerpt from *MEL* starting on p. 24.

Stiles B 237 <u>In the Arena: Good Citizens, a Great Republic, and How One Speech Can Invigorate America</u>, Pete Hegseth, New York, Threshold Editions, 2016, with dj. Churchill contribution: 'admonition' (Come on all), pp. 250–1, excerpted from *MEL* starting on p. 74.

Stiles B238 <u>The 'Broomhandle' Mauser</u>, Jonathan Ferguson, Oxford, Osprey Publications, 2017, card wrappers. Churchill contributions: 'Omdurman', p. 27, excerpt from *MEL* starting on p. 206; 'Omdurman', p. 28, excerpt from *MEL* starting on p. 207; 'Boer War', p. 29, excerpt from *MEL* starting on p. 366.

Stiles B239 <u>Seeing What Others Cannot See: The Hidden Advantages of Visual Thinkers and Differently Wired Brains</u>, Thomas G. West, Amherst, NY, Prometheus Books, 2017. Churchill's contribution: difficulty in school, pp. 169–70, excerpted from *MEL* starting on p. 52.

Stiles B240 <u>Much Promise: Successful Schools in England</u>, Barnaby Lenon, Melton Woodbridge, John Catt Educational, 2017. Churchill's contribution: learning English at Harrow, pp. 80–81, excerpt from *MEL* starting on p. 30.

Stiles B241 <u>Orders, Decorations, Medals and Militaria</u>, Auction Catalogue, Dix, Noonan, Webb, Mayfair, London, May 9 and 10, 2018, lot 43, pp. 43–45, 'Armored train derailment in Boer War', excerpt from *MEL* starting on p. 257.

Stiles B242F <u>I Ord Och Garning Winston Churchill I Urval</u> (In Word and Deed: Winston Churchill in Selection), Svante Nordin, Sweden, Timbro, 2019, 1st Swedish Ed., hardback, 'My Early Life' including Childhood in Ireland, Schooling, Omdurman, escape from Boers, the lower house and marriage, pp. 21–68, excerpt from *MEL*, translated to Swedish by Beatrice Cronstedt.

Stiles B243 <u>Winged Combat: My Story as a Spitfire Pilot in WWII</u>, William Arthur Bishop, Toronto, Harper Collins, 2022. Churchill contribution: 'admonition' (Come on all), p. 355, excerpt from *MEL*, p. 74.

iv. Anthologies and Selections

This section includes works included in either Cohen or Zoller, as well as anthologies not mentioned by either source. Where there is a Cohen number with an asterisk, it signifies where in Cohen's book it would be placed. Where no Cohen or Zoller designation exists, the volume will be labelled 'Stiles Anx' with sequential numbers.

Cohen A276.1 <u>A Churchill Anthology</u>, F.W. Heath, Ed., London, Odhams Press, 1962, *MEL* contributions: 'My Early Life' (Childhood, Harrow, Examinations, Mr. Gladstone in 1893, Swiss Holiday, Sandhurst, The Purity Campaign, Mrs. Everest, Cuba 1895, Royal Dinner Party, India 1895, The Bank of Observance, Reading and Religion, Sensations of a Cavalry Charge, A Living Wage, A Strange Correspondence, Candidate for Parliament, First Defeat, The Khaki Election, Member for Oldham and American Lecture Tour), pp. 17–72.

Cohen A276.2.a <u>Great Destiny</u>, F.W. Heath, Ed., New York, G.P. Putnam's Sons, 1965, 1st Am. ed., *MEL* contribution: 'My Early Life' (Childhood, Harrow, Examinations, Mr. Gladstone in 1893, Swiss Holiday, Sandhurst, The Purity Campaign, Mrs. Everest, Cuba 1895, Royal Dinner Party, India 1895, The Bank of Observance, Reading and Religion, Sensations of a Cavalry Charge, A Living Wage, A Strange Correspondence, Candidate for Parliament, First Defeat, The Khaki Election, Member for Oldham and American Lecture Tour), pp. 17–72.

Zoller A253 <u>A Man of Destiny: Winston S. Churchill</u>, by Editors of *Country Beautiful*, New York, Country Beautiful Foundation, 1965, 1st Am. ed., *MEL* contribution: 'My Early Life' (At 'The Little Lodge', Gaining a Prize, Death of His Nurse, The Well-to-Do), pp. 17–9.

Cohen A276.4* <u>Churchill in His Own Words: Years of Adventure</u>, F.W. Heath, Ed., New York, Capricorn Books, 1966, paperback, *MEL* contribution: 'My Early Life' (Childhood, Harrow, Examinations, Mr. Gladstone in 1893, Swiss Holiday, Sandhurst, The Purity Campaign, Mrs. Everest, Cuba 1895, Royal Dinner Party, India 1895, The Bank of Observance, Reading and Religion, Sensations of a Cavalry Charge, A Living Wage, A Strange Correspondence, Candidate for Parliament, First Defeat, The Khaki Election, Member for Oldham and American Lecture Tour), pp. 17–72.

Stiles An1 <u>Sir Winston Churchill Selections from his Writings and Speeches</u>, Guy Boas, Ed., London, Macmillan, 1966, 2nd Ed., with dj, *MEL* contribution: Childhood, To School, Harrow, Sandhurst, The Fourth Hussars, India, Omdurman, War correspondent: Prisoner of Boers, Escape, Relief of Ladysmith, The House of Commons, pp. 1–30, excerpted from *MEL* starting on p.15.

Cohen A276.3 <u>A Churchill Anthology</u>, F.W. Heath, ed., London, Odhams Book, Ltd., 1966, Bookplan Issue, *MEL* contribution: 'My Early Life' (Childhood, Harrow, Examinations, Mr. Gladstone in 1893, Swiss Holiday, Sandhurst, The Purity Campaign, Mrs. Everest, Cuba 1895, Royal Dinner Party, India 1895, The Bank of Observance, Reading and Religion, Sensations of a Cavalry Charge, A Living Wage, A Strange Correspondence, Candidate for Parliament, First Defeat, The Khaki Election, Member for Oldham and American Lecture Tour), pp. 17–72.

Stiles An2 The<u> Roar of the Lion</u>, London, Tandem, 1969, paperback, compendium of Churchill's writings and speeches including *MEL*. Churchill contributions (*MEL*): pp. 9–35 including Ireland, Mother, schooling, learning, Sandhurst; pp. 36–64, including India, Sudan, South Africa.

v. Reader's Digest

Churchill was exceedingly popular with the *Reader's Digest* organisation worldwide. They published complete versions or excerpts from *My Early Life* in both their magazine and book formats. 'C' items are in magazine (periodical) format, and 'B' items are in book format. Where the items are not found in Cohen, the nomenclature will be given as 'Stiles Cx', with sequential numbers indicating chronological order. As can be seen below, versions in German, Swedish, Spanish, Italian and French were produced.

Stiles C19 Reader's Digest, July 1949, Australian Issue, 'A Roving Commission', 32 pages.

C681 Reader's Digest, August 1949, Vol. 55, No. 328, 'Troublesome Boy, A Roving Commission', p. 101–4, excerpt from *MEL* starting on p. 53.

Stiles B245 Reader's Digest Condensed Books, Vol VII, Autumn 1951 Selections, The Reader's Digest Association, Pleasantville, NY, 'A Roving Commission', pp. 221–320, excerpt from *MEL*. (Two different bindings noted; distinct spines, one has brown lettering and a brown vertical box with titles inside; the other has green lettering and a green vertical box with titles inside.)

Stiles B18F Weltabenteuer Im Dienst (My Early Life) in Reader's Digest Auswahlbucher, Vol IV, 1957, Verlag Das Beste, Stuttgart, Germany, German ed., green cloth binding, front, gold embossed pomegranates centred, pp. 153–250 excerpt from *MEL*.

Stiles B18Fa Weltabenteuer Im Dienst (My Early Life) in Reader's Digest Auswahlbucher, Vol IV, 1957, Verlag Das Beste, Stuttgart, German Ed., orange leather spine and grey stripped cloth binding (front and back), pp. 153–250, excerpt from *MEL*.

Stiles B23 Reader's Digest Condensed Books, The Reader's Digest Association, 1958, London, 'My Early Life', pp. 231–318, excerpt from *MEL*.

Stiles B24F Le Mie Prime Guerre: Condensato del Libro My Early Life (A Roving Commission), Winston Churchill, William Faulkner, Milano, Selezione Reader's Digest, Italian, 1958.

Stiles B25F Min Ungdom (My Early Life) in Det Bastas Bokval, Reader's Digest Stockholm, Aktiebolag, 1959, Swedish, pp. 313–404, excerpt from *MEL*, green, tan and red boards, hardback with red dj.

Stiles B35F En Busca De Aventuras (My Early Life) in Biblioteca De Selecciones, Selecciones Del Reader's Digest, Madrid, Spain, 1963, Spanish, pp. 7–110, excerpt from *MEL*, hardback, tan leatherette half binding, front, gold design down edge of leatherette, gold wheat design, blue, buff, gold and green boards; back exactly the same as front; spine top to bottom, in gold rectangle wheat design, then a series of raised ribs with 6 blue background boxes bordered top and bottom with gold lines, within the boxes the titles of the condensed books, bottom has publisher's logo in gold within a box consisting of 2 gold lines top and bottom, and a single gold line on each side.

Stiles B36F <u>En Busca De Aventuras (My Early Life)</u> in <u>Biblioteca De Selecciones</u>, Selecciones Del Reader's Digest, Mexico, 1963, Spanish, pp. 275– 374, excerpt from *MEL*, hardback, pale blue boards with flower-like designs, leatherette spine.

Stiles B81F <u>Mis Anos Mozos (My Early Life)</u> in <u>Grandes Biografias, Selecciones Del Reader's Digest,</u> Madrid, Spain, 1971, Spanish, pp. 7–104, excerpt from *MEL*, hardback with dark blue boards, front patterned rectangle within the rectangle in gold script 'Grandes Biografias', at bottom in gold lettering 'SELECCIONES READER'S DIGEST'; spine with gold script 'Grandes Biografias', under that in gold bordered red box in gold lettering, 'Winston / CHURCHILL', under that 'CHARLES / LINDBER', under that 'RAMON / Y / CAJAL', under that outside the box in gold lettering 'SELECCONES / THE READER'S DIGEST'.

B196 <u>Reader's Digest 50th Anniversary Treasury</u>, Pleasantville, NY, Reader's Digest, 1972, 1st ed, with dj, Churchill's contribution: 'A Troublesome Boy', pp. 448–52, from Reader's Digest August 1949.

Stiles B98 <u>Family Treasuries of Great Biographies</u>, Vol. VII, Reader's Digest Association, 1976, Pleasantville, NY, 'My Early Life', pp. 7–110, excerpt from *MEL*, hardback with brown pebbled boards, front and back plain, spine with purple box with gold lines outlining box, within box in gold lettering the names of the authors; dust jacket buff with purple box on front with authors and titles; spine with authors in purple box; back images of all 5 authors.

Spectator, The 291
speeches *42*, 82, 83, 237, 287; Empire Theatre 264; first to Parliament 269
speechmaking 28
Spencer-Churchill, Lieutenant-Colonel Charles Richard John, Duke of Marlborough 'Sunny' 173
spontaneity 287
ss *Etruria* 32
Stanley, Albert Lord Ashfield 167
Stanley, Edward, Earl of Derby 162
Stanley, Lord Edward 162
Stewart, William S. 174
store, department 136, 209, 218
stories 285, 286, 287
Story of the Malakand Field Force, The 36, 58, 285; reviews *37–8*
storytelling 17–18
Strand Magazine 58, 60, 61
Stromberg, Kjell 297–8
style, personal 63
subscription (subscribers) 131, 229
success 18, 20, 32
Sudan 40, 43, 260, 300 *see also* Omdurman, Battle of
Sulzberger, C.L. 264
Sunday Times, The 50
Sweden 111, 297
Sword and pen: A Survey of the Writings of Sir Winston Churchill 275–6

teaching 26, 258
teams, writing 69–71
textbooks 258, 260
texts 147
The Scotsman 193
The Times Recorder 195–6
Theis, Otto F. 193–5
Themes from Experience: A Manual of Literature for Writers 262
Thomas Nelson & Sons 209, 218, 237

Thompson, H.W. 175
Times Book Club 131, 133–5, 229, 240
Times Herald 196–7
Times Literary Supplement 186–7, 288
Times, The 131
tours, speaking 82–4
trade depression 230–1
Traditions in Literature: America Reads 267
trains, armoured 148
translations 256, 297
Treasure Island 51
Trevelyan, George M. 164, 300–1
True Stories of Great Escapes 268

Uneasy Neighbors: Cuba and the United States 265
unhappiness 260
United States of America (USA) 82–4, 139
Unnatural History of the Nanny, The 268

Vancouver Sun 298
vanished age 288–9
version control 82, 103
versions, English and non-English 235–7
versions, English and non-English versions: anthologies 240; English language 237–40; excerpts 240; movies, tapes, DVDs etc 241; periodicals 241; *Reader's Digest* 240–1; translated editions 240
Vickers, Horace Cecil 173
videos 257
views, political 308
vocabulary 28
voice, human 291–2
voice, personal 63

war correspondence 71, 101 *see also* correspondents, war
Washington visit 56
Watson, P.N. 268
Watt, A.P. 83

Webb, Stanley James, Baron Passfield 175–6
Weidhorn, Manfred 275–6, 309, 310
Welldon, James 73, 157–8
Westerham library 166
Westminster, Duke of 161
While England Slept 297
Winnipeg Tribune 184
Winston Churchill 280
Woods, Frederick 32, 51, 67–70, 75, 237
word choices 295
word structure 128
words, sound of 71, 90, 285, 290, 311
World Crisis, The 286, 308; becoming a writer 55, 59; writing of *My Early Life* 68, 80, 84, 97

World of Polo Past and Present, The 268
worms 18
Worthington-Evans, Sir Laming 160
writing skills 262
writing styles 285–95
writing teams 69–71

Ybarra, Thomas Russell 197–8
Yorkshire Post 182–3
Young, G.M. 69
Young Winston 257
Young Winston's Wars: The Original Dispatches of Winston S. Churchill War Correspondent 1897-1900 58

Zoller, Curt J. 237